JAY GOULD

His Business Career

1867–1892

JAY GOULD

His Business Career

1867–1892

by

JULIUS GRODINSKY

PHILADELPHIA
UNIVERSITY OF PENNSYLVANIA PRESS

Published in Great Britain, India, and Pakistan
by the Oxford University Press
London, Bombay, and Karachi

Library of Congress Catalogue Card Number 56-12389

PRINTED IN THE UNITED STATES OF AMERICA
AMERICAN BOOK–STRATFORD PRESS, INC., NEW YORK

To My

Mimi

Preface

This volume is an examination of the policies of a businessman in the field of speculative or equity capital in the free enterprise era between the Civil War and the Theodore Roosevelt Administration. It is not a biography.

The research work for this volume has been financed in part from a grant by the University of Pennsylvania, Committee on The Advancement of Research.

JULIUS GRODINSKY

Philadelphia
1957

Index to Abbreviations of Companies

WHEN A COMPANY IS FIRST MENTIONED, ITS FULL NAME WILL BE USED. THEREAFTER, AS FOOTNOTED, THE ABBREVIATION WILL BE USED.

NAME OF COMPANY	ABBREVIATION
American Union Telegraph	American Union
Atchison, Topeka & Santa Fe	Atchison
Atlantic & Great Western	Atlantic
Atlantic & Pacific Telegraph	Atlantic & Pacific
Boston, Hartford & Erie	Boston
Burlington & Missouri River in Nebraska	B. & M.
Burlington & Southwestern	B.S.W.
Central Branch Union Pacific	Central Branch
Chicago & Alton	Alton
Chicago, Burlington & Quincy	Burlington
Chicago, Milwaukee & St. Paul	St. Paul
Chicago & Northwestern	Northwestern
Chicago, Rock Island & Pacific	Rock Island
Chicago, St. Paul & Kansas City	Stickney Road
Columbus, Chicago & Indiana Central	Indiana Central
Cleveland, Cincinnati, Chicago & Indianapolis	Bee Line
Delaware, Lackawanna & Western	Lackawanna
Denver & Rio Grande	Denver
Denver, South Park & Pacific	South Park
Gulf, Colorado & Santa Fe	Gulf
Hannibal & St. Joseph	Hannibal
Houston & Texas Central	Houston
International Great Northern	International
Kansas City, St. Joseph & Council Bluffs	Council Bluffs
Lake Shore & Michigan Southern	Lake Shore
Manhattan Elevated	Manhattan
Metropolitan Elevated	Metropolitan
Michigan Southern & Northern Indiana	Michigan Southern
Missouri, Iowa & Nebraska	Iowa
Missouri, Kansas & Texas	Kansas & Texas

NAME OF COMPANY	ABBREVIATION
Mutual Union Telegraph	Mutual Union
New York, Chicago & St. Louis	Nickel Plate
New York Elevated	New York
New York & Harlem	Harlem
New York & New England	New England
New York, New Haven & Hartford	New Haven
Pacific Mail Steamship	Pacific Mail
Philadelphia & Reading	Reading
Philadelphia, Wilmington & Baltimore	Wilmington
Pittsburgh, Fort Wayne & Chicago	Fort Wayne
Postal Telegraph	Postal
Quincy, Missouri & Pacific	Quincy
St. Louis, Fort Scott & Wichita	Wichita
St. Louis, Iron Mountain & Southern	Iron Mountain
St. Louis, Kansas City & Northern	Kansas City
St. Louis & San Francisco	Frisco
Toledo, Peoria & Warsaw	Peoria
Western Union Telegraph	Western Union

The Wabash, Erie, Pennsylvania, New York Central, and Delaware & Hudson, will be used at all times to identify these properties. The names of these railroads changed from time to time; but they were sufficiently well known by these names to justify their use.

Bibliographical Note

1. *Am. R. R. Journal* (*American Railroad Journal*). In the sixties and seventies this source made available a large number of annual railroad reports and of other documents pertaining to the railroad industry.

2. Burlington archives. The records of the Chicago, Burlington & Quincy Railroad throughout the period under consideration in this volume are deposited with the Newberry Library in Chicago, Illinois. They are a significant and valuable source of study, not only for American railroad historians, but also for students of American history in a variety of aspects. These papers reflect far more than the views, actions, and policies of an individual businessman—a description which characterizes most of the collections of business papers. In the Burlington archives are found the expression of conflicting views of officials of the Burlington and of many other railroads, some of them friendly and some unfriendly to the Burlington. Furthermore, these views are not screened, as are those normally presented before public investigating bodies. These papers reflect the hurried business judgments composed under the anvil of red-hot necessity, as well as the calm and deliberate judgments slowly matured over the course of years. They reflect, furthermore, no censorship or selection of material in such a way as to disclose favorable, and to eliminate or minimize unfavorable, conclusions. The dynamic aspects of a large and growing American business enterprise are presented in this unique collection of business documents.

3. *Chron.* (*Commercial and Financial Chronicle*). This weekly publication beginning in 1865 reflected the opinions of the financial community. Its editorials were frequently critical of the policies of particular railroad managements. There were from time to time, particularly in the late seventies and in the eighties, detailed studies of individual railroads, with emphasis on earning power and financial strength and financial weakness. Beginning in the late seventies, the *Chronicle* made available, more than any single source, the full, and in some cases only a

slightly abridged text of, railroad annual reports, as well as many other significant documents such as reorganization plans and reports of investigating committees.

4. Dodge papers. The papers of General Grenville M. Dodge are deposited with the Iowa State Historical Society in Des Moines, Iowa. Though they are not fruitful with respect to the business career of Gould, they do throw considerable light on the building program of the Texas & Pacific in the middle seventies; on the expansion of the Mexican railroads through the use of American capital; and on the strategic problems of the Union Pacific in the latter years of the administration of Charles Francis Adams, Jr.

5. The Minutes of the board of directors and of the executive committee of the Erie were examined in the offices of that railroad in Cleveland, Ohio.

6. H.V.P. This refers to the papers of Henry Villard deposited in the Houghton Library of Harvard University. These papers throw light on many of the business activities of Villard. They disclose in detail the conflict over control of the Kansas Pacific (1875 to 1879) between Villard and Gould. The papers also illustrate the way in which large amounts of foreign funds were attracted to the American railway industry through the initiative of American promoters and investment bankers. Also illustrated is the combination of investment and speculative motives that characterized the raising of funds for a growing industry in a dynamic economy.

7. Herapath's *Ry. Journal.* Herapath's *Railway Journal* is an English periodical devoted largely to the affairs of the British railroads. Because of the investments made by English investors in American railroads, the coverage also includes numerous American railroads. Aside from a number of documents made available from this source, the *Journal* is valuable because of the almost continuous optimism expressed over the future of American railroads. The analysis of financial prospects is on the whole superficial and reflects the kind of reasoning usually found in stock brokers' letters.

8. Joy papers. The papers of James Frederick Joy are deposited in the Burton Historical Collection in the Detroit Public Library, Detroit, Michigan. Particularly significant in the study of

Gould's career are the letters concerning the progress of the Wabash in its expansion stage in the Detroit area in 1879 and 1880. Significant also are the activities of Joy arising out of the reorganization of the Wabash in the middle eighties. Of interest also to the railroad historian are the numerous papers bearing upon the negotiations between Joy as the head of the Michigan Central and T. A. Scott and W. H. Vanderbilt of the Pennsylvania and the New York Central, respectively, in the early and middle seventies.

9. M.M. These are the letters between Collis P. Huntington, Charles Crocker, Leland Stanford, Mark Hopkins, and David D. Colton, deposited in the Library of the Mariner's Museum in Newport News, Virginia. These letters bear upon Gould partly in the relationship between Gould and Huntington in the middle seventies and again in 1881. In the early period Huntington's opinion of Gould and the references to the business conflicts between the Central Pacific and the Union Pacific are of value; and in the latter period, the letters between Huntington and Crocker reveal their determination to thwart Gould's ambitions to invade the Pacific Coast. Aside from the references to Gould, these letters are of value in tracing the unique methods used by Huntington in financing the Southern Pacific expansion program in the middle seventies, the Central Pacific's critical financial problems in 1872 and 1873, and the subsequent growth of the Southern Pacific's system between late 1878 and the early eighties.

10. Northwestern archives. A collection of letters in the seventies and eighties were found in the accounting offices of the Chicago & Northwestern in Chicago, Illinois. They reflect, though on a minor scale, many pressing business problems in the process of their formulation. They reflect also the opinion conservative businessmen held of Gould whom they considered primarily a speculator and stock trader. Probably through some oversight these letters were later destroyed. This author has photographic reproductions of some letters and typewritten copies of many others.

11. *R. R. Gaz.* The *Railroad Gazette* represents probably the most complete coverage of the affairs of the railroad industry in the seventies and eighties and in the early nineties. This is the

period covered by this study. Its discussions of the traffic problems of American railroads are the best available in secondary sources. Many of its editorial analyses cast interesting lights on significant phases of American railroad development. Its obituary notices on American railroad leaders are also valuable.

12. *Ry. Review.* The *Railway Review* was published in Chicago. Its discussions of the affairs of western railroads were frequently illuminating. The journal's value in reflecting western railroad affairs increased with the passage of time. The coverage was more complete in the eighties than in the seventies.

13. *Ry. World.* The *Railway World* began its publication in 1875. It was a successor to the *United States Railroad & Mining Register.* The *Railway World* in its earlier years supported the views of the Pennsylvania Railroad and of its President, T. A. Scott, especially in the Huntington-Scott struggle over the Southern 32nd Parallel Transcontinental Route in the seventies. During the eighties little is found in the *Railway World* that is not covered in the *Railroad Gazette.*

14. Union Pacific Historical Museum. Papers of the Union Pacific are deposited in the Omaha offices of that road. They have not, however, been made available for public examination. Mr. Paul Rigdon of that road sent the author a number of these letters bearing on Gould. The author expresses his appreciation of this courtesy. These letters are footnoted as "Union Pacific Historical Museum."

15. The *United States Railroad & Mining Register* was ably edited. Its contributions and opinions were valuable in the late sixties and the early seventies. The paper suspended publication in 1875.

Other sources used are newspapers in New York, Philadelphia, Chicago, and Boston, and a number of periodicals. These are footnoted. The most valuable of these periodicals is *Bradstreet's,* which began publication in 1879. A number of Congressional documents were useful, and these, too, are all footnoted.

Contents

MAPS

JAY GOULD

His Business Career

1867–1892

CHAPTER I

Introduction

THE bustling little town of Roxbury, New York, produced in the year 1836 a man who was to disturb the economic theories of this country, and to die, at the age of fifty-six, the possessor of one of the greatest single American fortunes. The youngest of six children, five of whom were girls, he was always soft-spoken, small, and frail. He had one wife, and two daughters, and four sons. There was no whisper of scandal about his private life. Although he loved fine houses, steam yachts, flowers, and formal gardens, he worked twelve, fourteen, sixteen hours a day and had few diversions. How could he have diversions? Once he went to Amsterdam to confer with Dutch bankers and investors. It took him an hour to conclude his business conference; in another hour he was back on his ship, impatient to get home to his family and to more complicated affairs.

Jay Gould, born Jayson, will always be a subject of controversy. Gould has been accused of betraying his friends, but he lived in an age when this was not uncommon. Daniel Drew and Jubilee Jim Fisk might easily have been in the penitentiaries to which some of Gould's friends did go, and to which some of his enemies gaily would have consigned him. On the other hand, he did keep many stanch friends. John Pierpont Morgan, with grim humor, called his (Morgan's) yacht *The Corsair*. Gould indulged in no such histrionics. When he testified, indeed, before a Senate Committee in 1883, he had to be urged to keep up his voice, for he could not be heard.

It will of course be obvious to any careful or even desultory reader that the ethical standards of his time, the business practices, would today scarcely be tolerated. Gould used every stock-rigging device then known, and some he originated or at least improved. Although the convertible bond and the proxy to control companies were by no means unfamiliar, Gould could use them as a dentist uses a drill, or as a butcher uses a cleaver.

The story of the Erie is so well known that the writer hesitates to include it. Yet the Erie was one of his failures. But he was young then, and perhaps he was associating with inferiors. Inferiors? He battled the Vanderbilts and C. P. Huntington and Charles Francis Adams, Jr. He controlled the telegraph business and the Manhattan Elevated, and he tried to corner gold, and came close to doing it. Gould was one of the first to recognize the power of that valuable house organ, the daily newspaper, He owned one, and controlled the financial and editorial pages of others.

Gould was born poor; his father was a respectable failure, but he rarely lacked money from the day he was seventeen. He was a surveyor, as Washington was, and a self-taught one, as Washington was not. He was not at all above making surveys of New York counties which would list the properties of those who could be useful to him, or of writing to newspapers which could help him and buying half a dozen subscriptions. There were financial transactions in his early life, when he was in the leather business, which seem dubious and to need explanation. One man shot himself in consequence of one of them. It may not have been Gould's doing; at all events he seems to have emerged from the debacle of a bad leather market with a substantial stake, and a thirst for greater enterprises.

His life was a progression. He began as a speculator, a stock-market manipulator. At the end, he was building railroads, not with a printing press but with steel, and seeing himself, as perhaps essentially he was, not a pirate, not as a conniving president selling his own stock short, not as a man who was running a road into the ground, in defiance of the bondholders, but as a builder of roads. "I am not interested in eastern roads," he said, once. "I am interested only in roads to the West—I am interested in Mexico."

Gould was scarcely more than five feet tall, with a predisposition to both neuralgia and tuberculosis. How interesting it might have been to see him, had he lived but a little longer, slipping gracefully away from that awkward behemoth, the Sherman Anti-Trust Law, yes, and engaging the great Morgan with his net and trident. The man who loved flowers, who was all his life the close friend of John Burroughs, the man who lived sedately and without much ostentation, and who had the adroitness, the ruthlessness and the splendid courage of the mongoose or the trapped tiger—this was Gould. He was trapped many times. His was no unbroken record of success. His failures were many but when he gasped out his life at last with his children around him, he could laugh at his enemies and perhaps at the gathering shadows, for he had achieved the success which apparently was his goal.

In considering Gould, it may first be useful to think of the time in which he lived. It was an age of individual enterprise. There was little government interference. Business ability had a chance. The local bank was ready to lend funds. A supply of labor was available. The essential thing was to keep costs low. The first to reduce costs was the successful man. There was Andrew Carnegie in steel, John D. Rockefeller in oil refining, Ogden Armour in meat-packing. In the railroad business there was James J. Hill, Albert Keep, C. E. Perkins, J. E. Thompson. These men made quick deliveries, sold dependable products, carried out their contracts—and reduced costs.

These things were not always enough. Open-mindedness and constructive imagination were necessary, too. There was George Westinghouse, who was not merely a great inventor but also a clever businessman, though not a good financier. Carnegie was no inventor, but he knew an inventor when he saw one, and hired him.

The merchandising faculty was also important. James B. Duke had this, and Rockefeller had it, and Marshall Field and Julius Rosenwald. In none of these fields did Gould show any particular ability. The Manhattan Elevated was not well run. The service on his railroad systems was poor. He was no innovator, no quick adopter of new ideas. He was of no help in developing the telegraph except for eliminating competitors—and after he had done that, improvements were fewer still.

Merchandising? There was no need to increase the demand for railway service. People were clamoring for it.

What did the man have, then? To understand his work, it is necessary to sketch briefly the evolution of American business. In the beginning, normally, every enterprise was a means of exploiting a local opportunity. Rockefeller opened a small refinery in Cleveland. Carnegie sold axles and forgings and fittings and bridge sections in western Pennsylvania. Even the Central Pacific was organized to do a local business between California and the silver country in Nevada. These small local companies grew largely by consolidation. At times this was the result of coercion; often it was the agreement of reasonable men.

When a company had many stockholders, the task was difficult. A first-mortgage bondholder, for instance, might have his own view of his own interests, and the second and third bondholders quite another. The interests of stockholders and bondholders might readily be at variance. A small decline might easily eliminate the stockholders' interest. It was not an easy task to buy control of a heavily bonded company with a widely scattered army of security holders.

If the company to be acquired had defaulted in its interest, the question presented was whether control should be acquired through the purchase of bonds or stock. In the years after 1865, when precedents had not been established, the rights of stockholders as compared with those of bondholders were not thoroughly known.

Suppose the businessman had solved the question of reasonable price: he then had to take into account the question of timing, for the price might not last for long. Surprisingly enough, there is little discussion of this problem in economic literature.

Gould's abilities lay largely in the field of corporate negotiation and security trading. At the age of thirty-one, in the fall of 1867, he went on the Erie board. Within less than six months he became both a corporate manager and a stock trader. Sometimes his interests in a corporation were primary; often his stock-market interests were primary, and he used his position on the board to further his stock speculations. In still other cases, he had a continuous interest in both his capacities.

Strictly speaking, he was not a good corporate manager. It was not until late in his career that he made any serious efforts to manage a property. After a short term as president of the Erie, he decided that he was not fit for such an office. After this, he accepted executive positions only temporarily, and usually because of financial necessity. In 1882, for example, he took over the presidency of the Wabash. On the other hand, he declined to become president of the Union Pacific, and he would not undertake the nominal management of his three major telegraph properties: the Atlantic and Pacific, the American Union, and the Western Union.

His great strength was in detecting opportunities to seize control and in his ability to maintain it. If this control led to a rapid rise in security values, frequently he sold out. The sale of his holdings did not necessarily mean the loss of control. He sold most of his Union Pacific stock by January of 1881, but he remained in control for another three and a half years. In 1882 he sold most of his stock in the Missouri, Kansas and Texas, although through a lease he dominated the destinies of that road for another six and a half years.

He was forced into the stock market, or perhaps it is more accurate to say that his earliest interest was the market, and this led him to corporate acquisition and expansion. His knowledge was profound. There is nothing in his environment, his education or his early training that explains this. Nobody knows how he may have learned it. Quiet, soft of speech, he was a secretive man. There were no public agencies to force him to publish any facts. There were no institutions representing security holders to compel him. There were courts and legislative bodies, of course, but these supplied relief only after the event. Judicial reviews and legislative inquiries produced a mass of facts and many curious and interesting stories. They rarely stopped the aggressions of an active businessman, and they rarely provided redress for the injured.

When Gould's activities brought him into public notice in the fall of 1867, he was already a master in the intricate field of corporation finance. He was only thirty-one, but he knew a great many devices, a great many methods of manipulation. He had mastered the complexities of the new banking system; he understood the still greater complexities of the depreciated currency and the gold market. He knew all this so well that he undertook to do what nobody else had done: virtually to produce a scarcity of gold. This meant the withdrawal of currency, deflation of purchasing power, the bankruptcy of traders and merchants, and general economic disruption. All this Gould accomplished.

In addition, he suddenly appeared as a master in the field of corporate expansion. He made a thorough examination of the intricate relations between the eastern trunk lines and their western connections. He must have consulted widely with many men, since he could not have found an answer in any published source.

Operating in his twin fields, corporate relationships and security manipulations, Gould displayed a streak of objectivity, of cold-bloodedness, of lack of emotion. Personal scruples seem to have been lacking in him. If a thing had to be done, it was done. There were legislators and judges to be bribed and bought. Gould outbid Vanderbilt.

The same objectivity was carried out in his personal relationships. He picked his associates carefully. When an ally no longer suited his needs, he dropped him—but he picked up many a former foe. Thus Richard Schell and H. F. Clark, who had opposed him in the Erie imbroglio in 1868, became his fast friends. An example of even greater significance was Russell Sage, who was his foe and afterwards his steadfast business friend. Gould could strike back at any time. He was patient, he was even-tempered, he was cool and calculating—and he picked his time to strike. In dealing with opponents, he honored only the letter of the contract and whenever possible he avoided contractual relations.

To his loyal followers, however, he was a man of his word. He never flinched from carrying out a promise. Even at the cost of heavy personal sacrifice, he would do this. "I never was with a more reliable and more considerate man than Jay Gould," [1] said a great railroad builder, General G. M. Dodge. Many others testified in a similar way. W. E. Connor, the stockbroker who in 1884 stanchly protected Gould's weakening speculative position, looked up to Gould as to one of the most loyal persons he had ever met. Sage could not praise Gould enough for his steadfast loyalty. Sidney Dillon, his associate in the Union Pacific from 1874 to 1884 and again in 1890 and 1891, was another Gould admirer. His operating chiefs: A. L. Hopkins, Solon Humphreys and others, repeatedly expressed their affection for him. E. H. Nichols, a railroad man who negotiated with Gould in several western railroad transactions, told a government investigating committee: "I never knew Mr. Gould to put his finger to anything that was not straight." [2] Isaac Jones Wistar, a distinguished and public-spirited citizen of Philadelphia, declared that Gould was "staunch and true." [3]

In every period of market reversal, when he was long of the market with securities bought on borrowed funds, Gould might sell, although he himself had recently recommended such purchases. He switched his trading position frequently. As a controller of a corporation, he would be on both sides of the market. In combination with other traders, with whom he formed market pools, he took trading positions which were tenable only because of his superior knowledge as a member of the board. To many, such transactions were utterly reprehensible. J. M. Forbes, a typical New England businessman and capitalist, characterized Gould as a "raider by profession." [4] Gould, nevertheless, was not a successful stock trader. What he gained by sharp practice, he frequently lost in a general smash.

His thorough knowledge of the art and practice of corporation finance did not make him popular. He was forever examining charters and leases and mortgages and bonds. He looked constantly for weak spots; he found them, and thus often acquired control. The subsequent rises in price would bring forth an army of enraged former security holders. Then he would sell out at the higher prices, and again they would be enraged. In short, he carried over into the field of corporate management the art and principle of security trading. An investor or speculator may admire a shrewd trader. When such a trader is also a director of a corporation, the holder of securities may well regard him somewhat differently.

Strange as it may seem, many of Gould's financial schemes were sound. He was an advanced thinker in the field of corporate finance, and he set precedents which were later followed by investment bankers and by state and federal legislators.

On the other hand, many of the things which Gould did can no longer be done. In the uncontrolled economy of his day he was a leader. He introduced many methods which now are disapproved. The railroad mortgages of the middle nineties contained many clauses designed to prevent some things which he had done; so do the state regulatory acts, and the Transportation Act of 1920.

As a trader he was not too successful. Although not a business manager, most of his personal fortune came from two large properties which he controlled and supervised: the Western Union and the Manhattan Elevated. He was successful as the operator of only a single railroad: the Missouri Pacific, over which he exercised an intimate supervision.

In the following pages an effort is made to trace the career of this leading trader, businessman, and capitalist in an era of unregulated business competition.

NOTES FOR CHAPTER I

1. J. R. Perkins, *Trails, Rails and War*, 263
2. United States Pacific Railway Commission, Testimony, Executive Document No. 51, Senate, 50th Congress, 1st Session, 1887, 4121, E. H. Nichols.
3. Isaac Jones Wistar, *Autobiography*, 495, Harper & Bros., New York, 1937.
4. Burlington archives, J. M. Forbes to .... Simpson, May 29, 1878.

CHAPTER II

The Pre-Gould Erie

IN OCTOBER, 1867, press dispatches carried the news that Jay Gould had been elected a member of the Erie board of directors. Gould was just past thirty-one, unknown in financial and business circles. However, his election was the beginning of a career that for a quarter of a century repeatedly stirred, stormed and shocked the financial and business world.

The Erie in 1867 was in a difficult strategic and financial situation. Its position was the outgrowth of fifteen years of evolution. The road was conceived as an ocean-to-the-Lakes carrier for the purpose of meeting the market needs of New York City and southern New York State. In this lay both strength and weakness. The state had advanced the road $3,000,000, but by the middle forties this investment was lost. With the further aid of public credit and wide use of private credit, the line was completed to Lake Erie at Dunkirk in the summer of 1851. No railroad up to that time had been built on such a comprehensive scale. Because of political considerations, however, the road was not built in accordance with strategic requirements. Since the Erie was the recipient of public aid from the State of New York, it was considered necessary so far as possible to confine its lines within the state. Despite the existence of sources of valuable traffic in the northern part of Pennsylvania, the Erie as originally constructed closely hugged the southern boundary of New York. Due also to the interplay of local political forces, the line at its western terminus did not reach the important traffic gateways of Erie and Buffalo but only the then relatively unimportant community of Dunkirk. Neither did it reach other important lake outlets. "The truth is," said a leading railroad journal of the day, "the moment the Erie Company [was] out of New York, it [was] out of doors." [1] Finally, the route in southern New York, selected partly because of local political influences, gave the Erie poor grades and made it for many years "an expensive line to work." [2]

The road, nevertheless, had excellent traffic possibilities. In November, 1853, just as its first major problems as a completed railroad were becoming critical, the board of directors issued a reassuring communication to the stockholders. The Erie, according to the management, had no competing water lines for the greater portion of its business. Its resources were "largely increased by the contributions of many tributary roads, which, like the country it penetrates, have had no other direct outlet to market, and it lies in the direct line of the greatest trade and travel which exists on the continent, with its terminus at the focus of that trade." [3] Stressing the Erie's location, the circular pointed out that the lateral tributary roads, except for the three most eastwardly ones, converged from north or south toward the Erie and had no other outlet. Short of the construction of a parallel road, a probability which was "nearly or quite impracticable," there could be no diversion of the business which these tributaries would throw to the Erie. The Erie, concluded the management in a peroration, must receive the business of all lines "without fear of diversion or competition," thus giving stockholders "a guarantee that they will receive an early and ample remuneration for their investment." [4]

These flattering possibilities contained some truth. The lateral roads were there, the traffic was there and constantly increasing, and there were no other through lines from lake to ocean. The New York Central from Albany to Buffalo was then in process of organization and its future could not be foreseen.

The Erie's possibilities were, however, immediately clouded by financial mismanagement, and in 1854 Daniel Drew was appointed treasurer to succeed the much criticized incumbent. Drew was skilled in the art of handling conflicting corporate interests. Shortly after his assumption of office and in return for his endorsement of some corporate paper, he took a mortgage on all the road's property.

In spite of this financial aid, the road remained on the verge of failure. In the face of the panic break of 1857, the Erie was again helpless and on September first of that year Wall Street was "in a state of delightful excitement." [5] The company needed $600,000 to pay interest on the second- and third-mortgage bonds. With the road's mortgage still in his possession, Drew, had he so desired, could have taken possession of the Erie. In spite of liberal terms, the road could make no further loans from individuals, and only at the last moment was it able to secure the help it needed from the banks. The reason for Drew's forbearance was not clear, although the report that Drew had made advances to the company in exchange for a pledge of 5,000 shares of Erie stock, and that he had bought and sold, and traded the stock, affords some clue.[6]

A new management assumed office after the crisis of 1857. It learned that capital improvements had been financed by short-term obligations. The road, because of the increase in business, had found it necessary to make terminal improvements; but the traffic expansion, upon which the terminal improvements were predicated, suddenly ceased late in 1857. The company again needed help, and it accordingly executed a chattel mortgage to its ever willing treasurer, Drew, to secure a six months' loan of $1,500,000. The loan, according to the newly elected president, had "completely destroyed the credit of the Company as soon as known . . . ,"[7] and the road after meeting its September interest payments permitted its floating debt to go to protest in October.

The president, who had criticized the financial practices of his predecessor, made determined attempts to solve the company's financial problems. Repeated appeals made to stockholders resulted in securing funds of less than $30,000 in the face of the liberal offer of $2,000 of fourth mortgage bonds for every $1,000 advanced. The floating debt was somewhat reduced, though Drew's hold on the Erie, through his possession of a chattel mortgage, was not removed. In violation of a provision of this loan, Drew, acting prematurely, initiated receivership proceedings in the late summer of 1859.[8]

The Erie reorganization of January, 1862, was careful of the rights of security holders. The financial structure, which had caused so much trouble, remained substantially untouched. The unsecured bonds, together with the accrued unpaid interest, were converted into preferred stock, and the property was left with a funded debt of almost $20,000,000, common stock of more than $11,000,000, and a new preferred stock of $8,536,000. In the following two years, partly because of war inflation, the road prospered. In the spring of 1864 the able war-time president, Nathaniel Marsh, died. During his administration, the road's traffic had been tripled; a new short line to Buffalo had been acquired; the valuable Long Dock property had been completed; an entrance to the Pennsylvania coal fields had been secured; the floating debt had been paid; and the mortgage debt reduced by several millions of dollars.[9]

Marsh had done his work well. Even now with the passage of time, it is difficult to judge how much of the road's prosperity was permanent, and how much the effect of temporary conditions. In part it came from war-time forces. The rate-cutting wars which had demoralized trunk-line earnings between 1857 and 1860 had ceased, only to be renewed after the war on a larger scale. Another contributing though temporary factor was the heavy flow of eastbound oil traffic from the newly discovered oil regions in Pennsylvania.

The oil traffic first began to affect the Erie's earnings in 1862. Although the Erie did not touch the oil fields, it did connect with the newly completed Atlantic & Great Western Railway,[10] a property that was destined to exert a far-reaching influence upon the fortunes of the Erie, the New York Central, and the Pennsylvania, and which for the next three years loomed up on the railroad horizon as one of its most brilliant constellations. When oil was discovered in Pennsylvania in 1859, the eastern roads had no wholly owned or controlled connections to the west beyond Buffalo and Pittsburgh. Of the three major eastern lines, only the Pennsylvania had taken steps to expand west. Though it recognized the importance of western outlets, it nevertheless hesitated to assume major financial responsibilities in acquiring such outlets. Through its president, J. Edgar Thomson, it had succeeded in extricating one of these western lines controlling a route to Chicago from a serious financial embarrassment. The Pennsylvania guided the road—the Pittsburgh, Fort Wayne & Chicago [11]—through receivership, but later sold the shares it had acquired in the reorganization. Another route to Chicago lay on the southern shore of Lake Erie from Buffalo to Chicago, and was controlled by a number of companies.

Despite the discovery of oil and the resultant increase in traffic, little construction by the eastern trunk lines followed. The decline in business after the panic of 1857 destroyed more traffic than the discovery of oil created. When military hostilities ushered in an extraordinary business expansion, little railroad building took place. Prices of materials were high and the supply of labor diminished by war-time enlistment and the diversion to military production.

One major route, however, was built: it served the Pennsylvania oil region. Promoters had long been at work on an interior route from southwestern New York across northwestern Pennsylvania to the Lakes. By further building and by connections with other roads, a new through route with the Mississippi and Ohio Valleys could thus be established. This route, penetrating the Pennsylvania oil fields, was completed by James McHenry, a successful English businessman and promoter, through the building of the Atlantic. Soon after its completion the road entered into a five-year traffic contract with the Erie.

The new road because of its large oil traffic was immediately profitable, and its oil business was a major factor in fattening the earnings of the Erie from 1862 to 1865. In addition to the oil traffic, the Atlantic's strategic location brought the business of many other connections to the Erie. The Atlantic in 1865 was thus a segment of a route reaching Cincinnati and St. Louis, with connections to Cleveland, Toledo and Erie. It also controlled most of the country's oil traffic. Little wonder then that observers were hopeful for its future. In view of its contract with the Erie, neither is it to be wondered that the optimism extended to that road.

The Atlantic's connection was indeed of the highest importance to the Erie, and Marsh, president of the latter, did not overlook its probable value. Besides contracting to pay the new line a bonus for eastbound traffic, he also made arrangements just prior to his death to procure a large increase in the supply of rolling stock in order to take care of future growth. An agreement was reached—whether by Marsh or his successor on behalf of the Erie is not clear—to supply the Atlantic with $5,000,000 of rolling-stock. The first published reference made to this contract appeared in a prospectus of the Atlantic's second-mortgage bonds, issued in London in the fall of 1864.[12] Early in the following year the London directors of the road listened to a report from an American representative, to the effect that the Erie was fulfilling its promise to supply rolling stock in accordance with the contract.[13]

To carry out this agreement, the Erie was again obliged to borrow, and by 1866 it was indebted to Drew for almost $2,000,000, the loan being secured by 28,000 shares of Erie. The Erie's floating debt now totaled $3,624,000. Informed observers were unable to understand why the Erie could not manage its affairs without continuous borrowings. When, in the fall of 1865, for example, a report spread that the Erie had made a loan of several millions abroad to pay a debt to an unnamed person (probably Drew), surprise was expressed. "It is really remarkable," declared a railroad periodical, "that this road [referring to the Erie], doubled in value by its connection with the Atlantic & Great Western, should flounder around as it does notwithstanding its enormous receipts." [14]

A break in the friendly relations with the Erie soon led the Atlantic to decide on a plan of construction and acquisition for creating a rival route to the seaboard. The London financial crisis of 1866 blocked its plans and left the road with a dangerously high floating debt. In the midst of these financial reverses, the Atlantic was suddenly confronted by a new problem. Its most important business—oil—was threatened by railroad competition, and its monopoly of the traffic was soon lost. By the summer of 1866 the Pennsylvania Railroad had finished its connection via a controlled line, the Philadelphia & Erie, to Oil City. This new route from the oil regions to New York City was shorter than the Atlantic-Erie route. In order to hold the business against this powerful competition, the Atlantic began a program of rate-cutting, thus initiating the policy which had such far-reaching effects a few years later on the growth of the Standard Oil Company. The cuts were reflected in a drop in the average rate per ton on the Atlantic from $3.70 in 1865, to $2.87 in 1866. Despite the fact that the tonnage increased almost 50 per cent, its earnings showed heavy declines.[15] The cutting of rates on oil traffic continued in 1867. In the fall of that year competition between the Atlantic and the Pennsylvania's line in the oil region broke rates from $2.60 to $1.44 per barrel, although later in the year the rates were increased.[16]

Similarly on the Erie the deflation of 1866, accompanied by sharp rate cuts in the first six months of the year, produced reversals in earnings. The road nevertheless, according to the president, was never in better condition to transact any business offered.[17] The investors, however, were not so well pleased. "It cannot be disguised," wrote one observer, "that very great uneasiness prevails in interested circles with regard to the condition of this road." [18] The business decline in 1866, together with heavy fixed charges that had been incurred to buy the new equipment for which there was now little use, as well as the poor physical condition of the roadbed, served to increase expenses in the face of a decline in gross. The company's floating debt again increased and in May, 1866, approximated $3,500,000. The Erie's finances were going from bad to worse. The company did not have funds to pay its employees, and its commercial paper was about to go to protest.

While the Erie was floundering in a mass of floating obligations, accumulated in consequence of its western connections, it was also preparing the way for further financial problems because of its eastern connections. The Erie had no controlled rail outlet to New England, the traffic from southern New England, the most populous part of the area, moving to New York City over the New York & New Haven.[19] In November, 1865, a corporation interested in the building of a line west to the Hudson River—the Boston, Hartford & Erie [20]—asked the Erie for help. Here was an opportunity for the Erie. A New England extension opened up the possibility of a large anthracite movement from northwestern Pennsylvania. However, there was also a risk. The Erie's financial obligations were heavy and additional commitments could not be lightly undertaken. For more than a year nothing was done. The Boston meanwhile applied for aid also from two anthracite producing companies, though this request proved similarly unavailing. It was not until the spring of 1867 that the Boston obtained help. An understanding was finally reached that if the State of Massachusetts lent $3,000,000 in State scrip, the Erie and the coal companies would supply $6,000,000.[21]

The coal companies for some unexplained reason were not willing to extend aid to the Boston. In April, 1867, a law was passed providing for a loan of $3,000,000 scrip secured by $4,000,000 of the Boston's bonds. Shortly after the passage of the law John S. Eldridge, president of the Boston, appeared before the Erie's executive committee with a proposal for an Erie guarantee of $6,000,000 of the Boston's bonds. The Erie management was cautious and was not prepared to plunge; there were advantages and disadvantages. On the favorable side the completed route which would probably give the Erie an annual gross of $2,000,000 was described as most direct, with but few short curves and steep grades. Between the Hudson River and Boston it would cross eleven railroads, thus facilitating the delivery of freight received from the Erie; while it would also bring much western trade to Boston and divert it from the route through New York harbor. Anthracite coal would be carried by a short non-congested rail route, as compared with the relatively circuitous route via Philadelphia and steamship beyond.[22]

There were also disadvantages. The cost of any project, no matter how attractive, may be excessive, and such was the case, not only with the Atlantic, but also with the Boston. To the north of the proposed line was the well-established Boston & Albany, connecting with the prosperous New York Central; the former, with more than half its line double-tracked, with superior buildings and depots, and with a line fully equipped, costing $17,000,000 compared with the proposed capital liability of $40,000,000, split evenly between stocks and bonds, for the Boston.[23]

In view of these conflicting considerations, the Erie's executive committee hesitated. It was prepared to recommend to the board that the Erie should guarantee $140,000 annually on the Boston's bonds for 1867 and also for 1868; subject, however, to numerous provisos: the Boston must sell enough bonds to finish the line to the Hudson River; it must make satisfactory arrangements to pay interest on the bonds until the road was finished; it must set aside enough of its gross revenue to meet the Erie's guarantee, and it must permit the Erie to fix rates and fares on interchange business and on coal traffic moving east from the Hudson River.[24]

Eldridge, in order to force the hand of the Erie and to compel it to come more actively to the support of the Boston, accordingly decided to buy Erie stock and get control. The picture was complicated. Cornelius Vanderbilt, who by this time had almost completed his control of the railroad triumvirate consisting of the New York & Harlem,[25] the Hudson River, and the New York Central, had bought heavily into the Erie. Control of that road would give him a monopoly of all railroad trunk lines entering New York City from the west. Vanderbilt, therefore, conducted a campaign for proxies, and Eldridge joined up with Drew to conduct a rival proxy fight. The Eldridge agent, however, sold out to Vanderbilt in a surprise move.

Gould at the time was, like Drew, a stockbroker. Although much of the Erie stock was held in the names of stockbrokers, the actual owners were others, many of whom were residents of England. They had not transferred the stock to their names, and title was transferred from one buyer to another by power of attorney. The right to vote the stock, since title was held in the name of the broker, was the property of the latter. Although Gould, as a broker, controlled Erie proxies, he did not have enough votes to insure control; but he apparently had enough to make it worth while to Eldridge. Even though Eldridge's agent sold out to Vanderbilt, Eldridge threw his support to Gould. And so, in the midst of these complicated and conflicting cross-deals, a part of the old board of the Erie retired in October, 1867, and a new group was added. In the overturn, Drew was dropped as a member of the board, and replaced by a nonentity; but within the next few days the latter resigned from the board and Drew took his place. What persuasive arguments Drew presented to Vanderbilt to permit the change are not known.

The new Erie board thus elected in the fall of 1867 was presumed to be Vanderbilt-controlled. The public eye was upon Vanderbilt and Drew—for many years, alternately, his associate, and opponent, both in the navigation, the railroad, and the stock-speculating business. Yet the financial press, the newspapers, and the railroad commentators, all relatively uninformed outsiders, were mistaken in their estimate of the controlling personalities. Drew, it is true, was preparing for a new stock-market foray similar to the one the year before in which he had made such a quick profit. Therefore in the battle of injunctions which soon followed, Vanderbilt sought to stop Drew. Vanderbilt's dangerous opponent was not Drew: Vanderbilt had overlooked the ingenious Gould. With all his sources of information, he was not able to detect his major foe for control of the Erie until it was too late.

Gould thus came to the directorate of the Erie at a time when its major western connection, the Atlantic, had gone into receivership. To balance this loss, the Erie apparently gained a valuable ally, the Boston, on the east. The Erie's newly elected president was Eldridge, the very man who was most interested in this eastern connection; in fact his primary interest lay in that property. The finances of the Erie, furthermore, with a floating debt of $6,000,000,[26] were bad. The road also was about to encounter for the first time the competition of a consolidated, singly controlled trunk line from New York City to Buffalo. The Erie's board was seemingly dominated by Vanderbilt, who also controlled the new competitive lake-to-ocean trunk line. Even though the Erie's traffic was large, its earnings were poor, and its property was in a disreputable physical condition. Though the road seemed to have an uncertain future, the Vanderbilt influence promised to enhance its value. Vanderbilt had multiplied the market price of the Hudson River and the Harlem stocks; he might do the same with Erie's. Strong cross-currents were at work, and diverse interests were endeavoring to acquire control for diverse purposes. In this competitive and speculative conflict, Gould emerged as the dominant personality.

NOTES FOR CHAPTER II

1. *Am. R. R. Journal*, June 6, 1857, 361.
2. This was the opinion of W. H. Vanderbilt, who was in a position to know; see *R. R. Gaz.* Nov. 20, 1875, 480, citing the report of the Dundee committee on the Erie.
3. *United States Economist*, Dec. 31, 1853, 198.
4. Ibid.
5. London *Times*, cited in *Am. R. R. Journal*, Oct. 10, 1857, 645.
6. *United States Economist*, April 11, 1857, 405.
7. *Am. R. R. Journal*, Jan. 23, 1858, 50.
8. Ibid., Oct. 22, 1859, 680.
9. Ibid., Aug. 6, 1864, 772.
10. Known hereafter as the Atlantic.
11. Known hereafter as the Fort Wayne.
12. *United States R. R. & Mining Register*, Nov. 5, 1864.
13. *Am. R. R. Journal*, June 24, 1865, 605.
14. Ibid., Sept. 30, 1865, 942.

15. Annual report, Atlantic & Great Western, for ten months ending Oct. 31, 1866, cited in ibid., June 1, 1867, 509-10.
16. State of Pennsylvania, Testimony before the General Judiciary Committee of the Senate, Charges by Railroads upon Freight and Passengers, 1867, 168, 169.
17. Annual report, Erie, 1866, cited in *Am. R. R. Journal*, May 25, 1867, 487.
18. *Am. R. R. Journal*, June 9, 1866, 555.
19. Known hereafter as the New Haven. In 1870 as the result of a consolidation, the name was changed to the New York, New Haven & Hartford. This road will also be known hereafter as the New Haven.
20. Known hereafter as the Boston.
21. Report on the petition of the Boston, Hartford & Erie Railroad Company by the Committee on Railways and Canals to the Legislature of Massachusetts, April 18, 1867, 19.
22. Boston *Commercial Bulletin*, cited in *Am. R. R. Journal*, Nov. 12, 1864, 1090.
23. New York *Tribune*, cited in *United States R. R. & Mining Register*, Aug. 29, 1868.
24. Erie, Minutes of Executive Committee, June 3, 1867, called to consider the application of the Boston, Hartford & Erie Railroad Company to guarantee $6,000,000 of its bonds.
25. Known hereafter as the Harlem.
26. *Commercial Advertiser*, cited in *United States R. R. & Mining Register*, Oct. 12, 1867.

CHAPTER III

Gould Acquires the Erie

ELECTED to the Erie board in October, 1867, Gould seemed to have no important role. To the public, to the railroad managers, and to speculators and investors he was unknown. Although for the previous eight years he had been a stockbroker, he had done little in the financial district to attract public attention. If he had been successful as a stock speculator, that fact could have been known only to his intimate associates. On the Erie he appeared to represent himself only.

Three groups struggled for control of the board. One was led by Eldridge, who was interested in the Erie only as a means of safeguarding his substantial investment in the Boston. Another was represented by Drew, who at that time had little Erie stock, and a third by Vanderbilt. Although Vanderbilt had been a railroad investor for more than a decade, it was only within the previous five years that he had become a railroad operator. His success in the short period was phenomenal. The Hudson River Railroad and the Harlem had been competitors. Prior to their acquisition by Vanderbilt, their properties had been in poor physical condition, and neither had an earnings record to qualify their securities as investments. By 1864 Vanderbilt, partly by a number of stock market deals, including the famous Harlem corner, had acquired control of both roads. The rise in stock values was spectacular. In 1867 he also secured control of the New York Central, operating a line from Albany to Buffalo.

With these three properties under his management, he had a through line from New York City to Buffalo. He then decided to acquire the Erie and secure control of all the main lines entering New York City from the west. Vanderbilt appeared confident of his position. Since Drew owed his position on the Erie board to Vanderbilt, he was presumably his friend. There was no reason why Eldridge, as president of the Erie, should oppose

Vanderbilt. Neither did Vanderbilt recognize any danger from Gould. He knew of Gould only as a stock speculator and believed that he was on the board only to aid his speculations in Erie stock.

Gould, however, unknown to Vanderbilt had already entered into close business relations with both Drew and Eldridge. With Drew he had concluded a joint trading account. And in order to increase his importance as a trader, he had also become a partner in a stock-brokerage house in which Henry N. Smith, a wealthy speculator, was the dominant personality. After Gould's entrance into this firm, its name was changed to Smith, Gould & Martin.

Gould's relations with Eldridge were even closer. Although the facts are not clear, the conclusion is nevertheless suggested that Gould's purchase of Erie proxies with funds advanced by Eldridge was responsible for the latter's elevation to the Erie presidency. Gould's promise to Eldridge of aid for the Boston as a consideration for Eldridge's aid to Gould was promptly carried out by the new Erie board. On October 8, the Erie executed a contract to guarantee interest of $4,000,000 on the Boston's bonds. The Boston agreed that by January, 1870, it would provide equipment sufficient to carry 300,000 tons of coal annually, and to set aside with the trustees for the bondholders revenue from the movement of coal sufficient to pay the interest on the bonds guaranteed by the Erie.[1]

Within a month following the election of the new board, Vanderbilt moved to exercise the power which he thought he had over the Erie directorate. In order to avoid a rate war between the Erie and the New York Central, Vanderbilt proposed a pool. Conferences were held, but due to the objections raised by the Erie, the proposal failed. The Erie contended that in the pool the New York Central wanted too much and offered too little.

Vanderbilt now perceived that he had made an error in permitting Drew to remain on the Erie board. He did not, however, see that his real opponent was not Drew but Gould. Failing to carry out his idea of a pool, Vanderbilt, resorting to the same policy which he had so successfully used with the Harlem and the Hudson River, decided to buy control of the Erie stock in the open market. His operations were secret. Nothing is known of the number of shares he had when in November, 1867, the negotiations for the formation of a pool collapsed, nor of the number of shares he bought from November, 1867, to February, 1868.

While Vanderbilt was thus busy with his plans to buy control of the Erie, the latter began a program of western expansion. In February, 1868, the Erie, forestalling Vanderbilt, reached an agreement with the Michigan Southern & Northern Indiana [2] to build a line to Chicago.[3] This new route would cut off the New York Central's lake shore route. Much of the traffic formerly moving over the New York Central would now move over the Erie; indeed some of the Michigan Southern's stockholders estimated that the new route would quadruple the interchange business of the road with the Erie and the Atlantic.[4]

This proposed arrangement stirred Vanderbilt to action. His experience had taught him that it was sound judgment to capture the enemy, and he decided therefore to take no chances. He would capture the Erie. In February he ordered his representative on the Erie directorate, Frank Work, to write to a leading director of the Michigan Southern to protest the proposed agreement with the Erie.[5] He then sent Work to the court of Judge Barnard to apply, in this and in later court appearances, for a series of injunctions. He wanted Drew enjoined from selling any more stock or convertible bonds and to return the Erie stock that he had sold in connection with his short-selling operations in the summer of 1866.[6] The complaisant judge granted all these requests. The court appearance of Work precipitated a sharp rise in Erie. Vanderbilt aimed the injunctions directly at Drew and the Erie board. He overlooked Gould and his creature—the executive committee. The committee had power to act between the dates of the board meetings, and it was therefore the committee, and not the board, that carried out the broad decisions of corporate policy.

The committee ignored the injunctions and recommended to the board that it be authorized to borrow in order to improve the road.[7] The board then authorized the committee to borrow such sums as might be necessary and the president and secretary "to execute all needful and proper agreements and undertakings for such purpose." [8] An elaborate statement by operating officers, explaining the need for improvements, served to justify the board's action.

The Erie apparently had arranged to sell bonds for the purpose of financing improvements. Appearances however were deceptive. Gould and his associates on the executive committee were engaged in stock market operations, and were selling Erie stock short. Vanderbilt on the other hand was buying. Since the bonds were convertible into stock, the sale of the bonds was only a deferred sale of the stock. It would have been simpler to sell the stock direct, but this method was possible only if the consent of two-thirds of the outstanding stock was secured. Since it was necessary to get an immediate supply of stock, such a course was not possible.

The sale of convertible bonds was, therefore, the only solution. The issue of bonds convertible into stock had been authorized by a state law of 1851, and many roads including the Erie had issued such bonds. On the very day that the board authorized the committee to issue the bonds, the committee authorized the treasurer to sell them and the treasurer shortly thereafter sold $5,000,000 to a broker, with Drew guaranteeing him against loss. The bonds were converted into stock, and the stock sold in the open market. The market in the Erie was active and strong, and Vanderbilt, confident of his strength, had issued orders to buy all the stock offered. The outpouring of this new block of 50,000 shares in a wild market, far from depressing its price, was followed by a rise.[9] There still remained $5,000,000 of Erie bonds authorized but unissued. On March 7 the treasurer sold the bonds and on the same day they were converted into 50,000 shares. Four days before, the court had enjoined Drew from selling Erie stock until he had returned 50,000 shares to the Erie treasury, and the Erie board from the issue of convertible bonds or stock. The tenth day of March was named as the day for a hearing before Judge Barnard. By that day, however, the 50,000 shares of Erie had already been delivered to the purchasers. Gould, Drew and associates had taken elaborate measures to appear obedient to the court injunction.[10]

Regardless of injunctions, the second block of Erie was successfully floated. When this second wave of stock struck the market, Vanderbilt was not so confident as he had been a few weeks before. Though the price of Erie momentarily dropped to 71, it soon rallied on the same day, March 9, and closed at 78. Before the end of the week, however, the price again dropped to 67½.

The sale of this second block of stock in violation of the court injunction was followed by some weird incidents. Vanderbilt, recognizing that the court injunction had been ignored and that he had been tricked, applied for a contempt order. Gathering hastily the corporate records, the books of account, and especially the cash proceeds of the sales of 100,000 shares of Erie stock, the Erie officials sped across the river in a ferryboat and moved the corporate offices to Jersey City. To say that the problems facing both contestants—Vanderbilt in New York and Gould and Drew in Jersey City—were novel and unprecedented, is to put the situation mildly. Vanderbilt's position was critical. His fortune consisted largely of the stocks of the New York Central and the Harlem, and the market for the latter stock was narrow. Since the corner of 1864 trading in Harlem shares was light, in an emergency only a few shares could be liquidated. It is probable that the market for New York Central stock would not have absorbed large sales. The trading and investment community was well aware of Vanderbilt's personal condition. Knowing that Vanderbilt had a large supply of New York Central, investors would not buy the stock except at reduced prices.

Vanderbilt had invested about $10,000,000 in Erie stock. Much of this stock he bought on credit, the loans being in large part secured by Erie stock. The Erie shares soon became partly unacceptable for collateral purposes,[11] and a number of stockbrokers failed. If the banks had eliminated the Erie stock from Vanderbilt's collateral, serious consequences might have ensued, and to save himself it might have been necessary for Vanderbilt to sell his New York Central and Harlem stocks. Such action would have produced a market crash and might have impaired Vanderbilt's personal fortune.

Had Vanderbilt flinched, had he been unable or unwilling to hold the price of Erie firm at or above 70; had he permitted its price to drop to its intrinsic value, probably about 50,[12] the disaster to him might have been irreparable. Vanderbilt did not retreat. The price of Erie was held at 70, and after the initial market shock in March and April, the prices of New York Central and the Harlem were also stabilized.

On the other side of the river in Jersey City the position of Gould, Drew and their associates was equally critical. They had violated an injunction and were in contempt of court. They could not appear in the State of New York to carry on the business of the Erie. The company had issued and sold 100,000 shares of stock illegally. A New York court had appointed a receiver for the proceeds of the sale of this stock, and a conflict between the management in Jersey City and the receiver in New York might make it difficult to operate the property. Though the company was incorporated in New York it could not perform its functions in that state. Its offices were located in New Jersey but it was not incorporated there. This was a defect; but it did not last long. Gould let it be known that the Erie had come to stay. Its existence in Jersey City would be a boon; it would bring in funds and increase the prosperity of both the city and the state. Within less than three weeks these arguments produced their effect. A law was rushed through the New Jersey Legislature and signed by the governor, making the Erie a corporation of New Jersey.[13]

Although the company could now legally do business in New Jersey, it was evident to Gould that its real place of business was in New York City. Since neither he nor any official of the company could return to that community without being taken into court and perhaps sent to jail, it was necessary to negotiate with Vanderbilt. Although Gould recognized that he could do little with Vanderbilt, he concluded realistically that he could do much with the New York State Legislature. In that body a bill was introduced to legalize the issue of convertible bonds. Vanderbilt opposed the bill and his representatives appeared in Albany to object to its passage. The bill was defeated in the lower house, and public-spirited citizens were relieved. The majesty of the law had been asserted and it was believed that the conspirators would be punished.[14] Gould, however, rose to the occasion. Appreciating his danger if the bill were lost, he appeared in Albany three days after its defeat in the lower house. There he was arrested and brought before Judge Barnard in New York City. He was then released on bail and after several contacts with the officers of the law, succeeded in getting sufficient time to complete his work with the New York State Legislature. He had with him a bag full of Erie money. Addressing himself to the efficient expenditure of this money among members of the State Legislature, he made certain that greenbacks flew thick and fast. Precisely how much he spent is not known, the estimates ranging from $300,000 [15] to $1,000,000.[16] Gould himself when asked five years later how much money he had spent to influence legislative or election activities, replied, picturesquely, "You might as well go back and ask me how many cars of freight were moved on a particular day." [17].

Whatever the cost, his success was unquestioned. The bill which had been lost in the lower house was amended, passed by both houses, and on April first signed by the governor. The law made it illegal for the Erie to use any money realized from the sale of convertible bonds, "except for the purpose of completing, furthering, and operating its railroad, and for no other purpose." [18] The issue of bonds and their conversion into stock, against which the injunctions had thundered, was now legal, providing, of course, that the money was used for specified purposes. Looking ahead to the perpetuation of his personal control of the road, and to anticipate further stock market forays by Vanderbilt, Gould succeeded also in inserting into the law a provision which forbade interlocking directors between the Harlem, the Hudson River, the New York Central and the Erie, and another clause forbidding any consolidation or pooling between the Erie and these lines.

This bill weakened Vanderbilt's trading position. Since he could not use the stock to control the policies of the Erie, he was no longer interested in holding any. He was therefore ready to trade with his opponents, and soon withdrew his suits. The way was thus laid for a settlement between the two contestants. The negotiations were lengthy. Drew was simple enough to assume that Vanderbilt's stock could be bought out only by using his own funds. Gould, however, had a richer imagination and a more comprehensive view of strategic possibilities. Though he had neither the funds nor the credit of Drew, he did have that quality which was then more important than either of these virtues. He had an understanding of the possibilities of corporation finance.

He knew that if he did not have adequate funds or credit, the Erie did, and that with the use of the Erie's assets, he could afford to make a proposal which would be more satisfactory both to Vanderbilt and Eldridge, to say nothing of himself.

A settlement was finally made in July, 1868, and Vanderbilt was amply provided for. Gould on behalf of the Erie agreed to purchase $5,000,000 par of Erie stock at $70 per share; payable $2,500,000 in cash and $1,250,000 par value in Boston bonds (guaranteed by the Erie) at 80. The Erie also paid Vanderbilt a bonus of $1,000,000 to induce him to withdraw the suits against the Erie, and Drew et al. Richard Schell, a relative of Vanderbilt's, and Frank Work, Vanderbilt's agent on the Erie board, had lost some money in speculating in Erie stock, and in order to reimburse them, the Erie agreed to pay them $429,000 in cash. During the course of the proceedings against the Erie in February and March, Peter B. Sweeny, high in the councils of Tammany Hall, had acted for a short time, under one of the numerous court orders, as a receiver for the Erie. "There had been nothing for a Receiver to receive, and as a balm for his not having had a chance at the Erie treasury," [19] the Erie paid Sweeny $150,000.[20]

In this settlement which Gould and Fisk later described as a "corrupt agreement," [21] Vanderbilt was given the opportunity to sell part of his Erie holdings. Gould, after having done most of the work in preparing the background for the settlement, was apparently overlooked—but only apparently. In the settlement he received the Erie. Vanderbilt elected two of his representatives, beneficiaries of the Erie settlement—Work and Schell—to the Erie board; while Gould and Fisk appointed themselves to serve on the Erie executive committee. Drew resigned and Gould and Fisk together with F. A. Lane, of Erie counsel, controlled the executive committee.

In the eyes of the law this arrangement had little significance. The directors were to be legally elected by the stockholders at their annual meeting, which would not be held until October. It would seem that Eldridge, the president of the Erie, might have had something to say about the Vanderbilt settlement. Eldridge's primary interest however was the Boston. No sooner did Gould settle with Vanderbilt than he made another settlement with

Eldridge. The Erie agreed to buy $5,000,000 of the Boston bonds at 80 if he would resign as president, and Eldridge accepted.

The Vanderbilt and Eldridge agreements required the Erie to raise approximately $9,000,000, as follows:

1. For 50,000 shares of Erie purchased from Vanderbilt at 70 ..	$3,500,000
2. For bonus to Vanderbilt	1,000,000
3. For compensation to Schell and Work	429,000
4. For "balm" to Sweeny	150,000
5. For purchase of $5,000,000 B.H.&E. bonds at 80	4,000,000
	$9,079,000

Gould well understood that the company which assumed this new burden was in fact, if not in law, a bankrupt. The Erie could not pay its floating debt. Its property was in poor physical condition, and to the already heavy fixed charges it had added the interest on the guaranteed bonds of the Boston—an incompleted road which had slight prospect of earning much to meet its interest. The Erie, however, under Gould's leadership, during the following nine months met all these obligations and in addition entered upon a large expansion program.

Gould's first step was the sale at a loss of Erie stock and the Boston bonds just purchased from Vanderbilt and Eldridge. Gould meanwhile faced an important personal problem. He was president, not by grace of shareholders' votes, but by an extralegal proceeding. Not until October could he be legally elected president. The campaign to insure his success was carefully prepared. Under the legal covering of a change in the by-laws, he announced on behalf of the executive committee, that the transfer books would be closed fifteen days earlier than in 1867.[22] This action prevented a number of stockholders from casting their votes. To make the prohibition against voting by other stockholders even stronger, he secured a by-law to make it illegal to cast any votes by proxy. Although the anti-Gould stockholders had not yet awakened to the situation, Gould took no chances.

He now took a further step. Trading upon the carelessness of the stockholders, he not only prevented those stockholders from voting who were unable to attend the meeting in person, but he also proposed to vote their stock himself. A large number of shares were held by foreign stockholders, many of whom had not taken the trouble to transfer the shares to their names. When

Gould, Drew and associates in March, 1868, converted the bonds into shares, they transferred the stock on the books of the company to the names of two brokers. When investors bought the stock, they did not transfer the stock to their own names. A power of attorney gave them title to the property. Gould voted all these shares in favor of his ticket.

By these devices, Gould, despite his small holdings of the company's stock, was able to control the election. To strengthen further his hold upon the company's management, his eye fell upon the Tammany politicians. The head of the Tammany ring was the notorious William Tweed, who had originally opposed Gould. Gould had previously approached Tweed to induce him to prevail upon Judge Barnard to issue an injunction, but Tweed had refused. When he was informed, however, the day following his refusal that he could make some money for himself, Tweed agreed, and thereupon asked Judge Barnard, as an act of friendship to him, to issue the desired injunction.[23] Tweed later received, apparently without any cash consideration, a block of Erie stock.[24] Tweed, together with Sweeny, his political ally, were elected to the Erie's board in October as part of the Gould slate. By elevating Tweed to the Erie board, Gould also secured the support of Judge Barnard. Barnard, who had supplied injunctions at Vanderbilt's request, would now supply injunctions at Gould's request.

By these means Gould and his allies were elected to the Erie board by a substantial majority. Gould was legally elected president, and Fisk, his coarse mouthpiece, was made a member of the board. Gould also controlled the executive committee, which was the governing body between board meetings, and Gould saw to it that there were few such meetings.

In the space of one year Gould had defeated Vanderbilt, the country's leading railroad man, and Drew, the country's leading railroad speculator. He had acquired full control of the Erie, one of the major eastern trunk lines, and had revealed to Vanderbilt clearly for the first time the identity of his railroad antagonist.

Even though master of the company's destinies, Gould had not yet solved its financial problems. His first task was to raise additional funds to keep the Erie afloat, to meet its operating expenses and to pay its floating debt. In view of the company's financial condition he could find no market for its securities through established banking channels. There was, however, always a speculative market for Erie stock. There may have been no earnings but there were hopes. Though the road could not sell the stock without approval of two-thirds of the stockholders, Gould, in charge of its affairs, could continue to sell convertible bonds. The executive committee had full liberty of action, and Gould dominated the committee. On August 5, 1868, the committee authorized the president to sell $20,000,000 of convertible bonds at prices and on terms he thought best. Between October 16 and 24, after the stockholders had elected Gould to the presidency, the company issued the bonds. They were promptly converted into stock and the stock sold at about 40, its current market price. According to Gould, the bonds were sold quietly by H. N. Smith of the brokerage firm of Smith, Gould & Martin.[25]

Even before these Erie securities were sold, and before Gould was elected president, he was already laying plans for a stock-market foray based upon another idea. He decided to exploit the strategic weakness of the national banking system. Bank reserves consisted of specie and legal tender, both of which were in short supply. The locking up of greenbacks for the purpose of reducing the supply of lendable funds for speculative purposes had been tried a number of times. Withdrawal of legal tender from circulation could be most effective in the fall months. At that time funds were normally withdrawn from New York City to the West to finance the fall movement of crops. The supply of money was thereby reduced and the price of current funds increased. Early in September, 1868, the supply of money appeared to be excessive. Any attempt to produce a financial crisis by withdrawing legal tender and thus accelerate a deflation, was likely, in the opinion of a critic just beginning its persistent quarter-of-a-century attack on Gould, to be temporary and the effect doubtful.[26]

During these weeks Gould and his group were selling the Erie shares which the road had purchased from Vanderbilt, and in addition borrowed more shares to sell short for their own accounts. The price of Erie, despite the rise in the general market, was down substantially from early July.

The money market, as well as the stock market, puzzled informed financial observers, who believed that money would continue easy. In the first week of October, however, money rates suddenly rose to 7 per cent. Monetary analysts now first recognized the fact that securities and national bank notes were being used to borrow funds. The proceeds of loans were taken in legal tender, withdrawn from the market and locked up by the borrower. And the borrower was Gould. The collateral for the loans consisted of property owned partly by Gould and partly by the Erie.

The stock market, however, was not convinced, and for the first three weeks in October prices advanced. Erie rose, too, fluctuating between 47½ and 50; thereafter, from October 20, Erie declined persistently. Rumors spread that the Erie had resumed the issue of convertible bonds, and the stock exchange appointed a committee to investigate. This action suited Gould's purpose well. He could now excite fear and stimulate further sales of Erie. He therefore informed the committee that since the end of the Vanderbilt litigation the road had authorized the issue of $10,000,000 additional convertible bonds, $5,000,000 of which had already been converted into stock. It would furthermore require strong efforts, he said, to prevent a default on the payment of Erie's acceptances due January first.[27] The Erie continued to drop and on October 30 the price reached 35¼. A few days later the selling spread to other securities but Erie remained steady. By the end of the month the truth was revealed. Gould and his group had withdrawn from $12,000,000 to $15,000,000 of legal tender.

The general stock market by this time was demoralized. Wheat dropped twenty-five cents a bushel, and cotton from three to four cents a pound. Government bonds declined 4 per cent in two days, and money rates soared from 7 per cent to 50 per cent, and then to 150 per cent. Gould in a few weeks had thus precipitated "the greatest difficulty which [had] presented itself in the commercial community in regulating the operation of the finances since the organization of the banking system." [28]

In the midst of this panic selling and shortly before Erie reached its record low, Drew entered the market. As a trader in Erie stock he was now an outsider. He had had little experience with Gould and, taking his public statements at their face value, sold 70,000 shares of Erie short at prices not much higher than 40. Large blocks of English-held Erie stocks were also sold. Since it took some time to mail the stock from England, the English shareholders were technically short of the market. In accordance with the rules of the Exchange, they were required to make immediate delivery. They therefore borrowed Erie shares, the loan to be repaid when the stocks arrived. This steady selling by the general trading public, by Drew, and by English sources did not, however, depress Erie any further. Yet pessimism was widespread and money tight.

All this was classical background for the execution of a typical Gould market climax. The funereal Friday gloom was followed by a Saturday financial blessing, for on that morning Erie suddenly shot upward from 36⅝ to 52½. On Monday, Erie, "amid one of the wildest scenes ever witnessed on the Stock Exchange, was run up to 61 in half an hour," [29] wrote the chronicler of the Erie's history, and the monetary stringency suddenly eased.

Gould had closed the trap and Drew was cornered. A man of affairs, long experienced in the intricacies of trading, Drew immediately recognized his danger. Against Gould, however, he was an amateur. Drew had heavy paper losses, and again, as in the Harlem corner a few years before, he refused to abide by his contracts and threatened suit. He asked Gould and Fisk to sell him the Erie stock necessary to deliver under his short contracts. If Gould did not have the stock, Drew insisted, he (Gould) could easily manufacture a supply through the now normal method of issuing convertible bonds.[30]

Gould did not relent and made no concessions to Drew. On the contrary, he picked up valuable information from him. Drew had been in touch with a representative of some English Erie stockholders represented in this country by August Belmont & Co.—a firm which had decided to bring suit against Gould and his associates. The day before their attorneys were to appear in court, Drew met Fisk and Gould privately. Unless he was given some stock to fulfill his engagements, Drew warned them, he would go over to the opposition.

Gould now had inside information. He knew that on Monday morning, November 16, Drew and English stockholders would begin judicial proceedings. On that day the Belmont counsel appeared before Judge Sutherland and asked for an injunction to restrain the Erie directors from issuing new stock or removing the company's funds beyond the jurisdiction of the court. The judge was asked to prevent Gould from doing in November what he had so successfully done in March. The court was also asked to appoint a receiver. Both petitions were granted.

Gould, however, taking advantage of the information Drew had imparted to him the day before, had anticipated the Belmont suit. As soon as Drew left, Gould ordered an Erie ferry superintendent to appear before Gould's new ally, Judge Barnard, early Monday morning and apply for a receiver. The revelations of the applicant probably did not surprise the judge, who immediately appointed a receiver, and the receiver was none other than Gould himself. Barnard on request also enjoined the parties in the Belmont suit from proceeding under their injunction.

Gould had created a complicated situation. The Erie had two receivers and was subjected to two sets of judicial injunctions. Delay was inevitable, a condition agreeable to Gould but not to Drew. Drew wanted some stock to settle his short contracts, but Gould's strategy frustrated his hopes.

Gould's ability in handling these complicated financial-legal problems was finally beginning to be recognized. In the accounts of the Erie incidents that had appeared in legal and lay periodicals, the writers described the work of Drew and Vanderbilt but scarcely mentioned Gould.[31] His discomfiting of Drew, however, brought him squarely to the forefront. His strategy in anticipating Belmont and Drew in the battle of judicial injunctions, in the opinion of a New York financial writer, exhibited "the presence of the master mind which [had] planned and carried out all the magnificent schemes connected with the speculation in Erie. However questionable these schemes, . . . their skill and success [exhibited] Napoleonic genius on the part of him who conceived them."[32]

Gould's strategy, however, was not yet fully unfolded. Two days after he had been appointed receiver, he appeared before Judge Barnard to relate that the Belmont counsel had raised some questions about the legality of the Erie stock issue. He wanted above all to make the stock legal, and therefore proposed that the court authorize the repurchase of this stock with company funds at prices less than par. The request was promptly granted. The judge thus authorized the use of Erie's money to repurchase stock at prices up to $100 a share, sold less than two months before at about $40 a share.

Even this was not the end. Gould moved swiftly from court to court, and soon discovered a federal judge—Blatchford—to serve as the vehicle for the issue of another extraordinary order. Upon application of a small stockholder, he appointed a receiver to administer the $8,000,000 of funds allegedly received by Erie from the sale in October of 200,000 shares of stock, and that receiver again was Gould. It is unnecessary to trace in detail the twists and turns of these judicial proceedings, as they are not relevant to the main issue. The point is that Drew did not get the Erie shares. Instead, he settled with Gould at about 57 or 58. Thereafter the price dropped to about 40 and Drew lost over $1,000,000.[33]

It is clear that Gould had impaired the value of the Erie stock. The stockholders were worse off than they were a year before Gould's acquisition of control. More than 300,000 shares of the Erie had been issued, and, except for some minor improvements and the $5,000,000 of Boston's bonds which were soon to pass their interest, the Erie treasury had nothing to show. Gould nevertheless succeeded in making a case for himself. In December, just before he turned to a series of new adventures, he issued an optimistic statement to the company's shareholders. The Erie, he said, had done many notable things: it had built a twenty-mile extension between Buffalo and Suspension Bridge to connect with other lines, from which it would get an increased annual gross business of from $1,000,000 to $2,000,000, it had built a short line between New York and Newburgh on the Hudson, and it had made a profitable contract with the United States Express Company increasing the compensation of the Erie. The executive committee had also directed the president to sue Vanderbilt to recover the $1,000,000 commission paid him in the July settlement and to force him to buy back $5,000,000 par of Erie stock for $3,500,000. Suits had already been begun against Drew to compel him to account to the Erie for about $1,000,000 of profits made from his lake steamships.

"Whenever the facts are fully known and the public becomes

aware of what is being done to make the Erie Railway the most magnificent and perfect railway line in the country and the pride of the City and State," declared Gould, "then the acts of the present managers will be appreciated." [34] Although the facts in the statement were correct, they were nevertheless facts which were carefully selected. The average stockholder, uninformed of business and economic backgrounds, had neither the experience nor the training to discriminate between important and unimportant matters. Although the facts presented by Gould were accurate, they did not embody the truth. The few improvements to which he referred represented an insubstantial investment compared with the millions which had been raised through stock issues and largely lost almost immediately thereafter; while further funds were lost through stock speculations of Gould, Drew, Fisk, Vanderbilt, Work, Schell, and others.

There was little doubt, however, that the public statement made by Gould in December was satisfactory to many shareholders. Gould had taken over a weak property; he was introducing improvements and would soon make the property profitable. Within the next few weeks he made an equally satisfactory impression upon representatives of the public interest. A state legislative committee, appalled at the outpouring of securities by the Erie, as well as by the Vanderbilt lines, made an investigation. Gould appearing as a witness proved to be "the most intelligent and thoroughly posted witness the committee have had before them." [35] Despite his multitude of speculations, his violations of court injunctions, his buying of judges and legislators, and his manipulation of the country's banking system, Gould was recognized as an able, well-informed, and intelligent business leader. He had severe critics but he also had loyal admirers. Still in his early thirties, he was a factor not to be ignored.

NOTES FOR CHAPTER III

1. Documents, Senate, Commonwealth of Massachusetts, Report of Testimony, Petition of Boston, Hartford and Erie Railroad Co., for State Aid, No. 133, p. 143.
2. Known hereafter as the Michigan Southern.
3. *Am. R. R. Journal*, May 23, 1868, 486-7. On February 18, 1868, the vice president of the Erie presented to the Executive Committee, the formal agreement with the Michigan Southern. See Erie, Minutes, Executive Committee, Feb. 18, 1868.

4. Letter of some Michigan Southern's shareholders to the New York *Herald*, March 3, 1868.
5. New York *Herald*, Feb. 20, 1868.
6. Ibid., Feb. 19, 1868.
7. Erie, Minutes, Executive Committee, Feb. 18, 1868.
8. Ibid., Feb. 19, 1868.
9. The sale of this 50,000 shares of Erie stock in the open market is dramatically described by an observer in William Worthington Fowler: *Ten Years of Wall Street*, 499-502, J. D. Denison, New York, 1870.
10. The steps taken to comply apparently with the injunction in letter, although violating it in spirit, has been described in great detail in a notable contribution by Charles F. Adams Jr. and Henry Adams, "A Chapter of Erie" in *Chapters of Erie, and Other Essays*. This story is based largely on testimony in the contempt proceedings before Judge Barnard. See, especially, the testimony as reproduced in New York *Herald*, April 23, 1868; May 1, 1868.
11. New York *Herald*, March 19, 1868.
12. This was the intrinsic value of Erie according to William Worthington Fowler: *Ten Years of Wall Street*, 501.
13. Trenton *Gazette*, cited in New York *Herald*, March 31, 1868.
14. A reporter for a leading New York newspaper wrote from Albany that the adverse report of the House Committee on Railroads on this bill was a "bright redeeming feature in the stupidly monotonous and forcedly virtuous career of the present session." See New York *Herald*, March 28, 1868.
15. Supreme Court, County of Delaware, Joseph H. Ramsey against Jay Gould, et al., Complaint 24.
16. Complaint of Erie in suit against Gould for damages, cited in *R. R. Gaz.*, July 16, 1872.
17. State of New York, Testimony before Select Committee appointed by Assembly to investigate Alleged Mismanagement of Erie Railway, 1873, 556-7.
18. *Chron.*, May 9, 1868, 587, citing the law.
19. Edward Harold Mott: *Between the Ocean and the Lakes*, 155, J. S. Collins, New York, 1899.
20. For discussion of the settlement, see ibid.; also Supreme Court, County of Delaware, Joseph H. Ramsey against Gould et al., Complaint 26.
21. Phila. *Public Ledger*, Jan. 15, 1871.
22. New York *Herald*, Aug. 22, 1868.
23. This was the testimony of Tweed before the Alderman's Committee, New York *Tribune*, Sept. 22, 1877.
24. The gift of Erie stock to Tweed is cited in *Boss Tweed*, by Denis T. Lynch, 297, Blue Ribbon Books, Inc., New York, 1931.
25. This is the testimony of Gould before the New York State Assembly, 1869, in Investigation of Increase of Stock of Railroad Companies, 51.
26. *Chron.*, Sept. 26, 1868, 390.
27. New York *Herald*, Oct. 27, 1868. Only a few weeks before, an authoritative English railroad journal in the course of a careful analysis of the Erie declared that the road should be an excellent dividend-payer. Referring to the status of the stock as a non-dividend-payer, it observed, "We do not suppose this will long be the case." Herapath's *Ry. Journal*, Oct. 3, 1868, 1022.
28. This is the language of a member of the House Committee on Banking and Currency, 40th Congress, 3rd Session, 1869, according to the *Congressional Globe*, Feb. 13, 1869, 1179.
29. Edward Harold Mott: *Between the Ocean and the Lakes*, 163.
30. *Chron.*, Nov. 21, 1868, 648.
31. See "The Erie Railroad Row" in the *American Law Review*, Oct., 1868, 41-86; "The Great Imbroglio" in the *Atlantic Monthly*, July, 1868, 111-21; "Erie Campaigns in 1868" in *Frazer's Magazine*, May, 1869, 568-84.

32. New York *Herald*, Nov. 19, 1868.
33. *Chron.*, Nov. 21, 1868, 653; New York *Herald*, Nov. 20, 1868.
34. *Am. R. R. Journal*, Dec. 12, 1868, 1248.
35. Testimony of Gould before the Senate Railroad Committee, investigating the over-issue of stocks by railroads, cited in New York *Tribune*, Feb. 6, 1869.

CHAPTER IV

Gould Expands the Erie

HARDLY had railroad men, investors, speculators, and bankers comprehended the stirring events of October and November, than Gould suddenly appeared in a new corner of the business world. Again he did the unexpected, again he appeared as an unsettling factor, again he adopted bold methods to carry out his objectives, and again he stirred up violent opposition to the use of such methods. The three New York and Philadelphia railroad trunk lines to Pittsburgh and Buffalo did not then wholly own or control their western connections. Informal understandings and written traffic contracts regulated the relations between the eastern lines and their western connections. There was little corporate control in the form of stockholdings and interlocking directors. There were four major traffic routes over which business moved between Philadelphia, New York, and the West. A brief sketch of these traffic routes is essential to an understanding of Gould's moves in December, 1868, and in the early months of 1869.

On the southern lake shore, a number of local roads connected Buffalo with Chicago. From Buffalo to Erie, from Erie to Cleveland, from Cleveland to Toledo, and from Toledo to Chicago, independent lines operated. These roads could form a through route and trade with the New York Central, or the Erie at Buffalo, or with the Atlantic at some point west of Buffalo.

To the south of this route lay the Atlantic—the road which had begun operations under such auspicious circumstances. Even though the road in December, 1868, lay in receivership, it had excellent traffic connections, and still moved much of the oil business from the oil region in northwestern Pennsylvania. It connected with the Erie in southwestern New York, and with other roads through which it reached the lines of the Pennsylvania Railroad. A third route, operating west from Pittsburgh, was owned by the Fort Wayne. In 1857 the road became financially embarrassed, and the Pennsylvania, in return for its aid, received more than a million dollars of the Fort Wayne's bonds, and a substantial block of its stock. In receivership the stock sold at about $8 a share, and the Pennsylvania would have had little difficulty in acquiring a controlling interest at this price.

The Pennsylvania's financial managers, however, lacked the imagination necessary to conceive of a railroad system as a national enterprise. In a spirit of commendable prudence the board refrained from expansion, and refused to increased its debt. In 1864, for example, the directors informed the shareholders that they had "kept steadily in view their original reluctance to incur a debt for the construction of their road. . . ."[1] Far from adding to its holdings in the Fort Wayne securities, the Pennsylvania by 1866 had liquidated its entire commitment. The Fort Wayne, meanwhile, had become a profitable enterprise.

Despite a written understanding concerning traffic interchange with the Pennsylvania, the Fort Wayne's management had become increasingly independent. At the height of the war inflation in 1863, the Fort Wayne discovered that the traffic was too heavy for the Pennsylvania to carry away eastbound, and that its capacity for moving this business exceeded that of the Pennsylvania. If, insisted the Fort Wayne management, the Pennsylvania could not increase its capacity in order to take care of these cars, then it would have to seek additional facilities via the Lake Shore route.[2] Aside from its ownership of a short route to Chicago, the value of the Fort Wayne to the Pennsylvania lay in its command of all but one of the entrances into Pittsburgh from the south and west, and this entrance was, strategically speaking, the least important.

The Fort Wayne operated in close harmony with another line—the Cleveland & Pittsburgh—which gave it an entrance into the oil refineries of Cleveland. The company, after an early receivership, was also profitable.

The fourth and most southern route connecting with the eastern trunk lines was partly controlled by the Pennsylvania. From Pittsburgh to Columbus the line was owned by a company incorporated in 1868—known as the Panhandle—as a successor in reorganization to a number of others which had been aided by the Pennsylvania. The line from Columbus to Chicago was owned by a number of other companies. In 1868 these were pieced together and merged into a new company, the Columbus, Chicago & Indiana Central.[3] The promoter of this combination was an Ohio banker, B. E. Smith, a man who in the sixties and seventies was an active figure in the mid-western railroad industry. The road could be used for a Chicago extension either by the Pennsylvania or by the Erie. Smith appreciated the road's strategic position, and was ready to listen to offers.[4]

The Indiana Central, in conjunction with the Toledo, Peoria & Warsaw,[5] offered the Pennsylvania also a short line between the East and the Mississippi River gateways. According to the management of the Peoria, the Pennsylvania in 1868 was about to organize the southern Panhandle-Indiana Central line into a new through route, and to perfect the route it had already spent about $2,000,000.[6] Through the Indiana Central, and via a number of leases and bond guarantees, the Pennsylvania controlled a line to St. Louis.[7]

Through the use of the northern Fort Wayne route and the southern Columbus route, the Pennsylvania therefore had outlets to Pittsburgh, Columbus, Indianapolis, St. Louis, and Chicago. In 1868 it was the only railroad with such connections.

Here, therefore, were four avenues for the movement of through traffic by the three eastern trunk lines: the New York Central, Pennsylvania and the Erie. Gould, in December, 1868, conceived the idea of seizing control of all these western routes. At this time Gould's activities were presumably concentrated on the Erie. The judicial battles over the injunctions and counter-injunctions were still raging, and leading New York papers were devoting columns to the details. To Gould, however, these details were history. Well supplied with funds realized from the transactions reviewed in the previous chapter, he was prepared to battle the Pennsylvania and the New York Central. The Atlantic had been in receivership for more than a year. McHenry, meanwhile, had decided to push his rate-cutting policy. With tariffs reduced to a fraction of existing figures, he believed that he could run so many trains that the track would be almost constantly occupied.[8] To accomplish this, however, he needed the co-operation of the Erie, while Gould, in charge of the Erie, needed the

Atlantic. Early in December, 1868, the Erie made a twelve-year lease of the Atlantic. The property was then in receivership, and to withdraw it from court jurisdiction required $1,600,000. The Erie advanced this amount on the annual rental account, and the receivership was lifted.

When the lease was made, the Erie was burdened with a heavy floating debt. Despite the fact that the New York State Assembly called upon Gould to reveal the Erie's current obligations, he succeeded in avoiding the issue. This debt, he informed the state legislators, was "so fluctuating and uncertain from day to day . . . that it [was] impossible to state the amount with any degree of accuracy." [9] McHenry, the largest stockholder of the Atlantic, was convinced, though he was not in the secrets of the Erie, that "large profits [were] likely to result to the Erie proprietors from the natural development under combined administration," [10] and that the whole Erie traffic would be given to the Atlantic.[11] He even expressed the surprising judgment that the Erie under Gould's leadership had charged operating expenses for capital improvements, and had thereby understated its earnings. If, he wrote, the Erie would abandon, as the New York Central and others had done, "the vicious system which [had] for many years governed the railways of America, of applying revenue to capital purposes . . . then it would be easy for it to fairly and faithfully make large and continuous dividends, . . ." [12]

McHenry, in leasing the Atlantic to the Erie, was convinced that he had prospects of increased returns. If, under the lease, the road earned more than the guaranteed rental, his stock might get a dividend. Although McHenry had hopes, Gould had realities; for he, on behalf of the Erie, controlled the policies of McHenry's Atlantic. With the leased line under his control, Gould had connections with all western routes. He could move in many directions and strike at vital points on almost all of the western routes. Late in December he took a train west. He came well advertised as the head of a group of eastern capitalists with large sums at their disposal. He struck his first blow at the Pennsylvania. The latter had just concluded a contract with the Fort Wayne to send its Chicago business over that line, and the Indiana Central, having thus lost the Pennsylvania's business, was willing to listen to the siren song of the Erie. Smith, president of the Indiana Central, was ready to trade, and quickly accepted the Gould bid for the stock of the road. Since it was agreed that the Erie should only lease the road, the agreement did not require Gould and the Erie to raise any funds. The contract was concluded with the directors of Smith's road to become effective only upon ratification by the stockholders. The Erie agreed to pay interest on the lessor's bonds and a dividend of 7 per cent on its stock.

The lease broke up the Pennsylvania's southern route to Chicago at Columbus, and weakened the Pennsylvania in competition with the Erie. The Pennsylvania management was aroused and forthwith abandoned its cautious expansion policy. Apparently under the influence of the expansionist in its management, Thomas A. Scott, it outbid Gould and the Erie. The Pennsylvania raced to the Indiana Central's stockholders, and before the end of January the latter rejected the lease made by the directors. They accepted a proposal to lease the road jointly to the Pennsylvania Railroad and one of its affiliates. The terms were favorable to the lessor, and the price of its stock jumped from 40 to 90.[13]

That the Pennsylvania acted defensively, without any knowledge of the leased property, is evident from the subsequent history of the lease contract. The Pennsylvania, upon assuming control, found the road "contrary to expectations, to be, to a considerable extent, in an unfinished and dilapidated condition, deficient in depot accommodations, with a limited rolling-stock largely out of repair, and shops entirely inadequate to place this machinery in good order." [14]

The Pennsylvania later tried to avoid some of the obligations imposed by the contract. In 1875 it defaulted on the lessor's bonds, and the company fell into receivership. To a leading metropolitan daily, this default struck "a serious blow at the value of the bonds of every leased railroad in the country"; and the Pennsylvania's attempted justification of the default was characterized as a "flimsy pretense." [15] After prolonged litigation the Pennsylvania finally concluded a contract which made life between the two corporations more harmonious.

While the Pennsylvania was negotiating with the stockholders of the Indiana Central to undo Gould's work, Gould suddenly struck a blow at one of its other connections—the Cleveland & Pittsburgh. The stock of that road was not closely held, and its control could not be acquired by negotiations with one man; a different technique had to be used. His sense of financial ingenuity, as usual, provided him with the necessary weapons. He first bought a large block of stock, not, be it observed, for the account of the Erie but for his personal account. What price the Erie would pay he would decide later. He could not, however, buy enough stock to control the election. The price of the stock was high, and to buy a majority of the stock quickly would probably elevate the price excessively. To get more votes at the forthcoming stockholders' meeting in January, he therefore took another step. There were many stockholders who, although refusing to sell their stock, wanted dividends and price appreciation—not voting power. They therefore sold their proxies. No serious study of the proxy market has ever been made, and even now little is known of the subject. In 1868 proxy selling was general, especially in England, and Gould, in his search for weak spots in the armor of corporate finance, seized upon the proxy market. For a few thousand dollars he secured a large voting power with which, in the language of a group on the Cleveland & Pittsburgh board that set out to defeat his machinations, he could "upset the value of property" in which he had a small pecuniary interest.[16]

At the annual stockholders' meeting of the road on January 6, 1869, Gould was set for his fight for control. He presented a series of resolutions. One resolution authorized a scrip dividend of 15 per cent; and another a cash dividend of 2 per cent on the scrip dividend. Still another authorized the issue of $1,000,000 convertible bonds to be sold at not less than 80; another abrogated the existing by-laws; another appointed an executive committee to make new by-laws, and to perform all corporate actions between sessions of the board without reporting to the board; while another appointed Lane, one of the big three of the Erie's executive committee, as financial agent of the road with the right to hold all of the company's securities and funds without bond; and still another, as a grand climax, appropriated $500,000 to be placed in the hands of Lane to pay attorney's fees and "to be otherwise used as he might deem expedient."

To make matters even more confusing, the majority of the

board as soon as organized appointed one of its members as secretary; and then excluded the secretary from the meeting. When the board adjourned, the secretary was given the resolutions to take with him without placing them upon record. Finally the board resolved, after adjournment, that it would meet again only upon the call of the president and with the approval of the financial agent.[17] Since Gould with his own stock and the purchased proxies controlled a majority of the votes, all the resolutions passed.

But, alas for Gould, he had not succeeded in securing control of the Ohio judiciary. In the state of Ohio he had no Judge Barnard, and against an independent judge, Gould was helpless. An opposition party, headed by the road's president, J. N. McCullough, was immediately formed. The president appealed to the court, and a few days after the stockholders' meeting, the court granted an injunction against the new board and appointed a receiver. The court also enjoined the directors, the executive committee, the financial agent and the treasurer, from performing any official act.[18] Gould was beaten and ready for a compromise. As the first step, his personally selected slate, the so-called "Erie board," resigned, and an executive committee consisting of the presidents of the Erie, the Cleveland & Pittsburgh, and the Fort Wayne, together with Samuel Tilden—the Democratic political figure—was appointed to decide all questions in dispute.[19] Despite resort to court action, and the bitterness engendered by Gould's tactics, the differences between the two groups were adjusted. The compromise board included Tilden and also George W. Cass, president of the Fort Wayne. McCullough was re-elected president, and though Gould was elected treasurer, he was not the controlling factor in the road's destinies. He had no executive committee to do his bidding, but he did, nevertheless, exert some influence. He was able, for example, to induce the board to give the Erie the right to reach Cleveland over its tracks.

Gould thus failed to capture the Cleveland & Pittsburgh, thereby tasting defeat twice in rapid succession. This road, as well as the Indiana Central, controlled considerable traffic. In January, 1869, when Gould controlled both, he diverted traffic from their existing eastern connections to the Erie, thereby swelling the latter's gross revenue. For years the road's gross had stood still, but in early 1869, due to its new western connections, the Erie, according to Gould, brought more freight into New York than the New York Central and the Pennsylvania combined.[20]

The big traffic prizes, however, were not these lines. The Fort Wayne and the independent lines forming the route along the southern lake shore were the major carriers. Since the stock of some of the roads was closely held, it was difficult to buy control of the shore route. One company was controlled by a Cleveland group represented by Amasa Stone and H. B. Payne, Cleveland capitalists, while Vanderbilt controlled another. Gould was buying stock of still another—the Michigan Southern—owning the line from Toledo to Chicago. He was also buying into the Toledo, Wabash & Western,[21] connecting the shore route at Toledo with the rich grain fields of the Middle West.

The corporate destiny of the Fort Wayne, however, was still uncertain; no group had yet acquired control. The favorable relations of this road and the Pennsylvania growing out of the traffic contract in December, 1868, were converted into hostility by the Pennsylvania's lease of the Indiana Central in the following month. The Fort Wayne's management in its annual report for 1868 stated that this lease gave the Pennsylvania "an alternative route to Chicago in which she has a very large sum of money invested, and upon such terms (for the present at least) as must make the officers of that Company very solicitous to augment the business of their new acquisition." Reference was made also to the aid given by the Pennsylvania to the project for the construction of a competitive, parallel line to St. Louis.[22]

Because of these strained relationships, Gould saw an opportunity to gain control of the Fort Wayne. To the Pennsylvania this road was the grand traffic prize of the West, and for some months, according to press reports, the Pennsylvania had been negotiating for some interest in the property. In the early summer of 1868, committees of both roads had conferred, and in the fall an agreement was reached. Cass of the Fort Wayne, however, put the document away in the safe to await his chances for the governorship of the state.[23] The Erie, even before the Gould control period, had also been negotiating. Cass was a shrewd bargainer and Gould recognized that if he desired control of the road he could make little headway by dealing directly with its board or its executives. The stock was widely distributed, much of it being owned in England. Negotiations with the stockholders were likely to be prolonged, and Gould had to act quickly. Gould, furthermore, did not control sufficient funds to buy the stock selling at high prices. He knew the Pennsylvania could outbid him and the Erie in a competitive fight for control. It had already taken away the Indiana Central and could probably repeat with the Fort Wayne. Since the annual meeting would soon be held, Gould had to use surprise tactics and act quickly. He decided therefore to use the proxy market.

His activities in the market did not go unnoticed. In mid-January, shortly after the Cleveland & Pittsburgh imbroglio, the Fort Wayne management issued a warning to its stockholders. They were publicly advised to hold their proxies, and in any event, to give them only to proper parties; as, "from present appearances, a desperate attempt [will] be made by other parties to wrest control of the road by the cheap method of purchasing proxies." [24]

By mid-February Gould was prepared. He had enough proxies to insure control.[25] Both the Fort Wayne and the Pennsylvania managements now sensed the danger, and both recognized their mutual interest. The Pennsylvania without the Fort Wayne might lose its most valuable Chicago connection, and suffer from new competition in the rapidly growing Pittsburgh area. Through traffic moving east over the Fort Wayne to Philadelphia might thereafter move over the Erie to New York. The Fort Wayne was originally laid out to connect with Philadelphia, and only about 10 per cent of its profits came from its New York traffic.[26] The capture of this road by the Gould-Erie group would substantially increase the Fort Wayne business moving to New York.

Cass of the Fort Wayne had met Gould on the battlefield of the Cleveland & Pittsburgh, and he did not want him to exercise any control over his road. The Fort Wayne was built to serve the state of Pennsylvania, and did not want its freight diverted to New York City.

The battle was soon joined. Cass, as well as Scott of the Pennsylvania, had assets of which Gould knew little. Though Gould had some influence in the New York Legislature, when compared with that of Cass and Scott of the Pennsylvania Legislature, it was relatively slight. Scott's position is well illustrated in an apt story. A member of the legislature of Pennsylvania, it was reported, once rose and moved to adjourn—if Scott had no more business to transact.[27] Such was the strength of the opposition which Gould had overlooked.

When in early February it became clear that Gould, through the use of the proxy market, had secured enough votes to elect a new board, Cass took the case to Harrisburg. He and probably Scott, also, pointed out that the capture of the Fort Wayne by the Erie group would divert business from Pennsylvania to New York. These and other arguments were persuasive, and in thirty-four minutes a bill designed to prevent Gould's control of the Fort Wayne passed both the House and Senate, and was signed by the Governor. The bill provided for four classes of directors of the Fort Wayne, and for the election of only one-fourth of the board each year.[28]

Gould was thus again defeated, though he was, as one observer expressed it, "outwitted, but not subdued." [29] Early in April he renewed an arrangement with the Michigan Southern—the road from Toledo to Chicago—designed to give the Erie access to Chicago. This was a renewal of the threat to the integrity of Vanderbilt's Chicago-Buffalo south shore route. Vanderbilt recognized the threat and tried to gain control of the Michigan Southern. A large interest in the road was held by LeGrand Lockwood, treasurer of the company, and a Gould ally. By the summer the shore lines were merged into a new company—the Lake Shore & Michigan Southern,[30] and Gould and Lockwood had entered into an understanding looking forward to a union of the Lake Shore with the Wabash in which Gould had a large interest.[31]

It was the gold panic of September which defeated this combination. The gold speculation, which has generally been interpreted as a Gould success, was in fact a calamity to Gould. One of its immediate effects was a stock-market shake-out which forced Lockwood, one of the leading Lake Shore stockholders, to sell his stock. It was Vanderbilt, the businessman with funds, and not Gould, the speculator without funds, who bought the distressed stock. Through this speculative windfall, Vanderbilt acquired control of the Lake Shore.

Gould had thus lost his battle for western outlets. The northern route had been captured by Vanderbilt, and the southern by the Pennsylvania. Though Gould had failed to acquire the third route, the Fort Wayne, he continued negotiations with Cass to use the road for a Chicago outlet for the Erie. So long as the Fort Wayne remained independent, there was hope that it might be induced to do business with the Erie, at least on equal terms with the Pennsylvania.

The Pennsylvania, as the months rolled by in 1869, discovered that the southern route via Columbus, despite newspaper and trade reports to the contrary, did not meet its needs. Aware as it was of the competition which an eastward extension of the Fort Wayne would create, it entered into negotiations for control of that road. The bargaining was hard and the terms stiff, but the Pennsylvania, having learned the disadvantages of excessive prudence, made up its mind to acquire the property. On the Fort Wayne stock which the Pennsylvania could have secured at nominal prices seven or eight years before, it was now obliged to guarantee dividends of 12 per cent. While the Pennsylvania agreed to pay only 7 per cent, the Fort Wayne paid a stock dividend in an amount sufficient to make the guarantee equal to 12 per cent upon the amount outstanding before the payment of the stock dividend.

The exhibition of childlike faith in the written pledged word of connecting properties was a policy which the Pennsylvania now abandoned. Gould and Vanderbilt were setting the tone for railroad policy. Local properties, prudently built, carefully financed, and slowly expanded within the limits of gradual increase in earnings, had been parts of a sound corporate policy. This policy was now abandoned. The risks of rapid, even promiscuous expansion were great, but the risks of slow, "sound," and "careful" expansion, as legitimate and useful as this policy might be in theory or in hindsight perspective, was one which no well-balanced trunk line could afford to follow. The Pennsylvania management, in reversing its policy, became one of the wonders of the railroad world. It expanded in all directions, almost regardless of cost. By lease contracts it acquired an outlet to New York City and many essential connections on the west, including not only the Fort Wayne, but the Cleveland & Pittsburgh as well. It built new lines, especially one in western Michigan known as the Grand Rapids & Indiana. It acquired substantial holdings in the old South, and it seemed for a time that it was about to become the leading trunk line in that region. Many of the controlled lines were unprofitable and did not earn their keep for years. Thus Gould, with hardly more than fifteen months of trunk-line railroad experience, had forced this revolutionary change of policy on two of the dominant railroads of the nation.

He accomplished little, however, for the Erie. His inability to capture control of any of the western connections made the lease of the Atlantic unprofitable. Early in April, 1869, therefore, he proceeded, without consulting McHenry, to change the terms of the lease. The lease had guaranteed the payment of interest on the Atlantic's bonds. The Erie proposed to change the coupons on some of the latter's bonds for the first-mortgage bonds of the Boston.[32] The bondholders rejected the offer and the company was returned to receivership. Two receivers were appointed and, strange to say, one of them was—Gould.

Gould as receiver could operate the Atlantic for the benefit of the Erie and pay no rent. Gould recognized that this was temporary, and that soon the Atlantic's bondholders would insist upon the cancellation of the lease. Early in June, 1869, an association of the company's stockholders let it be definitely known that the Erie "must either fulfil the conditions of the lease or give up possession of the Atlantic line." [33] Gould did neither. In fact he had a bill introduced into the New York Legislature to authorize consolidation of the Erie and the Atlantic. By the end of July he and McHenry had made an agreement by which the Atlantic's property would be sold under foreclosure to a new company, and thereafter leased to the Erie.[34] The bondholders of the Atlantic refused to support McHenry. More court battles ensued, and after a stirring battle between Gould and the Atlantic's security holders, the road was finally released to the Erie on condition that it work the line at cost until the foreclosure and sale of the lessor's property.

The Atlantic was therefore held in the interest of the Erie as a pawn in the expansion game of Gould. In this game, Gould and the Erie had been effectively checked and by 1870 the road had lost its struggle for westward connections. It was now stra-

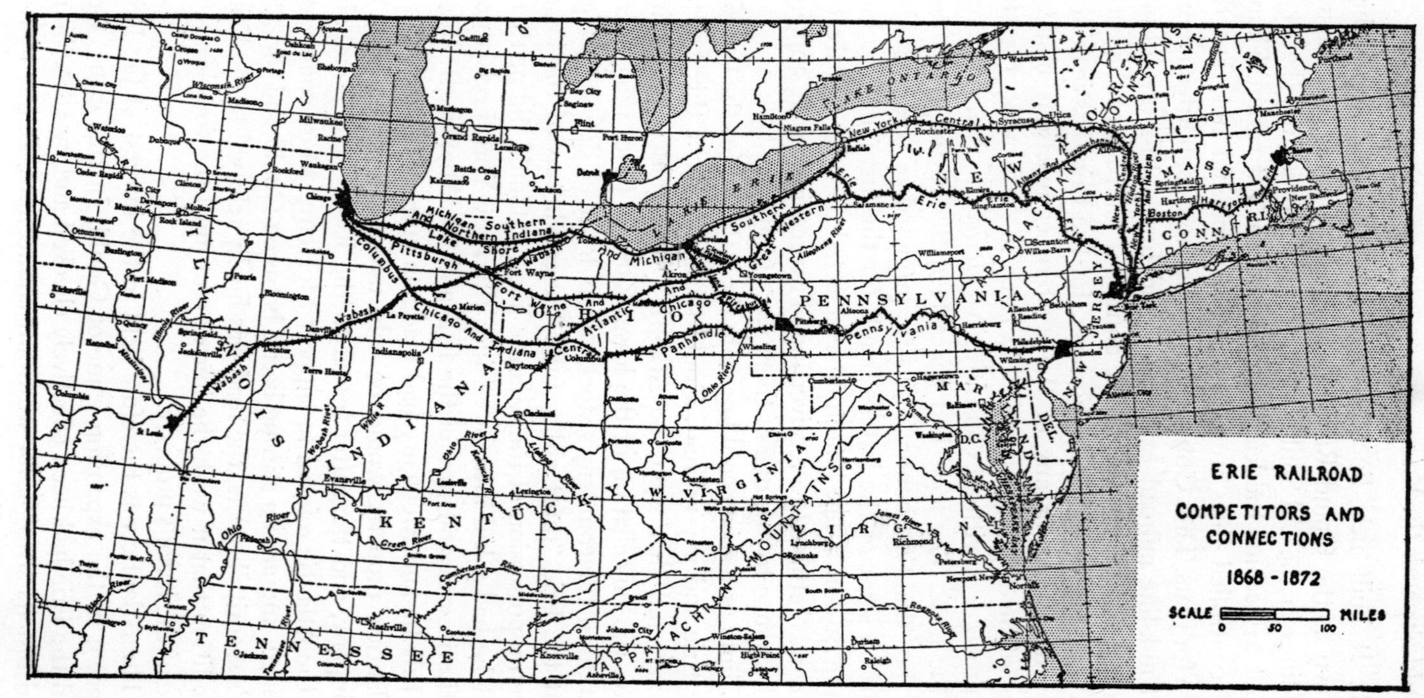
ERIE RAILROAD
COMPETITORS AND CONNECTIONS
1868 - 1872
SCALE
0
50
100
MILES
New York Central
Erie
Southern
Great Western
Michigan Southern And Northern Indiana
Lake Shore
Michigan
Pittsburgh Fort Wayne And Chicago
Columbus Chicago And Indiana Central
Atlantic And
Panhandle
Pennsylvania
Wabash
Albany And Susquehanna
New York And Harlem
Boston Hartford And Erie
PENNSYLVANIA
NEW JERSEY
NEW YORK
OHIO
INDIANA
ILLINOIS
KENTUCKY
W. VIRGINIA
VIRGINIA
TENNESSEE
MARYLAND
DEL.
CONN.
MASS.
R.I.
LAKE ERIE
LAKE ONTARIO
APPALACHIAN MOUNTAINS
Chicago
St Louis
Detroit
Buffalo
Pittsburgh
Philadelphia
New York
Cleveland
Toledo
Fort Wayne
Columbus
Indianapolis
Akron
Youngstown
Rochester
Syracuse
Utica
Albany
Schenectady
Binghamton
Elmira
Salamanca
Harrisburg
Altoona
Camden
Boston
Hartford
Springfield
Providence
Washington
D.C.
Baltimore
Richmond

tegically weaker than ever. Extending only to the Lake Erie ports, it was flanked on the north by the Vanderbilt lines and on the south by the Pennsylvania's. The Atlantic, the Erie's single western outlet, was in receivership; and its lease of that road was contingent upon its remaining in receivership. After reorganization the Atlantic would become an independent property, open upon equal terms to all of its connections. Despite the individual brilliance of his moves, Gould had failed. He had also lost to Vanderbilt. In this case his fondness for grand speculation had cost him the loss of the rich traffic prize in the form of the Lake Shore route.

In both cases he failed because, like conquering generals from time immemorial, he had started a battle with limited resources. Many aspiring conquerors have lost campaigns because of limited manpower and tools to finish their task. Gould had lost his campaign because of the limited funds of the Erie. The wonder is not that he lost the struggle for connections, but that, despite his limited resources, he even conceived the idea that he could possibly win. Though he lost the battle for the Erie, his influence on the railroad development of the country was permanent and far-reaching.

NOTES FOR CHAPTER IV

1. Annual report, Pennsylvania, 1863, 15.
2. Fort Wayne, report of superintendent, 1863, cited in *Am. R. R. Journal*, April 30, 1864, 437.
3. Known hereafter as the Indiana Central.
4. For details on the Columbus, Chicago & Indiana Central, see Logansport *Pharos*, cited in *Am. R. R. Journal*, Feb. 8, 1868, 145-6; and *Am. R. R. Journal*, April 25, 1868, 390-1.
5. Known hereafter as the Peoria.
6. Annual report, Toledo, Peoria & Warsaw, 1867, cited in *Am. R. R. Journal*, May 16, 1868, 462-3.
7. Ibid., Sept. 5, 1868, 847; Phila. *North American*, May 21, 1869, and July 8, 1869.
8. *R. R. Record*, Dec. 17, 1868, 505.
9. *United States R. R. & Mining Register*, March 27, 1869.
10. Ibid., March 13, 1869.
11. This statement was made in a message from New York to London after the lease of the road. See Herapath's *Ry. Journal*, Dec. 12, 1868, 1266.
12. Letter of James McHenry to the London *Times*, Feb. 15, 1869, cited in *United States R. R. & Mining Register*, March 13, 1869.
13. New York *Tribune*, Feb. 25, 1869. For details on the lease contract, see *Anglo-American Times*, London, cited in *United States R. R. & Mining Register*, Feb. 6, 1869; *Am. R. R. Journal*, Feb. 6, 1869, 149; and *The Road*, Feb. 15, 1875, 18.

14. Annual report, Pennsylvania, 1869, 17.
15. New York *Tribune*, April 5, 1875.
16. Ibid., Jan. 14, 1869.
17. *United States R. R. & Mining Register*, Jan. 16, 1869.
18. Ibid.
19. State of New York, Testimony before Select Committee appointed by Assembly to investigate Alleged Mismanagement of Erie Railway, 1873, 352-6.
20. State of New York, Assembly, 1869. Investigation of Increase of Stock of Railroad Companies, 57, Gould.
21. Known hereafter as the Wabash.
22. Annual report, Fort Wayne, 1868, cited in *Am. R. R. Journal*, April 3, 1869, 372.
23. New York *Tribune*, Feb. 28, 1869.
24. Ibid., Jan. 16, 1869.
25. *United States R. R. & Mining Register*, Feb. 13, 1869.
26. Phila. *North American*, Feb. 3, 1869.
27. This story was referred to by Chairman Tillman of a Congressional Committee investigating a strike on the Philadelphia & Reading. See Phila. *Press*, Feb. 18, 1888.
28. *Anglo-American Times*, cited in *United States R. R. & Mining Register*, Feb. 6, 1869; March 20, 1869; New York *Tribune*, Feb. 25, 1869; Phila. *North American*, Feb. 4, 1869.
29. New York *Tribune*, Feb. 25, 1869.
30. Known hereafter as the Lake Shore.
31. New York *Tribune*, Aug. 21, 1869; Oct. 14, 1869; Oct. 28, 1869; *Am. R. R. Journal*, Aug. 28, 1869, 979.
32. *Chron.*, April 10, 1869, 468.
33. London *Daily News*, cited in Phila. *North American*, June 16, 1869.
34. Erie, Minutes of Executive Committee, July 31, 1869.

CHAPTER V

Gould Manages the Erie

IMPORTANT as the problems of expansion were, it was still necessary to manage the day-to-day operations of the Erie. To accomplish this task satisfactorily, even though Gould and his associates had few Erie shares, a close control of the road's management was indispensable. The policies that Gould adopted to make this possible aroused storms of criticism and condemnation. A representative of the English Erie shareholders, for example, in referring to some Gould move in the courts, observed that this action appeared to him "to be an outrage on private rights perpetrated in the name of the law, such as has no parallel in modern times in any civilized country in the world." [1] This statement, although written in the heat of a stirring controversy, had some substance of truth. Control was so ingeniously arranged and so comprehensively executed, that Gould could and did ignore the views, to say nothing of the rights, of the stockholders, and resisted for almost his entire administration the efforts of city, state and federal courts to unseat him. In October of 1868 he surrounded himself on the Erie directorate with two leading Tammany politicians, Tweed and Sweeny, and secured an influence in the state courts by granting Judge Barnard a free gift of a liberal amount of Erie stock. He also required every member of the board either to sign a pledge to support his policies or to resign.[2] To prevent interference, he arranged with his Tammany associates to pass a bill so that at each shareholders' annual meeting only one-fifth of the board would be elected. This classification, Gould informed the Erie shareholders in all seriousness, probably would "secure to the property a responsible, experienced and intelligent management, and be the means of preventing in the future the sudden changes in the policy of this magnificent railway, peculiar to it in the past while it was a mere creature of Wall Street speculation." [3]

Thus protected, Gould did not find it necessary to hold any board meetings. In May, 1869, the English stockholders who had bought so much of the stock at high prices organized with the hope of transferring the stock to their names, thereby securing representation on the board. Gould was concerned over this assertion of independence. At the 1869 annual meeting, therefore, new members were elected who more than ever made the board a Gould rubber stamp. One member was an assistant treasurer of the Erie, another the father of the transfer clerk and himself an Erie employee, another the secretary of the company, another its supply agent, and still another an employee of the Fisk-controlled Narragansett Steamship Company.[4]

Here was an almost unassailable combination. Gould controlled the board, and even if he owned none of the stock, his hand-picked board could not be supplanted for five years. Though the stockholders owned the stock, Gould had the votes. In 1869 the stockholders began a long struggle to compel Gould to allow them to vote. Unfortunately they labored under a heavy handicap. Gould owned a judge, and the early battles were therefore decided in Gould's favor. Tammany Hall, furthermore, controlled the law-making bodies and its leaders served on the Erie board. Gould, however, was not satisfied that the Tammany influence was sufficient to block adverse legislation. To make certain that hostile laws would not be passed, he engaged legislative agents and spent a "good deal" of money in electing "friendly" men. Money so spent, said Gould, was well "invested."[5]

Even with the development of corporate law and practice over the following eighty years it would be difficult to conceive of a more workable combination to perpetuate the control of a corporation with thousands of shareholders, in the hands of a small group, in the face of opposition of the bulk of the shareholders. Modern corporations, it is true, hold their control by the right of proxy freely granted to the officials on the basis of confidence in their management. In this case, however, neither the approval of the stockholders nor the grant of their proxies was essential. The English shareholders soon learned that any stocks which they delivered for transfer could and would be seized by the controlling clique.

The property which Gould took over in the fall of 1868 did

not in the three and a half years of his incumbency, upon any proper basis of accounting, earn its interest charges. In charge of this financial derelict, he was able nevertheless in the opening weeks of 1869 to make his drive to capture the western connections. By February the Pennsylvania had stopped him, and by May it had captured control of the lines operating west from Pittsburgh. The south shore route from Buffalo to Chicago was, however, still open.

In order to use that route for the benefit of the Erie, Gould conceived the idea of acquiring a controlling interest in the Wabash and of sending its business over the Lake Shore. The traffic of the former was a grand prize. It could be sent east via Toledo over the Lake Shore or over other connections. Gould planned to unite the two roads, and thus organize a through route between New York, Chicago, and the Mississippi River. Such a combination would block the Vanderbilt-Chicago-New York City route via the Lake Shore and make the Erie a strong competitor for western business.

The initial movement made by Gould to carry out this proposal was in the stock market. By August, 1869, he had bought almost 12,000 shares, and the Lake Shore 15,000, making a total of about 27,000 out of 75,000 outstanding. It is probable, furthermore, that some large stockholders of the Lake Shore also bought heavily into the Wabash.[6]

By the summer of 1869, with the business and earnings of the Wabash rising, Gould's plan of consolidation was about to be consummated. By early August, when he was elected to the Wabash board, the consolidation of the two roads was accepted in railroad circles as a fact.[7] Concurrently with this decision, an agreement was reached with the Erie to lay an extra rail on its line between Buffalo and New York City in order to facilitate the interchange of business between its broad-gauge line and the Lake Shore's narrow-gauge line. It was also proposed that the Erie issue bonds to finance the construction of a third rail.[8]

Gould had thus momentarily achieved the realization of his project for a through western connection of the Erie. The agreements had been made between the boards of directors and some of the leading stockholders, and could be made final only after approval of the stockholders.

In carrying out this project Gould was obliged to carry a heavy financial load. Though he had pledged at least 11,900 shares of Wabash as margin for a bank loan,[9] he did not hesitate to assume additional responsibilities. Presumably to strengthen the position of the Lake Shore-Wabash project in Pittsburgh, he bought 64,000 Cleveland & Pittsburgh shares, which he deposited with a bank as collateral for another loan. It is not clear whether the stock was bought and the loan made by Gould personally or by the Erie.[10]

To increase the price of Wabash stock, Gould took steps to increase its eastbound wheat traffic. This move in turn led him to the wheat export market. If the wheat were used domestically probably little would flow eastbound over the Lake Shore, but if it could be exported, both the Lake Shore and the Erie would receive a long haul. To stimulate exports, Gould was led to think in terms of speculation on a scale of grandeur rarely equaled in American financial history. Foreign merchants paid for American wheat in gold. If the value of the American dollar in terms of gold could be weakened, foreigners would buy more American wheat. No railroad, no individual and no government had control over the price of gold; its price was determined in the open market.

Gould nevertheless conceived the idea that he could raise the price of gold. The country had suspended specie payments and currency was not freely exchangeable for gold. There was a price for gold just as there was a price for any other commodity. In transactions within the country, national currency known as greenbacks were used in settlement of contracts. The national law, however, did not operate abroad, and since foreign trade was therefore conducted in terms of gold, foreign merchants were necessarily interested in the price of gold. To facilitate their operations, a gold market had been established.

Even though international operations were conducted in gold, the American producer exporting cotton, corn or wheat, for example, required payment in domestic currency. The merchant serving as middleman between the American seller and the foreign buyer sold his merchandise for gold. Normally two weeks elapsed between the sale of the goods by the American producer to the American merchant and the receipt of gold by the merchant from the foreign importer. In this period, needed to assemble the goods at the port of export, to complete the bill of lading and to arrange the necessary letters of credit, a drop in the price of gold might cause losses to the American merchants. Prudent merchants, to protect their margin of profit, borrowed gold and sold it on the open market.

To facilitate these operations a reasonable market supply of gold was required. Since interest on government bonds and customs dues was payable in gold a large amount of gold was held in the federal treasury. If a substantial part of the gold outside of the treasury could be controlled by one group and lent to the merchant short sellers, that group could victimize the business community by bidding up gold in the face of frantic buying by businessmen who had sold gold short. To accomplish this successfully, however, the supply of gold controlled by the Treasury must during the period of operations be kept out of the open market.

On the basis of economic and financial conditions, such an operation in the summer and fall of 1869 had little promise of success. The trend of gold was downward. In the summer of 1869 gold was selling at about 135 and many people familiar with existing conditions believed that the price would drop to 120. Prior to 1869 exports of merchandise had been declining. In the spring of 1869, due to large exports from the good American crop, the trend began to turn, and the outward movement of gold dropped sharply. "Everybody," wrote an observer in a leading financial monthly [11] in the summer of 1869, "believed in lower gold prices," while a financial weekly declared that because of the better credit standing of the government, the gold premium would "permanently range at a lower level." [12] Trade and psychological factors combined to produce a feeling of confidence in the value of the currency. Merchants sold gold freely and speculators added their contribution.

Gould, however, was thinking things over. He believed it was possible to create a scarcity of gold, just as a year earlier he had produced a scarcity of legal tender. Though he had ample banking credit in Wall Street, he decided to assure himself an even better line. He therefore bought some stock of the Tenth National Bank. Logically speaking, a bank is a curious mechanism:

What a person can *not* do, a bank can do. A bank in 1869, for example, could multiply a dollar of its assets by four or five. Gould more than understood the possibilities; he decided in fact to surpass them. He would either draw checks against nonexistent assets which the bank for a while would courteously tolerate as an "overdrawn" account, or he could ask the bank to "certify" checks against assets which he would deposit later. How much "later" was not clearly specified, but perhaps enough later to enable him to complete his transactions and to harvest his profit. And in an emergency there was no reason why he could not use the Erie credit for his own personal purposes.

He could not, on the other hand, fight off the government of the United States, and it was therefore essential that the Treasury's gold be kept off the market. In early summer, 1869, Gould quietly began his gold-buying campaign. He bought steadily, though owing to the large supply the price did not rise. The Secretary of the Treasury was buying government bonds and selling gold. During the spring he sold $1,000,000 gold weekly, and in July $3,000,000.[13] The price of gold fell to 138, and in late August to 131. With this weakness in the gold market came weakness in wheat, and wheat prices declined 25 per cent. Traders refused to buy and grain receipts at ports dropped sharply.

In order to increase the traffic strength of the Erie at its eastern end, Gould now decided to acquire control of a newly completed road—the Albany & Susquehanna—which furnished access to the anthracite market of eastern New York and southern New England. Shortly before the road was completed in January, 1869, the stock was selling at about twenty-five cents a share. A large block was then owned by Joseph Ramsey, president of the road. The Erie had no stock ownership in the company. In an effort to gain control, the Erie managers quietly bought a large amount of stock held by cities along the line. Then followed a number of bold maneuvers in the courts, with a view of placing the road in receivership and seizing control through the instrumentality of a complaisant judge. The scheme was admirably conceived and its execution was carried out under dramatic circumstances.[14] The opposition, however, proved to be unusually stubborn. Ramsey, raised in the school of hard railroad experience, met force with force. In August the road was in receivership, and the battle for control between Gould and Ramsey was still on.

Early September found Gould in the midst of a combined stock market-gold-railroad-control campaign of spectacular proportions. If he could force the merchants and traders who were short of gold to cover; if he could advance the price of gold to about 150 and keep it there for a number of weeks, his grand speculation had some chance of succeeding. The volume of export wheat over the new through route would increase. The Lake Shore stockholders who owed no allegiance either to him or Vanderbilt would follow Gould's lead and approve the consolidation with the Wabash. The Erie's traffic would be increased and its strategic position strengthened. The road would control a line from the grain fields of Illinois and Indiana and from the city of Chicago to New York City and to the large markets of eastern and central New York and of southern New England.

To achieve all this it was necessary that the price of gold be advanced. If the price should fall Gould would lose in his gold speculations and, what was probably even more important, in the stock market. Since his stocks had been bought on margin, a price decline would eliminate his margin and lead to their loss. To save himself, it might even be necessary to sell his Wabash and his Albany & Susquehanna holdings. Such an eventuality would probably defeat the proposed Wabash-Lake Shore consolidation.

In late August and early September, however, the price of gold did not move up. In order to advance the price it was necessary, first, to buy more gold. Gould's resources being insufficient, he took Fisk into his confidence and Fisk became a partner. Beyond all, however, it was essential before he or Fisk bought more gold that the Treasury should not sell. In order to assure himself of the government's view on this subject, he decided to make approaches to the President of the United States, and to this end he struck up a friendship with a relative of the President, Abel R. Corbin, a brother of Mrs. Grant.

Gould urged upon the President the desirability of raising farm prices, then as always a popular policy. After some hesitation, the President seemed to agree: at least, so thought Gould. He believed the way had been cleared—that the Treasury would not throw its gold on the market, and early in September he and Fisk sharply stepped up their scale of gold buying until they had acquired enough to control the market. They lent so much gold to merchants and other short sellers that the short interest in gold grew to "enormous" proportions.[15] Merchants and speculators were certain that the weakness of the summer months would continue, and they kept on selling. Gould stated that on the day of the panic the gold short interest exceeded $200,000,000; yet in New York City the gold and gold certificates did not exceed $20,000,000.[16] The sharp rise in the price of gold in September aroused the President. Complaints from legitimate export and import merchants came in volume. Various activities by Gould's confederates, furthermore, made the President suspicious, and becoming aware that Mrs. Grant's brother was involved in gold speculation, he requested that she write to her brother to desist from any participation in the gold market. Corbin, an unsteady old man, showed this letter to Gould on Wednesday night, September 22. Corbin was hot and excited, Gould calm and steady. Before the market opened on Thursday, Gould, saying nothing about this letter, informed Fisk that the time had now arrived to advance the price of gold sharply and to force the short sellers to settle. He instructed Fisk to *buy* gold in volume. From a mass of conflicting evidence, it appears that Gould induced Fisk to fabricate some document which indicated that Fisk was *buying* gold on behalf of another broker. Be that as it may, Gould maintained on Thursday and early Friday an *appearance* of buying gold; actually he was selling. Under the impetus of heavy buying by Fisk on Friday morning, gold moved from 141⅝ to 144. Thereafter in a matter of minutes the value of gold rose by millions of dollars, and by noon sold at 160. Shortly thereafter a bid appeared at 162½. Within a few minutes the wires carried the news of the sale of Treasury gold. With scarcely any transactions on the way down, gold dropped sharply to 140 and then to 133.

The stock market, in which Gould was heavily committed, also cracked. During the month of September the price of the Erie, of the Cleveland & Pittsburgh, and of the Wabash declined sharply. Gould as a stock trader had heavy losses. Since he had bought on margin, his account was undermargined and he could not pay his brokers' loans. His brokers could have sold his stocks, applied the proceeds to his loans and then sued for the unpaid balance. Gould was not to be so easily caught. He still had control of the Erie and he shifted some of the Erie stocks from his personal account to that of the Erie,[17] and with the help of his controlled judge, enjoined his creditors from selling the pledged securities. This saved him from his stock-market creditors but did not protect him from his gold-market creditors. A large part of the losses fell upon Fisk who had bought much of the gold at high prices as agent for several brokerage firms including Smith, Gould, Martin & Company. To protect itself the latter firm repudiated Fisk's transactions.

Despite this repudiation every dealer, including Gould and his brokerage firm, had to make a settlement with the Gold Board through the Gold Exchange Bank by submitting daily a statement of debits and credits. Every dealer except Smith, Gould, Martin & Company submitted a statement. Feeling against the firm was "intensely bitter." [18] Gould remained calm and defied the board, the bank, and his fellow dealers. The latter had their rights, Gould had his judge—Judge Cardoza—a newcomer to the Gould-Tweed financial and political set-up. Cardoza issued an injunction against the Gold Exchange, restraining it from buying or selling gold for the account of Smith, Gould, Martin & Company. A collection of other injunctions was secured and Gould was saved from his gold-market creditors.

Gould's speculations had, however, failed, and this failure led to the collapse of the railroad route between the seaboard and the Mississippi. When Gould promoted the Lake Shore-Wabash consolidation in the summer of 1869, Vanderbilt recognized that he himself had only a minority interest in the Lake Shore. He soon perceived the weak points of the opposition. Discovering that LeGrand Lockwood (a brokerage associate of Gould in the Wabash-Lake Shore speculation) personally, as well as the brokerage firm of Lockwood & Company, had bought Lake Shore stock on borrowed funds, he took the offensive and, in the extravagant language of a contemporary commentator, "with all his vast resources in hand, batteries unlimbered, and military chest full to the brim," [19] moved to acquire the Lake Shore.

Late in August, after the announcement of the Lake Shore-Erie contract, he opened his attack on the Lake Shore. The stock was then selling at 110. Vanderbilt threw large blocks on the market, and the price sagged to the middle 80s. Sales of New York Central and of Harlem produced sympathetic selling in other stocks. In the middle of the panic break, Lockwood sold 25,000 shares of Lake Shore for $2,000,000 but was unable to deliver the stock. The lending banks refused to hand over the stock in exchange for checks, and insisted upon legal tender.[20] In this emergency, Lockwood, according to some reports, asked Gould for help,[21] but Gould, because of his financial troubles, had to exercise all his ingenuity to remain solvent. The Lockwood firm failed with heavy liabilities. It owed the Lake Shore more than $1,000,000,[22] and, according to one report, a number of Ohio capitalists had deposits with the firm of about $500,000 each.[23]

The failure of Lockwood was an opportunity for Vanderbilt. He borrowed $10,000,000 from Baring Bros., and with part of the loan purchased 70,000 shares of the Lake Shore from Lockwood.[24]

Even with this acquisition, it was doubtful whether Vanderbilt could defeat the Wabash consolidation. Some of the large shareholders of the Lake Shore were convinced of the wisdom of the Wabash-Lake Shore union. The Lake Shore, furthermore, had contracts with Lockwood & Company for the purchase of Wabash stock. Early in October the Lake Shore board met behind closed doors, and appointed two Vanderbilt men to positions of influence. Despite this, the board approved the proposed Wabash consolidation, and submitted the plan to the stockholders at a special meeting to be held on December 29. The stockholders rejected the proposal. Gould and the Erie had lost again, and Vanderbilt and the New York Central were victorious.

Shortly before that failure Gould also lost control of the Albany & Susquehanna. Ramsey had enlisted the services of J. Pierpont Morgan, then a local banker, who was soon to make his mark in national affairs. With Morgan's help a court decision was handed down which ousted the Gould board and legalized the Ramsey-Morgan board.[25] Under Morgan leadership, the road was leased to the Delaware & Hudson at a guaranteed rental of 7 per cent upon its stock. The price of the lessor's line shot up to

125. Gould probably did not profit, as he had sold his stock in the panic.

The Erie now had no outlets east of New York or west of Buffalo. In the battle for connections, it was its competitors who had won, and the Erie was permanently weakened. Gould's personal losses were heavy. In the stock-market movements of the next two years he did little except to organize small speculative market pools. His impaired financial condition was further revealed by the unimportant role he assumed in the acquisition of control of a road which, although having no relation to the Erie, did connect with the Wabash. The Hannibal & St. Joseph [26] controlled a short line from the Mississippi River gateways of Quincy and Hannibal to St. Joseph and Kansas City, and in the late sixties had no rival in a territory more than a hundred miles wide between the Mississippi and the Missouri Rivers. Between 1865 and 1871, the stock sold at prices warranted neither by its earnings nor its assets. The high price invited substantial selling from large stockholders of the Chicago, Burlington & Quincy,[27] who were also large and in most cases original stockholders of the road.[28]

This was the stock which the Tammany ring, led by Tweed and Sweeny, guided largely by Smith, the brokerage partner of Gould, bought heavily in the prosperous summer of 1871. It is significant that officers of the Burlington were informed that the Hannibal stock-buying clique included Tweed, Sweeny and others, with no mention of Gould.[29] When the Hannibal was finally acquired by the Tammany group in 1871, Smith, not Gould, was appointed president, and although Gould was elected to the board of directors he owned only a nominal number of shares.

While Gould engaged in these successful battles to acquire connections, he did not overlook the detailed problems of managing the Erie as a railroad property. Here again Gould revealed his inability to disassociate corporate and personal interests. A managerial policy, sound in itself, was impaired and occasionally destroyed by its prostitution to considerations of personal profit. He would propose a sound move in the interests of the Erie, but in executing it he could not overlook the exploitation of an opportunity for personal gain.

Even before the stockholders had elected him to the presidency in October, 1868, such an opportunity emerged. The executive committee had authorized him as president to terminate a contract with the United States Express Company and to make a more favorable one.[30] Accordingly Gould and his associate Fisk informed the express company that its annual rent to the Erie would be increased by $500,000. When the express company refused, it was told to leave the Erie. Gould informed the company that the Erie would organize a new express company, and the stock of the United States Express Company dropped from 60 to 16. At the lower price Gould bought the stock,[31] signed a new contract and sold the stock on the advance. The profits from this market transaction were reported to be approximately $3,000,000. Gould in reporting this transaction to Erie stockholders did not misrepresent the fact. He wrote that the Erie had made a new contract with the United States Express largely increasing the Erie's compensation. While the fact was correct, the truth was not. It was a half-truth, which is often more dangerous than a falsehood.

More important to the Erie than the express business was the rail traffic. After disruption of friendly relations with the Atlantic in the fall of 1865, the Erie made repeated efforts to strengthen its traffic position in the Pennsylvania oil region. In 1867 numerous proposals for the acquisition of various railroads in that territory for the increase in oil traffic were considered by the board and the executive committee.[32] Though the oil business was increasing, the rates, largely because of McHenry's rate-cutting policy in the Atlantic, were declining. Shortly after Gould became president, the Atlantic's receiver laid a proposal before the Erie for the acquistion of a controlling interest in some pipe lines in the oil regions. The executive committee, significantly enough, referred to the proposal to the president.[33] The Erie did nothing but its president, Gould, acting through his personal account, did much. Together with others, he bought more than half the stock of the most important pipe-line company in the region—the Allegheny Transportation Company.[34]

Meanwhile the war initiated by McHenry had spread, and rate-cuts, drawbacks and rebates soon characterized the oil business.[35] All participating lines made efforts to stop the war, and by September, 1868, the Pennsylvania, the New York Central, and the Atlantic finally banded together and reached an agreement. "To avoid needless and harmful depreciation" in rates on oil, the contract of September 24, 1868, provided for pooling of the oil traffic, prohibition of drawbacks, and the equalization of rates, the intention of the parties being that all shippers should "be placed upon a perfect equality." [36]

The contract had only one signature—that of Scott of the Pennsylvania, and thereby hangs a tale. Gould, owing to his control of the pipe lines through his holdings in the Allegheny Transportation, was obviously unprepared to sign a non-discrimination contract. Shortly after the date of the agreement a letter from McHenry to the Atlantic's president emphasizing the former's rate-reduction philosophy appeared in the public press. A rate of one cent per ton mile (the current rate then was about three cents), he observed, would greatly increase railroad profits.[37]

By the time this letter appeared, Gould had secured full control of the Erie's destinies, and was ready to co-operate with McHenry. The drastic rate war of October, 1868, followed. Less than two months later the Erie's lease to the Atlantic gave Gould power to exploit the Atlantic's oil traffic. Gould put the oil business of the combined Erie and Atlantic into the hands of Henry Harley—a man long experienced in this field. Rebates and drawbacks were freely used for competitive purposes. In this rivalry the Erie was not successful. Early in 1872 just before the negotiation of the South Improvement Company's contracts, the Erie's oil business had dwindled to nominal proportions.

The delivery of the oil traffic on the eastern end of the Erie posed still other problems. Additional facilities at these termini were essential to handle the business. The Long Dock terminal being inadequate, the Erie purchased from Gould the property of the Weehawken Docks Company. This was a simple contract, but, because of Gould's inside position, the Erie was obliged to pay "an extra price." [38] On the plea that additional building space was necessary to take care of the larger flow of business, the Erie leased the Grand Opera House from Gould at a rental beyond any true rental value. Since the $300,000 cash needed to purchase the property was "borrowed" from the Erie as a prepayment of the Erie rental, the Opera House had cost Gould little.[39]

The situation at Buffalo meanwhile confronted the Erie with a critical problem. The capture of the Lake Shore by Vanderbilt was followed by the closing of the south shore route. To open an alternative route, Gould revived plans for construction of a parallel road between Buffalo and Suspension Bridge. Early in 1867, prior to the Gould regime, the Erie management had already agreed upon the building of such a connection with the Great Western.[40] The road was now completed and the new company which built and owned the line leased it to the Erie. Even before it was finished, Gould entered into negotiations for a through line via the north shore to Detroit.[41] The stock of the new company was issued as a bonus, and part of it in some inscrutable way fell into the hands of Gould and Fisk.[42]

Since it was clear that Vanderbilt would not permit the Lake Shore to deliver any business to the Erie, sound judgment dictated the wisdom of co-operation and the avoidance of slashing price wars. Rates on the Erie were low. What the Erie needed, observed a leading railroad journal, was "not so much more business, as business that [paid]." [43]

This, however, was precisely what Gould was unable to give the Erie. Early in 1870 the road was offering large drawbacks on westbound traffic. In February, Gould, W. H. Vanderbilt (son of Cornelius, and vice president of the New York Central), and Thomson, for the Erie, New York Central, and Pennsylvania respectively, in a move to stabilize rates, agreed that no contract would be recognized by trunk lines except at rates in the printed schedule, and that any officer who quoted rates below such schedule would be dismissed from the service.[44] This agreement like so many others, proved to be temporary. Early in June a fierce rate war began and within a few weeks livestock from Buffalo to New York City was reduced from $120 to $40 a car. A few days later the reduction of rates by the Erie to $1.00 a car was followed by the fantastic spectacle of the movement of sheep and hogs from Buffalo to Suspension Bridge at one cent apiece.[45] All roads connecting with New York City were soon drawn into this struggle.

The war was too fierce to last and by late August the contestants were ready to settle, Gould taking the lead. A conclusive settlement was reached in late December. A circular signed by Gould, Scott, and W. H. Vanderbilt prohibited the offering of rebates to shippers. All parties were enjoined to carry out the agreement in good faith, so that all shippers could be placed "on a perfect equality."[46] This agreement also lasted only a short time. By December, 1871, the Erie and the Lake Shore were carrying cattle from Chicago to New York at $80 per car, one-half the usual rate, and were paying drawbacks on grain.[47] Powerful competitive factors in the major industries—iron, oil, wheat, livestock, lumber, coal—produced continuous rate disturbances.

Although neither Gould nor Vanderbilt was able to control the rate structure, both had full power to improve the physical property, raise the standard of maintenance and increase the operating efficiency of their respective properties. Vanderbilt accomplished these results on every property he acquired—the Harlem, the Hudson River, the New York Central, and the Lake Shore. On these lines he performed outstanding services in reducing unit costs and raising standards. The Erie's physical property in the years following the death of Marsh at the height of the Civil War inflation, had deteriorated, the speculative conflicts of the Erie managers leaving them little time for cultivation of the art of railroad operation. Of equal importance was the fact that the road was not supplied with sufficient funds to finance the provision of rolling stock and other essentials to improve operating standards.

After Gould succeeded in acquiring control of the Erie, he had also adopted policies designed to improve the road's physical condition and to reduce costs. He made an active study of the efficiency of iron versus steel rails and discovered the superiority of the latter. In view of their high cost, however, he was constrained, to use his own language, "to investigate whether a middle course could not be adopted with advantage and economy."[48] He learned that a mill in Trenton, New Jersey, owned by one of the leading iron manufacturers of the time, Abram S. Hewitt, had been experimenting on the manufacture of iron rails with steel heads. Hewitt was a distinguished citizen, a member of one of the country's leading iron firms, Cooper & Hewitt, becoming later one of the public-spirited men of the day, successively a congressman and the mayor of New York City. The Erie became joint owner with Cooper & Hewitt of the Trenton Mill, which rolled steel-headed rails for the account of the Erie. Hewitt was confident of the success of these rails. In December, 1870, he expressed his optimism in a letter to the Massachusetts Railroad Commissioners, declaring that the Erie, under Gould, had been able through the use of these rails, to reduce the needs of new rails from 2,000 tons to about 600 tons monthly.[49]

Trade and financial journals vied in commending the high operating standards of the Erie management. Even the popular organs joined in their praise. After reviewing Gould's annual report of the Erie in glowing terms which "in comprehensiveness, compactness and clearness . . . [was] almost as much a 'Public Document' as that of the Treasury or General Post Office," an eastern weekly observed that the Erie's managers had made the road "the great aorta of the heart and metropolis of the Western World.[50] In the summer of 1871 a leading eastern railroad journal called attention to the fact that four "elegant" drawing-room coaches were being built for the Erie to operate between New York and Niagara Falls over the new extension from Buffalo. These new coaches, it was declared, were to "surpass any others yet made. . . ."[51]

Gould was thus in the opinion of many of his contemporaries in and out of the railroad field an able operating man. This reputation, however, was not deserved. He was, rather, a skillful publicity writer and an excellent salesman. His ability in relating favorable, and in glossing over unfavorable, facts, his skill in doing a little along the path of righteousness and in enlarging that little into much, were unique. He did indeed build a few iron bridges, and though he made it appear that he would build more, he didn't. He also built a number of elegant passenger coaches which were used for advertising purposes on the Niagara branch. Although he laid only a few steel or steel-headed rails, Hewitt, the able iron and steel manufacturer, lent his willing pen to the glorification of his improvement program.

It must have been surprising to cursory observers that despite all the deeds detailed by Gould, and in spite of the even more extravagant expectations which he raised, the Erie remained an inefficient property. In the spring of 1871 a newspaper reporter observed that the equipment handling milk traffic, one of its most lucrative forms of business, was still old and dilapidated. Some of the cars had been used for fifteen years, the brakes were nearly worn out, and the cars appeared to be "ready to break down at any moment. . . ."[52]

At the end of three and a half years of Gould power, the Erie was a physical wreck. It "was an incomplete concern, its track disconnected at different points, largely single track, no terminal improvements or facilities, defective machinery, iron rails, largely wooden bridges, in a condition that it could not be worked with economy: . . ."[53] Such was the language of Hugh Jewett, president and receiver of the road and an experienced railroad operator, who took over the executive responsibilities after the departure of Gould and the McHenry satellites who followed him. Jewett's conclusions were confirmed by another railroad man who, in the interests of his English clients, made an elaborate survey of the property. The Erie, he wrote, needed iron to replace its wooden bridges. It lacked steel rails and durable sleepers, and it badly needed an improvement in its grades. Its terminal arrangements were inadequate. The road, furthermore, had only a single track, while the New York Central had four and the Pennsylvania two tracks, and in many places a third. The New York Central with its additional tracks between New York and Buffalo was able to reduce the running time of trains and the cost of freight transportation. The absence of double tracks on the Erie, on the other hand, led to delays, expense and operating risks. The absence of improvements increased substantially the road's operating expenses.[54] Thus in his first venture as an executive of a major road, Gould as an operating man was a failure.

Despite the issue of a mass of new securities he did little to improve the property, and in fact devoted but little time to the details of railroad operation. Occasionally in later years he expressed pride in his ability to operate a railroad with the help of only a few associates. His forte, however, was not in detailed operation but rather in the shifting of control of properties.

Long before this was generally known, groups of security holders were attacking the Gould control. Early in March, 1872, he was ousted; but before he left he negotiated a number of transactions of more than ordinary profit which put him in funds to finance other enterprises. The first involved an Erie lease of two small railroads, which afforded an outlet to another road—the Northern Central—for its business from Pennsylvania to eastern New York and New England. Because of the increase in coal traffic in the intervening years, the leases had become profitable to the Erie. Late in 1871, representing himself as an Erie agent, he bought control of both lines, and then, by defaulting on the rental, forfeited the leases. In view of the strategic position of the roads, he found it easy to sell the stocks to the Northern Central at a profit of more than $2,000,000.[55]

The Northern Central transaction was accompanied by two others, both profitable to Gould. Shortly before a small oil road, the Union & Titusville, was completed, the Erie board authorized its president to enter into an agreement for the operation of the completed line.[56] After the road was finished, the president (Gould), ignoring the authorization of the board, acquired a trifle less than 50 per cent of its stock. When the line was opened in February, 1871, its competitor, the Oil Creek & Allegheny River, closely affiliated with the Pennsylvania, cut rates sharply.

Gould had a loss on his hands. The stock had no market. The competitive line, however, was well known in Philadelphia where the stock in the spring of 1871 sold at more than $50 a share. In August the Gould line was leased to the Pennsylvania affiliate, and in December the lease was transformed into a merger. Gould's stock, with a nominal nuisance value, was exchanged for almost 8,000 shares of a stock with a market value of about $50 a share.[57]

At about the same time, another transaction, the lease of the Cleveland & Pittsburgh to the Pennsylvania, was completed. This gave the Pennsylvania its entrance from the east into Cleveland, enabling it from that day to this to bid for a share of the rapidly growing traffic of the Cleveland industrial area. Just how Gould and his associates acquired the block of the Cleveland & Pittsburgh is not known.[58] When in consequence of the lease Gould and his associates were placed on the former's board of directors, they represented not the Erie, but their own personal interests. The combined holdings of the Pennsylvania and the Gould group were not sufficient to assure approval of the lease. To obtain additional votes, about 10 per cent of the company's proxies were bought and the stock transferred to the names of the Gould group,[59] while to make ratification certain, another financial device was adopted, a device which bore all the earmarks of Gould's ingenuity. The notice of the special meeting to be held on November 21 was issued on November 3. The transfer books were closed on October 30, ostensibly only for the 2 per cent regular quarterly dividend. Actually, it turned out that when the announcement was issued on November 3, the transfer books had also been closed on October 30 for the purpose of voting on the proposed lease contract.

The lease was duly ratified. Since the number of shares held by Gould is not known, the extent to which he benefited from the lease cannot be determined. Neither is it known to whom and at what price he sold his Cleveland & Pittsburgh stock. Since he was elected to the Cleveland & Pittsburgh board he must have had some holdings.[60]

From these transactions, completed by the end of 1871, Gould realized substantial profits. He also owned at this time considerable real estate, most of which, however, was heavily mortgaged. The large collection of securities of Erie auxiliaries afforded him some additional income. Neither the real estate nor these securities were sufficiently liquid to permit their use as collateral to finance stock-market operations. In the Erie there were no further profits to be made. The property was in poor condition, its financial position was desperate, and its stocks and bonds were being offered in the markets at lower and lower prices. Moreover, the stockholders who for so long had been deprived of any representation on the board were now engaged in a contest which grew more and more unfavorable to Gould. At the New York State election in the fall of 1871, his political friends were overturned and the new state officials appeared willing to cooperate with anti-Gould factions. His famous judicial associate, Judge Barnard, had been ousted, while a number of groups of shareholders were organizing for the attack. Gould finally succumbed. He resigned—but he did so under conditions which enabled him to escape the legal effect of his breach of trust. He had lost much of his profits gained in 1868 and 1869. He had never regained for the Erie the losses which during his administration he had inflicted upon it. Despite these violations of his corporate trust, however, he succeeded in avoiding any legal responsibility for his defections, and in the end he resigned his control of the road in such a way as largely to enhance his personal fortune.

NOTES FOR CHAPTER V

1. Charles Burt, in *R. R. Gaz.*, Aug. 13, 1870, 469.
2. Heath et al. vs. Erie Railway Co. et al., Circuit Court S. D., N. Y., April 27, 1871; in *Federal Cases* Vol. XI, 976, Bill of Complaint.
3. *United States R. R. & Mining Register*, Feb. 26, 1870.
4. Heath et al. vs. Erie Railway Co. et al., Circuit Court S. D., N. Y., April 27, 1871; in *Federal Cases* Vol. XI, 976, Bill of Complaint.
5. New York *Tribune*, April 12, 1873.
6. Amasa Stone and H. B. Payne of Cleveland, H. F. Clark, Augustus Schell and J. H. Barker of New York, interested in the Lake Shore in 1869, and elected to the Wabash board in 1870, were the leading factors in the ill-fated expansion of the Wabash in the early seventies. On the basis of this and other evidence it can be inferred that these capitalists owned large blocks of Wabash stock.
7. In the Burlington archives, for example, there is a letter from J. N. Denison, treasurer of the Burlington, to J. F. Joy, president, Aug. 23, 1869, in which Denison called attention to the fact that the Wabash had consolidated with the Lake Shore on the basis of a joint capital of $50,000,000 with a debt of $35,000,000, and in a letter to Forbes, Aug. 25, 1869, Denison refers to an article in the *Wall Street Journal* (sic) in which the terms of exchange of the securities of the two roads are described.
8. Erie, Minutes, Executive Committee, Sept. 10, 1869.
9. Supreme Court, County of Delaware, Joseph H. Ramsey against Jay Gould et al., Complaint 66-67.
10. Cass, president of the Fort Wayne, in a letter to S. J. Tilden, March 18, 1872, stated definitely that in 1869, the Erie controlled a majority of the stock of the Cleveland & Pittsburgh. Cass in 1869 was on the board of the Cleveland & Pittsburgh, and therefore was in a position to know the facts. This is according to the New York *World*, March 20, 1872. Late in September, 1869, the Erie sued to prevent the Union Bank of New York City from selling stock which had been placed as collateral for a loan by the Erie. Included in this collateral were 64,000 shares of the Cleveland & Pittsburgh, and 11,900 shares of the Wabash. In May and June of the same year in court proceedings initiated by Gould to prevent the Wabash from increasing its outstanding stock, Gould, and not the Erie, appeared as the owner of 10,000 shares of Wabash. Furthermore, in the minutes of the board of directors and of the executive committee of the Erie, no mention is made either of the holdings of Cleveland & Pittsburgh or of the Wabash. If Cass is correct in his statement that the Erie in 1869 did control a majority of the Cleveland & Pittsburgh stock, it may be inferred that Gould, in order to extricate himself from the financial predicament he was in after the Black Friday in September of 1869, transferred both his stock and his loan from himself to the Erie. A financial newspaper stated editorially that the borrower from the Union Bank was a brokerage firm of which Gould was a member, but that Fisk in his affidavit insisted that the Erie was the real owner of the Cleveland & Pittsburgh stock. See *Stockholder*, Oct. 5, 1869, 760-1.
11. *Bankers' Magazine*, Nov. 1869, 385.
12. *Chron.*, March 27, 1869, 390.
13. New York *Tribune*, July 9, 1869; July 21, 1869.

14. For details see Charles F. Adams, Jr. and Henry Adams: "An Erie Raid," in *Chapters of Erie, and Other Essays*, 135-2.
15. New York *Tribune*, Sept. 27, 1869.
16. Gold Panic Investigation, Report No. 31, House of Representatives, 41st Congress, 2nd Session, 1870, 134, Gould.
17. Supreme Court, County of Delaware, Joseph H. Ramsey against Jay Gould et al., Complaint 66-7.
18. New York *Tribune*, Sept. 29, 1869.
19. *Stockholder*, Nov. 9, 1869.
20. Ibid., Oct. 5, 1869.
21. New York *Commercial Advertiser*, Oct. 5, 1869.
22. *R. R. Record*, Jan. 20, 1870, 482.
23. New York *Commercial Advertiser*, Oct. 4, 1869.
24. New York *Tribune*, Oct. 1, 1869.
25. The People vs. Albany & Susquehanna Railroad Company, I Lansing, 309, Supreme Court, N.Y. State.
26. Known hereafter as the Hannibal.
27. Known hereafter as the Burlington.
28. Burlington archives, Denison to Hall, May 10, 1871.
29. Ibid., Denison to John C. Green, Aug. 1, 1871.
30. Erie, Minutes, Executive Committee, Aug. 1, 1869.
31. See Alvin F. Harlow: *Old Way Bills*, 317, Appleton-Century, New York, 1934; *Chron.*, March 6, 1869, 301; New York *Tribune*, Feb. 25, 1869; March 1, 1869. Many details of the raid on the express stocks are found in Cincinnati *Gazette* of March 8, 1869, cited in Chicago *Tribune*, March 12, 1869.
32. Erie, Minutes of Executive Committee, June 26, 1867; Aug. 14, 1867; and Minutes, Board of Directors, Oct. 2, 1867.
33. Erie, Minutes of Executive Committee, Aug. 19, 1868.
34. J. T. Henry, *History of Petroleum*, 531-2, Jas. B. Rodgers Co., Philadelphia, 1873.
35. For rate cuts 1867–69, see State of New York, Railroad Investigation, 1879, 2739, Diven.
36. This contract is in the files of the Erie, Cleveland, Ohio.
37. New York *Herald*, Oct. 7, 1868.
38. Heath et al. vs. Erie Railway Co. et al., Circuit Court S. D., N. Y., April 27, 1871; in *Federal Cases* Vol. XI, 976, Bill of Complaint.
39. Ibid.
40. Erie, Minutes, Executive Committee, March 27, 1867.
41. Joy papers, Gould to Joy, Sept. 2, 1870.
42. State of New York, Railroad Investigation, 1879, 2468-9, Guppy.
43. *R. R. Gaz.*, Jan. 6, 1872, 422.
44. Joy papers, H. E. Sargent to W. H. Vanderbilt, Feb. 21, 1870, telegram from Vanderbilt to Sargent of the same date, and printed circular marked "General Notice, Feb. 21, 1870."
45. *R. R. Gaz.*, July 2, 1870.
46. Ibid., Dec. 24, 1870, 294.
47. Joy papers, J. M. Walker to Joy, Dec. 8, 1871.
48. Annual report, Erie, 1869, cited in *Am. R. R. Journal*, Jan. 29, 1870, 119.
49. *R. R. Gaz.*, Jan. 28, 1871, 414.
50. *Frank Leslie's Illustrated Newspaper*, Feb. 12, 1870.
51. *R. R. Gaz.*, June 17, 1871, 140.
52. New York *Tribune*, April 18, 1871.
53. State of New York, Railroad Investigation, 1879, 1371, Jewett.
54. For details on the report of this railroad man, Captain H. W. Tyler, see *R. R. Gaz.*, Nov. 21, 1874, 451; *Am. R. R. Journal*, Nov. 28, 1874, 1508; Dec. 5, 1874, 1540.

55. State of New York, Railroad Investigation, 1879, Vol. V, 534.
56. Erie, Minutes, Board of Directors, Aug. 18, 1870.
57. *Am. R. R. Journal*, Dec. 30, 1871, 1462; *The Road*, March 1, 1875, 35.
58. For details on this point, see *supra*, note 10.
59. This percentage represents the estimate of a writer in the New York *Commercial Advertiser*, Nov. 3, 1871.
60. For some of the details on the Cleveland & Pittsburgh lease, see New York *Commercial Advertiser*, Nov. 3, 1871 and Nov. 4, 1871.

CHAPTER VI

Gould Leaves the Erie

In May, 1869, Gould was at the peak of his control of the Erie. He had disenfranchised the holders of almost all of the foreign stock, more than half of which was held by residents of England. They had bought the stock and secured title through a blank power of attorney, but Gould by various pretexts had made it impossible for them to cast their ballots. Furthermore, the Classification Act had just been enacted and this assured Gould's group a term of office for at least five years. It was at just about this time that a group of English shareholders, spurred on by the drop in the price of Erie stock, decided to secure a voice in the management of the company equal to their shareholdings.[1] They organized a London protective committee, and arranged to transfer their stocks on the Erie's books in the names of two English citizens, Robert Amadeus Heath and Lewis Raphael. A power of attorney made out in their names was attached to the stock certificates and sent to a New York City banker.

Months passed before the committee was well organized and before the mechanism to effect the desired transfer of the stock was well established. Meanwhile Gould proceeded with the elaborate speculations that culminated in the gold panic of September, 1869. Before the English shareholders could make a move to assert their influence over the affairs of the Erie, a new opponent of Gould, Ramsey, the belligerent president of the Albany & Susquehanna, made an unexpected assault upon the Gould clique. The Gould group had made a determined effort to acquire control of his road. Before the struggle was decided, Ramsey suddenly took the offensive, bought some securities of the Erie, and in November entered suit with the view of ousting the Erie board. Ramsey was one of the rare opponents of Gould who familiarized himself with Gould's operations. He engaged counsel, a former Erie attorney, who in the opinion of Judge

Barnard had a valuable knowledge of Erie's history,[2] and with his help drew up a bill of complaint. Realizing he could accomplish little through Judge Barnard, he selected an independent judge, Judge Murray in Delaware County, before whom he submitted his charges. Judge Murray promptly issued the requested orders, suspended Gould, Fisk, Lane and others from the Erie board, forbade their doing any business for the Erie, and stopped all operations of Gould in selling stocks or interfering with the books and business of the Erie. He also appointed a referee to take testimony and establish the facts in the case.[3]

Gould was not prepared for this move, having taken no counter-measures to ward off the blow, played for time. Although Judge Murray had issued the order, Gould was determined that it would not be served. For three days court officials pursued him. He was ejected from the Erie's offices. At home he concealed himself. On one occasion the court official caught him as he was entering his carriage, but before he could serve the paper he was seized from behind by Gould's escort, who was aptly compared to the private armies retained by medieval knights.[4]

Judge Murray became indignant over this judicial farce, and on December 10 called a hearing to ascertain why the suspension order should not be made permanent and why the summons, complaint, order of suspension and the injunctions should not be served on Gould and his associates by leaving them at their respective residences. In the existing state of Gould's affairs, execution of this order would have been serious. His losses suffered in the gold panic had not been retrieved. With the help of his judicial associate, Judge Barnard, Gould evaded the trap set by Ramsey. Through some legal legerdemain he succeeded in securing an order from Judge Barnard enjoining Ramsey from proceeding with his suit. Furthermore Gould, as he had so often done before and was destined to do many times in the future, took the offensive. He induced Barnard to dismiss Ramsey's complaint and to hold Ramsey in contempt for bringing a suit a few weeks later in defiance of an earlier order of the judge. The Ramsey litigation lasted fourteen months and during this period Ramsey was free from injunctions only five days.[5]

Meanwhile the Heath and Raphael group had begun action to

force the Erie to transfer their stock. Their request was refused and litigation followed. The American counsel for the English group then decided to make an attempt to induce the assembly to repeal the Directors' Classification Act. He had preconceived opinions of the integrity of American legislative bodies, but was soon disillusioned. Later he wrote to his clients that he had been told by a member of the assembly that if he "had let it be understood that [he] had brought $20,000 to smooth the way, [he] should have made more progress.[6]

It was clear to the Heath and Raphael group that nothing could be accomplished in the state legislature. The initial attempt to get the names of the English stockholders on the Erie's books through the orderly normal process of transfer had been rejected. The next move, made in the spring of 1870, produced a notable display of legal and financial pyrotechnics. To make their stock marketable under the rules of the New York Stock Exchange, it was necessary to register the stock. As protection against duplication of security issues, the rules required that the shares be certified on their face that they were registered in accordance with its regulations. Unregistered shares were accordingly unmarketable. The shares owned by the Heath and Raphael group were part of the stock registered by the Erie with its registration agent, the Farmer's Loan & Trust Company. In order to identify them as genuine a block of 60,000 shares was deposited with the Erie. From this point the fireworks really began. No sooner were the certificates left in the Erie's offices than Gould and Fisk sped away to the offices of Judge Barnard. On a flimsy pretext the judge was induced to take the stock away from the jurisdiction of its English shareholders and appoint a receiver. The receiver delivered the shares to Gould, and Gould gave the receiver a new certificate.

Here was another opportunity. Gould at this time (the winter of 1870 and 1871) though still in debt was trading in securities. His old brokerage firm had been dissolved and had been replaced by the new firm of Willard, Martin & Balch. Though it is not clear what Gould's speculative position was at this time, it is certain that he needed funds and that the deposit of the English stock offered him the means of financing his needs. Of the 60,000 shares obtained by Gould from the receiver, 30,000 were so mutilated as to make it impossible to register them with the trust company.

Without the consent of the board or of the executive committee, Gould as president issued $3,000,000 of convertible bonds, converted the bonds almost immediately into stock, delivered the stock to the trust company for registration, and then sold the stock at current market prices. Though Gould never paid the Erie for any of the stock, the brokerage house did. How much it paid is not known.

To what extent Gould benefited from this raid cannot be ascertained, but the loss to the English shareholders is certain. They rushed back to the courts and asked Judge Blatchford to discharge the receiver. This was a reasonable request and the judge directed dissolution of the receivership and restoration of the Erie stock to its legitimate owners. The Erie raised no objection to the order—a puzzling reaction for Gould, who never surrendered without a struggle. The puzzle, however, was soon solved. Judge Blatchford's order of dissolution was to take effect on March 11, 1871. Two weeks before that time Gould had asked the ever ready Judge Barnard to appoint a new receiver for the stock. Judge Blatchford's order could not be executed because the receiver against whom it was issued had no stock. The stock was now in the hands of a new receiver who held some subordinate position on the Erie.

Judicial proceedings were protracted. Orders were issued against Gould to deliver the stock to the rightful owners and to reimburse them for losses incurred, but on one pretext or another Gould postponed final action until December of 1871. By that time, having completed the Cleveland & Pittsburgh and the Union & Titusville stock transactions, he was in funds, and in accordance with the order of the court he delivered the 60,000 shares to their legitimate owners. Since the Heath and Raphael group were about to get the right to vote their stock, they were in sight of victory, and furthermore, since an independent attorney-general and a new state assembly had been elected, they were also reasonably certain of securing the repeal of the Directors' Classification Act.[7]

When the English stockholders were thus on the eve of success, another move was begun to oust Gould from control of the

Erie. The new group was led by McHenry, the promoter of the Atlantic. The road's property by this time had been taken out of the receiver's hands. The reorganization, at least in London financial circles, had been hailed with relief. A journal, long an authority on British railway news, expressed the belief that investors would soon learn for the first time of the earning power "of this fine property." [8] McHenry was quoted as stating that after allowing for a 60 per cent operating ratio there would be a large and increasing margin for dividends.

Plans were laid to make the road independent of the Erie. Narrow-gauge connections were to be made with the Pennsylvania for a line to Philadelphia, and with the New York Central for a line to Buffalo. A short extension from the controlled Cleveland & Mahoning would bring the road into the Baltimore & Ohio network and open a route between Cleveland, Baltimore and Washington.[9]

The reorganized Atlantic moved fast in expanding its local traffic. McHenry was determined to exploit the possibilities of the oil business, and to free the road from its exclusive dependence on the Erie for outlets to the oil-consuming markets. Accordingly, he laid plans for the extension of system lines in the oil region of northwestern Pennsylvania.

As president of the road, McHenry chose General G. B. McClellan, a man of national reputation and distinction. Associated with McClellan in the road's reorganization in 1871 were Senator Thurman, and a banker, W. B. Duncan, of Duncan, Sherman & Co., a banking firm with good London connections. It was to this bank that J. S. Morgan had sent his son, J. Pierpont, to get his banking experience. McHenry organized a directorate of exceptional strength including Hewitt, the iron manufacturer, Lloyd Aspinwall, a capitalist held in high regard in financial circles, and J. H. Devereux, an able railroad man of Cleveland.

The company's past financial troubles were conveniently laid upon the shoulders of the Erie. No longer, declared McHenry, would its earnings fall into the Erie treasury "whence they have not hitherto been readily extracted, . . ." [10] Great hopes were entertained for the company's future earnings, provided it could be relieved of the dishonesty and inefficiency of the Erie management. An analyst in an elaborate article in an English railroad journal concluded that if the road were worked in conjunction with the Erie, but with the same honesty and regard for the interests of the stockholders as other trunk lines, it could earn a "handsome dividend." [11]

In view of this optimism it is not surprising that the road's capital structure was not seriously disturbed. The company was reorganized in a period of national prosperity when traffic was expanding and railroad mileage increasing. The reorganization increased the company's capital account from $59,000,000 to $93,000,000, its debts alone equaling almost $140,000 per mile.[12] The road was further handicapped because it ran against the prevailing direction of traffic. With the exception of Cleveland, it had no termini at any major traffic producing centers. To make matters worse, the new property was organized at the time when a business genius, John D. Rockefeller, was making plans to control the oil business and to dominate the oil traffic. Despite the unfriendly feelings between the Atlantic and the Erie, the latter was the major eastern railroad outlet for the former's oil business. The growing oil-refining industry of Cleveland secured most of its crude oil from the region served by the Atlantic. The latter therefore had a large east- and west-bound oil business, carrying crude oil west and refined oil east. By the fall of 1871, however, its position had changed for the worse. The Lake Shore by a short extension had succeeded in securing access to the oil regions, and since it could now send oil over its own system lines to Cleveland and to New York, it need no longer depend upon the Atlantic. Rockefeller, furthermore, had acquired Cleveland refineries formerly owned by men who were directors of the Lake Shore, and because of these acquisitions, Henry B. Payne and Amasa Stone were now stockholders of the Standard Oil and of the Lake Shore. Such a business arrangement meant more traffic for the Lake Shore and less for the Atlantic. The Lake Shore-New York Central system, instead of being a friendly connection of the Atlantic, became an unfriendly competitor.

About the same time, the Pennsylvania, moving to increase its competitive strength in the oil business, secured access to Cleveland and the profitable Rockefeller oil traffic over the Cleveland & Pittsburgh.[13] In a few months after reorganization, the Atlantic was thus faced with powerful competition on its most profitable business.

Since McHenry was determined to fight for a larger share of the oil business, a rate war was inevitable. Though rates were low at the time, the new war reduced them further, and by 1874 a railroad commentator declared that the Atlantic did its business "at an astonishingly low cost," and accepted business at "an extremely low price."[14]

Despite his insistence on the necessity for independence of Erie associations, McHenry discovered in a few months that there was no alternative, and that friendship with the Erie was inevitable. He therefore made up his mind to acquire an influence over the affairs of the Erie, but to do this it would be necessary first to oust the Gould clique. His opening gun was fired in a circular dated December 12, 1871, and addressed to the Erie shareholders. He had already rescued the Atlantic, he declared, and he now proposed to rescue the Erie by removing the present Erie directors. To achieve this purpose it was necessary that he buy Erie stock and get some proxies. In order to get financial help, he allied himself with an English financial house, Bischoffscheim & Goldschmidt, specializing in railroad securities.

Except for the common aim, the ousting of the Gould party, there was little sympathy between the McHenry and the Heath and Raphael groups. The amount of Erie stock held by McHenry was slight, while the holdings controlled by Heath and Raphael were substantial. The latter looked askance at McHenry, believing that he was interested chiefly in the Atlantic. Upon request of the Heath and Raphael group, Attorney-General Barlow had agreed to begin proceedings in the state courts against the Erie board. The McHenry group, making a more seductive approach, induced General D. E. Sickles, American Ambassador to Spain, to take an interest in its "public-spirited" activity to oust the nefarious Gould. Sickles asked Barlow to represent McHenry and his London banker in the United States, and Barlow accepted.

Early in 1872, repeal of the Classification Act was considered certain. In December of 1871, furthermore, the federal court finally convinced Gould of the necessity for permitting the transfer of a large block of Erie stock to its lawful English holders, almost all of whom were associated with the London Protective Committee, as the Heath and Raphael group was now called.

At about this time, when it appeared reasonably certain that Gould could be removed by the use of legal methods, the affairs of the Erie took a new turn. A member of the Erie's original executive committee trio, Lane, conceived the idea that in order to enhance the credit of the Erie, it would be wise for the Gould-controlled directory to resign. So convinced was he of the wisdom of this proposal, that a bribe was also considered acceptable. Whether Lane or some other party suggested the idea to McHenry cannot be satisfactorily determined. In any event McHenry was offered the Erie board for $1,500,000, and after some negotiation, the amount was reduced to $300,000.[15] Had it not been for the well-known fact that McHenry was so anxious to acquire control of the Erie to help the Atlantic, it is probable that the proposal to buy the resignations of the board would not have been considered.

The Erie by this time was physically and financially an empty shell. It was borrowing from day to day and on the very morning of the day on which the Gould group left the Erie board, its floating debt was $3,930,000. The debt had been negotiated with bankers and others who were personal friends of Gould's and who had no interest in the affairs of the company. A new non-Gould management would therefore be requested to pay this floating debt immediately. Erie's treasury assets of stocks and bonds were pledged as collateral for loans.[16]

In the face of this dreadful financial condition, with the credit of the Erie about to collapse, with receivership impending, with a heavy floating debt payable on call in the hands of creditors who had no reason to support the Erie, the board, in the early hours of the day of March 11, 1872, finally resigned. Barlow sent McHenry a wire, "Complete victory. . . . Gould removed. I congratulate you." [17]

In this startling removal, the stockholders were not consulted. The Heath and Raphael group were dissatisfied. Had they known the truth, had they known of some of the conditions under which the Gould group resigned and the McHenry group took charge, they would have been even more dissatisfied, perhaps to the point of declining to co-operate. The Atlantic claimed that the

Erie owed it between $1,000,000 and $1,200,000.[18] What is even more significant, the money which had been used to induce the Erie board to resign was to be reimbursed to the McHenry group from the Erie treasury. In October, 1872, when the McHenry board was in control of the Erie, McHenry's London banking house collected $400,000 for "special" expenses paid on account of the resignation of the Erie board.[19]

Neither did the Heath and Raphael group know that the Gould surrender was conditioned upon an understanding between Gould and General Sickles on behalf of the Erie, "that bygones should be bygones." [20] Even so, they decided only reluctantly to co-operate with the McHenry group.

On acquiring control, McHenry was immediately confronted with grave financial problems. On the very first day after the Gould overthrow, the Erie's floating-debt creditors pressed for immediate payment. Thus, the first Gould surrender of control of a majority property was accompanied by a floating debt—a phenomenon that was destined to recur on many subsequent occasions. Each fresh group of investors was surprised over the existence of a floating debt well secured; in fact, secured in such a way as to diminish the security of the company's mortgage debts, in which more was invested than in the floating debt.

There were no funds available to pay the Erie's call loans, and McHenry's banking firm in London played the role of the protective shepherd which Drew had played a few years before. Word was rushed to London that funds were necessary, and through McHenry, the firm immediately advanced $2,000,000 secured by Erie bonds. Shortly thereafter, the same additional amount was made available. Later, the same firm sold a block of Erie consolidated bonds, from the proceeds of which it retained a large sum as a commission for the sale of the bonds and for its services in ousting the Gould-controlled Erie board.[21]

The Gould tyrant was now overthrown. The Erie itself was still a financial derelict. The Atlantic was of no financial aid to the Erie. The Erie furthermore had lost valuable traffic from the lines sold by Gould to the Northern Central. The Erie was desperate, unable to pay a large call loan, with scarcely sufficient funds to maintain itself on a day-to-day basis. The Gould overthrow brought hope to the hearts of thousands; informed opinion, however, was not entirely misled. Traders and investors who observed affairs carefully had ample notice of the character of the change. One of the leading eastern railroad journals declared that the overthrow was "much like that of sneak-thieves purloining the plunder of high-way robbers; . . ." [22] and an observer in Philadelphia characterized the overthrow as a "gamble and a sham." [23]

A large part of the financial world, however, construed the overthrow as a prelude to greater things. The remarks of a Philadelphia commercial weekly were typical. "The blow has at last fallen with crushing force upon the Erie Ring, which has gone down, stunned and helpless, never to rise again." [24] Traders, speculators and investors on world financial markets—London, Paris, Frankfort, New York—rushed to buy Erie. They ignored realities and looked solely to future blessings. They would buy now and assure themselves of participation in the road's coming prosperity. This sort of guessing contest is characterized as discounting the future. When in the future the expected good things come to be true, the price of the stock no longer rises. Many people believe this now, and many believed it in 1872. In the week before the overthrow, the stock fluctuated in a narrow range, but in the week following the overthrow, the stock advanced in heavy volume. In four days following the Gould removal, almost 300,000 shares (out of 780,000 shares outstanding) exchanged hands; [25] while in eight days following the ouster, six-sevenths of the stock was traded. In London the price advanced further and dealings in the stock on the Exchange were described as "enormous." [26]

Both the overthrowers and the overthrown, the rescuers and the rescued, participated in these heavy trading transactions. By its optimistic reports the new Erie executive committee (controlled by McHenry) fanned speculative hopes. It reported, for example, that after an examination of the books it had discovered that Erie earnings had been underestimated. The news was widely publicized both in this country and abroad. In the rise of Erie stock, McHenry's banking firm benefited handsomely. Between the dates of the overthrow in March and the annual stockholders' election in July, McHenry's bankers traded in and out of Erie a half-dozen times, while other bankers and the Heath and Raphael group also took part in the speculative excitement.[27] Gould also participated in this speculative enthusiasm. Late in March he announced that he had conveyed the title of the Grand Opera to the Erie. The property had cost him nothing and it had been rented to the Erie at a high rental. As a result of this "Opera House comedy," [28] Erie rose from less than 51 on the twenty-third of March to almost 66 on the twenty-sixth. In the heavy trading English and German investors bought, and Gould sold. Gould realized profits of $3,250,000 on the advance.[29]

While these profits were being taken the Erie itself remained in a desperate condition. No economic theory explaining values over either long-term or short-term or in static or dynamic markets can explain these fluctuations in price and value which have no relationship to the world of realities. Under the influence partly of misrepresentation and partly in hope of Erie prosperity, shareholders the world over bought Erie stock. Hope, however, could not induce traffic to flow to the Erie, nor raise rates, nor re-establish and maintain earnings.

As railroad operators in charge of the destinies of both the Erie and the Atlantic, the McHenry group, aside from maintaining the company's solvency, had two major problems to solve. First it was essential to secure permanent control, for McHenry, like Gould after the Vanderbilt settlement in July of 1868, had not been elected by the stockholders. To secure permanent tenure, a circular issued in London stated that it was considered desirable to place the Erie's shares in the hands of a committee in exchange for the committee's certificates.[30] A London Erie office was organized, known as the "London Directors." This was an extralegal organization with no relationship to the Erie, and was not responsible for any of its promises or for any of its contracts. The stockholders nevertheless were asked to deposit their stock, and to sign an agreement by which the expenses of this group would come out of the Erie treasury. Those who deposited their stock surrendered their voting power. The "London Directors" were controlled by McHenry and his banker. After their experience with Gould, many stockholders again surrendered their independence to a new controller. Most of the English stock, however, was controlled by the Heath-Raphael group whose main object was to unseat Gould. Though McHenry had accomplished this, they liked neither him nor his extralegal methods. The alternative to co-operation with McHenry was an open fight, and so, true to banking instincts, they co-operated by surrender, thereby giving McHenry a proxy of 150,000 shares. With this help McHenry was successful. At the annual election in July, 1872, although having little stock of his own, he secured an Erie board of his own choice.

In order to recover misappropriated funds, the McHenry-controlled Erie management instituted legal proceedings. It discovered, however, that Gould was more than a match in ingenuity and judicial experience. Since the Gould overthrow in March, the Erie's books had been examined. The Erie informed the court that in the three and a half years of Gould's control more than $40,000,000 par value of Erie stock had been sold, and of the proceeds the road had received only a nominal amount, whereas Gould and his group had received more than $12,000,000. Since the Erie books were in wretched shape little could be proved in court. The sales of the Erie shares had been accounted for on the books of brokerage houses, primarily Smith, Gould, Martin & Co. These books, however, were not in the hands of the Erie nor could it gain access to them. The suits dragged along and nothing happened.

Meanwhile, with the Erie under McHenry's control, the construction program of the Atlantic lagged. The declaration of peace between the warring trunk lines in March, 1872, after the South Improvement fiasco which appeared to give each line, including the Erie, an opportunity to get a fair share of the growing oil traffic, had broken down. The Pennsylvania and the Lake Shore were getting more oil business at the expense of the Atlantic and the Erie. Early in August, McHenry arrived in the United States to unify more closely the operations of the Atlantic and the Erie and to wage a war for control of the oil traffic. Since McHenry was interested in immediate financial aid to help him in this struggle, he preferred to make a deal with Gould now and get less, than to engage in litigation and some years later get more.

Gould by this time had realized handsome profits from his trading in the Erie stock and had again become, for the first time since the gold panic in September, 1869, one of the leading traders of the day. In his trading activities Gould fell out with his business partner, Smith, and they took opposite sides in the market. While Gould bought, Smith in conjunction with Drew sold short. Gould soon learned that Smith was short of Chicago and Northwestern.[31] He had also discovered a bull pool in that stock. Early in 1872 a Vanderbilt group, Clark and Schell, were engaged in a campaign to acquire control of the Northwestern [32] and, to carry out their objective, had borrowed several millions from Europe.

Gould's discovery of the short position of Smith and Drew was a stroke of fortune to Clark and Schell. With all their borrowings, the price of Northwestern in September and October did not materially advance. Gould brought the good news of the existence of the heavy short interest in Northwestern to the two operators and an alliance was formed among the three. The Northwestern market began to move mysteriously. "The eccentric career of the stock," declared one market observer, was "a conundrum to the street." [33]

Smith by this time had heavy paper losses on his short sales. Realizing that Gould had trapped him, he thought for a way out of his predicament, and his thoughts fell on the books of the ex-brokerage firm of Smith, Gould, Martin & Co. Here, he thought, was the incriminating evidence that would send Gould to the penitentiary. If bail could be made heavy enough, Gould might be hustled off, and in his absence a break in the market would enable Smith to buy back the stock he had sold short, and thus avoid the heavy losses that then confronted him. The Erie management was also confident that if the books of the brokerage firm could be produced, a conclusive case against Gould could be made. Smith accordingly located the missing books, and delivered them to Barlow, Erie's counsel, who after an examination, was convinced that he had proof to convict Gould. Since Sickle's release of Gould in March, 1872, had not been approved by the board of directors,[34] Barlow contended, it was void.

Barlow now moved quickly and by November 22 the order for Gould's arrest was ready. The Gould complaint reiterated not only the old charge that the Erie had sold more than 400,000 shares and had received little of the proceeds, but it also included a new complaint, viz., that Smith, Gould, Martin & Co. owed the Erie $3,000,000. Gould, according to the complaint, had transferred this amount to himself on the ground that the Erie owed him this sum. The complaint added some new details of Gould's wrongdoings. On one occasion, he lost over $359,000 speculating in Reading stock, and on another over $13,000 in New York Central—both losses being charged to the Erie.[35]

Gould knew what was going on. For days he had been closeted with Clark and Schell planning details of the Northwestern market movements. On November 22 the stock opened at 98½, and after declining to 95, suddenly rocketed on a purchase of 4,700 shares. In the afternoon about thirty minutes before the close of trading, the sheriff appeared in Gould's offices. When Gould left to go to the sheriff's office, Northwestern was selling at 105. Shortly thereafter, when trading closed for the day, the stock was bid 200 with none offered.[36] Gould's bail of $1,000,000 was immediately provided by his partners, Clark and Schell, and Gould was released. On the day following the stock was bought in for the parties short who had failed to deliver on their contracts. The price moved on successive transactions as follows: 155, 200, 199, 200, 206, 212, 230, 225, 229, and 230. 64,000 shares were bought in for the account of two firms that did business for Drew, and it was estimated that Drew lost about $2,000,000, and Smith even more.[37]

Though the arrest of Gould was tragic to Drew and Smith, it was an occasion for rejoicing to the Erie. "The criminals may be brought to justice," [38] was the triumphant cry of that organ of railroad opinion that had picturesquely condemned the Erie rescue of March, 1872. This, however, was a pious hope. Gould was indeed arrested and the charges against him were serious.

The directors and managers of the Erie in 1872 were anxious for a settlement. Gould was out on bail. The Erie directors were willing to negotiate—and so was Gould. Gould had in his possession a motley collection of securities. He also owned real estate in Rhode Island, New Jersey, Pennsylvania, New York, and elsewhere. Neither securities nor real estate had cost Gould much. The securities which were associated largely with the operation of the Erie seemed to have considerable value. Concerning these properties, according to the Erie's counsel years later, it appeared to the Erie to be "of vital importance that the title and possession should be acquired by the company as soon as possible without awaiting the result of the long litigation and the complications which [might] arise in the meantime pending litigation." [39] Here is the typical philosophy of compromisers. A fight in court would take too long and might result in failure. Peace might be long postponed. Indeed, to the weak heart and laggard soul, it might never come. In the interests of a quick peace and an immediate settlement, therefore, let the aggressor be mollified and his terms accepted.

So on December 18, 1872, the great compromise was arranged. Gould turned over to the Erie a mess of securities. The famous Opera House was valued at $1,500,000, while other pieces of real estate were inventoried at the same amount.[40] Another asset turned over to the Erie was $1,000,000 of the stock of the United States Express Company which had a contract with the Erie; but the stock was destined never to be delivered to the Erie since Gould never had the stock. He had only a contract with the company by which the company, in return for certain considerations, had promised to deliver the stock. Gould passed this contract over to the Erie, but since Gould had not carried out the conditions of the contract, this item of $1,000,000 in the settlement was worth nothing.[41]

The settlement, contrary to the so-called rescue in March, was hailed on all sides as genuine. The Erie management was happy —so happy that it made no investigation of the value of the securities. Reflecting their judgment that large sums had been recovered for the road, the board directed the opening on the books of a Reclamation Account with a credit balance of approximately $9,000,000. Even as late as the spring of 1874, the road's management stated that in order to improve the Erie's bad physical condition, it had charged expenses for repairs to the Reclamation Account.[42]

The actual value of the securities which the Erie received in exchange for relieving Gould from liability for damages was not recognized for some years. All authoritative evidence assured the investors, traders, and speculators that the Erie had been enriched. The Erie was badly in need of funds and the new wealth would add to the value of Erie shares. Immediately, and in excited trading, the price of Erie rose sharply to reflect the increased value of the company's assets. Gould added to the trading excitement. Resorting to his technique of indirection and suggestion, he arranged an interview and raised buoyant hopes for the future. Since he was allied with Clark, president of the Lake Shore, the Erie now could negotiate a traffic route with that line, and eliminate its dependence upon the Atlantic. The credit of the Erie, he said, had been "renewed tenfold." And finally Gould came to the vital point: the Erie board, he said, would give him the first market bid for 200,000 shares, although just how the board could control the market was not explained. Gould had not finished his list of imaginative suggestions; he hinted that he would use his influence with the Northwestern to send traffic over the Erie.[43] Thus the Lake Shore and the Northwestern would become new and powerful Erie allies—and all through Gould's influence. His purchase of all or part of 200,000 shares of Erie would of course elevate the price of Erie.

The very next day, however, Barlow, Erie's counsel, brought the traders back to a sense of reality. He denied the entire Gould tale of the preferred market for 200,000 shares, and the various agreements between the Erie and other roads. What Gould meant by his lurid suggestion of a bid for 200,000 shares is not clear. Perhaps it was designed to lead people to believe that he was about to execute an order for the purchase of Erie stock large enough to induce a rise in price of substantial proportions. Gould did have some stock, for in a letter to the president of the Erie on the day before the settlement he wrote that he had "a large pecuniary interest" in the Erie.[44] But the reported call for 200,000 Erie was probably a Gould canard.

Whatever the truth, the settlement produced a lively market. The reaction was not as powerful as it had been in March. Despite the official seal set on the claim of large Erie recoveries, there were many doubters. Expectations of the Erie increase in traffic and earnings, so widely entertained in March, had not been fully borne out by events. In the ten days of heavy trading following the December settlement, Erie advanced from 52 to about 60. Perhaps Gould made some profits, though they were not large.

It was not until the summer of 1874, largely through the work of accountants who examined the books of the Erie on behalf of the London shareholders committee, that the real value of the property delivered by Gould was determined. Plenty of hindsight criticism soon developed. Additional suits against Gould began to drag their way through the courts. Meanwhile the company dropped into receivership. The receiver, who was also president, finally submitted for the court's approval terms of another settlement. By this time (1876) Gould had recovered his losses and had become a leading railroad man. By the terms of this settlement, he was able to afford the Erie some real value and the court therefore approved the settlement. Gould gave the receiver 5,000 shares of United States Express and about $500,000 of Northern Central bonds, and he also relieved the Grand Opera House of its mortgage.[45]

Gould's escape from the legal obligations imposed upon him by his misappropriations is a tribute partly to his resourcefulness and partly to his ability to interpret the motives of human nature. Although the value of Erie recoveries in the first settlement were indeed small, the recoveries made by the Erie were more than nominal. An officer of the road some seven years after the first settlement estimated that the securities (not the real estate) were probably worth not more than $200,000.[46] The recoveries in the second settlement, however, were substantial. They were made at a time when Gould was able to pay. He had bided his time and, as a result of protracted negotiations, settled at a time when the drain on his personal wealth was slight. He secured exemption from all future litigation, and the court stamped its approval upon the terms of the final settlement.

The settlement, however, was by no means a net loss to Gould in the record of dealings between the Erie and himself. To the very last day of Erie's record as a solvent enterprise, Gould was able to act for profit to himself. When the Erie capitulated and confessed its inability to solve its financial troubles without the help of the courts, and petitioned the courts for receivership in May of 1875, Gould was forewarned. According to one account Gould precipitated many suits, which in May, 1875, led to the receivership.[47] According to another he received advance information from a brother of the Erie's president. In possession of this advance information Gould sold Erie stock short. As a result of the receivership, the stock broke in a few days from 30 to a low of 18. Gould gave his informant $150,000 for services rendered.[48] Gould, except for the formal conclusion of the second Erie settlement in February of the following year, waved farewell to the Erie.

NOTES FOR CHAPTER VI

1. The first announcement of this move is found in the London *Times*, cited in Phila. *North American*, May 28, 1869.
2. New York *Commercial Advertiser*, Feb. 8, 1870.
3. New York *Tribune*, Nov. 25, 1869.
4. Ibid., Dec. 6, 1869.
5. This was the statement made by Francis C. Barlow, attorney-general, in a letter to the New York *Tribune*, March 2, 1871.
6. *R. R. Gaz.*, Aug. 13, 1870, 469.
7. This account of the struggle of the Heath and Raphael group to register and transfer its shares is based upon an account in the *American Law Review*, January, 1872, pages 230 to 254, and the proceedings before the Master in Equity before Judge Blatchford, as reproduced in the New York *Herald* in various issues of July, 1871. Additional details will also be found in the New York *Tribune* of March 4, 1871.
8. Herapath's *Ry. Journal*, cited in *Am. R. R. Journal*, Aug. 26, 1871, 957.
9. Cleveland *Herald*, cited in *Am. R. R. Journal*, Aug. 16, 1871, 1019; *R. R. Gaz.*, Sept. 9, 1871, 265.
10. Circular of James McHenry, cited in *R. R. Gaz.*, Jan. 20, 1872, 31.
11. *London Railway News*, cited in *United States R. R. & Mining Register*, July 29, 1871.
12. *R. R. Gaz.*, July 29, 1871, 202.
13. See Chapter IV, pp. 88-9.
14. *R. R. Gaz.*, Dec. 19, 1874, 495.
15. Edward Watkins, an able representative of the Erie security holders, declared that $250,000 was paid to buy the resignation. See *R. R. Gaz.*, Nov. 6, 1875, 456.
16. Details of this debt are given in State of New York, Testimony before Select Committee appointed by Assembly to investigate Alleged Mismanagement of Erie Railway, 1873, 144-5; see also State of New York, Railroad Investigation, 1879, 3590, Barlow.
17. *The Road*, Nov. 15, 1875, 307.
18. State of New York, Testimony before Select Committee appointed by Assembly to investigate Alleged Mismanagement of Erie Railway, 1873, 94.
19. Report of London accountants investigating the Erie, cited in *R. R. Gaz.*, Oct. 31, 1874, 422.
20. This is according to Sir Edward Watkin, cited in *The Road*, Nov. 15, 1875, 307; see also, State of New York, Testimony before Select Committee appointed by Assembly to investigate Alleged Mismanagement of Erie Railway, 1873, 493.
21. State of New York, Testimony before Select Committee appointed by Assembly to investigate Alleged Mismanagement of Erie Railway, 1873, 152-3.
22. *R. R. Gaz.*, March 16, 1872, 118.
23. Phila. *Public Ledger*, June 20, 1872.
24. Phila. *Commercial List & Price Current*, March 16, 1872.
25. *Financier*, March 16, 1872, 221.
26. *R. R. Gaz.*, March 23, 1872, 128.
27. Phila. *Public Ledger*, June 20, 1872.

28. This is the descriptive phrase used in New York *World*, March 26, 1872.
29. Ibid.
30. *Chron.*, March 30, 1872, 406.
31. Known hereafter as the Northwestern.
32. The president of the Burlington stated early in March of 1872 that the Vanderbilt interests had acquired a majority of the Northwestern's stock. Joy papers, Walker to Joy, March 7, 1872.
33. New York *Tribune*, Nov. 1, 1872.
34. Ibid., Dec. 6, 1872.
35. The complaint is summarized in New York *Tribune*, Nov. 23, 1872; see also, New York *Herald*, Nov. 23, 1872.
36. This account is based on current press reports, and on Gould's statement to a newspaper reporter of the New York *Tribune*, Nov. 25, 1872. It differs from a recital in the *Wall Street Journal*, July 4, 1924. This writer, "H. A.," writing from memory, has recalled many interesting incidents in American financial history. In this account some of his facts are inaccurate.
37. *Ry. Review*, Nov. 30, 1872, 5.
38. *R. R. Gaz.*, Nov. 30, 1872, 514.
39. State of New York, Railroad Investigation, 1879, 3856.
40. State of New York, Testimony before Select Committee appointed by Assembly to investigate Alleged Mismanagement of Erie Railway, 1873, 314-5.
41. State of New York, Railroad Investigation, 1879, 1459-61, Jewett.
42. *R. R. Gaz.*, April 18, 1874, 143.
43. New York *Tribune*, Dec. 20, 1872.
44. State of New York, Railroad Investigation, 1879, Vol. 5, 532.
45. *Ry. World*, Aug. 12, 1876, 522; *R. R. Gaz.*, Aug. 21, 1875, 350; for settlement of Feb. 1, 1876, see State of New York, Railroad Investigation, 1879, 1392-3, 1459, Jewett.
46. State of New York, Railroad Investigation, 1879, 2503, Guppy.
47. Ibid., 1558-9, Jewett.
48. This account is based upon *The Road*, April 1, 1876, 72. This account is supported by Collis P. Huntington in a letter to David C. Colton, May 28, 1875, that Gould made "very large amounts" on the fall of Erie. This letter is found in the Mariners' Museum, Newport News, Va., known hereafter as M. M.

CHAPTER VII

Gould Acquires the Union Pacific

When Gould left the Erie in 1872 he was again a man of wealth. He had lost a fortune in the fall of 1869; he made another in the winter of 1871–72. He was now in funds, and could resume his activities in the business and speculative markets of the day. He was still in the brokerage business with Smith, and with him he engaged in transactions involving the locking up of currency with a view of affecting both the gold and the securities markets. Little is known about Gould's operations in these fields.[1] He could not, however, long remain in action purely as a trader. In that role he was not at his best. He found it essential to operate in the securities of a given company, and by participating in its management to master the details of its business. With such knowledge, he could trade against the general run of traders.

His first spectacular success after the Erie epilogue, in trading in securities from the inside, with the aid of those familiar with the operations of the company, was in the Northwestern stock.[2] It took only a few weeks to find another, and his choice fell unerringly on the leader in the speculative markets of the day—the Pacific Mail. Gould thus for the first time entered the transcontinental transportation industry. The Pacific Mail, long a prosperous company, had fallen from its high estate. Competition of the transcontinental railroad had wrecked its earning power and its stock had become a speculative football. Gould began to trade in this stock in the fall of 1872. The existing management, led by A. B. Stockwell, was tainted with fraud and dishonesty, and by early 1873 the company was in a critical financial condition.

The annual election took place in May and here Gould showed his hand. Though his name did not appear, his influence was clear. C. J. Osborne, a newly elected member of the board, was the senior partner in the brokerage firm of Osborne & Chapin, of which Gould was a partner. Another member was Sage, who like Gould combined the functions of stock-market trading and business activity. At this time Sage was already a veteran market operator, and in his career had realized heavy market profits and had suffered heavy losses. Sage, however, was more than a stock trader. He made heavy investments in corporations, accepted directorships and assumed managerial responsibilities. In many of his corporate connections he was active in financial machinations, and was frequently the center of dramatic struggles initiated by dissatisfied security holders. He possessed one advantage over many businessmen and market operators—he always managed to maintain an ample supply of cash; and this gave him an undeserved reputation for conservatism. A standard biographical source book, for example, describes him as "one of the shrewdest and most conservative of all great financiers." [3] He was passably shrewd, but only his heavy losses in the panic of 1884 taught him conservatism. Indeed, he was one of the country's great risk-takers, and though constantly fishing in speculative waters, had the happy faculty of assuming his risks in a low-priced market.

This was the man with whom Gould allied himself. It was the votes cast by Gould that elected Sage to the Pacific Mail board.[4] The other new board member was Trenor W. Park, with whom Gould had done some speculative business, and upon whom he thought he could rely to do his bidding. The new management was elected by minority holders, and the methods were partly the same as those used in the Erie election of 1868. It was a typical Gould board; outside of the president—and he did not last long—the members were traders and stockbrokers. After some curious transactions, Sage became president of the company. The new management was not successful, the finances of the company turned for the worse, the price of Pacific Mail stock dropped sharply, and Gould's holdings showed him a heavy loss.

It was at this time that Gould made his original commitments in Union Pacific stock. The Union Pacific had completed its transcontinental line four years before. Of the original group, Oakes Ames became financially involved and made a composition with his creditors, though after his death in 1873 his sons so skillfully conducted the estate that they succeeded in retrieving substantially all of the lost ground. Oliver Ames, however, continued to hold his shares. Three other members of the board also lost heavily. When these people retired from the road's management in January of 1871, the company was left with a floating debt of $5,000,000 maturing in three months, secured by collateral with a market value about one-third less than the loan, and $10,000,000 of income bonds maturing between 1872 and 1874. The stock sold down to 9, the income bonds to 32, and the land grant bonds to 53.

The break in market prices was due in *part* to the publicity given to the company's finances. This road, like most of the railroads of the time, was built from the proceeds of bond sales. Although bondholders provided funds for a road's construction, they were rarely afforded the opportunity of participating in its future profits. Strange as it may seem, the bondholders took almost all the risk, and except for their limited contractual return, they enjoyed none of the profits. The common stock controlling the voting power represented normally only a nominal cash investment. Paradoxically enough, the issue of many rather than fewer shares of stock was widely denounced as an evil. In some cases the promiscuous issue of shares was followed by bankruptcy, in others by success. In neither case did the number of shares manufactured by promoters and financiers have any effect on subsequent earnings. A road could have earned and paid as much on one share as it could, and did, on thousands and in later years on millions of shares.

This increase in the number of shares outstanding did, nevertheless, lead to curious results. The law had evolved a quaint idea that a stock had a value independent of the earnings, finances, and physical condition of a railroad. The stock had a par value—presumed to represent the value of assets which the corporation had received in the form of cash, property or services. In fact, the company in return for its stock rarely received cash or property. The services received were valued in terms of pieces of paper called stocks, and the millions of dollars of par value stock—purely nominal value—were normally retained in one way or another, directly or indirectly, by the promoters of an enterprise. Even such an acute critic of financial excesses as Charles Francis Adams, Jr., remarked with the mellowed maturity of many years of experience, "I do not think the stock-watering system amounts to much one way or the other." [5]

This system, which corresponded to the realities of the time, was denounced by the consuming and shipping public. Some of the promoters became wealthy and their success was attributed to overcapitalization: that is to say to the issue of an excessive number of shares. Just as serious was the charge that rates were in some inscrutable way based neither upon costs nor competition, but upon the desire, even upon the necessity, of earning a return on the par value of the shares. This belief was not supported by experience. Some of the roads, such as the Atlantic and the Erie which had issued many shares, were in almost continuous insolvency; while others, such as the Lake Shore, the Fort Wayne, and the New York Central which had also issued many shares, were prosperous.

Of these overcapitalized companies the public spotlight in the early seventies was concentrated upon the Union Pacific. Oakes Ames had used political pressure in the halls of Congress, and a Congressional investigation had followed. The crude attempts to influence legislation by distribution of stock created a storm of excitement. Investor confidence was impaired and the price of the Union Pacific stock dropped. The Union Pacific furthermore was not living up to informed expectation. The increased traffic that was generally expected to follow the completion of the transcontinental route had not materialized.

The financial difficulties of the road in 1871 gave capitalists, not formerly connected with the management, the opportunity to acquire control. Aside from local groups there were at this time three major financial interests. Gould, as president of the Erie, had made an unsuccessful bid to set up a fourth group. A New York party was built around the aged Cornelius Vanderbilt, who was now through his individual stockholdings in control of the New York Central-Lake Shore route from New York City to Chicago. A second, which had already made its mark in the business life of the country, was known loosely as the Boston group and included such men as James F. Joy, John M. Forbes, and the Ameses. They had financed many middle-western railroads, including the Michigan Central, the Hannibal and the Burlington. The third group hailing from Philadelphia was loosely described as the Pennsylvania Railroad party. The bid made by Gould early in 1869 to wrest control of the Pennsylvania's western allies had invigorated the expansionist elements in the Pennsylvania management, and as the year 1871 drew to a close, the road completed a vast expansion program from Chicago and the Mississippi River to New York City. In the central transcontinental area Scott, its vice president, was also a member of the board of the Kansas Pacific which controlled the line from Kansas City to Denver. That road had also an important local traffic, and by 1870 had become a leading cattle-carrier. Although Scott did not control the Kansas Pacific, he did, as a director, represent an important Philadelphia stockholding interest. Only a link between the Kansas City and St. Louis was needed to give the Pennsylvania a line extending from Denver to New York City.

In 1871 the Pennsylvania group succeeded in taking control of the Union Pacific. Scott, together with George M. Pullman, and Andrew Carnegie, at that time a leading manufacturer of railroad supplies, became a member of the board. Scott's election as president was considered by some as a turning point in railroad history, one of the best-informed railroad journals of the day observing that in consequence of this step the Pennsylvania Railroad would "be likely to control all the transcontinental traffic for many years to come." [6]

The Pennsylvania, however, soon relinquished its control. As the date for the annual election of the Union Pacific in March of 1872 drew near, a managerial struggle developed. It was probable that the Vanderbilt group had by this time begun to recognize the influence which its major competitor was attaining in transcontinental territory. With the Pennsylvania in control of the Union Pacific and the Kansas Pacific, it was probable that it could swing eastbound traffic away from Omaha and divert it to Kansas City. Such a diversion would decrease the competitive strength of the New York Central and increase that of the Pennsylvania. Less traffic would move from Omaha to Chicago for delivery to the New York Central's Lake Shore route, and more would move to Kansas City and from that point to St. Louis for delivery to the Pennsylvania. The Vanderbilt system, be it remembered, had no line to St. Louis.

At the annual meeting in March of 1872, therefore, the expected happened. The Pennsylvania's representatives were dropped from the Union Pacific board and those of the Vanderbilt group took their place, Clark, a son-in-law of Vanderbilt, assuming the presidency.

The Pennsylvania group meanwhile expanded in the Missouri valley and in the Southwest. By interlocking directorates and traffic agreements, a through route between St. Louis and Denver was established, thus creating a line between Denver and New York. Scott was also elected president of two roads—the Texas & Pacific and the Atlantic & Pacific—which were planning to build to the coast.

Thus the three major financial groups of the late sixties and early seventies participated in one or more of the transcontinental routes. Yet none of them realized their transcontinental ambitions. Where they failed, Gould succeeded. His capture of the transcontinental routes was one of the major events in American business history, and his acquisition of large stock interests at a slight cost was indeed a compelling tribute to his genius in the arena of corporate consolidation. After the depression swept the country in the wake of the panic Gould was able to retain and expand his holdings. The two most powerful financial interests, those allied with the Pennsylvania and with the Vanderbilt-New York Central groups, were obliged to scuttle their extra corporate cargo and to limit themselves to their primary commitments in the territory between the Mississippi and the Atlantic seaboard.

Gould's first commitments in the transcontinental railroad situation were made in the spring of 1873, and years later he described the circumstances in which he made his original commitments.

"In the spring of 1873," he testified before a Congressional committee, "I met Mr. Clark and Mr. Schell at Chicago. Mr. Clark was the president of the road and he and Mr. Schell (Augustus Schell, treasurer of the Lake Shore & Michigan Southern) had been out over it and were on their return trip. . . . And they spoke so highly of the property that it induced me to send an order down to New York to buy that stock. I was on a trip over the Chicago & Northwestern, and I sent an order down, I think, to begin at 35 and buy the stock; buy it on a scale down. Well, it seems that Mr. Clark was then ill. He returned, and when I was off up in the woods he grew worse, and his brokers discovered that he would have to die, and they took the opportunity to sell his stock, and my orders caught it. After I got home the stock kept going down, and I got alarmed about it and began to inquire into the condition of the property. . . ." [7]

Gould's tale probably was factually correct. This statement was not, however, strictly truthful. Gould knew of the poor financial condition of the Union Pacific, the floating debt, the notes held by directors and the early 1874 maturity of the income bonds. This was all public property. He did not disclose to the Commission that at that time he had an important stock interest in the Pacific Mail, that his representatives were on the board of the Pacific Mail watching his interests, and that shortly after his acquisition of the Union Pacific stock, Sage, a fellow broker who had been nominated to the Pacific Mail's board through the help of his votes, became president of that company. Gould, probably, already had conceived ideas of the suppression of the competition between the Pacific Mail and the Union Pacific. If rates could be harmonized in such a way that the competition of the water route was eliminated, it was clear to Gould that an influence on the board was essential. That in turn could only be attained by a substantial interest in the stock. He was aware of the financial position of the Union Pacific and of the risks he was assuming.

Neither was it correct to say that Clark's death depressed the price of the Union Pacific. A week after his death, the stock after moving down from 26⅛ to 24½, returned to 26⅛; but two weeks later it sold at 29. The price declined because of the general market trend, and the threat of legal action by the government. In the midst of his buying program, the attorney-general filed a bill against the Union Pacific, its construction company, and a large number of individuals, suggesting that the court, among other things, declare that the Land Grant bonds and the Income bonds had been unlawfully issued. The price of Union Pacific stock declined the day after from 30½ to 25¼.

Meanwhile Gould had become interested in a relatively small property in New Jersey, the New Jersey Southern. Between the New York metropolitan area and the Delaware and eastern Maryland peninsula there was a profitable traffic in fruit, vegetables, fish and oysters which was controlled almost entirely by another road. Although the New Jersey Southern alone reached no important sources of traffic, it could by construction and acquisition provide the basis for a new route to compete for this profitable business. At its northern terminus, in December of 1870, it had made a contract with the Narragansett Steamship Company, controlled and operated by Fisk, Gould's Erie associate, by which it had an entrance into New York harbor, while at its southern end, another small road gave the company a connection with the Delaware Bay. The purchase of ferries and the acquisition of small roads in Delaware and Maryland and some further construction would produce the competitive through route.

In October of 1872, Gould and a new board of directors was elected, Gould becoming president. The road had outstanding both first and second mortgage bonds. The interest on the first mortgage bonds both in 1871 and 1872 had been earned by "a considerable sum." [8] Gould soon after his election issued an optimistic statement, so characteristic of his accession to power of a new property, promising "to make the road second to none of the great lines running to New York." [9] The route that Gould established was a queer-looking affair, consisting of portages and ferries, three-fourths rail in two separated parts, and one-fourth waterway across three bays. Despite all these disadvantages, the Gould management made some efforts to negotiate a new Baltimore-New York through line.[10]

To finance the formation of this route Gould in May, 1873, created a third mortgage with an authorized issue of $8,000,000 of bonds, of which $7,000,000 was reserved for the refunding of outstanding bonds. He then offered for sale the other $1,000,000 and also 10,000 shares of stock at par. The financial proposal was a failure and he succeeded in selling none of the bonds.

When the panic hit the country the road was in an unfinished state. It had a floating debt which could not be met; it had fixed charges that could be paid only from the movement of through business, and this could be secured only if arrangements with connections could be made. To perfect the through route and restore the finances of the company required a heavy investment. Gould, after the panic unable to supply the funds, promptly threw his commitment overboard. In October, 1873, at the end of his first year as president, he resigned, and arranged a default in the payment of interest on the road's first mortgage bonds. Before this final gesture, however, he provided himself with a strategic position in the road's financial structure. To secure a loan of $600,000, he acquired valuable collateral, especially the common stock of the Long Branch extension.

Gould was also confronted with losses arising from the Northwestern corner of December, 1872. In the settlement Smith and Drew paid him a large sum to discharge their outstanding short contracts. To make this corner effective, and to maintain a high price for the stock, he was obliged to buy a large number of shares. It is probable that the Clark-Schell group, knowing of Gould's anxiety to corner the stock, permitted most of the floating supply to pass into his hands. In any event, Gould was unable to sell all his Northwestern stock after the corner was completed. Though for months he tried to unload, he was not successful. More than four months later Gould, according to one observer, was still carrying most of the stock on his shoulders—after the manner of the mythological Atlas.[11] In the panic he sold as much of the stock as he could "to anyone who would take it. The whole operation was a most disastrous speculation for him." [12]

In disposing of his Northwestern and other stocks, thus lightening the burden of his financial obligations, he showed his superiority as a businessman and as a trader over most of his contemporaries. Neither Scott in his ramified operations in railroad and industrial lines, nor McHenry and his associates in their numerous adventures, nor Jay Cooke in his support of the Northern Pacific, displayed Gould's ability to dispose of part of a cargo in order to protect the rest. Scott's losses were particularly severe. The Pennsylvania Railroad, as the result of an elaborate examination by a stockholders' investigating committee, withdrew from the South and West, to confine its activities to the territory north of the Potomac and the Ohio and east of the Mississippi.

Gould, on the other hand, saved his Union Pacific commitment. Though his paper losses were heavy and he had some trouble in negotiating his loans, he managed to survive. Gould's personal secretary, and long his intimate associate in many of his operations, stated years later that the panic left Gould "comparatively a poor man. . . . I doubt if any man parted with more cash and securities than did Mr. Gould by reason of the catastrophe." [13]

Gould's main object in the months after the panic was to save the Union Pacific. The immediate and pressing problem was the floating debt maturing in August. If it could not be paid or funded into other securities, the road would go into receivership. Probably Gould would then follow in the path of Cooke to find a refuge in the courts, or he might lose his hope of securing a commanding influence in transcontinental railroad properties and thus follow in the footsteps of Scott. He did neither. In conjunction with other directors, he succeeded in transforming the floating debt into a longer-term bond issue.[14]

Gould then undertook to handle the income bonds maturing in 1874. The retirement of this obligation had long been considered by the Union Pacific management, and under Clark's leadership plans had been laid for its refunding. The management was embarrassed, not only by the short maturity but also by the high interest rate of 10 per cent. These plans called for a 7 per cent gold bond to take care of both the income bond and the floating debt.[15] Clark was not successful, and neither at first was Gould. Vexatious legal proceedings were begun to block the new plans, and investor opinion began to reflect the impending inability to meet the $10,000,000 maturity. The future looked gloomy.

Congress had passed a law in March of 1873 withholding the payments due the Union Pacific by the government on account of government freight, as part payment for interest on United States government bonds lent to the road to help finance its construction. Long negotiations failed to bring about a satisfactory result, and in July of 1874 the Union Pacific began suit to recover the amount retained by the government.[16]

In the first half of 1874 these depressing influences reflected themselves in the stock market. The price of Union Pacific dropped, and Gould bought more stock. In the spring his election to the board occasioned little notice. The new president was Sidney Dillon, who now for the first time became associated with Gould. Dillon was primarily a railroad contractor and builder, of the firm of Dillon, Clyde & Company. At that time he was described as a man who had constructed probably as many railroads as any other living man.[17] He did not, as did Drew, Smith and others, cross Gould's path in strictly financial matters. To such men Gould exercised an exceptional loyalty and from them he also drew a corresponding measure of personal loyalty and support.

In the midst of the depression, however, things began to assume a more favorable aspect. The sharp contraction in production and consumer demand which had prostrated most of the country had not as yet reached the Far West. The silver business was good and gave the Union Pacific a heavy volume of traffic at attractive rates. In 1873, moreover, the California cereal grain crop proved to be large, far in excess of the crop for the preceding year. The Union Pacific could say, therefore, as it did in the summer of 1874, that while other roads were showing a loss in traffic, the Union Pacific showed "no falling off whatever." [18] Also, because of the absence of competition, local rates were exceptionally high.

Gould meanwhile had resumed his trading activities. After having failed to gauge the major turn in the security markets in the fall of 1873, he reappraised the minor trends successfully. In the new environment he traded well, adapting his trading program to the new financial and business background. He took his losses promptly, reduced his liabilities, and confined his investment holdings to a few securities—primarily the Union Pacific and the Pacific Mail. In the secondary rally in the security markets late in December of 1873 and early in January of 1874, he took a heavy short position, and by the late summer of the year, he and his trading associates were given credit in some circles for having realized $5,000,000 in trading operations.[19]

During the same period Gould and his associates were working on a plan for the exchange of the income bonds for new sinking fund bonds. By the middle of September the exchange was accepted by a large percentage of the bondholders. This news, despite the existing reaction in the stock market, boosted the price of Union Pacific stock. "The principal feature of the stock market was Union Pacific, . . ." [20] declared a watchful Philadelphia analyst in September. This phrase was significant in its description of the existing market and was a prelude to many a stirring Gould market in the years to come.

In the fall of 1874, however, Gould was not yet ready to lead the market with Union Pacific, since a number of problems required solution before the stock could be utilized for market purposes. First was the competition with the Kansas Pacific. The road was still controlled by the group of Philadelphia capitalists, led by Scott, now president of the Pennsylvania Railroad. Although the Pennsylvania group no longer exercised a commanding influence in western railroads, Gould thought it wise to conciliate Scott. With this group as friends, he could look forward to securing some part of the westbound business of the Pennsylvania for the Union Pacific. He, therefore, welcomed harmonious relations between the Union Pacific and the Kansas Pacific, and after lengthy negotiations succeeded in perfecting a temporary agreement for dividing the business of the two roads.[21]

Both shared now in the transcontinental traffic and both took immediate advantage of the elimination of competition by raising their rates. This was the first of a number of steps Gould took to stabilize competition between the two lines. Every step, including this, the first one, seemed to have every reason for success. The stock-market effects were consistently favorable, and the competitive position of the roads always seemingly improving. Yet the business realities were so deep-seated that in each case the remedy, short of final and complete consolidation, did not succeed.

Gould had succeeded in elevating rates on traffic moving between interior points, on traffic, that is to say, exempt from water competition. The rates on business subject to water competition, however, were still depressed by the fight with the Pacific Mail. In order to improve the earnings and outlook of the Union Pacific it was essential to minimize, and if possible, to eliminate this competition. Although Gould was not on the Pacific Mail board, his brokers, Smith and Osborne, were. The Pacific Mail by early 1874 had recovered some of its credit standing.

Gould early in 1874 began negotiations with the company for a contract to minimize competition. Preliminary soundings failed. A senate committee meanwhile recommended that the subsidy to the Pacific Mail be eliminated, and the price of its stock slumped.

This was followed by events which throw a lurid light upon the affairs of corporations whose executive officials are primarily stockbrokers or bankers. The annual meeting of the Pacific Mail was held late in May. Early in the month, both Sage, president, and Rufus Hatch (also in the brokerage business), vice president and managing director, issued optimistic statements. Sage declared flatly that the Pacific Mail was "destined to become the great steamship company of the United States." [22] Under the impetus of these optimistic observations, Pacific Mail rose from 37 to 45.

At the annual meeting held in the last week of the month the management was re-elected. The Gould representatives on the board were charged with working in his interests. Gould had been trading heavily in Pacific Mail, and he had sold out since Sage had informed him of the "worthlessness" [23] of the stock. Just when this conversation took place is not known, but from this time on, it seems probable that both Gould and Sage, president of the company, were on the short side of the market.

Meanwhile a rate war between the Pacific Mail and the transcontinental railroads sharply reduced rates between New York City and San Francisco. Furthermore, the Pacific Mail succeeded "in diverting nearly all the China trade via the Isthmus" [24] (of Panama). The earnings of both the Union Pacific and the Central Pacific were reduced. Huntington, the dynamic personality behind the latter road, had supported a new line of English steamships established early in the summer. Though the failure of the venture left the Pacific Mail in a strategic position, Gould took steps to exert pressure on its management. The depression had left many idle ships in British harbors. Gould bought a number of them at the prevailing low prices and organized a new enterprise, with the board of directors consisting of members of the Union Pacific board and of other American and English capitalists. Though Huntington refused to support this new venture, Gould persisted. Taking advantage of the harmonious relations existing with Scott, he asked him to arrange a steamship service between Philadelphia and Liverpool to serve as the Atlantic division of his new West Coast shipping enterprise. It may be questioned whether Gould ever entertained the idea that the project would be a successful competitor of the Pacific Mail. The competitive threat, however, was part of his technique. If he could not succeed in negotiating directly, he threatened competition and then immediately backed up his threats by appropriate action. Sage, as president of the Pacific Mail, made light of this new venture, describing it as "ridiculous." [25]

Nothing came of it. Huntington refused to endorse it, and Sage refused to be frightened. Huntington continued to press his negotiations with the Pacific Mail for a new contract. He was primarily interested in diverting transcontinental traffic from the water to the rail route. If this could be accomplished, the Central Pacific would raise rates on through traffic destined for points far beyond the eastern end of its line.

While these negotiations were progressing, the rumor spread that a member of the board of the Pacific Mail was selling its stock short. A special meeting was held and it was resolved that it was "highly unbecoming" for any director "to persistently sell the stock of the Company short." [26] Sage denied that he was guilty of this practice. There is little reason to doubt, particularly in view of the events of the next few weeks, that Gould and his brokerage associates were responsible for the rumor.

Huntington, however, was not interested in these stock market machinations. Having been rejected by the Pacific Mail, he made up his mind to organize a competitive project. He revived Gould's plan and jointly with Gould organized a new company—the Occidental & Orient Steamship Company. It was capitalized at $10,000,000, but the original stockholders put up only $300,000 in cash. The company used chartered vessels; it owned none of its own. The enterprise proved highly profitable.

The organization of the competitive steamship line exerted the necessary pressure on the Pacific Mail. Before the end of the year an agreement was finally reached with the railroads guaranteeing the company a monthly rental.

This contract created a working arrangement between the water and rail routes, and removed the fear of rate wars. To Gould such an alignment was not satisfactory. A contract, he recognized, could be canceled with or without reason. He decided to get control of the Pacific Mail. However, the time was not yet ripe. The stock was reasonably but not cheaply priced. To buy at existing prices a controlling interest, say 100,000 shares out of a total of 200,000 outstanding, would have cost about $4,000,000. The board meanwhile was not satisfied with the denials of Sage concerning the short selling of its stock, and another special meeting was held late in November. Sage took the aggressive. There were members of the board, he said (referring probably to the Gould representatives), who were selling the Pacific Mail stock. (Informally, after the board meeting he stated that he had referred to the Gould representatives, Osborne and Smith.) The latter retaliated; the retaliation, revealing the hand of Gould, declared that Sage, knowing of the Pacific Mail's floating debt, had sold all of his Pacific Mail, and had sold additional shares for short account. Sage denied the accusation, and Osborne then delivered the telling blow. He read a letter from Gould which insisted that Sage had a short account at Osborne's office. A dramatic scene ensued. Sage insisted that the accusation was false. The board however was not convinced. At an informal meeting held later with Sage absent, it was resolved that if Sage did not resign he would be removed. A few days later Sage resigned.

Sage's retirement from the presidency and the public revelation that the directors were selling the stock short, further depressed the price of the stock. Gould in the press of the day was advertised as a bear on the stock. He also had company from the president and perhaps other members of the board. Under these conditions there was no reason to suspect that a buying movement in Pacific Mail would develop. So, if Gould wanted to buy the Pacific Mail, the way was open. Following the break in December Gould and his associates saw their opportunity and bought into Pacific Mail at prices almost as low as those reached in the panic. Gould thus was able to acquire a strategically valuable property at a low price.

In the meantime Gould had increased his Union Pacific holdings. Early in 1875 he owned 100,000 shares, Dillon owned another 26,000 shares (out of 367,000 outstanding). The fortunes of the road were improving, both gross and net in the first two months exceeding that of the corresponding period of 1874. The property's capacity for carrying business was substantially beyond the volume of business done, and with no "considerable" additional expense and with no increase in its outstanding debts, the company could double its volume of business.[27]

Gould was careful to make these favorable facts available to the public. The monthly earnings were published immediately.

Late in February the president took occasion in a statement to the bondholders on the successful exchange of the sinking fund bonds for the old maturing-income bonds, to express optimism. Stressing the growing importance of the local traffic and the retention by the Union Pacific of the mineral and coal-bearing lands, he went into details to describe the increase in ore and bullion traffic, which, from rather ambiguous figures, indicated a 100 per cent increase in 1874 over 1873. He also explained that coal could be mined on the company's land at low prices. Furthermore, because of the absence of the "violent competition" existing in the East, the traffic yielded a good profit. These facts, concluded the president, "warrant the steady rise in market value" of the company's bonds.[28]

The way was thus prepared early in March of 1875 for a market movement. On the third of March it was announced that Gould and his associates had been added to the board of the Pacific Mail. The rate war between rail and ship was over, and rates were sharply increased.[29] The market responded to the new transportation environment. The Union Pacific, in control of the Pacific Mail, was now free to increase its rates without fear of competition from the steamship route. With the volume at high levels and moving at monopolistic rates, the earnings picture of the Union Pacific was bright. On the morning of March 4, the day after the assumption of Gould control of the Pacific Mail, excitement on the New York Stock Exchange was "intense." Nearly everybody, according to one observer, began to trade in Pacific Mail and in Union Pacific. Soon after the opening of the Exchange, "there followed such a scene of frantic excitement, as has seldom been witnessed on the Stock Exchange." The trading in these two stocks was in "immense" volume. The same observer asserted that the "Pacific Mail will be lifted from the slough of despond . . . and again assume its proper attitude." At least, he continued, with a commendable hedge, this was the promise.[30]

The financial future of both the Union Pacific and the Pacific Mail were to be revolutionized. Shortly after the buoyant market of early March in these two stocks developed, the annual report of the Union Pacific made its appearance. Gould, speaking through this document, informed the stockholders that the importance of the road's increasing mineral traffic could hardly be overestimated. He again described the increasing production of the silver and gold mines. The establishment of friendly relations with the Pacific Mail was stressed as "a very important matter," enabling the Union Pacific to charge "remunerative" rates for freight and passengers.

The support of the Union Pacific, furthermore, would be helpful to the Pacific Mail. Though the latter's current liabilities were probably in excess of the current assets, Gould upon taking control early in March, expressed the utmost optimism: "I will see the company through financially," he remarked to one of the Pacific Mail officials.[31] The association of the company with the Union Pacific deeply impressed financial observers. It was recognized that the company was "likely to become the mere tender of the Union Pacific . . ." but under the auspices of the latter company, and with some freight guaranteed for its steamers and with some reduction in expenses, it was "better even thus to lose its significance than to be the football of brokers and speculators."[32]

The sponsorship of the Union Pacific soon brought about results. By a new arrangement between the steamship company organized under the joint Gould-Huntington leadership, and the transcontinental railroads, the two steamship lines alternated on the United States-Oriental service. The ships would run in conjunction with the overland railroads and the Pacific Mail. The railroads would divide earnings on through business between China and the United States. Gould would benefit both from his Union Pacific and his Pacific Mail.

By the end of April the hopeful predictions, combined with the favorable contracts (some of which on close analysis seemed flatly to contradict each other) produced a rise in prices. The Union Pacific moved from a trifle more than 40 to almost 80, and the Pacific Mail from the lower 30s to slightly more than 45. On July 1, the Union Pacific declared its first dividend of 1½ per cent quarterly which was increased to 2 per cent on October 1.

The Union Pacific, both in volume and in price appreciation, overshadowed the market. The stocks of Union Pacific and of the Pacific Mail combined frequently accounted for more than 50 per cent of the transactions in all stocks on the Stock Exchange. Gould by the early summer of 1875 had established his position as a force in railroad and speculative activities. Since his original association with the Union Pacific, the price of the stock had more than quintupled. From a low of 14 in 1873, it had in less than two years advanced to almost 80.

Traders and investors alike profited from Gould's leadership. The Pacific Mail, "just hovering on the verge of bankruptcy, according to its own published statements, at the touch of [Gould's] magical wand, suddenly [began] to participate in the success of its recent competitor (Union Pacific) . . . ," observed a conservative railroad journal, accustomed to weighing its words carefully. The primacy of Gould, as the leader of the class of businessmen whose operations are closely associated with their stock-market activities, was now established. "The truth is," said the same commentator, "that one man holds almost undisputed sway over the movements of the Stock Exchange. . . . No such example of one-man power has ever been known in Wall Street. . . . Under these extraordinary circumstances, to write of the New York Stock Market is simply to describe the movements of Jay Gould." [33]

NOTES FOR CHAPTER VII

1. See *Financier*, April 13, 1872, 294; April 20, 1872, 311; Sept. 21, 1872, 217; and Chicago *Tribune*, Sept. 25, 1872, for some details on the operations of Smith and Gould.
2. See Chapter VI, pp. 105-6.
3. *Dictionary of American Biography*, Vol. XVI, 292.
4. This is the statement of Gould in a letter read at the Pacific Mail board meeting in December 1874. New York *Tribune*, Dec. 4, 1874.
5. Transportation Interests of the United States and Canada, Report No. 847. Senate, 51st Congress, 1st Session, 1890, 150.
6. *R. R. Gaz.*, Feb. 11, 1871, 467.
7. United States Pacific Railway Commission, Testimony, Executive Document No. 51, Senate, 50th Congress, 1st Session, 1887, 446, Gould.
8. Annual reports of the road, cited in Phila. *Press* by a contributor, Dec. 8, 1873.
9. *Chron.*, Oct. 19, 1872, 523-4.
10. *American Railroad Manual*, 1874, 185.
11. New York *Tribune*, April 28, 1873.
12. This is the opinion expressed in *Bradstreet*, Sept. 17, 1881, 179.
13. Murat Halstead and J. Frank Beale, Jr.: *Life of Jay Gould*, 82, Edgewood Publishing, Philadelphia, 1892.
14. United States Pacific Railway Commission, Testimony, Executive Document No. 51, Senate, 50th Congress, 1st Session, 1887, 446-7, Gould.
15. Credit Mobilier and Union Pacific, Report No. 78, House of Representatives, 42nd Congress, 3rd Session, 1873, 416, Clark.

16. New York *Tribune*, June 5, 1876.
17. *R. R. Gaz.*, Nov. 2, 1872, 477.
18. *Ry. Monitor*, Aug. 15, 1874, 217.
19. New York correspondent of the Boston *Bulletin*, cited in *Stockholder*, Aug. 25, 1874, 593.
20. Phila. *North American*, Sept. 14, 1874.
21. *R. R. Gaz.*, Oct. 10, 1874, 398.
22. New York *Tribune*, May 6, 1874.
23. This is the word used by Gould in a letter to his two broker representatives on the Pacific Mail board which was read at a special meeting of the board late in November of 1874. An account of this meeting is found in the New York *Tribune*, Dec. 4, 1874.

    Huntington stated flatly that Gould was largely short of Pacific Mail. He added, "I thought at one time I would sell short but did not; and I shall not. . . ." (Huntington to Leland Stanford, Nov. 28, 1874, M. M.).
24. Letter of Jay Gould (not addressed but evidently to E. H. Rollins, treasurer of Union Pacific) Aug. 28, 1874, in Union Pacific Historical Museum.
25. New York *Tribune*, Sept. 22, 1874.
26. Ibid., Nov. 9, 1874.
27. This is the estimate made in the Report of the Government Directors, Union Pacific, for 1875, Executive Document No. 127, House of Representatives, 44th Congress, 1st Session, 1876, 7.
28. *Chron.*, Feb. 27, 1875, 202.
29. For details on rate increases, see Chicago *Tribune*, March 30, 1875, *Ry. World*, Feb. 12, 1876, 102, statement of T. A. Scott.
30. Phila. *North American*, March 5, 1875.
31. *The Road*, March 15, 1875, 56.
32. Ry. *World*, March 27, 1875, 193.
33. Ibid., July 17, 1875, 449.

CHAPTER VIII

Gould Utilizes the Union Pacific

GOULD in the spring of 1875 occupied a unique position in the railroad and financial life of the country. For a relatively small price he had secured working control of the eastern part of the transcontinental railroad—the Union Pacific. He had acquired the stock toward the end of the stock-market boom, and despite his heavy paper losses, he was able by judicious trading to maintain his financial position sufficiently to enable him to retain his stock. Unlike Huntington, he did not have the extensive support of banks and of dividends on his stock. Furthermore, the road whose control he held so carefully throughout the panic days had been acquired and lost by three dominant financial groups on the eastern seaboard.

The Union Pacific was now prosperous; its floating debt was paid, and its pressing bond maturities removed. With his control of the New York-San Francisco water line, and the eastern link of the transcontinental rail route, he dominated the rate structure. In this regard, observed Huntington, he had "a power equal to the control of the whole link." [1] Gould, as the largest stockholder, could now become an investor and reap the fruits of his activities. He was not, however, prepared to play the role of a passive investor.

The main avenues for financial and corporate strategy aside from the Union Pacific itself lay, first, in the independent Kansas Pacific and its controlled line in Colorado, second, in the contractual relations between the dominant Western Union Telegraph and the transcontinental railroads, and third, in the competitive coast-to-coast water-transportation service.

The Kansas Pacific in the spring of 1875 had fallen into financial difficulties. Shortly after the panic of 1873 the company had confessed its inability to meet its interest charges. In the spring of 1874 an arrangement was made by which the unpaid interest was funded into long-term bonds. Despite its financial weakness the Kansas Pacific was a valuable property. It had adequate terminals, both in Denver and in Kansas City. It served a rich agricultural territory in central Kansas. At Kansas City it connected with a group of roads with which it formed through routes to St. Louis and beyond. Through a wholly owned subsidiary, the Denver Pacific, it connected with the Union Pacific's main line at Cheyenne. The Union Pacific refused to grant rates to and from points west of Cheyenne that would enable the Kansas Pacific to participate in the business. This was apparently in violation of the Act of 1864 which required the Union Pacific to charge the same rate per mile on traffic interchanged with its competitive connections (including the Kansas Pacific) that it charged on its own business. This the Union Pacific declined to do.

The Kansas Pacific and the Union Pacific were active competitors. The Union Pacific moved its business over its line to Omaha. The Kansas Pacific endeavored unsuccessfully to move some Pacific Coast business over its line via Kansas City for interchange with the Union Pacific at Cheyenne. The Union Pacific furthermore controlled the Colorado Central which owned a small line from Denver north to Longmont. The Union Pacific by completing this line north to Cheyenne could compete actively with the Kansas Pacific for local Colorado traffic.

It would be in the interest of both roads to co-operate in order to remove this competition. Gould early in 1875 therefore worked out an apparent solution. A new company was to be organized, to control both the Union Pacific and the Kansas Pacific. One-half of the stock would be issued to persons named by the Union Pacific, and the other half to be exchanged for the stock of the Kansas Pacific.[2] This scheme soon collapsed and a rate war followed.

The war brought the Kansas Pacific a large volume of business from eastern Colorado, and from some points on the main line of the Union Pacific. To hold its long-haul traffic to its main line to Omaha, the latter had to meet the rate cuts of the Kansas Pacific. On through business moving beyond its own line at Omaha it could not readily do so since at that point it traded with three well-managed properties: the Northwestern, the Chicago Rock Island & Pacific,[3] and the Burlington. Shortly after the completion of the transcontinental line, these three roads connecting Omaha with Chicago formed the famous Iowa Pool for the handling of the Union Pacific traffic. The pool was the envy of the railroad world. The lines divided the through business in accordance with agreements that in the 1870s were generally observed.

Neither the Northwestern (aside from some common holdings by leading shareholders in a small trans-river road) nor the Rock Island had any interest in lines west of the Missouri River and did not therefore compete for traffic with the Union Pacific. Since the Burlington also terminated at the river, it similarly offered no competition. Members of its board, however, owned most of the stock of the Burlington & Missouri River in Nebraska,[4] and also served on its board. This road, serving southern Nebraska paralleling the Union Pacific and connecting with it at Kearney, was a valuable feeder of the Burlington. The bulk of its traffic moved to points east of the Missouri River and could be traded with the Burlington at E. Plattsmouth, Nebraska, a few miles below Omaha—the point of interchange between the Union Pacific and the Burlington. The latter gave the B. & M. a drawback on all business, and almost all of its eastbound traffic accordingly flowed over the Burlington. In addition to its local business the B. & M. wanted a share of the transcontinental traffic, and it therefore insisted that the Union Pacific quote similar rates on traffic of both roads moving either over the B. & M. via Kearney, or over the Union Pacific via Omaha. This the Union Pacific declined to do. The Pacific Railroad Acts, however, anticipated competition and not monopoly. Hence, the B. & M. in co-operation with the Kansas Pacific, supported a bill in Congress—the so-called pro-rata bill—to compel the Union Pacific to charge the same mileage rates for traffic of all roads moving over its lines. Under such conditions, traffic would flow east from Kearney to Omaha over the Union Pacific or to Plattsmouth over the B. & M.; and also east over the Kansas Pacific via Cheyenne, and the Denver Pacific to Kansas City.

Gould transformed the local struggle in southern Nebraska into one of larger proportions. Despite the fact that the Burlington traded on a friendly basis with the Union Pacific at Omaha, it, so argued Gould, endorsed the pro-rata bill. According to Gould, the Burlington was thus supporting a measure designed to reduce the volume of business interchanged between it and the Union Pacific in order to increase the volume it interchanged with the B. & M. The Union Pacific and the Burlington had always been friends—so ran the Gould argument—but that friendship was no longer dependable. "With one hand we are offered friendship and peace; and with the other Enmity and War." [5] Although this was not Gould's language, it reflected his views. Gould, by holding the Burlington responsible for the policies of the B. & M., charged that it was reducing the business of the Iowa Pool lines. He thus paved the way for the development of adverse interests between the Burlington on one hand, and the Rock Island and the Northwestern on the other.

The Burlington denied Gould's contention, insisting that it neither controlled the B. & M. nor had anything to do with the pro-rata bill. The B. & M. refused to back down. Its general manager, Charles E. Perkins—a man destined to assume the leadership against Gould in western territory—never flinched. The struggle between them exerted an outstanding influence on the growth of the West. Perkins refused to be upset by Gould's threats to force the Burlington to break up the traffic arrangement with his road. Nothing, he wrote, "nothing but cold cash" could induce his road not to exhaust its legal remedies. His road, and not the Union Pacific, was the injured party, and had his road been properly treated the pro-rata bill would never have been proposed. Perkins, through an intermediary, advised Robert Harris, president of the Burlington, to write the Union Pacific a good stiff letter. Such a letter would "do more to maintain friendly relations than any show of weakness." [6]

In the midst of this struggle over the pro-rata bill the relative position of the two major contestants was suddenly changed. Taking advantage of a sharp break in the stock market early in 1877, Gould purchased large blocks of the shares of both the Northwestern and the Rock Island. He believed that by buying these stocks he could separate the business interests of these two roads, members of the Iowa Pool, from those of the remaining member, the Burlington. At the annual meetings of the Northwestern and the Rock Island shortly thereafter, Gould and two of the Union Pacific board members (Dillon and Oliver Ames) went on the boards of both roads; while three of the board members of the Rock Island and Northwestern joined the board of the Union Pacific.

Gould understood that trading at Omaha with the Iowa Pool lines was essential to the welfare of the Union Pacific, and the conviction grew upon him that in order to depress the Omaha-Chicago rate structure, it was necessary to break up the Iowa Pool. Of the Pool roads, the Burlington was the only one that competed with the Union Pacific in Nebraska—through the medium of the B. & M. To exert pressure on the Burlington, Gould had to deal with two strikingly different personalities. The president of the Burlington was Harris, a temperamental compromiser. His business philosophy was best expressed in his own language. In a letter to Schuyler Colfax, vice president of the United States during Grant's administration, he described himself as an opponent of rate wars. On "throat-cutting," as applied to railroads, he wrote, "count me out first, last and always. I object to murder in all its forms and especially to suicide, and appreciate the military maxim:

> 'He who fights and runs away
> Lives to fight another day.' "[7]

Harris was inclined to be timid and was frequently ready to compromise a position in advance, even before he was attacked. He saw the attack coming, but instead of preparing a defense he devised a compromise.

Perkins, the other leader of the Burlington camp, had an iron backbone. Gould's threats had little effect upon him. Both in public utterances and in private communications he defied Gould's dire warnings, referring to them frequently as "bulldozing."

Shortly after his election to the Northwestern and Rock Island directorates, Gould left for New York, and early in April he met with the representatives of the B. & M. and of the three Iowa Pool roads. There he proposed to settle the open questions between the Union Pacific, the B. & M. and the three Iowa roads in one grand all-embracing transaction, to be known as the Quintuple Contract. The B. & M. would surrender its demands for interchange with the Union Pacific, and both would agree not to extend their lines in competitive territory until 1884 without a mutual understanding. The traffic of the B. & M., Gould further proposed, should be divided among the three Iowa roads. This was another of Gould's gestures. It was a specious proposal which had all the elements of fairness. He probably knew that at the proper time he could observe the letter of agreement and yet destroy its spirit.

The proposals appealed to Harris, and during the next few days in May and June he evolved one compromise after another. While they did credit to his ingenuity, they showed clearly his fear of Gould's tactics. He was certain that the Northwestern would yield to the Gould pressure, and that this road in conjunction with the Rock Island would break up the Iowa Pool. "All my action," wrote Harris, "is based upon this idea." [8]

The views of Harris influenced the Burlington's board, and on April 13 Harris and Perkins were instructed to prepare a financial and traffic report. Harris carried on extensive negotiations with officers of the other two Iowa lines. Many proposals were made, amended and later rejected. Harris stressed his fears of the possible losses to the Burlington and insisted that the B. & M. should not endanger the pool.

Perkins, however, would make no concessions on behalf of the Nebraska. It is not certain that this opposition alone would have defeated the Quintuple Contract. Gould, however, by a tactical trading blunder helped Perkins, overreaching himself in trading, as he so often did. Gould induced Dillon, president of the Union Pacific, to route some of its traffic via the Missouri Valley lines. From Council Bluffs south to St. Joseph and Kansas City extended the line of the Kansas City St. Joseph & Council Bluffs.[9] East from St. Joseph to Quincy at the Mississippi River was the Hannibal, and that road connected in turn with the Wabash which owned a line to Toledo. "A very large portion" of the Union Pacific's eastbound business was diverted to this route, for the purpose of affecting the Quintuple negotiations.[10] An official of the Rock Island who learned of this was thereby convinced that the Quintuple Contract would not incline the Union Pacific to give the Iowa roads any practical advantages. This opinion was shared by Harris of the Burlington.[11]

Slightly more than a month later the Northwestern and the Rock Island abandoned further negotiations for the signing of the Quintuple. The Iowa Pool was saved. Perkins's stand was justified, and his views served as a precedent to guide subsequent corporate conflicts between the Burlington and Gould.

Gould had lost his fight to break up the Iowa Pool—and it was the Burlington that had defeated him. Gould, however, did not long remain quiet under the sting of this defeat. Even while the Quintuple negotiations were in progress, he had moved south to deliver a blow on the Burlington's flank. The Burlington's lines in southern Iowa terminated on the west at E. Plattsmouth, Nebraska, where connection was made with the B. & M. The Burlington over its own lines did not reach Kansas City, the gateway to the rapidly expanding Southwest. The direct connection for the Burlington's business between the Mississippi River and Kansas City was the Hannibal, which gave access also to St. Joseph—another lucrative traffic-producing center. In 1871 the Boston interest, including a number of Burlington directors, sold out their stock control to the Tweed-Sweeny group. Nevertheless the Burlington's officers were confident that the management of the Hannibal was friendly and would continue to be so. The Hannibal in fact could not afford to be otherwise, since the Burlington's connection was "worth more than any other or all others" the Hannibal could make.[12]

The Burlington had an opportunity in the middle seventies to acquire control of the road at a low price. Some officials favored the acquisition, while others, including the president, opposed it. The road, though financially weak, was of strategic value not only to the Burlington but also to other lines. Gould made a spectacular bid for control of the road, but at the last moment a group of wary stockholders beat him.

The struggle to outflank the Burlington by the capture of the Hannibal involved a simultaneous effort to acquire control of the Kansas Pacific connecting with the Hannibal at Kansas City. With the Kansas Pacific and the Union Pacific under common control, traffic could be diverted to the Kansas City route, and away from the Iowa lines at Omaha. The Kansas Pacific, freed from Union Pacific control, could be bought either by the Atchison or the Burlington. The latter could connect with the Kansas

Pacific at Kansas City either by buying an existing road between Omaha and Kansas City, by acquiring the Hannibal, or by building a new line. The Atchison of course joined the Kansas Pacific at Kansas City.

The finances of the Kansas Pacific meanwhile had taken a turn for the worse. The company had been unable to meet its interest payments on the funded coupons and in December of 1876 a receivership followed. Two receivers were appointed; one, Carlos Greeley, was the road's second largest stockholder and also held a large part of the floating debt. The other was Henry Villard. He represented the German bondholders of the Kansas Pacific. In October of 1873 he had been elected a member of the Committee of Bondholders, and early in 1874 had returned in that capacity to the United States. He had been a Civil War journalist, had dabbled a little in financial matters and by this time had enlisted the confidence of German investors and large German financial institutions. Villard as receiver acted in a twofold capacity. He administered the road's affairs as receiver and looked after the interests of the bondholders as a member and later as chairman of a bondholders' committee of nine.

Greeley represented the holders of the bonds secured by a mortgage on the Eastern Division, while Villard represented chiefly the holders of the bonds secured by a mortgage on the western end—known generally as the Denver extension.

Financially, possibilities fitted in well with Gould's unique temperament. Most of the funds needed to build the road had been furnished by the bondholders. A floating debt, substantial enough though small in comparison with the sums furnished by the bondholders, was held largely by the road's directors. Gould perceived an opportunity of using a bit of money to facilitate control of a property in which others—the bondholders—had invested much more. A little money at the right time and in the right place could go a long way in the hands of an astute trader. And Gould could certainly qualify. To take care of the floating debt Gould worked out a Funding mortgage. This suggestion was accepted by the board of directors in exchange for a promise by Gould, Oliver Ames and the Union Pacific to relieve the directors, if there was any default on the first mortgage bonds, of a large portion of their personal liability for the floating debt. The Funding mortgage was secured by collateral including the stock of the Denver Pacific.[13] Upon default of the Funding mortgage, the Union Pacific could take control of the Denver Pacific and thus eliminate the Kansas Pacific's ability to compete with the Union Pacific on Pacific Coast traffic. Thus, Gould with no proprietary interest in the Kansas Pacific secured a strategic position in its affairs. Gould also made short-term advances to the Kansas Pacific secured by notes maturing in February of 1877. Furthermore, the sharp decline in the prices of Kansas Pacific securities afforded Gould the opportunity to buy at exceptionally low prices. For some of the income bonds, for example, he paid only about twelve cents on the dollar.[14]

Gould soon thereafter entered into a struggle to acquire control of the Kansas Pacific through his ownership of part of the floating debt, part of the Funding mortgage, and a substantial block of the road's junior securities. These latter he acquired in the open market. Villard was his major opponent. He represented the interests of the first mortgage bondholders. Gould's devious shifts and successive trades and proposals were met by the firm insistence of Villard that the bondholders' interests must be protected. In order to force Villard to settle on his own terms Gould exerted pressure in a number of directions. In the fall of 1877 a contract was signed with the Iowa Pool lines to encourage the movement of business via Omaha and away from the Kansas Pacific line. This contract was made, according to Villard, "preparatory to a desperate raid on our (Kansas Pacific) Colorado business. . . ." [15] Gould also threatened to move all the Colorado business the Union Pacific could control east to Kansas City via the Atchison. Gould next completed the unfinished line of the Colorado Central from Longmont to Cheyenne, thereby completing for the Union Pacific a through Denver-Omaha route competing with the Denver-Kansas City line of the Kansas Pacific. Soon after the completion of this connection a profitable bullion traffic which had moved east over the Kansas Pacific was diverted to the Union Pacific.[16]

The immediate result was a rate war on Colorado business. Chicago-Denver rates fell so low that the Union Pacific carried through freight from Omaha to Cheyenne destined to Denver for one mill per ton mile, as compared with the local rate of from twelve to eighteen times that amount.[17]

Villard, as leader of the mortgage bondholders, fought back. He went ahead with plans to foreclose the Denver Extension mortgage. Had this been carried out Gould's investment in the junior securities of the road would have been worth very little. Villard, furthermore, made a strong effort to interest officials and large holders of the securities of the Atchison, Topeka and Santa Fe [18] and the Burlington to co-operate with him in acquiring control of the Kansas Pacific. William Endicott, a wealthy capitalist of Boston, Forbes of the Burlington, T. H. Nickerson, president of the Atchison, were among those whom Villard approached. These and a number of their followers bought some of the mortgage bonds of the Kansas Pacific and promised support to Villard in reorganizing the road. Early in 1878 Villard had already devised a plan of reorganization involving foreclosure and the elimination of Gould's junior holdings as part of a decision "to fight Gould to the last." Forbes was impressed by the prospect of a successful reorganization thereby strengthening a competitor of the Union Pacific. Beyond offering prayers for Villard's success, and the purchase of a relatively small amount of Kansas Pacific first mortgage bonds, Forbes was not prepared to go.

Villard had one more piece of ammunition with which to fight Gould. He announced his determination to press forward with his effort to push through Congress the so-called pro-rata bill. This would have forced the Union Pacific to make such rates as would have enabled both the B. & M. via Kearney and the Kansas Pacific via Cheyenne to obtain a part of the transcontinental business. The Union Pacific would lose, and the Kansas Pacific and the B. & M. would gain.

Meanwhile Gould and Dillon approached Villard in an effort to enter into negotiations in order to reach a solution on the outstanding problems between the two roads. One agreement had been made in the summer of 1877; but this did not last long. Villard and his chief associates refused to negotiate. "It is clear to my mind that we can have no more agreements with Gould, because we cannot believe anything he says," [19] wrote one of Villard's chief negotiators. Gould, according to Villard, was furious over Villard's refusal to negotiate. He finally responded to this sturdy defense of Villard by applying to the court to dismiss him as a receiver. Late in 1877 the court discharged both Villard and Greeley as receivers. Gould meanwhile intensified the rate war. The Union Pacific, wrote Villard in February of 1878, "seems to be now making war on us in earnest." [20]

By the spring of 1878 Gould and his associates—a number from St. Louis—had bought heavily of the junior securities of the Kansas Pacific. Villard meanwhile had induced many investors both in this country and Germany to invest substantial sums in the first mortgage bonds. In order to unify the interests of the holders of the junior securities, Gould conceived the idea of pooling their holdings. Gould, furthermore, convinced Villard that in order to harmonize the interests of the junior and senior securities, he should join the committee administering the pool. The pool was formed in April, 1878. The holdings of the junior security holders were exchanged for the stock of the pool. The precise plan for the exchange of these securities as published by the Pacific Railway Commission was as follows:

PLAN FOR THE EXCHANGE OF KANSAS PACIFIC [21]
JUNIOR SECURITIES FOR STOCK OF THE POOL

Securities of Existing Kansas Pacific	Par Value of Existing Securities	Rate of Exchange	To Be Received in New Stock
Stock	$ 9,600,000	12½%	$1,200,000
Floating debt	1,200,000	par	1,200,000
Unsubordinated income bonds	227,000	50%	113,500
Subordinated income bonds	4,048,350	30%	1,214,350
Second land grant bonds	1,055,000	50%	527,500
Arkansas Valley Railway bonds	570,000	50%	285,000
Leavenworth branch bonds	630,000	50%	315,000
	$17,330,350		$4,855,350

Following the organization of the pool, Gould entered into active negotiations to reorganize the road. In consideration of Villard's agreement to join the pool, Gould on behalf of the Kansas Pacific, since he owned the largest part of the pooled securities, offered Villard a plan of reorganization, favorable to his clients. Gould, however, exacted a price. He agreed to make these concessions only in consideration of an arrangement by which the management of the road would be placed under Union Pacific officers. Only in this way could the war between the two lines in the courts and in the marts of business be settled, their relations harmonized, and the rates restored to profitable levels.

Gould had long bargained with Villard, who had made few and insubstantial concessions. Gould could wait no longer. The Kansas Pacific in the spring of 1878 was in financial trouble. A large amount of its notes were indorsed personally by members of the board and assumed by the Union Pacific, so that the Union Pacific in effect saved the junior security holders of the Kansas Pacific. Gould and his associates on the boards of both the Kansas Pacific and the Union Pacific used the credit of the strong Union Pacific to sustain the financial life of the Kansas Pacific in the junior securities of which Gould and his group had a large interest.

The Kansas Pacific, furthermore, was renewing its pressure in both the halls of Congress and the judicial chambers to force the Union Pacific to trade with it on fair and equitable terms. There appeared to be reasonable prospects that the Union Pacific would be required to reduce its rates on business carried for the other line. In the winter of 1877–78 Congress appeared determined to compel the Union Pacific to interchange business with the Kansas Pacific on a non-discriminatory basis. It was not clear, however, which road would gain. Legal compulsion on the Union Pacific might bring about an even more intensified warfare. The sensible business solution would be a union of interests, a communion of management, the elimination of rate wars, and a permanent restoration of the rate structure.

The concessions Gould gave to Villard enabled him to take steps toward his final goal. Once having cleared the way by his agreement with Villard, he moved with his customary energy and decision. He drew up a contract for a union of the two roads and their respective Colorado subsidiaries—the Colorado Central and the Denver Pacific. These properties, together with the Omaha Bridge which connected Omaha and Council Bluffs on the eastern end of the Union Pacific, were placed "under the general direction of the Union Pacific," to "be managed, operated and controlled as one property." [22] It was a remarkable business contract, embracing the largest pool ever proposed west of the Mississippi River covering nearly 2,000 miles of road, and under the terms of which the revenue of all the lines was consigned to a common fund. The contract was followed shortly by a rearrangement of the directorate of the Kansas Pacific. The new board included largely the holders of the common stock and junior debt securities.

The agreement was concluded early in June. On June 20, Gould held a secret meeting of the representatives of the Pool of the road's junior securities. Villard was not present at this meeting. At that meeting the group arranged to press forward with a foreclosure suit under the terms of the Income mortgage. Villard discovered this move almost immediately. This effort constituted a violation of the pooling contract. The break between Villard and Gould was again renewed. Gould, wrote Villard, is "again going back on us . . . he and the rascally St. Louis people, . . . had formed a regular conspiracy in the west to break the contract and cheat the bondholders." [23]

A long and desperate struggle between the two opponents followed. It went on for months. Gould fought to acquire control of the Kansas Pacific through the junior securities. Villard was insistent upon reorganizing the road in the interests of the first mortgage bondholders. "We, that is the bondholders, are trying to overcome Gould, & Gould is trying to overcome us," [24] declared Villard. Villard moved quickly to secure control of a majority of the Denver Extension mortgage bonds. Through New York and German bankers he succeeded in securing the deposit with his committee of a substantial percentage of the bonds. The bonds were deposited with Villard's committee of nine and exchanged for certificates of interest. He then instructed counsel to press for foreclosure. He also renewed his efforts to induce the Atchison and the Burlington to co-operate with him in controlling the Kansas Pacific. Alternatively as another possibility he endeavored to bring the Kansas Pacific and the Atchison under one control. He also considered plans of building a connection between Denver and Ogden, thereby using the threat which Gould so successfully utilized only a year later in forcing the Union Pacific to acquire the Kansas Pacific on Gould's terms.

Gould now proposed to buy the Extension bonds deposited with the Villard committee at prices substantially below par.

Having thus secured the bonds, Gould would control the foreclosure sale and acquire the property. Villard was furious. His language was reminiscent of the palmy days of the Erie. Gould, according to Villard, was faithless. No longer could he place "implicit trust in an associate who had so betrayed his confidence." His committee meanwhile went ahead with its plans for foreclosure, and by late August was able to arrange for the selection of a purchasing committee to buy the road at the foreclosure sale. The majority of the bonds had already approved the plan.

Villard, even though no longer a receiver of the Kansas Pacific, enjoyed the confidence and loyalty of the bondholders. He had defeated Gould. He had defeated a combination to exclude them from the management of the property and to turn it over to the junior security holders. Gould on the other hand was patient and he decided, if possible, to outwit, outwait and outbargain the Villard followers. Since, despite the removal of Villard as a receiver, the Denver Extension group proceeded with its plans to foreclose the property and thus to take control, Gould decided to make another proposal. He offered to merge the Union Pacific with the Kansas Pacific, but this was forthwith rejected by Villard.

The Villard group meanwhile went ahead with its plans. At a bondholders' meeting, a committee of three submitted a plan of reorganization. The plan would give control to Villard's Denver Extension bondholders. Toward the end of 1878 it seemed probable that Gould would lose his long battle over the control of the Kansas Pacific.

While he was thus struggling with these land-transcontinental problems, he could not afford to lose his interest in the water route, via the Isthmus of Panama. Indeed, when he assumed control of the Union Pacific in the spring of 1874, this problem seemed to be of paramount importance. The Panama route by aggressive rate-cutting could divert the Orient and the Central and South American traffic from the overland route. It could also attract business between the two coasts, and in view of the war of rates which perennially raged in the eastern trunk-line territory, especially on eastbound business, it was possible to attract business to the water route at points as far inland from the

Atlantic coast as Chicago and St. Louis. In order to meet competition the transcontinental railroads were compelled to reduce through rates.

Gould in the spring of 1875 had apparently solved this problem by acquiring control at a low price of the competitive water route. Through interlocking directorates between the Union Pacific and the Pacific Mail, it appeared within the power of Gould and his group to maintain rates and to guide the flow of traffic either on rail or on water as considerations of profit might indicate. In carrying out his plans, however, Gould soon encountered the physically tiny but financially powerful Panama Railroad, operating a line across Panama, thereby serving as a link in a transcontinental water-rail-water route.

Early in 1875 at the annual meeting of the Panama road, the board representatives of the Pacific Mail were dropped. Park, the fiery midget of Vermont and California, was elected president, and the war between the Panama Railroad and the Pacific Mail-Union Pacific combination began almost immediately. After the election of the new board, a resolution was passed that after the end of ninety days, the present contract regulating the division of profits with the Pacific Mail, made late in 1874, be abrogated. The Pacific Mail on its side, to add to the bitterness of the conflict, notified the Panama that it would waive the ninety days' notice required for cancellation and that it would immediately ship oriental traffic over the overland railroad. The Panama Railroad thereupon threatened to organize a rival steamship line. Whereupon the vice president of the Pacific Mail declared that a new steamship line would not take in sufficient revenue to pay the wages of the engineers.

A rate war seemed inevitable. Yet before the end of the month a basis of settlement was apparently reached with the Union Pacific. This contract, according to one source, meant that any rates between the Pacific and Atlantic coasts, not prohibitory, could be charged. It was soon discovered, however, that the contract did not cover the unfortunate Pacific Mail. "It is hardly credible," said one journalistic observer, "that this line has been slaughtered, as it is understood that a majority of the stock is in the same control as the railroads." [25] The price of Pacific Mail dropped. Gould was primarily interested in Union Pacific, his financial stake in its stock being uppermost in his mind. He was, therefore, willing to subordinate the Pacific Mail in which he had a small commitment, to the Union Pacific in which he had a large one.

Soon, however, trouble developed. Within two weeks negotiations were discontinued. Gould insisted that the rail-water route carry bulky traffic, and that the land route carry the lighter more valuable traffic. Park, on behalf of the Panama Railroad, was adamant in the support of his stand. He was not prepared, he said, to let Gould manage the Pacific Mail-Union Pacific combination and leave the Panama road with only the low-class, relatively low-profit business.[26]

Gould was not ready to make terms with Park. Although he had had some trading and speculative experience with Park, he had not tested him in the industrial world. Gould, far from proposing any settlement, announced that he was ready for a war on the Panama Railroad, and threatened to initiate court proceedings against the property because of certain alleged charter violations which had been publicly spread many years before.

The Pacific Mail stock continued to drop and early in June reached a low of 32. A few weeks later Gould, twisting another screw in order to gain better terms from Park, negotiated a contract between the two transcontinental railroads (the Central Pacific and the Union Pacific) and the two steamship companies (the Pacific Mail and the Occidental & Oriental Steamship Company). The steamship lines operating in conjunction with the railroads would offer alternative service between New York City and the Orient; and each line would get an annual subsidy from foreign governments. The railroads would guarantee the Pacific Mail's ships 600 tons of freight semi-monthly.[27]

Park however would not budge, while Gould, on behalf of the Union Pacific and the Pacific Mail, continued to negotiate. Early in September another transaction was announced. This time it was a five-year contract by which the business was to be divided between the transcontinental railroads and the Panama Railroad. Of the California business, the Panama would get one-fourth, and of the Central American business, one-third.[28]

This agreement, like so many others publicly announced with many flourishes, was never approved. These announcements were usually followed by significant movements in the prices of the Pacific Mail. It is probable that both sides were buying and selling Pacific Mail in a response to their knowledge of the negotiations. From month to month the speculative interest in Pacific Mail was maintained. On October 19, on a report that the Pacific Mail had sold some ships for $700,000, the stock moved up over two points on a volume which represented almost 50 per cent of the total trading on that day. In the following three days on reports of a favorable financial statement submitted to the board of directors, but not yet made public, the stock in heavy trading advanced another three points.

In November of 1875 these negotiations came to an abrupt halt, and the price of Pacific Mail stock dropped again. At about the same time the directors of the Panama appointed a committee to provide ships in order to engage in business between New York and San Francisco, and between Panama and Central America, and authorized also the issue of $4,000,000 of bonds to raise the necessary funds.[29] According to one story, published many years after the event, by an observer who had apparently unusual sources of information, Park is said to have sold 60,000 shares of Pacific Mail short in anticipation of the injury which a Panama-controlled steamship service would inflict upon the Pacific Mail.[30]

The Pacific Mail (Gould, of course) immediately applied for an injunction to restrain the Panama Railroad from entering the steamship business. Though the injunction was granted, the Panama company was firm. Recognizing that the Pacific Mail was not independent, it was determined to break the connection with the Union Pacific.

Although Gould succeeded in enjoining the operation of the steamship service by the Panama, he had in reality accomplished little. Informed observers soon became aware of the likelihood that Park could legally carry out his purposes by operating the service through a separate company. In mid-March Park announced that the new company, the Panama Transit Steamship, would have its first ship ready by the first of April. A price war between the two steamship companies followed. The Pacific Mail lost heavily and in May, 1876, at the time of the annual meeting, the company was faced with impending bankruptcy.

Gould had promised a year before to solve its financial problems. Now he took no interest in the company. He did not even attend the board meetings and made no plans and offered no suggestions to remedy conditions. Recognizing that Park would make no concessions, he saw clearly that a war of rates between the Union Pacific and the Pacific Mail was inevitable. There was no point in maintaining his hold upon the company while the war with Park and his companies continued. Gould therefore quietly allowed, and perhaps encouraged, the Pacific Mail to increase its debts. At the annual meeting held soon thereafter, Gould and his group were ousted, and Park and his group elected. The Gould venture in the Pacific Mail was, therefore, a failure.

In his moves to dominate the Pacific Mail and the Kansas Pacific and to bring the Burlington to terms, Gould dealt with established companies and with well-known relationships. He dealt with railroads or with competitors of railroads, with properties which exerted a definite influence on the business life of the Union Pacific, in which his interests mainly rested. There was sound basis for his agreements with railroads and steamships, and there was general expectation in informed quarters that to promote the welfare of the Union Pacific, such moves were essential.

However, few expected Gould to use his connections with the Union Pacific to make his entry into the telegraph business and to challenge that imposing telegraph citadel, the Western Union Telegraph Company.[31] His attack on the powerful telegraph monopoly was made with a small, almost insignificant competitor—the Atlantic and Pacific Telegraph Company.[32]

In the competitive race in the telegraph business, the Western Union by the middle sixties had secured a dominant role. Its pre-eminence was due in part to its foresight in negotiating railroad contracts. To the railroads, telegraph service was indispensable. For financial and other reasons, however, they hesitated to build their own lines, and so as a general rule they owned little telegraph property. In February, 1879, for example, it was reliably declared that less than half a dozen railroads owned any wires.[33]

Although competition was open to all comers, the Western Union succeeded in getting most of the railroad contracts. Having made a contract with the Western Union, a railroad was not permitted to make a contract with any other telegraph company. Among the few properties which were obliged by law to do their own telegraph business were the Pacific railroads.

The Union Pacific, like most of the roads, soon found that it had plenty of railroad problems to settle without trying to master the telegraph business. Early in its history, accordingly, it took advantage of an opportunity to get out of this business. A small rival of the Western Union—the Atlantic & Pacific—established a line from Chicago to Omaha. In order to serve the region west from that point, it purchased the line of the Union Pacific for 24,000 shares of the Atlantic & Pacific stock—stock which had been sold at ten cents on the dollar.[34] Soon afterward the company made contracts with the Huntington road for service to the coast.[35]

To the Atlantic & Pacific the purchase price was nominal, and to the Union Pacific the stock was without much value. The company operated at a loss, and neither the Union Pacific management nor any of the financial analysts paid any attention to the stock as an asset. Gould was not guilty of such an oversight. Through a syndicate consisting of himself and other members of the board, he bought the road's holdings at $25 a share, assuredly a reasonable price for a deficit company. Next, he canceled the Western Union's contract with the Atlantic & Pacific. Then followed the execution of a contract with a newly organized cable company, the Direct United States Cable, which for the first time challenged the monopoly of the Anglo-American Telegraph.

Meanwhile Gould set out to increase the efficiency of the telegraph service of the Atlantic & Pacific. In his search for technical improvements, Gould encountered the then young inventor later to become so famous, Thomas A. Edison. In 1870 Edison had devised and patented a scheme for sending two or four messages simultaneously over one wire, the ownership of which he shared with a partner. Edison tried to sell his device to the Western Union, but though that company made an initial payment, it refused to go through with the agreement. Gould, learning of the patent, had one interview with Edison and for $30,000 bought his share in the famous quadruple. A few months later he assigned the patents to the Atlantic & Pacific.[36]

Gould was now ready to strike at the business Goliath, and in February of 1875 he opened hostilities. His company reduced rates between Boston, Albany and Washington and intermediate stations to a uniform basis of twenty-five cents. The next day the Western Union met the cut. A few months later he struck another blow. Capitalizing on his close business relations with Scott, he succeeded in negotiating a contract with the Pennsylvania Railroad by which the latter agreed to permit the Atlantic & Pacific to erect new wires along its entire line and connections.[37]

Then Gould suddenly stopped. He did not extend the war of rates. The Western Union however stood firm; it was not frightened. Gould again stood face to face with the aged Commodore Vanderbilt. The Commodore in 1869 had bought a substantial interest in Western Union,[38] and soon thereafter applied his policies of corporate management. Dividends were passed and earnings used to finance improvements. The standard of service was raised and rates reduced. In its corporate strategy the Western Union was Commodore Vanderbilt. Gould comprehended the situation quickly. He could make no impression with a rate war, and Vanderbilt made no move to buy him out. Clearly, that was Gould's intention, and he became anxious, if not solicitous, about his investment in the Atlantic & Pacific stock. He took the initiative in his plan to palm off the company on the Western Union. Talking through the vice president in charge of operations, he publicly disseminated statements on the large savings that a consolidation would create. Union of the two companies, it was asserted, would save $1,500,000 a year.[39]

Gould then entered into negotiations with prominent shareholders of both companies. By the end of 1876 he had accumulated between 70,000 and 80,000 shares of Western Union stock, and reports spread that a consolidation with or sale to the Western Union was already made.

The nature of these negotiations has never been revealed. Vanderbilt was not disposed, after his experience with the Erie, to make life any easier for Gould or his clique, and he refused to budge. Early in September, after several weeks of negotiations, it was announced publicly that the consolidation of the two properties had been formally abandoned.[40] For the remainder of the year Gould, finding it difficult to frame a policy, did little. Then death came to the elder Vanderbilt in January of 1877, and Gould's mind was set. Recognizing that with Vanderbilt's death went also the backbone of the enemy's leadership, he resolved to resume the struggle on a broader, more aggressive basis. (Hereafter, except where otherwise mentioned, Vanderbilt refers to W. H. Vanderbilt.)

He found an ally in the Baltimore & Ohio, then engaged in a railroad rate war in eastern territory. The war involved an old principle. Baltimore and Philadelphia served, respectively, by the Baltimore & Ohio and the Pennsylvania railroads, insisted that their lines be permitted to carry freight to and from these cities at rates lower than those charged by the New York Central and the Erie on New York City business. This was necessary, so it was contended, in order to equalize the lower ocean rates and other services which tended to favor New York City as a shipping center. Gould, overlooking no opportunity, took advantage of this opening, and succeeded in diverting the competitive aggravations from the railroad to the telegraph field. He was able, in short, to utilize the antagonisms of the railroad rate war as a tool in his telegraph war. The Western Union was a Vanderbilt property.

A thrust at the Western Union was a thrust at Vanderbilt. Gould asked John W. Garrett, the fighting president of the Baltimore & Ohio, to serve on the board of the Atlantic & Pacific. The contract of the Baltimore & Ohio with the Western Union was not as ironclad as the typical arrangement, and there was good legal ground for believing that the contract could be canceled. Gould asked Garrett to do this very thing, thereby bringing the Baltimore & Ohio's line into the fold of Gould's telegraph company. He pointed out that the Western Union's stock was watered, and that, therefore, with the help of Garrett's property, competition would be facilitated.[41]

In mid-February, 1877, a few weeks after the death of the elder Vanderbilt, the new policy of Gould's telegraph company was formally announced. The board of directors was enlarged, adding Garrett and Jewett, president and receiver of the Erie. Two of the four trunk lines were now represented on its board. The board was further strengthened by the election of Huntington, the dominant power in the affairs of the Central Pacific, and

C. K. Garrison, who held the controlling interest in the Missouri Pacific. Another newcomer was James R. Keene, a speculative trading capitalist, just arrived in the East after making a series of successful trades in the gold and security markets in California. He had some loose cash, and Gould induced him to take a speculative flier in Atlantic & Pacific. Keene shortly thereafter brought Sage into the venture.

Shortly after the organization of the new board, the company announced its expansion program. To finance this new program the board authorized the sale of 200,000 shares of common stock at $20 a share. It also ordered a sweeping reduction in rates. The new rate structure produced losses for both companies,[42] as Gould had intended. In announcing the heavy rate cuts, he informed the public that he was working for the public welfare, thus following the same technique that he had pursued a few years before as president of the Erie. He had then been fighting the New York Central-Vanderbilt monopoly, and was now fighting the Western Union-Vanderbilt monopoly. The Atlantic & Pacific, said a Gould-sponsored statement of the board of directors, had "been the pioneer in extending the benefits of cheap telegraph communication to the public. Whenever they [Atlantic & Pacific] have been in competition with the Western Union, a reduction of rates has been the result." [43]

Gould now massed his fortunes to attack the very heart of the power of the Western Union—the exclusive railroad contract. His first shot was the cancellation of the Baltimore & Ohio-Western Union contract, and in February the Baltimore & Ohio transferred its telegraph business from the Western Union to the Atlantic & Pacific. His next blows were delivered in Ohio and Indiana where the Atlantic & Pacific had executed contracts with a number of railroads which then had exclusive arrangements with the Western Union. The Atlantic & Pacific was stopped by injunctions and the exclusive contracts upheld.[44] He then turned to the Northwestern and the Rock Island to whose boards he had just been elected. On these roads he held minority interests, and although he promised much, he accomplished little. About the same time he entered into active negotiations with the Erie whose president was also on the board of the Atlantic & Pacific. Although at times success seemed close at hand, the Erie finally decided to retain its Western Union management. In short, the Western Union's exclusive railroad-telegraph contracts were almost universally sustained.[45] The Western Union, nevertheless, for the first half of 1877 failed to earn its dividends. The fortunes of the Atlantic & Pacific meanwhile, in the language of the president of the Western Union some years later, were "at low ebb." [46]

Vanderbilt, son of the Commodore and his successor in business, obviously could have exploited these weaknesses for the benefit of the Western Union. Since his fortune was tied up largely with the earnings and value of the New York Central system, his interest in the Western Union was not his primary one. He owned most of the stock of the New York Central and a large block, not a majority, of the stock of the Lake Shore, whose earning power had not yet been well established. Shortly before the death of his father in January, 1877, the eastern rate war broke out anew. Its effects were particularly damaging on account of the deepening depression. The spring of 1877 was severely gloomy. Railroad earnings fell and stock prices dropped to new lows. The prolonged railroad rate war intensified the existing pessimism. Early in April, however, both the railroad and the financial worlds were surprised by the sudden ending of the rate war. The principle of rate equality between eastern ports which Commodore Vanderbilt had espoused and which was so glowingly endorsed by his son was surrendered in the new agreement of April 5. Vanderbilt "virtually [yielded] all that [Commodore Vanderbilt] won," observed a financial writer.[47]

To Gould this settlement was a signal, representing a beacon on the right path to negotiations with Vanderbilt. William H., unlike his father, was not temperamentally constituted to fight a battle to its bitter and necessary conclusion. He had developed the conservative instinct of the investor and could not appreciate the importance of changing values and of changing economic forces. He would not turn away from approaching personal loss at the expense of a corporation and its bond and stockholders. On the other hand, he had the instinct of self-preservation. He usually waited for the attack, and if he was attacked, he defended himself. If the losses were too severe, he habitually compromised with or appeased the aggressor. Gould understood these habits of mind. Vanderbilt's surprising concession in the agreement to end the rate war in April, 1877, taught Gould how to play his cards in the approaching negotiations designed to unload the weakening Atlantic & Pacific upon the shoulders of the powerful Western Union.

In addition to the New York Central and the Lake Shore, Gould in dealing with Vanderbilt also had to take into consideration two additional sets of railroad properties. First was the north shore line from Chicago to Buffalo via Detroit. From Detroit to Buffalo two properties competed for the through business. One was the Great Western, in which Vanderbilt had no interest. The other was the Canada Southern, a line with exceptionally low grades and with low operating costs. It was built by a group of promoters with whom Drew was associated; but almost before the road was opened for through business, the panic of 1873 deprived it of financial support. At Detroit these two roads were fed with eastbound traffic by the Michigan Central, which for many years prior to 1873 was financially one of the strongest in the country. It was also essential for Vanderbilt to cultivate friendly traffic relations with a railroad from Chicago to Omaha in order to command a part of the eastbound transcontinental business of the Union Pacific.

Gould, aware of these relationships, used them skillfully in his negotiations over the Atlantic & Pacific. In April of 1877, within a few days after Vanderbilt negotiated the eastern railroad rate agreement, Gould, taking advantage of a sharp market break, bought enough shares of the Rock Island and the Northwestern —two of the three Omaha-Chicago roads—to get him on the boards of both.

No sooner had he found a place on these boards than the report spread that he had acquired control of the majority of the stock of the Michigan Central as well as of the Canada Southern. The sharp drop in the price of the former's stock lent color to the story. Many of the old stockholders sold,[48] though Moses Taylor, the veteran president of the National City Bank, held on. So did Samuel Sloan, the vigorous chief of the Lackawanna, and indeed in the early market break of the stock, he even added to his holdings.[49] In the spring of 1876 Taylor made up his mind to use his influence to elect Sloan as the successor of Joy to the presidency of the road. In June of 1876 the Taylor ticket, with Sloan at its head, was easily elected.

By the time the 1877 annual election approached, the affairs of the Michigan Central had not improved. An open proxy fight developed. One ticket was headed by Dillon, president of the Union Pacific, and an intimate Gould associate. Such a group might divert the Michigan Central business from the Canada Southern to the Great Western and, combined with a rate war, might succeed in impairing the value of the Vanderbilt holdings in the Canada Southern.

Even though the Gould ticket opposed the existing Sloan-Taylor management, there was no community of interest between it and the Vanderbilt ticket. Sloan himself was not averse to admitting Vanderbilt to the board; indeed he believed that such a representation would improve the competitive situation and facilitate the organization of a pool between the Michigan Central and the Lake Shore.[50]

As the time for the annual election drew near, Sloan lost some of his earlier confidence. Although he and Joy were working hard to line up the proxies, the climax took place in the home of Taylor in New York City. The balloting was as close as Sloan had feared. Taylor, true to the type of conciliatory and peace-loving interests of the investment banker, insisted that harmony must prevail on the Michigan Central's board. He was anxious to be rid of speculators and therefore wanted no representative of the New York Central on the board. In view of the conservative Vanderbilt following this might appear strange, though it is not so strange when it is understood that Taylor believed Vanderbilt's proxies would include those of Sage, Dillon and Gould. Taylor had received information from certain stockbrokers that Vanderbilt had written Gould asking him about his proxies.[51] Gould, however, was playing a careful, complex game, and Vanderbilt, neither for the first nor for the last time, seemed entirely unaware of his real motives.

A few days before the election, Vanderbilt called upon Taylor at the latter's home. On the occasion of his first call, June 19, in a talk which lasted an hour and a half, Vanderbilt denied that he wished to acquire control. He wanted only some representation on the board of directors. In the discussion Vanderbilt at no time mentioned Gould's name; but while the discussion was proceeding, a messenger arrived with a telegram from Gould addressed to Taylor, in which Gould inquired whether Taylor was certain that without Gould's proxies he was sure of electing his ticket. The Gould messenger informed Taylor that Vanderbilt had telegraphed him that he had enough votes to control the election.

On the evening of the twenty-first Vanderbilt again called upon Taylor, and again Vanderbilt explained that he wanted only to be represented on the Michigan Central's board. He now recognized that the promised hope from Gould would not be realized. Vanderbilt himself had only 30,000 proxies, while Taylor had 80,000; and with Gould and Dillon, respectively, controlling 40,000 and 25,000, Vanderbilt concluded to throw his support to the Taylor ticket, thus insuring the defeat of the Gould combination. When Taylor informed Vanderbilt that he could not promise him representation on the board, Vanderbilt, with a dramatic gesture, declared to Taylor, "There are the proxies, you can use them." [52]

Since both the Gould and the Vanderbilt proxies were turned over to Taylor, the Taylor-Sloan ticket was re-elected to office by a sweeping majority. In consequence of the proxy battle, Vanderbilt recognized that Gould held the deciding position in a contest for control. The Taylor following did not consist entirely of strongly held stocks, and an increase in the price of the stock would probably bring about selling from holders who had carried it all the way down, and, who on the way up, would be able to recover a portion of their cost. Some of the stock sold by disappointed investors might therefore be bought on the open market. Under these circumstances it was probable that the support of the Gould and Dillon proxies would probably exert the controlling influence in the annual election of the Michigan Central in the summer of 1878.

It is probable that in the summer of 1877 when negotiations were proceeding for the union of the two telegraph companies, such a possibility was presented to Vanderbilt. Gould, in trading on behalf of the Atlantic & Pacific, held the whip also over Sage who with his speculative associate, Keene, was a large holder of the Atlantic & Pacific stock. The stock was only 20 per cent paid up, and in view of the company's deficit, an assessment would soon be necessary—an outcome which was more than Sage had bargained for.

It is therefore probable that Gould presented Vanderbilt with a proposal somewhat as follows: *I will sell to you, Mr. Vanderbilt, sufficient stock to enable you to acquire a controlling influence in the Michigan Central, and in turn you will purchase from me and my associates the controlling influence in the Atlantic & Pacific.* It is also probable that Gould might have induced Dillon to agree to sell his large holdings of the stock of the Canada Southern to Vanderbilt.

In the Michigan Central's annual election of June, 1878, the control was passed to Vanderbilt. As late as April Vanderbilt kept repeating the denials he had made in the summer of 1877, that he was not buying control of the property and that if control did pass to him, it would be accomplished through proxies. The fact remains nevertheless that he had been buying stock steadily since July of 1877, and it is significant to observe that this was shortly before the execution of the agreement for the sale of the Atlantic & Pacific to the Western Union.

A final agreement in the form of a consolidation and pooling arrangement for the sale of the Atlantic & Pacific to the Western Union was made in August, 1877. Although the one was not necessarily contingent upon the other, the president of the Western Union was sufficiently realistic to understand that a pooling agreement, unless it was accompanied by control, would not be kept. The Western Union bought more than 72,000 shares at $25 per share, payable partly in cash and partly in its own shares; the president piously expressing the hope that the pooling agreement and stock control would stop "wasteful competition." [53] If the current report can be accepted that Sage, Keene and associates controlled 58,000 shares out of the 72,000 involved in the agreement, then they must have looked up to Gould with a sort of reverential awe. The Atlantic & Pacific was weak financially. With the optimistic expectations entertained so lavishly early in the year almost gone, and with the monthly statements indicating an inability to earn even operating expenses, Gould succeeded in unloading this property in exchange partly for cash and partly for the stock of one of the best investment properties on the Stock Exchange.

As a result of this transaction, Gould enlisted the services of two powerful associates. The Atlantic & Pacific was the first transaction in which Sage joined with Gould since the latter exposed the former in the Pacific Mail. Only two months before, Gould in entering the Rock Island board did not take Sage with him. After the telegraph agreement, Sage's membership with Gould on corporate boards was almost a universal rule. The salvage of the Atlantic & Pacific investment cemented a life-long friendship between the two men.

The immediate results of the agreement were satisfactory to all concerned. The short-period results of most of Gould's moves were usually satisfactory, thereby enabling him from time to time, as changing circumstances required, to obtain the support of leading personalities. He could drop them later as changing circumstances again dictated. When he needed a public propagandist, Fisk was at hand; when he needed strong leaders and market supporters, Keene and Sage were at hand; when he needed citizens of eminence and respectability, Cyrus W. Field and Joy were available.

While Sage and Keene benefited from the unloading of the semi-defunct Atlantic & Pacific onto the Western Union, the Western Union stockholders were not harmed. In fact the immediate effect was favorable. Western Union which late in July sold below 62, sold late in August, soon after the consolidation, more than 20 points higher. This consummation was of course gratifying to Vanderbilt and he was congratulated by both his friends and enemies. Perhaps he felt like Neville Chamberlain when he returned to England after concluding the Munich Pact in September, 1938. He had saved the peace for his own people and had given his enemies the opportunities they desired. The latter advantage, in either case, except for a few farseeing souls, was not appreciated. Vanderbilt set an unfortunate example twice in one year in appeasing his enemies. The Atlantic & Pacific contract was especially unfortunate. It put promoters on notice that if they could produce sufficient noise and disturbance and exert sufficient loss on another property, their own loss would be temporary, since they would eventually be taken over by the corporate Santa Claus. Vanderbilt did not learn this lesson immediately. Not until the summer of 1884 did he take firm ground, as his father always had done, in rejecting compromises with corporate racketeers.

It is probable that after his disposition of his Atlantic & Pacific stock, Gould's major holdings consisted of his large block of Union Pacific—more than 50 per cent of the total outstanding—and his increasingly large holdings in the junior securities of the Kansas Pacific. In the latter part of this Union Pacific period, from the fall of 1877 to the winter of 1878–79, Gould accomplished little. In these years, as indeed during most of his Union Pacific association (1874–84), his control was almost absolute. Charles Francis Adams, Jr., when president of the road in 1885, expressed the opinion, "that some years ago Mr. Gould was the Union Pacific Railway Company. His will was just as much law in it as the will of the captain of a frigate on board his ship. Mr. Dillon (president) was his representative. Mr. Dillon never consulted anyone except Mr. Gould, and Mr. Gould was in the custom of giving orders without consulting Mr. Dillon at all. These orders were implicitly obeyed." [54] In his efforts to exploit the possibilities arising out of his domination of the policies of the Union Pacific he was not successful. Neither did he succeed in building up the earnings of the Kansas Pacific. On the eastern end of the transcontinental line, his program must also be set down as a failure. He made no impression on the Omaha-Chicago roads; his moves to exercise an influence in the corporate policies of the Northwestern and the Rock Island produced only slight results. At the eastern terminus of the Kansas Pacific in Kansas City, his efforts were similarly unsuccessful. He also failed in his grab for the Hannibal.

By the fall of 1878, moreover, the value of Gould's Union Pacific holdings became questionable. The dividend due in July, 1878, was passed. This was due largely to a law which obliged the road to pay 25 per cent of its net earnings into a federal subsidy sinking fund. In October the road resumed dividends, but on a basis reduced from 2 per cent quarterly to 1½ per cent quarterly. Though for months the price of the stock ranged between 65 and 70, it was reported that bankers would lend money on the stock as collateral only at a marked-down price of 30; and at that price the paper profit of Gould's Union Pacific disappeared.

To some extent the lack of interest in Union Pacific stock was due to the concentrated ownership of more than a majority in the hands of one man: Gould. It was due also to the baneful influence of Gould's financial and speculative methods. The collapse of the Pacific Mail after his retirement in the spring of 1876, his lack of faith toward his railroad associates in the directorate of the Atlantic & Pacific, his chicanery in undermining the Hannibal, and his faithlessness in dealing with Villard in the negotiations for the reorganization of the Kansas Pacific gave him and his controlled Union Pacific a bad name. No intelligent trader would trade in a stock, a large part of which was controlled by a leading operator whose career marked him as one who would not hesitate to use any means to achieve trading results. And his methods induced the average investor to shun the purchase of a stock over which Gould exercised all but complete control.

Furthermore, the earnings of the Union Pacific were no longer rapidly expanding. In the fall of 1878 a government source informed the investing public what the railroad world already knew. The physical condition of the Union Pacific, reported the agency, was not satisfactory; its "deficiencies [were] many and apparent," and the management gave no evidence that it was "the work of any superior organizing mind." [55]

Gould's financial position late in 1878 was made more serious by errors in trading judgment. Gould was optimistic on the grain roads, and when in the summer of 1878 reports of heavy crop damage broke the price of the granger (i.e., the Northwestern grain carriers) stocks, his losses were heavy. Gould shared the common gloom arising from the drop in stock prices, and in the fall of 1878, just as the market was about to move up under the influence of the approaching resumption of specie payments, he revised his trading position, and sold granger and other stocks short. A well-known railroad capitalist and a close observer of stock-market affairs declared that Gould at that time was a "very great bear" and that he was spending the greater portion of his time depreciating the value of the Northwestern and St. Paul securities.[56]

Gould's trading judgment was wrong. The preparations for specie resumption were carefully made, and the damage to the grain crop proved to be exaggerated. A good crop combined with a short crop in Europe brought in a large supply of gold. The price of the dollar in terms of gold rose, and by the end of the year the dollar sold at par with gold. The stock market began the rise which did not end until the summer of 1881.

The upward market movement, furthermore, was well led and well organized. Keene, Gould's trading associate in the Atlantic & Pacific speculation, was the leader of the traders operating for the rise. Keene was favored by Gould's trouble with his trading associates. Late in 1878 his former trading allies became his enemies. Keene, understanding the weakness of Gould's trading armor, moved to break him financially. The path seemed easy. Gould's heavy holdings in Union Pacific and Kansas Pacific were pledged to secure loans—mostly due on demand. The Union Pacific market was not too good; the Kansas Pacific market was nominal. Keene invited Gould's creditors to a conference to settle with Gould, and all except Sage accepted. The demands for immediate settlement upset Gould and it was reported that he sold 40,000 shares of Union Pacific. Another meeting was called and according to one story, Keene at this meeting delivered an ultimatum: Gould must leave Wall Street forever—or be irretrievably ruined. Gould agreed but Sage saved the day. Learning of Keene's tactics, he went into a towering rage, declaring that Keene had gone too far, and that he would back Gould to the end. He did. The next morning Gould gave Keene a check for $2,000,000. The check bore the name of Sage, and Gould was saved.[57] Though the details of Gould's finances are not available, enough is known to assert that Gould was in real financial danger. Patrick Geddes, a private banker in New York and a large stockholder in a number of western railroads, wrote confidentially to a business associate that Gould's cash means were very much reduced, and that he was told that Gould was no longer feared or followed.[58] Another influential railroad stockholder, W. L. Scott, of Erie, Pennsylvania, reflected financial opinion when he observed in a letter to the president of the Northwestern that if any reliance could be placed upon what everyone says, Gould in the fall of 1878 had lost from a million and a half to three millions of dollars and that he was then in a tight position.[59]

In the winter of 1878–79, therefore, Gould as a trader was in an unenviable position. He had a large block of Union Pacific stock, the price of which was stable only because he did not and could not sell any more of his holdings. His Kansas Pacific securities had slight value, and the threatened foreclosure of the Denver Extension mortgage promised to eliminate even that. On the other hand, the securities which he had sold short had advanced. Hence, his paper profits on his securities owned were elusive; while the losses on his securities sold short were real and heavy. His reputation among traders meanwhile reached a new low. "He is a man who can't make any money himself," said one trader, "and doesn't want to see anybody else do so." [60] And another, described in the press as one of the three greatest Wall Street operators, declared, "Nothing that Gould undertakes will ever amount to anything." [61]

Out of this drab outlook in the winter of 1878 and 1879, Gould by brilliant maneuvering, and by shifting into new fields with speed and decisiveness, succeeded in the course of the next three years in reaching the pinnacle of business power and influence. In these years his moves were almost uniformly successful, and before the end of the period he became in many respects the leading railroad man of the land and undoubtedly one of its most powerful financial leaders.

NOTES FOR CHAPTER VIII

1. Huntington to Hopkins, April 19, 1875, MM.
2. This agreement is critically analyzed by one of the muckraking journals of the day, *The Road*, May 15, 1875, 118-19. The writer was presumably the editor, T. S. Fernon, who for many years was an able observer of the growth of the Pennsylvania Railroad, and who was familiar with the work of Scott. Referring to Gould and Scott as "that brace of local filibusters," he concluded that the transaction was primarily "a Gould-Scott job." See for summary of plan, *Chron.*, May 15, 1875, 476-7.
3. Known hereafter as the Rock Island.
4. Known hereafter as the B. & M.
5. Burlington archives, letter of S. H. H. Clark, General Superintendent, Union Pacific, to W. B. Strong, General Superintendent, Burlington, April 14, 1876.
6. Ibid., Perkins to Strong, undated but probably between April 14 and 20, 1876.
7. Ibid., R. Harris to Colfax, March 12, 1877.
8. Ibid., Harris to J. N. A. Griswold, April 7, 1877. The letter was marked "Not Sent."

9. Known hereafter as the Council Bluffs.
10. Burlington archives, Harris to Griswold, May 17, 1877, expressing the view of an official of the Rock Island. George Tyson, an officer of the B. & M., in a letter to Perkins, May 21, 1877, repeats the same story. Harris in a letter to Perkins, May 16, 1877, credits Riddle of the Rock Island with the opinion that Gould and Dillon desire "very much" that the route via the Council Bluffs, the Hannibal and the Wabash shall participate largely in the business to and from the Union Pacific. These letters are found in Burlington archives.
11. Ibid., Harris to Perkins, May 16, 1877.
12. Ibid., Walker, president, Burlington, to Griswold, Chairman, Jan. 19, 1875.
13. This account of Gould's relation to the Funding mortgage is based on statements by Villard in the affidavit filed in the suit begun by Gould to oust Villard as a receiver of the Kansas Pacific. The affidavit is in the H.V.P.
14. This was told to a banker who was close to the Burlington management by a New York attorney, who had drawn foreclosure bills on two Kansas Pacific mortgages. Burlington archives, P. Geddes to Forbes, April 21, 1878.
15. H.V.P., T. F. Oakes to Villard, Nov. 30, 1877, Box 7.
16. *Ry. Review*, Dec. 29, 1877, 225.
17. Report of Government Directors, Union Pacific, 1878, 148.
18. Known hereafter as the Atchison.
19. H.V.P., Horace White to Villard, July 5, 1877, Box 108.
20. H.V.P., Villard to Robert Carr, February 5, 1878, Box 117.
21. United States Pacific Railway Commission, Testimony, Executive Document No. 51, Senate, 50th Congress, 1st Session, 1887, 165.
22. *Chron.*, June 22, 1878, 626, for the text of the contract; and in the Report of the Government Directors of the Union Pacific, 1878, 151-2.
23. H.V.P., Villard to Mrs. Villard, June 25, 1878, Box 7.
24. Ibid., Villard to John Evans, Nov. 19, 1878.
25. Phila. *North American*, April 24, 1875.
26. New York *Tribune*, Nov. 30, 1875, contains the statement of Park in an injunction suit begun by the Gould interests to stop the Panama from operating steamships.
27. New York *Tribune*, June 22, 1875.
28. *Financier*, Sept. 4, 1875, 169; *Chron.*, Sept. 4, 1875, 231.
29. *Ry. World*, Nov. 20, 1875, 759.
30. *Wall Street Journal*, Sept. 17, 1925.
31. Known hereafter as the Western Union.
32. Known hereafter as the Atlantic & Pacific.
33. This was the statement of Norvin Green, president of Western Union, made before the Senate Committee on Railroads, Senate Report No. 805, 45th Congress, 3rd Session, Feb. 13, 1879, in connection with a resolution authorizing an investigation into the expediency of authorizing railroads to build and operate telegraph lines for commercial purposes, p. 1. For details on railroad telegraph contracts, see Testimony before Committee on Post Offices and Post Roads, on the Postal Telegraph, Report No. 577, Senate, 48th Congress, 1st Session, 1884, 19, 128, 186; Bradstreet, Aug. 15, 1885, 98.
34. Land-Grant Telegraph Lines Report No. 3501, House of Representatives, 49th Congress, 2nd Session, 1886, 24, Reiff. According to *Federal Reporter*, Vol. 1, 746, 1880, the Union Pacific received only 17,800 shares.
35. *R. R. Gaz.*, April 30, 1870, 102.
36. New York *Tribune*, April 20, 1877; Mary Childs Nerney, *Thomas A. Edison*, 178; Harrison Smith, New York, 1934.
37. *Am. R. R. Journal*, May 22, 1875, 667; *R. R. Gaz.*, May 22, 1875, 211.
38. The circumstances under which Vanderbilt bought into the Western Union are described in Testimony before the Senate Committee on Education and

Labor as to the Relations between Labor and Capital, Report No. 1262, Senate, 48th Congress, 2nd Session, 1885, 948-9, Green.

39. New York *Tribune*, Aug. 17, 1875.
40. New York *Tribune*, Sept. 6, 1875.
41. Testimony before Committee on Post Offices and Post Roads, on the Postal Telegraph, Report No. 577, Senate, 48th Congress, 1st Session, 1884, 131-2, Garrett.
42. This opinion was expressed by Green some years later in Testimony before the Senate Committee on Education and Labor as to the Relations between Labor and Capital, Report No. 1262, Senate, 48th Congress, 2nd Session, 1885, 919-20; and in Testimony before Committee on Post Offices and Post Roads on the Postal Telegraph, Report No. 577, Senate, 48th Congress, 1st Session, 1884, 228.
43. *Ry. World*, Feb. 24, 1877, 174.
44. Federal Cases, Vol. XXIX, 791; *R. R. Gaz.*, Feb. 16, 1877, 78.
45. For a list of cases sustaining these contracts see Competing Telegraph Lines, Minutes of a Hearing before the Committee on Railroads, Report No. 805, Senate, 45th Congress, 3rd Session, 1879, 24-6.
46. Testimony before Committee on Post Offices and Post Roads on the Postal Telegraph, Report No. 577, Senate, 48th Congress, 1st Session, 1884, 250, Green.
47. *Chron.*, April 7, 1877, 309.
48. Even conservative investing institutions were selling; as revealed, for example, in a letter to Joy, Jan. 7, 1876, by Sloan, who stated that the Aetna Insurance Company of Hartford, Connecticut, had sold 500 shares of Michigan Central, and in another letter on the following day in which Sloan informed Joy that the same company had sold another 500 shares. These letters are found in the Joy papers.
49. Joy papers, Sloan to Joy, Oct. 5, 1875.
50. The possibility of a pool is expressed by Sloan to Joy, in a letter of April 22, 1877, Joy papers.
51. These views of Taylor are expressed in a letter, Taylor to Joy, June 21, 1877, in the Joy papers.
52. Ibid., June 22, 1877.
53. Annual report, Western Union, 1877, cited in *Chron.*, Oct. 13, 1877, 355.
54. Adams, to Isaac Bromley in Union Pacific Historical Museum.
55. Report of Government Directors, Union Pacific, 1878, 139, 141.
56. Northwestern archives, W. L. Scott to Albert Keep, Sept. 6, 1878.
57. This story appeared in Phila. *Press*, Dec. 3, 1892, after the death of Gould. The correspondent of this paper for almost a decade had revealed an extensive acquaintance with many details of Gould's business career. It is of course not possible to vouch for the accuracy of the story.
58. Burlington archives, Geddes to Forbes, Feb. 1, 1879.
59. Northwestern archives, W. L. Scott to Keep, Sept. 6, 1878.
60. New York *Times*, Jan. 30, 1879.
61. *Public*, April 15, 1880, 345.

CHAPTER IX

Gould Merges the Union Pacific

THE transformation of Gould from a trader into a business leader of national proportions was one of the most startling events in American business history. His accomplishments in the three years of 1879, 1880 and 1881 were unprecedented in the business and financial life of the country, and in a sense have never been repeated since that time. Gould, unlike Harriman twenty years later, did not have the support of commercial and investment banks, nor did he have any aggregation of investment capital at his command. Gould financed his startling success of corporate acquisitions primarily by stock-market profits. He borrowed funds from the bank on margin in the same way that the ordinary stock-market trader does, and he pyramided his borrowings along strictly conventional lines. By the skillful shifting of his security holdings he was able to exercise dominant control over a surprisingly large number of corporations. He succeeded indeed in lifting himself up by his financial boot straps. The effect of his activities on the business as well as the economic life of the country was far-reaching. He became the competitive bull thrown into the stabilized china shops, overturning rate compacts from the Rockies to the seaboard. He built new roads into territories long considered monopolistic havens by others, thereby setting off a long train of economic factors in the form of competitive building, overexpansion, heavy financial losses and pronounced railroad rate reductions.

The event that enabled him to assume leadership in the railroad industry was the sale of a large block of his Union Pacific stock. In the fall of 1878 when his trading losses were heavy, and when his major, almost his sole, asset consisted of his large block of Union Pacific, he had made an effort to sell some of it to the Northwestern and the Rock Island. The two companies were asked to buy about 10,000 shares each with the understanding that both should have representation on the Union Pacific's board. Both roads, however, concluded that they would consider no proposal that did not include the Burlington, their sister road in the Iowa Pool, on an equal footing. They therefore asked Forbes of the Burlington whether it would be wise or practicable for the three pool roads to entertain such a proposal. Forbes rejected the idea and instead raised the question whether the funds might not be more profitably applied to buy and hold each other's securities rather than those of the Union Pacific. The natural alliance, Forbes thought, was with the pool lines instead of with the Union Pacific. Instead of the pool roads aligning themselves with the Union Pacific, he believed that the existing alliance between themselves should be made more permanent. Forbes preferred to use the five-million-dollar surplus of the Burlington to buy into the Rock Island and the Northwestern rather than to buy the Union Pacific stock at 66. Forbes moreover reflected his usual suspicion of the ambitious Gould, and observed that the proposed transaction was made to bring on some negotiation, and that there was no foundation for the judgment that Gould meant to sell his stock.[1]

Gould did not thus succeed in selling his Union Pacific stock. Nevertheless in the face of his paper losses and of the 50 per cent bank write-down of his Union Pacific collateral, he loomed up in the middle of February, 1879, as a leader in the infant bull market. On February 17 the financial community was treated to a typical Gould sensation. Less than four years after the market stir generated by the Pacific Mail-Union Pacific alliance, he announced the sale of a large block of Union Pacific to a syndicate led by Sage and Keene at a price of from $65 to $70 a share. The effect on the Union Pacific stock was immediate. It opened at 68¼ on the morning of the seventeenth, and within a few minutes moved to 78⅜. Not until late in the day was the news of the sale published. The transaction was negotiated and completed in secrecy.

Gould's financial problems were solved overnight. His losses on the short side of Northwestern were settled by delivery of Union Pacific at prices below the market.

Though newspapers and periodicals freely discussed Gould's future actions, nobody correctly envisaged the extraordinary turn his career was about to take. He moved simultaneously in the field of corporate acquisitions on a widespread front from the eastern seaboard to the base of the Rocky Mountains in Colorado. For convenience of discussion these operations will be divided into the following groups: those affecting the transcontinental railroads from the Missouri River to eastern Colorado; those affecting the middle-western roads from the Missouri River to Chicago and Toledo; those affecting the southwestern railroads from St. Louis and Kansas City to El Paso, Texas, and the Gulf of Mexico; and finally those affecting the eastern roads from Buffalo to New York and to New England. The transcontinental roads will be examined in this chapter, and the other roads will be separately considered in successive chapters.

The transcontinental scene in 1878 and 1879 was still dominated by the conflict between Gould and the Burlington. The latter recognized more than ever that it was essential to build a line to Denver. From Kansas City it could reach Denver either via the Atchison or the Kansas Pacific, and from Omaha it was dependent for access to that rapidly growing traffic center upon the circuitous line of the Union Pacific. Forbes was therefore interested in the acquisition of the Kansas Pacific as a means of giving the Burlington its Denver connection. Forbes, however, was not aggressive. The environment of depression continued to weigh heavily upon him. When John Duff, a leading railroad speculator of Boston, asked him to aid Villard to secure control of the Kansas Pacific, Forbes declined. He suggested that Villard open the way with the Atchison, and after he had the road carefully examined by railroad experts, and "*without committing* ourselves to it," it would be worth taking individually an interest in the Kansas Pacific.[2] Though his conclusion was well worthy of his New England conservatism, it was not of course a solution to the reorganization battle and offered no hope to Villard.

Forbes was not, in short, a professional risk-taker. Though he was anxious to negotiate a trade, he was not ready as a businessman to assume a heavy risk in the heart of a depression in order to accomplish a far-reaching business goal.

Gould, on the contrary, united both of these abilities. He was at once a professional risk-taker and a businessman. As a trader, he put up his own funds and enlisted the active support of other speculators. As a businessman he examined an existing railroad or drew plans for the building of a new one; he then reached independent judgments based upon the existing and prospective value of a railroad as an active business unit. While Forbes was examining and hesitating, Gould assumed the offensive, invested his funds, shouldered the burdens and dictated the pattern of business diplomacy.

The Kansas Pacific was not the only property that Forbes was examining in the spring of 1878 as a means of protecting the strategic position of the Burlington. He had his eye also upon the St. Joseph & Denver City. Harris in the fall of 1877 had expressed fear that the Union Pacific in control of that road could coerce the Iowa lines into taking positions they would not otherwise take. It would then be as much to the interest of the Union Pacific to trade at St. Joseph as at Council Bluffs.[3]

While Forbes was making preliminary inquiries into the value of the Kansas Pacific and the St. Joseph & Denver City railroads, Gould suddenly struck in southern Nebraska. A gentleman's agreement between the Union Pacific and the B. & M. had for a number of years stabilized their competitive positions in the region south of the Platte River. In May, 1878, Gould broke the peace by filing amended articles for the organization of subsidiary corporations to cover the territory with new roads. Forbes was not yet ready to start a war of competitive construction. Villard, who according to a Burlington official knew what Gould wanted, offered to negotiate a settlement. Villard thought he could come to an agreement with Gould on the division of territory, but he accomplished nothing and the Burlington party struck back. Early in July the B. & M. announced its intention to build roads further west in southern Nebraska.[4]

Neither the Burlington nor the Union Pacific, however, was ready for actual warfare. Though they had revealed their intentions to build, they refrained from putting those intentions into action. Neither party dared to commit itself, and their announcements accordingly were not followed by the laying of rails.

Meanwhile Forbes maintained a continuous interest in the St. Joseph problem. The bridge at that point was owned by a company then in receivership. Control of both the bridge and of the St. Joseph & Denver City was for sale. In the negotiations that followed Gould got in ahead and bought both the railroad and the bridge.

The grand traffic prize to the Burlington, however, was neither the bridge nor the road, but rather the Kansas Pacific. In February, 1879, after the sale of Union Pacific stock to the syndicate, Gould retained his Kansas Pacific holdings. Although the finances and earning power of the road were weak, strategically it was important. If Gould secured control, he had hopes of uniting it with the Union Pacific on a basis which would make its stock and junior bonds valuable. The competitive and strategic problems were complex. On the east, the Pennsylvania under the guardianship of Scott was an ever-threatening factor, and on the west, the aggressive Atchison presented other competitive possibilities. The Pennsylvania ended at St. Louis, while the Atchison began at Kansas City. If the Pennsylvania should acquire control of the Missouri Pacific, and the Atchison work in harmony with the Pennsylvania, a new competitive through route could be established. Such a combination could damage the Kansas Pacific. It was also possible that the Baltimore & Ohio, whose financial condition was of the best, might join with the Missouri Pacific and thus weaken Gould's rapidly growing power over the traffic movements between Kansas City and the Middle West. The Baltimore & Ohio, through corporate and individual holdings of its officers, had a heavy interest in the Ohio & Mississippi—then in receivership—which extended its system from Cincinnati to St. Louis.

As it turned out, none of these possibilities materialized. Garrett of the Baltimore & Ohio displayed his aggressive expansion plans in his independent fight against the telegraph, express, and sleeping-car companies. The Pennsylvania management was still haunted by losses occasioned by the rapid expansion from 1869 to the panic. The deficits on some of its leased lines were substantial, and only the able management of Scott and the heavy volume of local traffic enabled the company, in the depression years, to maintain its credit rating.

On the western end of the line Gould was also confronted by critical problems. In Colorado, the interest centered around the rapidly expanding mining business in an area in which Leadville was the major producer. The wealth of the region and the inward tide of immigration increased through the spring and summer of 1879 and between March and October probably 20,000 people entered the area.[5] The mining boom found two local roads in the construction stage. Former Governor Evans, promoter of one road, the Denver and South Park,[6] had the loyal support of a majority of its stockholders who had pooled their stock with a trustee. The other road was the Denver & Rio Grande,[7] which had been projected as a north-and-south line from Denver to El Paso. Through the Kansas Pacific, Gould had relations with both roads. The Denver, which had been pushing south in 1878, found its career expansion blunted and later diverted by the powerful onrush of an able Boston group of managers and capitalists. The Atchison starting as a local road in eastern Kansas had developed great expansive power, and by 1876 it had reached Pueblo. A conflict developed between the Atchison and the Denver, and a lease of the latter by the former in October, 1878, apparently settled all outstanding problems. These indications, however, were deceptive. Both the lessee and the lessor had pushed west to pre-empt the San Juan mining region's traffic by building lines to Leadville. There was, however, only one practicable route, and that lay through a gorge in the Arkansas River Valley. Both roads disputed for possession of this right of way, and in September 1878 the court declared that both contestants could build duplicate lines. Sensible business judgment rose above legal permission, and shortly after the decision was rendered, both properties agreed upon a compromise. The lease soon followed.[8]

To Gould, in the winter of 1878–79, this union of interests between the Denver and the Atchison appeared dangerous. Villard was still insisting upon the foreclosure of the Denver Extension mortgage. A traffic agreement between the Kansas Pacific and the newly formed association of the Atchison and the Denver would impair the earnings of the Union Pacific, and an agreement with the Burlington on the east would strengthen the combination. The new route could compete in eastern Colorado and move the profitable ore and bullion traffic over its own lines to Kansas City there to be forwarded over the Garrison-owned Missouri Pacific for further movement to St. Louis.

Gould in the winter of 1878–79, as he looked out upon this rapidly changing scene of railroad strategy, was relatively helpless. He had little cash and purchasing power. It was his sale of Union Pacific stock in February, 1879, which gave him both. With this new supply of cash and credit Gould attacked the Kansas Pacific problem with renewed energy. Late in December, 1878, Villard appeared before a federal court and denounced the pooling agreement of 1878 between the Union Pacific and the Kansas Pacific. The pool, he insisted, worked to the disadvantage of the Kansas Pacific; it should be set aside, since it was "vicious" in itself and "monstrous" in its provisions for the future. The court postponed a decision to the March term of the court.

Gould was then planning the sale of his Union Pacific stock, and he knew that he would soon have cash. He recognized also that Villard's legal position had been established, as one observer stated it, "beyond the possibility of further dispute." [9] The power of the Denver Extension bondholders to shut out by foreclosure proceedings the Kansas Pacific's junior security holders was now unchallenged. Gould had lost his battle to extract concessions from Villard, and he therefore opened negotiations to ascertain a basis for settlement. He had little time to lose since it was possible that during the March judicial term Villard, if his interests were not settled, might destroy the 1878 pool, foreclose the mortgage and wrest control of the property. A plan was finally evolved. Gould agreed on behalf of the junior security holders to pay all the interest arrearages on the Denver Extension bonds in cash, and to reduce the interest on the new bonds, to be exchanged par for par for the old, from 7 per cent to 6 per cent. This proposal Villard accepted, and the Denver Extension bonds which two years before had sold at 35, advanced to 102. Villard's leadership in his struggle was generally recognized. "It may be doubted," declared one contemporary writer, "whether any other great railroad property in this country, which has been actually in the hands of a receiver, can show so remarkable an advance as this." The bondholders united, continued the writer, in crediting Villard with this achievement.[10]

Control of the road now rested with its junior securities, held largely by the Reorganizing Pool. After considerable negotiation, Gould bought out the other Pool investors, thereby securing a majority of the road's junior securities. Subject to the agreement with Villard, Gould now took control of the reorganization.

The significance of this development was not appreciated by the financial community. The Gould-Villard arrangement was construed as a victory for Villard. Actually, it was. The transfer of ownership of the Kansas Pacific junior securities to Gould was also construed as a defeat for Gould since, after all, title to the junior securities did not increase their value. The announcement of these Kansas Pacific arrangements, therefore, led to a sharp break in the price of its stock.

Gould, however, knew better. With Villard's threat of foreclosure removed, with most of the junior securities securely in his hands and with the merger of the road with the Union Pacific a distinct possibility, he decided to acquire more junior securities by open market purchases. Early in March Gould made his peace with Villard. Under the influence of Gould's buying, the price of the stock moved from less than 20 to a high of 58½ in late April. In the spring of 1875, and now again in the spring of 1879, the speculative following expressed thanks to Gould for profits rendered and received.

Gould by the early summer of 1879 had acquired a majority of the stock of the Kansas Pacific and had successfully reorganized the road. In his effort to unite it with the Union Pacific, however, he had not succeeded. In order to strengthen his hand in negotiating with the Union Pacific, he decided to improve the competitive position of the road. He therefore set before him the double task of breaking the Atchison lease of the Denver and acquiring control of the Denver Pacific. The latter road—the Kansas Pacific subsidiary in eastern Colorado—competed with a Union Pacific system line. The stock of the Denver Pacific at that time had little value; the road was in receivership, and paid no interest.

The steps Gould took to acquire control of the latter were carefully made, each being well adapted to an immediate end. No observer or critic understood the meaning of each step as it was made. Strangely enough he first worked through the Kansas Pacific. Almost as soon as its reorganization took place, he proposed a new financial scheme. A consolidated mortgage was authorized, designed to facilitate the conversion of existing bonds into new consolidated bonds—a scheme similar to the one that Gould had proposed in the summer of 1873 for the New Jersey

Southern. The proposal was not attractive to the first mortgage bondholders, though the junior creditors gladly exchanged their pooled securities for bonds which were part of a larger issue and secured by a blanket mortgage. Such bonds had a wider and more active market than the numerous classes of existing bonds. Gould and his leading allies, Sage and Dillon, received these bonds in exchange for their pooled junior securities. Gould and Sage were named trustees of the consolidated mortgage. Slightly less than 30,000 of the 40,000 Denver Pacific shares outstanding, as well as some relatively worthless securities of smaller properties, were deposited as additional security for the new mortgage bonds.[11] The two trustees and the additional collateral security appeared to be relatively unimportant, and at the time were overlooked. They eventually proved to be the key which unlocked the mystery of the new mortgage. The Denver Pacific stock seemed to be without value. In July, 1879, the court, at the request of the bondholders, had ordered the foreclosure of the mortgage and the sale of the property. When, therefore, Gould a few weeks later purchased a big block of the Denver Pacific bonds held in Amsterdam, the brokers in that city were "astonished." [12] Gould, however, had his reasons, and he was careful not to enlighten the astonished brokers. His negotiations for the acquisition of the bonds were rapid and conclusive. "I got in there [Amsterdam]," said Gould some years later before the Pacific Railway Commission, "in the morning at ten o'clock, and got my breakfast, and let them know I was there and they met me at eleven o'clock, and at twelve o'clock I bought them out and paid them." [13]

Gould, as the largest holder of the bonds, could control the impending foreclosure, thus eliminating the value of the stock. This obvious view was of course the one assumed by the average observer. Gould did not follow this view, and before the end of the calendar year he had devised an ingenious scheme by which the *seemingly* worthless stock became even more valuable than the *seemingly* worthless bonds.

While negotiating for the Denver Pacific's securities, Gould did not overlook the necessity of breaking the Atchison's lease of the Denver. In the spring of 1879 William J. Palmer (president of the Denver) and his party, which included an agent of Perkins, continued to press forward with the fight against the lease. The lessor insisted that the lease was invalid, and that it had a prior claim to the right of way through the canyon. The lessee disputed both claims. The security holders of the lessor declared furthermore that traffic was being diverted to the South Park. This claim was also denied by the lessee. Suits and countersuits, the appointment of receivers, the seizure of parts of each other's property, the ordering of the militia for action in the event of violence, the holding of the lessor in contempt of court, were actions reminiscent of the Erie-Vanderbilt struggle.

The Burlington watched this struggle with keen interest. Perkins thought of making peace between William B. Strong of the Atchison and Palmer of the Denver, and then contracting for the joint ownership of the road. "I don't know but my imagination may be heated," wrote Perkins, "but I can't help believing that would be a wise combination." [14] Perkins's mind went even beyond the idea of the union of these two roads; he believed that the interests of all the Boston roads should be harmonized, a consummation which would have had serious repercussions on Gould. For Boston, wrote Perkins, was a pet aversion to Gould; a Boston railroad seemed to have "the same disagreeable influence upon him that holy water [was] said to have on his great prototype." [15] The Atchison, meanwhile, defeated in court in its efforts to control the right of way through the Grand Canyon, appealed the decision. Its position remained uncertain, and in order to assure control of the mining region it made a bid for the stock control of the Denver. Gould, appreciating his danger, entered the lists as a competitor. In this struggle Gould was successful. Late in September he succeeded in buying one-half of the Denver's voting trust certificates at 22, payable at his option either in cash, Kansas Pacific stock at 66, or Kansas Pacific Consolidated bonds at 88.[16]

At the same time, the Atchison lost also in its attempt to control the other potential line to Leadville—the South Park. That road had earned scarcely more than its operating expenses, but in the summer of 1879 its earnings began to rise. The stockholders became optimistic and raised the offering price to the Atchison. The latter refused to pay. Gould meanwhile increased his stock holdings by purchases from counties in the territory served. His influence over the road's policies grew, while the Atchison's influence disappeared.

Gould had out-traded his opponent on all points. He now had an interest in both the north and south lines into the Leadville district, thereby increasing the strategic power of the Kansas Pacific. In the fall of 1879 the boom was at its height. The South Park began payment of dividends, while the earnings of the Denver rose. Gould, therefore, controlled an important volume of business for his Kansas Pacific, and what was more important, the volume gave promise of increase. Although the road was still operating at a loss in the fall of 1879, its traffic position was improving. Gould believed his position was sufficiently strong to enable him to solve the competitive problems between the Union and the Kansas Pacific on the basis of consolidation. The idea was not new, it had been discussed for some years.

Accordingly in September he again proposed the sale of the road to the Union Pacific. The Union Pacific board considered the price suggested by Gould excessive and accordingly rejected his proposal. The board based its policies upon the questionable assumption that the road would continue to make interchange agreements with existing lines.

When his proposals to unite the two roads were rejected, Gould left for the West. By this time, late in September, he had working control of the new Wabash system, which was building a line, a circuitous one it is true, to Chicago, while Gould was negotiating for a connection from Toledo to Detroit. He was also engaged with Vanderbilt, the controlling interest in the New York Central system, in a struggle for other Wabash connections, which was to end soon in victory.[17] Other than the Wabash, only the Missouri Pacific and the St. Louis & San Francisco [18] connected Kansas City and St. Louis. The latter's line was indirect and unprofitable. The Missouri Pacific, however, controlled a direct line. Gould's rapid moves in the preceding few months had impaired its competitive position. In control of the Kansas Pacific, Gould could divert eastbound business at Kansas City from the Missouri Pacific to the newly organized Wabash. At St. Louis, as the dominant factor in the affairs of the latter, he could divert westbound business to the competitors of Garrison's Missouri Pacific.

Garrison was not the type of man to take this turn of affairs calmly. On the western end of the Missouri Pacific there were a number of unfinished stubs, which had attracted his attention as they had Gould's. They were either in receivership or in financial difficulties. Garrison, in May of 1879, had bought the controlling interest in one of these small lines—the Kansas Central—which owned a line west from Leavenworth, Kansas. By relatively short connections with the Union Pacific and the B. & M. he could make serious inroads into the business of the Kansas Pacific.

Another of the unfinished stub ends in Kansas was the Central Branch Union Pacific.[19] Despite its name it had no corporate relationship to the Union Pacific. Its promoters had planned to connect it with the Union Pacific, but when the Kansas Pacific was extended to Denver, the stock lost most of its value, and in the language of one of its builders, the stock then was not worth ten cents on the dollar.[20] In 1877 a new management led by R. M. Pomeroy took hold. Even though the property was in receivership, the management initiated an expansion policy, and in 1879 organized a company to build a line to Denver. Because of its heavy debt and the few shares outstanding, a relatively small drop in profits eliminated its per share earnings, while a relatively small rise rapidly sharply increased those earnings. The heavy grain crop of 1879 accompanied by a rise in prices multiplied its earnings per share.

Despite its expansion policy, the large stockholders were willing to sell. At least four buyers appeared. Vanderbilt, in his hit-and-miss fashion, declared that he was anxious to buy, presumably as part of his plan to deliver a blow to Gould in the war over the Wabash. Perhaps he also wanted to strike at the Kansas Pacific in order to bring pressure on Gould in the East. Against Vanderbilt and his wealth appeared the veteran manipulator, Garrison, and the sharp bargainer, Gould. Garrison saw in the Central Branch an opportunity to extend the Missouri Pacific from Kansas City to Denver. Such an extension would reduce the traffic of the Kansas Pacific, impair the market value of its stock, and thus prejudice his plan of merging that road with the Union Pacific. Gould therefore was forced to buy: defensively, to protect the Denver business of the Kansas Pacific, and offensively, to give him another weapon with which to fight the Union

Pacific. The Burlington also appeared as a buyer of the Central Branch.

Gould opened negotiations with the controlling holders through Oliver Ames who had inherited a large block of stock from his father, one of the founders of the Union Pacific. Ames traded shrewdly and succeeded in selling the stock to Gould at a fancy price averaging $239 per share. Gould transferred these shares to the Union Pacific at the cost to him.

Garrison's ambition to expand his Missouri Pacific west of Kansas City was thereby blocked, if not stopped. He could now expand only through the construction of new lines. Directly and through agents Gould had been negotiating for control of the Missouri Pacific for some weeks. Some of these interviews were stormy. Garrison insisted there was no basis for a compromise, and that he was determined to expand west of Kansas City. Gould's acquisition of the Central Branch, however, changed the situation in his favor, and after negotiations which lasted three months, the trade was finally made. The price he paid for the stock was, on the basis of established earnings undoubtedly excessive, as it had been for the Central Branch. The road, however, was strategically located, and with a large flow of business, earnings on the small stock issue promised to increase rapidly and enhance the value of each share.

Gould now dominated both of the direct Kansas City-St. Louis lines. To perfect his trading position with the Union Pacific it was necessary for him to control also the road in southern Nebraska and northeastern Kansas, which gave the Union Pacific a short line to St. Louis. The key to this situation lay at St. Joseph, Missouri. The St. Joseph & Denver City and the bridge at St. Joseph were the two vital properties. By June, Gould in a trading duel with Forbes of the Burlington had succeeded in buying control of both.

By the first week of December, 1879, Gould had thus strengthened the strategic position of the Kansas Pacific at its eastern end. To complete the southern ring around the Union Pacific, he now proposed to extend the recently acquired Missouri Pacific from Atchison to St. Joseph, and the Central Branch to a connection with the Kansas Pacific, thus making a new short route from Denver to the Missouri River.

To hem in and to demoralize the Union Pacific even further, Gould also proposed to extend the Kansas Pacific to Ogden, there to connect with the Central Pacific. This new line might lead to a war of rates, and Gould's record in the railroad world was sufficient evidence to any doubter that he would not hesitate to carry such a war to its uttermost lengths.

These were the plans that confronted the Union Pacific board late in December. The board was on the defensive, and it was not necessary for Gould to make the advances. He knew his power and awaited offers; the offers soon came. The Union Pacific proposed a consolidation with the Kansas Pacific, and on Gould's terms. The board was willing to exchange a share of stock of the Union Pacific—a solvent dividend paying security—for a share of the Kansas Pacific, for years a non-interest-paying property and in receivership, and recently reorganized. Gould, however, was reluctant and refused to consolidate. He wanted to convert the Kansas Pacific-Missouri Pacific system into a new transcontinental route. He therefore refused to sell; the Union Pacific insisted. The board took the ground that Gould "was bound by his previous conversations to give [the Union Pacific] the preference, and to let the [Union Pacific] take the property if [the Union Pacific] could agree upon the terms." [21]

Gould understood the strength of his position. He knew that while the Kansas Pacific was not financially strong, as a threat to its competitor it had the strength of Samson. If its terms were not met, it could lay low both the strong and the weak. Another overland line would, it is true, perpetuate the insolvency of the Kansas Pacific; but in due course it would also insure the insolvency of the Union Pacific.

With the Union Pacific on the defensive and begging for terms, Gould's dramatic sense must have been stimulated. Far more important, however, was the stimulation of his ingenuity and financial resourcefulness. Aside from the Kansas Pacific he had a number of other poverty-stricken roads that he was determined to exchange for the high-grade Union Pacific stock. First, was the apparently worthless stock of the Denver Pacific, and second, that valueless stock of the St. Joseph bridge and road, though in later years both came to be valuable. The latter had a strategic value as part of a short Union Pacific route to St. Louis. The former

—the Denver Pacific—had slight value except as a competitive bludgeon in the hands of Gould. If its stock could be released from the trust and placed in the treasury of the Kansas Pacific, no violation of the trust would result; the stock would be returned to its rightful owner, the Kansas Pacific. Furthermore, with the stock in the Kansas Pacific treasury as a free asset, it could be exchanged if the Union Pacific was willing, for Union Pacific stock, and Gould would see to it that the Union Pacific was willing. Upon receipt of the Union Pacific stock by the Kansas Pacific, the latter could exchange it for the securities of the St. Joseph properties which were held by Gould.

Gould's immediate task, therefore, was to remove the Denver Pacific stock from the trustees of the consolidated mortgage. Since judicial proceedings are slow and long-drawn-out, the release of stock from a trust within a few days is usually a difficult task. In this case, however, the legal machinery moved fast, and within ten days, as officially described by the Pacific Railway Commission, "A suit was manufactured, in which the Kansas Pacific Railway Company was made the plaintiff, and Jay Gould and Russell Sage the defendants, and the entire machinery of complaint, answer, trial, decree, and execution was carried to a finish. . . ." [22] The court ordered Gould and Sage, trustees for the consolidated mortgage bondholders, to return the Denver Pacific stock to the Kansas Pacific treasury.

The way was thus opened for the merger on Gould's terms. The contract was made on January 4, 1880. The Kansas Pacific and the Denver Pacific stocks, together with the Union Pacific stock, were exchanged par for par into the stock of a new company—the Union Pacific Railway Company. Though the operating mileage and the gross revenue of the Union Pacific was increased, its finances and earnings were weakened.

In these negotiations, Gould resumed the trading position he had so often occupied on the Erie—that of representing both buyer and seller. He owned almost one-half of the Kansas Pacific and was also a small holder of the Union Pacific stock. Adverse interests on the Erie had produced stinging denunciations from Adams in his famous Chapters on the Erie. Strange to say, however, the Union Pacific-Kansas Pacific-Denver Pacific merger brought no such criticism from this source. The Union Pacific, insisted Adams, gave no "larger consideration" for Kansas Pacific than the Missouri Pacific was willing and anxious to give. "It cannot be fairly argued," he maintained in defending the merger before the Pacific Railway Commission in 1887, "that the director of one railroad company, who is likewise interested in the stock of another railroad company of which he is also a director, is called upon to sell to the first company his interest in the securities of the second company for a less price than someone else is willing to give. He is merely called upon not to take advantage of his position as a director to get for his property more than it would bring in the outside market." [23]

Whatever ground there may be for this fine-spun distinction, the effects of this, and of the Erie, transactions were the same. Gould's business strategy in the Union Pacific trade was almost perfect. He threw the Union Pacific board suddenly and almost without warning into a defensive position from which there was no retreat. He left no basis for either compromise or alternative.

The merger of the Union Pacific and the Kansas Pacific revolutionized Gould's bargaining power against the Atchison. Except for that road he exerted an influence in every line in eastern Colorado.

Although early 1880 found the Denver still in receivership and under lease to the Atchison, the stockholders had repudiated the lease. In the face of adverse legal decisions, the Atchison refused to surrender its right to expand into the rich mining areas of southern Colorado. The relative privileges of both lessor and lessee had not yet been judicially decided, and the court had appointed a commission which was still holding hearings and gathering evidence. The mineral traffic of the disputed region was described in the 1880 annual report of the Denver as "a principality in itself." The area had gold, silver and lead, as well as "enormous" coal fields, and was a "vast store-house of splendid timber." [24] The Atchison was determined to press the issue. While the court proceeded leisurely to gather the facts and formulate an opinion, it took more advanced ground, renewing its threat to build a line from Pueblo paralleling the Denver road.

Gould, however, was not idle. While his trunk line opponent was making its thrust, he was preparing a counterthrust. Sharpening his effective weapon—the threat of parallel construction—he announced the organization of a new property (naming it the Pueblo & St. Louis), to build a line paralleling the Atchison from Pueblo to Ft. Dodge, Kansas, a distance of about 266 miles. On the west of the Atchison, he announced that the line of the Denver would be further extended without delay to Utah and beyond. These additional extensions by the Denver and the Pueblo & St. Louis would create "much the shortest route from St. Louis to the heart of Colorado, . . ." Gould as a promoter-salesman described the prospects of the new road in glowing terms. The line, he declared, would be built at such a low cost that it would realize handsome profits at rates very much lower than those which the Atchison had been compelled to charge "in order to sustain such a heavy load of capital." [25] Gould offered $1,500,000 of the capital stock of a construction company to finance construction. The proposed new road was described in the Gould-owned New York daily as one calculated to open to the Denver "the entire Gould system east of the Missouri and Mississippi Rivers." [26]

Here was a typical Gould master stroke. The Atchison was too busy fighting its way into the Southwest to bother much about its eastern lines. It had accordingly left that flank open; there Gould made his attack. Gould as usual was acting in the twofold capacity of a stock operator and a businessman. In the former his campaign was immediately successful: the price of the Denver's voting certificates which he had bought in the fall at 22 advanced rapidly to 50 in January, 1880, and to 75 in February. As a railroad man his major objective was the termination of the war of duplicate construction. The Atchison was poised for a Pueblo-Denver line; the Denver for a Pueblo-Kansas line; the Burlington for a Nebraska-Denver line, and the Union Pacific for an extension into the mining region of southern Colorado. Gould took the lead in stabilizing this competitive clash which promised to unsettle the territorial equilibrium in the trans-Missouri River area. He controlled for the moment the corporate destinies of the Denver and could therefore dominate its construction policy. He was also the leading figure in the Union Pacific management and could regulate its decisions. By his threat to parallel the Atchison line in Kansas, he had brought this management to think in terms of conciliation and peace.

Gould still had the Burlington to consider. The officials of that road were convinced that an extension to Denver was essential to its welfare. The Burlington's officials understood that the building of a Denver line would intensify the war of duplicate construction. In view of the complex building and territorial problems on the middle and eastern end of its lines, peace if attainable on reasonable terms was desirable. If the roads in eastern Colorado would deliver eastbound business to the Burlington at the Missouri River, the Burlington would take the risk of not building—at least for the present.[27]

An agreement reached early in March, 1880, set the pattern for railroad development for many years in eastern Colorado and in New Mexico. The Denver agreed not to build east of its north-south line; while the Atchison agreed not to build west of that line, nor north into Denver. For a cash consideration representing the cost of construction, the Atchison also surrendered its incompleted line into the mining regions, while Gould, speaking through the corporate instrumentality of the Denver, agreed to surrender the building of the line paralleling the Atchison from Pueblo east.[28] The Union Pacific agreed that it would not construct or promote the construction of any competing line in Colorado south of the latitude of Denver on the Kansas Pacific. The Union Pacific and the Atchison, furthermore, agreed to divide the westbound mountain traffic *equally;* and to divide the Denver traffic, one-quarter to the Atchison and three-quarters to the Union Pacific. The eastbound traffic of Colorado and New Mexico originating west of the Denver-El Moro line of the Denver would be divided equally between the Union Pacific and the Atchison. All the three lines agreed also not to interchange traffic with any new railroad line. An oligopoly thus set itself up to dominate the Colorado railroad business. In still another understanding the B. & M. agreed with the Union Pacific not to extend to Denver; the Union Pacific in turn agreed to surrender the idea for which Gould fought in the spring of 1877 in the Quintuple negotiations, thereby permitting the Burlington to carry all the business of the B. & M. The Union Pacific also approved the pooling of its business at the Missouri River with all its eastern connections, including the Burlington.

These were agreements with fundamental implications for the

territorial development of the West. The Denver-Union Pacific-Atchison agreement which ran for ten years gave the Denver the business of the southern Colorado mining region, and the Atchison the traffic of the rich Arkansas Valley. The agreement also gave the traffic of New Mexico to the Atchison, thus opening the way for the latter's construction of a new route to California.

One more major competitive problem to the Union Pacific remains for consideration, viz., the water route via the Isthmus of Panama. In non-railroad hands the Pacific Mail controlling that route was a dangerous rate-cutter. Gould had no intention of letting it remain independent of railroad control. When he left its directorate in the spring of 1876 the company had a floating debt, of which he and Dillon, president of the Union Pacific, were the major holders. It is probable that Gould had contemplated the use of the floating debt as a means of reacquiring control of the company at a slight price. If this was his plan, he made a serious blunder. His efforts in this direction were blocked by the astute Park. The relinquishment of control of the Pacific Mail by Gould and his associates was followed by the ascendency of Park and his associates. No sooner had the new group acquired control than it addressed itself to the payment of the floating debt, each member of the new board subscribing individually to a fund which provided sufficient funds for its liquidation.[29]

Gould was defeated. For the moment he had no ready-made plans with which to counter the thrust of Park. The result was a rate war between the Pacific Mail and the transcontinental railroads which soon spread to the Pacific where the Pacific Mail competed with the Occidental & Oriental—the line organized by Gould and Huntington to compete with the Pacific Mail for a share of the business of the far east. The rivalry between the ships of these two lines led to "ruinous prices" and to "a life and death fight."[30] It was not until the summer of 1877 that an arrangement between the land and the water route was perfected. The contract which terminated the war suppressed competition. The Pacific Mail limited its coast-to-coast runs in exchange for a subsidy from the railroads. Although the business was to be solicited jointly by the steamship line and the railroads, the latter in the case of any difference had the right to make rates.[31]

Despite these arrangements with the railroads, the Pacific Mail was able to discharge neither the advances made by the members of its board, nor its floating debt to the Panama. The stock meanwhile had become a low-priced speculation. The company paid no dividends, and there was no reasonable prospect of payment. Much of the stock was held by speculators who had bought at higher prices and who would not sell at the lower prices, and in part by traders buying and selling for quick turns. At the annual election in the spring of 1878 a group of outsiders led by Henry Hart, who had bought some of the stock at higher prices, seized control.

Gould was still an outsider, having rebought none of the stock which he had sold early in 1876. Developments in the Pacific Mail probably led him to believe that under the new conditions it was not wise to reacquire any interest. Control under the existing conditions would hardly be worth while since the Panama by insisting on the payment of the floating debt could make the stock worthless. Instead of trying for control, therefore, Gould went off on a different tack. He decided to abandon the subsidy contract between the railroads and the Pacific Mail, and late in July, 1878, the Union Pacific gave the Pacific Mail notice that within sixty days it would cancel the contract. This was followed by one of those sudden moves which made it so difficult to follow Gould and to anticipate his next step. The Union Pacific changed its tariffs and classifications, increasing rates on many commodities from 50 to 100 per cent, at the same time eliminating its open tariffs under which the shippers were permitted to ship either by water or rail. It further announced that if any shipper agreed to move all of his freight by rail, especially low rates would be made. The scheme, which was not submitted to the board of directors, was devised by two freight agents and approved under verbal authority of the president and one of the directors.[32] Presumably the director was Gould. Even before this advance, transcontinental freight rates were the highest in the country.

Gould had gone too far. Shippers refused to make special contracts with the transcontinental roads, and many decided to send their freight over the Pacific Mail. Early in August, after the increase in railroad rates, the Pacific Mail vessels filled up rapidly and the line made arrangements to run extra ships. A Pacific Mail director, enthusiastic over its prospects, said the company had determined to make no further contracts with the Union Pacific, and to operate its lines for the benefit of New York and California merchants on business principles.[33] With the shippers refusing to accept the transcontinental roads' offer of lower rates in exchange for the exclusive movement of business over their lines, it became inevitable that either a price war or a pooling agreement had to follow. The negotiations were long and involved. By the end of that year another pool-subsidy agreement was arranged. The railroads agreed to increase the subsidy formerly paid the Pacific Mail, and the latter in turn permitted the railroads to fix rates.[34]

The contract was hardly made before it was canceled. From time to time during the year negotiations were resumed. As the months rolled on in 1879 and early in 1880, it became evident that existing differences could not be reconciled, and finally in January of 1880 another war of rates broke out. The Pacific Mail reduced its first class New York to San Francisco passenger fares from $130 to $75. The Central and Union Pacific requested the roads east of Omaha to meet the cut by a corresponding reduction. The eastern roads refused. The Central Pacific then abandoned competition on first-class traffic, but slashed rates on coast-to-coast emigrant business to about one cent a mile.[35]

The renewed competition was a serious threat to the earnings of the newly consolidated Union Pacific. Despite these impending disasters to the Pacific Mail, the price of its stock rose in spectacular fashion. Early in 1879 the stock had sold at a record low of little more than 10, while in March, 1880, it reached almost 60.

The key to this mystery was then being fashioned by Gould. While the stock speculators were selling, Gould was buying. And while critics and analysts were expatiating upon the dissolution of the Pacific Mail, Gould was planning to restore its power to earn profits and to pay dividends. He spent much time in 1879 in an effort to reconcile divergent interests, and early in the following year he succeeded in effecting an arrangement to which all companies were able to subscribe. The new Pacific Mail board elected in March contained representatives from all groups. The independently minded management of the Pacific Mail was ousted, Gould and Sage having bought up enough of the stock at the low prices prevailing in 1879 to enable them to take control. The rate war was eliminated, competition was suppressed, and a new contract providing for a fat subsidy to the Pacific Mail and the granting of rate-fixing power to the railroads was concluded.[36]

Gould had won a notable success, and again everybody was happy. Those who had bought the Pacific Mail as a market speculation had a handsome stock-market profit, and those investors who had bought Pacific Mail as an investment were the beneficiaries of handsome dividends. The public interest, if not ignored, was certainly not consulted. A resolution was introduced into the Senate to investigate the pool. Although there was much discussion in Congressional circles and in the trade press, nothing was done.

To Gould the prospects were attractive. He had removed the last competitive obstacle to the progress of the Union Pacific, and on land as on water the Union Pacific had little opposition. It was free to charge rates on the basis of what the traffic could be made to bear. Although transcontinental rail opposition was being threatened, it was not yet serious, and of course there was only slight possibility in the immediate future of any new steamship competition. Thus the way was open for the formulation of investment judgment that the Union Pacific stock was a high-grade security. The price rose rapidly to new highs of between 100 and 130. Some of the stock cost Gould less than 10; while other shares cost him even less. With the suppression of competition, managed almost entirely by Gould, the stock looked good.

In 1881, a year after the merger, when the facts were clear to everyone, Union Pacific stock was "greedily bought" by Boston capitalists at over 130. "They have eyes and they see not." The investor's eyes sought only the past. The Union Pacific stock seemed to pass "into the ranks of the few dividend-paying stocks possessing a sufficiently solid position to withstand the brunt of bad times." [37]

Not so to Gould. After the merger he was again the dominant

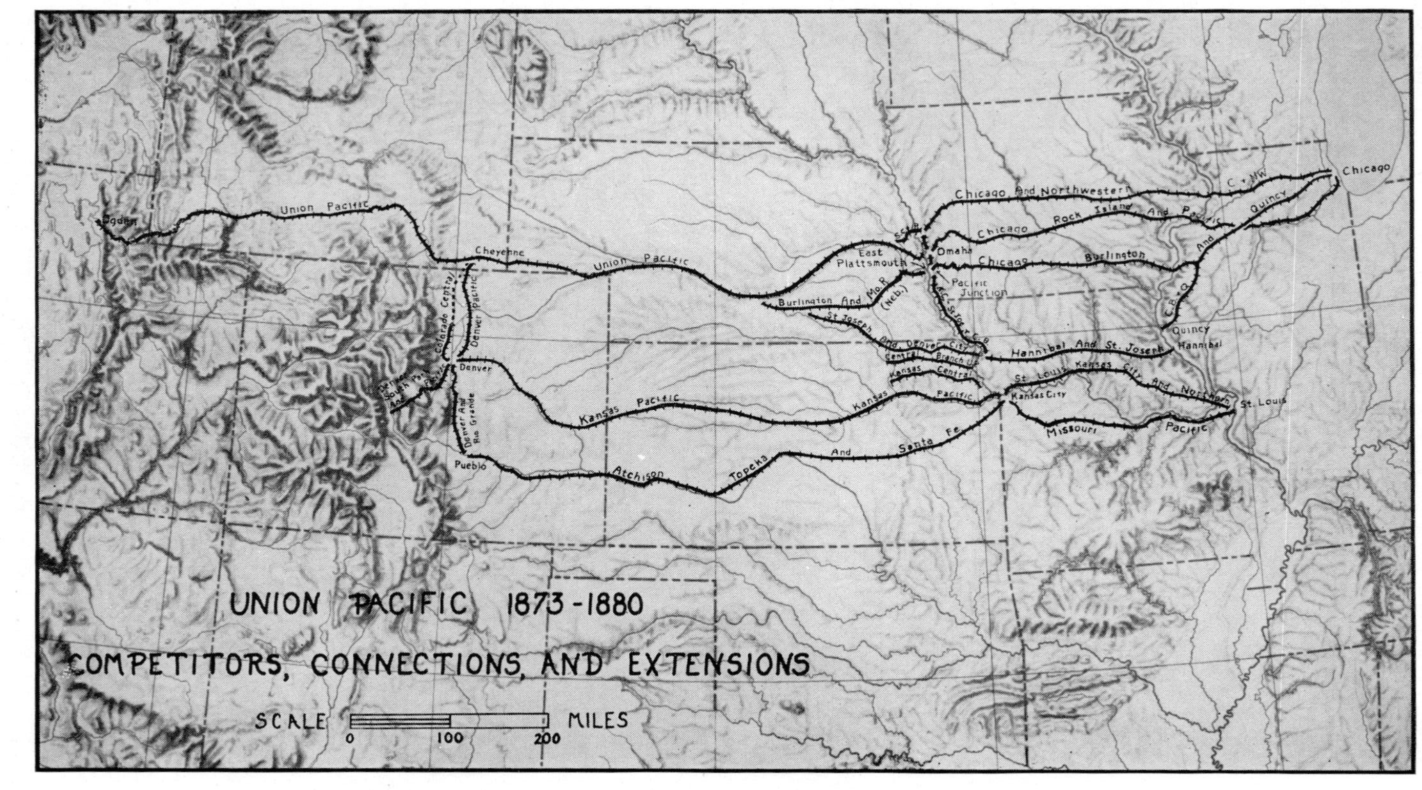
UNION PACIFIC 1873-1880
COMPETITORS, CONNECTIONS, AND EXTENSIONS
SCALE
0
100
200
MILES
Ogden
Union Pacific
Cheyenne
Union Pacific
Colorado Central
Denver Pacific
Denver
Denver And Rio Grande
Pueblo
Kansas Pacific
Atchison Topeka And Santa Fe
Chicago
Chicago And Northwestern
C. + N.W.
Chicago Rock Island And Pacific
Chicago Burlington And Quincy
C. B. + Q.
Quincy
Omaha
East Plattsmouth
Pacific Junction
Burlington And Mo. R. (Neb.)
St Joseph And Denver City
Hannibal And St. Joseph
Hannibal
Central Branch U.P.
Kansas Central
St Louis Kansas City And Northern
Kansas City
St. Louis
Missouri Pacific

factor. His eyes were wide open. He saw, and he sold. He supplied the investors with stock and they supplied him with cash.

NOTES FOR CHAPTER IX

1. Burlington archives, M. L. Sykes, secretary of the Northwestern, to Forbes, Oct. 28, 1878, and Oct. 30, 1878; Forbes to Perkins, Oct. 30, 1878; and Forbes to Griswold, Nov. 10, 1878.
2. Ibid., Forbes to Tyson, March (day not given), 1878.
3. Ibid., Harris to Griswold, Sept. 28, 1877.
4. *Am. R. R. Journal*, July 6, 1878, 763; *R. R. Gaz.*, July 5, 1878, 338.
5. This is the estimate of Bradstreet, Jan. 28, 1882, 53; although current newspaper estimates were substantially larger.
6. Known hereafter as the South Park.
7. Known hereafter as the Denver.
8. The lease contract is in *Ry. World*, Nov. 30, 1878, 1153-4; and *R. R. Gaz.*, Nov. 29, 1878, 583.
9. New York *Times*, March 9, 1879.
10. *Public*, March 13, 1879, 176.
11. American Exchange, cited in *R. R. Gaz.*, May 16, 1879, 275-6.
12. Phila. *North American*, Oct. 17, 1879.
13. United States Pacific Railway Commission, Testimony, Executive Document No. 51, Senate, 50th Congress, 1st Session, 1887, 465, Gould.
14. Burlington archives, Perkins to Forbes, May 31, 1879.
15. Ibid., Perkins to Tyson, May 31, 1879.
16. For details on the purchase contracts, see American Exchange, cited in *R. R. Gaz.*, Sept. 26, 1879, 516; Denver *Tribune*, cited in *Ry. World*, Oct. 18, 1879, 996.
17. See Chapter XI, pp. 211-9, for details.
18. Known hereafter as the Frisco.
19. Known hereafter as the Central Branch.
20. United States Pacific Railway Commission, Testimony, Executive Document No. 51, Senate, 50th Congress, 1st Session, 1887, 4009, Henry Day. Day was one of the builders of the road.
21. Ibid., 662, F. L. Ames.
22. Ibid., Report of the Commission, 63.
23. Ibid., 4156, Adams.
24. Annual report, Denver & Rio Grande, 1880, cited in *R. R. Gaz.*, June 17, 1881, 330.
25. Printed circular of the Pueblo & St. Louis Railroad, Jan. 15, 1880, found in the Burlington archives.
26. New York *World*, Jan. 30, 1880.
27. Burlington archives, Perkins to Forbes, Jan. 30, 1880. Perkins sketches the argument for peace.
28. On this contract see New York *Tribune*, Feb. 3, 1880; *R. R. Gaz.*, Feb. 6, 1880, 83. For more of the details of the contract, see General William J. Palmer, *A Decade of Railroad Building*, by George L. Anderson, Colorado Springs, 1936, 117.
29. New York *Tribune*, June 10, 1876; *R. R. Gaz.*, June 16, 1876, 269.
30. *Ry. World*, Jan. 27, 1877, 81.
31. Contracts Between Southern Pacific Railroad and Other Companies, Executive Document No. 60, House of Representatives, 49th Congress, 1st Session, 1886, 12.
32. Report of Government Directors, Union Pacific, 1878, 145.
33. *Ry. World*, Aug. 10, 1878, 769.

34. For details on these negotiations see New York *Tribune*, Dec. 17, 1878. The contract is found in Contracts Between Southern Pacific Railroad and Other Companies, Executive Document No. 60, House of Representatives, 49th Congress, 1st Session, 1886, 12.
35. A good account of this rate war is found in *Ry. Review*, Feb. 21, 1880, 1887. See also *R. R. Gaz.*, Feb. 27, 1880, 120.
36. For details of this contract see Contracts Between Southern Pacific Railroad and Other Companies, Executive Document No. 60, House of Representatives, 49th Congress, 1st Session, 1886, 9.
37. *Economist*, May 17, 1884, 602.

CHAPTER X

Gould Acquires the Wabash

The second major field of Gould's corporate activity in the three boom years of 1879, 1880, and 1881 was the rich traffic-producing area between the Missouri River from Kansas City to Omaha and the Great Lakes at Chicago, Toledo and Detroit. This region was featured by the hottest kind of railroad competition. Through lines, branches, lines running counter to the main direction of traffic, and roads partly finished abounded. Most of the feeders and branches had passed their dividends, and a substantial majority had defaulted on their interest. Some of these were of no strategic importance; others, although in or bordering on receivership, controlled valuable terminal facilities or short connections between rapidly growing traffic centers. It was therefore difficult for a few groups to acquire control and thereafter maintain a competitive equilibrium. There were too many roads and too many conflicting groups; but it was possible for one person or group to acquire a few strategic lines and use them to disturb the rate structure, to break the pools, and to produce business chaos. This is what Gould accomplished in this region.

Gould's capture of a number of main lines dominating the Kansas City-St. Louis area, and of the strategically located Wabash extending from St. Louis and the upper Mississippi River gateways to the Great Lakes at Toledo was both surprising and spectacular. No one suspected his invasion of this region, and his arrival led to fantastic estimates of future possibilities. Control of the Wabash led him into territory crossed by eastern trunk lines, and their connections enabled him to invade some of the richest traffic areas of the country, as well as to challenge some of the major trunk lines in their own territory. The upper and lower Missouri valleys together with the lower Great Lakes area—all directly invaded—had transportation problems of their own, and it is to these problems that attention must be directed. Only by understanding them can the business significance of Gould's actions be appreciated.

By the middle seventies a notable difference between the development of the middle-western roads north and south of Chicago had emerged. Between Chicago and the Mississippi and Missouri Valley crossings the railroads were financially strong, while in the rich wheat and corn fields in central and southern Illinois, and in Indiana and Missouri, they were generally weak. Of this latter group the Wabash occupied a strategic position. In the early seventies the road reached four gateways on the Mississippi River: St. Louis, Hannibal, Quincy, and Keokuk. Its freight traffic was described in one authoritative trade source as "enormous." Its line was the shortest route from Toledo to points in Missouri and Kansas, and from Buffalo to St. Louis the line was one hundred miles shorter than the route via Chicago. "Only Central Route to the West" was the challenging description the Wabash used in its advertising program.[1] In addition to these main lines of traffic, it controlled also five considerable branches which were "accessible by a very large proportion of Central Illinois."[2]

The Wabash was the only road of those operating east from St. Louis which reached the upper gateways of the Mississippi and also Toledo. In addition it was the only St. Louis road connecting with the Great Lakes east of Chicago. The improving technology of steam railroad operation had during the previous few years reduced the unit costs and the selling prices of railroad services, while the price of water transportation over the Great Lakes had not been proportionately reduced. Shippers of wheat and corn thus found it more profitable to pay the rail rate on traffic to Toledo instead of to Chicago in order to avoid the water haul from Chicago to Toledo. The higher rail rate to Toledo was more than compensated by the savings in the water rate from Chicago to Toledo. In the years prior to the panic of 1873, the growth of this all-rail grain traffic substantially enlarged the business of the Wabash. The Wabash, nevertheless, in the next few years fell into financial difficulties, and shortly after the panic the road went into receivership. Despite this and other receiverships in the same area, competition was so severe that rate wars were the normal order of the day. The roads could not settle their rate problems, even in the face of a general agreement in eastern trunk-line territory. The Wabash took the lead in these rate wars, so much so indeed that it came to be characterized as the "Ishmaelite of corporations." [3] In the middle seventies the road, adhering to these rate-cutting practices, followed the shortsighted policy of capturing traffic by taking full advantage of its strategic location. Such a policy was dangerous. The Chicago-Missouri Valley roads, i.e., the Burlington, Rock Island, Northwestern and Alton, interchanged traffic at Chicago on a friendly basis with non-competitive connections: the Pennsylvania, Michigan Central, Baltimore & Ohio, and the Vanderbilt lines. The western roads traded their eastbound traffic for the westbound traffic of the eastern roads. If the Wabash took the Kansas City and St. Louis traffic east to Toledo, it interchanged business on an unfriendly basis with competitive connections; for, on business moving between Chicago and Toledo, the Wabash competed with its eastern connections.

Despite the rate wars, the Wabash was able by the fall of 1877 to reorganize its property. Although the plan was adopted under the laws of Ohio and the property returned to its stockholders, the title was not entirely clear, and a number of suits tended to obscure its financial future. The price of the stock, therefore, even after the reorganization, dropped to exceptionally low levels. Its physical condition meanwhile was not enviable. Even as late as 1880 the road needed sidings, second track, improved terminals, and additional equipment. Many of its cars were not owned, and were held under car trusts.[4] The company, furthermore, was manipulating its accounts while awaiting a return to better times. In a public statement issued in March, 1878, for example, it reported earnings for the previous year of over $168,000; yet in a lawsuit a few months later, the treasurer revealed a deficit of over $570,000.[5]

The road was finally returned to its shareholders in February, 1878. The board of directors included Field, who, like Gould and Sage, was actively interested in stock-market trading. Field was a large holder of cable companies' stocks and of a wide assortment of railroad securities. He was a recognized leader in speculative circles and his following included Tilden, the Democratic candidate for President in 1876. In the dreary days of 1877, when the financial fate of the Wabash hung in the balance, an investigation of the Wabash led to the purchase by Field of "a considerable amount" of its common stock, some at less than one dollar a share.[6] This turned out to be an important factor in Gould's acquisition of control of the road in 1879 and 1880. Field was primarily a stock trader and only incidentally a railroad man. When the price of Wabash stock advanced, Field was a seller, and he sold just at the time when Gould was a ready buyer. The president of the road was James A. Roosevelt, a member of the brokerage and banking community of New York City. The new management did not modify the road's traffic policies.

Thus during the depression period, the Wabash, in and out of receivership, under one management or another, was at all times a trouble maker. It could not refrain from the temptation to take advantage of its location.

In the fall of 1878 the Wabash management changed again. The new president was Commodore Garrison, who was then in full control of the Missouri Pacific. Early in 1877 he also acquired an interest in the other direct St. Louis-Kansas City connection—the St. Louis, Kansas City & Northern [7]—and a few months later his son, W. R. Garrison, vice president of the Missouri Pacific, was elected a member of the Kansas City board. The new management revived a long discussed project—the construction of an extension from its line in northwestern Missouri to Omaha. Such a connection would enable the road to compete with the Iowa Pool for traffic to the Mississippi Valley and beyond, and open up a line from Omaha to St. Louis, sixty miles shorter than any existing route.[8] The traffic from Omaha to St. Louis via the proposed extension could move east over any one of the numerous connections at St. Louis, including the Wabash.

Garrison in the fall of 1878 thus controlled the Missouri Pacific, held a substantial stock interest in the Kansas City, and headed the management of the Wabash. While the Kansas City was pushing a line to Omaha, Garrison, as president of the Wabash, decided to build a new line to Chicago. He was a realistic trader and, like Gould, he had learned not to place undue reliance upon the promises of others in open competitive battles. In 1878 he learned this lesson again. Despite the traffic agreement which the Kansas City had with the Alton for the interchange of Kansas City business, the latter decided to extend its own line west to that point. Garrison, in order to fight the Alton, decided to get to Chicago by the purchase of a small road with a terminus about one hundred miles southwest of Chicago.

Although Garrison had expansionist tendencies, the directors of the Wabash were not fighting railroad businessmen. Either they were representatives of bankers interested in the preservation of creditor rights, or men with memories—memories of the ill-fated extensions of the road in the early seventies. A number of the directors, large stockholders, had vivid recollections, some by personal experience, of the disastrous results which followed that expansion program. They were fearful of the consequences of the new program and therefore sold the bulk of their stock.[9]

Garrison, however, convinced of the necessity for a Chicago line, made it clear that, in charge of the destinies of the Wabash, he would press on with the program. The Illinois Central objected strenuously. If the Wabash built to Chicago, it would build to St. Louis. After weeks of negotiation, a settlement was reached and both roads surrendered their construction programs. "We may congratulate," remarked one observer, "the Wabash and Illinois Central roads on their sober second thought. . . ."[10]

Garrison by acquiring control of the Wabash had placed himself in a position which Gould had vainly contrived to secure. By controlling the two direct lines from Kansas City to St. Louis and the Wabash from St. Louis to a point not far distant from Chicago, Garrison was able to outflank the Omaha-Chicago line of the Iowa Pool roads. By controlling the Wabash, Garrison also could trade with the Hannibal and with the Kansas & Texas at the Mississippi River connections. If skillfully handled, this would give him a controlling influence in the St. Louis railroad strategy. At Kansas City his roads connected with the Kansas Pacific and the Atchison, and if he could make a satisfactory arrangement with the bondholders of the former he could reduce Gould to a position of impotence. Villard, on behalf of the Kansas Pacific's Denver Extension bondholders, could foreclose the mortgage and make Gould's junior securities relatively valueless.

Garrison's election to the Wabash presidency was therefore recognized as presaging a great change in western railroad strategy. It "is a great step in the consolidation of the greatest railway combination ever known," sweepingly announced one financial analyst.[11]

Despite the belligerence of Garrison and the weakened position of the Kansas Pacific, Gould within a period of four months succeeded in transforming the entire railroad picture in the lower Missouri Valley.

On the face of things the Wabash in 1878 was financially undesirable and the general run-of-mine investor and speculator could see little in its future. The road was not earning its fixed charges. Its prospects, however, were improving. Local traffic in the later months of the year showed exceptional increases, due largely to the heavy grain crop which benefited the freight receipts of all middle-western roads. While the Wabash in June did not earn enough to meet its pay rolls, traffic in the following weeks swelled to "immense proportions."[12] Despite the heavy demand for wheat, its price was extremely low, and for that reason railroad rates could not be increased. The heavy traffic brought little in higher profit.

That Gould was interested in the unprofitable Wabash, now securely in the hands of Garrison, was apparently suspected by nobody. No observer believed that Garrison would relinquish his plans for expansion and turn his major acquisitions over to Gould. Garrison was not an appeaser and was not frightened by bogies and threats. From the time he fought Cornelius Vanderbilt in the early fifties to the very moment of his acquisition and extension of the Wabash, he was aggressive. At this time, however, he had other projects in mind.

Gould understood the strategic possibilities of the Wabash. Although the Wabash receiver had been discharged for more than a year, title to the property was not yet free. While he was negotiating for the purchase of Garrison's holdings, suits arising out of the receivership and foreclosure were still pending. Despite its clouded legal position and in the face of poor earnings, the price of Wabash stock shortly after the sale of Gould's Union Pacific in late February began to rise on heavy volume. In the first two weeks of March, however, the renewal of legal proceedings reduced its price from 23 to below 18. On the decline as well as on the previous advance, the volume of trading was unusually heavy. On some days during this period the stock, which prior to that time had a quiet market, became the second most active on the exchange. When the stock market turned weak, it was Gould who received credit for the decline. Only ten days after the sale of the Union Pacific stock, a weak market was ascribed to Gould, whose short-selling operations, according to one authoritative source, "seemed to be gathering momentum from its recent successes."[13] Gould's smoke screen thus promoted his accumulation of Wabash and facilitated his negotiations for the purchase of Garrison's holdings.

So, protected by the speculative judgments of the day that he was interested neither in Northwestern nor in short-selling operations, Gould proceeded quietly to accumulate a large amount of Wabash stock. The first public news of the changing picture came on April 6, when the market was active and excited. A large subscription to the new government 4 per cent bonds was the motivating optimistic factor. Late in the day on news of the resignation of Garrison as president, the price of Wabash suddenly dropped to 19. It was thought that he had sold his stock before resigning, but not until about a week later was it learned that Garrison had sold. Even then it was not known that Gould and his associates had secured control. A week after Garrison's resignation Wabash resumed its upward price trend, and on the thirteenth of April, in heavy trading making it the second most active stock, the price rose to almost 21. Next day the trading was again heavy, but the price of Wabash remained about the same. Gould thus had a period of about two months in which to accumulate Wabash stock on the open market. His handling of this problem must be considered as masterful. His activity was kept secret; even the most penetrating of financial and market observers did not suspect the truth.

Gould's buying was aided by the management's passive policy over the lawsuits against the company. The officers made no move to protect the suits against the Wabash for receivership and foreclosure. Field, who early in 1878 had become a director of the Wabash, felt these legal actions keenly. He believed that the Wabash should enter suits for conspiracy against those who were manufacturing claims against the road in order to depress the value of its securities. In the fall of 1878, however, Field relinquished his Wabash directorship. These lawsuits kept the price of Wabash securities low, thus reducing the price Gould had to pay in order to acquire control. Short-sellers and nervous stockholders hurried to sell, and in conjunction with sales by large capitalists, who sold because of fear of the results of the Garrison expansion program, a substantial supply of stock at low prices was available. It is probable that by the first week in April, when Garrison resigned, Gould had purchased control of the Wabash. Based upon a price of about twenty for the stock, a majority interest cost him less than $2,000,000.

In assuming control, Gould took pains to select a proper managerial leadership. This was one of Gould's strong points. He was usually careful to select just the right man for the right job and to keep that man only as long as necessary to do that job. The Wabash had long been a speculative property. Gould was now planning an expansion program and was anxious to build up a strong following which would enable him the more readily to secure the necessary capital. Gould therefore chose Field to head the Wabash. Field, though not a railroad man, had many supporters among moneyed men who trusted him and looked to him for leadership. He was still a holder of Wabash stock. The Wabash under the leadership of a man with the background and reputation of Field would probably be able to enlist the support of an army of security holders. Field at first refused to accept this new responsibility. Precisely what proposals Gould made to Field to induce him to change his mind are not known. In any event on the sixteenth of April, 1879, he agreed to become president on condition that he receive no salary, and that he serve only until a good man with railroad experience be secured.[14]

In order to strengthen the board, Gould succeeded also in enlisting the services of Joy—another strong personality, and for many years a leader of the Boston group which had promoted many prosperous lines known collectively as the Joy roads. Gould recognized Joy's ability and appreciated the value of his following.

Despite his disassociation from active participation in the affairs of major roads, Joy continued his interest in the transportation problems of Detroit. He was convinced that the Vanderbilt monopoly of that city's transportation facilities was inimical to its best interests. Joy saw in the Wabash an opportunity to develop competition with the Vanderbilt lines. He had already made a beginning in this direction. From a point at the eastern tip of Indiana (Butler) to Logansport, a road under construction since the Civil War years had been finished just prior to the panic. Together with four other roads it formed a short route between Detroit and Indianapolis. Strategically the road was highly important to a number of eastern trunk lines as a southwestern traffic outlet. Its usefulness to the Lake Shore, for example, is revealed in the statement of the general manager in 1875, that the value of this connection to that road had been "thoroughly demonstrated." [15] The road became financially embarrassed and late in 1877 Joy, on behalf of himself and other bondholders, bought control at a foreclosure sale. A relatively short extension would bring this road into Detroit, and, in conjunction with the enlarged Wabash, give Detroit a new line to Chicago. Joy was not interested in the Wabash and he therefore refused Gould's request that he join the directorate. Gould's declaration that the Wabash would proceed immediately to make a Toledo-Detroit connection, however, won Joy over. Even then he joined the board only with the understanding that he would not share any of the responsibility for the road's finances.[16] Joy's acceptance of a place on the Wabash board was a momentous event. Joy had a host of friends in England who trusted him and willingly bought Wabash securities because of his association with that property. Gould's selection of Joy as one of his associates on the Wabash reflected again his uncanny genius in selecting the right man for a particular purpose.

In addition to Field and Joy, Gould enlisted the services of his two close associates, Sage and Dillon, now recognized as his partners in most all of his corporate affiliations. Two additional personalities with a broad background of railroad experience in the new Wabash system completed the board's new personnel. A. L. Hopkins was an able operating man who had served in an important capacity on the Wabash, and the other, Solon Humphreys, was a New York banker intimately acquainted with the financial problems of the Kansas City—soon to serve as the western part of the new Wabash system. With Sage, Dillon, Field, Hopkins, Humphreys and himself, Gould created a powerful executive committee. "It would not be easy," wrote one commentator, "to combine more intellectual and financial strength and railway experience" than in these six.[17] A New York daily assured its readers in analyzing the significance of the new Wabash board that "The country will wait for some time to behold a man more gifted than Mr. Jay Gould." [18]

In order to exploit the traffic advantages of the Wabash, Gould decided to acquire one of the lines connecting the Wabash at St. Louis with Kansas City and therefore with the Kansas Pacific. This was a momentous step pregnant with far-reaching consequences. The through Kansas City-Toledo route would make the participating roads competitors of most all of the east-west roads from Chicago east.[19] To place the Wabash with a St. Louis-Kansas City line would stir up violent competitive conflicts, and in the picturesque language of a railroad traffic man, "would establish a bridge over the 'bloody chasm.'" [20] Garrison's control of the Kansas City line was slight. A large block of the stock of this road was held by Humphreys who had long been on the board of directors. A number of financial institutions who were bondholders in the predecessor of the Kansas City company had received stock of the successor company in the reorganization of the early seventies. Institutions were not anxious to retain the stock of such a financially weak company. They were therefore ready to sell at any substantial price advance. They thus supplied Gould with considerable stock in the spring and summer of 1879. The number of shares held by Garrison is unknown. The Kansas City's stock in the early months of 1879 was even more laggard than the Wabash, with the price fluctuating aimlessly at about 10 to 12. Its market movements in March and April suspiciously resembled those of the Wabash, and on both active and on quiet market days, the stock of the road turned over in heavy volume. Late in April it became particularly active and for a time was one of the market leaders.

Gould's acquisition of control of the road in the summer of 1879 was not to the liking of Garrison, nor was it accomplished with his consent. Gould by his spectacular market successes in the Kansas Pacific, Union Pacific and Wabash, had attracted an important speculative following, many of whom as stockholders of the Kansas City were ready to respond to his leadership.

When Gould in the midst of a rising stock market submitted a plan for the union of that road and the Wabash on the basis of an exchange of stocks, little opposition was encountered, and by the fall of 1879, the consolidation was an accomplished fact.

The strength of this new corporate alliance between the Wabash and the Kansas City was soon sensed by informed financial observers. The election of Gould and his associates to the Wabash board was "full of speculative significance and interest," declared a leading metropolitan daily paper.[21] As on so many other occasions, Gould was able to raise visions of future possibilities in the minds of his contemporaries. The common ownership of the Kansas City and the Wabash was pictured as foreshadowing a new through route from the Atlantic to the Pacific which would include the Erie, the Atlantic—then in receivership and still independent of the Erie—the Wabash, the Kansas City, the Kansas Pacific, and the Union Pacific. An authoritative Chicago railroad journal concluded a description of the change in management and the execution of some trackage agreements between the Wabash and other roads with the observation that the Union Pacific managers had thereby achieved "a direct outlet under their own control from Kansas City to the Lakes." [22]

In less than three months after Gould had apparently retired from the transcontinental business, he had returned stronger than ever. What he had failed to do as a representative of the Union Pacific in fighting the Iowa Pool, he had now as an individual market trader succeeded in doing. In control of the new through line from Omaha and Kansas City to Toledo, Gould could now outflank the Iowa Pool roads. The local business of the Wabash and of the Kansas City was large and growing, and the two roads, according to journalistic observers, could also command a part of the large amount of freight delivered by the Union Pacific and Kansas Pacific to connections at Omaha and Kansas City.[23] With this volume of eastbound traffic under his control Gould could seemingly ignore the Iowa Pool lines and cut rates on transcontinental business. If he reduced rates on business moving east from Omaha and Kansas City, he could divert some share of the traffic of the Iowa lines to the route under his control. At the eastern end where the Pennsylvania, the Baltimore & Ohio, and the Lake Shore were eager for their share of the transcontinental traffic, competition would also enable him to play off one road against another. A diversion from the Burlington lines to the new Wabash route would cost the eastern trunk lines some of the transcontinental business formerly received at Chicago, but part of the loss they could make up if they succeeded in negotiating a new traffic alliance with the Wabash route at Toledo.

The heart of Gould's new railroad route, aside from its broad transcontinental implications, lay at St. Louis. Although the rates between Chicago and Omaha were relatively high, the eastbound rates from Chicago in comparison with those from St. Louis were low. This was due to the application by eastern trunk lines of the mileage principle. Commercial interests, which had long contended for lower rates eastbound from St. Louis, argued that a rate structure based upon the "mileage principle" would give St. Louis, as well as the railroads, considerable advantages.[24]

Hence any move made by Gould to assert the rate equality of the St. Louis roads would prove to be popular with the local community. Gould, alive to these opportunities, acted speedily, and the early results were successful. In scarcely more than a week after he took control of the destinies of the Wabash, he carried the fight into the camp of his enemies. The Wabash offered to carry freight from the eastern seaboard to the Missouri River points at the prevailing Chicago rates. Here was a direct attack on the rate structure of the Iowa Pool lines. In order to compete, it was necessary that the Pool lines carry freight from Chicago to the Missouri River points for nothing, unless their eastern connections at Chicago agreed to share in the rate cuts. Almost immediately the joint executive committee of the eastern trunk lines, the agency through which the eastern railroad pool had been operating since the spring of 1877, met but no settlement was reached. Three days later the committee meeting again decided upon halfway measures and tried to compromise. The Wabash, however, was insistent. "If our demands be granted by the commissioner," declared the Wabash management, "our recent rates will be withdrawn; if they are not, the war has just begun." [25] Despite mounting public opposition, the eastern pool had worked well but a concession made to Gould promised to upset the delicate balance. The age-old question now confronted those who in the interests of peace appease the aggressors. If the demands of the Wabash were met, and the existing key rates reduced, what additional concessions would other roads make and what additional breaks in the rate structure would follow?

This embarrassing problem obviously did not concern Gould who was strengthening his lines in order to make even further demands and thus strengthen his position. His bargaining power was improved by the heavy volume of eastbound traffic then moving. Business over the mid-western roads, including the Wabash, was rapidly reaching record proportions, and the Pennsylvania and the Baltimore & Ohio, in order to secure a long haul, made a bid for the Wabash business.

The failure of Cornelius Vanderbilt to expand the Lake Shore south and west from the main Toledo-Chicago line gave Gould also the opportunity to exert pressure on that road. For some years the Lake Shore had close traffic relations with the Cleveland, Cincinnati, Chicago & Indianapolis,[26] extending southwest from its main line at Cleveland. Although title to the stock of the road was in question, its properties appeared to be under the control of the Erie, and the union of these two lines threatened to deprive the Lake Shore of a major connection for its southwestern business. The Bee Line, furthermore, had been a serious competitor of the Wabash in the latter's own local territory and was described by a contemporary observer as "for years the main obstacle to the success of the Wabash. . . ." [27]

Through the growing strength of his traffic position, Gould was able to negotiate to a successful conclusion a pooling arrangement, long under consideration between the Wabash, the Bee Line, and another road. These three lines agreed for a five-year period to divide their earnings, and to authorize an executive committee to maintain rates and divide traffic.[28] Gould thereby acquired a whip hand over Vanderbilt in directing the flow of southwestern traffic to or from the Lake Shore at Toledo.

Thus fortified, the Wabash early in July renewed its demand for rate equality. Gould, on behalf of the road, insisted that more transcontinental traffic westbound be moved over the Wabash route via Toledo and less over the competitive route via Chicago and the Iowa lines. The trunk lines ignored the request. The Wabash management, however, was not discouraged, since by adjustment of rates it could get a proper share of the Pacific coast business. That clearly meant a rate war for which the eastern trunk lines were not yet ready.[29]

Gould and his Wabash were therefore appeased. Albert Fink, commissioner of the eastern trunk-line executive committee, recognized again, as he had two months before, the justice of the Wabash claim. The trunk lines agreed to route over the Wabash any freight so designated, and to give it a higher division of the new New York-St. Louis through rate. Thus the eastern lines agreed to give the Wabash both more business and a higher price. It was even reported that the New York Central-Lake Shore route had agreed to deliver all of its California-bound freight to the Wabash at Toledo and that other trunk lines would do the same.[30]

Gould by the early summer of 1879 had therefore re-established himself as a dominating force in the American railroad industry. Profits from his railroad holdings and security trading gave him the necessary cash and credit to enable him to proceed with other far-reaching plans. His profits were large in the Wabash and in the Kansas City, and even larger in the stocks and junior bonds of the Kansas Pacific. No sooner was he in control of the new railroad enterprises, than he turned to the task of exploiting their telegraph possibilities. Failure to achieve more than a temporary defensive success with his Atlantic & Pacific in 1877 was due partly to the judicial interpretation of the Western Union exclusive railroad-telegraph contracts. Only a few months after his surrender of the Atlantic & Pacific, the United States Supreme Court changed its mind, and thereby changed the law of the land. In October of that year the court asserted the jurisdiction of the federal government over all forms of communication and declared that the jurisdiction of the federal government extended to the telegraph business. If a railroad made a contract with a telegraph company giving the latter exclusive permission to build a right of way on its railroad lines, the contract could not be invalidated by federal or state action. If, however, the railroad with which the telegraph company had the contract voluntarily agreed to permit another telegraph company to build a line on its right of way, the courts of the country could not interfere.[31]

Under this interpretation of the Western Union railroad contracts, Gould could, as the controlling factor of a road, make an agreement with any telegraph company for another right of way, and thus invite wholesale duplication of the telegraph system. Gould was not the man to hesitate to take such a far-reaching step merely because it might be uneconomic.

His first move to build up a new competitive telegraph system was, as usual, unobtrusive. Late in April, 1879, he appeared as one of the three incorporators of the Union Telegraph Company with a nominal capital stock of $10,000,000. Gould took half of the stock, and D. H. Bates and C. A. Tinker each took one-quarter. Bates was superintendent of the Atlantic & Pacific; and Tinker held the same position on the Baltimore & Ohio's telegraph property. Neither of these two incorporators had any funds; and Gould provided them with the means to finance their subscription. Only a small amount of cash was thus raised. Funds needed to finance construction and expansion came from bond and stock sales of a construction company. This imposing capital stock of $10,000,000 must not, of course, be taken seriously. It was no index to the cash, property or services invested in the enterprise. The nucleus of the new corporation was a small competitive line, the Central Union Telegraph, which began business about six months before. Although it had few miles in operation, it had an ambitious program. The promoter of the company, a Mr. Owen, had vainly tried to interest the Western Union. The company did not consider the venture seriously, and a person connected with the Western Union said, "I don't believe it is a legitimate enterprise. I believe that persons interested in it never intend to build the line." [32] Other and more impartial observers took more kindly to Gould's telegraph venture. A Chicago railroad trade journal, reflecting probably the judgment of those who yearned for more telegraph competition, remarked that there was "every reason to believe that this [was] no blackmailing scheme organized with the especial object in view of selling out as soon as perfected at a handsome figure; but one that [was] a bona fide effort on the part of the railroads to secure to themselves the profits obtainable from their own resources." [33] The project was described as one which would connect with the Wabash line, and extend over the roads just passed under Gould's control and beyond to San Francisco. Again Gould displayed his ability for leading informed people to think of his ideas in terms of extravagant hopes and possibilities.

A few weeks later, on May 15, Gould broadened the project by the incorporation of the American Union Telegraph, capitalized at $13,000,000. Through a construction company he sold securities to the general speculative public. He immediately expressed the same underdog psychology that had been so successful on the Erie more than a decade ago. He thundered against the "great monopoly"; he would slay the monopolistic devil.[34]

His next competitive move was shrewdly made. Taking advantage of the newly rendered Supreme Court law of the land, he had the Wabash make a contract with the new American Union for a competitive and duplicate right of way over its line. He even tried to outdo the law of the land, and ousted the Western Union from the lines of the Wabash. The Western Union raced to the court for protection, and the court declared that while the Western Union could not be excluded from the lines of the Wabash, neither could the Western Union through its exclusive contract exclude the American Union. Both companies could build duplicate lines on the railroad right of way.[35] A few weeks later Gould followed an identical policy over the lines of the Kansas City. He ousted the Western Union and made a contract with the new American Union. Again the Western Union asked for an injunction and again the court refused.[36]

While these court struggles were going on, Congressional action strengthened Gould's position almost as much as the Supreme Court had in October of 1877. After extensive hearings and prolonged parliamentary moves Congress, in the form of a rider to an army bill, authorized the railroads to do a commercial telegraph business.[37] This permitted Gould, through his railroads and in conjunction with the American Union, to enter into competition with the Western Union in all parts of the country. The interesting speculative opportunities which this legislative permission made possible was foreseen in the hearings held when the bill was under consideration. "If the most unconscionable of all stock-jobbers," declared counsel for the Western Union before a Congressional committee in February of 1879, "had sought to provide himself with a club for the threatening of his enemies could he have devised anything more happy than the option which this bill gives to parade from time to time a possible combination of railroads to imperil the value of telegraph franchises, and, consequently, the market value of stocks?" [38]

With this legislation and the new court decisions to sustain him, Gould initiated a program of telegraph expansion. He discovered that a considerable mileage of poles and wires was owned by the railroads and operated by the Western Union on terminable leases. Wherever possible, the American Union acquired control of these lines and built new ones. In his efforts to penetrate the larger cities of the country, he encountered other difficulties. It was necessary to secure consent of the local council, and frequently exceptionally high prices were insisted upon by the city solons. Such was the case in Philadelphia. In other cities, the situation was such that the American Union had to use physical force to achieve its end. In Buffalo, for example, competition led to the cutting of wires and poles and to other riotous proceedings.[39]

At the same time Gould took steps to give the American Union a transatlantic cable service independent of any connection with the Western Union. To expedite matters he arranged for the organization of a French cable company with which, on behalf of the American Union, he made an exclusive and preferential business arrangement.

Nevertheless, the Western Union still refused to take the new movement seriously. The steps so far taken by Gould were indeed only beginners. He had spent most of July in Europe negotiating other transactions and had not yet had the time to divulge his major aims. The Western Union directors on the other hand believed that upon his return from Europe Gould would concern himself with his railroads, and that the American Union—the "opposition company" [40]—would soon be broken up.

By midsummer of 1879 Gould's power as a factor in the telegraph industry and as a leading force in the middle-western railroad picture was strong and growing. Through his surprising acquisition of two financially weak but strategically located railroads between Kansas City and Toledo, he had succeeded in wresting notable concessions from the powerful eastern trunk-line pool. He was preparing further blows against one of the most powerful non-railroad enterprises of the day—the Western Union.

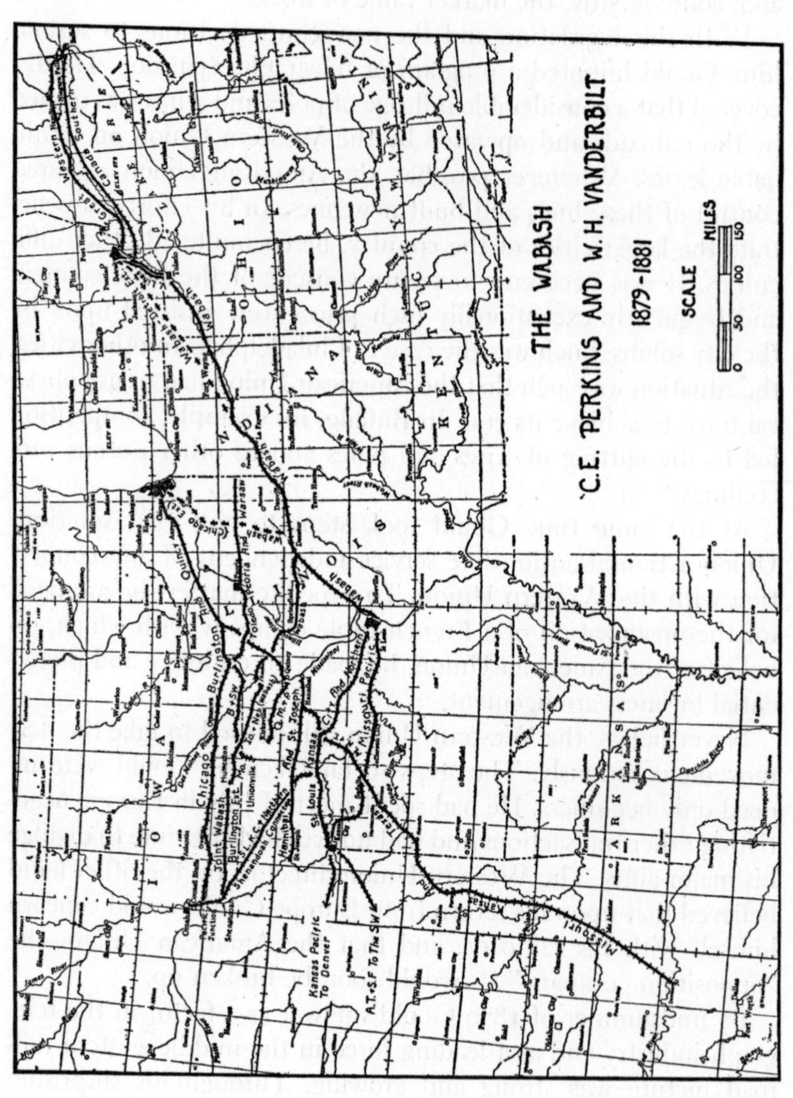
THE WABASH
C.E. PERKINS AND W.H. VANDERBILT
1879-1881
SCALE
MILES
0
50
100
150

That concern was represented on its board by strong financial interests: Vanderbilt; Morgan of Drexel, Morgan & Co., one of the leading firms in the railroad and government bond financing field; Taylor, the aged and eminent executive and major owner of the National City Bank; and Edwin D. Morgan, formerly Governor of New York and one of the wealthy and influential men of the time. Against all of these, Gould was about to pit his individual leadership, his comparatively limited resources, and his amazing resourcefulness and ingenuity, financial and trading ability. While he expanded his telegraph enterprise, he flung the Wabash strategic influence into the camp of eastern railroad and financial magnates. By ruthless pressure he extracted concessions that brought him to a position of leadership and influence in the eastern railroad community. He could no longer be ignored in any eastern or middle-western railroad strategy, and neither, for other reasons, could he be ignored in far-western affairs. And only a few months before he had been widely advertised as ready for enforced retirement.

NOTES FOR CHAPTER X

1. Buffalo *Commercial Advertiser*, cited in *R. R. Gaz.*, Aug. 13, 1870, 464-5.
2. *R. R. Gaz.*, June 29, 1872, 273.
3. *Public*, Oct. 25, 1877, 265; see also *Ry. Review*, April 26, 1879, 173.
4. *R. R. Gaz.*, March 25, 1881, 171.
5. New York *Tribune*, June 18, 1878.
6. This statement was made by Field in State of Massachusetts, General Court, Joint Committee on Claims, New York & New England Railroad second mortgage bond sale. Hearing on the petitions of Cyrus W. Field and others before the Joint Committee on Claims, 1886, hereinafter referred to as the New England Bond Investigation, 522.
7. Known hereafter as the Kansas City.
8. *Am. R. R. Journal*, Jan. 18, 1879, 76.
9. This account of the expansion program of Garrison is based on the following: New York *World*, Nov. 22, 1878; Chicago *Tribune*, Nov. 27, 1878; *R. R. Gaz.*, Nov. 29, 1878, 579.
10. A New York newspaper, cited in *Ry. World*, Dec. 28, 1878, 1251.
11. *Public*, Nov. 28, 1878, 339. The announcement of the Garrison management served as the occasion for a comprehensive editorial analysis of the Wabash in *R. R. Gaz.*, Nov. 29, 1878, 579.
12. This statement was made by a local newspaper in the heart of Wabash territory, the Lafayette *Journal*, cited in *R. R. Gaz.*, Sept. 13, 1878, 452.
13. Phila. *North American*, Feb. 27, 1879.
14. So stated by Field in New England Bond Investigation, 522.
15. Joy papers, John Newell to Joy, Sept. 8, 1875.
16. *Ry. Review*, May 3, 1879, 186; London *Railway News*, Oct. 11, 1884, 580.
17. *Stockholder*, Nov. 18, 1879, 98.
18. New York *Mail*, cited in *Stockholder*, Oct. 2, 1879.

19. See *supra*, p. 191.
20. State of Missouri, Statements and Testimony of Railroad Managers and others before Committee on Railroads and Internal Improvements of the Extra Session of the 34th General Assembly of Missouri, Jefferson City, 1887, 376, W. M. Sage of the Rock Island.
21. New York *Tribune*, April 22, 1879.
22. *Ry. Review*, May 3, 1879, 187.
23. In fact the interchange traffic of the Union Pacific was relatively small. In 1880, for example, California freight reaching the trunk lines was about equal to the business of Evansville, Indiana; to one-quarter that of Cleveland; to one-seventh that of Pittsburgh; and to one-fifteenth that of Buffalo. The rail freight received by the trunk lines from Chicago every five days was more than that received from California in the whole year, *R. R. Gaz.*, April 7, 1882, 210.
24. Memorial of the Merchants' Exchange Freight Committee, cited in *Public*, Dec. 21, 1876, 393.
25. New York *Tribune*, April 29, 1879.
26. Known hereafter as the Bee Line.
27. *Public*, July 31, 1879, 71.
28. *R. R. Gaz.*, Aug. 1, 1879, 422; see also New York *Tribune*, July 29, 1879.
29. This new demand was so astonishing that the well-informed *Railroad Gazette* refused to believe it. "The story seemed to be of a piece with many others that [had] been widely published recently—that is, without any foundation in fact or reason other than somebody's desire to get certain roads talked about." *R. R. Gaz.*, Aug. 1, 1879, 416.
30. See for these negotiations New York *Tribune*, July 25, 1879; July 28, 1879; *Public*, July 31, 1879, 71.
31. Pensacola Telegraph Co. vs. Western Union, 96 U.S., 1 (1877).
32. New York *Tribune*, April 30, 1879.
33. *Ry. Review*, May 10, 1879, 198.
34. This is the language used in the stock prospectus of the American Union, according to counsel in a suit against the Western Union merger, New York *Tribune*, Jan. 29, 1881.
35. Western Union vs. American Union Telegraph, Circuit Court, Indiana District, in *Federal Cases*, Vol. XXIX, 190-1.
36. New York *Tribune*, Aug. 2, 1879; *R. R. Gaz.*, Aug. 8, 1879, 431.
37. Land-Grant Telegraph Lines, Report No. 3501, House of Representatives, 49th Congress, 2nd Session, 1886, 26, 31, Reiff.
38. Competing Telegraph Lines, Minutes of a Hearing before the Committee on Railroads, Report No. 805, Senate, 45th Congress, 3rd Session, 1879, 16-7, G. P. Lowrey.
39. *R. R. Gaz.*, Sept. 19, 1879, 503. In Philadelphia, clashes with local municipal authorities accompanied the competitive struggle of the American Union against the Western Union, according to the Philadelphia *Times*, Aug. 20, 1879.
40. New York *Tribune*, Aug. 8, 1879.

CHAPTER XI

Gould Tempts W. H. Vanderbilt

IN EXPANDING the Wabash in eastern territory, in carving out new through routes for the movement of traffic via Chicago, Toledo and Detroit, Gould clashed head-on with Vanderbilt—probably the country's wealthiest railroad stockholder. His holdings in 1879 were concentrated largely in the New York Central, the Harlem, and the Lake Shore. In addition he had large commitments in the New Haven, New England (successor of the old Boston, Hartford & Erie), Michigan Central, Canada Southern, and Northwestern.

In American business and railroad history he must be set down as a classic example of one who failed to exploit his business strength in a free competitive battlefield. He rarely took the initiative to seize a vantage point from which he could dictate the detailed negotiations; he was almost always on the defensive. In such a position repeated attacks by his opponents forced him into a negative strategy. He was unable to develop mature and well-conceived plans to overcome his opponent so as to make him, and not himself, sue for terms of peace. And when the opposition persisted in its aggressiveness, he frequently sued for peace. He thereby became one of the country's greatest business appeasers. In one contest after another Vanderbilt made the concessions necessary to the termination of a business war. In the struggle over the export differential rates, in the telegraph war between the Western Union and the Atlantic & Pacific, which have already been reviewed, the contest was settled upon terms adverse to those interests represented by Vanderbilt. He was the stronger party in the telegraph contest, and by no means the weaker in the differential; yet in both he refused to fight a protracted war and reluctantly accepted terms which produced a temporary peace.

Vanderbilt furthermore could not adopt a definite policy and patiently, consistently, and with perseverance continue that policy until its logical, and if necessary its bitter, end was realized. He acted in spurts; sometimes he moved haltingly and then suddenly he rushed ahead with celerity and decisiveness. He could not be depended upon to follow a policy rigorously, once he had adopted it. It was not a mere change of mind dictated by changing circumstances which was such an emphatic side of his character, but rather the lack of fortitude necessary to hold out against a combination of adverse circumstances. He would savagely assail a company, a line of corporate policy, and even a particular personality, and a short time later make peace with the person or situation thus assailed.

Although some of Vanderbilt's actions and policies have already been examined, it is in connection with Gould's exploitation of the Wabash in eastern territory that his peculiar business characteristics were revealed against a comprehensive background of railroad strategy.

The consolidated Wabash in the hands of Gould was a dangerous business weapon. It was the only railroad which connected Kansas City, St. Louis, and the upper Mississippi River gateways with the Great Lakes at a point east of Chicago. The Wabash, therefore, was at the same time an eastern and a western road. Its traffic and rate policies affected the rate structure of at least two important traffic regions.

In the East the road connected with all major eastern trunk lines. It competed with the Pennsylvania's affiliates from Indianapolis to St. Louis, crossing its leased lines at numerous points in Indiana and Illinois. At Toledo it joined with the Vanderbilt system, and by a short extension, could reach the lines of the Atlantic which were soon again to be united into the Erie system. The Wabash, furthermore, by some new construction could connect with Detroit and there enter traffic relations with two lines which extended to Buffalo and beyond to New England.

The Wabash had the power, therefore, by pursuing diverse policies, to divert a large volume of eastbound business to any one of a number of lines. It could follow a traffic policy which would tend to harmonize conflicting interests, and, even at the expense of a loss in volume, tend to stabilize the rate structure, or it could exploit its strategic location even at the expense of slashing rate reductions, in order to collect the largest volume of traffic for its lines.

Of the three trunk lines which connected with the Wabash, the one which appeared most likely to be challenged by Gould was the Vanderbilt system. As owner of the short line along the southern shore from Buffalo to Chicago, and as the holder of the two outlets from Detroit, it was, strategically speaking, a powerful middle-western system. In its lack of connections with the Southwest, it had, however, a vital weakness. Only two independently owned railroad outlets into this region remained—the Wabash and the Bee Line, in neither of which the Lake Shore had any stock interests. The Lake Shore received a heavy volume of traffic from the Wabash at Toledo, and if Gould, in charge of its destinies, decided to follow an aggressive policy in the east he could divert traffic from the Lake Shore to another line. And he decided to do just that.

By the summer of 1879 when Gould opened up with his attack on the Vanderbilt system in the Middle West, Vanderbilt had invited a new competitive enemy by expanding his holdings in Burlington territory through his acquisition of a substantial stock interest in the Northwestern. As a counterweight, Forbes and Perkins of the Burlington considered the idea of buying some shares in the Pennsylvania. Forbes however was cautious and merely suggested that it would be a good plan to cultivate friendly relations, believing that all the objectives of an alliance with the Pennsylvania, such as those suggested by Perkins, could be secured without any stock holdings.[1]

At the very time when Vanderbilt was acquiring his Northwestern securities, thereby inviting the enmity of the Burlington, he was attacked by Gould in the east. Despite his power and influence, Vanderbilt found himself on the defensive, just as Garrison and the Union Pacific board were then being forced into the same position.

Though the Wabash had a heavy volume of traffic, it was nevertheless forced by circumstances to do business at low rates. It served a territory which was criss-crossed by trunk lines fighting eagerly for a share of the through traffic. Since it had relatively little local business *entirely* free from the competition of other lines, it was unable to make up, on that traffic, what was lost on the competitive traffic. Nearly everywhere it competed with roads which carried business to the Lakes by shorter routes. Rates were therefore low; in 1878, for example, its ton-mile rate was only 0.83 cents. Competitors in southern and central Illinois, unaffected by trunk-line competition, had rates which ranged from 1.06 cents to 1.44 cents.[2] An increase in the rate level appeared to be the wisest policy. A small rise on existing traffic would produce more profits than lower rates accompanied by more volume. Gould, however, had no intention of promoting rate stability. He saw opportunities for increasing the business of the Wabash and of other properties which he then controlled, and perhaps of still others which he was planning to control. He obtained results on one property by exploiting another. Such a policy, however, made stabilization impossible; his move was met by a countermove, and a war was on.

Peace between Gould and Vanderbilt was further obstructed by another difference. Joy had joined the Wabash board and lent his prestige to the Gould group because of his interest in a connection between Detroit and Chicago, independent of Vanderbilt. To complete such a line it was first necessary to gain access from Detroit to Toledo; but both of the Detroit-Toledo roads were owned by Vanderbilt. East of Detroit connecting that city with Buffalo were two trunk lines: one, the Great Western, was independent of Vanderbilt; the other was the Canada Southern whose interest had been guaranteed by the New York Central. Another line, the Grand Trunk, connecting Detroit with Portland, Maine, took steps to secure a Chicago connection. Its efforts in that direction were, however, blocked by Vanderbilt. Gould meanwhile had taken steps to carry out his promise to Joy to build a Detroit line. The road would be built, he declared, as rapidly "as new money can do the job." [3] Arrangements were made with the Great Western to allow the Wabash to use its Detroit terminal facilities, and a contract was negotiated with the Grand Trunk to permit it to use the proposed extension.[4] Differences developed almost immediately and the agreements were never ratified. Gould thereupon reached another understanding with the Great Western, informal in character, and not reduced to writing, for the joint construction of the Detroit line. This contract also was never consummated. Meanwhile discussions continued with Vanderbilt. Nobody, declared Gould, would profit from the construction of a parallel line, while everybody, he argued suavely, would be best served by the existing Vanderbilt road. Vanderbilt refused, however, to lease either of his two properties on any terms, though he would grant trackage facilities. A contract was drawn up affording running rights to the Wabash, Grand Trunk and Great Western. Gould laid down his customary ultimatum: accept or refuse in seven days. Vanderbilt refused, and the refusal, strangely enough, arose from an insubstantial difference of opinion over the valuation of the property.[5]

Negotiations were now terminated. A subsidiary company controlled by the Wabash was organized; a bond issue was created, and Gould, Sage, Dillon and Joy subscribed liberally. Adequate capital thus flowed into the venture; and the public was soon provided with a badly needed competitive facility. Gould and Vanderbilt, meanwhile, made a strong fight to seize the line which for some years had served as part of the through route between Indianapolis and Detroit. The road made connections with the Vanderbilt line, the Pennsylvania and the Baltimore & Ohio. With this road in his hands, Vanderbilt would have had the beginning of an extension into middle-western territory in western Indiana, from which he could, either by construction or acquisition, acquire a route to St. Louis. To Gould the road was equally strategic. With this property in his possession he would have a connection to northeastern Indiana from which the Detroit line could be built without passing through the congested Toledo terminal facilities.

In the contest for control, Gould was the victor. His shrewdness in selecting Joy as a member of the Wabash board of directors was now revealed, for in the reorganization of the road, Joy and his associates had acquired a majority interest. Because of its light traffic density, and the competition of surrounding trunk lines, rates were exceedingly low. The Wabash nevertheless agreed to lease the property at a relatively high rental.

The acquisition of this road made it impossible for Vanderbilt (except of course by the construction of new mileage) to invade Wabash territory. Vanderbilt meanwhile backed down in his fight with the Grand Trunk. Concluding that he could gain nothing by holding up its line to Chicago, he accordingly sold the small road which enabled the Grand Trunk to complete its Chicago line.

While Vanderbilt was thus surrendering to the Grand Trunk, Gould was making grand promises to the Great Western. He convinced that road that a vast flow of traffic from the Wabash would eventually move over its tracks via the new Detroit line of the Wabash. The two roads agreed to divide the through rate, but not on the basis generally used, of their contribution to the joint service, either in terms of mileage or in the use of terminal facilities. The Great Western would haul the Wabash cars over its line for a low price per car. The latter would thus have a through route to Buffalo and the use of the terminal facilities of the Great Western both in Detroit and Buffalo. It would also be able without consulting the other Buffalo roads to fix rates to that city.

This agreement was criticized by a group of the Great Western's stockholders. The management, however, justified the contract. The defense was a tribute to the matchless skill of Gould in presenting to his allies for the moment business promises in terms of business realities. Said the Great Western management, ". . . the Wabash Railway of today is not the Wabash of yesterday. The Wabash of today is, if not the greatest, one of the greatest systems of railway communications in the world." The road, it argued further, by a connection with the Union Pacific, was part of a route which reached halfway to San Francisco. Finally, continued the statement, one of the directors of the Wabash is "the principal of that line," referring of course to the Union Pacific.[6] This statement was made at a time when Gould had sold out a large block of his Union Pacific, when he was busily engaged in forming a combination through the Kansas Pacific to compete with the Union Pacific and to force it to take over this competitive system. The complex adverse interests which Gould was then building up against the Union Pacific was not observable, even by well-informed people in the railroad industry.

Gould had again put Vanderbilt on the defensive. Vanderbilt now recognized that he could not have both the heavy volume of Wabash eastbound traffic and a monopoly of the Detroit business. Gould had already diverted some business away from the

Lake Shore; for some months "large quantities" of freight had been moving over the Pennsylvania.[7] By October Vanderbilt had made up his mind that he could have the Wabash business at Toledo only if he made the necessary concessions. Late in that month, the traffic executives of the Wabash and of the New York Central conferred,[8] and by this time presumably the agreement for traffic interchange was almost ready. Gould, however, was not yet ready to settle; for he had new demands of a financial character.

Vanderbilt owned such a large proportion of the stock of the New York Central that the property was looked upon as a family road. Vanderbilt personally had been criticized for corporate errors and abuses. In 1879 these criticisms were brought to a head by a committee of the New York State Legislature in the so-called Hepburn investigation. Vanderbilt felt this criticism keenly and he appeared unable to stand up against the resolute attacks of public opinion. He did not have the stern fabric of his father, who could follow his sound business instincts regardless of the opposition. Perhaps it might be more charitable to say that in view of the passage of the four or five depression years, the currents of public opinion could no longer be ignored. Whatever the true cause may be, Vanderbilt decided to sell a large block—250,000 shares—of the New York Central stock.

Suddenly, while these negotiations for the sale of the New York Central stock were pending, a panic broke out on the Stock Exchange. The reported sale of the New York Central stock under these distressing circumstances could hardly be believed, a keen newspaper critic of Gould stating that the reported story of the sale was made up out of "whole cloth." [9] The story was created, so it was declared, only to precipitate a break in the stock market.

In the midst of these discussions, carried on for the Wabash by Field, came the news that Gould had bought the Missouri Pacific. The position of the Wabash was greatly strengthened. Except for the Alton and the weak and recently reorganized Frisco, Gould controlled all the lines between St. Louis and Kansas City. He now controlled more eastbound traffic, and his bargaining power with Vanderbilt was thereby enhanced. He now demanded as a price for his Wabash business that he be given a participation in the syndicate then in process of formation for the sale of the New York Central stock and a membership on the New York Central board. He threatened, upon learning of Vanderbilt's objection to his terms, to send both the Wabash and the Union Pacific business over the Baltimore & Ohio.[10] A few days after the market break, Vanderbilt sold $25,000,000 of the New York Central stock to a Drexel, Morgan syndicate, which included Gould and his two associates, Sage and Field.

Gould's prestige was increased by his association with one of the country's leading bankers. He was now in the best of company. His banking associations promised to facilitate the financing of many transactions that characterized his activities in the next few years. This new banking connection soon helped him to secure another bit of profitable financial business. Huntington decided to sell 50,000 shares of the Central Pacific, with a six months' option for another 50,000. A number of financial houses, including Kuhn Loeb & Co., and Fisk & Hatch, were in the syndicate; so was Gould.

To some writers the New York Central agreement was looked upon as marking a union of the two great railroad interests which for so long had been hostile. Gould, it was said, was the most important railroad man in the country. One, in a burst of reckless enthusiasm, gave him credit for controlling more than 10,000 miles, including the Northwestern, the Rock Island, the Hannibal, and numerous other properties; [11] while another referred to the "practical consolidation" of the Gould and Vanderbilt interests.[12] The potential power of the Gould-Vanderbilt alliance impressed not only outside observers but some railroad men as well.

Despite so many appearances to the contrary, Vanderbilt had not made a close alliance with Gould. Their traffic interests still clashed on many points. Vanderbilt had fought a long and losing battle against Gould. He had neither invaded the enemy's territory nor paralleled the line of his opponent by new construction or the acquisition of existing railroads. At no time did he threaten to enter Wabash territory to exploit the immense bargaining power of his westbound traffic, as Gould exploited the power of his eastbound traffic. Vanderbilt, in short, appeared to have been worn out by Gould's aggressive tactics, and he was sorely tempted to accept the proffered olive branch. He finally succumbed to the alluring prospect of corporate peace and the prospect of a steady flow of eastbound traffic at Toledo.

After the consummation of the New York Central transaction, Vanderbilt was loquacious. He talked at length to newspaper reporters and his philosophy was well expressed in one of these interviews. "It was a choice," he said, "between continuing the competition for western connections and making its members my friends. I thought it wise to do the latter." [13] Vanderbilt was again appeasing Gould, although Gould was not long to be appeased.

Vanderbilt was optimistic, and was certain he had made an agreement which would benefit his system. Here is what he said: "We protect the main line by making the interests of those who have tributaries to it identical with our own." He admitted that the New York Central was more important to the Wabash than the Wabash was to the New York Central. Nevertheless, he continued, "By bringing them in we prevent any cutting off of the tributaries; we stop any attack on the main line by uniting and pouring into the Central all their business." [14] Gould must have given Vanderbilt abundant assurances of the flow of traffic that would soon overtax the Lake Shore's line from Toledo. Informed commercial judgment seemed to be equally optimistic over the favorable effects upon the city of New York. One New York commercial journal with a wide following was certain "that New York would be greatly benefited by a connection through the Central with the great Wabash Railroad system." [15] Perhaps the situation can best be summed up by a remark filled with wisdom made by an observing stockbroker. A fellow broker had asked him why Vanderbilt had sold his large block of New York Central stock. His reply was suggestive. "Oh; I suppose he wanted peace." [16]

In the traffic contract between the Wabash and the New York Central, completed early in January, 1880, both roads agreed to establish a new through line, to be operated under the joint management of three fast freight lines. The equipment was to be used solely between Boston, New York City, and the western termini of the Wabash.[17]

Not many weeks passed before Gould made it clear to the railroad world, including Vanderbilt, that he had no intention of trading eastbound business exclusively with Vanderbilt. Early in March of 1880, the Wabash called a stockholders' meeting to approve a bond issue for the purpose of financing the building of a Chicago line. The Wabash, it was clear, would trade its eastbound business at Chicago as well as at Toledo. The Grand Trunk meanwhile had finished its new, although roundabout, line to Chicago.

Vanderbilt proposed to fight both the Grand Trunk and the Wabash. Accordingly he petitioned the court to enjoin the construction of depot facilities by the Chicago & Western Indiana—a new terminal company to serve both of those roads—and at the same time attacked the validity of a city ordinance which authorized the company to use the city streets. Both the Vanderbilt and the anti-Vanderbilt groups resorted to physical violence. Engines and rails were displaced, and a number of people had their heads broken by brickbats.[18] Eventually, Vanderbilt accomplished little and succeeded only in delaying the completion of terminal facilities from April to August. When they were finished, the Wabash and another small road, the Chicago & Eastern Illinois, leased the properties of that terminal company and guaranteed the interest on its bonds. The Grand Trunk contract with the terminal company remained unchanged.

The Chicago terminal war was accompanied by the passenger war of 1880 to 1882, which introduced a new railroad technique that was to be followed on an ever-widening scale during the next decade. Railroad wars in the previous quarter of a century had been fights for business, with each participating road attempting to get more of the available traffic. Gould's Wabash line from St. Louis to Chicago, however, was circuitous, and there was little expectation that through a rate cut he could get any increase of business. If a rate war would cost him little, however, it would cost his competitors a great deal. Vanderbilt, on behalf of the Lake Shore, was not the only one who wanted to keep Gould out of Chicago. The Illinois Central and the Rock Island were in full agreement with Vanderbilt. The passenger fare war, however, was designed not so much to get more business for the Wabash, as it was to enforce a policy on a competitor. In the rate struggles of the eighties and the early nineties, many such wars occurred. Almost a decade after Gould began this policy, an association representing the railroad industry denounced such wars in no uncertain terms. "No common carrier," it wrote, "can be justified in engaging in a general rate war to punish an adversary or to redress a wrong." [19]

Although by the fall of 1880 the Wabash had been in Chicago for six months, it could do little business until it had station and terminal facilities. Suddenly, without any previous negotiations, the Wabash struck, and cut passenger fares drastically. Gould, for the Wabash, lost the first round. The Alton—a Chicago line—controlled also a line from St. Louis to Kansas City, between which points the Wabash had the short route. The Alton, by cutting its Chicago-St. Louis-Kansas City rate, therefore, hurt the Wabash more than itself. Within a week, a conference in which Gould for the first time represented the Wabash apparently settled the war. The participating roads, which included the Missouri Pacific as well as the Wabash, agreed to pool their passenger and freight business through the existing Southwestern Association. Since this new grouping resembled the Iowa Pool which had for so many years stabilized the Chicago-Omaha business, railroad people were happy over the outcome. It was even believed that the Iowa Pool and the new association might consolidate.[20] The Wabash, strange to say, even though represented by Gould, agreed to accept any division of business to be decided at an arbitration meeting to be held later. The business of the Wabash, in view of the rapid expansion of its system, was increasing. Since the arbitrators were to meet every six months and establish a new basis for division of the traffic, the Wabash expected to gain from the pool arrangement.

Despite the clear advantages of arbitration to the Wabash, the prospect of agreement with a Gould-controlled line was too good to be true, and Gould himself soon regretted his amiability. The terms of the settlement had been indefinite and the railroad officials present at the peace meeting disagreed on the meaning of its terms. In two weeks the war broke out anew and continued for more than a year and a half; it was not settled finally until June, 1882.

Gould's rate wars and Vanderbilt's battles were only part of the many activities in which he engaged in order to build up a new railroad grouping in eastern territory. Gould was convinced that to increase the competitive strength of the Wabash in this region, a large increase in through traffic was essential. He could trade better, he believed, and fight with greater expectation of success, if he could control and deliver more through traffic. It was not until some years later that he learned, as did so many other railroad men, that he had grossly overestimated the value of such traffic. He expanded the Wabash, seemingly in all directions, but actually in response to the hypothesis of the value of through business.

Thus, for example, Gould decided to carve out a new north-and-south route between the Southwest and the Middle West. To accomplish this he bought a number of short and financially weak lines, two of which were secured largely through the intermediary of Drexel, Morgan & Co. The bonds were eliminated in foreclosure, and the Wabash obtained control by issuing its own bonds secured by a mortgage on the acquired road. Although part of the securities during the preceding two years had been bought by Gould, most of them were purchased by the Wabash directly from the bankers. The Morgan firm in London, recommending the exchange of the securities for the bonds of the Wabash, declared that the latter was "a sound investment security." [21] Some years later when the Wabash collapsed, criticisms were freely made that securities of these roads and many others were purchased by Gould and sold to the Wabash at inflated prices. There is little evidence to support this conclusion. The high prices paid for many of these short lines were the result of an illusion concerning the value of through traffic, an illusion which was shared with Gould by many other railroad men and railroad investors.[22]

These new through routes were for the most part established in a slipshod fashion and with almost no examination of their traffic possibilities. The struggling bankrupt lines from which these routes were built appeared to find a haven of safety in the arms of the Wabash. Gould thought that consolidation would strengthen the weak roads and make them profitable as part of a unified system. Some railroad men were in agreement with this opinion although there were others with wide traffic experience who were convinced that consolidation was no Aladdin's lamp, and of itself could not revolutionize the earning power of insolvent roads.

Gould purchased a number of other lines which appeared to have little except nuisance value. One road, for example, had practically all eastbound business. It had no western connections, and its cars westbound moved "absolutely empty." [23]

While building the Wabash system in the West, Gould was developing a new program in the East. In that region he entered upon a program of buying the stock of the Delaware, Lackawanna & Western [24]—one of the anthracite carriers serving the northeastern Pennsylvania mines. Its lines extend l west to Binghamton, New York, and east to the seaboard at Hoboken, New Jersey. The road was a competitor of the Pennsylvania and worked closely with the New York Central on traffic to Buffalo and the West. If it were extended to Buffalo, Vanderbilt's New York Central would be hard hit, although the Wabash would not necessarily be helped.

In the summer of 1880 Gould's hand in this new railroad strategy was revealed. On heavy trading volume the price of the Lackawanna stock rose rapidly, and in August came the announcement of the incorporation of a wholly owned subsidiary for the purpose of building a Buffalo extension. The incorporators of the new railroad included Gould, his two major associates on the Union Pacific, Dillon and (Frederick L.) Ames; his associate on the Wabash, Humphreys; General Eckert, president of the American Union; and Sloan, the aggressive president of the Lackawanna. Sloan had met Gould a decade earlier on the Erie battleground. Then they were business enemies, now they were allies. Their interests had clashed; now they harmonized. Business deals, like political deals, make strange bedfellows.

The Buffalo extension was a surprise to both railroad and financial groups but Gould's interest in the venture was an even greater one. With the completion of the Detroit extension early in 1881, the Wabash had a connection with the Great Western and could now send its traffic over that road to Buffalo. In anticipation of this lucrative business, the Great Western refused to merge with the Grand Trunk, since such action might lead the wily Gould to change his mind and transfer the Wabash business to another line, perhaps to Vanderbilt. A few weeks after the organization of the new company for the Buffalo extension, the Wabash, the Lackawanna, and the Great Western entered into a traffic alliance for a through route to the seaboard.

The Wabash accordingly was about to become a competitive line in eastern trunk-line territory, and its financial outlook appeared to be favorable. A leading eastern railroad journal reported Chicago opinion as believing that the various combinations in which the Wabash was then engaged would make it "one of the most important and formidable of any in the West." [25] A well-informed middle-western railroad authority remarked emphatically that the Wabash system had been skillfully devised, and that while under good management and favoring circumstances the road would thrive, under adverse conditions it could "hardly suffer more than the older lines with which it [was] throwing itself into competition." [26]

Despite his brilliant success in the handling of the Wabash, Gould's policy was unsound. His projects involved largely a diversion of traffic from existing lines. It is probable that had Gould made a co-operative arrangement with the existing Chicago roads, the traffic could have been equitably divided with profit to all.

This, however, was not Gould's strong point. In these negotiations he could not resist the temptation to look upon railroad projects as an opportunity for beating his competitors. Under such circumstances a war of rates was logical. In the Wabash territory rates on Missouri River traffic were cut immediately after his acquisition of power in April of 1879, while on Chicago traffic the passenger war broke out in 1880. On the east, the projection of the new extension from Binghamton to Buffalo exerted an important effect in precipitating the rate wars which began in June of 1881. The trunk lines asserted they would make no concessions to the new Lackawanna until through competition it was demonstrated that it could force a division of the business.

These rate wars, furthermore, hit the Wabash at its weakest point. Under independent operation before Gould control, the road had already suffered from rate reductions. "About a cent and a quarter per ton mile," remarked an editorial analyst, "is the best medicine for this company. It would do more good than a thousand miles of new branches and connections with every city in the Northwest."[27] In 1881, again at the height of its power, the Wabash, even at the expense of less traffic, needed higher rates. The full extent of the Wabash influence, its strength and weakness, cannot however be understood without a knowledge of its activities on the western end of the line. Here Gould also had the opportunity to display his ingenuity on a broad panorama. The corporate and personal opposition encountered in the West was more formidable than that displayed in the East. There he found no Vanderbilt prototype whom he could lure into making temporary agreements. Though the opposition was vigorous, the results were paradoxical. Despite the stubbornness of Gould's opponents, the losses on the western lines of the Wabash were smaller than those on the eastern. The moves made by Gould on the west nevertheless exerted a vital effect on the later evolution of American railroads.

NOTES FOR CHAPTER XI

1. The views of Forbes are found in Burlington archives, Forbes to Perkins, May 6, 1879, and May 8, 1879.
2. *R. R. Gaz.*, Nov. 29, 1878, 579.
3. Joy papers, Gould to Joy, May 1, 1879.
4. Ibid., Francis Grey to Joy, June 2, 1879; Wager Swayne to Joy, May 17, 1879.
5. Ibid., Humphreys to Hickson, July 24, 1879; Sept. 25, 1879; Field to Vanderbilt, July 24, 1879.
6. Statement by the president of the Great Western at the general shareholders' meeting on proposals for the fusion of the net receipts of the Great Western and the Grand Trunk, cited in Herapath's *Ry. Journal*, Oct. 4, 1879, 1080-2.
7. *Public*, Oct. 23, 1879, 262.
8. New York *Tribune*, Oct. 28, 1879.
9. New York *Times*, Nov. 22, 1879.
10. *Am. R. R. Journal*, Jan. 16, 1880, 57.
11. Phila. *North American*, Nov. 28, 1879.
12. *Am. R. R. Journal*, Dec. 18, 1879, 1421.
13. New York *Tribune*, Nov. 27, 1879.
14. New York *Times*, Nov. 27, 1879.
15. *Bradstreet*, Nov. 29, 1879, 4.
16. New York *Tribune*, Nov. 27, 1879.
17. Chicago *Times*, Dec. 2, 1879, states that the new freight line would provide 6,000 additional cars to be run exclusively over the New York Central and the Wabash; but *Ry. World*, Jan. 17, 1880, 57, states that the lines would not run exclusively over the Wabash. It appears that the 6,000 new cars would be used solely on the Wabash; and the existing equipment used over other lines as well. See New York *Tribune*, Jan. 14, 1880.
18. This is the description of Sir H. Tyler, president, Grand Trunk, cited in *R. R. Gaz.*, Nov. 12, 1880, 596.
19. Decision of Executive Board of Interstate Commerce Railway Association in

application of the Chicago & Alton, and the Chicago Burlington & Quincy for a reduction in lumber rates, cited in *R. R. Gaz.*, June 7, 1889, 379.

20. *R. R. Gaz.*, Oct. 29, 1880, 573. A full account of the misunderstanding between Gould and other railroad officials as to the terms of the settlement is found in the minutes of an adjourned meeting of General Managers and General Passenger Agents, held on Nov. 8, 1880. This document is in the Burlington archives.
21. Herapath's *Ry. Journal*, July 16, 1881, 865.
22. Differences of opinion on the value of the acquisition of bankrupt roads by the Wabash was referred to by a traffic official of the Rock Island, in State of Missouri, Statements and Testimony of Railroad Managers, and others before Committee on Railroads and Internal Improvements of the Extra Session of the 34th General Assembly of Missouri, Jefferson City, 1887, 434.
23. *R. R. Gaz.*, Sept. 26, 1879, 515.
24. Known hereafter as the Lackawanna.
25. *R. R. Gaz.*, Sept. 24, 1880, 512.
26. *Ry. Review*, Sept. 25, 1880, 496.
27. *R. R. Gaz.*, Nov. 29, 1878, 579.

CHAPTER XII

Gould Battles C. E. Perkins

WHILE on the eastern railroad chessboard, Gould encountered the hesitant and shifting personality of Vanderbilt, on the western end he clashed headlong with the sturdy and vigorous leadership of Perkins. While some of Perkins's activities have already been examined in a previous chapter, it is essential at this point to sketch his character more comprehensively against the framework of railroad relationships in which he and Gould acted as main characters in the dramatic corporate and territorial conquests in the years beginning with the railroad boom of 1879. Perkins was one of the business statesmen of his day. He had neither the flair for dramatic action that characterized Gould nor the penchant for ceaseless publicity of the widely advertised "Empire Builder" of the Northwest—James J. Hill. Neither was Perkins an independent leader in his own right as a majority stockholder nor as a leader of a substantial minority interest. Prior to his elevation to the presidency of the Burlington in 1881, he could rarely move independently of the views of a number of stalwart forceful and influential men on its board. Regardless of his personal judgments, therefore, it was impossible for him to move with the speed and dexterity of Gould. Perkins, furthermore, by 1880 had not yet attained a position of executive leadership in railroad affairs; and in this respect he was unlike his arch-competitor, Gould. It was necessary as superintendent and later as vice president of the B. & M., and subsequently as vice president of the Burlington itself, to harmonize and co-ordinate his views with those of his peers and superiors. He exerted little influence in the formation of the early Burlington line between Chicago and the Mississippi River and in its later extension to the Missouri River at Council Bluffs.

Despite the fact that after the panic of 1873, Perkins's judgment came to be increasingly solicited and respected, the dominant factor in laying down the managerial policies of the road was that of Forbes. Forbes's mind was constantly haunted by the losses which had been incurred as a result of the overexpansion in the boom years from 1868 to the panic. As a holder of every railroad stock except the Union Pacific,[1] his losses must have been heavy. He was sarcastic and even cynical in his comments on promoters and bankruptcy-stricken railroad enterprises. His idea was stability, to be achieved by agreements among railroads to respect each other's territory. When he joined the Burlington's board his first step was to say to the Burlington and the Rock Island: Let us make the public pay a fair dividend, try to agree on a division of territory, and not intrude on each other's territory.[2] In charge of the corporate destinies of the Burlington, he was almost always in dread of extensions and acquisitions.[3]

Forbes did not modify his cautious policy until Gould's moves in the eighties forced a change upon the Burlington management. In defending his conservative actions over the previous decade, Forbes wrote that while the policy of respecting each other's territory had hitherto worked well, the activities of Gould in "making combinations in all directions" made it necessary for the Burlington in self-defense to combine with the Rock Island and defy Gould and Vanderbilt and "all other outside influences."[4]

Perkins however recognized as early as 1877 that the time had come for a change. He saw, as had the Pennsylvania management ten years before, that it was unsafe for a road to depend for traffic connections on alliances with independently owned and managed railroads. In a series of comprehensive reports and memoranda characterized by intimate knowledge and clear thinking, he analyzed the strategic location of the Burlington and the necessity for taking action either by acquisitions of existing properties or by construction of additional mileage to complement the system and to unify and integrate the property.

His recommendations, while an executive of the B. & M., were for years not accepted by the Burlington management; but under the spur of Gould's belligerence, they finally became its settled policy. After much hesitation and reluctance, the Burlington under the leadership of Perkins finally launched out in the great policy of expansion which carried it to the foot of the Rocky

Mountains at Denver and north and west in a wide area in Nebraska and Wyoming to a connection with the Hill lines in southern Montana. Although Perkins was not the father of the Burlington's stem of the sixties, he was surely the creator of the Burlington system of the eighties.

In enlarging the road by acquisition and construction, however, Perkins did not show the same genius for financial trading which characterized the activities of Gould. He could not map out a plan of acquiring securities at low prices in order to build up a system which was strategically essential to a well-rounded program of system building. Neither did he have the ability to negotiate for securities carrying control of desirable properties and of concluding trades rapidly in a period of general business uncertainty. Perkins was too keen a student of operation and administration, and too familiar with the physical necessities of railroads to reach a snap judgment on the strategic value of a desirable property. Exhaustive examinations made by himself and his associates preceded his decision to expand. Even when acquisitions were essential in self-defense against attacks made by others, the necessity for thorough reports was not overlooked. Once his mind was made up, he acted decisively though not obstinately. In the midst of changing circumstances, he at times changed his mind, the better to accomplish a final result. However, once he recognized that a given policy was sound, and necessary to the achievement of a particular objective, he no longer hesitated. His execution of the project was carried out without fear or compromise, and no threats could move him. Next to Cornelius Vanderbilt and Huntington, Perkins was the most determined and redoubtable foe that Gould met in his business career of railroad expansion.

While the gloom of the depression in the seventies was still thick, Perkins's mind was turning to the immediate and future status of the Burlington as a first-class railroad system. The Burlington was financially secure; its debt was low, its earnings stable, and its stock was paying dividends. However, new forces were in the making and in a number of memoranda Perkins reduced to writing his ideas on the railroad network as they appeared to him toward the end of the depression in 1878 in the Mississippi and Missouri Valleys. They have a significance far greater than their value to the fortunes of the Burlington road and even to the country's railroad properties as a whole. The main line of the Burlington at that time extended from Chicago to Quincy with an offshoot to Burlington. From that point the lines extended through southern Iowa reaching the Missouri River at Council Bluffs and connecting also at Plattsmouth with its Nebraska affiliate. The system lines extended north to Council Bluffs in part by trackage over the Council Bluffs railroad. At Quincy the Burlington connected with the Hannibal which extended across Missouri to St. Joseph and Kansas City. The Burlington also interchanged traffic with the Kansas & Texas at Hannibal a few miles south of Quincy. The road was a desirable outlet for the southwestern business of lower Kansas, southwestern Missouri, the Indian Territory and Texas. The Kansas & Texas did not, however, reach Kansas City.

From upper Mississippi River points three unfinished lines had been projected into the area served by the Burlington. Each had encountered financial difficulties and had been precipitated into receivership. The traffic on the first road, the Quincy, Missouri & Pacific,[4a] was "very light."[5] If extended farther west, it would however penetrate southern Iowa, served exclusively by the Burlington. The second road, the Missouri, Iowa & Nebraska,[6] was launched under auspicious circumstances with support of reliable capitalists, including Carnegie and Smith (the influential banker of Columbus, Ohio), both of whom served on the board of directors, and with the reported support of the Pennsylvania Railroad.[7] The third road, the Burlington & Southwestern,[8] was projected as a competitive line of the Hannibal. In addition to its main line from Burlington, Iowa to St. Joseph, Missouri, another extension was to be pushed southward to Kansas City, and still another further south to serve southwestern Missouri. Like the other two small lines the road was not finished, and by 1878 it had been extended to a point one hundred miles away from Kansas City. And like the other two lines, it was also in receivership. Perkins was convinced that the Burlington must have a Kansas City connection and must control also the country between its Iowa lines and the main line of the Hannibal. To accomplish this it would be necessary to acquire the Quincy, the Iowa, and the B.S.W. If these roads were not taken they would gradually push on to trouble the Burlington. "If we do take them now," he wrote, "when they are bankrupt and before others are awake to the value of that region, we control that country and can extend these roads at our leisure." After discussing alternative policies, Perkins concluded that it was desirable also for the Burlington to acquire control of the Hannibal.[9]

Such were the well-conceived plans of Perkins, recently elected vice president of the Burlington. They were not, however, the plans of Forbes and the board of directors. When Gould in the summer of 1879 invaded the Burlington territory through his capture of the Wabash and the Kansas City, the interrailroad competitive situation was still the same. The Burlington had bought control of none of the local or through roads, and had made no definite proposals for their acquisition.

In 1879 Gould moved to acquire control of almost all of these lines. Between the summer of 1878 and the spring of 1879, the owners of the Quincy entered into negotiations with both Gould and Perkins. Little is known of the Gould proposals. It seems that his bargaining tactics were shifty and difficult to follow. One of the Quincy men told Perkins late in June that "they were not solid in their love for Jay Gould & C.–," and Perkins observed that the Quincy people began to see how Gould had pulled the wool over their eyes.[10] Nevertheless Gould finally acquired control by a lease to the Wabash. With the Wabash in possession of one of the three stubs, Perkins believed that the probability of its acquisition of the others would be lessened.[11]

Perkins's judgment proved to be incorrect. Although one of the other short lines—the Iowa—was not as valuable to the Burlington as the others, the battle for control turned out to be significant and dramatic, and ultimately paved the way for a territorial understanding between the Burlington and the Wabash in southern Iowa and northern Missouri. By November, 1879, the Burlington had acquired enough of the bonds to lead Perkins to conclude that the trade was practically closed. Gould, however, discovered that the general manager of the Iowa, who owned a large interest in the Peoria—the line connecting with the Iowa at Keokuk—as well as a large block of the Iowa's bonds, was anxious to promote a new through line consisting of the Peoria and the Iowa. Perkins observed the interest of the Iowa's manager and pointed out to Forbes that probably the Burlington could acquire that road only if it bought at the same time control of the Peoria. Though the Peoria would make no positive contribution to the earning power of the Burlington, defensively it would be of considerable aid. The Peoria, Perkins pointed out, crossed the Burlington at four places, where it made rates and demoralized business generally. To get rid of this competition would be a considerable gain.

Gould early in 1880 succeeded in convincing some bondholders, who had agreed to sell to the Burlington, to sell instead to the Wabash.[12] His ability to secure control over the Iowa was the result of his understanding of the ambitions of the Iowa's general manager to secure a new line from Omaha to the east, of which the Iowa and the Peoria were constituent parts. A plan between the Wabash and the Iowa was arranged in which both agreed to extend the line west to a junction with the Wabash, and to exchange the securities of the short line for those of the Wabash, providing the directors and shareholders of both roads approved. If such approval could not be secured, then the Iowa obligated itself to lease its line to the Wabash. A number of other provisions were inserted by which the bondholders were guaranteed a fixed interest and afforded the hope of securing additional contingent interest upon some income bonds. In response to the Iowa manager's fear that the company might not be able to complete the line because of legal obstacles that might be presented by its minority bondholders or stockholders, the Wabash, in the event of such contingency, accepted the responsibility of completing the extension. Although this ingenious contract was signed by the president of the Peoria, the chairman of the executive committee of the Wabash, and by the trustees for the reorganization of the Peoria, the contract bears all the earmarks of the trading genius of Gould.

By March, 1880, Gould had acquired control of both the Iowa and the Peoria. No sooner had he obtained possession than he decided to extend the former to the Missouri River and thus invade the territorial preserves of the Burlington. The new line in conjunction with the Wabash would make a reasonably short route from Omaha to Wabash points between St. Louis, Peoria, and Toledo.

To the Burlington the loss in local Iowa traffic from the proposed westward extension of the Iowa was far more important than the loss of through traffic. This local business was both large and profitable. Indeed the two-hundred-mile stretch east of the Missouri River was the heart of the Burlington territory, and was described by a railroad authority as "one of the most productive districts in the world." [13]

Gould's invasion of this territory was therefore a vital thrust at the pillars of the Burlington's earning power. Perkins made it clear to Gould that the Burlington would fight if he carried out his competitive threat. To permit a big company like the Wabash to knock the Burlington down without hitting back, declared Perkins, would be fatal and would only cause others to do likewise. The best way to strike the Wabash, he thought, would be to parallel the road from Peoria east to the state line and there connect the Burlington with the Pennsylvania Railroad.[14]

While the battle between Perkins and Gould was thus being joined in southern Iowa, important developments were taking place with respect to the Hannibal—an important competitor of the Wabash. In the summer of 1879 the president of the Hannibal, fearful of the strength of the Wabash, proposed to Perkins that the Burlington lease the Hannibal upon the basis of 40 per cent of its earnings. The specter of Gould crossed his mind; he did not know whether Gould had secured a controlling interest in his road, or whether a contest between Gould and himself was in the offing. He therefore thought that no one, not even the members of the two boards, should know that he and Perkins were conferring. At the annual election in early November, Gould and Sage were elected directors of the Hannibal. Although Gould did not have a controlling interest in the stock, his election to the board was forced upon the Hannibal under the cumulative voting laws of Missouri.[15]

The election took place at about the time that Gould acquired the Central Branch and the Missouri Pacific. The successive corporate acquisitions of Gould put the Burlington in a dangerous position. To all appearances its lines were almost completely shut off from access to the lower Missouri Valley below Council Bluffs. The Wabash had secured control of two of the three unfinished stub lines which threatened to invade the rich Burlington territory in southern Iowa, and Gould on behalf of the Wabash was dickering for control of the third line. Ownership of the latter would provide the basis for a new line from Burlington territory in the upper Mississippi Valley to Kansas City.

Meanwhile the extent of Gould's control over the policies of the Hannibal was not immediately clear, although prudent management dictated the advisability of preparing for the worst. And the worst was the Gould exploitation of the road with its short line to Kansas City and its valuable terminal facilities. When the news came in early November that Gould had purchased the Missouri Pacific it seemed momentarily that the worst had indeed occurred. Something like consternation struck the camp of the Burlington. "Gould moves so rapidly," exclaimed Perkins, "it is impossible to keep up with him with Boards of Directors." [16] He wondered how far Gould would try to use this power in order to whip other roads into subjection. It would be something of an undertaking, he thought, for either one of these properties to fight Gould single-handed. Perkins was sounding a call for united action against the common enemy, his appeal sounding very much like those made by Churchill in 1939 and 1940 to the neutral countries in western Europe to unite against the common enemy. The rule of self-help was followed in 1939, just as it was in the railroad battles of 1879 and 1880. If Gould should join wholeheartedly with Vanderbilt (Perkins was writing at the time when the Gould-Vanderbilt negotiations for a Lake Shore traffic contract were under consideration), it would make trouble for all the roads. In such an event an alliance with the Pennsylvania would be a natural result, but Perkins had it on good authority that Gould had joined with T. A. Scott, president of the Pennsylvania, in the construction of the Texas & Pacific extension to El Paso, and what that union of interests implied, Perkins did not know.[17]

Of one thing Perkins was certain: that the Gould control of the Union Pacific and of other short lines made it important to do something toward the purchase of the Council Bluffs. This road—another Joy property—had long served as an important factor in the traffic of the Burlington in western Iowa and Missouri. Extending from Council Bluffs to Kansas City, Missouri, it gave the Burlington access not only to the important river gateways of St. Joseph, Atchison and Leavenworth, but also by trackage rights afforded it a convenient line into Council Bluffs. Toward the end of the depression of the seventies, the growth of these lower Missouri River cities had taken a surprising spurt. The Burlington management recognizing the value of the road had long endeavored to acquire control. Shortly after becoming president of the Burlington in 1878, Forbes, desirous of minimizing risks, opened negotiations for a lease based upon its earnings, and the opportunity to acquire the road at a reasonable price slipped by. Its stock could have been bought at one time for little or nothing by guaranteeing the bond interest.[18]

When Gould almost a year later bought the Missouri Pacific, the Council Bluffs was still independently owned. Gould made an immediate bid for control, and an officer of the Union Pacific informed at least one newspaper reporter early in December that within forty-eight hours Gould would own the road and shut the Burlington out of Council Bluffs.[19]

This officer however was talking without full knowledge of the facts. Perkins recognized the strategic importance of the Council Bluffs line, and had little difficulty in convincing Forbes of the necessity of acting promptly to secure control. In late November, shortly after Gould's purchase of the Missouri Pacific, Perkins initiated an exhaustive investigation into the merits of the line. A steady stream of reports from officials of the Burlington and the Council Bluffs, and of outside parties as well, supplied Perkins with the facts upon which the Burlington management should act. Against the advantages to be realized in the purchase of the road—advantages that have already been summarized above—was the heavy cost of the road. Only a few years before, the company's income bonds and common stock had sold at nominal levels, and prior to 1879 the common stock had earned practically nothing. Early in the negotiations the traffic manager of the Burlington had expressed the thought that the purchase of the road on the basis of about $30,000 a mile would be self-sustaining; but less than two weeks later the assistant general manager had no hesitancy in approving the purchase of the road at about $50,000 a mile. This looked like a large sum, he added; but, he continued, "I believe we had better do it rather than let it go into the hands of other rival lines." [20] A new road from Council

Bluffs to Kansas City could have been built for approximately \$21,000 a mile. The price which the Burlington finally paid for control, \$125 (in its own stock) for the stock and income bonds of the acquired road,[21] was probably the highest price in terms of asset value and earning power which up to that time the Burlington had ever paid for control of any road. The Burlington's hand was forced. It was now defensively following in the footsteps of Gould—buying roads with poor earnings at high prices.

By this purchase the Burlington had at least kept open one road to Kansas City. On the other hand, the Burlington after a prolonged contest lost control of another friendly connection with which for some years it had interchanged traffic to and from Texas and the Southwest. Despite this strategic position and the heavy volume of business, this road—the Kansas & Texas—fell a victim to depression influences. In an effort to stave off receivership it made a valiant effort to reach a voluntary agreement with its bondholders, offering to fund part of the interest in the form of preferred stock.[22] This and other plans were unsuccessful and finally a receiver was appointed. The receivership however lasted only a short time and was succeeded by one of those unique schemes arising so often from desperate financial necessity. When the receivership was terminated the property instead of being turned back to its stockholders was placed in the hands of a trust company assisted by an advisory committee of seven. The road then issued income bonds to fund its past due interest and floating debt, the trust company agreeing to apply the revenue after operating expenses to the payment of interest.[23]

The company in 1879 had a heavy debt outstanding consisting of more than \$14,000,000 of consolidated mortgage bonds in addition to a small amount of prior liens and a substantial block of junior income bonds. Of the consolidated bonds approximately \$6,000,000 had been deposited with a committee of Dutch bankers. Both Gould and the Burlington management were in contact with these bankers known as the Amsterdam Committee. Gould had visited Amsterdam in the summer of 1879 in connection with his purchase of the Denver Pacific bonds, and there is little doubt that at that time he communicated with the Dutch bankers and exchanged opinions about reorganization plans.

Some months before this trip to Europe, competitive buying for the securities of the road took place and at least one New York newspaper declared that there was "no doubt" that Boston capitalists were buying its bonds and stocks.[24] At the annual election a number of Burlington representatives were elected to its board, and reports even spread that the road might be leased to the Burlington. These rumors were not correct, though the Burlington's management was in touch with the Amsterdam Committee, competing with Gould for control of the property. This competitive rivalry, all things considered, should have ended in a victory for the Burlington, one of the most prosperous roads in the Middle West, and one of the few that had escaped the panic and depression years financially unscathed.

Despite these advantages the struggle to control the Kansas & Texas was lost by the Burlington. For against the group of capitalists was matched an individual who was constantly in search of strategic flaws and possessed of an almost bewildering knowledge of the intricacies of corporation finance. In view of the heavy debt of the Kansas & Texas, the Burlington management was not willing to pay anything for the common stock, and accordingly planned to acquire control through a mortgage foreclosure which would make the stock valueless. By the fall of the year the Burlington had finally made a definite offer, expressing its willingness to guarantee a return of 4 per cent upon the bonds. Forbes believed that the bondholders would take this guaranty of the Burlington in preference to a 5 per cent offer of the Wabash. He was savage in his attack on the Wabash guaranty proposals. "It is an *edifying* spectacle to see hungry capitalists hankering after guarantees of bankrupt roads by other bankrupts. It is like the blind leading the blind and the lame carrying the lame." The Burlington had no intention of competing with the Wabash "and other such adventurers" in a race to lend corporate credit to weak lines, even though the stockholders of the Kansas & Texas were urging an alliance with the Burlington.[25]

In October, the Dutch bondholders finally declined the Burlington offer and insisted upon a 5 per cent guaranty.[26] Even though these terms were attractive they believed that more could be secured from Gould, and in fact shortly after rejection of the Burlington's guaranty, the Wabash did offer them 6 per cent.

Shortly after the rejection of the Burlington offer, the price of the Kansas & Texas stock rose sharply in one day from 22 to more than 25, and on the next day to 29. Informed financial judgment could not understand the reasons for the sudden elevation of a stock which had long been considered as worthless. "It would require," remarked one commentator, "a very powerful microscope to discover one-tenth of that price in the present value of that stock." [27] Gould's connection with the buying movement was of course unsuspected, and he was thereby able to repeat his experience earlier in the year with the Wabash, the Kansas Pacific, and the Kansas City. Looking for no bargains and taking the market price as representative of the values he sought to acquire, he bought at the market price and paid high prices which no conservative management would care to pay. It must be remembered, however, that he was an individual, acting in his individual capacity as a market trader, and risking his personal funds. Although the price was high, he achieved his major purpose of acquiring a majority of the stock of the road.

Gould's conquest of the Kansas & Texas was rapid indeed. By the following January he had installed his board of directors, and by May he had induced the stockholders to approve a lease of the property to the Missouri Pacific. The lease was an ingenious document conceived in the best tradition of Gould's financial technique. Under the terms of the contract, the lessee although agreeing to pay interest from the earnings realized by the lessor, guaranteed nothing; it agreed only to turn over any surplus in earnings to the lessor's shareholders.[28] At any time and whenever the interests of the lessee so required, the lessee could return the property to the lessor. In making this lease the bondholders were not consulted, and they might therefore well challenge its legality. A foreclosure sale could still pass title of the property to the bondholders who could then trade with the Burlington. Gould was well aware of these possibilities, and he recognized that in order to insure the Missouri Pacific control of the Kansas & Texas, it was essential that the trust company return the property to the shareholders. In October, 1880, accordingly, Gould in his capacity as president of the Kansas & Texas tendered the trust company $800,000 in cash; this amount, together with an additional $250,000 cash in the lessor's treasury, was sufficient to honor the unpaid interest coupons, thereby removing the existing default. Gould therefore demanded restoration of control of the road to the stockholders. He informed the trust company that as soon as this restoration was effected, a fund of $5,000,000 already subscribed would be spent in realizing the company's original hopes of extending its line to the Rio Grande. In demanding the return of the property upon payment of the defaulted interest, Gould was on solid legal ground; and the court therefore ordered restoration of the Kansas & Texas to its stockholders. The request of Gould, as president of the road, for the return of its property, wrote the judge, "would seem to be a reasonable demand. . . ." [29] Gould had now secured another notable victory without putting up any funds (since he could now sell the Kansas & Texas stock at a profit) without assuming any liability, and with the assumption of no corporate liability by the lessee, which he personally dominated.

The control of the Kansas & Texas was now in the hands of people who were not interested exclusively in its affairs and who had greater commitments in other roads with which the newly leased line was affiliated. The lessee nevertheless was given a blank check in dominating the lessor's policy, in construction of extensions by the lessor, in the diversion of traffic from the lines of the lessor to the lessee or of other lines in which the owners of the lessee were interested, and in the preparation of books of account in such a way as to increase or decrease public earnings in order to satisfy the paramount interest of the lessee. With the Missouri Pacific in control of the Kansas & Texas, the latter's business could be diverted from the Burlington to other Gould lines. Not long after the passage of control, for example, the Kansas & Texas, in face of the fact that the largest shippers preferred the Burlington, diverted almost all of its Texas-Chicago livestock to the Wabash.[30]

By the end of 1880, therefore, the Burlington, as the result of its prolonged competitive contest with Gould, had succeeded only in the capture of control of the Council Bluffs, although it was probable that it might still be able to play some role in the determination of the policies of the Hannibal. That road meanwhile (for the year 1880) was trading about one-half of its interchange business with the Wabash.[31] In view of the close relations which had for so long existed between the Hannibal and the Burlington, such a high percentage could have been secured only by diversion of business from the latter. The Hannibal furthermore threatened the Burlington with an extension of its line from Quincy to Chicago.

At the same time Gould was negotiating for control of the B.S.W. The Burlington officials, well acquainted with the condition of that road, refused to bid up its price even in the face of its possible acquisition by Gould. Forbes, cautious as ever, believed that the Burlington could take care of the Kansas City business by making some combination with existing roads. If, however, that proved to be impossible and the Burlington was forced to build, the new road would have to be something a good deal better than the B.S.W. could "*any how be made.*" If, he concluded, there was any reasonable chance of the Burlington being required to build a good road to Kansas City, then it had better avail itself of the then existing low prices of money to build immediately and take the chance of acquiring the road later.[32]

By the summer of 1880 it had become clear to Gould that, in view of his control of the two St. Louis-Kansas City short lines, a third outlet to Kansas City in the form of a financially unproductive property was not essential to his system-building plans, and although no agreement with the Burlington had yet been made, a sale to Gould and his group was off. The relationships between the Burlington and the B.S.W. were such as to make the Burlington feel safe that the B.S.W. would pass into its hands at a reasonable price.

Under these circumstances Perkins could take the initiative in the campaign of challenges and counter-challenges which charged the atmosphere of personal and corporate negotiations between Gould and Perkins and between the Burlington and the Wabash. Perkins threatened to get control of the B.S.W. and build an extension to Kansas City if reasonable terms could not be made with the Hannibal, and Gould served a counter-threat that in that case the Hannibal would build to Chicago.

Despite their verbal exchanges, neither Perkins nor Gould for the moment made any aggressive moves. On both sides steps were taken to secure peace with honor, and to find a friendly way out of a threatened corporate war with the minimum injury to each of the contestants. Early in July Gould took the initiative by writing confidentially to Perkins that he thought the Burlington and the Wabash might get together to stop the Hannibal line to Chicago. In communicating this information to Forbes, Perkins suggested that if the Burlington could acquire control of the B.S.W. and buy the Iowa from the Wabash, the country could be divided so that both contesting systems could make a profit. There was more profit, wrote Perkins, to the Burlington and the Hannibal in maintaining the one line to Chicago and Kansas City than in extending the B.S.W. west and the Hannibal east.[33] Perkins in his reply to Gould nevertheless continued to advert to the danger of the Hannibal's Chicago extension.[34]

These friendly interchanges were followed by a meeting between Gould, Perkins, and Dillon of the Union Pacific. At this meeting these three "in a very friendly spirit," to use the language of Gould, arranged all matters west of the Missouri River.[35] Gould reported that he had advised the Hannibal to make what he considered "a perfectly fair adjustment" with the Burlington, and had recommended that the Wabash make a strong alliance with the Burlington at Peoria such as Perkins "intimated would be satisfactory." Though the Wabash people said they were committed as part of their purchase of the Iowa to include the extension across the state of Iowa to a connection with their Omaha line, they agreed on the other hand that they would go no further than the extension to Omaha, thus protecting the Burlington system in the rich country of southern Nebraska. This was as far, said Gould, as he had been able to commit the Wabash people up to this time, and he suggested therefore that T. J. Coolidge, a member of the Burlington board and president of the Atchison, who had arranged the Gould-Perkins-Dillon meeting, come to New York to consider these problems with the Wabash directors in order to work out a satisfactory adjustment.

Perkins meanwhile had talked with the leading Hannibal stockholders and officials of the road, and although Gould was ready to conclude an agreement upon the basis of the status quo, the Hannibal stockholders were not satisfied and as an alternative suggested that the Burlington buy a controlling interest in the Hannibal stock. Perkins, however, was not interested and remained confident that a trade could be made on the basis of the status quo for a three-year period, an interval sufficiently long to enable the Burlington to consider maturely the idea of building an extension to the foot of the Rockies.

All these prolonged negotiations, however, achieved no immediate results. Both camps were probing each other's strength and weakness, and neither was prepared to make the concessions necessary to a trade. Perkins revealed not the slightest intention of compromising the main objective of keeping the Wabash out of its Iowa territory. Neither was Gould prepared to surrender his objective of securing a new short line for the Wabash system. By September Perkins concluded that the negotiations would lead nowhere and that it was necessary for the Burlington itself to take the offensive in order to bring Gould and the Wabash to terms. Perkins therefore informed Humphreys of the Burlington's intention to build the road paralleling the line of the Iowa, and Humphreys replied that he would build lines in Nebraska.[36]

This defiant attitude of Humphreys—and Humphreys to the realistic mind of Perkins reflected the policies of Gould—had to Perkins only one meaning: Gould either could not or would not make peace, and since it was unlikely that he could not make peace, Perkins concluded that he simply would not. Despite the imminence of the railroad construction war, Perkins still had some hope. He believed there was one, and only one, compromise left that both parties could afford to accept. The Wabash had insisted that it wanted only a through line to connect the line of the Peoria with Omaha, and that it had no design upon the Burlington's local business. The Burlington also wanted a through line through southern Iowa connecting with the Burlington's lines at the Mississippi River junctions in order to facilitate the movement of its traffic from the Southwest and from southern Nebraska. The needs of both lines would be served by the construction of one road to be owned half and half by each of the two parties and to be managed under a contract which would protect the Burlington against branches that would interfere with its local traffic and tend to demoralize rates. The local business on the new line would belong one-half to each party.[37]

Almost at the same time Gould in a conversation with Coolidge had made a similar suggestion. He developed the idea that the connection of the Iowa could be owned in common in return for an agreement by the Burlington not to invade Colorado or Kansas for a period of ten years. Perkins admitted that to let the Wabash come into the Burlington's Iowa territory, even on joint ownership "*without our building anything in retaliation* [*was*] *a dangerous precedent—& a backdown.*" He was ready, however, to make this agreement as the easiest way out of the difficulty. If, however, said Perkins, he were as rich as Vanderbilt and owned half of the Burlington, he would fight Gould and whip him; but he wasn't certain that the mass of Burlington stockholders would favor such a program.[38]

Meanwhile, Coolidge, frightened by the renewed threat of the outbreak of a competitive construction war, had also suggested to Perkins that some compromise be worked out with the Wabash. Although Perkins was ready for business on any fair basis, he questioned the wisdom of any compromise if it involved the extension of the Wabash through Burlington territory. Even if the Wabash did not interfere with the Burlington's local traffic, a compromise, in Perkins's judgment, might be regarded as a bad precedent. But if Coolidge's suggestion meant the negotiation of "a general treaty," by which the Wabash, the Burlington and the Union Pacific would guarantee the status quo, and by which the Burlington would agree not to extend its lines to Denver in exchange for a "fair share" of the business of the Atchison and of the Union Pacific, a basis could be laid for a general all-around understanding.[39]

Perkins's perspicuity and his statesmanlike sense of business realities led him to make a fruitful suggestion striking directly at the heart of the subject. "Mr. Gould's power [is] so great and his influence [extends] over so many corporations that I think he personally should also be party to such a contract if practicable." [40] Gould however was too shrewd and too familiar with the tactics of trading ever to commit such a blunder. He rarely assumed any personal responsibility for contracts which expressed his personal judgments of corporate policies, but rather made them through the instrumentality of a corporation which apparently was the one most directly affected. Usually other companies in which he had stock interests, directly or indirectly, were also affected, and his interests in such concerns frequently made it essential to change the contract, or even to nullify it. In substance, although not in form, Gould was usually the most important factor in the contract but personally he never appeared as such. The Union Pacific contracts were signed by Dillon as president; the Western Union contracts were signed by Green as president; and the Wabash contracts by Humphreys as president. Perkins's suggestion for a Gould signature to any agreement which might be made was therefore sound, but it passed unheeded by Gould.

Perkins moreover was not certain that Gould meant business and he still feared a renewed contest for territory. If this contest continued, insisted Perkins, "the fences [were] down"; and the company which moved slowly or timidly must in the end be submerged. To protect corporations from each other, it was important to respect territorial rights. Throwing down the gauntlet indirectly and without naming Gould, he declared that the Union Pacific had been among the first to insist upon the recognition of the rule of territorial rights; and the Burlington had accepted it. The present disagreements with the Wabash, he declared, had grown "wholly out of its unwillingness to accept this rule."

In a burst of personal frankness worthy of Pepys' Diary, Perkins related that the Burlington was not entirely blameless, since it should have insisted upon applying this rule one or two years before, when the Wabash first invaded the Burlington territory by building an extension to Council Bluffs. Applying this to the Burlington, Perkins stated that that road could not accept the rule west of the Missouri, for example, if there was to be no such rule east of the river. If therefore the Wabash extended into Burlington territory because it could get half of its business, then there was no territorial law, and the Burlington must then build to Kansas or Colorado or wherever it could find business.[41]

The unyielding stand taken by Perkins finally impressed Gould. A meeting attended not only by Gould and Perkins but also by officials of the Union Pacific and the Wabash was held in New York from October 19 to October 22. No longer could Gould prolong negotiations by shifting the responsibility to the other two roads. No longer could he say that he had tried unsuccessfully to induce this or that official to do so and so. All policy-making officials were present, Dillon representing the Union Pacific and Humphreys the Wabash. The solution was found in the idea that had been independently suggested by both Gould and Perkins. The Iowa's extension was to be built by an independent company for joint account, the Wabash and Burlington putting in half the money and having an equal voice in its building and management. Each road felt that it was surrendering something. The Wabash believed that it was surrendering the business that it might have obtained by building new lines in Iowa and Nebraska, while the Burlington believed that it gave up much that might have been secured by going into Kansas and Colorado. The Burlington "*knows*," wrote Perkins, that by this compromise it must lose a certain amount of business which it formerly had. In the general territorial understanding the Burlington agreed to abandon opposition to the construction by the Wabash of a number of small branch lines; while the Wabash and the Union Pacific in turn agreed not to extend their lines into southern Nebraska. The Burlington agreed not to build to Denver, thus protecting the Union Pacific, and the Wabash agreed to build no more main or through lines in southern Iowa, thus protecting the Burlington.[42] Despite the sacrifices made in the form of a loss of future potential business, the Burlington management had nevertheless secured what appeared to be a definite territorial settlement, an absence of competition on its rich local traffic in southern Iowa, and—what promised to be the grandest prize of all—the assurance of rate stability.

The superior business ability of Perkins, as compared with that of Vanderbilt, is revealed in the final outcome of this dispute which threatened to develop into such a far-reaching program of competitive and duplicate building in the territories of the Burlington and of the Wabash. Gould had forced Vanderbilt to follow a policy highly advantageous to Gould, personally, and also to his corporate interests. This policy, however, had not saved Vanderbilt from Gould competition. Perkins made no gestures. He made it known to Gould that if he acted to harm the Burlington, regardless of the harm done to the Wabash, Perkins would act to hurt the Wabash regardless of the injury to the Burlington. While Vanderbilt had twisted himself into an entangling alliance with Gould, Perkins sturdily maintained the corporate independence of the Burlington. Perkins made it clear to Gould and his associates that if any violation of the territorial agreement of October, 1880, was made, the Burlington would retaliate and invade the corporate domain of Gould's Union Pacific in Kansas and Colorado by extending its own line to Denver.

There is no doubt that Gould recognized the potential dangers arising from a Denver extension of the Burlington. The high rate structure of the Union Pacific was protected by the absence of competition in its local territory, a large part of which would be invaded and subjected to competition by a Burlington line. Gould's primary interest, however, was no longer in the Union Pacific. By the spring of 1881 he had sold out his stock and, in so far as his railroad interests were concerned, was most interested in his southwestern system. The peace agreement of October, 1880, afforded the Wabash the opportunity to build some small local extensions in southern Iowa. Gould taking advantage of this loophole, proposed early in 1881 to build a north-and-south line in Iowa across the Burlington territory to the state capital at Des Moines.[43] Although this was a violation of the spirit if not the actual provisions of the agreement of the previous fall, the Burlington overlooked the incident.

There was still no certainty that the Burlington would ever push its line west to Denver and engage in competition with the Union Pacific. In the fall of 1880 there existed a difference of opinion on its board of directors with respect to the wisdom of such a connection. Some members believed the extension was essential to the welfare of the Burlington, and in fact inevitable; while others held the view that in the interests of harmony such an extension should not be built.

Neither Forbes nor Ames, however, could exert any control over Gould's activities in behalf of his new southwestern system. The Union Pacific was to Gould a secondary interest; while the Missouri Pacific, the parent of the southwestern roads, was his primary one. The Missouri Pacific extended from Kansas City to St. Louis, connecting at that point with a number of roads from Arkansas, Texas, and Louisiana. The main flow of the Union Pacific traffic, however, terminated at Omaha; and in order to tap this rich volume of business, Gould decided in the summer of 1881 upon building an extension of the Missouri

Pacific from Atchison to Omaha.[44] Such a line penetrating the territory west of the Missouri River would serve some of the richest Burlington counties,[45] and might therefore encourage the Burlington to break with the Union Pacific and finally to push west to Denver. The first intimation of this new move by Gould came to the attention of Perkins in June of 1881, for in the middle of that month Perkins wrote a letter to Gould marked "Private," referring to reports concerning the intention of the Missouri Pacific to extend its lines into Nebraska.[46] Gould informed Perkins a few days later that the reports were correct and that the Missouri Pacific had decided to extend to Omaha. Gould insisted that the proposed extension was necessary to perfect the system of the Missouri Pacific and to preserve a connection with eastern Nebraska and the Union Pacific at Omaha; and that the Burlington, since it had annexed two small independent lines over which the Missouri Pacific had formerly secured access to Omaha, had no right to object. Indeed, insisted Gould, since the Burlington's absorption of these lines, the business of the Missouri Pacific had "gradually shrunk to small proportions." [47]

The danger of Gould's actions to the Union Pacific was obvious. For a number of years the Burlington had considered plans to extend its lines west from southern Nebraska to the foot of the mountains at Denver. Partly in deference to the views of Forbes and partly because of the repeated promises made by Gould to preserve inter-corporate peace—concessions and promises which sounded pleasant to the ears of conservative leaders in the Union Pacific and the Burlington camps, this project had been repeatedly postponed. The last promise of inter-corporate peace had been made by the Union Pacific in the agreement of October, 1880, an agreement which from the standpoint of the Burlington was designed to stabilize territorial competition in southern Nebraska. The peace was now about to be disturbed by an individual who, although exercising an influence on the policies of the Union Pacific, owned only a few shares of its stock.

Gould's policy of extension through the corporate instrumentality of the Missouri Pacific was strongly opposed by Dillon, president of the Union Pacific, who declared in a letter to Perkins that the Missouri Pacific's proposed construction had been undertaken without his consent and against the protest of himself and of the Union Pacific's directors in Boston.[48] Those directors who had stoutly maintained their conservative views, and who had always desired the maintenance of peaceable relationships between that road and the Burlington, set to work to prevent the Burlington from denouncing the 1880 territorial agreement, and to frustrate the Burlington's extension west to Denver. Frederick L. Ames, a leader of the conservative group of the Union Pacific, interviewed Sidney Bartlett of the Burlington board. Dillon followed with a letter to Bartlett in which he again pointed out that he had "earnestly" objected to the proposed construction of the Omaha line, and that it would be unjust to the Union Pacific to hold it responsible "for action taken which it could not and can not prevent and which it did not and does not favor." [49] Approaches to the Burlington were also made by Vanderbilt who at that time had "a very large interest" in both the Burlington and the Union Pacific. He followed the line of reasoning developed by Dillon, and insisted upon the reasonableness of a point of view which permitted differences to arise between the two companies because of an "individual action" in which the Union Pacific had no interest and in which it took no part. Vanderbilt, ready as ever to conciliate, expressed his willingness to co-operate in protecting the mutual interests of both roads.[50]

However, the day of conciliators and peacemakers had passed. Leaders on both sides refused to budge. Gould as president of the Missouri Pacific insisted that the Burlington had acquired the old Joy road on the east side of the Missouri River from Omaha to Kansas City, thereby securing an advantage over the Missouri Pacific in competition for the Omaha traffic. The Missouri Pacific, he insisted, was therefore "in a battle and it must free itself at any cost of money or peace." [51] Perkins was equally firm and determined. In his earlier experiences with Gould he had been somewhat hesitant. After his initial contacts early in 1874, he had, however, maintained consistently an attitude of opposition to Gould's policies. Forbes, on the contrary, had championed efforts at reconciliation. Recognizing that his policy had failed, he was no longer willing to make peace overtures and he therefore rejected the conciliatory advances made by Vanderbilt. In forthright language, reflecting the determined convictions of Perkins, Forbes informed Vanderbilt that agreements "must depend not on their legal or technical validity, but upon the honest purpose and determination of persons participating in their formation, to live up to them." [52] Perkins's policy of dynamic defense against the Gould policies in the form of a Burlington offense eventually won out in the Burlington camp. On July 20, 1881, the board resolved that the road's vice president, Perkins, be instructed to notify the Union Pacific that the organization of a company by some of its leading directors to build a road in eastern Nebraska was an abrogation of the agreement with the Burlington.

Although Gould recognized the determined character of the decision, he refused to make concessions, and indeed, in accordance with his usual policy, he decided to meet threat with threat. He insisted that if the Burlington extended its line to Denver, thus competing with the Union Pacific, Gould acting not through the Union Pacific whose interests were endangered, but rather through the Missouri Pacific, would transfer the latter's business between Hannibal and Chicago to the competitors of the Burlington. The Missouri Pacific would also build an independent line of its own to Chicago and extend a series of lateral lines into Nebraska. "We wish peace," wrote Gould to Perkins, "but we are ready for war if you insist on making it. Carrying out your menace of extending your line to Denver means war." [53]

Perkins was equally firm and defied Gould to do his worst. The war threatened by Gould, Perkins replied, began not with any act of the Burlington but by the act of Gould and his associates in building a road "where the October agreement was intended for the present to prevent one from being built." It is true, he declared, that if the Burlington took no notice of the proposed Omaha extension, there would be for the time no war; but this was true of all threatened railroad or other wars where one party submits; "but responsibility for the war can hardly be charged to the party attacked if he refuses to submit." Gould's position as peacemaker was curtly rejected by Perkins. "As to who has been the peacemaker in the past and who is responsible for the present difficulty, the record speaks for itself. It shows that we have never received anything at your hands for which we have not given a very full consideration." [54]

The course of the Burlington was now set. The policy of Perkins had won. All doubts about the Burlington's Denver line were now resolved. In preparation for the major change in policy involving the road in a broad expansion plan to the west, the executive management was changed. Forbes moved up to the chairmanship of the board and Perkins was elevated from vice president to president. He had always been the constructive and aggressive element in the company's directorate and managerial hierarchy. Now he was for the first time in full charge of the company's executive policies. The management, in the expressive language of a contemporary newspaper, had finally "put on their war paint." [55]

The Burlington was ready for war. Despite the acquisition of several financially unproductive roads, its credit remained excellent. The margin of safety for its fixed charges was substantial, and it continued to pay dividends. The management therefore found no difficulty in financing the Denver extension, and construction once begun was carried on actively. By May of 1882 the last rail was laid and through trains ran from Chicago to Denver. Shortly thereafter, in the spring of 1883, the Denver completed its extension from Denver to Ogden. A new transcontinental route, competing directly with the Union Pacific, was thus established. Gould who was serving on the board of the Union Pacific thus seriously impaired its strength and earnings. The Colorado business, which since the Union Pacific's merger with the Kansas Pacific in 1880 was so largely controlled by the Union Pacific, was hereafter to be shared with the Burlington.

The Burlington extension also damaged the fortunes of the Wabash. The Union Pacific, controlling without competition the middle transcontinental line between Ogden and Omaha, distributed its eastbound business between the Iowa lines at Council Bluffs and the Gould-controlled lines at Kansas City. The Kansas City route was circuitous and not as desirable as the direct line to Chicago. Gould in control of the Union Pacific and of the Wabash, could, without danger of retaliation, route some of the former's business over the latter's lines east of Kansas City. With the Burlington soliciting traffic over the direct line from Omaha to Chicago, the competitive pressure exerted

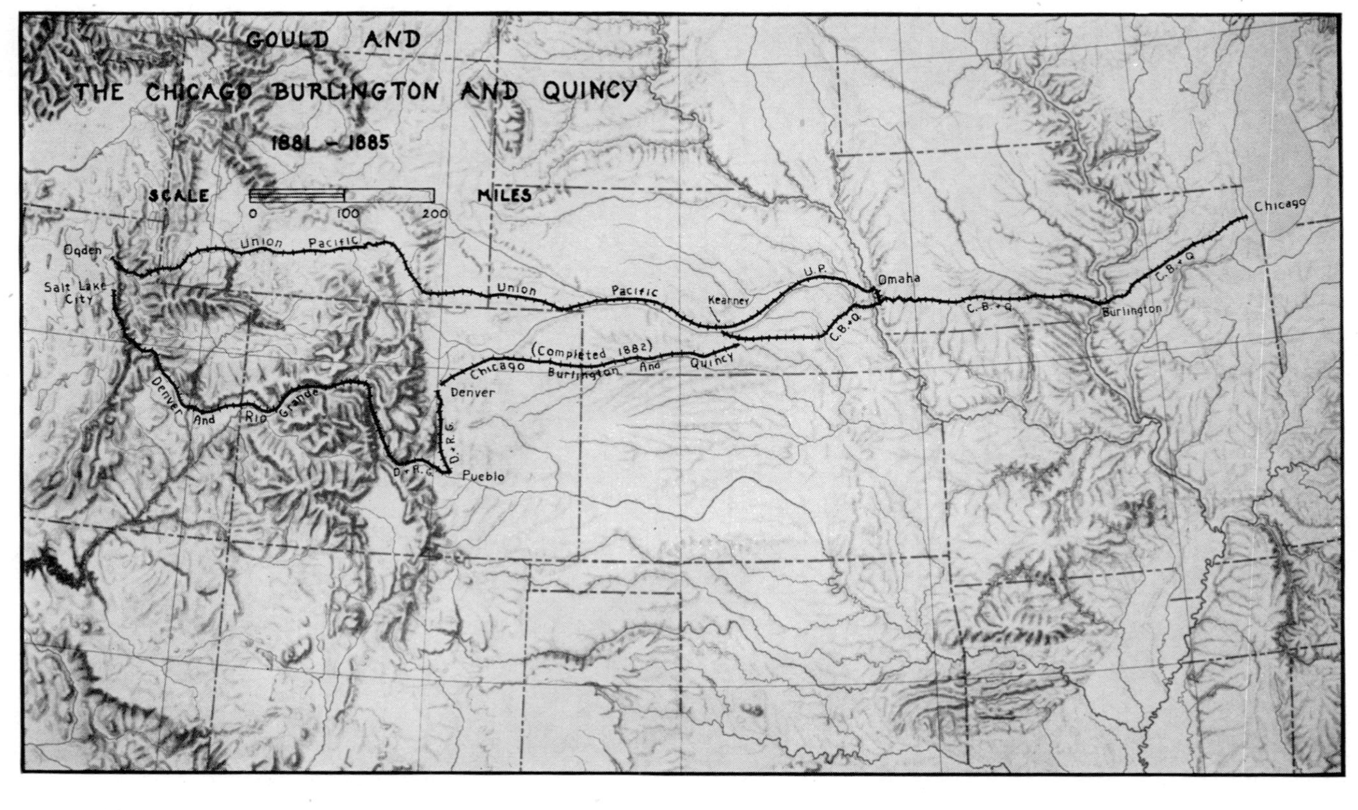
GOULD AND
THE CHICAGO BURLINGTON AND QUINCY
1881 – 1885
SCALE
0
100
200
MILES
Ogden
Salt Lake City
Union Pacific
Union Pacific
U.P.
Kearney
Omaha
C.B.+Q.
C.B.+Q.
C.B.+Q.
Burlington
Chicago
(Completed 1882)
Chicago Burlington And Quincy
Denver
Denver And Rio Grande
D.+R.G.
D.+R.G.
Pueblo

upon the Union Pacific to give the same standard of service made it difficult to continue to send any significant volume of business via the Kansas City gateway. The Wabash could not meet the service standard set by the Iowa Pool roads.

Furthermore, under this new competitive arrangement, the Union Pacific was forced to give its connections at Omaha, including the Burlington, more eastbound business. Only in this way could it secure a share of the westbound business of the Burlington and of the other Iowa lines. If it continued to send traffic east via Kansas City and away from Omaha, it would have to receive from the Wabash at Kansas City westbound, as valuable traffic as it delivered to the Wabash at Kansas City eastbound. The major trend of traffic through the Kansas City gateway was south and west and not north and west. The Union Pacific, therefore, was forced to deal preferentially to a greater extent than ever before with its Omaha connections, since thereby it secured more westbound business than it could by trading at Kansas City.

By renewing this competitive struggle with the Burlington, Gould injured both the Wabash and the Union Pacific. He succeeded however in selling his Wabash and Union Pacific holdings before these adverse results were reflected in published financial statements. Later he bought these stocks again. The problems which he inflicted upon the Wabash and the Union Pacific produced losses for both roads. By the fall of 1881, however, his railroad activities had assumed new shape, and he had become interested in still other properties. These new phases of his activities will be examined in the following chapters.

NOTES FOR CHAPTER XII

1. Burlington archives, Forbes to Simpson, May 29, 1878.
2. Ibid., Forbes to Lucius Tuckerman, March 20, 1880; also Feb. 14, 1880.
3. Ibid., Tyson to Perkins, March 18, 1878, for example, observed in referring to the proposal to co-operate with Villard in acquiring the Kansas Pacific, that Forbes dreaded the idea of any more extensions; and, Tyson continued, that the Burlington could not forego the advantages which the troubles of other roads offered it of securing a large future business. Tyson also remarked that if the Kansas Pacific could be controlled, the Atchison could also be secured.
4. Ibid., Forbes to Tuckerman, March 20, 1880.

4a. Known hereafter as the Quincy.

5. Ibid., T. J. Potter to Perkins, Jan. 13, 1886. This observation was made by

an informed traffic officer of the Burlington in the middle eighties after the rapid increase in traffic in the Middle West. Clearly the traffic density in 1878 was no higher than it was in 1886.

6. Known hereafter as the Iowa.
7. Burlington archives, Perkins to Brooks, Feb. 6, 1871.
8. Known hereafter as the B.S.W.
9. The long memorandum in which he outlined his views was undated; but from internal evidence in the document, it appears that it was written in 1878.
10. Burlington archives, Perkins to Forbes, June 29, 1879.
11. Ibid., May 30, 1879.
12. Ibid., Perkins to W. W. Morsman, Feb. 1, 1886.
13. *R. R. Gaz.*, March 26, 1880, 169.
14. Burlington archives, Perkins to Forbes, Aug. 30, 1880.
15. Ibid., Nov. 8, 1879.
16. Ibid., Nov. 19, 1879.
17. Ibid.
18. This was the opinion of Perkins expressed in ibid., Perkins to Forbes, Nov. 12, 1879.
19. Chicago *Times*, Dec. 2, 1879.
20. Burlington archives, Potter to Perkins, Jan. 4, 1880. The recommendation for the purchase of the road at about $30,000 a mile was made in a letter from Smith, Burlington traffic manager in Chicago, to Potter, under date of Dec. 24, 1879.
21. Ibid., Forbes to Charles Merriam, May 7, 1880.
22. *R. R. Gaz.*, Nov. 28, 1874, 468.
23. Poor's *Manual of Railroads*, 1878–9, 820-1; New York *Tribune*, Feb. 1, 1879.
24. New York *Tribune*, March 10, 1879; see also Phila. *North American*, March 12, 1879, and April 12, 1879.
25. Burlington archives, Forbes to Geddes, Aug. 28, 1879.
26. Ibid., telegram, W. J. Ladd to Perkins, Oct. 14, 1879.
27. New York *Tribune*, Oct. 22, 1879.
28. St. Louis *Republican*, cited in *R. R. Gaz.*, June 4, 1880, 310.
29. New York *Tribune*, Nov. 18, 1880.
30. Burlington archives, E. P. Ripley to S. Frink, general freight agent, Missouri Pacific, March 24, 1882.
31. Ibid., J. S. Cameron to Perkins (month not given) 1880.
32. The above quotation from, and the summary of the views of, Forbes are taken from ibid., Forbes to William Endicott, July 11, 1880.
33. Ibid., Perkins to Forbes, July 7, 1880.
34. Ibid., Perkins to Gould, July 7, 1880.
35. Ibid., Gould to T. J. Coolidge, Sept. 10, 1880.
36. Ibid., Humphreys to Perkins, Sept. 13, 1880.
37. Ibid., Perkins to Forbes, Sept. 16, 1880.
38. Ibid., Sept. 26, 1880.
39. Ibid., Perkins to Coolidge, Sept. 26, 1880.
40. Ibid.
41. The views of Perkins and the above quotations are taken from ibid.
42. On provisions of the agreement, see New York *Tribune*, Oct. 21, 1880; and *Public*, Oct. 28, 1880, 280.
43. *Public*, Jan. 27, 1881, 52. For further details on these plans, see also *Ry. Review*, April 2, 1881, 185.
44. That the Missouri Pacific's decision to build the Omaha extension was motivated by the desire to furnish an outlet of the Missouri Pacific's business from the south and southwest to Nebraska, is referred to by a railroad man

in State of Missouri, Statements and Testimony of Railroad Managers and Others before Committee on Railroads and Internal Improvements of the Extra Session of the 34th General Assembly of Missouri, Jefferson City, 1887, 35.

45. Burlington archives, Perkins to Forbes, Jan. 30, 1884.
46. Ibid., Perkins to Gould, June 15, 1881.
47. Ibid., Gould to Perkins, June 20, 1881.
48. Ibid., Dillon to Perkins, July 28, 1881.
49. Ibid., Dillon to Sidney Bartlett, July 28, 1881.
50. Ibid., Vanderbilt to Forbes, July 26, 1881.
51. Phila. *North American*, Sept. 27, 1881.
52. Burlington archives, Forbes to Vanderbilt, July 30, 1881.
53. Ibid., Gould to Perkins, Aug. 4, 1881.
54. Ibid., Perkins to Gould, Aug. 8, 1881. The other quotations indicating Perkins's point of view are taken from the same source.
55. Boston *Transcript*, Aug. 18, 1881.

CHAPTER XIII

Gould Moves into the Southwest

PREVIOUS chapters have examined Gould's railroad acquisitions in the trans-Missouri area and in the region between the Missouri and the Great Lakes at Chicago and Toledo. In this chapter his activities in the region south of the Missouri to the Gulf of Mexico and west of the Mississippi will be considered. In this broad territory his activities were as unexpected as his acquisitions revolving around the new Wabash through route from Toledo to Omaha. The surprise turned in the next few years, however, to a sensation, when it was discovered that Gould had actually built up a permanent railroad system, and had not bought the securities for trading and speculation. The Gould system of railroads was confined largely to the properties in the Southwest, and embraced southern Missouri, Louisiana west of the Mississippi River, and the states of Arkansas, Texas, and Oklahoma, to which was later added a large mileage in southern Kansas and a small mileage in eastern Colorado.

In the two decades preceding Gould's entry into this area, many railroads were built which with few exceptions were conceived as parts of through routes destined to connect the Gulf ports with St. Louis and the upper Mississippi River gateways. In almost all cases, however, the panic left the lines unfinished. Substantial parts of the existing mileage, moreover, could not be economically operated because of the inability either to forward local traffic to the market or because of inability to carry traffic over their lines from important points of interchange to competitive markets.

A survey of the railroad map in the late seventies discloses this unfinished stage of development. In New Orleans, with the aid of local subscriptions, the New Orleans Pacific was organized to build from New Orleans to Shreveport, but by the spring of 1879 little construction had been completed. Another local property, also a victim of the panic and a remnant of an ambitious transcontinental route, fostered by one of the ablest groups of railroad capitalists in the country, was the Texas & Pacific. With the aid of a land grant, the line was planned to extend from the Louisiana-Texas boundary to San Diego. After earlier failures, the project was undertaken by (T. A.) Scott, then vice president of the Pennsylvania, in the year 1872. With the help of a construction company in which, among others, Carnegie was interested, plans were made for financing its construction. The check given to these plans by the panic proved to be permanent. By 1879 the road extended only from Shreveport to Forth Worth, and from Texarkana west to Sherman.

At its northeastern terminus at Texarkana—at the intersection between the states of Texas and Arkansas—it connected with the St. Louis, Iron Mountain and Southern,[1] a road built in the early sixties to serve an important iron-ore region in southeastern Missouri. Under the leadership of Thomas Allen, a prominent citizen of the state, it was extended to eastern Arkansas, and by 1873 constituted a direct link between Texas and St. Louis.

On the western end of the region, there were two major properties. One was the Kansas & Texas, extending from the upper Mississippi at Hannibal to northern Texas. The other property, spanning southern Missouri, was the Frisco whose predecessor company, the Atlantic & Pacific railroad, had been planned as a transcontinental route along the 35th parallel. Its ambitions were also frustrated by the collapse of 1873; construction languished; Scott and his group relinquished the direction of its management, and the railroad remained in its incompleted state.

These properties obtained connections to southern Texas through the International Great Northern,[2] a consolidation of two corporations that had been promoted by a number of leading capitalists, including Taylor of the National City Bank who according to a New York daily was "a controlling spirit" in the road's management.[3] The road was designed as a through route to the Rio Grande, connecting on the north with the Texas & Pacific, and through the latter with the Iron Mountain. On the south the financial crash left that line with a number of stub ends in Texas many miles short of its destination on the Rio Grande. So distant did this objective appear in 1879 that a correspondent of a metropolitan newspaper writing from Waco, Texas, stated that it would "be a long time before [the International] [would] be built to the Rio Grande." [4] Yet in two years Gould succeeded not only in accomplishing that purpose but indeed far more.

The northern railroad link of this vast southwestern area was owned by the Missouri Pacific. Its line south of the Missouri secured the entrance to St. Louis from the west. Within one year after Gould secured that road, he acquired working control of a substantial proportion of all the lines and terminal facilities in the Southwest. The conquest was rapid; indeed in American railroad history there had probably been no other system built in such a short time by the use of such simple means with the aid of so few banks, bankers, or security issues.

The financial condition of nearly all of the southwestern roads was similar to that of the Wabash: they were heavily bonded, and their interest charges were high. Although the territory was rapidly growing, the future of the transportation industry was uncertain. Even in the midst of the inflationary markets in the early seventies, it was difficult to sell stock for cash, and the slaughter of financial values in the years following 1873 made it impossible to sell stocks with uncertain earning power. Of these roads the Iron Mountain and the International were in receivership. Although the Texas & Pacific succeeded in avoiding this desperate remedy, it was not in good financial condition.

In the summer of 1879 while Gould was negotiating traffic alliances for the Wabash and in executing those projects which allied him momentarily with Vanderbilt and while he was consummating his plans for the merger of the Kansas Pacific and the Union Pacific, he was also bargaining with (T. A.) Scott for resumption of the construction program of the Texas & Pacific. To build the road west from Fort Worth to El Paso either for connection there with the Southern Pacific or for its extension west to San Diego required considerable funds.

These funds could not yet be raised by the sale of bonds to simon-pure investors. The Chesapeake & Ohio late in the year 1879, for example, had unsuccessfully tried to sell an issue of $1,250,000. Money for construction was forthcoming largely from capitalists who were willing to take extra risks in return for extra gains. Through the use of a construction company, a railroad building program could be financed by bonds with stock as a bonus. The bond was the investment with a risk, and the stock the compensating prize. The necessity for this device was appreciated even by some of the shipping interests. Early in 1880, for example, a trade journal in the iron and steel industry—probably the greatest customer for railroad service—stated that the extra cost arising from the use of the construction company could "scarcely be said to be dishonest, as no intelligent investor [bought] the bonds of a railroad in ignorance of the fact that the stock issue [brought] no money into the treasury." [5]

In 1879–80 the Texas & Pacific could raise no money and the road was apparently destined to remain a property of only local significance. Congress refused to extend aid. If it did not build west to El Paso and beyond, its traffic might be decimated by the aggressive expansion of Huntington. If he built north to a junction with the Atchison, or south to a junction with an east-and-west Texas road, the Texas & Pacific would be left with little through business. It was a bleak prospect.

Help suddenly arrived from a most unexpected quarter. That which Congress was unwilling to do, and (T. A.) Scott and his Philadelphia followers unable to do, Gould was both willing and able to do. Fresh from his conquest over Vanderbilt and the Union Pacific, his prestige and influence soaring not only because of these successes but also by his purchase of the Missouri Pacific, he was able to unite a number of wealthy capitalists in a proposal to raise the Texas & Pacific out of its doldrums. The syndicate organized to finance the building of the westward extension included Sage who had proved to be Gould's stanchest friend in the bleak days of the fall of 1878 and in the first few weeks of 1879. It included also George M. Pullman, the leading factor in the railroad sleeping-car business; (W. L.) Scott, long interested in railroad promotion and construction, a confidential adviser of Vanderbilt and a member of the New York Central stock syndicate of 1879; and C. F. Woerishoffer, a stockbroker and active trader in New York City, associated with Villard in the Kansas Pacific deals, and with a large speculative following. Other capitalists brought both cash and distinction. The syndicate and the construction company were organized in December, 1879, and the construction company's contract with the railroad for building the extension from Fort Worth to El Paso was signed in January, 1880.

Even though investors were not yet ready to buy bonds, speculators for more than six months had been reaping good profits from the speculative boom. The markets had been rising since the fall of 1878, but between July and late November, 1879, a boom swept over the speculative markets unequaled for more than six years both in scope and enthusiasm. The Texas & Pacific stock paid as dividends by the construction company to its shareholders could, therefore, be sold on a rising market.

Both shippers and stockholders were satisfied with the results of the work of the Texas & Pacific syndicate. The opening up of new territory through new construction was greeted with almost unrestrained enthusiasm. "Already," wrote one observer, "the effect is magical." New cities were springing up by the hundreds.[6] Security holders were happy. The price of the Texas & Pacific stocks and bonds rose; the price of the stock of the construction company rose even more rapidly. Eventually the original shareholder of the construction company realized a profit of 700 per cent on his investment.[7] A few months after the consummation of the contract, (T. A.) Scott, as president of the Texas & Pacific, informed the stockholders that the contract when completed would leave the road with $3,000,000 first mortgage bonds in its treasury and a surplus of about $600,000 in income and land-grant bonds. Since the company had no floating debt, "this reserve of securities [would] not only insure a well-constructed and fully equipped road, but [would] enable your company [Texas & Pacific] to maintain the very strong financial position which it [then enjoyed]." [8] This was Scott's last message. The next annual message appeared over Gould's name.

The backers of the New Orleans Pacific, controlling the right of way from New Orleans to Shreveport now looked to Gould, the new Moses, to lead them out of the wilderness. The president of that property opened negotiations with Gould, to whom, in the words of an observer of the railroad industry writing from New Orleans, "so many languishing enterprises have recently looked, and not in vain." [9] To get the road built, the owners would make almost any concession. Little more had been accomplished than the grading of one hundred miles. The property nevertheless had considerable value. It had a land grant, a feature that kept alive many an otherwise hopeless project. To the speculative mind, inflamed by the market profits already made and being made, a land grant attached to a railroad charter was more valuable than the prospective railroad itself. Gould, a master of speculative psychology, did not overlook this possibility. First, jointly with (T. A.) Scott, he bought the creditors' claims on the New Orleans Pacific at fifty cents on the dollar, payable in first mortgage bonds of a newly organized company.[10]

More important, however, was his discovery of another land grant. Although (T. A.) Scott had been in control of the Texas & Pacific for some years and had taken an active interest in the affairs of the New Orleans Pacific, he had not discovered the importance of the grant. It was owned by a company, the New Orleans, Baton Rouge & Vicksburg, popularly known as the Backbone. It had been organized to build a road from New Orleans to a connection with the Texas & Pacific at Shreveport, but on the other side of the Mississippi River. Conditioned upon completing the road in five years, it had in 1871 received a large federal land grant. At the end of the period, the company having built nothing, the state legislature forfeited its charter. A federal court, however, declared the action unconstitutional. Gould wanted that land grant; even more, he wanted it transferred to the New Orleans Pacific. Congress was asked to repeal the land grant of the Backbone and to grant it to the New Orleans Pacific. A Louisiana senator introduced the bill but nothing came of it.

This did not discourage Gould; he probably expected it. To achieve his aim of placing the mythical Backbone road and its real land grant in the hands of the New Orleans Pacific, he resorted to private trading, an art in which he had few equals. (W. L.) Scott, a Vanderbilt ally, was permitted to participate in Gould's construction companies. Since Gould was soon to declare himself again an open foe of Vanderbilt, if he wanted to enlist (W. L.) Scott's aid, he had to act quickly. Gould, for the construction company, negotiated with (W. L.) Scott on behalf of the railroad company. Since (W. L.) Scott was reaping profits from his construction company commitments, negotiations were stimulated and an agreement reached. A majority of the stock of the Backbone had been pooled in the hands of (W. L.) Scott and an associate, the president of the road. By the end of 1880 the road had transferred its land grant to the New Orleans Pacific, and the latter in turn conveyed it to the controlling construction company.[11]

Gould in executing his construction plans in the early eighties —and there were many of them—was prompt and aggressive; but in the building of the New Orleans extension, unaccountable delays were encountered. Despite the fact that the construction company was organized in February, the contract with the railroad for building was not made until late July, and the actual work did not begin until late fall. In fact, Gould was arranging to secure control of the New Orleans Pacific. The transaction by which he acquired control was an ingenious contrivance. The construction company—the American Railway Improvement Company—bought the road's securities and then reoffered them for sale to the stockholders of the Missouri Pacific, the Kansas & Texas, and the Texas & Pacific.[12] The stockholders of Gould's southwestern lines thus became partners in the construction enterprise. The speculation was successful, and Gould's following had further reason to hail their chief. There was accordingly no opposition from dissatisfied stockholders to the merger of the road with the Texas & Pacific. (T. A.) Scott was enthusiastic over the New Orleans extension. Local business alone, he averred, would "more than provide for the fixed charges on the construction bonds of the company. . . ."[13]

To Gould the new line was the missing link in his southwestern system. To the Texas & Pacific it was the short line from New Orleans to St. Louis, and the Iron Mountain was dependent upon the Texas & Pacific for the movement of a large volume of long-haul traffic. On this business the Iron Mountain competed with the circuitous route of the Kansas & Texas, over which by combining several roads the traffic could reach Missouri and Illinois. To induce traffic to move over its line, the Kansas & Texas cut rates and gave rebates.[14] Allen, the leading factor in the destinies of the Iron Mountain, had unsuccessfully urged Commodore Garrison when he was piloting the destinies of the Missouri Pacific, to buy control of the Kansas & Texas. While Garrison declined Allen's advice, Gould later accepted it. The reader has already been acquainted with the inimitable way in which he secured control.[15] Gould's acquisition of the Kansas & Texas was a blow to Allen. By adjustment of rates and services the Gould group could now divert business from Allen's line to their own Kansas & Texas. Besides the Texas & Pacific, other roads contributed to the business of the Iron Mountain. The International owned a line to Houston. Another road just finished, the Texas & St. Louis, fed the Iron Mountain with traffic at its southwestern terminus, thus giving it a profitable long haul. When late in 1879 and early 1880, it became apparent that the Texas & Pacific would build west to El Paso, and that both the International and the Kansas & Texas would build south to the Rio Grande, the future of the Iron Mountain looked bright indeed. In its annual report for 1879 the management, reviewing these developments, concluded hopefully that they would bring the road "increased traffic." [16]

By 1880 the Iron Mountain had solved its financial problems. To strengthen its position, Allen made a proposal to aid the Texas & Pacific to build its Fort Worth line. He was too late. (T. A.) Scott had already reached an agreement with Gould, and organization of the construction company for the building of the extension soon followed. This action threatened the friendly relations of the two roads. To counteract the effect of the loss of the Texas & Pacific traffic, the Iron Mountain tried to arrange a plan with the International, by which the latter would be extended to Laredo, on the Rio Grande.

While Allen had his eyes fixed on the south, Gould suddenly moved on the north. Again revealing his appreciation of strategic railroad values, he noted that the Iron Mountain did not reach its St. Louis connection over its own lines. Its southwestern line terminated at a small point in Missouri from which it reached the Illinois side by a ferry. From a point on the Illinois side to a point nine miles north to East St. Louis was a small terminal road known as the East St. Louis & Carondelet which was used as a connecting road between lines ending in or near St. Louis and the eastern lines. This terminal road fed the Wabash and other roads with traffic originating on the lines of the Missouri Pacific and of the Iron Mountain. Early in February the Wabash purchased control of the property. Allen was now caught in a vise. He had to work with Gould to secure an outlet for the traffic coming to and from St. Louis, or, at great expense, build a direct connection with the St. Louis Union Depot.

By early summer of the same year Gould had surrounded Allen's Iron Mountain, both on the north and west—on the north by the capture of the terminal line, and on the west by the capture of the Kansas & Texas. On the south he had already acquired a large block of Texas & Pacific, and through the construction company he was getting more. Allen still had available the river route from New Orleans and a large territory in Louisiana accessible to such transportation. There was also the friendly International, which formed in connection with the Iron Mountain, "nearly a bee line" from St. Louis to Austin.[17] The International meanwhile was making its own building plans. Late in May, 1880, when the security markets were telling their tale of prosperity, and of even more optimistic anticipations, it announced its oft-renewed determination to build to the Rio Grande. It would, however, start prudently and build immediately only to San Antonio.[18] Taylor was still a large stockholder. Henry Marquand, vice president of the Iron Mountain, and next to Allen its largest stockholder, had been one of the promoters of the road, and although he had retired from the management in 1873, still retained his stock ownership.

Despite this announcement, construction of the extension lagged. Completion of the line would have helped the Iron Mountain, potentially the most strategic link in Gould's southwestern system. Although there is no evidence to explain this unexpected delay, inferences can be drawn. Gould, Sloan, and Taylor were now closely associated in the affairs of the Lackawanna, having already reached an agreement on the building of the Buffalo extension. Perhaps Gould worked the Wabash charm on these men as he had on Vanderbilt of the New York Central and Francis Grey of the Great Western. If you work with me in the Southwest and work the International in my interests, Gould may well have said to Sloan and Taylor, the Wabash will give you part of its "vast" traffic at Buffalo, thus making the Lackawanna's proposed Buffalo extension profitable. This is only an inference, but the fact is that the International did not build its Rio Grande extension. Before many months Gould struck another blow at the Iron Mountain. In early autumn the New Orleans Pacific after long delays finally began its building program. The line from New Orleans to Shreveport cut "right across the southern end of the Iron Mountain, by which there was a strong possibility that still another slice of [its] cotton business would be taken away." [19] In December Gould sprung the trap by buying the controlling stock interest in the International. So unexpected was the event that the report was at first denied. Though the surprise was complete, the report was accurate.

Allen's Iron Mountain was now surrounded. Although in control of the short line from the Southwest to St. Louis, it had lost much traffic and was destined to lose more. Though its competitors were many, the majority wound up under the control of Gould. Allen, however, could still fight. He could ally himself with the Texas & St. Louis and build a Rio Grande extension. The latter line in fact was then endeavoring to raise money for that very purpose. He could alternately attach himself to the Gulf Colorado & Santa Fe, secure an outlet to Houston and then become a formidable competitor of Gould.

Allen, however, refused to fight. "I could have gone on an indefinite time," he declared, "but the prospect of having to fight singlehanded the combined money and influence of a combination such as that of Messrs. Gould, Sage, Dillon and their associates, was not very encouraging, especially as I could not feel the necessity for carrying on the struggle. I thought that by selling out to them I would be able to secure harmony." [20] In the race for "harmony" by appeasement, he had thus outmatched even Vanderbilt. Yet Allen was more logical than Vanderbilt. Unlike Vanderbilt he expected nothing from Gould except a check for his stock. Allen had decided to enter the public service and in November had been elected to Congress. He had therefore neither the time nor the inclination to fight. Gould dealt generously with his surrounded business enemy, and in December purchased Allen's 40,000 shares for a trifle less than $2,000,000—a price above the market—and an additional 20,000 shares from Marquand, vice president. Gould also bought stock in the open market, bringing his total holdings to 70,000 shares,[21] out of a total of approximately 227,000 shares outstanding.

By the end of 1880, through transactions negotiated largely by himself, Gould had secured a controlling influence in all the railroads terminating at St. Louis from the west, with the exception of the Alton and the Frisco. The latter, however, entered the city over the tracks of the Missouri Pacific. The stock interests of the Gould-acquired roads could be joined in a common effort only through the personal decision of Gould. Of one road he was president, while of another he was a member of the board; of one road he had little stock, while of another he had much. He owned a majority of the stock of the International, but he owned less than a majority of the stock of the Iron Mountain, while of the Texas & Pacific he owned only a minority. Of Missouri-Pacific stock he had a high percentage. In every road, however, with the single exception of the Texas & Pacific, he was the dominating influence.

It was logical that Gould should make the Missouri Pacific the parent of his corporate brood, since it was the only member of the family which he dominated by the ownership of an overwhelming percentage of the outstanding stock. The company, however, because of its lopsided financial structure, was ill-adapted to serve as a corporate vehicle for consolidation. Against more than $15,000,000 in bonds, it had only $800,000 in stock. The stock of such a company could scarcely command an active market and trading in the stock was bound to be slight. Neither could its value for collateral purposes be substantial. If the company was to be used as a medium for effecting the unification of all of Gould's southwestern lines, it was therefore imperative to widen the stock base; i.e., to issue more stock.

Gould lost little time in solving the problem. To create a legal basis for an enlarged stock base, he turned to the corporate subsidiaries of the Missouri Pacific. Most of these were part of the road when Gould bought the stock from Garrison. A number of others were either bought by Gould at low prices or were newly organized for construction purposes.[22] These companies and the parent were merged, the transfer of titles being accomplished by an increase of the capital stock from $800,000 to more than $12,000,000. This transaction, while attracting but slight comment, had nevertheless a revolutionary effect on Gould's plans. With a large base the stock could be widely distributed, and the price per share brought down to a level at which public buying could be attracted. It was now a stock which could be actively traded and which could be accepted in a consolidation exchange.

Before he could take any further steps toward corporate union, however, it was necessary to remove the only remaining adverse interest—that of the Texas & Pacific. (T. A.) Scott was still president, the offices of the company were still located at Philadelphia —far removed from the center of Gould's operations. Since the time when Gould and Scott were first thrown together in the battle over the Fort Wayne in 1869, they had made many market and corporate trades. They had not, however, jointly managed a corporation, and their ideas of administration and operation clashed in the Texas & Pacific. It grew more and more evident in the early weeks of 1881 that one or the other would have to give way. The climax came in April, 1881. A meeting of the board of the Texas & Pacific was held in Philadelphia at the home of (T. A.) Scott, attended by Gould and his chief financial adviser, Sage; General Dodge, supervisor of the road's construction program; Major Bond, vice president of the Texas & Pacific and president-elect of the Philadelphia & Reading, and by Scott himself. The following day another meeting was held and decisive action taken. Scott resigned and sold to Gould his 40,000 shares of the Texas & Pacific stock and some bonds as well. A check was drawn to Scott's order, Scott delivered the securities and the transaction was completed. Gould sold the bonds and kept the stock.[23] And in the twenty-four hours following, Gould rearranged the executive officers and assumed full control.

Gould was now the dominant, even if not the majority, stockholder in all these southwestern roads. He had, furthermore, a handsome profit. The stock market, after hesitating awhile early in 1880, again became buoyant in the fall, and in the spring of 1881 it was in the midst of a speculative boom. Gould could have sold out and realized heavy profits. On the other hand, he could unify the roads, build up a new system and control a large part of the business of the southwest. Although he dominated most all of the western approaches to St. Louis, he had plenty of competition in the southern and central parts of Texas. If he were to remain an important factor in the business, it was necessary that he unite his southwestern properties into a smooth working unit.

To accomplish this purpose, the co-operation of the other shareholders of each road must be secured.

Even before the acquisition of the Texas & Pacific securities from (T. A.) Scott, Gould had made inquiries to test the terms upon which stocks of the various properties could be exchanged. At no time did he consider the use of any complicated financial methods to effect the consolidation. There were no proposals for the issue of collateral trust bonds, for the pledging of traffic agreements, or the creation of special classes of voting stocks. The first proposal for the union of the Iron Mountain, the International, and the Texas & Pacific met with a chilly reception.

The Scott-Texas & Pacific transaction greatly improved the prospect for consolidation. It fired the imagination of traders and investors, and the southwestern stocks became the leaders in the market. The International in two days jumped 20 per cent on a few transactions, and the Texas & Pacific as well as the Iron Mountain stocks also advanced rapidly to record high prices.

Gould immediately took advantage of this excitement. He first proposed that the Iron Mountain and the Texas & Pacific be exchanged share for share. A group of the latter's stockholders, particularly those from Philadelphia, demanded better terms and insisted upon an advantage of 5 per cent over the Iron Mountain, while the latter's officers argued for an allowance of about 1 per cent. Gould was equally interested in both roads, and he decided to accept any terms acceptable to these parties. In late April an agreement for the absorption of the Iron Mountain by the Texas & Pacific was apparently reached,[24] but within a few days the agreement was broken. The Philadelphia group in the Texas & Pacific declared that the road had no competition, while the Iron Mountain had; also it had a valuable land grant, whereas the Iron Mountain had none. Negotiations accordingly collapsed.

This did not long deter Gould and he decided to ignore the Texas & Pacific. The sensational advance in the prices of Iron Mountain and Missouri Pacific stocks of which he had heavy holdings led him to work out a union of the two lines alone. Within less than a week an exchange offer was completed on the basis of three shares of Missouri Pacific for four shares of Iron Mountain. Although the Missouri Pacific thus secured a large majority of the stock of the other road, Gould's holdings in the

Missouri Pacific were, to the extent of this exchange, diluted. Instead of owning between 80 and 85 per cent of the stock, he probably owned after the exchange less than 60 per cent.

Through ownership of the enlarged Missouri Pacific, Gould now controlled the direct route from St. Louis to Texarkana, where connection was made with the Texas & Pacific, which in turn connected with the New Orleans Pacific whose extension was soon to be completed to New Orleans. Gould thus controlled a through route from St. Louis to New Orleans. He had not, however, unified his lines farther to the west. The lease of the Kansas & Texas to the Missouri Pacific had given Gould access to the upper Mississippi River gateway from the Southwest. The International, however, had not yet been fitted into the consolidation scheme. Gould's handling of this problem was another tribute to his detailed knowledge of railroad strategy of the region —acquired in such short period. The International and the Kansas & Texas had been competitors for the building of the extension to the Rio Grande and their interests might again conflict. Gould united them and avoided any potential clashes by turning over the International stock to the Kansas & Texas. The exchange of two shares of the Kansas & Texas for one share of the International reflected the market price of the two stocks. Since Gould owned a large majority of the International's stock, he could by a few transactions so determine the market price as to facilitate the acceptance of his proposals. Consolidation of the two properties was therefore easily effected.

His mastery over the southwestern railroad system was, however, not as yet complete. While the International gave an outlet to Houston, system access to the neighboring port of Galveston was still denied. A small line, the Galveston Houston & Henderson, connected the other Houston railroads with Galveston. Like so many strategically located properties, this tiny road in the fall of 1880 had long been in financial difficulties. Two bankers, N. A. Cowdrey and P. F. James, had in 1871 purchased the property in foreclosure. In January, 1880, the property was surrendered to the mortgage trustees who assumed the responsibility to pay interest.[25]

Gould watched these proceedings closely. Again, he and not his competitors recognized the possibilities. Taking advantage of a dispute between Cowdrey and James, Gould in conjunction with Sage bought Cowdrey's bonds. He then purchased additional bonds in the open market in amounts sufficient to acquire a majority. Once in this key position Gould and Sage carried out a transaction of a kind which made them so detested. They elected themselves trustees, foreclosed the mortgage and bought the property at the sale. Then they executed a squeeze: they made an offer to the minority bondholders requesting them to scale down their principal by 20 per cent and reduce their interest from 7 to 5 per cent. The offer was refused and another legal battle was on.[26] Gould nevertheless retained control. He was free to switch the property to any corporate member of his southwestern railroad structure, and finally decided to turn over the stock of the reorganized road to the International. The road itself was leased to the International.

Even before these corporate realignments were formally completed Gould loomed up in a new character. For more than ten years he had been a railroad negotiator and consolidator. He had bought and sold railroad properties, and he had planned many consolidations. Though he had failed in some, he had succeeded in others. Beginning with the fall of 1880, however, he became a leading railroad builder. Into areas which had vainly appealed and begged for new railroad facilities he came as a rescuing angel. In areas in the Southwest where his influence was felt in the construction of new railroad lines, he was no longer a speculator; he was no longer a trader; he was no longer a negotiator. He was now a builder of new roads not only in the Southwest, but also in the Rocky Mountain country, the Middle West and the East.

Gould's southwestern system was created by acquisition, by construction of main lines to complete unfinished through routes and by the building of feeders to accommodate the increasing population and wealth of the territory served. The parent company was the Missouri Pacific which in the course of years acquired all of the stock of the Iron Mountain. Because of opposition from some of the Philadelphia stockholders, the Texas & Pacific never became a fully controlled subsidiary of any of the Gould lines.

By the end of 1881 Gould's southwestern system controlled more than 5,000 miles of line, and about 475 additional miles

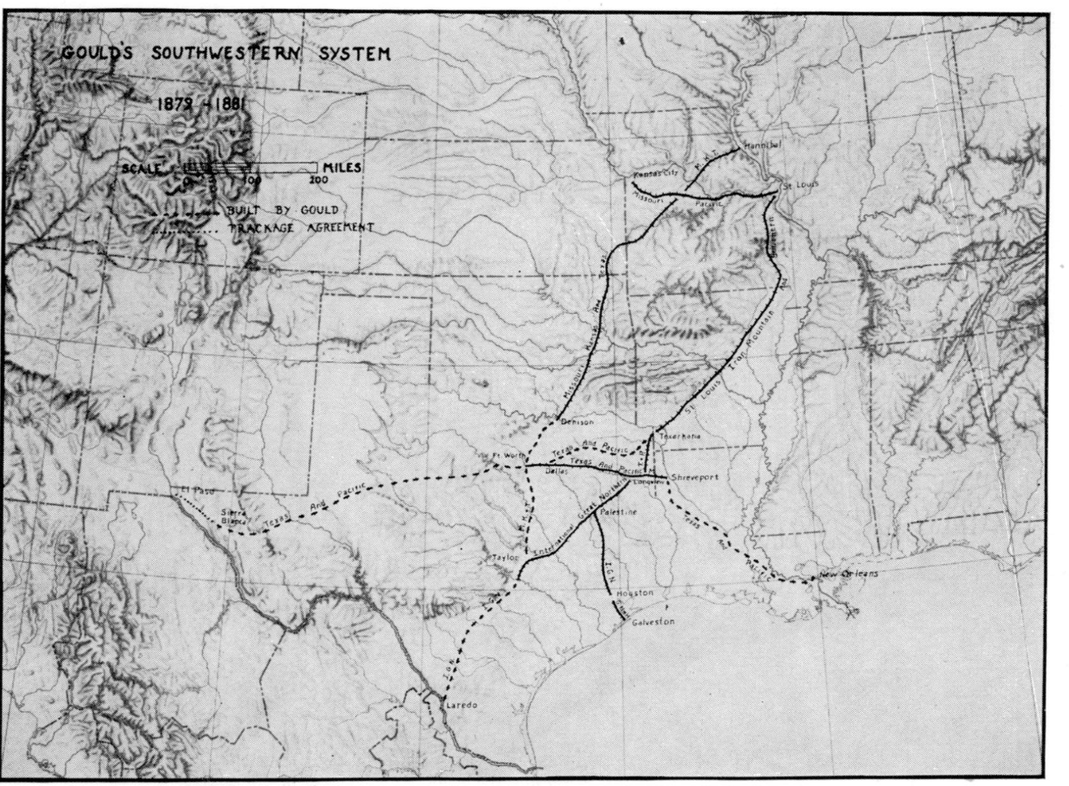
GOULD'S SOUTHWESTERN SYSTEM
1879 - 1881
SCALE
0
100
200
MILES
BUILT BY GOULD
TRACKAGE AGREEMENT
Hannibal
Kansas City
St. Louis
Missouri
Pacific
Missouri Kansas And Texas
St. Louis Iron Mountain And Southern
Denison
Texarkana
Ft. Worth
Dallas
Texas And Pacific
Shreveport
Longview
Palestine
International Great Northern
Taylor
I.G.N.
Houston
Galveston
New Orleans
El Paso
Sierra Blanca
Laredo

were in the process of construction.[27] The system served the area north of the Southern Pacific in Texas, east to the Mississippi River, west to the Texas-New Mexico boundary, and south of the Missouri River from St. Louis to Kansas City. Though the roads were operated under one management, the accounts were separately kept and cleared through the parent company—the Missouri Pacific. To this system other lines were later added, and while some of the lines, notably the Kansas & Texas, were lost, the southwestern roads remained the major heritage of Gould's railroad holdings. To the surprise of most current observers, he did not dispose of his holdings in Missouri Pacific. He traded, he bought, and he sold, but he always kept control.

Despite the size of the system and the great possibilities in the boom years of 1880 and 1881, the eventual losses to outside investors exceeded the gains. The Texas & Pacific, when Gould acquired control, had no floating debt, and was earning and paying interest on underlying bonds. Within a few years the company passed through receivership and was reorganized. The Kansas & Texas, on whose bonds the Dutch bondholders had refused a 4 per cent guarantee by the Burlington, passed through receivership. The International was involved in a series of financial and legal struggles which impaired its value. The Missouri Pacific, however, enlarged by the acquisition of the Iron Mountain and by its ramifications throughout the South and West, remained intact during Gould's life. In 1881 at the peak of the boom, however, the southwestern roads appeared only to be a small part of a much larger system controlled directly or indirectly by Gould. He was one of the most important—indeed from some standpoints *the* most important—leader in the railroad industry, as well as the leader in the stock-trading community.

NOTES FOR CHAPTER XIII

1. Known hereafter as the Iron Mountain.
2. Known hereafter as the International.
3. New York *Tribune*, May 24, 1882.
4. Ibid., May 31, 1879.
5. *Iron Age*, Jan. 1, 1880, 14.
6. Stated by a correspondent of the *Wall Street News*, cited in *Ry. World*, June 26, 1880, 613.
7. New York *Times*, Jan. 10, 1885.
8. Annual report, Texas & Pacific, 1880, 25.

9. *Ry. Review*, April 17, 1880, 184.
10. *Chron.*, April 24, 1880, 434; *Ry. World*, May 1, 1880, 421.
11. A detailed account of Gould's negotiations with the Backbone is found in the New York *Times*, Jan. 10, 1885; and a comprehensive description of the transfer of the Backbone's land grant is found in Bradstreet, March 21, 1885, 180.
12. Annual report, Texas & Pacific, 1880, 28-9.
13. Ibid.
14. Phila. *North American*, Dec. 16, 1880.
15. See Chapter XII, pp. 234-7, for details.
16. Annual report, Iron Mountain, 1879, cited in *Ry. Review*, April 10, 1880, 176.
17. St. Louis *Republican*, cited in *Ry. World*, Nov. 25, 1876, 766.
18. *Ry. World*, Feb. 14, 1880, 157.
19. Statement of Allen in *Ry. Review*, Dec. 18, 1880, 664.
20. Ibid.
21. *Chron.*, Dec. 18, 1880, 653.
22. The best connected account of these lines is found in the Report of the Reconstruction Finance Corporation on the Missouri Pacific, 1935, 7, mimeographed.
23. Phila. *Press*, April 13, 1881; Phila. *North American*, April 13, 1881. For an account of some of the personally interesting aspects of this purchase, see J. R. Perkins: *Trails, Rails and War*, 259.
24. *Ry. Review*, April 29, 1881, 242.
25. Galveston *News*, cited in *R. R. Gaz.*, Jan. 9, 1880, 23-4; *R. R. Gaz.*, July 16, 1880, 386; Sept. 24, 1880, 511.
26. New York *Times*, June 30, 1882.
27. *Ry. World*, Dec. 31, 1881, 1265.

CHAPTER XIV

Gould Acquires the Western Union

To Gould's astute mind, the expansion in the railroad industry inevitably led to expansion in the telegraph industry. Under the Supreme Court ruling, a new railroad was a new telegraph customer. Gould, as the controlling factor in a railroad, could contract with Gould, the controlling factor in the new American Union, for telegraph service to compete and perhaps supplant the Western Union.

In building up the competitive position of his American Union to a point of effective striking power, Gould was challenging one of the country's largest corporate enterprises. The Western Union was a prosperous dividend payer, and in the expanding telegraph industry it had little competition. Its contracts with the railroads, long judicially regarded as exclusive, at least prior to a Supreme Court decision in 1879, had made the pathway of competitors difficult. Since its organization in 1856 it had absorbed numerous companies and now only a few outside its corporate family remained. Gould's effort to break the Western Union's grasp on the industry with his Atlantic and Pacific had failed, and the company met the same fate as all predecessors. It was bought out by the Western Union.

Aside from its excellent financial condition, its real strength lay in its railroad contracts. It was precisely this citadel of Western Union strength which Gould attacked. No sooner was he in control of a road than he challenged the Western Union contract. Vanderbilt fought back with injunctions, the same weapon that his father had wielded more than a decade before in the Erie battle. The father, however, struck on the offensive; the son, except on rare occasions, acted on the defensive.

The Western Union's financial strength, paradoxically enough, proved to be a fatal weakness in the contest with its rival. Its controlling stockholders came from eastern financial groups. Vanderbilt was looked upon as the leader of the rank and file of the conservative-minded investor-stockholders. Another large stockholder with an investor following was Edwin D. Morgan, no longer active in business and now primarily interested in preserving his income by a continued flow of dividends. Taylor of the National City Bank was another large stockholder. Western Union was thus controlled by conservative interests, cautious in their make-up and careful to maintain the company's financial position and earning power. The managers were not dynamic businessmen; they were passive investors ready to sacrifice corporate verities in return for immediate income. This defensive policy was a weakness of which Gould in 1880 and 1881 took advantage, even as Cornelius Vanderbilt had with the New York Central in 1866 and 1867.

The Western Union, sure of its monopolistic position, belittled the new American Union. Its board members did not appreciate Gould's capacity for bold action in unexpected quarters. Little fight could be expected from Vanderbilt. Other members of the board had had but slight experience with Gould, and had not yet listened to his vague and alluring promises. Vanderbilt paid scant attention to the growth of the American Union since Gould kept him busy in the railroad field. In an effort to defend himself against Gould in the railroad arena and perhaps to take the initiative, Vanderbilt ranged far and wide. Gould foiled him at almost all points.

Gould first made a number of small acquisitions. He then went after bigger game. The Baltimore & Ohio which in 1879 was operating its own telegraph system had an excellent credit standing. It was not overcapitalized. Its stock for this reason alone had a good credit standing. A record of dividend payments justified its position as a high grade investment. Garrett, president, leading stockholder and for many years its policy-maker, was a strong and independent character. He early determined to operate, so far as possible, his own telegraph, express, sleeping-car and other auxiliary services. Earlier, in the seventies, he had allied the Baltimore & Ohio's telegraph system with the Atlantic & Pacific, and when in 1877 it sold out to the Western Union, he took advantage of some "peculiar phraseology" [1] in the agreement with the Atlantic & Pacific and prevented the transfer of its wires to the Western Union. To Gould the prospect of getting the road's telegraph business for the account of the American Union was attractive; he had little difficulty in convincing Garrett of the virtue of joining hands with that company. Playing on Garrett's prejudices, he roundly denounced the telegraph monopoly. Garrett became a member of the American Union's board, and bought stock in the company.[2]

Garrett was again in fighting trim; he was again challenging the great monopoly. Since he did nothing by halves, his support of Gould's American Union was wholehearted. No sooner had the company received Garrett's aid than the stations of the Baltimore & Ohio, "as if by magic," [3] were decorated with American Union signboards. The four thousand miles of lines thus added to the American Union were a significant acquisition, constituting early in January, 1880, about one-third of the total wire mileage of the American Union system.[4]

Despite the alliance with the Baltimore & Ohio, Gould's American Union at the turn of the year 1880 was not in a powerful position. The Western Union still maintained most of its railroad contracts and owned or controlled the telegraph wires located on the main railroad lines, thus maintaining a significant advantage over competitors. The American Union could not erect wires along main railroad lines, and its wires were "largely along the wagon-roads, or alongside and just outside the fence lines of the railroads." [5] The American Union was knocking at the gates of the monopoly but had not yet penetrated its defenses.

Before the new year was many weeks old, however, the position of the American Union was strengthened. As a result of the merger with the Kansas Pacific in January, the enlarged Union Pacific now owned the Kansas Pacific from Kansas City to Denver, the Denver Pacific from Denver to a connection with its old Omaha line, and a number of other smaller railroad properties. The system lines also reached important local points in wide areas in which there were almost no other lines of telegraph communication. By early 1880 despite the succession of Western Union injunctions, the American Union had completed lines to both Omaha and Kansas City. Over the main line of the Union Pacific from Omaha to Ogden was a telegraph wire owned by the company and used for its own railroad purposes. Another wire originally built by the Union Pacific was leased in 1869 to the Atlantic & Pacific, the controlling interest in which was acquired by the Western Union in 1877. Still another was built and operated by the Western Union. On the Kansas & Pacific and other roads included in the new Union Pacific, the Western Union used the wires under an exclusive contract. One line of wires was set apart for use by the railroad, and the others were owned and operated by the Western Union. The American Union wires connected with all of these. Gould decided to bid for the entire telegraph business and eliminate the Western Union from the Union Pacific system.

A few weeks after the Kansas Pacific merger he outlined a policy to be executed immediately. In control of the American Union he asked the Union Pacific to accept and transmit telegraph messages on the same basis as the Western Union. Under the new Supreme Court doctrine, the Union Pacific was at liberty to accede to this request. The Western Union's exclusive contract was no longer a hindrance. If the Union Pacific accepted, it would have a contract with both the Western Union and the American Union. The Western Union probably expected Gould to go so far and no further. Gould as usual did the unexpected. He wanted more for his American Union than another contract competitive with the Western Union. For the American Union to build a parallel line along the railroad's right of way would have been expensive. Gould therefore aimed to eliminate the Western Union from its position on the Union Pacific and allied lines, and to put the American Union in its place. To do this it was necessary to invalidate existing contracts and to seize the occupied property of the enemy immediately, and not await, with all the attendant delays, the directions of the courts of the land.

Gould opened operations by engaging as counsel John F. Dillon (full name is repeated to avoid confusion with Sidney Dillon), who was then beginning a long and distinguished career in his service. With his help, Gould was able to interpret contracts in diametrically opposite ways at different times in accordance with his changing interests. He asked John F. Dillon (and his associate, Sidney Bartlett) to pass upon the legality of the 1869 lease of the Union Pacific's wires to the Atlantic & Pacific. John F. Dillon did not long delay his reply, and his opinion was, of course, favorable to Gould. Gould had first instructed the American Union at Omaha to ask the Western Union, controlling the lines west of Omaha, to handle the former's telegraph messages. The Western Union, on the conditions laid down by the American Union, had refused. John F. Dillon and Bartlett were asked whether the Union Pacific legally should not be operating its own lines. Could the Union Pacific, asked Gould, turn over by lease or otherwise, its telegraph wires to the Atlantic & Pacific? Counsel replied in the negative. The Union Pacific had issued bonds secured by a mortgage on its railroad and telegraph lines. The Union Pacific owned the telegraph, and it was therefore the duty of the Union Pacific under its charter to operate the telegraph. It could not refuse to receive and send messages for the American Union Telegraph without violating its duty.[6] This legal interpretation was subsequently approved by a federal judge.

A year later Gould wanted help of the same counsel. By that time he had succeeded in making a new contract between the Union Pacific and the Western Union. He now controlled the Western Union, and the Union Pacific was no longer operating its own telegraph line just as it operated no line a year before. What was illegal for the Union Pacific in February, 1880, became legal one year later. Counsel had overlooked in 1880 a section of the Act giving the Western Union certain rights, but in 1881, with the aid of Gould, counsel discovered this section of the Act. This gave the Western Union new rights, and enabled Gould to conclude his ardently desired contract with the Union Pacific.

Gould in February, 1880, was not as yet solicitous about the rights and privileges of the Western Union. He was, however, deeply concerned with the privileges and profits of the American Union. Fortified with the opinions of John F. Dillon and Bartlett, and operating through the Union Pacific, he prepared his campaign. Secretly, he installed new transmitting batteries at the eastern termini of the Union Pacific at Kansas City and Denver. Suddenly, in late February, he cut the Western Union lines away from its main batteries at these points, and connected the secretly constructed batteries with the Union Pacific wires.[7] The seizure was carried out without interruption from the Western Union. "Last night," wired an officer of the American Union on the twenty-seventh of February, "I took possession of all lines on the Union Pacific." It was a short, prosaic and ordinary business message; but it ended the first round in another corporate battle, with Gould on the aggressive.

The struggle, recognized almost immediately as one "of large proportions," [8] was transferred to the courts. The Western Union was deprived of connections to the Pacific coast, and from the mountain sections it could reach the East only over the telegraph wires of the Atchison. The federal judge, to whom the Western Union appealed for an injunction to restrain the moves of Gould's corporate satellites, agreed with the views of John F. Dillon and Bartlett that the contract by which the Union Pacific had leased its wires to the Atlantic & Pacific was illegal; he did not agree with the moves of Gould in transforming these views into action. The Atlantic & Pacific and therefore the Western Union, insisted the judge, had acquired some property rights. The company was entitled to "due process"; and the court ordered the Atlantic & Pacific to repossess its property. Also, said the court, the Western Union had an interest in its own line on the Union Pacific which the court was determined to protect, and accordingly ordered the restoration of that line. The arbitrary seizure of the telegraph wires by Gould was "not calculated," said the court, "to create the most favorable impression on a court of equity. . . ." [9]

It was probable that Gould entertained no serious desire to create a favorable impression upon the court of equity. To him the court battle was only incidental, since victory was to be won not in the courts of law, but on the Stock Exchange. Gould was interested neither in buying nor in winning a lawsuit. His ambition, dating back to 1874, was to acquire control of the profitable telegraph business, a purpose which could be consummated only by seizure of control of the Western Union. Court battles were of importance to him only in so far as they enabled him to achieve this major purpose. If he could litigate the Western Union stockholders into uncertainty by keeping the case in court, his objective would be realized. It was not until early fall that the court handed down a final decision to the effect that although the Kansas Pacific had the exclusive use of one wire it could not interfere with the Western Union in the use of the other two. The Western Union was happy; the decision, it proclaimed, was "a substantial victory for the Western Union and [left] them in uninterrupted possession of their lines on the railroad named." [10]

Although competition between the two telegraph companies meanwhile increased, there was no serious rate war. The Western Union followed its historic policy of reducing rates as technological improvements and enlarged sales reduced costs. These rate reductions [11] were no more substantial than those which had occurred from time to time over the preceding ten-year period.

A genuine rate war did not develop. Gould's Atlantic & Pacific Telegraph experience had taught him a lesson. Losses of the Atlantic & Pacific had been heavy, and equally heavy losses might make it impossible for him to continue active competition with the well-established Western Union. The Western Union, even at the height of the American Union's power in the summer of 1880, had many offices at non-competing points. Gould appreciated that a war which would bear heavily upon the earnings of the American Union would bear lightly, in view of the heavy volume of non-competitive business, on the Western Union. The American Union, therefore, did not repeat the experiment of a war of rates.[12] Even though no such wars occurred, the effect on Western Union earnings was substantial. Meanwhile the loss of its monopolistic position on the Gould railroads was becoming serious. The Western Union knew that it was in for a fight. Gould had succeeded in impairing the trade position of the Western Union as no competitor had ever done before. As Gould kept adding to his railroad empire in 1880, the Western Union's monopolistic position, achieved by virtue of its railroad contracts, was steadily weakened.

The relationship of these railroad acquisitions to the future earnings of the Western Union was well recognized. Many of its stockholders therefore sold part of their holdings and retained smaller portions which they believed they could hold during a period of depressed earnings. In dealing with the threat of the American Union, the Western Union board was divided. It was a fatal division especially in the presence of such a watchful, ingenious, and informed antagonist as Gould. Instead of uniting against the common enemy, the board fought amongst themselves. A faction led by its president, Norvin Green, was all for fight. He was in favor of stripping down, of reducing expenses, of throwing off the luxurious fat, and of engaging in a knock-down-and-drag-out fight with Gould's American Union.[13] For such a battle the American Union had many advantages, but the Western Union had many more. In addition to the thousands of non-competitive points, it could offer the best services between the large industrial and commercial cities. It had few fixed charges, and could therefore pass dividends and use its resources to wage the battle of competition. Another group, led by Vanderbilt, was in favor of conciliation. There was an army of approximately 2,200 shareholders who, as usual, were interested only in immediate results. They were investors who had bought their stock for income. They wanted dividends, not rate wars. Like the democracies of recent years, they wanted peace.

It was a distressing situation and the alternative was not clear. Before the Western Union could chart a policy, Gould was already executing one in the stock market. In conjunction with a number of other traders, including Keene who had made a number of successful trades, Gould formed a stock pool in order to depress the price of Western Union. He convinced his associates that with the American Union becoming ever more aggressive, the Western Union earnings were bound to decline. This was not yet clearly recognized by the average investor and trader, who respond only to facts and tendencies which are visible clearly to all who read and run. The Western Union early in 1880 was selling at a high price. The general market was strong; in such a market it was easy for Gould and his group to build up a large short interest. Late in April of 1880 the price of Western Union's stock declined sharply. The decline was a "puzzle" to the financial district. The report was current that Gould had bought 100,000 shares from Vanderbilt, but this Vanderbilt denied.[14] In the following months the decline continued, and stories of dissension among board members became a matter of public notice.[15] The annual election was approaching and a contest over corporate policy impended. Gould, watching the progress of this contest, discovered that several members of the board had sold large blocks of stock. Some of the sellers believed that after the price dropped they could buy the stock back and then vote it at the election. They were thus unconsciously allying themselves with Gould who, in order to strengthen his hand, entered the proxy market. That market was distinct from the market for the stock. When the speculators returned to the market to rebuy the Western Union they had sold, in order thereby to vote the stock at the election, they discovered that the proxies had been bought by Gould. Buying by short sellers also occurred about this time. Meanwhile the price rose to about 105.

Despite the rise, the bear pool remained intact. In the rising market, prices of good stocks advanced, while the price of Western Union suddenly dropped. In the first week of December it fell below 90. Then came the real news: the Western Union published its earnings and revealed the almost complete disappearance of the previous year's surplus of $1,600,000. This was followed by a dividend reduction. Little wonder, to use the language of Vanderbilt, that the stockholders "were getting very uneasy." [16] Reports and rumors spread thick and fast. "A thousand rumors of the disastrous condition of the company, of the impossibility of its standing against the rivalry of the American Union, and of the implacable hostility of the latter, were skillfully circulated; and the two companies, Mr. Vanderbilt controlling the one and Mr. Gould the other, entered on a war of rates, which it was declared was to be fought to the end." [17]

The price of the stock dropped further and in a few days it sold at 82½. There, for three or four days it seemed to be stabilized, but on December 17, 1880, in the midst of a buoyant market and in heavy trading, Western Union fell to 78. The bear traders, now set for the kill, stood ready to purchase the stock at the depressed prices and to take their profit. The price, however, did not budge. At the turn of the year it suddenly jumped from less than 81 to almost 87. "As an exhibition of superb manipulation," remarked one financial analyst, "this price movement has never been surpassed." [18] Who was doing the manipulating, nobody knew—at least nobody who was willing to inform the outside public. The same writer who observed the manipulation reported that the "average operator" was convinced that the rise was due to the purchases of Vanderbilt.[19] The traders themselves who were (outside of the negotiating parties) the closest observers of market happenings knew as little as anybody else. They were described as being "very bitter." [20] They had been told, so they complained, to buy when prices were high, and were told later to sell when prices were low.

Even the members of the bear pool, those who organized for the sole purpose of making a profit out of the movements in Western Union stock, were discomfited. When they tried to rebuy stock at the low prices of mid-December, they discovered little stock offered for sale. The market shot up rapidly as soon as they entered substantial buying orders. Gould alone benefited from this remarkable operation. When his associates in the bear pool were selling, or at best, when they were not buying for the purpose of completing their short selling contracts, Gould was buying. In all he bought more than 90,000 shares, and he was therefore, late in December, 1880, the largest single shareholder. In the strong investment market he sold his Union Pacific stock at high prices and invested part of the proceeds in Western Union.

The Western Union board in late December, though not aware of this development, was acutely aware of two others. The first was the status of the Pennsylvania Railroad contract. The road had never signed an exclusive agreement with the Western Union and felt at liberty to offer a competitive contract for the use of its right of way on its lines east of Pittsburgh to both of the leading telegraph companies. Gould on behalf of the American Union accepted a contract [21] on the basis of a price so high, according to an official of the Baltimore & Ohio, that for the mere right to locate its poles and wires on the road, the company agreed to pay the Pennsylvania an annual sum which if capitalized would have equaled the entire cost of its own line on that road.[22] Having given the American Union a new contract, the Pennsylvania in September, 1880, notified the Western Union that existing arrangements would end on the first of January, and began negotiations for the erection of a line of its own telegraph poles on the northern side of the right of way. Finally, on the sixth of January, with the Western Union defending its exclusive contract, which it insisted could not be canceled at the pleasure of the railway company, the Pennsylvania gave notification that existing arrangements would end forthwith.[23] The Western Union took the case to court asking that the Pennsylvania be compelled to uphold existing contracts.

In December, while the Pennsylvania problem was approaching a climax, Gould struck another blow. Neither of the rival telegraph companies controlled the cable business, although each had established a working arrangement with an independently owned cable company. After a number of rate wars amongst themselves, the cable companies on September 24, 1880, entered into an agreement for the pooling of receipts and the fixing of minimum rates.[24] Of these companies the Anglo-American Cable, with four cables and a capitalization of $35,000,000, worked with the Western Union; the Direct Cable, with one cable and a capitalization of $6,500,000, worked with the Atlantic & Pacific; and a French cable company, with one cable and a capitalization of $10,000,000, worked with the American Union. All these concerns were controlled by foreign capital. To the ordinary mind this fact might seem unimportant. To Gould, however, it fitted well with a far-reaching plan of international significance. In the Erie regime of the late sixties and early seventies he never overlooked an opportunity to champion the Erie as the savior of railroad competition in New York City. Only the Erie, he said, stood in the breach and saved the city from the grasping Vanderbilt monopoly. Now, in 1880, Gould thundered against the foreign cable monopoly. He would promote a national independent cable enterprise; he would break the monopoly; he would reduce the artificially maintained rates. The average capitalization per cable of the existing companies exceeded $8,000,000, he said, and he would build a cable for $3,000,000.

In late December he was ready for action. He organized a construction company with a capitalization of $10,000,000 to build a new trans-Atlantic cable, and called immediately for 70 per cent of the subscription. His success was astonishing, and in forty hours the money was raised.[25] The Gould cable company—the American Telegraph & Cable—was a new threat to the Western Union, since it would be able to break up the existing rate structure and thereby reduce Western Union revenues.

Although by the end of 1880 the Gould telegraph combination had potentialities of becoming a powerful enterprise, it was not as yet a profitable one. Indeed the American Union's receipts had never equaled its expenses, although at the time of the consolidation with the Western Union it was just about paying its way.[26]

The future of the American Union, however, in the opinion of its owners and managers was bright. The president thought that it could earn 20 per cent on its investment. Gould was more conservative; he believed that it would earn about 6 per cent. The company's connections with his railroads, Gould was convinced, would make the American Union highly profitable. "My own ownership in great roads," he declared, "my directorship and control in others, enabled the American Union to make contracts of incalculable value." [27]

Despite the dangerous growth of this competitor, the Western Union board was still in the throes of internal conflict. It had not as yet been able to lay down any general policies. While the board was wrestling with its problems, a ray of sunshine suddenly appeared. This turned out to be Gould himself. Through Dillon, president of the Union Pacific, the information was relayed to Vanderbilt that Gould was ready to talk terms. Negotiations opened with Gould's usual deftness. He was the largest Western Union stockholder. Though he appreciated that the Western Union might decide to fight, he knew that an important group wanted peace. Through Dillon he informed Vanderbilt that he would not oppose an "amicable settlement." Gould thus succeeded, as he had a little more than a year before in the Union Pacific merger, in placing the other party on the defensive. Holding the whip hand in the negotiations, he was ready to see Vanderbilt if Vanderbilt was agreeable, and Vanderbilt was agreeable. To use his own language, Vanderbilt on Sunday night, January 9, at his home, agreed to talk terms to "the great Mogul." [28]

The negotiations were conducted with the same skill and rapidity that had characterized his negotiations in the Union Pacific merger. The troubles of the Western Union, Gould demonstrated, could easily be solved. He was all sweetness and amity. He, the chief enemy of the Western Union only a few days before, was now its chief proprietor. He was willing to adjust, arrange, compromise. "We were taken by surprise," said Green, the leader of the fighting party,[29] and, continued Green, though the board could have said it was not ready for agreement, it still had 2,000 shareholders to consider. "We could not afford to forego an opportunity so unexpectedly offered, and we accepted the negotiation." [30] The Western Union board in 1881, like

Joseph Stalin in August, 1939, was presented with a gift of peace. All of the acute problems, all the frightful ills which might arise from an impending war, now disappeared.

Negotiations proceeded swiftly. Gould as master of the situation aimed to please everybody. He was anxious to please the stockholders of the American Union. He had only a fair amount of its stock and bonds. A good price for American Union would indeed enhance his own holdings; but even more important, would assure the loyal following of his associates. He also aimed to please the minority stockholders of the Atlantic & Pacific. Should they profit they would attribute their success to Gould. Finally, he aimed to please both himself and the 2,000 stockholders in the Western Union.

In the transaction that was finally made, the "actual value" of the American Union entered but slightly into the calculation of the Western Union board, anxious as it was to rid itself of a competitor and to enter upon a corporate career of harmony and dividend payments. Gould in satisfying the board arranged also for the satisfaction of all corporate interests. The Western Union issued $15,000,000 of stock to pay for the securities of the American Union, a price equivalent to about twice its original cost.[31] Another $8,400,000 in stock was paid for the Atlantic & Pacific stock, giving the latter a price of 60, in contrast to the price of 25 paid in the agreement of 1877. Finally, to make everybody happy, the Western Union declared a stock dividend of $15,500,000. This was surely a piece of curious historical irony. The stock dividend represented earnings invested in the property and never capitalized, of approximately $17,000,000. Although the Western Union's practice of reinvesting earnings was begun on a small scale in 1866, it did not reach substantial proportions until the advent of Cornelius Vanderbilt in 1869. It was the soundness of his financial policies which made the Western Union stock dividend possible, and it was Vanderbilt's son, William H., who handed over a large part of the value which his father had created, to his father's arch-foe—Gould.

Before the end of the month the transaction was completed. On February 5, 1881, Gould and his ally, Sage, were elected to the board of the Western Union. Thomas T. Eckert, president of the American Union, was also elected a director, and appointed vice president and general manager of the property. Green, who had been prepared to fight Gould and his American Union, was too able an executive to be dismissed. Gould retained his services, and he continued as president of the enlarged property.

Gould was now the largest stockholder and the policy-maker of one of the most influential and profitable companies in the country. As a gatherer of news, through its contracts with the Associated Press, the company had no rival. It also did a large part of the railroad-telegraph business of the country.

The American Union-Western Union consolidation produced a storm of protest. From journals of financial opinion came strong condemnations of the financial phases. One described the combination categorically as "another immense stock-watering upon which the people must pay dividends," and estimated the capital actually invested in the system at about $25,000,000 as compared with $80,000,000 in outstanding securities.[32] The business and commercial public also were up in arms. The Cotton Exchange of New York, for example, talked of organizing an independent company. Committees from the Cotton and Produce Exchanges of New York met with committees from the Chicago exchanges. They spoke hopefully of organizing an independent company, and followed with the announcement of the organization of the Merchants' Telegraph Company which in Chicago alone raised $500,000 in stock subscriptions.[33] In the halls of Congress there were voices loud in protest. Aside from local reactions, they took the shape of a bill to aid a company to build lines and to authorize the government to permit it to use public and private lands, post roads and bridges.[34]

Although the government accomplished nothing, private enterprise was active and new competition was not long in coming. Within less than six months after the merger, the Postal Telegraph, destined to remain as the only surviving competitor of the Western Union, was organized with Keene as president. Keene was Gould's most prominent associate in the Western Union's bear pool of the preceding year.

If the public and Gould's enemies were dissatisfied with Gould's work, the telegraph stockholders were well pleased. From the shareholders of the American Union and the Atlantic &

Pacific came no bleat. They had received handsome treatment indeed and were content. To them Gould was a hero; they could thank him for spectacular profits on their stockholdings in the short period of less than a year. From the stockholding group of the Western Union, two legal efforts to test the validity of the merger evolved. One was brought by Rufus Hatch, a speculator who had frequently tilted with Gould and usually came out second. The day before the agreement of consolidation he bought 100 shares of Western Union, and four days later he bought 400 more. The judge before whom the suit was brought had little difficulty in throwing out the case. Hatch, he said, came into the court with "unclean hands" and therefore had no standing.

The other suit was brought by William S. Williams, a small stockholder of the Western Union. Williams insisted that the stock dividend was illegal; that the Western Union had overvalued both the American Union and the Atlantic & Pacific. In the long judicial contest, Williams won in the lower court but was overruled in the higher court. There remained no doubt of the legality of the Western Union stock dividend.

Long before its legality was affirmed, Gould, through the Union Pacific, signed a contract demonstrating the potentialities of the new corporate telegraph union. The Supreme Court had declared that a railroad, despite an exclusive contract, could make a contract with another telegraph company. To Gould this was not satisfactory. By the summer of 1881 he had sold his Union Pacific stock, but not his Western Union. The Union Pacific contract was valuable to the Western Union and he did not propose to lose it. With the help of counsel, he discovered a legal foundation for the doctrine that the Union Pacific did not violate the law by leasing its wires to the Atlantic & Pacific; that in fact it could make any contract, as binding as necessary, with its successor, the Western Union. In the new contract, the Union Pacific turned over its wires to the Western Union and agreed to do business with no other telegraph company. To make the provision doubly sure, the Union Pacific agreed that if any question of interpretation arose the Western Union could prosecute the case in the name of the Union Pacific.[35]

By the end of 1881 it was clear that despite all protests, public and private, from commercial and business organizations, and from the general press, the consolidation was permanent. Gould lost no time in perfecting his grasp on the cable business. No sooner was the Western Union agreement consummated than he canceled the American Union-French company and the Atlantic and Pacific-Direct Cable contracts. Both cable companies were astounded, and promptly entered suit. Gould's legal victory was clear-cut and decisive. On technical grounds a contract which appeared to be a contract became only a legally voidable arrangement. Gould's skill in nullifying written and binding agreements was again demonstrated.

Gould meanwhile went ahead with his plan for laying new cables. The recently incorporated American Telegraph & Cable signed up with the Western Union. As soon as the cables were completed the latter would get the business; how much, the public did not know. A mysterious contract was arranged, part of the consideration being a Western Union guarantee of the cable company's bonds and 5 per cent on the stock. When the construction company was organized it was proposed that the new cable company issue $10,000,000 of stock. Although that public announcement was never changed, the subscribers, when asked to exchange their certificates for new stock, discovered that the stock had been increased to $14,000,000. This was welcome news and no stockholder could object. When finally they received their certificates, they got another surprise; they were asked to sign a paper stating that they had read the contract between the Western Union and the American Telegraph & Cable, and that they had approved of the contract. This was a move by Gould to reveal in his quiet way his growing power over the world's cable business. One innocent shareholder, not appreciating the nicety of the arrangement, asked for the privilege of reading the new contract. The contract, he was informed, was not shown to anybody; but " 'it was all right,' " he was told, and of course he signed.[36]

The Western Union had thus increased its fixed charges by $700,000. What did it get in return? In 1881 it received nothing. By the summer of 1882 the cable company at a cost of $6,000,000 finally put two cables to work.[37] Gould's opinion of the probable cable costs were amply justified. The Western Union, however, paid a return of 5 per cent, not on the $6,000,000 cost of the cables but on the cable company's stock of $14,000,000. Whether Gould personally benefited is not so clear. Gould was a heavy stockholder in Western Union, and it is conceivable that he may have lost as much from the reduced earnings on Western Union as he may have gained from the guaranteed return on his cable securities.

By late summer of 1881 the American Telegraph & Cable completed its cable, and a rate war broke out immediately. Furthermore, the new cables soon broke down and were lost. Gould competition was thus temporarily removed but the established cable companies had received a shock. They knew by the short experience what was in store for them. Gould dominated the land wires, and in the course of the next few months made it clear that he would not hesitate "to work serious injury to the old cable company by subjecting them to great embarrassment." [38] The Gould pressure was again successful, and in March of 1882 a pooling and rate-fixing agreement among the cable companies was reached. All companies pooled their business; rates were doubled; and everybody was again happy. The Western Union, however, obtained a cut on messages from all the cable companies.[39]

In all these complicated telegraph and cable negotiations, in the courts and in business circles, Gould showed excellent judgment. By patience, by a knowledge of the weakness of the opposition, by taking full advantage of all the openings offered by the law in the technical interpretations of business contracts, he overcame almost all opposition. In the face of storms of public protest, despite suits in the courts, despite competition from new telegraph companies, he succeeded. The path was long and rocky, and was strewn with many a serious obstacle. The cost for a time seemed heavy. Rates were reduced, losses in earnings were substantial, and dividends were cut, but in the end Gould beat down almost everybody, including the United States Government. And from a host of competitors, only the Postal Telegraph and its allied Commercial Cable survived.

NOTES FOR CHAPTER XIV

1. Phila. *Press*, July 20, 1881.
2. Testimony before Committee on Post Offices and Post Roads, on the Postal

Telegraph, Report No. 577, Senate, 48th Congress, 1st Session, 1884, 56-7, Reiff.

3. Phila. *Press*, July 20, 1881.
4. New York *Tribune*, Jan. 7, 1880.
5. This was the statement of a former superintendent of a division of the Western Union, in the New York *Times*, Aug. 15, 1881. Norvin Green, president of the Western Union, stated that the American Union built its lines just outside of the railroad right of way of one of the lines from Chicago to Omaha. Testimony before Committee on Post Offices and Post Roads, on the Postal Telegraph, Report No. 577, Senate, 48th Congress, 1st Session, 1884, 222.
6. Land-Grant Telegraph Lines, Report No. 3501, House of Representatives, 49th Congress, 2nd Session, 1886, VIII.
7. New York *Tribune*, March 3, 1880.
8. *R. R. Gaz.*, March 5, 1880, 136.
9. *Federal Reporter*, Vol. 3, 417, 1880; the other cases involving the seizure of the telegraph lines are in ibid., Vol. I, 745; Vol. III, 423, 430.
10. *Railway World*, Oct. 9, 1880, 976.
11. New York *Times*, Dec. 3, 1879; *Bradstreet*, Dec. 6, 1879, 4.
12. This was the opinion of John Van Horne, operating vice president of Western Union, expressed in Testimony before Committee on Post Offices and Post Roads, on the Postal Telegraph, Report No. 577, Senate, 48th Congress, 1st Session, 1884, 192. It was the opinion of Green, president of Western Union, in Testimony before the Senate Committee on Education and Labor as to the Relations between Labor and Capital, Report No. 1262, Senate, 48th Congress, 2nd Session, 1885, 894. He also stated in the New York *Tribune*, Jan. 16, 1881, that with the American Union there had never been a war of rates; that for fourteen years Western Union had reduced rates; a reduction, he said, that was "accelerated at times by competition." Albert P. Chandler, connected with the Atlantic and Pacific since 1875 as secretary, treasurer, vice president and president, stated in an affidavit that the American Union did not "to any considerable extent" lower the previous rates; see New York *Tribune*, Jan. 26, 1881. William Holmes, superintendent of the Tariff Bureau of the Atlantic and Pacific, said, in the same source, that reduction in rates since the establishment of the American Union averaged 25 per cent; but in the New York *Times* of the same date his remark is clarified. He there stated that the American Union did not reduce rates "between points of competition" until Dec. 16, 1880. This was just two weeks before Gould met Vanderbilt and arranged a plan of consolidation.

    These views conflict with the statements made in secondary sources which refer to extensive rate cuts of the American Union. See Anna Youngman: *Economic Causes of Great Fortunes*, 96; Murat Halstead and J. Frank Beale, Jr.: *Life of Jay Gould*, 360; Henry Clews: *Twenty-eight Years in Wall Street*, 629, which states that the American Union "cut the rates until the older and larger corporation found that its profits were being reduced towards the vanishing point." These secondary sources probably received their impressions from some reckless statements made in the newspapers.
13. *Public*, Sept. 23, 1880, 198-9, refers editorially to Green's views.
14. New York *Tribune*, May 1, 1880; New York *Times*, April 30, 1880; *Bradstreet*, May 1, 1880, 4.
15. *Bradstreet*, Sept. 22, 1880, 5.
16. New York *Tribune*, June 2, 1881.
17. *Bradstreet*, Jan. 15, 1881, 24.
18. New York *Tribune*, Jan. 4, 1881.
19. Ibid., Jan. 6, 1881.
20. Ibid., Jan. 14, 1881.

21. Testimony before Committee on Post Offices and Post Roads, on the Postal Telegraph, Report No. 577, Senate, 48th Congress, 1st Session, 1884, 128, G. G. Hubbard.
22. Ibid., 125, J. K. Cowen.
23. Phila. *Press*, Jan. 5, 1881.
24. Details on this pool noted in the decision of the French Court of Appeals in the case of the Anglo-American Telegraph Company Limited, vs. La Compagnie Francaise Du Telegraph de Paris, cited in *London Railway News*, May 12, 1888, 780-3.
25. *Ry. Review*, Dec. 25, 1880, 677; see New York *Herald*, Dec. 19, 1882, on the cable developments.
26. This is the judgment of Thomas T. Eckert, president American Union, as reported in New York *Tribune*, May 18, 1881.
27. New York *Tribune*, May 20, 1881.
28. Ibid., May 17, 1881.
29. This was the statement made in Green's argument before the Senate Committee on Miscellaneous Corporations, cited in New York *Tribune*, Feb. 10, 1881.
30. Ibid.
31. This is the opinion of Green in the New York *Tribune*, May 17, 1881.
32. *Chron.*, Feb. 19, 1881, 206.
33. New York *Tribune*, Feb. 6, 1881.
34. New York *Times*, Jan. 21, 1881.
35. Land-Grant Lines, Report No. 3501, House of Representatives, 49th Congress, 2nd Session, 1886, 4-5, D. H. Bates; 138, Wm. F. Frick. The contract is found in Report No. 3501, 43-7.
36. New York *Herald*, Dec. 19, 1882.
37. *Chron.*, Dec. 24, 1881, 716; Testimony before Committee on Post Offices and Post Roads, on the Postal Telegraph, Report No. 577, Senate, 48th Congress, 1st Session, 1884, 134, Garrett.
38. Message from the President of the United States, transmitting a communication from the Secretary of State, in response to a Resolution of the House of Representatives in relation to modifications of the Stipulations which the French Cable Company made with this Government, Executive Document No. 46, House of Representatives, 47th Congress, 2nd Session, 1883, 25. This is the language of the Report of the Board of Managers of the French Cable Company, June 30, 1882.
39. Text of the pool is found in ibid., 5-15; for details on the pool see New York *Times*, May 16, 1882; Dec. 28, 1885.

CHAPTER XV

Gould Acquires Manhattan Elevated

THE Manhattan Elevated,[1] even more than the Western Union Telegraph, occupied a position of monopoly. While the latter encountered considerable competition, the Manhattan had a complete grasp of the rapid-transit facilities in New York City. It was, furthermore, a monopoly conferred by law through a grant of the franchise contract. Nevertheless, despite its strategic competitive position, it was financially weak. Unlike the Western Union it had no record of dividend payments, and its property was covered with mortgages. From its very inception its solvency was questionable. At an early stage in its career, its leading stockholders had sold out their holdings and announced publicly that the company's position was desperate. Vanderbilt expressed his conservative instincts by refusing to make financial commitments in such a risky scheme. The earliest promoters in fact sank two million dollars in the first Manhattan company organized in 1875. The original proposal of building two rapid-transit systems was abandoned, whereupon two other companies were organized to do the job. These promoters also took a severe financial drubbing. The depression in the seventies bore heavily upon them and a decision of the Court of Appeals subjecting the rapid-transit properties to the burden of real-estate taxes constituted another blow which the original stockholders were unable to absorb.

Field, on the lookout for a property with speculative attraction, seized upon the stock of one of these lines—the New York Elevated [2]—and succeeded in purchasing stock at almost nominal levels. The other property—the Metropolitan Elevated [3]—was more conservatively financed and was supported by stronger financial groups, its stock being owned largely by a construction company—the New York Loan & Improvement Company.

For reasons which are not entirely clear, the New York, shortly after acquisition by Field in May of 1877, prospered more than its competitor, the Metropolitan. Within less than two years after he acquired control, both the gross and net showed excellent increases; the financial condition was improved, the standard of service was raised, and the price of the stock increased ninefold.[4] The Metropolitan, although not as prosperous, was a vigorous competitor. A curious mistake made by the Rapid Transit Commissioners in 1875 drove these competitors into a hasty alliance. The Commissioners had authorized the New York to pass over part of a route already granted by charter to its competitor. They proposed that both roads build part of the structure in common, but such a solution from an operating standpoint would have been impracticable. Serious friction between the two companies had meanwhile developed. The regulatory authorities, after examining the problem, refused to devise a practical solution, and said in effect, "Gentlemen, go settle this among yourselves; it is a matter we cannot deal with." [5] Though this legislative mandate was of no help, the companies in response to pressing business necessities did find a way out; they eliminated competition by adopting a lease contract. In this agreement the strong company did not lease the weak one; neither did the one secure a primacy over the other. It was indeed legally impossible, in view of the prohibition against the consolidation of parallel and competing lines, for one company to acquire the other.

Field had a major interest and was the dominant factor in the New York. Why Field should have permitted the prosperous New York to enter into an ill-starred corporate union upon the same terms granted to the less prosperous competitor cannot easily be deduced.

The old Manhattan Company was now converted into a holding company. Though it held no stock of the operating companies, it did hold a lease of their properties. In consideration of the lease, the holding company issued to each lessor company $6,400,000 of stock, and guaranteed the interest on their bonds as well as a 10 per cent annual dividend on their stock.

The new combination, from a standpoint of long-term values,

may have been sound. Perhaps in the course of time the traffic would build up and the earnings advance to a point where the guaranteed dividends would be covered out of earnings. At the time of the lease neither property was finished; another $10,000,000 needed for further construction was to be provided by the two lessors and handed over to the lessee.

The inability of the new combination to increase its earnings in the early stages was overlooked by the speculative market. Speculators were attracted to the new venture which eliminated the conflicts between the two competitors. The price of Manhattan stock rose rapidly. The managers of the property, however, soon became aware of the difficulties of the new combination. Questions were raised over the legality of the leases, and legislative interference was anticipated.[6] The optimistic anticipations of speculators were soon removed by the financial realities. By the turn of the year, it became evident that the Manhattan would be unable to meet its dividend guarantee. Major stockholders in the lessor roads who had received the Manhattan stock in exchange for the lease had by the spring of 1880 sold out.[7] They had transferred the risk to the speculative public. Many had bought the stock because of suggestions made in the press both by Field and Tilden, yet both of these speculative leaders had sold their holdings. Tilden in fact made a wholesale clean-up of all his holdings not only in the Manhattan but also in the New York. According to current accounts which received widespread publicity both in this country and in England, Tilden in liquidating his holdings violated his pledged word to Field. This revelation did not apparently surprise English informed public opinion. One leading British railway journal observed some years later that even "such friendship as that of Damon and Pythias might not be proof against the temptations of the 'almighty dollar' in Wall Street." [8]

As the weeks rolled on in 1880, and as the financial problems of the elevated system became more generally realized, the price of Manhattan stock continued to drop. The belief spread that the stock was worthless. Field, for example, was reported to have been short about 10,000 shares.[9] The company's officers, one after the other, retired from their position of leadership and publicly voiced their pessimism. Early in 1881 even the representatives of the uninformed security holders, the financial press, were convinced that there was little value in the stock. "As to the Manhattan," wrote one observer, "it is difficult to see what value that [had] at all, for that [was] water pure and simple."[10]

In this campaign of gloom, the promoters of the Manhattan, Field, Tilden and Garrison, advised their followers to sell at low prices, even though little more than a year before they had advised buying at high prices. The Manhattan was deficient in earnings, it was asserted, and it would be unable to pay its July 1 interest and dividend guarantees.

In the midst of this plague of bad news, Sage appeared in mid-April as a savior. He had a plan. He had bought a large block of Manhattan in the twenties, and with his plan he thought he could save both his investment and the Manhattan. He proposed that the company issue $2,000,000 of preferred stock to its stockholders, and that if the stockholders were unable or unwilling to buy, the stock would be bought by a syndicate which had faith in the value of the property. The syndicate also offered to make good the deficiencies of the lessee for a period of two years. The lessee would be provided with funds out of the proceeds realized from the sale of the preferred.[11] The plan was sound in the sense that it was designed to bridge the gap between the construction stage and the time that the property would be completed and its earning power could respond to the influences of expanding demand and cost reduction.

Whatever chance for success the plan of Sage may have had, was rudely interrupted by a new development. The president of the Manhattan and some of his directors had called upon the mayor for relief from a rising tax burden and had submitted a statement revealing a loss of about $500,000, excluding some additional taxes recently proposed. If the company paid taxes in full, it would be unable to pay interest. There still remained in arrears taxes for the two previous years of $960,000. If the city insisted upon payment of taxes the company would go into bankruptcy. The net income, he said, was much less than in the previous year. The city, however, was obdurate and refused to accept the appeal of the company for a tax reduction.

This was the situation when Gould's daily organ—the New York *World*—began its determined attempt, persistently prosecuted for the next few months, to undermine both the legal and financial position of the company. The company was friendless. According to the president's statements, it was dropping into insolvency, and a default on July 1 was imminent. Influential quarters insisted that the stock was all water. Even the company's legal position was assailed; the company though incorporated to build elevated lines had not done so. It was now merely an agency for the leasing of the properties of two other corporations which had built the lines.

In the midst of these uncertainties, the company was suddenly attacked from an unexpected source. Those interested in the Metropolitan had arranged to raise the cash to enable the Manhattan to meet its July first guarantee. Before these plans could be perfected, before any move could be made to aid either the Manhattan or the Metropolitan, the attorney-general suddenly asked the court to vacate the Manhattan charter and to appoint a receiver. The company, he declared, had forfeited its franchise, had no legal existence and therefore had no power to lease the property. Furthermore, it was insolvent. The company, authorized by its charter to issue $2,000,000 stock, had issued $11,000,000 additional, and the shares issued to the lessors as a consideration for the lease of their properties, said the attorney-general, was "one of those gigantic swindles upon the community. . . ." [12]

One would expect that such an action would drive the stock to exceptionally low figures. It did no such thing. Even though the move was a surprise, the stock moved up first from 26 to 29, and then fell back to its opening figure. Nobody could "make head or tail of it . . ." declared a New York financial writer. "Being utterly worthless, it is being used as a stock-jobbing football by speculative gamblers." [13]

To make the situation even more confusing, the attorney-general suddenly stopped proceedings in the courts of New York City, abandoned the charge of legal invalidity and presented a complaint alleging insolvency as the sole cause for receivership before a court in upper New York State presided over by Judge Westbrook. This lawsuit was accompanied by others initiated by seemingly independent bond- and stockholders of both the lessors and the lessee. The instigator of these suits was then not known. As in March of 1868 the leadership of the anti-Vanderbilt forces appeared to fall upon Drew, so the leadership in 1881 appeared to fall upon Field who, however, upon his return from abroad, denied any responsibility.[14] That there was "some cunning hand pulling the wires against these companies" [15] was generally believed. Weeks passed and litigation increased in scope and complexity before the hand of Gould was finally revealed.

Gould from time to time lent a helping hand to increase the market confusion. He and his two lieutenants, Sage and Dillon, bought large blocks of Manhattan and Metropolitan,[16] but they were not held very long. Gould was not yet sure of his ground. His immediate aim was to place the company in receivership, and thus prevent the New York from reacquiring its valuable property. By the middle of June the leadership on both sides became clear. Field for the New York was "breathing out threatenings and slaughter against all enemies, his eye being evidently most steadily fixed on Mr. Gould." [17] It was clear, also, that Gould was against the New York. Whether he was for the Metropolitan or the Manhattan was not so obvious. He apparently had decided to interest himself in both companies. If the Manhattan disappeared, he could acquire the Metropolitan and compete with Field's property. He could then by the reduction of fares or the creation of operating obstacles exert pressure on his competitor. He might even force a merger—on his own terms. To reproduce the line of thought of a New York press critic, he could make a drive against the Manhattan and when the stock was pressed down to a low price by threat of dissolution, "well-informed" people would push the price up, a compromise would be arranged, and the company would be set up on its feet.[18] In fact, Gould played on both sides, and he acquired a heavy interest in both properties. "My theory was," he said a few months later, "that which ever side won I would have the same interest at stake." [19]

He went ahead carefully with his plan, selecting first the proper judge. The new judge was not tied up with a political boss who accepted stock in the company for services duly rendered. He was a complaisant person, one who was impressed by personal business success. He was, furthermore, a judge whose credibility knew almost no bounds.

It is impossible to invade the inner workings of the relationship between the attorney-general and Gould's retinue of associates and employees. Why the attorney-general presented a complaint which was drawn by the lawyers for Connor, Gould's stockbroker, cannot be explained.[20] The attorney-general neither profited from the Gould stocks nor was he a party to any of Gould's transactions. There was no doubt, however, that he followed Gould's wishes, or at least fulfilled his desires, first in presenting a complaint and secondly in placing it in the hands of a suitable judge. To make it more certain that the Manhattan would get no relief, and to assure default on July 1, thus precipitating the Manhattan into insolvency, Gould arranged a number of other legal side shows. A small bondholder of the two lessor lines asked the trustees of their outstanding bonds to request the court to enjoin the lessee from paying any dividends on the stocks of the lessor properties. The distribution of dividends "utterly destroys the lien of the bondholders . . . and is a gross and inexcusable waste of the mortgaged property," said his lawyer.[21] The request was rejected. The bondholder on his own account then asked the court to enjoin the dividend payments. The request was granted. Regardless of plans made by the Metropolitan security holders to advance funds to the Manhattan to enable it to pay dividends and thus to keep it solvent, Gould made his point, and the company was judicially insolvent.

The fears of the past six weeks were now realities. The Manhattan was a helpless wreck, and the financial journalists were unanimous in their belief that the end had come. They were sure that the Manhattan's lease would be broken. The stock then would "be worth fully the ragman's price for the paper on which it is printed, but hardly more." [22] Gould's organ, the New York *World*, speaking through the "Wall Street Gossip," column, stated flatly that the "Complete wiping out of the Manhattan company and its stock would be a great blessing to Wall Street." [23]

It was generally agreed that the Manhattan was insolvent, and should be placed in receivership. Receivership, however, had a weakness: it left the way open to the recapture of the New York by Field. This was a consummation, which, at all costs, Gould must prevent. The New York was the profitable arm of the Manhattan system; without it the stocks of the other lessor and the lessee would be worth little. Gould therefore arranged the receivership to prevent this evil. A group of nominees from which a receiver would be appointed was presented to Judge Westbrook. All were Gould men, and from this list two were selected. One was John F. Dillon, the attorney for the Union Pacific, who had rendered such valuable service in interpreting the federal law for the benefit of the Western Union, and who was soon to perform some equally clever legal legerdemain for the Manhattan. The other was Hopkins, the operating vice president of the Wabash. Both were loyal followers of Gould; both were on his pay roll; both constantly saw Gould on the Manhattan and other business.

By this receivership, Gould further increased his bargaining position against Field who could not secure repossession of his New York until he traded with the receivers. Field remained in a threatening and fighting mood, but Gould knew his man. Field, like Vanderbilt, fought intermittently. He would blaze forth in a rising flame of anger, but the flame gradually died out and soon became a dead fag-end of ashes and dust.

In order to improve his position Gould deemed it wise, if not indeed essential, to secure a position of commanding influence in the policies of the Metropolitan. If he secured control of this property he might be able through his technique of threats of competitive construction, to bring Field to heel. Gould believed that in control of the Metropolitan he could induce Field to pool his New York with the Metropolitan. To get a controlling influence of the policies of the Metropolitan seemed on the face of things well-nigh impossible. Gould had only a nominal interest, perhaps one hundred shares of the stock. Though Sage had been a speculative leader in the stock, he, too, had relatively few shares. The controlling interest was held by Sylvester H. Kneeland, who had bought heavily at high prices. Kneeland was discouraged. The price of his stock had declined and he was uncertain of the future. He was also appalled that Field might seize control of the New York and operate it in competition with the Metropolitan. Sage, therefore, presented himself to Kneeland in the role of a rescuer. Gould, said Sage, could, if given a chance, "build up the company." [24] These were small words but they were pregnant with possibilities. If the ticket for the Metropolitan board were made up as Gould wanted it, then, assured the bland Sage, "he thought they could handle Mr. Field." [25]

Gould acted well the part of the bashful young lady. He was not interested in the property; in fact, he would not even allow his name to be used on the ticket. It was a beautiful case of self-effacement. The case was so convincing indeed that an independent judge three years later, upon the basis of all available evidence, concluded that Gould was not interested in the Metropolitan board and that he was only induced to join it by the other party under conditions laid down by himself.

Thus early in July the shy Gould and his ticket was elected by a vote of 45,000 shares out of 52,000. Gould and his associates had only a nominal interest in the stock. His associates owned nothing; Kneeland's shares qualified them as board members. It is strange how extensive grants of power are freely surrendered and freely extended. Gould made no agreements; he made no conditions that had any standing whatsoever in the courts. He had a reputation for being a dangerous man. He had succeeded in one ingenious trade after another in taking advantage of every opportunity afforded by a corporate or financial set-up. Despite this record he was entrusted with an extraordinary grant of power. No questions were asked and no assurances were given. Kneeland accepted Gould's terms, placed him and his group on the board and in return received nothing except the assurance made by Sage that he, Gould, would "build up the property."

Gould now had some influence in two of the three properties. Through the receivers, he could control the policies of the Manhattan; through his personally picked board of directors he could influence the policies of the Metropolitan. He had, however, no influence on the affairs of the New York, and Field on behalf of that company insisted that there were only two policies to follow. Either the lease agreement must be carried out and the guaranteed dividend paid, or the New York must repossess its property. In view of the inability of the lessee to carry out the former alternative, Field in mid-July moved to adopt the latter. The Manhattan now owed the New York close to half a million dollars for unpaid interest and dividends. While the New York had always earned the guaranteed dividend, the Metropolitan had earned barely enough to meet its interest.[26] Field therefore asked the receivers for an order directing the return of the New York to its owners. This the judge refused to do and instead issued an order to show cause why the property should not be returned. The order was returnable the next day; though many weeks passed before the order was returned. Upon one pretext or another the date was suspended, giving the patient Gould his opportunity to do battle with the belligerent Field.

In this contest, Field was on strong ground, and certain of success. Gould, as usual, had a financial trick in his bag. Though it was not a new one, Field had long recognized its importance. In May, 1881, shortly after the attorney-general had taken legal action against the Manhattan, he had solicited an opinion from John F. Dillon on the potential claim of the lessee against the lessors for further consideration for its issued stock. The Manhattan stock had been exchanged for a lease of the properties of the New York and the Metropolitan. The original stockholders of the New York, including Field, who had received $6,500,000 of stock had sold out. Did not the Manhattan, therefore, have a claim against the New York for the stock which it had issued and for which it had received nothing? Early in August while Judge Westbrook, on one pretext or another, was postponing the hearing on the show-cause order for the return of the New York, the Manhattan shareholders announced that they would sue Field and other original shareholders on the ground that they were personally responsible for the par value of the stock which they had received. Since Field had fortified himself with John F. Dillon's opinion that he was not responsible,[27] he had no fear, and therefore laughed at the threat. Alas! He did not know what John F. Dillon, egged on by Gould, could do to his own legal judgments. All that he needed was a delicate hint from Gould and forthwith he interpreted the facts to suit another point of view. Gould knew John F. Dillon well; better than did Field. And Gould, when he heard of Field's reactions, informed him that unless he approved a reasonable settlement, there would be "enough lawsuits to last him the rest of his life." [28] A reasonable settlement, of course, was one in which Field surrendered part of the earnings of the New York to help the Metropolitan and the Manhattan.

The fight was now joined. Field would not resign the presidency, he said, until his fight for regaining possession of his property was finished.[29] The hearings before Judge Westbrook on the order for the return of the property were again postponed. On September 30, the ninety days' grace under the lease contract expired, and on that date, the lessor was entitled to recover its property. At twelve o'clock noon, on the twenty-ninth, while Field was making preparations to take possession, another blow was suddenly struck, this time apparently on behalf of the Metropolitan. The Manhattan now proposed to sell receiver's certificates to raise money to pay the lessors. In that event the New York would not immediately repossess its property. The Manhattan, however, would be saved, and the Metropolitan protected from irretrievable loss. The stage setting was beautifully arranged. It was announced that persons interested in the Metropolitan would buy the receiver's certificates. The judge arranged a meeting in the Western Union Building in an office adjacent to Gould's private office. The order was granted and it appeared for a time that the money would be provided to pay dividend and interest arrears and thus hold the elevated system together. The receiver's certificates, the issue of which was approved by the credulous judge, turned out to be a financial absurdity. Instead of being secured by a lien on the properties of the two lessor companies, the certificates were secured only by a charge on the net earnings of the lessee. To make doubly certain that the certificates were valueless, it was provided further that they could not be sold below par. They were "not worth anything," said Field, "I wouldn't give a dollar for as many as a jackass could draw downhill." [30] He was sure, he continued, that he would have his property the next day. He did not get his property the next day. The day was spent before the judge in presenting petitions. The petitions were uniformly pessimistic of the future of the Manhattan.

The proceeding was a farce and apparently accomplished nothing. As a matter of fact, as in other instances in Gould's career, it accomplished everything. Informed security holders were now again unanimous, as they had been in the early summer, in the belief that the position of the Manhattan was hopeless. The company would soon lose the New York. It could raise no money through the sale of receiver's certificates and therefore could not pay its accumulated unpaid obligations. If Field seized the property, the Manhattan would have no equity and its common stock would be valueless. The price of the stock continued to drop and Gould and Sage told Kneeland privately that the Manhattan was at the end of its rope.[31] Although Kneeland and his group did not sell, many others did. When everything seemed blue, when the market was ready to plumb new and unknown depths, the decline suddenly stopped. What happened in December of 1880 to the price of Western Union happened in October, 1881, to the price of Manhattan. Gould played his hand skillfully. Every interested party, friend and foe, united publicly in declaring that the Manhattan had no future. Its disappearance was certain. The newspapers, the stockbrokers, the financial journals, and the responsible trade sources all chimed in. It was a symphony of fatalism. While everybody croaked and sold, Gould said nothing and bought. In the last week of September, he owned no shares of Manhattan. By the eighth of October he appeared as the owner of 20,000 shares, and also transferred 28,000 of his business associate, Connor. Gould therefore controlled 48,000 shares out of a total of 128,000 outstanding.[32] One month later Gould's ticket was elected to the Manhattan board. Again there were the familiar names of Gould, Sage and Dillon, to which were now added the elevated specialists, Field and Garrison. In view of the formidable market problems still remaining before full control could be assured, Connor, the stockbroker expert, was also added.

While Gould now controlled the Manhattan he did not control the New York, the most profitable part of the system. Since business transactions of this kind are normally carried out in secret, the positions of Gould and Field during this period are difficult to trace. Here was a mixture of secrecy and public profession which seems hard to reconcile. A financial paper throws some light on the mystery by its reference to a report that Field aided Gould in exchange for a Gould tip to buy Western Union.[33] Two days after the new Manhattan board was organized, Field was elected to the directorate of the Western Union. After the election he had a friendly interview with Gould, a fact known to newspaper reporters. Field and Gould were still at odds over the Manhattan—Field insisting that his property be returned to him, and Gould that precisely the contrary be done. Field's election to the Western Union board was therefore surprising, and "what were supposed to be two opposing forces in the elevated railroad system, were smoking the pipe of peace around the executive board of the telegraph company." [34]

Although conciliation seemed to pervade the Manhattan atmosphere, the conciliation, it became clear, would be made on Gould's terms. Field would do the giving and Gould the receiving. In some undisclosed way, it appeared that the New York would not be operated as a separate property; rather that it would be included in the existing Manhattan system. Optimism rapidly supplanted pessimism. The price of Manhattan which in late September had dropped to below 18 now jumped rapidly, and Gould's 20,000 shares which had cost him $30 a share were at this time worth $54.

Strange to say, Field was adamant and not disposed to relinquish control. "I shall fight," he insisted on the thirteenth of October, in the midst of developments bright for the fortunes of the Manhattan, "until I regain possession of my property. I am in favor of peace, but sometimes it is necessary to conquer peace." [35] Field was no doubt sincere in his determination to fight out the issue. He did not, however, know his man. He was not the shrewd judge of the strength and weaknesses of his associates and antagonists that was Gould. His mind could not conceive the range of Gould's mind, and it never dawned upon him that Gould could play his game with Judge Westbrook as he had with Judge Gilbert in the Erie days, and with Judge Donohue in the transfer of the Denver Pacific stock from Gould as trustee of a Kansas Pacific mortgage to Gould as the owner of the Kansas Pacific stock.

Gould retained his ability in the art of judicial interference. In the Manhattan negotiations with Field this form of business skill gave him such a vantage point as to make his position almost unassailable. The counsel for the receivers of the Manhattan was General Wager Swayne who did little legal business other than that for the companies controlled by Gould. While the Manhattan was in receivership he saw Gould once or twice weekly on railroad business. Swayne was also in constant touch with Judge Westbrook throughout the weeks of the Manhattan receivership, and consulted him in connection with the prolonged negotiations over the order directing the return to Field of his New York property. Early in September when Judge Westbrook was preparing to hold hearings on Field's motion for reacquisition, he wrote to Swayne suggesting arguments to be presented on behalf of the Manhattan. "Should not," wrote Judge Westbrook, "also the claim be made that the Manhattan Co. has a counter-claim to be sent in the shape of unpaid stock?" [36] And some two weeks later, only a few days before the expiration date of the ninety-day grace period, the judge wrote blandly to Swayne that if the payments on arrears under the lease contract were made on October first, the last date possible, "it would have a most happy effect." He had already informed Hopkins, one of the Manhattan receivers, both by wire and by letter of the necessity of securing this result. "I am willing to go to the very verge of judicial discretion," he wrote to Swayne.[37]

In these negotiations Gould through the receivers' counsel was duly informed of events to come before they were publicly announced. The judge informed both Swayne and John F. Dillon—the other Manhattan counsel—what he intended to do, and what decisions he intended to write. Neither Field for the New York nor the attorney-general for the state, had this way of knowing the mind of the judge. The innocent attorney-general complained, but did nothing. When upon one occasion, he said, the roads made an agreement among themselves as to what kind of order should be entered, they hurried off to the judge but gave no notice to the attorney-general, and after the judge granted the order, they raced back to the attorney-general for his approval. The judge, complained the attorney-general, "graciously" informed him that the order ought to be granted. Did the attorney-general object to the granting of the order? He did not. He seems to have had no iron in his soul and despite his temperamental bleatings made more than six months after the event, he complied with the wishes of the judge and said nothing to the people whom he represented, nor to the representatives of the security holders of the Manhattan.

With Gould thus safely established in the judicial citadel, Field had only a slight chance to regain his property without a prolonged contest. Moreover, he was not prepared to fight against the powerful forces represented by Gould. He, like Vanderbilt, felt more dangers than he saw, and he saw more dangers than existed. It was easy for Gould to use a goblin story to frighten Field, as he had Vanderbilt. Field's goblin at which he had laughed earlier in the summer was the threat to sue him personally for his proportionate part of the six and one-half million dollars of stock of the Manhattan given to him in 1879 in consideration of the lease of the New York.

It was on the twenty-first of October that the long-repeated Gould threat to make Field liable was finally converted into a finished weapon. This was the day that the judge after so many weeks of delay finally denied Field's request to restore his property. The judge's reasoning was almost as astonishing as his decision and conveyed a clear indication that Gould's mind had some part in its making. It was another counteroffensive of the kind which Gould had so extensively used in previous campaigns. The judge declared that the New York had been guilty of adopting those very measures which had been followed by Gould and his little army of subordinates and satellites. The New York, said the judge, having by its deeds encouraged the nonpayment of interest and dividends by the lessee—the Manhattan Company—ought to be estopped from setting up this very nonpayment as a ground for forfeiture of the lease. Further, the judge intimated that the lessee might have a claim against the lessors for the full payment of the $13,000,000 of stock. Some months before John F. Dillon had advised Field that such a claim was untenable. Now in his capacity as receiver of the Manhattan and legal adviser to Gould, he performed a neat somersault and asked for permission to sue for the recovery of $6,500,000 from each lessor. The application was promptly granted.[38]

To Field, the decision of the judge refusing to return the New York "was a surprise and a disappointment." [39] The probable claim of the Manhattan shareholders (now primarily Gould) had the intended effect. It made Field surrender to Gould. Field, without waiting to consider the possible alternative, rushed to his new and gracious friend, and proposed a settlement. Gould of course was happy to please. In twenty-four hours Field proposed, and Gould disposed.

There was no trouble about the Metropolitan. Even though

Gould and his group owned relatively few shares, they still controlled the board. The consent of that company through the board was, therefore, easily obtained. Though the settlement called for payment in full of the interest on arrears of the bonds of both lessors, the quarterly dividends on the guaranteed stock for the six months ending October 1 were not to be paid. In a new lease the New York would get a guaranteed dividend of 6 per cent and the Metropolitan 4 per cent, payable only if earned by its own lines. The Manhattan stock would also get 4 per cent. Any surplus earnings would be divided equally between the three companies.

Although the Manhattan was still in receivership and, according to the attorney-general, insolvent, the stock market refused to accept the logic of these facts. In three weeks the price of the stock advanced more than 200 per cent. The market indeed told the truth. The attorney-general soon surrendered to Gould. "The Attorney-General has informed us," blandly stated Gould to a newspaper reporter, "that he would not stand in the way of our project—our settlement. The property of the Manhattan Company was given back to the company by the receivers with his declared consent." [40] This was the public statement made by Gould; but Gould, through Judge Westbrook, had carefully arranged the setting and the attorney-general innocently enough played his part as planned. The termination of the receivership was quietly arranged before the judge (it took just three days), and the judge sent the order over to the attorney-general for his signature. So, complained the latter some months later, there was, therefore, "nothing left for me . . . except to submit to what seems to have been disposed of substantially in my absence." [41] Gould, of course, did the disposing.

Although Field was a peacemaker, and willing to share with the Manhattan the profits of the New York, the security holders of the Metropolitan were not so ready to forgive and forget. They did not want to be blessed as peacemakers. Kneeland, unlike Field, did not propose to surrender. He was enough of a financial man of affairs to understand that under the new agreement the Metropolitan would probably get nothing. In charge of its policies, the Gould-controlled directorate could adjust revenues and expenses in such a way as to leave no profit to the shareholder.

Kneeland resorted to the courts and thus opened another chapter in the history of the prolonged litigation which characterized the progress of Gould's effort to acquire the mastery of the city's rapid-transit facilities. Kneeland sued to upset the agreement: it was a violation of the 1879 lease and represented an organic change in the corporate structure of the company—a change of such significance that it could be made only with the approval of the shareholders. Gould immediately took countermeasures. He divided the stocks of the lessor companies into two classes—assented and nonassented. The stockholders of each of the lessors would exchange their certificates for new stock with the reduced rate of payment. The stock was called "assented" stock. Gould then proposed to list the assented stock on the New York Stock Exchange; and to make *only* the assented stock good for delivery on that exchange. Furthermore both of the lessor companies would pay no dividends on the other class—on the stock which had not "assented." This was an ingenious but highhanded proposal which destroyed the market value of the nonassented stock. After considerable hesitation, the governing committee of the Stock Exchange refused to list the new certificates.

Gould with the help of his two major allies, Sage and Dillon, and of his newly discovered ally, Field, replied with a countersqueeze. He decided to negotiate with the Stock Exchange as he had with so many railroads. He would issue threats; if the Stock Exchange would not agree to his request, he would organize a competitor. He announced that he would build a new structure, establish a new trust company and a new bank, and would go into the business of managing a competitive stock exchange. The threat was not taken seriously. Gould, as usual, said little while Field, as usual, was choleric. He was furious with the Stock Exchange and he used violent words in denouncing its action in refusing to list the stamped certificates. "It was," he asserted in referring to its action, "the greatest outrage ever perpetrated. . . ."[42] This temperamental outburst must have made Field feel better. Gould, however, remained cautious and cagey, and it was not long before he recognized that he had gone too far and that he had better make an arrangement more agreeable to Kneeland. Accordingly the three puppet boards of directors approved a new plan providing for the organization of a new company. Kneeland resorted to court action to invalidate the proposal. The judge, however, decided that the Metropolitan board had acted in "good faith." [43] The new agreement was therefore valid.

Kneeland, although defeated, fought on. The new chapter in the elevated litigation had indeed only begun. Kneeland thought that he could take a page out of Gould's book of tricks. If the Manhattan charter had been considered illegal by one attorney-general in May, 1881, Kneeland believed it might be considered illegal by another in January, 1882. He therefore requested the new attorney-general to enter suit for the dissolution of its charter. Gould's counsel who had worked so assiduously in May, 1881, to establish the illegality of the company's charter, worked with equal diligence in January, 1882, to establish its legality. Out trotted the innocent holder-widow and the orphan-vested rights argument. The Manhattan company, it was declared, had 486 stockholders, every one of whom had become such since May, 1879, when the original lease was consummated.[44] Although it is not clear how many stockholders the Manhattan Elevated had in May of 1881, it is probable that there were more than 486. These stockholders, however, had followed the advice of Field and Tilden, and were therefore entitled to no organized vocal protection before the law. Most of the 486 stockholders eight months later had bought their securities, under the leadership of Gould and Sage, and they were properly represented.

The new shepherds turned out to be more successful than the old. Kneeland's request to the attorney-general to bring suit to annul the Manhattan charter was turned down. Kneeland, again defeated, decided to await the annual meeting of the Metropolitan's shareholders. At that time he could cast his ballots and the ballots entrusted to him by the majority of the company's shareholders in favor of the elimination of the existing Gould-controlled board. The meeting was scheduled for the first week in July. Since almost all of the Metropolitan's stockholders had refused to exchange their stock for the stock of the new company, they were receiving no return on their investment, but since they held a controlling interest, they were certain they could recapture control in July.

In acting on this hypothesis, they recognized their inability to appreciate the limitless resourcefulness of Gould. They awaited patiently a fateful June day, but Gould was awaiting a fateful July day. Early in June the Metropolitan board met and adopted a resolution changing the date of electing new directors to the date of the Manhattan election, which was the second Wednesday in November. The new Metropolitan board, therefore, could not be elected until that time. The Gould stroke came as a surprise. It was furthermore resolved that the Metropolitan shareholders could not vote until they were registered on the books and this they could not do unless they exchanged their old for new certificates.

Kneeland again refused to surrender and the fight was renewed before the attorney-general. Kneeland won the first round of the battle. After considering the matter for some weeks, the attorney-general agreed to bring action to remove Gould and his associates from the Metropolitan board.

There was little time to lose. The meeting of the Metropolitan board was scheduled for November 8, and in order to reinstate the Metropolitan shareholders in their position of power and responsibility, it was necessary to secure legal action before that time. The suit, however, was not begun until the fourth day of November.[45] The temporary injunction was issued and the election proceeded in accordance with the wishes of the electorate. The true ownership was thus revealed. Of 65,000 shares outstanding, a little over 5,000 were cast for the Gould ticket. "We have lost the election," declared Sage. . . . "There will be more litigation or a compromise."[46]

There was now the prospect of open competition between the two rapid-transit lines. Ordinary businessmen would probably have engaged in a competitive battle. Perhaps the standard of service might have rapidly increased; perhaps one of the contestants might have early introduced electric power to supplant steam power; perhaps there might even have been a break in passenger fares. Both Kneeland and Gould, however, were heavily involved financially in one or another of the companies, and both were engaged in a struggle to acquire a larger share of an existing earning power.

There was therefore no war of rates, but there was a war of negotiation and litigation. Gould asked Judge Donohue to issue an injunction to restrain the new Metropolitan board from issuing any certificates with a 10 per cent guarantee by the Manhattan. This was the original guarantee which the Manhattan had made on the stocks of both the lessor companies in May, 1879. The judge, as usual, was gracious to Gould and issued a preliminary injunction. Three weeks later he continued the injunction.[47]

Meanwhile negotiations proceeded in an effort to reach an agreement. It was understood that the Metropolitan as an independent competitor would serve the financial interests of neither side. Field was elected to handle the discussions. Field, however, was not a good negotiator. He had none of the patience and tact with which Gould carried on his dealings, nor did he know when to delay and when not to delay; when to remain silent and when not to remain silent. Field's plans for settlement were repeatedly rejected by Kneeland, and he finally declared that he was disgusted and would bargain no more. For more than a year the group led by Gould and Kneeland were unable to accomplish any results and in fact were unable to compel the other to enter into negotiations.

The financial status of the Manhattan, according to the books of account as they were published under Gould's supervision, did not appear to be particularly good. The fixed charges were earned only by a fair margin. It appeared by the summer of 1882 that the company, after meeting all expenses including depreciation, was not far from insolvency. An acute critic questioned, after an elaborate analysis of the company's revenue and expenses, whether any sane person could claim that the Manhattan was worth anything.[48] A heavy burden against the company arose from its accumulated unpaid taxes (an accumulation which was partly responsible for its insolvency in the summer of 1881). Gould, however, succeeded in inducing the state legislature to propose a compromise with the company. The bill was condemned by the Mayor and Comptroller of New York City, who pointed out that the bill incorporating the compromise would enable the company to cancel its obligations by paying about 50 per cent less than any other railroad. "The bill," declared the city officials flatly, "is legislative robbery. It deprives the city of half a million of money now due to it, puts a premium on defiance of the law, and compels every citizen to contribute toward the payment of the taxes of the elevated railroad companies for 1880 and 1881." [49] A legislative compromise was nevertheless arranged and the accumulated burden of taxation upon the elevated properties was eased.

During this period of judicial uncertainty which lasted until April of 1884 both parties made no move. The fruitless effort of Field to reach a negotiated compromise was not followed by any important moves of Gould, and it was not until late in April of 1884 that the court of highest jurisdiction finally handed down its decision. For the first time in the history of Gould's career, the court condemned his policy of not subjecting corporate actions for stockholders' approval. By the purchase of proxies, by the sudden closing of transfer books, by secret actions unknown to creditors and stockholders, Gould had committed shareholders to important lines of policy without consulting them. Federal and state judges had repeatedly handed down decisions judicially denouncing certain phases of his policies, but at no time had they flatly declared an agreement illegal because the stockholders had not been asked to approve it. In this decision the court stated that the board had no power to nullify a lease without the approval of the shareholders, and that even though there was no fraud involved, the agreement was voidable because of the interlocking directorate between the three companies. Gould usually was careful with the help of able counsel to set up financial combinations which although objectionable to security holders were not tainted with fraud. This case was no exception. The court declared however that there was objection to the manner in which things were done; the actions complained of represented attempts "to use the form of law to coerce the stockholders of the lessor companies into ratifying the merger agreement." [50]

The agreement by which the Manhattan leased the Metropolitan was pronounced invalid. The lease agreement of October, 1881, was judicially declared a radical change in the terms of the lease, and the complaining lessor company, the Metropolitan, was therefore entitled to a judgment relieving all the parties from the terms of that agreement.

Kneeland, after a two-and-a-half-year struggle, had won a judicial victory over the Gould-Sage-Field combination. A victory in the courts was not, however, a victory in business. Kneeland was soon to learn of the resourcefulness of his wily opponent. The decision was not to be made in the courts but in the stock market. Gould's first counterattack was a skillful bit of corporate financial jugglery. The Manhattan, still in control of the New York, was financially sound because the New York was sound. The Manhattan was entitled to the surplus earnings of the New York after the payment of the dividends on the latter's preferred. Gould now proposed that the Manhattan surrender the property of the New York, and the latter to surrender its claims against the Manhattan. In order to make this exchange attractive to the shareholders of the Manhattan, the New York agreed to give to that company's stockholders its own 6 per cent junior stock. After the distribution of a 6 per cent dividend on the New York stock by the stockholders of the Manhattan, the excess earnings would be divided pro rata among the stockholders of both companies. It was a truly ingenious device. The assets of the Manhattan which made the stock of that company so attractive to Kneeland and his associates was based upon the earning capacity of the New York whose property was no longer in the hands of the Manhattan. Although the Manhattan lost the earnings from the New York, the Manhattan stockholders did not lose those earnings. The Manhattan stockholders gained, and the Metropolitan stockholders lost.

The agreement between the Manhattan and the New York was made possible only through concessions made by Field, president and major stockholder of the New York, who had so indignantly opposed the previous moves of Gould. Since October of 1881, when the lease of 1879 was abrogated and the new merger agreement approved, he had reversed himself and co-operated with Gould. Despite the superior earnings of the New York over the Metropolitan, he had made repeated concessions on behalf of the stockholders of the latter.

In trying to force Kneeland to a decision, Gould resorted to other steps. He recognized that his arch-opponent was engaged in heavy speculative activities, and he therefore endeavored to force his hand by depressing the price of those securities in which he was interested, particularly the stock of the Metropolitan. The stock was therefore raided, and according to one authoritative source, every Gould broker early in 1884, after the adverse decision in the elevated railway case, was advised to sell short in order to make a profit in thirty days.[51]

Gould meanwhile opened negotiations with Kneeland. He was still anxious to maintain a monopoly of the city's rapid-transit facilities. Gould at this time was in a critical financial position and his whole fortune was at stake in the panic markets of April and May of 1884. In these anxious days when every day, indeed almost every hour, depressed the value of his holdings and impaired the margin of his collateral loans, he was unable personally to give the necessary time to negotiate with Kneeland. The Manhattan board had appointed Field and himself to reach an agreement with Kneeland, but Gould authorized Field to act for him. Field proposed that the Metropolitan could have its lines returned, or have them leased back to the Manhattan. If Kneeland favored a lease, the Manhattan would pay the earnings of the Metropolitan to the stockholders of that company up to 8 per cent on the latter's stock, with the balance to go to the Manhattan.[52]

For the next six weeks nothing was accomplished, and it appeared that further court action would be necessary in order to stabilize the relationships between the two roads. By the end of June, however, a final settlement was surprisingly reached. It was Gould who created the conditions essential to a final settlement. The sharp May break had embarrassed Kneeland and many of his followers, and they were therefore forced to sell part of their Metropolitan holdings.

A number of new personalities came into the Metropolitan picture. One was a stockbroker, William K. Souter, who had correctly interpreted the downward swing in the security markets which developed in the summer of 1881. He had long been bearish on Missouri Pacific, and had openly expressed his opinion for many months prior to the break in May, 1884, that the Gould stocks were too high. Another personality was H. O. Armour, brother of the Chicago meat packer, and a man who had established himself in the New York financial community.

These two men, together with an active trader who frequently represented Gould in stock transactions, John D. Clayback, were appointed a committee of the Metropolitan board to reach an understanding with the other two companies for a union of interests. Again Field on behalf of the New York made the necessary concessions. In this last and successful proposal, a single class of stock was created. Of a total issue of twenty-six millions of the new Manhattan stock, each stockholder of the old Manhattan received approximately 85 per cent of his holdings in new stock; of the Metropolitan 110 per cent, and of the New York 120 per cent. The following table shows the distribution:

DISTRIBUTION OF STOCK OF THE MANHATTAN ELEVATED AMONG THE SHAREHOLDERS OF THE THREE COMPANIES

Name of Company	Old Capitalization	New Capitalization
Manhattan Elevated	$13,000,000	$11,000,000
Metropolitan Elevated	6,500,000	7,150,000
New York Elevated	6,500,000	7,800,000

Though the earnings of the New York substantially exceeded those of the Metropolitan, it received only a slight preference in the distribution of the new stock. The reasons prompting Field to make this concession are not clear. Field himself, when asked to express an opinion about the plan, remarked, "I am the victim, led to the slaughter, as usual." [53]

The directors of the three companies ratified the proposal and, except for the approval of the shareholders, which was soon forthcoming, the three-year contest was at an end. Gould had succeeded through a series of court actions in acquiring control of a holding company which had been condemned as a financial derelict. It was overcapitalized. It could neither pay its taxes nor its fixed charges. The owners of the prosperous lessor company insisted that its properties be returned. The holding company was placed in receivership and there seemed to be no hope for it. The price of the stock sank to record low levels. Gould at that very time, however, bought it in wholesale quantities. Threatening judicial action, he enlisted the support of his former antagonist who controlled the most profitable part of the elevated system to aid him in acquiring a monopoly of the city's rapid-transit system. For another two and a half years his financial mastery was challenged in the courts. Although he lost the court battle, he won the financial battle. At the very moment when he was deeply involved, when his solvency was questioned, and when he appeared to be on the brink of financial disaster, he succeeded in eliminating all opposition.

He was now master of the rapid-transit lines of New York

City. It was only necessary for him to comply with the forms of the law, and this he was always able to do. It was necessary that he respect the declarations of the court made in 1884 invalidating the 1881 lease agreements. The court had condemned the interlocking directorates and it was therefore essential to eliminate this condition. Before the agreement was submitted to the stockholders for approval accordingly the board of the New York resigned. The new board consisted of confidential representatives of the old board. Of the thirteen members of the new board, six were made stockholders less than three weeks before they became directors. To them was transferred exactly two hundred shares in all, varying from ten to fifty shares each. On August 1, 1884, the New York stockholders' meeting was held. Within fifteen minutes the polls were opened, the election held, and the polls closed. Within a few minutes after this, the new noninterlocking board held a meeting, elected officers and ratified the agreement. Two weeks after the new "independent" board had made necessary ratifications, it resigned. The new board represented the interests of the Manhattan.[54]

Gould's position was now financially and judicially unassailable. His patience and resourcefulness had proved adequate to solve a complex task. He had employed methods condemned in the public press and in financial circles, and his use of the forms of the law to carry out his policy had involved a judge and an attorney-general. Their actions were exhaustively reviewed by a legislative committee. No collusion and fraud were found, but only incompetence and credulousness. Gould had displayed in these negotiations a mastery of financial and trading technique and a knowledge of relations between the ill-formed corporation law of the day and corporate finance which have had few parallels in American financial life. In the control of the policies of the Manhattan, he shared his power only with Field who was the only large stockholder whose views he had to entertain seriously. Field however was no match for Gould in the financial and trading world. Field after the final settlement in the summer of 1884 waxed enthusiastic over the Manhattan's future, switching from indigo pessimism to rainbow enthusiasm. While Gould was liquidating his speculative commitments in the 1884 and 1885 markets, Field was becoming actively engaged in the speculative commodity and security markets. He continued to increase his holdings in Manhattan, and bought heavily on margin account. In the fall of 1886, after the stock had risen from about $40 to $175 a share, he boasted openly that the Manhattan's franchise alone was worth $50,000,000 and that this, apart from any other property of the company, was worth about $200 a share.[55] He also became an active speculator in the commodity markets and it was the collapse of these markets in the spring of 1887 that led to his downfall.

Field's financial position in the spring of 1887 was made even more critical by the speculative activities of his elder son, Edward M. Field, through whose brokerage firm the elder Field tried to corner the market in the Manhattan stock. Field apparently had some desire to emulate the speculative career of Gould. Gould having retired from speculative activities in December of 1885, Field, it seems, had ambitions to succeed him. He did not, however, have Gould's ingenuity and resourcefulness. When Gould was financially cornered he found ways of extricating himself; usually acting decisively before a financial crisis all but overwhelmed him. He left himself in a vulnerable position in the summer of 1884, it is true, but his resourcefulness combined with the stupidity of his trading opponents enabled him by a narrow margin to escape disaster.

Field had none of this ability. The break of the wheat corner in the spring of 1887 almost ruined him. Although his losses cannot be ascertained, it was certain that he stood in need of cash to settle his obligations. He had at the same time approximately 75,000 shares of Manhattan. Had he been able to liquidate at the current price of $175 a share his problem would have been solved. He was no more able to do this, however, than was Gould in the winter of 1878–79 with his Union Pacific. While Gould found a market for most of his Union Pacific, Field did not find a market for his Manhattan.

What occurred between Field and Gould will never be known. Field apparently approached Gould for financial help. Gould, not being in the speculative markets and having no stocks on margin, was reported to have had about $6,000,000 in the bank.[56] June 24, 1887, was a tragic day for Field. That day's market fluctuations were among the most remarkable in stock-market history.

Commercial conditions were improving, stimulated by a large crop and an extensive foreign demand. Suddenly and with no warning the stock market on that day broke into a wild retreat. In a matter of minutes the price of Manhattan in the morning dropped 25 per cent, Missouri Pacific 12 per cent, and Western Union almost 10 per cent. Money rates suddenly rose to 25 per cent. In the afternoon the market reversed itself. What appeared to be a panic for those who held stocks turned out to be a panic for those who sold stocks.

One is tempted to conclude, as have so many commentators in secondary sources in after years, that Gould led Field into a speculative trap and then cornered and smashed him. Perhaps that may be the fact. On the basis of evidence available, however, that conclusion cannot be substantiated. A bitter and most consistent daily newspaper critic of Gould maintained precisely the opposite. The writer stated that Gould only "pricked the bubble"; and he pricked it in such a way that a crash which would have ruined one or more financial institutions was averted.[57] Field personally denied in a statement to a newspaper reporter the accuracy of all the stories that necessity had forced him to sell.[58]

Whatever the truth, whether Gould planned Field's debacle, or whether he was a victim of Field's financial blunder—it is the judgment of the writer that the latter hypothesis represents more nearly the truth, it remains true nevertheless that Gould now controlled the Manhattan. Before the end of June, Field sold his remaining 25,000 shares of Manhattan to Gould; and in possession of this large block of Manhattan stock Gould feared no rival.

Gould had become the undisputed master of an enterprise which had a monopoly of the rapid-transit facilities in the largest city of the country, and he never surrendered its control. Its earning power increased as the demand for transit services expanded. Its financial position was strengthened; its credit was enhanced; strong bankers of the day bid for the opportunity to purchase its securities and conservative investors bid for the opportunity to invest in its bonds. The stock was placed on a dividend basis, and the property proved to be, together with the Western Union and Missouri Pacific, the basis of Gould's business empire in his lifetime and one of the prime pillars of his estate after his death.

NOTES FOR CHAPTER XV

1. Known hereafter as the Manhattan.
2. Known hereafter as the New York.
3. Known hereafter as the Metropolitan.
4. *Chron.*, Jan. 18, 1879.
5. State of New York, Railroad Investigation, 1879, Vol. V, 134-5.
6. New York *Tribune*, Feb. 5, 1880.
7. Field, in ibid., March 25, 1880, said he had none of the Manhattan stock. Ibid. of April 3, 1880, said he formerly owned 13,000 shares.
8. London *Railway News*, Sept. 6, 1884, 391.
9. *Wall Street News*, Oct. 9, 1880.
10. *Bradstreet*, April 16, 1881, 232.
11. New York *Times*, April 16, 1881.
12. New York *Tribune*, May 19, 1881.
13. New York *Herald*, May 19, 1881.
14. *Bradstreet*, May 21, 1881, 312.
15. Ibid.
16. Ibid., June 18, 1881, 376.
17. Ibid., June 25, 1881, 392.
18. New York *Herald*, July 9, 1881.
19. New York *Tribune*, May 7, 1882.
20. This statement was made by the New York *Times*, Jan. 21, 1882.
21. Ibid., May 19, 1881.
22. Phila. *North American*, July 9, 1881.
23. New York *World*, July 6, 1881.
24. New York *Tribune*, Dec. 4, 1883.
25. Ibid.
26. New York *Times*, July 26, 1881.
27. Ibid., Dec. 30, 1881.
28. New York *Tribune*, Aug. 13, 1881.
29. *Chron.*, Sept. 10, 1881, 282.
30. New York *Tribune*, Sept. 29, 1881.
31. Ibid., May 6, 1882.
32. New York *Times*, Oct. 9, 1881.
33. *Wall Street News*, Oct. 22, 1881.
34. New York *Tribune*, Oct. 14, 1881.
35. Ibid., Oct. 14, 1881.
36. Ibid., May 7, 1882.
37. Ibid.
38. Ibid., Oct. 22, 1881.
39. This was the language used by Field before the legislative investigating committee inquiring into the actions of Attorney-General Ward, and Judge Westbrook. See ibid., May 9, 1882.
40. New York *Times*, Oct. 28, 1881.
41. New York *Tribune*, May 7, 1882.
42. Ibid., Nov. 23, 1881.
43. *Chron.*, Dec. 24, 1881, 717.
44. Ibid., Jan. 21, 1882, 86.
45. The complaint before the court is an interesting document and is found in full in New York *Herald*, Nov. 5, 1882.
46. Ibid., Nov. 9, 1882.
47. A note on the order of Judge Donohue continuing the injunction is found in *Chron.*, Dec. 9, 1882, 658.
48. New York *Times*, July 23, 1882.
49. New York *Tribune*, June 1, 1882.

50. Ibid., April 16, 1884.
51. *Bradstreet*, May 10, 1884, 296.
52. This is the account of the negotiations between Field and Kneeland, as reported by Field in a statement to a newspaperman. New York *Tribune*, May 21, 1884.
53. New York *Tribune*, June 6, 1884.
54. This account of Gould's compliance with the forms of law is based upon the New York *World*, May 31, 1885.
55. New York *Times*, Oct. 24, 1886.
56. This is the estimate of Phila. *Press*, Sept. 1, 1887.
57. New York *Times*, June 17, 1892.
58. New York *Tribune*, June 29, 1887. In addition to the current press reports for an account of this incident, see also "Recent Movements of the Stock Market," by Cuthbert Mills, in *North American Review*, Vol. 146, Jan. 1888, 51.

CHAPTER XVI

Gould Creates Empire—East

In 1881 Gould reached the height of his business career. He dominated the policies of corporations which controlled more railroad mileage than any other single person or group of persons. By the sale of a block of Union Pacific in February of 1879 he had revolutionized his position. At one stroke he paid his heavy trading losses and acquired a substantial cash balance. How he used these funds in 1879 to acquire the Wabash and the Kansas Pacific and to reacquire dominant control of the Union Pacific has already been described. In the following year at small cost he secured control of the southwestern railroads, and in 1881 he utilized his railroad control to conquer the Western Union. Later in the same year, he climaxed this brilliant three-year period with his mastery of the Manhattan Elevated.

Early in 1879 the country was in the last stages of a prolonged depression. Even though business was moving forward, the speculative and investment public was not yet ready to buy securities. Gould, however, was and his initial purchases at the low prices of the spring of 1879 laid the basis for his rapid rise to power.

The railroad system under his influence was truly awe-inspiring. In the Far West in 1881 he was the policy-maker (although at that time he held little of the stock) of the Union Pacific—the country's premier transcontinental carrier. Together with his associates he held also the controlling influence in the stock of the leading water competitor of the overland railroads—the Pacific Mail. At its eastern terminus on the southern flank, the enlarged Union Pacific connected at Kansas City with two other Gould-controlled lines to St. Louis, the Missouri Pacific and the Wabash. On the face of things he was in a position to divert the Union Pacific's eastbound traffic to these two roads. His southwestern system furthermore controlled almost all the through routes from the Rio Grande to St. Louis.

In each acquisition Gould secured new allies who believed in him and looked to him for financial help. In every case they secured some help—initially. He was aggressive here, he compromised there. Whether he fought or compromised he exerted a permanent influence on the American railroad structure. He built new lines, initiated and stimulated forces leading to the building of additional lines by other roads, established through routes, and promoted alliances some of which have lasted until the present day. Out of his incessant activities and the development of complex adverse interests, there grew consolidations, contracts and corporate re-groupings that changed the face of American railroad and business life.

The railroad system which Gould built up in 1881 was unique. Nothing like it had ever existed before and nothing like it has ever appeared since. This was not a one-man domination such as in the late sixties and early seventies Cornelius Vanderbilt had erected. Vanderbilt took an active managerial interest in these properties and assumed responsibility for their operation. Gould from 1874 to 1879, it is true, followed a like policy with regard to the Union Pacific. He had, however, an urge for expansion and a love for securities operations which could not be satisfied by his control of a given corporation, no matter how complete that control was. If he discovered that negotiations with competitors could not be consummated, if he could not secure business or corporate advantages by direct negotiation, he almost instinctively thought of the stock market as an aid.

By 1879, however, he recognized that the exclusive control over a given property handicapped his trading operations. He could not use his capital represented by the stock to facilitate his market moves and to settle his trading accounts, and he therefore sought for close allies. These allies were carefully selected for definite purposes. The two most important and those who remained with him until the end were Sage and Dillon. Sage was an experienced veteran market operator. The conversion of the Atlantic & Pacific Telegraph speculation from a prospective loss into a handsome profit made Sage a hero worshiper of Gould. From that day on his loyalty to Gould was never disturbed. Dillon was a railroad builder, and served as president of the Union Pacific during the Gould regime from 1874 to 1884.

This combination of Gould, Sage, and Dillon, occasionally designated as the Wall Street trinity, was a mark of Gould triumph in his years of expansion. Sage was the market trader, Dillon the corporate manager, and Gould the policy-maker. If corporate acquisition was preceded by a stock-market campaign involving the intricacies of corporate relationship and of stock-market technique, Sage's work was essential. His was the responsibility of examining the technical position of a stock, and of its distribution among traders and investors, of determining the floating supply, and of discovering the brokers. If the leading stockholders in an enterprise sought after by Gould were members of the stock-trading fraternity, Sage aided in the negotiation. So it was that Sage played the leading role in delivering the Metropolitan directorate to Gould, even though the latter owned none of the shares.

In addition to Sage and Dillon, Gould added to the board of each new corporation the names of others who served some temporary, although important purpose, and they remained just so long as they served that purpose. When disagreement developed they were dropped. Sometimes the same person appeared in a number of Gould enterprises because in each he could accomplish that which was needed. Field and Joy from time to time made many valuable contributions to Gould's career. Other important characters were added from time to time. There was Connor, the loyal stockbroker who stood unflinchingly behind him in the dark days in the early summer of 1884. Connor greatly admired Gould, and even after their business friendship clouded, his personal loyalty never wavered. An even more brilliant trader associated with Gould for a while was Woerishoffer, a Gould opponent in the Kansas Pacific reorganization. Thereafter Gould permitted Woerishoffer's brokerage house to serve as a fiscal agent for a number of Gould's construction companies. Woerishoffer also took an active interest in the sale of the Denver's securities, but in these transactions he and Gould broke relations and they finally became foes. In the break of May, 1884, it was Woerishoffer who led the bear contingent and inflicted heavy trading losses on Gould, only to fall victim to Gould's superior strategic conceptions. Hopkins, another ally, remained for many years the able executive of the Wabash. Sloan, long a stormy petrel in eastern railroad affairs, was another able associate. He fitted in with Gould's plan to extend the Lackawanna to Buffalo and worked closely with him in rate-cutting tactics in eastern territory.

These business partners were more than fellow directors or business managers and operators. They were men of capital and of influence. Some who served on the Gould boards, like the presidents of the eastern trunk lines, Huntington of the Southern Pacific, and bankers like Morgan and Taylor, were not his associates. They collaborated because at that time his interests were theirs. Morgan and Taylor, for example, appeared on the Western Union board because they were large stockholders. The former appeared on the New York Central board with a Gould associate—Humphreys of the Wabash—because he (Morgan) was the banker of both the New York Central system and of Vanderbilt, the largest owner of the New York Central stock.

In explaining Gould's successes in the early eighties, mention must also be made of his press organs. One was the New York *World*, which he bought from (T. A.) Scott, a purchase which Gould tried valiantly to make appear as unimportant. "It was really a mere accident," he insisted.[1] Be that as it may, it was nevertheless true that he obtained much free publicity through the paper, and that many transactions were facilitated by its news and editorial columns. For some time, through a loan to its publisher secured by the controlling stock, he had a voice in another New York paper: the *Tribune*.[2] Furthermore, one of his helpful associates in the early eighties, Field, owned still another New York paper—the *Express*—which he bought at a "fabulous" price,[3] and which he later united with the *Mail*.

Gould's associates, those who worked with him as managers of his properties, as advisers, financial aids, stock-market operators and traders, were usually stockholders. They served as directors primarily because of their ownership in the property. Some of them were paid executives such as Hopkins of the Wabash and (John F.) Dillon and General Wager Swayne, counsel of the Union Pacific. Dillon resigned a judgeship in the West to come East to take a law professorship at Columbia University, but the real inducement was said to be the position of counsel to Gould's concerns at an annual salary of $10,000.[4] Most of his associates, however, Field, Humphreys, Sage, Sloan, Marquand, and Hopkins, helped Gould carry the burden of corporate ownership, thus enabling him to spread his funds over many properties and yet retain control.

The greater part of his railroad empire, even at the peak of his influence in 1881, was kept together by minority holdings, and occasionally by no holdings at all. Only in three major properties did Gould act as a proprietor interested permanently in the welfare of its business. He never relinquished his stock control of the Missouri Pacific, the Western Union, and the Manhattan. Of these, only the Missouri Pacific was a part of his railroad net. This road became in the spring of 1881 the parent of his southwestern railroad group. He had decided even at this early period to subordinate the interests of the other properties to those of the Missouri Pacific; his interest in the road therefore resulted in a network of adverse influences that crossed and recrossed his railroad empire.

It was difficult for a student of current affairs in 1880 and 1881 to observe the corporate tendencies in Gould's system. Gould moved rapidly from one situation to another. Scarcely a week passed, remarked a contemporary observer, that he did not accomplish something. Acquisition was piled upon acquisition, and rate wars, negotiations and competitive transactions followed each other in rapid succession. Hardly was one sensational development completed, than another was thrown into the hopper of current market news.

Underneath these events numerous adverse interests crisscrossed the corporate structure. In many sections of his empire one set of influences worked in one direction for one company and worked in another direction for another. A policy that favored one group distressed another. The clearest conflict arose between the two corporations in the transcontinental route from Ogden to the Great Lakes at Toledo and Detroit. From the flow of traffic over the Union Pacific-Wabash route, maximum results had been anticipated. This route was important to the Wabash because of the large flow of business expected from the Union Pacific at Omaha.[5] If the lines acquired by the Wabash, many of which had little local traffic, were to be made productive, the through traffic had to be increased.

The through business, however, was subject to sharp competition. To competitive points the traffic was frequently hauled at low rates. If all traffic were carried on the basis of such rates, many of the strongest roads would find themselves in financial difficulties. Quaint theories of railroad costs were evolved to justify the transportation of through traffic at competitive rates; rates which were far below those charged on noncompetitive traffic. These theories survive to the present day. The through traffic, it was argued, had to be carried by somebody. If a particular road did not carry it, another would. The road refusing to carry the business at low rates would then have no revenue instead of a little revenue.

Since the through traffic did not, however, produce revenue in accordance with expectations, the value of local business came to be more appreciated. The local traffic in the middle seventies, for example, probably saved the Central Pacific and Huntington from financial disaster. The increase in the local business of the Union Pacific in 1874 and 1875 increased the earnings of the road and made Gould's stock commitment good. Local traffic in southern and western Pennsylvania aided the Pennsylvania Railroad in overcoming the losses occasioned by the high-priced leases of the late sixties and the early seventies while in the late eighties about 90 per cent of its business was local.[6]

Many of the newly acquired Wabash lines had little profitable local traffic, and they therefore looked forward to a large increase in through business to come largely from the Union Pacific at Omaha. Since the latter and the Wabash were under common influence through the Gould holdings it was reasonable to look forward to such results. Gould in fact did in the early stages of the formation of the route divert much of the Union Pacific traffic.[7]

The diversion could not, however, long continue. If relationships were closely examined, these hopes for large diversion could not bear analysis. The Union Pacific was a westbound as well as an eastbound carrier. Its traffic was preponderantly eastbound. The road, therefore, had a large flow of westbound empty cars. In order to fill those cars, it was necessary to secure business from its eastern connections. To secure traffic westbound from its connections at Omaha, it had to give them eastbound traffic. So long as there was no transcontinental competition the consideration was unimportant. With the completion of the Atchison and the Burlington systems to a connection with the Denver this principle could not be overlooked. Little of the Wabash traffic moved west. The Iowa Pool roads, on the other hand, carried a large volume of westbound business. At Chicago the Lake Shore, Pennsylvania, and Baltimore & Ohio brought a heavy tonnage of such business. If the Union Pacific delivered its eastbound traffic to the Wabash, then the Chicago-Omaha lines would deliver the traffic received at Chicago to its competitors. By the summer of 1882 both the Atchison and the Burlington had completed routes competitive with the Union Pacific over which, via connections, they were able to carry traffic between the Missouri Valley and the Pacific coast.

The Wabash was destined to receive relatively little eastbound transcontinental business. The Missouri Pacific system in order to aid the Wabash urged its shippers to move business by that road. Billing arrangements to facilitate the movement of traffic from Dallas to Chicago over the Missouri Pacific-Wabash route, for example, were uncovered by the Burlington in the fall of 1882. This policy having never been disclosed, the latter's traffic official wrote frigidly to the Missouri Pacific, "I presume these things are in accordance with the policy of your company." [8] To avoid retaliation by the Burlington, the Missouri Pacific could not therefore continue its policy of traffic friendship for the Wabash. The Missouri Pacific, Iron Mountain, and Texas & Pacific also produced a volume of eastbound business which was traded at St. Louis. To get westbound business at St. Louis from the Pennsylvania, the Illinois Central, and other lines, it was necessary to trade some of their eastbound traffic. In order to increase the earnings of the Missouri Pacific, Gould sacrificed the Wabash in which his holdings were light.

In the southwestern group, the heart of his system, another set of adverse influences developed. In northern Texas the lines of the Kansas & Texas and of the Texas & Pacific met and crossed each other. While this connection facilitated the movement of joint traffic, the traffic movements could be adjusted to favor one road at the expense of the other. Both local business and business received from connections (including that coming north from the International) could move further north either via the

Kansas & Texas or via the Iron Mountain. On the southern end of the southwestern railroad system, other possibilities of clashing traffic influences existed.

Gould in control of these properties could build up the earnings and improve the market value of the stock of one road, thereby impairing the earnings and reducing the market value of the stock of another. To sustain one part of the system he was forced to injure others. It may be asked why investors of the time did not understand these influences at work. People bought then, and buy largely now, in response either to psychological hopes or to established records. Speculators prefer the former standard, and investors the latter. The values of the new Wabash and of the southwestern railroads were established in a market boom. In such a period speculators are apt to forget past records and to make their commitments in a spirit of abounding hope. Investors, on the contrary, frequently make their commitments on the basis of past earnings and tend to overlook the pernicious evils of static conditions. A property which has done well in the past will, it is assumed, do well in the future. The Union Pacific having paid dividends in depression years was such a property. In 1880 it had absorbed its major competitor and its revenues were rising. Since it had paid dividends in depression it could surely pay dividends in prosperity. The stock was therefore eagerly purchased.

The Wabash, on the other hand, did not have the credit standing of the Union Pacific. Its securities therefore could not be as easily sold. Gould had to watch the market for Wabash securities, since he might easily saturate it with new offerings. Demands for capital by the Gould roads in 1880 and 1881 were so large and insistent that it was necessary to secure additional supplies in Great Britain. Because of their losses in Erie in the seventies, Gould was *persona non grata* with British investors. Nevertheless he did succeed in selling securities by a circuitous way to a large British clientele.

Some of the capital necessary to build up the Wabash system had to be financed through the sale of securities. The construction of the Chicago line and of the Detroit extension, for example, required the expenditure of "a vast amount of money." [9] Accordingly the Wabash created a general mortgage, authorizing the issue of $50,000,000 of bonds, of which $33,000,000 were reserved to retire existing bonds at maturity, and the balance for equipment, improvements, and other purposes. Mortgage restrictions upon the issue of bonds and the use of the proceeds were exceedingly lax, and the abuses flowing from the grant of such wide authority to borrowing corporations led to the emergence of the Morgan restrictive mortgages of the nineties.

These Wabash bonds and other securities were sold in England through the good offices of the Great Western. The renewed Gould-Vanderbilt rift had been followed by a new Great Western-Wabash arrangement from which the Great Western expected much. The profits from the Wabash contract were stressed both in railroad circles and in the British press. Whatever benefits the Great Western had already realized from the Toledo junction, declared its president, were to be "infinitely enlarged by the direct connection now contemplated at Detroit." [10] When a British paper, described sarcastically as a "society journal," remarked that any railroad (referring to the Wabash) of Gould or Field should be "fought shy of," one of the leading railroad journals replied that this was not a correct statement. Field was no longer a member of the board of the Wabash, and although Gould was a member, Humphreys, who was a member of the New York Central board, was president and directed its policies. There was therefore nothing in the traffic agreement with the Wabash to create antagonistic interests between the two roads.[11]

Gould was playing his game well. His technique of creating an interest through the distribution of statements, which were factually correct but did not contain the essential truth, was again at work. Although the prospect of a wholesale diversion of business from the Vanderbilt lines to the Great Western was expected, yet in the period of slightly less than two years between the time of the first Wabash-Great Western understanding and the opening in the summer of 1881 of the Detroit connection, Gould never committed himself. At no time did he state the precise volume of business that the Wabash would give the other line. Neither for that matter did the president nor any other responsible official of the Great Western make such a statement.

So convinced was the Great Western of this financial Utopia

to be realized from its relationship with the Wabash that it co-operated with the latter to finance its needs. A few months before the completion of its Detroit extension, the Wabash opened a London office on the premises of the Great Western, with the latter becoming the agent for the former in England. Headed by a local judge, a group of Gould-directed agents moved to England and on the ground of the profitable character of the traffic contract between the two companies sold Wabash securities. The judge, in the language of a Great Western stockholder who led a revolt against the management, "succeeded in placing an enormous amount of [Wabash] stock in England on the faith of the brand which [the Great Western] placed upon it." [12] The circularization and selling efforts of the Gould agents must have been well directed and far-reaching in their effects. An Englishman some years later made a number of observations which bear the earmarks of intimate acquaintance with the subject.

"The brokers' circulars, which find their way through the post into every country house and rectory, were at one time full of Wabash. Not one person in a thousand had the least idea where the road was, or whence it drew its traffic, or what sort of men conducted its affairs. The advertisements and circulars gave a brilliant account of it; there had been a consolidation, new regions were to be opened up, tremendous interest might be expected. It was an old story; but why should anybody invent a new story when the old succeeds so well? People rushed in to buy the shares with their eyes shut." [13]

Of the $17,000,000 of Wabash general mortgage bonds sold, about $11,500,000 were disposed of in Great Britain at a price of from 80 to 95.[14] A precise estimate of the amount of Wabash stock sold in England is not available, although the English stockholder critic of the Great Western management in 1882 described the amount as "enormous." [15]

Gould meanwhile suddenly appeared on the eastern railroad scene as the head of a new combination to fight the Pennsylvania Railroad. The eastern territory was the fourth major division of his railroad operations—his activities in transcontinental, middle-western and southwestern areas having already been examined in previous chapters. The Pennsylvania had aided Gould's American Union; but now that Gould had the Western Union, he no longer needed the Pennsylvania's help and could afford to become its foe. Even while the Pennsylvania was working hand in glove with his American Union, Gould was working secretly on a scheme damaging to that road. The latter used, but did not own, a link essential to the operation of its through line from New York to Baltimore and Washington. The connection between Philadelphia and Wilmington was owned by the Philadelphia, Wilmington & Baltimore.[16] The Baltimore & Ohio encountered great difficulties in doing business in Philadelphia and New York, and could reach New York only over the Pennsylvania or by a complicated and unsatisfactory water route. In 1880 when the Reading and the Central of New Jersey jointly completed a new Philadelphia-New York City route, however, the impasse seemed about to be broken. The Baltimore & Ohio could now send its New York City business over a route independent of the Pennsylvania. The latter, however, was determined to prevent its competitor from using this new Bound Brook route, so named from the fact that this town served as a connecting point between the Reading on the south and the Central of New Jersey on the north.

The Pennsylvania, therefore, did everything possible to obstruct the movement of freight over the Baltimore & Ohio's new route. Here was another unique opportunity for Gould. If he could acquire control of the Wilmington, he could at one stroke cut off the Pennsylvania on the south, and induce the Baltimore & Ohio to shift its telegraph lines from the American Union to the Western Union. North of Philadelphia lay the Reading—the country's heaviest anthracite carrier and the major competitor of the Pennsylvania in the Philadelphia area. Despite these advantages, this property under the brilliant and erratic business personality of F. B. Gowen was in receivership. If Gould succeeded in cutting off the Pennsylvania on the south, he would thus be fighting the Reading's persistent enemy. There was therefore every reason for the Reading to permit the use of its tracks as a part of the Philadelphia-New York City route.

The Reading's tracks on the north terminated at Bound Brook and from that point to Jersey City extended the lines of the Central of New Jersey. That road was also in receivership, a victim, like the Reading, of expansion in an inflation period under the leadership of an inveterate optimist—John Taylor Johnston. The receiver, Francis S. Lathrop, a conservative operating man, kept no construction account and charged the cost of betterments to operating expense. In settlement of some outstanding differences over a market battle with Keene, Gould, having secured a stock interest in this road, approached a large stockholder and pictured the alluring possibilities of a union of the road with the Wabash. Gould's charm was again successful and he and his group were admitted to the board.[17]

Gould, however, had not yet shown his full hand. He was still the friend of the Pennsylvania, which then had no fear of its insolvent competitors, the Reading, and the Central of New Jersey. It was also satisfied with its southern extension, the Wilmington, a prosperous road whose stock was controlled by relatively few shareholders. Approximately 85 per cent was held in Boston; [18] with the largest block held by Nathaniel Thayer, one of the Boston group of railroad capitalists.

Gould co-operated with Garrett for acquisition of the Wilmington. The syndicate included his major-domos, Sage and Dillon, Garrett, and two major banking houses, August Belmont, and Drexel and Company. Gould approached Thayer who had no particular love for him. In a loose business deal, highly characteristic of Gould's methods, though utterly unlike the careful procedure of Thayer, the latter nevertheless, although owning only 6,000 shares, agreed to sell to the syndicate 120,000 out of a total of 235,901 shares outstanding at a price of 70.[19]

All was now ready and the trap was about to be sprung. Gould was prepared to step into the eastern railroad picture at the head of a powerful combination to challenge the Pennsylvania. Late in February, 1881, he announced the acquisition of the Wilmington. The blow was unexpected, and it took the railroad and financial world by surprise. Comment was confused, but observers were certain that Gould had again triumphed. One commentator, whose views reflected the judgment of the commercial as distinguished from the financial interests, took it for granted that the Gould and Garrett syndicate "had arranged, beyond all question, for the majority of the stock." [20]

Here was a combination in the making. Gould, in co-operation with leading bankers and the Baltimore & Ohio, was on the point of aligning a number of strategic roads into a new through route. He was about to unite into a single common business interest two financially weak properties—the Central of New Jersey and the Reading—with two strong properties—the Baltimore & Ohio, and the Wilmington—and thus head a group which would offer the Pennsylvania its most serious eastern competition in the inner gates of its citadel at Philadelphia.

In less than two weeks after the Gould-Garrett syndicate had apparently purchased control of the Wilmington, the Pennsylvania officially announced that it had acquired control. Gould had bought from Thayer but Thayer no longer had the loyal support of the stockholders. He had acted without their knowledge, and had not informed them of the agreement he had made to sell their stock to Gould. They accordingly organized an independent shareholders' committee and communicated with the Pennsylvania.[21] The Gould syndicate had offered 70 for the stock; the Pennsylvania offered 78 and finally paid 80.[22] The non-Thayer stockholders delivered their stock to the Pennsylvania and the transaction was completed. Gould's plan thus failed, and the proposed eastern railroad combination headed by himself and Garrett never materialized. The able institution known as the Pennsylvania Railroad had again triumphed.

While thus working with Garrett to form a north-south route through the purchase of the Wilmington, Gould was working with his competitor to form an east-west route. Within a few days after his election to the board of the Central of New Jersey early in 1881, he proposed that the Pennsylvania help him form a new route between New York City and Toledo to make a connection there with the Wabash. Leaving no stone unturned to utilize the strategic location of the Central of New Jersey, he thus proposed to re-establish the through route in the central part of Pennsylvania contemplated by McHenry in 1865. The new line would extend west to a small point in eastern Pennsylvania (Haucks); the Reading would carry it farther west to Milton; the Pennsylvania system would take it to Redbank, near Pittsburgh. From Redbank to Youngstown, Gould would build seventy miles of track, and from Youngstown by traffic arrangements he could reach Toledo and the Wabash. He proposed that the Pennsylvania help the Wabash to carry through traffic between the East and the Middle West, thereby to some extent at least diverting business from its own lines.

Although the Pennsylvania did not immediately accept the idea, neither did it forthwith reject it. Another conference was held in mid-April. Early in May a decision was apparently reached. It was announced that the necessary papers would be signed immediately.[23] President Roberts, however, was not so sure. He took a firm stand in refusing to permit the use of a system line to compete with the main line of the road. Gould was ready with his usual technique: If the Pennsylvania did not sign, he declared, he would create another through route. In western Pennsylvania and eastern Ohio there were a number of financially weak, broad-gauge roads, some of which were owned by Humphreys, president of the Wabash. These roads would be converted into standard gauge, and by short extensions tied in with the Wabash, thereby connecting the latter with Buffalo.[24]

Although the evidence is not clear, Roberts was not impressed and refused to yield. The board, however, took a hand. Early in June a contract was finally signed giving the Wabash the necessary trackage rights for the movement of through business on condition that the Pennsylvania secure a division of the through rate.[25] Gould made his usual glowing promises. The through route promised to divert Wabash business from the Vanderbilt lines at Toledo, not to the Great Western at Detroit, but to the Pennsylvania for a connection with the Central Railroad of New Jersey. Such action would indeed constitute a blow to the Vanderbilt system, and perhaps explained the willingness of the Pennsylvania's board to ratify the trackage agreement.

No sooner was the Pennsylvania trackage contract signed than Gould finally acted to conclude a contract for the distribution of the Wabash eastbound business at Toledo and Detroit. The traffic was to be divided equally between the Lake Shore at Toledo and the Great Western and the Canada Southern at Detroit; each road to get one-third of the Wabash business. The contract was a blow to the ambitious hopes of the Great Western. There is little reason to doubt that the Great Western officials had expected far more than one-third.[26] On the other hand, the distribution of two-thirds of the Wabash business to the Vanderbilt lines could not be interpreted as appeasement. Though

Gould frequently compromised and agreed to make concessions to secure elsewhere even more concessions, he did not appease. He presumably gave Vanderbilt two-thirds of the Wabash eastbound traffic in order to secure a fair share of his westbound traffic, which moved over the long haul of the Wabash to St. Louis and beyond over the network of Gould's southwestern lines.

Hardly had this allocation been made than a new disturbing factor emerged. Because of Vanderbilt's concessions, the rate structure in eastern territory had been stabilized since the spring of 1877. Vanderbilt had agreed to a system of freight differentials, which made the cost of railroad transportation more expensive to New York than to Philadelphia and Baltimore. In the traffic boom which followed after the cessation of the depression influences in the fall of 1878, the growth of New York traffic lagged behind that of Philadelphia and Baltimore. In the boom of 1881, the loss of traffic was accentuated. In addition, the New York Central lost business to its competitors.[27] Vanderbilt, attributing the latter's gain to secret rate reductions, retaliated, and in June, 1881, cut rates openly. The war that followed proved to be the most savage up to that time in the history of the country. For some nine months the war went on. The loss in earnings, remarked one of the railroad presidents, an acute observer of current affairs, was "so much money thrown into the sea. Nobody has got any advantage from it, and no company has obtained any advantage over any other company, for we have all carried about the same proportions of traffic as would have been carried if all had been getting reasonable rates." [28]

The war almost immediately changed the relative importance of the contracts, routes and other arrangements which Gould had established in the first half of the year. The break in rates combined with the relatively poor grain crop in 1881 diminished the value of the Wabash traffic alliance to the Great Western. The latter had agreed to carry the Wabash cars over its own tracks at a relatively low price.[29] The new influences reduced the Wabash contract to its proper proportions.

In the midst of the rate war, Gould in conjunction with Sloan decided to carry out a long considered plan of extending the Lackawanna to Buffalo. Gould and his associates were elected to the

Lackawanna's board. Taylor's death in 1882 left Sloan as the most influential person in its management, and Sloan and Gould became close allies. The Wabash in the area between St. Louis and Toledo meanwhile cut rates. When therefore, in the summer of 1881, it was decided to press forward with the construction of the Lackawanna extension, Vanderbilt laid plans for a long contest. Although he maintained a common directorship with Gould on the Western Union, he steered clear of him in his railroad connections. With Gould and the Lackawanna at Buffalo, the New York Central would lose that road's profitable westbound anthracite coal business. Vanderbilt's reaction was vigorous and his policies exerted a profound effect on the growth of the New York Central system.

By this time Gould had broken relations also with Garrett of the Baltimore & Ohio. His initial move to swing Garrett into his camp by the formation of the Washington-New York City route having failed, Gould tried desperately to buy out the Baltimore & Ohio's telegraph system. Garrett not only refused to budge; he went further, and decided to compete with Gould's telegraph property.[30] Gould now carried the fight to the camp of the enemy. Looking for the enemy's weak point, he thought he found it in the Ohio & Mississippi, a line which provided the Baltimore & Ohio with its Cincinnati-St. Louis outlet. The Baltimore & Ohio owned a few of the other's securities, but the Garretts personally were the largest owners of the second mortgage bonds, and "by far the largest stockholders in the company."[31] Other substantial blocks were held in England by those who believed in Garrett and in the future of the Baltimore & Ohio.

Gould's plan to capture the road was conceived in secrecy. He issued neither warning nor threat. On the day before the election, Gould and his retinue of lawyers descended upon Cincinnati and upon its courts. Gould found little difficulty in locating weakness in his enemy's armor. Garrett held the proxies for 7,000 shares. That was not right, said Gould, for he, Gould, had borrowed those shares and was entitled to their votes. He therefore solicited an injunction to stop Garrett from voting them. Garrett proposed also to vote on some of his bonds. The by-laws of the company explicitly provided that bondholders could vote, but Gould wanted Garrett enjoined from voting. Garrett proposed that the board as usual appoint the tellers; Gould insisted that the shareholders do the appointing, and that the board be enjoined. The judge issued the injunctions. Garrett, however, sent his counsel over and gave the judge more facts, and early next morning he dissolved the injunctions, and the election proceeded. The vote was close; the Gould trinity, to which was added Humphreys of the Wabash, had 120,920; but the Garretts had 153,500.[32]

Gould by his shifts from one party to another, by his efforts to advance the interests of the Western Union, and by depressing the rate structure of the Wabash in order to advance the earnings of the Missouri Pacific, had made enemies of both Garrett and Vanderbilt. Some permanent effects soon became evident. In order to secure westbound traffic in exchange for that lost as a result of the Lackawanna extension, Vanderbilt decided to make common cause with the Reading. There was no physical connection between the New York Central and the Reading, but if a traffic arrangement could be made a connection could be built. Vanderbilt had learned from long experience that a contract made with a road in which he had no stock interest could at some critical moment be impaired or invalidated. He therefore decided to acquire an interest in the Reading.[33]

While Vanderbilt was negotiating with that road, Gould suddenly delivered another blow in a totally unexpected corner, this time in New England. Except for the move to control the Boston, Hartford and Erie in 1868, Gould had made no attempt to establish a foothold in New England territory. That road, soon after its dealings with the Gould-Fisk group then in control of the Erie, fell into financial difficulties and was precipitated into receivership. (Cornelius) Vanderbilt was then a dominant factor in another New England road—the New Haven—and he gave the stock to his son, William H. The old Commodore, in consequence of the trade with Gould over the control of the Erie, had also acquired ownership of a substantial block of the Boston's bonds which he also gave to his son. These bonds were later exchanged for the stock of the successor company in a reorganization following a receivership. (W. H.) Vanderbilt thereby became one of the road's largest stockholders.[34]

By January, 1882, the route from Boston to the Hudson River, for so many years under construction, was finally finished. The road was in good physical condition. For more than a decade it had paid little interest on its large debt and had used its earnings to build up the property. Late in 1881 the Railroad Commissioners of Massachusetts expressed the opinion that the road had "the best line of single track in New England." [35]

Although the road had a through route from Boston to the Hudson River, thus enabling it to bid for through traffic to the west, its connections with New York City were in no way improved. New York was reached via the New Haven, a property in which Vanderbilt exercised an important though not a controlling influence. The road's managers, therefore, felt that a connection with New York independent of the New Haven was indispensable to its success. To reach the city several alternatives were open. It could build an extension from Danbury, Connecticut, to the Manhattan Elevated, which by the end of 1881 was securely under Gould's control. Secondly, it could connect at another point with a small line known as the New York City & Northern, a financially weak property which, because of its location and lack of connections, seemed doomed to a life of continuous poverty. A short extension by this road would enable the Boston to reach New York City and thus compete with the New Haven monopoly. And in the third place it could reach New York over Vanderbilt's New York and Harlem.

Here were the elements of a free-for-all fight. The New Haven, on whose board of directors Vanderbilt sat, controlled the New England-New York City business, and it seemed that with the aid of the eastbound traffic flowing over the Vanderbilt lines, sufficient inducements could be made to trade some traffic for an agreement by the New York & New England [36] to move its New England business south over the Harlem. Furthermore, Vanderbilt was an important stockholder in the line. Gould, on the other hand, had no interest in the road, or at least so it appeared.

In the contest for control of the road Gould's promises rose superior to Vanderbilt's realities. While Vanderbilt was in secure control of his properties—the Lake Shore, the Harlem, the New York Central, and the Michigan Central—Gould had only a tentative and incomplete control over his. While the New England's management was succumbing to the Gould touch, while arrangements were being made to sell a block of the stock of the road to the Gould group at a price substantially below the prevailing market price, and while the road's directorate was being changed to include Gould and his associates, the public was informed of the extraordinary prosperity which was bound to ensue. "We have now," said a member of the board, "secured a position of power and influence and traffic, making this line second to none coming into the city. . . ." To another board member of some years' standing, the new alliance with Gould "made his head swim," [37] referring of course to the great possibilities from the Gould combination. Even the Governor of Massachusetts was convinced. "Strong men," he wrote, referring to Gould and his associates, "have it [the New England] in hand. Its prospects were never better; and, though large expenditures must still be made to perfect it, there is reason to count on its future appreciation and ultimate great value." [38]

Gould had won again. Vanderbilt had lost again. At the annual election of the New England in December, the Gould triumvirate were elected to office. To this group was added Field who, through his union with Gould in the Manhattan merger a few weeks before, had become a new associate. In addition, two others were introduced: Roberts, president of the Pennsylvania, and Jewett, president of the Erie. A consistent journalistic Gould critic believed that this board was "a pretty clever stroke on the part of Gould." [39] The new combination, it continued, would give the Erie a new direct route to New England. The New England would get both the business of the Erie and that of the Pennsylvania because the two roads were represented in the new board. It is strange to a point that passes understanding, that an able and well-informed journal, which had for more than a decade been unstinting in detecting the flaws of Gould's corporate structures, could fall into this habit of believing that mere representation on a board was sufficient to divert business. Gould promises to support such views were issued in rapid succession. The Gould trio and Field agreed with the road's president to build a New York City connection. Seven million dollars were needed to finance the program. The Gould group, shortly after the stockholders' meeting at which they were elected to the board, subscribed to $7,000,000 of the company's bonds. This subscription was not honored.[40]

Entrance into the heart of New York would be secured by using the lines of the Manhattan. A central depot to take care of the passenger business of the Wabash and the Lackawanna, as well as that of the New England, would be erected. Both the president and the board looked forward with confidence to the success of the program, the former asserting that the new combination "meant simply this—that we should have a double-track steel road fully equipped from the heart of the city of Boston through our principal cities to New York, and also to the Hudson River." [41] And the stockholders at the meeting which placed the Gould combination in office by formal resolution requested the directors to secure a New York City line other by lease, purchase, or construction.

All this and more Gould promised to secure. Just what his objectives were in making these promises is difficult to determine. He and Vanderbilt were then engaged in a major struggle and perhaps he entered New England as a means of embarrassing Vanderbilt. Vanderbilt himself made some half-hearted and ineffectual attempts to invade Gould's territory. He entered into negotiations, for example, to capture control of the Texas & St. Louis, a road which was beginning to edge into the territory of Gould's Iron Mountain. Perhaps both contestants interested themselves in properties located far outside their main areas to increase their trading strength.

NOTES FOR CHAPTER XVI

1. New York *World*, May 13, 1883.
2. Boston *Herald*, cited in *Ry. Review*, Jan. 17, 1880, 33. According to a member of the Burlington board, the New York *Tribune* "was entirely" under the control of Gould, who owned a majority of the stock. Burlington archives, Griswold to Perkins, Dec. 13, 1876.
3. New York *Herald*, Sept. 28, 1882.
4. *Ry. Review*, Jan. 17, 1880, 33.
5. Even such an able railroad man as Perkins of the Burlington believed that Gould could pour traffic from the western roads over the Wabash. Perkins expresses this judgment in a letter to Geddes, Nov. 24, 1879, found in the Burlington archives.
6. Transportation Interests of the United States and Canada, Report No. 847, Senate, 51st Congress, 1st Session, 1890, 220, George B. Roberts.
7. Burlington archives, Potter to Perkins, Aug. 30, 1880.
8. Ibid., Ripley to Frink, general freight agent, Missouri Pacific, Oct. 11, 1882.
9. Hopkins, 1st vice president, Wabash, in New York *World*, cited in *R. R. Gaz.*, Oct. 29, 1880, 567.

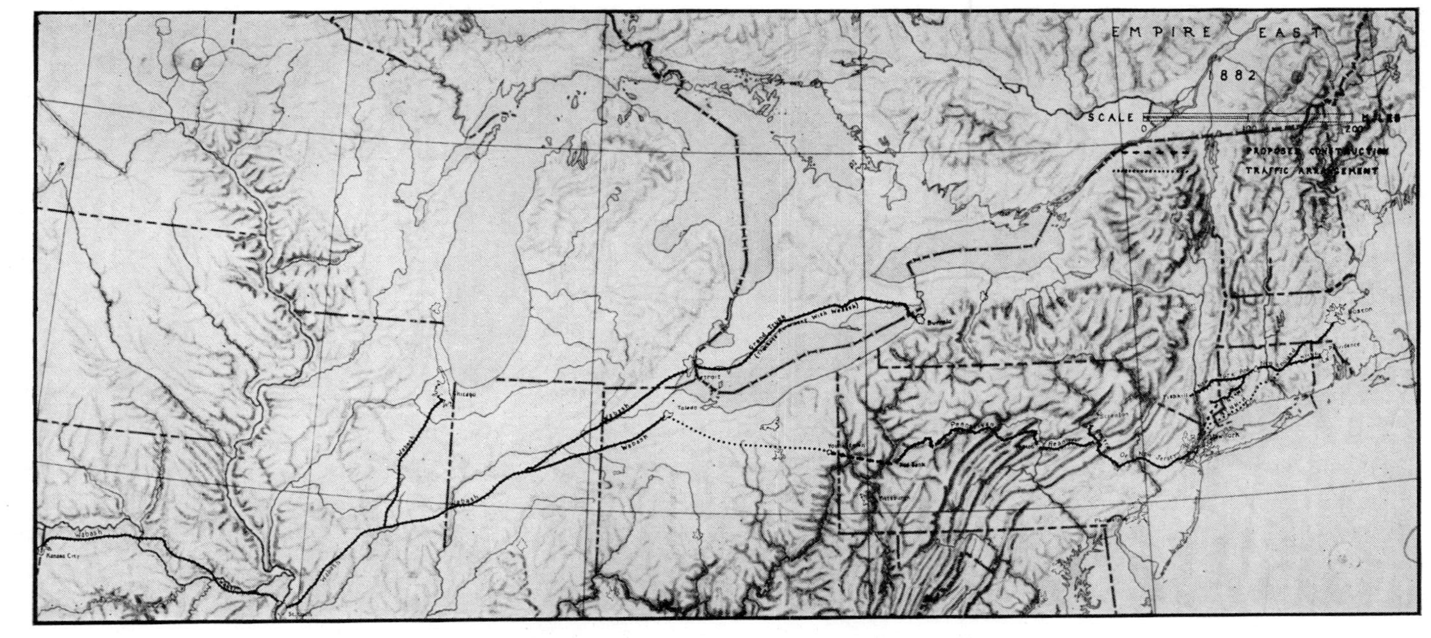
EMPIRE EAST
1882
SCALE
0
100
200
MILES
PROPOSED CONSTRUCTION
TRAFFIC ARRANGEMENT
Chicago
Detroit
Toledo
Buffalo
Wabash
Kansas City
Boston
Providence
New York

10. Statement by the president, Great Western, at the semi-annual shareholders' meeting, cited in Herapath's *Ry. Journal*, Oct. 23, 1880, 1199.
11. Herapath's *Ry. Journal*, July 10, 1880, 782.
12. R. R. *Gaz.*, May 19, 1882, 309.
13. *Quarterly Review*, July and Oct. 1884, 81, "The Romance and Reality of American Railroads."
14. *North American Review*, Jan.-June, 1888, 182, "A Chapter of Wabash," by an anonymous author.
15. R. R. *Gaz.*, May 19, 1882, 309.
16. Known hereafter as the Wilmington.
17. This account of Gould's original purchase of this stock is taken from the Chicago *Tribune*, Jan. 12, 1882.
18. This is the statement of Phila. *North American*, Dec. 16, 1880.
19. Burlington archives, Forbes to Perkins, March 9, 1881. Forbes was present at the Wilmington stockholders' committee meeting, at which the stock was sold to the Pennsylvania, and for this reason his statement of the position of Thayer can be accepted as reasonably reliable.
20. *Bradstreet*, March 12, 1881, 156.
21. The committee's circular is summarized in *Ry. Review*, March 5, 1881, 187.
22. This is the price as stated in Burlington archives, Forbes to Perkins, March 9, 1881.
23. R. R. *Gaz.*, May 6, 1881, 256, citing a wire of May 3 from Philadelphia.
24. Phila. *North American*, May 11, 1881.
25. Ibid., June 9, 1881. As late as 1923 the Pennsylvania Railroad management actively canvassed the idea of establishing a through freight route almost identical with this route negotiated between Gould and Roberts. See "Investigation of Railroads, Holding Companies and Affiliated Companies," Additional Report of the Committee on Interstate Commerce, pursuant to Senate Resolution No. 71, Senate, 76th Congress, 3rd Session, 1940, 1136.
26. R. R. *Gaz.*, May 19, 1882, 304.
27. On the important grain traffic, for example, in the first five months of 1881, the New York Central's proportion dropped from 51.5 per cent in 1880 to 38.8 per cent; while the traffic of its competitors, the Erie and the Pennsylvania, rose, respectively, from 30.4 per cent to 37.7 per cent, and from 16.9 per cent to 21.8 per cent. *Public*, June 30, 1881, 406.
28. Sir Henry Tyler, president, Grand Trunk, cited in R. R. *Gaz.*, April 14, 1882, 222.
29. Ibid., May 19, 1882, 403.
30. For details, see Chapter XXIII, pp. 462-3.
31. Letter from a former Ohio & Mississippi director to the New York *Tribune*, Oct. 22, 1877.
32. On this incident, see *Ry. Review*, Oct. 15, 1881, 573; New York *Tribune*, Oct. 14, 1881; New York *Times*, Oct. 14, 1881.
33. For details on this acquisition, see Chapter XVIII, pp. 361-2.
34. For details on the Vanderbilt holdings, see Phila. *North American*, Jan. 3, 1884; New York *Tribune*, April 14, 1886; New England Bond Investigation, Field, 533.
35. This was the statement made to the president, according to the Phila. *North American*, Dec. 9, 1881.
36. This was the name of the successor company to the Boston, Hartford & Erie, and known hereafter as the New England.
37. New York *Times*, Dec. 7, 1881.
38. *Ry. Review*, Jan. 14, 1882, 25.
39. *Chron.*, Dec. 10, 1881, 634.
40. New England Bond Investigation, Henry L. Higginson, 209.
41. New York *Tribune*, Dec. 7, 1881.

CHAPTER XVII

Gould Creates Empire—West

IN THE West even more than in the East, many opportunities called for fundamental decisions of policy. This was particularly so in the building of new lines to open up territory rich in raw materials. In the Northwest as well as in the Southwest, the economic future of thousands of communities depended upon rail facilities. Of the promoters and capitalists who supplied this demand, Gould was in many respects the most important. He, as much as any other person in the early eighties, laid down the rails —the symbol at that time of a changing civilization.

Before he was well on his way in working out his western empire building policies, however, he executed a brilliant stroke of corporate strategy in the very center of his expanding system at St. Louis. In this way he enhanced his competitive strength and secured a controlling position in this vital terminal area. A bridge to connect St. Louis with East St. Louis across the Mississippi River was long considered a vital necessity. In 1868 the Illinois & St. Louis Bridge Company was formed to make this hope a reality, and in 1870 J. S. Morgan & Company of London bought $2,500,000 of its bonds with an option to buy the remaining $4,000,000 within thirty days. Of the amount issued, St. Louis subscribers took $1,200,000.[1]

In addition to the bridge, a tunnel to connect with the railroads and a depot was also built. The tunnel was equipped with a steel double track and operated in connection wth the bridge, and the latter guaranteed its interest and principal.[2] Like so many other sound projects, this enterprise despite its inherent value was doomed to failure because of timing blunders. The bridge was built at the wrong time and incurred a heavy load of fixed charges on the basis of inflated prices. It began to do business when interest remained and business declined. The company soon paid the penalty of financial miscalculation: the interest was passed, receivers were appointed, the property was sold at foreclosure to a group representing the bondholders, and the stockholders were eliminated. New first mortgage bonds were exchanged for the old, and new preferred stock was issued for the junior bonds.[3] The common stock of the new company—the St. Louis Bridge Company—was transferred to the committee on reorganization to be used in any way it thought necessary.[4] The committee was controlled by the banking firm which originally sold the bonds.

By 1881 the earnings of the company were sufficient to cover interest charges and part of the preferred dividend. The property was of great strategic value to Gould's system. The Wabash lines from the east terminated at East St. Louis. The Missouri Pacific, soon to become the parent company of a group of railroads in the far-reaching stretches of the Southwest, terminated at St. Louis. Approximately 80 per cent of the freight carried by the bridge was interchanged for these two properties.[5]

A pretty problem in corporation finance now emerged. Here was a bridge and a tunnel essential to Gould's roads. The reorganized companies had a bonded debt, while a banking firm held the stock for the benefit of the security holders. How could this property be purchased in behalf of the two railroad connections in such a way as to give Gould the controlling interest in the terminal facilities? To the lay observer the solution would appear to rest in the purchase of the stock from the reorganization committee. That solution, however, would require the purchaser—in this case Gould—to put up cash or other valuable consideration. Gould, however, did not adopt such a simple device. Indeed, although he was anxious to acquire control, he made no overtures for the purchase of the stock. Instead, resorting to his threat technique, he announced that he was building a competitive bridge across the Mississippi forty-five miles above St. Louis at a point where the Wabash east-and-west lines could be connected by a short extension. The new line was advertised "as the most important link in a great transcontinental route." [6] A charter for a bridge was requested from Congress and construction proceeded rapidly.

Gould's tactics were successful. The St. Louis Bridge Company surrendered, and Gould stopped construction on the competitive bridge. The Wabash investment in this line was impaired, and a few years later its receivers dropped it forthwith. The St. Louis bridge and tunnel properties were leased jointly to the Missouri Pacific and the Wabash, the lessees guaranteeing the interest on the relatively small issue of the first mortgage bonds as well as a dividend at the rate of 5 per cent on the first preferred for the first two years and 6 per cent thereafter, and 3 per cent on the second preferred.[7] The lease guarantee contract made no reference to the common stock. Terms of the settlement were described by the London Morgan firm prosaically and somewhat wistfully as "somewhat less favorable than hoped"; but, in view of agitation for another bridge, the firm had no hesitation in recommending acceptance of these terms.[8]

What did Gould personally secure? Apparently nothing, though as in the Erie-Vanderbilt settlement, actually he secured almost everything. In the St. Louis bridge deal, the bondholders of the old property received a return on their investment and Gould received the property; that is to say, the common stock. For this, presumably, he agreed to induce the directorates of the Wabash and the Missouri Pacific to become lessees of the bridge and tunnel properties and to pay the rent. The common stock had no earnings; indeed, based upon existing earnings it had a deficit value, though that was quickly changed. With a monopoly in a vital terminal area he could adjust the tolls for railroad interchange and transfer service on such a basis as to make the bridge company's common stock valuable.

The adverse results which flowed from this power became visible only gradually. In 1880 and 1881, however, Gould in the eyes of the citizens of St. Louis became "a sort of patron saint."[9] In addition to the acquisition of his major transportation properties he undertook also the purchase of interests in a number of important industries in St. Louis.

Another St. Louis acquisition, vital to the city's prosperity, revolved around the Mississippi River barge transportation business. For years champions of water service had looked upon transportation down the Mississippi as a means of reducing rates. Gould acquired an interest in two of the barge companies and by the summer of 1881 succeeded in consolidating them into a new enterprise. Gould controlled five out of the nine members of the board. In view of the fact that the through eastbound freight rates from St. Louis and Chicago to New York had been adjusted by the settlement made in the spring of 1877, railroad rates appeared to be high. This factor combined with the large grain crop in 1879 and 1880 led to a revival of water transportation down the Mississippi.

Anticipation of prosperity for the water lines was soon disturbed by the succession of rate wars in eastern trunk-line territory which by the summer of 1884 reduced the rates on wheat and other commodities to new low levels.

While Gould was thus promoting so many business interests in St. Louis, his activities in other parts of his railroad empire in the West did not diminish. In fact it was there that Gould became for the first time in his career a great railroad builder. His building activities in the East were relatively unimportant, consisting mostly of connecting links in trunk-line railroads.

In 1880 and 1881, however, he emerged as one of the leading, and for more than a year, the leading railroad builder of the land. In the West he enlisted many millions of new capital for the building of roads, and many communities looked to him for their economic salvation. He also made heavy commitments in industries closely associated with railroads and other forms of transportation. To get an adequate supply of locomotive fuel he acquired interests in numerous coal mines. In Iowa and Illinois he and Sage organized coal ventures most of whose production was taken by the Wabash, and in the Indian Territory he organized another coal company which for a number of years not only supplied all the Texas railroads with coal but in addition sold a large tonnage in the commercial and non-railroad markets.[10]

It was, however, primarily into the field of railroad building that Gould poured millions of his own money and the money of an army of followers. In the Far West the Union Pacific in 1879 had already entered upon its feeder-building policy which some years later was so sharply criticized as a major factor in the breakdown of its finances. A contrary policy, refusing to furnish transportation service to productive farm, forest, and mining areas would probably have promoted an even greater flood of criticism. Perhaps construction was carried out too hastily or in advance of actual traffic needs. The essential soundness of the policy, however, both to the railroads and to the public, cannot be fairly challenged.

In addition to the branch building policy, the Union Pacific in 1880 and 1881 entered upon an expansion program in the Northwest. In order to give the Union Pacific access to the Columbia Valley, a new company—the Oregon Short Line—was organized. Stockholders of the Union Pacific were given rights to buy one $1,000 (face value) bond, plus five shares of stock of the new company for $1,000. For a guarantee of the Short Line's bonds, the Union Pacific received one-half of the stock. The venture was one of the major construction programs of the early eighties. Eventually the line was turned over to the Union Pacific and proved to be a profitable addition, though for a few years it was a drag on earnings.

At the same time another extension into new and productive territory was undertaken. Some years before, a promoter had conceived the idea of building a new road from the main stem of the Union Pacific north to Butte, Montana, at that time the center of a rapidly growing copper industry. This road, the Utah & Northern, was originally built as a narrow-gauge line, and though still uncompleted in the fall of 1880, was described in the territory served "in the highest terms of its equipment and management." [11] The leading spirit in its promotion, Colonel Joseph Richardson, ran out of funds just at the time when, because of the rapid increase in copper production, the unfinished road developed earning potentialities. Here was an opportunity too good for Gould to overlook. He and his associates on the Union Pacific agreed to buy the unfinished property and to supply the funds to complete construction. Richardson sold his interest in the property and in return received some of the bonds. To Gould this was a cheap price since, in effect, the property cost him nothing. He had the road create a bond issue, sold some bonds to raise funds to complete the extension and transferred a small block to Richardson. Two hundred and fifty miles of additional construction was then completed in the scheduled time of eight months.[12] The construction of the line which had languished under an indigent proprietor was thus completed in short order under a prosperous successor. At about the same time the Union Pacific, to get a more direct route to Denver, built a Denver cut-off from the main line, thus enabling it to carry its Denver traffic more efficiently and at lower cost.

The cut-off was part of a general program of construction and expansion in central and eastern Colorado. By the fall of the year the road was in the midst of a program designed to penetrate the rich mining districts tributary to Denver. Early in 1880, as part of the settlement between the Denver and the Atchison, the Union Pacific had agreed not to build or promote the building of a parallel or competing line to the Rio Grande from its own lines above Denver to any point in Colorado south of Denver and the main east-and-west line of the Kansas Pacific. Nothing was said in the agreement about the South Park—the line which provided a short route from Denver into the Leadville mining regions. In the construction contest between the Denver and the South Park, personal enmities and bitter feuds had developed. An agreement in October, 1879, had appeared, however, to have achieved an equilibrium; the roads agreed to divide the business, and under a schedule of reasonable rates they would be able to earn a return upon their investment.

The two roads, however, did not reckon with Gould. In accordance with his usual skill in solving strategic problems of this character, he had wormed himself into a position of controlling importance in both the Denver and the South Park. His acquisition of the Denver stock has already been noted. Gould acquired the South Park's stock in a series of steps. In 1877 the South Park was short of cash. In that year the business depression was at its high and it was difficult to raise funds. Here Gould, acting through the Kansas Pacific, took South Park stock on behalf of that railroad in payment of freight bills for transportation services rendered to the South Park. Again Gould served as a source of speculative capital, and a part of the profit later made by selling the stock to the Union Pacific was in consideration of the speculative risk assumed in the depression period. Then, in 1879 through some patient planning, Gould secured another block, about one-fourth, of the South Park's stock. This acquisition was made in a trade with the stockholders of the controlling construction company. Personal and corporate interests were so intermixed that one finds it difficult to determine where the one interest begins and the other leaves off. Gould agreed that if the construction company sold him the South Park's stock, the Kansas Pacific and Union Pacific "would forebear certain discriminations" against the construction company. In December of that year Gould bought an additional number of shares from one of the Colorado counties.

The remaining South Park shares, except for a small amount owned by a New York investment banker, were placed in a pool, with instructions to the trustee to sell all or none. Before the end of 1879 the South Park had become profitable. Both Palmer for the Denver, and Gould on his own behalf, bid for the South Park stock. These bids were met by high asking prices. Gould finally (November, 1880) wired Evans, president of South Park and agent of the pool to which the citizens had trusteed their stock, to make an offer. The offer to sell at $100 per share was promptly accepted by Gould.[13] A few weeks later Gould sold (at the same price) all the stock to the Union Pacific.

To the lay observer it might occur that with Gould interested in both the Union Pacific and the Denver, a period of peace would follow. One would be justified in drawing such a conclusion from the terms of the territorial agreement of 1880 which had forbidden the Union Pacific to build south into the territory of the Denver. No such peaceful interlude occurred. The Union Pacific declared that the agreement did not prevent it from expanding. True, the agreement did enjoin the Union Pacific from taking such action, but it did not mention the South Park. It was not the Union Pacific which would build into the Denver's territory; it was the South Park that would do so.

By early summer of 1881 the battle was again joined. The Union Pacific through the South Park and another subsidiary surrounded and tapped the Denver at all important points, including Leadville. The Denver retaliated and not only built into Union Pacific territory, but also took extraordinary steps to prevent that road from getting into Leadville proper.

These construction programs in Colorado and Utah, although charged with dramatic interest, were nevertheless local in character. It was in the Southwest that Gould's construction program blossomed and flowered in all its imperial glory. There the main lines of development were still unfinished. Railroad tracks did not extend to the natural termini which the trade and commerce of the country and of its neighbor, the Republic of Mexico, required.

In this region Gould initiated his program almost immediately after he acquired control. The population and wealth of the Southwest were then rapidly increasing. "South-westward the star of empire wends its way," [14] remarked one observer. Gould recognized the opportunity to pre-empt desirable traffic-producing territory and laid his plans with almost dazzling speed. Through his general manager, he announced in February, 1881, his intention to build more than 900 miles of track before the end of the year. About half would be built in Missouri and Kansas, and the other half in Texas.[15]

Another campaign of construction was projected in Arkansas. At the close of 1879 the state had less than 500 miles of railroad. No sooner did Gould acquire control of the Iron Mountain than he called a stockholders' meeting to approve his plans for new construction. The meeting approved an increase of the company's debt and a contract with a construction company. Gould's rapid-fire action made a deep impression. One board member declared in a burst of enthusiasm: "The road has suffered long for the want of branch lines, and it is now proposed to secure them. This is one of the results of placing live men in the directory. Those western men are able enough, but so very slow." [16]

It was in the vast stretches of central and southern Texas, however, that Gould's projects made the deepest impression on contemporary economic life and on the growth of American railroads. Two competitive lines—the Kansas & Texas and the International—which had nurtured ambitions many years before to build connections with the Rio Grande, were by 1880 in the control of Gould. Within less than a month after he took charge, he began a program which soon fulfilled the ardent hopes of their early promoters and the yearning desires of the people for new railroad facilities. A few days after the court authorized the return of the property to its shareholders, the Kansas & Texas called a special stockholders' meeting. The outstanding stock was increased to $25,000,000, and the Gould policy to extend the road 500 miles to Laredo on the Rio Grande was approved. The money needed to finance the program was quickly subscribed.[17]

Gould had now perfected a physical union of all his southwestern lines, and controlled alternative north-and-south routes to northwestern markets. Adverse interests therefore became inevitable since traffic that moved over one route was bound to benefit one road and hurt another. Gould could select that route which benefited himself and his favored railroad most, and this is precisely what he later did.

While he was planning these lines between Kansas, Missouri, and Texas, he prosecuted with even greater energy the building of the El Paso line of the Texas & Pacific. In this wild building rush into and through the Southwest, Gould finally stubbed his toe. He met and failed to overcome the determined opposition of that great American builder and borrower, Huntington. It is a question whether the present generation has succeeded in overcoming the clouds of suspicion and exaggeration overhanging Huntington's business career, engendered by bitter political and newspaper attacks on his business monopoly in California, to a point sufficient to recognize his work as the leading railroad builder in American history. Huntington was the cart horse of the vast Central Pacific-Southern Pacific system. He called himself vice president, and permitted Leland Stanford to serve as president. Stanford was the smooth talker, the publicity agent, and the mouthpiece of Huntington and his associates. Huntington, however, was the driving factor and the creative genius that built more miles of railroad in the United States than any other individual. He was also the financier. By personal credit and by transferring loans from bank to bank and from person to person, he succeeded in financing the only single major railroad construction program in the depression of the seventies. Furthermore, by continuing to pay dividends for most of those years on more than $50,000,000 of Central Pacific stock representing only a slight cash investment, he succeeded in accomplishing that which only a handful of others were able to do. He succeeded also in buying up practically every railroad competitor in California, and in acquiring at almost nominal cost the control of all railroad approaches as well as almost all the waterfront terminal facilities of the San Francisco area.

In 1881 he, like Gould, was building rapidly. He was then rushing to completion the Southern Pacific lines from the Colorado River to El Paso. For some years T. W. Pierce, a promoter and capitalist (connected neither with Huntington nor Gould), had been energetically prosecuting other plans for the building of a through line between eastern Texas and El Paso. It was expected that this line when completed would have close business relations with the Texas & Pacific, and in some quarters a merger between the two companies was contemplated.[18] When therefore in the summer of 1881 it appeared likely that Huntington would join with Pierce and other groups in building and expanding into southeastern Texas and Louisiana, Gould sensed the danger. Huntington might move all the way east to New Orleans, or even worse, northeast into Gould's territory.

Gould recognized the character of the opposition. He knew Huntington; he had previously negotiated with him. He therefore did not hesitate; he did not wait; he issued no threats; he well knew that threats had little meaning to a man of Huntington's rugged character; he arranged no parleys, and he called no conferences.

The major Pierce railroad property—the Galveston, Harrisburg & San Antonio (in July, 1881, Huntington bought control of this property)—terminated on the west at San Antonio. When Gould, in February of 1881 through the International, began to build west, the Pierce road followed suit. After duplicating each other's lines for about twenty-five miles the tracks diverged. Gould saw no purpose in following the other road west to El Paso, thus duplicating Texas & Pacific in which he had such a large interest. When therefore he headed straight for Laredo on the Rio Grande while his competitor moved north and west to El Paso, Gould decided to act in the interests of the southwestern system as a whole and to ignore the separate interests of each road. Since the International was building one line to the Rio Grande, a line of the Kansas & Texas to the same area would be an economic waste. A special shareholders' meeting called to approve the change in the latter's extension program produced no opposition. Building on the Kansas & Texas was stopped at a small point in Texas, many miles short of its goal on the Rio Grande. The system was benefited but the Kansas & Texas was hurt. Representatives of the road seven years later criticized the action, but in 1881 it was approved and any potential future danger was lost sight of in the enthusiasm of the moment.

While Gould was thus successful in solving his internal system problems, he became acutely aware of the growing danger arising from the Huntington-Pierce moves. For the first time since his clash with Cornelius Vanderbilt in 1868, he had encountered an aggressor who asked for no terms and sought no settlement. Gould instead of seizing the offensive was compelled to search for defense weapons. He first looked for a flaw in the Huntington set-up. The Southern Pacific was building roads under territorial law but through land covered by a grant given by Congress to the Texas & Pacific. The Supreme Court of New Mexico, therefore, granted Gould's Texas & Pacific a temporary injunction to restrain the Southern Pacific from operating approximately 130 miles and to recover that part of the road built through the land embraced in the grant to the Texas & Pacific.[19] Since the Southern Pacific stock was held by Huntington and his associates, Gould's favorite battle ground—the New York stock market—was of no use. He therefore resorted to his other club of compulsion—the building of parallel and duplicate lines.

Toward the end of the summer he massed his forces for invasion of the enemy's territory. It was truly an imposing aggregation of properties which he proposed to unite. To retaliate against Huntington's move into Texas and Louisiana, he planned to move into California. He consolidated his forces first on the western end of the Union Pacific. From the end of a small Union Pacific controlled road in southern Utah—the Utah Central—he planned to build west.[20] Far to the west the Union Pacific acquired control of a small road—the California Central—with a right of way into San Francisco, thus promising to give Huntington's Central Pacific its first competition in that city. Through a number of new companies, in effect divisions of the California Central, the latter would be extended to the Nevada boundary line, there to connect with the western extension of the Utah Central. Through these lines and extensions Gould's Union Pacific would have a line to San Francisco independent of Huntington's Central Pacific.

These arrangements, far-reaching as they were, by no means represented the climax of Gould's plans. He proposed to unite in one combination all the other roads with transcontinental ambitions. As potential transcontinental roads, they were potential competitors of the Union Pacific, but Gould proposed to make them friends. One, the Texas & Pacific, was building rapidly west to El Paso, there to connect with the Atchison. Over the latter and over one of its affiliates by trackage rights, the Colorado River could be reached. In the last week in August, 1881, Gould finally proposed an agreement for the grand alliance directed against the Central Pacific—Southern Pacific's California monopoly. Included were the Texas & Pacific, the Atchison, the Atlantic & Pacific (the Atchison's affiliate), and the Union Pacific.

Here was the first vital threat in Huntington's business experience to his Pacific Coast monopoly. However, he did not flinch. Yankee realist that he was, he made no appeasing gestures. He moved quickly, by sending out parties to survey a duplicate line east of Ogden. Huntington preferred a connection with the Burlington, while C. F. Crocker, a Central Pacific vice president, insisted upon a more northerly approach via the Northern Pacific.[21] It was believed that the new road could be built at a cost of one-third that of the Union Pacific. As soon as the Union Pacific and its allies moved west of Ogden to parallel the Central Pacific, Huntington made it clear that the Central Pacific would move east of Ogden to parallel the Union Pacific. The Union Pacific, declared Huntington, had been "cavorting" around too much in the West. "Their people have gone in our bailiwick," and they don't belong there, he concluded.[22] Gould's transcontinental ambition was frustrated. He was then heavily involved in many unfinished railroad and market operations. The eastward extension of Huntington's lines into trans-Missouri territory would precipitate rate wars, reduce the earnings of his Texas & Pacific, and upset local rates in many parts of his southwestern system. Gould realized that he had met a man of tested mettle, of financial strength and of independent character. Huntington was supported by the energetic Crocker, vice president of the Central Pacific. Give Dillon "pretty square talk and tell him that all this stuff and talk about building parallel to us will not be tolerated." [23] And toward Gould, Crocker advised Huntington "to do more *watching* than 'praying.' " [24]

The negotiations for a settlement were carried on in Huntington's office in New York between Huntington, Gould, Sage, and Dillon. These rivals soon composed their differences. Huntington joined the Western Union board, thus becoming, momentarily at least, a Gould ally. What is more important an agreement was reached that appeared to harmonize the competitive relationships of their respective properties.

The agreement reached in November, 1881, was one of the most famous of its kind. Huntington had already built ninety miles east of El Paso, and it was agreed that the Southern Pacific and Texas & Pacific would use this stretch on equal terms. The gross from the Pacific Coast through business would be shared by the Texas & Pacific and the Huntington lines. Huntington would complete this road south and east from El Paso and agreed not to build north and east from that point. The Texas & Pacific relinquished its claim to its land grant, right of way and franchises west of El Paso to the Southern Pacific. So long as the agreement was fulfilled, the Texas & Pacific promised not to extend its road west of El Paso. Similarly, the Southern Pacific agreed, subject to the same condition, not to parallel the Texas & Pacific east of El Paso.[25]

For Gould it was a defensive move. It protected his Texas & Pacific while it also gave him the opportunity to share in the business to the Pacific Coast. In return he gave Huntington the opportunity to share in the business to New Orleans, then served from the west only by the Texas & Pacific. The restrictions on the territorial expansion of both the Southern Pacific and the Texas & Pacific permanently modified the railroad map of the Southwest. Huntington never pushed ahead with any extensions from El Paso north and east. Similarly the Texas & Pacific never built west of El Paso.

The agreement between Gould and Huntington for the division of traffic between New Orleans and the Pacific Coast lasted as long as the business of the two parties made it wise to do so. Like so many diplomatic agreements, the arrangement proved to be no more than an armistice. It provided a waiting period during which both contestants resumed their business and construction plans unimpeded by the other's threats or counterthreats. The agreement did not deter Huntington from completing two years later a new through route to New Orleans by which he turned the flank of the Texas & Pacific. Huntington thereby exerted an important force in the middle eighties in breaking up the finances and earning power of the Texas & Pacific.

This outcome, however, was not then anticipated in any quarter. Financial judgment did not look forward to any adverse results. The union of the Gould-Huntington interests was expected to boom the business of the Texas & Pacific. In Philadelphia, a city in which through the activities of (T. A.) Scott heavy investments were made in the road, the expectations were expressed in optimistic language. One of the leading papers declared flatly that the agreement would "soon more than double the present earnings." [26] A lengthy description of the property in Gould's New York press organ was climaxed by the assertion that "immense traffic" in California breadstuffs would move over it to New Orleans.[27] Field in one of his voluble moments misled his followers, and presumably himself as well, by waxing enthusiastic over the new route. Its possibilities, he said in his personal press organ, could "scarcely be over-estimated." [28]

The optimism bubbled over into the stock market. In heavy volume the price of the Texas & Pacific in a weak market rose substantially. Activity at these elevated prices facilitated the sale of Gould's holdings. Prices registered at that time were not again to be duplicated in Gould's lifetime. Much if not all of the stock which he then sold he later repurchased, and at critical times he managed to keep sufficient of the stock to retain control, even through financial reorganization.

The vast Gould program, part of which led to the contest with Huntington, was in geographical scope, in the number of individual railroad companies, and in the speed with which construction was carried on simultaneously in so many sections of the country, unprecedented in American life. He had now for the first time in his career the opportunity to profit from railroad building.

Profits from this source had for many years been realized through construction companies. The construction company was an old device. In return for the railroad's stocks and bonds, the construction company agreed to build the road, whereupon it made arrangements with contracting firms to do the actual building. Usually the par value of the securities paid by the railroad to the construction company substantially exceeded the cost of construction. Normally the bonds raised the required funds; the stock represented consideration for promotion services. After the line was completed and the construction company dissolved, the latter declared a liquidating dividend payable in its assets—those assets consisting usually of all or at least a large part of the stocks of the railroad company. In this way the stockholders of the construction company with only a small cash outlay secured control of the railroad company.

The earlier companies found it difficult to sell their stock to outsiders. Between 1873 and 1879 there was little construction and few construction companies. It was Gould who was responsible for their increased use in the late seventies and early eighties.

Gould carried the construction-company device to greater lengths than ever before. First, he made an active market for its stock, something which Huntington, for example, had never been able to do. Second, he used the stockholders of his railroad companies as a means of floating the stocks of his construction companies. He sold rights to buy the securities, either of the construction companies or of the railroads. The ventures were profitable and Gould thus increased his speculative following. He made profits for himself, and at the same time enabled those who accepted the subscription privileges to make profits also.

His first important venture into this field was unusually successful. The Pacific Railway Improvement Company contracted to build the Rio Grande division of the Texas & Pacific between Fort Worth and El Paso. Gould succeeded in attracting to the board of this construction company not only his permanent associates, Sage and Dillon, but also Huntington. Shortly thereafter he brought out the stock of the American Railway Improvement Company which had the contract for the Texas & Pacific's New Orleans extension. The first company having proved so profitable, Gould found little difficulty in attracting a following for a new one. Subscribers included capitalists from New York, Philadelphia, and Baltimore.[29] The stock was offered for subscription not only to the stockholders of the Texas & Pacific, but also to those of the Kansas & Texas and the Missouri-Pacific.

By the summer of 1881 the stocks of both construction companies had advanced to high levels. The Pacific Railway Improvement was quoted at $260, a premium apparently due to the fact that the work of construction was expected to last for several years. Events soon proved this to be a false hope, since the line to El Paso which was scheduled for completion in the fall of 1883 was in fact never built to its destination. Owing to the aggressive eastward building program of Huntington, the El Paso extension was constructed much faster than anticipated, and by fall the building program was over. The stock of the American Railway Improvement also proved a bonanza. In the summer of 1881 it was quoted from $215 to $225 a share—a substantial premium.

Another company, the International Railway Improvement, took over the building program in Texas of the International and of the Kansas & Texas. This company was also profitable. Upon liquidation within less than a year after its organization, it paid a dividend of 25 per cent in bonds of the Kansas & Texas, even though only 60 per cent of the stock was paid in. The profits were "remarkably large," declared Field, by this time a confirmed Gould follower.[30]

In the East the expansion program of the Lackawanna was also carried out through the medium of a construction company. A few months after its organization the shares of this company, the Central Railway Construction, were quoted at a 40 per cent premium above par.[31] Field's press organ again hailed the speculative hero, and described this construction company stock as the best subscription on the list.[32]

Examination of the famous Gould empire of 1881 is thus concluded. It was an empire built around Gould's personality, and not necessarily around his stockholdings in each road. Whether he held a majority or minority interest, or no interest at all, his influence was predominant. His was the decisive word in the determination of major corporate policies. It is, therefore, sound to conclude, regardless of the number of shares which Gould personally held, that he was master of their destinies. In control of this vast system of railroads, terminals, bridges, and of telegraph lines, of elevated street railroads, of river and lake transportation, to say nothing of his miscellaneous industrial enterprises, Gould was one of the decisive factors in American business life. An idea of his far-reaching influence in the railroad industry alone can be realized from the following computation showing his railroad empire at its peak at the end of 1881.

Gould's Railroad Empire, December 31, 1881	
Central of New Jersey	557
Delaware, Lackawanna & Western	776
Denver & Rio Grande	1,065
International Great Northern	776
Missouri, Kansas & Texas	1,286
Missouri Pacific	904
New York & New England	478
St. Louis, Iron Mountain & Southern	723
Texas & Pacific	1,392
Union Pacific	4,269
Utah Central	280
Wabash	3,348
	15,854
Total miles in country 104,813[33]	

The mileage represented 15 per cent of the mileage of the country's railroads. Not until the days of E. H. Harriman, twenty-five years later, was any railroad system established with the same relative importance in mileage. Gould, however, had another property—the Western Union—which exerted an influence as great as did the railroads in their respective spheres. Through its contracts with the country's railroads, the Western Union made large-scale competition difficult and expensive. His control of the Manhattan in New York City was also made complete in 1887, when the removal of Field left no one on the board to oppose his policies.

This system was established in little more than two and a half years. In the fall of 1878 his hold on the Union Pacific was shaky. Though he held a substantial percentage of Union Pacific stock, he could not liquidate his holdings. Through the skillful use of a relatively small sum raised by the syndicate sale of this stock, he laid the foundation in the next few months for the country's most extensive and diversified corporate empire. In point of control over the corporate and business life of the country, Gould had no equal. His empire of control was not a permanent arrangement. Many parts of the corporate fabric were weak; others were indeed not integral parts at all; still others were bought for speculative and stock-market purposes. Many shrewd observers in succeeding months insisted that no part of this far-flung empire was bought with any permanent purpose in mind.

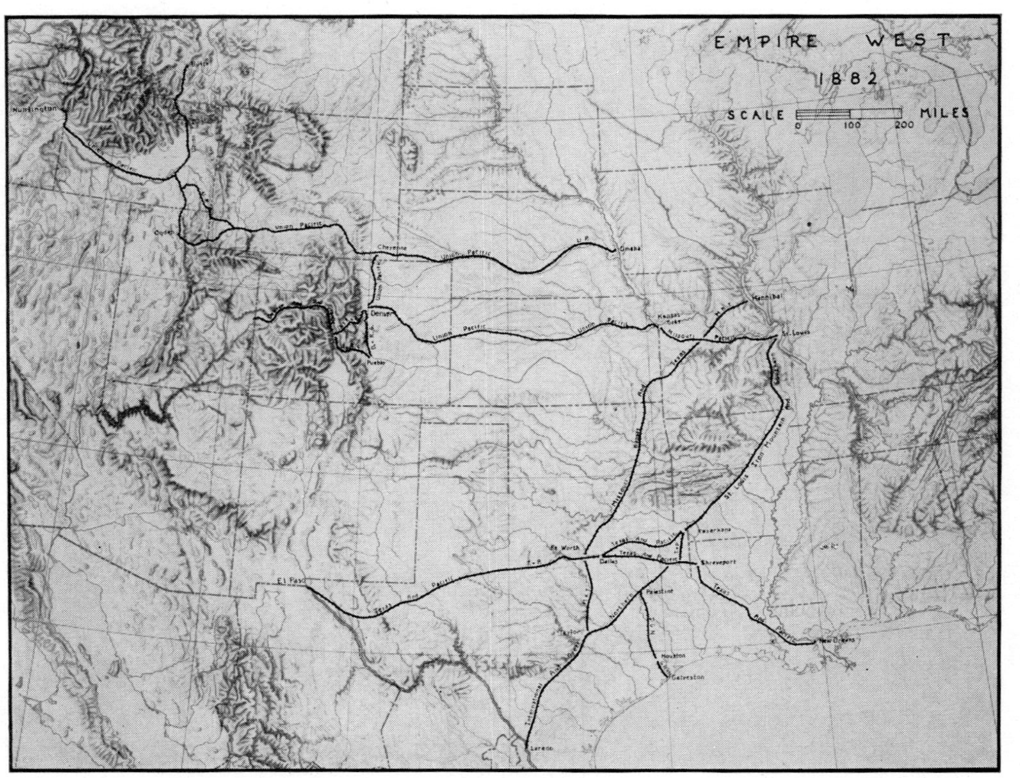
EMPIRE WEST
1882
SCALE 0 100 200 MILES
Huntington
Ogden
Union Pacific
Cheyenne
Omaha
Denver
Pueblo
Hannibal
St. Louis
St. Louis Iron Mountain
Texarkana
Shreveport
Ft. Worth
Dallas
El Paso
Texas and Pacific
Palestine
Houston
Galveston
International
Laredo
New Orleans

Nevertheless at its peak in 1881 it gave Gould unprecedented financial power; and to other observers he seemed, in the few years following the establishment of this empire, to be the country's uncrowned business dictator.

As the year 1881 passed on into the pages of history, Gould was by no means ready to sit back and rest. He was deeply involved in trading operations. Misjudging the trends of the markets from the summer of 1881 on, he adopted a trading strategy that almost resulted in disaster. It was not long after the end of the brilliant year of 1881 that, in recognition of his overexpanded position, he began to contract his corporate system, to sell out here and there, to reduce his obligations, and to cut his losses, and in other cases to cash in on his gains. In other parts of his system he expanded continuously. Both in the East and in the West, and in the wide stretches of the Southwest, he came into repeated conflicts with existing companies and railroad systems, and with towering and aggressive personalities. In these conflicts he was by no means successful. In some cases he lost heavily, and in others he won. Regardless of immediate results, however, he exercised a commanding influence in the country's financial, business, and economic life.

NOTES FOR CHAPTER XVII

1. *Am. R. R. Journal*, April 9, 1870, 400.
2. R. R. Gaz., Aug. 1, 1874, 297.
3. Ibid., Dec. 27, 1878, 629.
4. Herapath's Ry. *Journal*, June 25, 1881, 778.
5. R. R. Gaz., July 8, 1881, 375.
6. New York *Times*, March 11, 1889.
7. The terms of the contract are given in *Chron.*, June 18, 1881, 659; and in R. R. Gaz., July 8, 1881, 375.
8. Herapath's Ry. *Journal*, Aug. 13, 1881, 999.
9. This is the expression used editorially in Phila. *Press*, April 6, 1881.
10. Phila. *North American*, May 31, 1883.
11. *Am. R. R. Journal*, Oct. 16, 1880, 1147.
12. This account of the Utah & Northern is based upon the Phila. *North American*, Nov. 8, 1880; and United States Pacific Railway Commission, Testimony, Executive Document No. 51, Senate, 50th Congress, 1st Session, 1887, 2173, John Sharp.
13. Ibid., 1851-4, Evans.
14. Ry. *World*, Dec. 15, 1880, 1226.
15. This program is described in detail in the St. Louis *Republican*, cited in Ry. *Review*, Feb. 12, 1881, 87.
16. New York *Tribune*, Jan. 8, 1881.
17. Ry. *World*, Nov. 20, 1880, 1113.

18. This is the opinion expressed, for example, in *Ry. Review*, April 17, 1880, 184.
19. *Ry. World*, June 11, 1881, 564.
20. Crocker to Huntington, Oct. 7, 1881, M. M.
21. Ibid., Aug. 5, 1881, M. M.; the Northwestern also offered a route over one of its Missouri Valley lines, Crocker to Huntington, Oct. 8, 1881, M. M.
22. *Ry. Review*, Sept. 24, 1881, 535.
23. Crocker to Huntington, Sept. 30, 1881, M. M.
24. Ibid., no date, but written some time in October, 1881, M. M.
25. See No. 62, House of Representatives, Committee on Public Lands, 48th Congress, 1st Session, 1884, for details on the Texas & Pacific Land-Grant and the Gould-Huntington agreement.
26. Phila. *North American*, Nov. 5, 1881.
27. New York *World*, Dec. 18, 1881.
28. New York *Evening Mail & Express*, Nov. 17, 1881.
29. A list of principal subscribers to the stock of the American Railway and Improvement Co. is found in the Dodge papers in the Iowa State Historical Society, Des Moines, Iowa.
30. New York *Evening Mail & Express*, Oct. 6, 1881.
31. Prices of construction company shares are taken from *Bradstreet*, Aug. 6, 1881, 82.
32. New York *Evening Mail & Express*, Oct. 26, 1881.
33. Mileage from Poor's *Manual of Railroads*, 1882.

CHAPTER XVIII

W. H. Vanderbilt Takes the Offensive

By the sophisticated onlooker, particularly the trader and banker, Gould's empire was viewed with suspicion. Most observers were convinced that Gould was still the same as before, that what he bought at low prices he would sell at high prices. Almost every market break was credited to Gould; he was selling his stock or some other stock, or he was shifting his interests in such a way as to facilitate the purchase of a low-priced stock in order to make a market for some other security. At the same time railroad men felt the lash of Gould's whip. Dealing with stocks he acted as a trader; in the field of railroad strategy he was a man of business and as such pressed ahead aggressively, and repeatedly forced issues. He changed the railroad map; he carved new traffic and corporate alliances; he built thousands of miles of road. Railroad men, in considering long-term policies, therefore, had to consider Gould's activities. Even though Wall Street men looked upon him as a trader, as one of their kind, railroad men could not operate without considering his intentions and activities. They could no more ignore him as a trader than they could ignore him as a railroad builder, promoter, or executive.

Both railroad men and traders were correct. If Gould was selling stocks, he may have been selling only part of his holdings. Even though he sold all the stocks of some parts of his empire, he kept other parts intact, and perhaps sold the stocks of still other parts only in such amounts as not to disturb either the majority interest or a controlling minority interest. Even if he sold a controlling interest, he still managed to maintain an influence over corporate policy. If he did not have enough votes to elect a majority of the board of directors, he might have sufficient votes or proxies to elect himself and one or more of his associates.

Even though he owned few shares in a road, he might be able to determine its corporate policy.

In 1881 and 1882 Gould's system consisted of three major parts. In the East it was built largely around the Wabash. In the West the Union Pacific was the basic property, while in the Southwest the system was built around the Missouri Pacific with which the Iron Mountain had been almost completely merged. Of these the most complex in the early and middle eighties was in the East, where the four major trunk lines that still dominate this area had already been established. The Pennsylvania, with its through lines between Chicago, St. Louis, Philadelphia, and New York, was the most complete system. The other three trunk lines were as yet incomplete. The Erie, handicapped by a succession of blunders and misdeeds, had no through line of its own to Chicago. Though the Baltimore & Ohio had completed its Chicago line in 1874, it had not built to Philadelphia and New York. The New York Central, though stronger than either the Baltimore & Ohio or the Erie in control of traffic routes, was weaker than the Pennsylvania. It extended only to Buffalo from which point, through the Lake Shore holdings of Vanderbilt, it reached Chicago. The system, however, had no outlet to St. Louis, Cincinnati, and Indianapolis. On the other hand, it occupied a position of strength in the rich traffic area between Chicago and Detroit where the dominant line, the Michigan Central, was controlled by Vanderbilt. The Wabash struck out from its major point of interchange in St. Louis like the vanguard of an aggressive army with its spearhead at Toledo. In the territory between Toledo and St. Louis, it reached more important traffic centers than any road, with the exception of the Pennsylvania.

The Wabash distribution of its eastbound traffic among three major lines in 1881 was made shortly after the trunk-line territory was struck by a violent rate war. Since most of its traffic was competitive, the effect on the Wabash was tragic. Its financial, as contrasted with its traffic, fortunes were at the mercy of railroad rates. More than any other property in the East, its earning power depended upon rates for through traffic. The Wabash, furthermore, on its line from Chicago to Kansas City, was engaged in a passenger war.[1] While the gross revenue enriched by the heavy through business fed by Gould's southwestern system was increasing, the profit was declining. Gould, however, did not publish the current month-by-month net earnings. He reported gross earnings only, and these revealed growth. In January, 1881, the preferred stock began to pay quarterly dividends, though conservative judgment did not merit such action. Gould, however, had a personal stock-market position to consider, so he paid the dividend—with apologies. Admitting that the earning power was not satisfactory, he held a number of nonrecurring factors responsible.[2]

Matters did not improve and it was evident as the months rolled on that earnings were declining. Nevertheless, the Wabash preferred dividend due in November, 1881, was paid as usual though the dividend was not earned, and neither was the interest. The cash necessary to pay the dividend was borrowed from Gould and his associates. Before the end of the month the financial condition of the Wabash became generally known, and the price of the stock dropped sharply. By the end of the year the road did not have cash sufficient even to pay interest. Humphreys, president of the Wabash, resigned, and Gould succeeded him.

This is an excellent example of Gould's corporate technique. Gould and Sage, in control of the financial policy of the property, had made advances to the company to enable it to pay an unearned dividend. In a declining market, the payment of the dividend maintained the price of the stock. Gould and Sage, who made small loans to facilitate the payment of a relatively small dividend, sold out most of their holdings at high prices. After thus disposing of his stock, Gould, far from resigning from the board, assumed the presidency of the road. In doing so he consulted no stockholders, called no stockholders' meeting, and took counsel only with himself and possibly with a few of his fellow directors.

Gould's assumption of executive power in the affairs of the Wabash passed over almost unnoticed. The break in its securities had come before he assumed power, and perhaps he was considered by some investors as a rescuing angel. The poor earnings were not made public until the following April when the public was informed that a rise in the year's gross of about 16 per cent was accompanied by a decline in net of more than 20 per cent. The deficit after fixed charges amounted to $1,412,000.

While the investors in Wabash were being harmed, the Wabash itself as a factor in the railroad business was losing none of its strategic importance. Vanderbilt was now convinced of his mistake in co-operating with Gould. He recognized that Gould's cat-and-mouse policy of dangling traffic possibilities, first before the Great Western, and then before his lines, had extorted concessions from each. He therefore decided to strengthen his system in one of its most vulnerable points—the area between Cleveland, Toledo and St. Louis. The Bee Line owning roads to Cincinnati and Indianapolis and a 50 per cent interest in a line to St. Louis had long been a dividend-payer. Because of its excellent earnings and dividend record, its stock sold at a high price—apparently too high to please Commodore Vanderbilt. While he was awaiting the opportunity to acquire the stock at lower levels, McHenry in 1873 on behalf of the Atlantic bought a large block of the stock sufficient to insure control. Amid much legal confusion involving considerable litigation, control of the road in 1874 passed to the Erie. The Erie's title, however, was not clear, and a group of stockholders resisted the proposed transfer of control to that road.[3]

Precisely how Vanderbilt acquired a controlling interest in the Bee Line is not known. The negotiations were secret, and the event of actual control in the fall of 1881 was a complete surprise, especially to the Erie, which gave the Bee Line four times more traffic than did the New York Central.[4]

In view of the 50 per cent interest of the Pennsylvania in the road from Indianapolis to St. Louis, Vanderbilt's control was incomplete, and for traffic purposes, ineffective. Joint control of a property in the interests of neutrality, experience had already demonstrated, meant an unenterprising management. Fortunately, the Pennsylvania was willing to step out.

Vanderbilt was now in control of a through line from the Lake Shore to St. Louis. He could, therefore, more effectively fight the Wabash, since he could now exercise a strong influence on the movement of its traffic by cutting eastbound rates from St. Louis.

The expansion of Vanderbilt into the area southwest of Toledo was only part of the battle with Gould. Gould, operating through the Central of New Jersey and Lackawanna, was negotiating traffic alliances designed to divert traffic from the Vanderbilt properties. The Lackawanna's Buffalo extension was aimed at a large flow of New York Central traffic from the Lackawanna. Vanderbilt, in a fighting mood, did not propose to accept this loss meekly and took measures to parry the blow.

In the Pennsylvania anthracite region south of the territory served by the Lackawanna, the Reading originated a heavy volume of westbound traffic which it delivered at Williamsport, Pennsylvania, to the Pennsylvania system. To recoup the New York Central for the anthracite traffic lost by the building of the Lackawanna's extension, Vanderbilt proposed to divert the Reading's westbound business at Williamsport from the Pennsylvania system. The New York Central in turn would divert its eastbound business to Philadelphia from the Lackawanna-Pennsylvania Railroad route to the Reading.[5] Though the New York Central did not physically connect with the Reading, such a connection could apparently be made at reasonable cost.

To carry out his program Vanderbilt thought it essential to secure a large stock interest in the Reading. The road was in receivership and a contest for control was then in progress. Gowen, a brilliant attorney, a remarkable phrase-maker, a man who carried conviction and thrilled audiences, a man who in many respects was more of a political leader than a business executive, was the leader of one party. He had built up the combined Reading Railroad and coal system. Its original plans for a trunk line to the west were replaced by a policy to insure domination of the coal mines in the Schuylkill area in eastern Pennsylvania. Coal lands were bought with borrowed funds at top prices prevailing in the late sixties and early seventies. The slump in prices after the panic of 1873 broke the back of the Reading, and in 1880 it went into receivership.

An important group of security holders, who had no faith in the brilliant but erratic genius of Gowen, supported Frederick S. Bond—a man sympathetic to the interests of Gould. Here Vanderbilt saw an opportunity. Having learned from his experience with Gould, he resolved to intercede in the family troubles of the Reading, and decided to support Gowen. In July, 1881, shortly after the Pennsylvania-Wabash-Central of New Jersey traffic contract was concluded, he assumed the initiative and asked Gowen to meet him in Saratoga. A bargain was struck. Vanderbilt agreed to use his influence to elect Gowen, and Gowen agreed, if elected, to send the Reading's anthracite business over the New York Central.[6]

At the annual meeting of the Reading in January, 1882, the balloting was close. The final vote revealed that Vanderbilt had purchased a large block of Reading stock on his own account and had secured the proxies of a number of important groups. With Vanderbilt's help Gowen was elected to the presidency of the Reading.

This new community of interests produced far-reaching results in the eastern railroad industry. Only a few months before, Vanderbilt had insisted upon the importance of the differential problem to New York. Within two weeks after Gowen's election to the presidency of the Reading, Vanderbilt changed his mind. Withdrawing his opposition to the demands of the Philadelphia and Baltimore roads, he joined with the other trunk lines to submit the differential question to a special commission. The war that had been raging since June, 1881, was settled, and the old rates were re-established. This agreement also provided for the first time for the pooling of eastbound freight in trunk-line territory.[7]

Vanderbilt, meanwhile, made arrangements to secure a physical connection with the Reading. A small property with a charter was acquired; a number of new companies were organized; and plans for the building of additional trackage were made. By these means, the Reading at Williamsport was connected with the New York Central in southern New York, thus creating a new route for the westbound movement of anthracite over the Reading-New York Central lines. The cost was heavy. Although the initial mortgage amounted to $2,500,000, Vanderbilt finally invested about $20,000,000 in the project.[8]

Vanderbilt was now assured of westbound coal business to replace that lost to the Lackawanna's extension. The gain to the New York Central, however, was a loss to the Pennsylvania, and the latter was therefore determined to block the new Gowen-Vanderbilt combination. A curious corporate mélange soon emerged—a situation so relished by the ingenious mind of Gould. Gowen, in control of the Reading management, was anxious to work with Garrett of the Baltimore & Ohio, and Garrett was equally anxious to work with Gowen. Both wanted to get to New York City but that goal could be realized only by the acquisition of the Central of New Jersey. Gould early in 1882 was still in control of that line, even though he had sold most of his stock. Instead of retiring from the Central of New Jersey, however, he suddenly became active. Although only a year before he had fought the Pennsylvania through his effort to capture the Wilmington, he now became its great friend and ally. Since acquisition of the Central of New Jersey by the Reading would increase their competitive strength, the Pennsylvania was determined to block the union. The Central of New Jersey had outstanding about 185,000 shares—which could be increased only with the consent of two-thirds of its stockholders, and about $8,000,000 of callable bonds. An ingenious scheme was devised—a scheme which for surprise, secrecy, and boldness rivaled even that of the great bond-stock conversion of the Erie in 1868. With the support of the influential Pennsylvania Railroad [9] a bill was quietly pushed through the New Jersey legislature—"a brief and apparently unimportant bill" [10]—to authorize the company to sell 80,000 shares of common stock to finance the retirement of the bonds. If the Gould group bought all the stock, it would have the controlling interest. It was a lovely scheme and almost succeeded. According to one source, the Gould group had planned to buy the entire block before the Garrett party could get a single share, although this report was denied by the vice president and a board member.[11]

In the legislature Gould in co-operation with the Pennsylvania was influential. The president and receiver of the Central of New Jersey, Judge Lathrop, knew every legislator personally. This friendship did not, however, extend to the governor, and the bill was vetoed. The assembly then passed it over the governor's veto, and the case went to the courts. Gould was unfortunate with the courts of New Jersey in 1882 as he had been with the courts of Ohio in 1869, and after considerable delay the new stock issue was enjoined. For the first and last time the Pennsylvania and Gould were jointly and simultaneously defeated.

Gould's influence in the Central of New Jersey was now approaching its end. Although he had but little financial interest in the property and had no system use for it, he did not give up without a fight. The Garrett-Gowen party appealed to the receiver for the necessary authority for a stockholders' meeting. The law as usual was technical. There were many delays and not until late in May did the court order a stockholders' meeting for the specific purpose of electing a new board. Even as Gould surrendered, he kept on fighting. In exchange for some stock, he agreed to support the Baltimore & Ohio in its efforts to acquire a line into New York City, while Garrett agreed to make "certain concessions" in shaping the policy of the Baltimore & Ohio Telegraph. What that statement meant, however, was not clear.

Within little more than a year after his appearance in eastern territory, his influence as a factor in the determination of policy was revealed in its correct proportion. The through route via the Central of New Jersey and the Pennsylvania traffic contract was only a market hoax enabling him to make an excellent trade of a large block of Central of New Jersey. It was a skillful piece of work, requiring patience in accumulation of the stock, careful negotiations with a leading trunk line to make the Central of New Jersey to appear what it was not—a part of a new through route between the Lakes at Toledo via the Wabash and the eastern seaboard, and patience and skill to distribute the stock at higher prices in the summer and fall of 1881.

In his capacity as a factor in the affairs of the Lackawanna, however, Gould's position was more permanent. When the extension was first projected in the summer of 1880, it was not clear how he would connect his Wabash at Toledo with the new extension in Buffalo. In April, 1881, however, a new project promised to modify traffic alignments in such a way as to give the Wabash the desired connection. At that time a syndicate led by George I. Seney, Samuel Thomas, and C. S. Brice organized a new company, the New York, Chicago & St. Louis,[12] popularly known as the "Nickel Plate," to build a line from Buffalo to Chicago, designed to parallel the Lake Shore. When completed the road would make an ally of the Lackawanna or the Lehigh Valley—the latter an anthracite carrier which through a trackage arrangement with the Erie also reached Buffalo.

The road was extravagantly built, a typical product of a construction company arrangement. Brice was the major beneficiary of the venture. Although he did not have $500 in ready cash, he managed to subscribe to $500,000 of the construction company's stock.[13]

Since it was built not to operate a line or necessarily to do a railroad business, but to force another group to buy it and leave the promoters with a profit, little stress was placed upon good construction. The more cheaply the line could be built, the greater the promoters' profits. Consequently the road was poorly built. Vanderbilt himself, in a sarcastic and savage interview, expressed his opinion of the property thus: "It is a poor piece of work," he said, "and you can't tell me anything else, for I know it to be a fact. I hear that on the trial trip they went over some parts of the road at the rate of nearly a mile a minute. Well, somebody else will strike some of their elegant trestle work some of these days and go over it a mile a minute and faster too. . . . No man or set of men with sound sense could expect to build such a road and operate it to make it pay. . . . They seem to think that because the Lake Shore, an old well-established road in splendid working order, is doing a large and successful business, they can rush right in with a half-built road and do likewise. . . ." [14]

By October of 1882 the road, although it had not yet acquired Chicago terminal facilities, was about finished, and it appeared clear that by early November it would be ready to do business. The promoters were in touch with the Lehigh Valley, and according to its vice president, there was "a tacit understanding" that upon its completion, it would buy the property. "One thing is certain," stated this official, "our people fully [intend] to buy the Nickel Plate." [15] Representatives of the road may have also negotiated with Gould, for on a trip to the West in late October, Gould, accompanied by the vice president of the Wabash, remarked to some of his friends that he had been invited to examine the road and give an opinion.

How much truth there was in these rumors and reports it is impossible to say. The property was in poor financial condition. By early summer of 1882, the price of the stock having declined substantially, it is probable that Gould was anxious to acquire control, though he was not willing to pay a high price for the stock of a road which was not earning its interest. Gould, however, denied any such intention. "I don't meddle with Eastern lines at all," he declared, "and never had a dollar's worth of interest in the Nickel-Plate Railroad, nor did I ever have any negotiations with anybody with a view to secure it." [16]

It is impossible to state the precise moment at which Vanderbilt decided to acquire control. Only a few weeks before he bought the stock of the company, he had denounced the road as a high-cost, poorly operated machine. On the face of things it probably would have been well to leave the property alone and to take the chance of acquiring it in receivership. Gould, however, had repeatedly shown his ability to use a property aggressively for the purpose of tearing down values, and it was probable that the Nickel Plate in the hands of Gould could be made the basis for a new major trunk line in eastern territory.

These are only inferences, and the truth may be found elsewhere. In any event, Vanderbilt late in October suddenly purchased control. The acquisition, however, was not as surprising as the high price paid. According to one account, written many years after the event, the promoters were close to bankruptcy, and had the contract not been made, Thomas and Brice would have been paupers.[17]

Vanderbilt did not include the Nickel Plate in traffic routes in such a way as to shut it off from alliances with other roads. The Wabash and the Lackawanna were free to make arrangements with it, although to promote stability in the rate structure Vanderbilt insisted that the Nickel Plate should get its percentage of the regular rate.[18] Vanderbilt had thus checked the Wabash at Toledo and he must also have believed that he had prevented it from extending its rate cuts to the territory east of that point. The unsettling influence of the Wabash on the fortunes of the New York Central system was by no means exhausted. The 1881 contract for the distribution of Wabash eastbound traffic proved unprofitable to all concerned. Shortly after he assumed the presidency of the Wabash, Gould gave notice of his intention to abrogate the contract, an action which had far-reaching consequences. Proposals for many years had been repeatedly made to merge the Grand Trunk with the Great Western. The latter's friendship for the Wabash blocked the union. The Wabash contract cancellation destroyed that friendship. In May, 1882, the old board of the Great Western resigned and a new one pledged to carry out the merger with the Grand Trunk was elected.

This corporate union destroyed the profits of the traffic interchange between the merged system and the Vanderbilt lines. Since the new system competed for business at Chicago with the Lake Shore, it was to the interest of the Grand Trunk (as the new system now was called) to carry freight over its own lines from Chicago through Detroit to Buffalo and the East. On westbound traffic it was more advantageous to carry the business over its own long haul to Chicago. It was therefore no longer profitable for the Michigan Central, as part of the Vanderbilt system, to divide its eastbound business between the Canada Southern and the Great Western in exchange for the westbound traffic delivered by the latter. With the Great Western now part of a competitive system, Vanderbilt decided to acquire control of the Canada Southern and to divert all of the Michigan Central's business over that line, thereby moving the eastbound and westbound business over a combined system route between Chicago and Buffalo via Detroit.

Unification between the Canada Southern and the Michigan Central was finally consummated in November, 1882. Vanderbilt found it impossible to induce the stubborn Hollanders who had a controlling interest in the Canada Southern to sell their stock. Nevertheless they had confidence in Vanderbilt and raised no objection to the execution of a twenty-one-year agreement by which the Michigan Central agreed to operate the Canada Southern, with the earnings of the two roads paid into a common treasury.[19] This agreement proved to be a permanent influence in the financial and industrial life of the country. The Canada Southern-Michigan Central route between Buffalo and Chicago became in the course of time an indispensable part of the enlarged Vanderbilt system. The event might have happened normally without the encouragement of Gould and his ambiguous traffic policies, but in fact it was the dillydallying and the shift of traffic agreements and business loyalties between the Great Western and the Vanderbilt interests that produced the new alliance.

The new Grand Trunk system became an ally of the Gould lines. It was the only independent connection between the Lackawanna at Buffalo, completed just about the time of the execution of the Michigan Central-Canada Southern agreement, and the Wabash at Detroit. The power of Gould through the Wabash to throw traffic over either the Vanderbilt lines at Toledo or the Grand Trunk at Buffalo was now curtailed. The strategic bargaining strength of the Wabash was reduced and that of the Lake Shore increased.

Under these conditions it would have been prudent for Gould to aid in stabilizing the railroad rate structure and in that way improve the earnings of the Wabash. Gould, however, repeating his decision of 1879 and 1880, did not choose that path. For more than a year following the 1882 agreement, eastern rates had been well maintained. Albert Fink, the able chairman of the association which supervised the operation of the pool, remarked late in that year that the trunk lines since the middle of March had "very effectually maintained" their tariffs.[20] Gould, however, was not content with the arrangement, and could not forego the advantage of every opportunity for scalping business. He was soon to discover that Vanderbilt had made his last gesture of concession.

Fink early in 1883 had referred charitably to some irregularities which appeared to disturb the picture of rate harmony. The truth was more serious than that pictured by the tactful chairman. Gould, followed by Vanderbilt, had indeed introduced practices which violated, in spirit if not in letter, the entire intent of the pool. The rates applied only to through traffic from Chicago to St. Louis to the seaboard, and not to intermediate points. A western road at St. Louis in billing its eastbound traffic was therefore free to make rates to these intermediate points at a figure less than the mileage proportion of the through rate. Combined local rates, contrary to railroad experience, was therefore less than the through rates. This practice, known as short billing, was a form of deception and was so denounced by Fink.[21]

Another practice, equally repugnant to the spirit of the pooling agreement, was reported to Fink by the Wabash. Complaint was made that the Vanderbilt line out of St. Louis made half-number waybills which were not reported to the pooling commissioner. Investigation confirmed the truth of the charge; but it was discovered that the Wabash had also adopted this practice but on a much larger scale. Inasmuch as under the terms of the pool each St. Louis road received an equal amount of traffic, carriage of unreported freight was another deception upon the other members of the pool. "This is," remarked Fink, "perhaps, the most utterly scandalous of the many scandalous tricks that have been played in the traffic departments of the railroads. The St. Louis railroads are virtually partners, and the failure of one to report any of the pooled business is equivalent to one partner's pocketing a payment due to the firm." [22]

The 1881 rate war meanwhile had produced heavy financial losses to Gould's eastern railroads. Two of them—the Wabash and the New England—were embarrassed at once by an abundance of traffic and a scarcity of earnings. Following Gould's assumption of the presidency of the Wabash in 1882, there were continued reports of declines in earnings. Gould denied such reports. Similar denials came from the New England. Both roads were choked with business, but the business was moved at low rates.

The financial condition of both these Gould lines, however, grew more desperate. Publication of the Wabash annual report for 1882 revealed a condition which shocked both speculators and investors. While the gross revenue rose sharply, the company did not earn its fixed charges. The road was face to face with receivership, and unless outside aid could be secured a flight to the courts for relief against pressing creditors seemed inevitable. Gould could have abandoned the line just as he had others; as only the year before he had dropped the Central of New Jersey and its projected through route in eastern territory.

The Wabash, however, although financially decrepit was an invaluable aid to Gould. He was primarily interested in his southwestern system, and for that very reason he was interested in the Wabash. Jointly with the Missouri Pacific, the Wabash controlled the St. Louis terminal facilities and made through routes and joint rates. In control of both lines, Gould could keep rates of the southwestern roads high and the rates of the Wabash low. In behalf of his southwestern lines it was essential to keep the eastern rate structure unbalanced, since low rates on the Wabash meant higher rates for the Missouri Pacific. This is what informed critical judgment for some years could not comprehend. Observers predicted a conclusion upon a balanced eastern rate schedule, even when it was essential to Gould, as master of the Wabash, to unbalance that schedule. Gould therefore decided to maintain control of the Wabash. In view of its inability to cover its fixed charges, his retention of the line posed a definite problem.

His resourcefulness had rarely failed him in the past and it did not fail him now. After he bought a large block of the stock of the Wabash at the prevailing low prices, he proposed a lease of the road. To insure approval of the idea, he obtained first the support of a group of foreign shareholders, with the Morgan-London firm cabling its approval.[23] The lease was to the Iron Mountain (a lease to the parent Missouri Pacific would have been illegal), most of whose stock was owned by the Missouri Pacific. The lease did not guarantee the unconditional payment of the fixed charges of the Wabash. In form it was a net earnings lease similar to that of the Kansas & Texas. If the road had any earnings, the lessee generously permitted the lessor to keep those earnings; but if the lessor had no earnings, then the lessee could, if it wished, lend money to enable the lessor to pay its fixed charges. The lessee was free at any time to decide that it no longer felt it wise or advisable—these terms being defined in the light of their own interests—to pay the lessor's fixed charges. Little wonder that Sage, ever the confidant of Gould, exclaimed in high glee that the lease would "be a great thing for all of us—there is no doubt about that. Why, it will be another Kansas & Texas lease—that's it. We shall give the Wabash its net earnings but nothing more. We shall guarantee nothing." [24]

The lease served Gould well. The southwestern lines and the Wabash were now operated as one. Though Gould solved his immediate problem of preserving the solvency of the Wabash, he accomplished little in preserving the eastern rate structure. The competitive situation in the summer months became more and more critical. Late in the spring the Lackawanna made a bid for a heavy sugar contract. It organized a fast freight line with the Nickel Plate and the Grand Trunk, thereby offering a through line to Chicago, and with the help of Vanderbilt's Bee Line, it was able to establish a route to St. Louis. Suddenly early in May, Vanderbilt announced that he would refuse to haul Lackawanna cars over his St. Louis line, thus forcing the Lackawanna to withdraw from the business. Vanderbilt thus had thrown off the mask of friendship.

Intra-industrial warfare soon became so keen that the eastern railroad presidents finally decided to try to restore stability. In a meeting held a few weeks after Vanderbilt's action, they charged the Grand Trunk with having participated in the Lackawanna's rate cuts, a charge which the Grand Trunk denied. The meeting accomplished nothing. A renewed effort was then made to induce the Lackawanna to join the pool, but the Lackawanna refused.

Gould was momentarily placed on the defensive. His thrust at Vanderbilt for his refusal to carry the Lackawanna's cars to St. Louis was ineffective. After weeks of negotiation he succeeded only in making a deal with the Grand Trunk for the formation of a new route, consisting of the Grand Trunk to Detroit, the Wabash beyond Detroit to a small point in northern Illinois, and the Baltimore & Ohio from that point to Chicago. Although the Lackawanna could now compete for Chicago business, the route was circuitous and could operate successfully only by virtue of a differential rate.

Meanwhile the war of rates which so many had dismissed as of slight consequence was about to be converted into a struggle of major proportions. The Lackawanna first reduced rates on westbound business. The New York Central and the Erie followed. The Lackawanna stoutly maintained that it was not cutting rates, and continued to report its traffic to the Joint Executive Committee operating the eastern trunk-line pool.[25]

The prospect of a wide-open rate war appeared imminent. A meeting of eastern presidents was again called, and again nothing was done. Another meeting at which the presidents met representatives of their western connections soon followed. The Vanderbilt lines insisted that they were the greatest sufferers. Various proposals to settle the difficulties were made. No agreement was reached and the meeting finally ended in talk. No effective sanctions were provided, and there was nothing to induce Gould to change his rate-cutting tactics. The Lackawanna remained outside of the pool—and Gould was free through rate cuts and other devices to capture as much traffic as competitive conditions permitted.

In the first week of November still another meeting of eastern presidents was called. All roads recognized that the Lackawanna was at fault. A decision was finally reached: the Grand Trunk and the other lines agreed that if the Lackawanna continued to cut rates, the pool lines would neither make through lines with it, exchange through cars, nor maintain through connections.[26]

Regardless of consequences, the pool was forced to act, for now a new factor of major importance had entered the picture. Vanderbilt, after many years of experience with concessions, had decided to engage in an aggressive war on his own account. Early in November both of his lines—the Lake Shore and the New York Central—began to cut rates in order to recover traffic lost to competitive roads.

The pool moved fast. The commissioner, acting upon instructions of the president, informed the Lackawanna that all its western connections including the Grand Trunk would discontinue traffic arrangements. A week later the Lackawanna apparently surrendered by agreeing to divide traffic and maintain rates. Negotiations were immediately opened in order to decide on the division to be made to the new member.

On December 31 the executive committee of the pool offered the Lackawanna an allotment which would give it 50 per cent more net than it had earned in the first ten months of the year. The Lackawanna not only declined the offer, it even refused to arbitrate. Owing largely to the numerous contracts made at reduced rates, it was now carrying a much larger volume than in the first ten months of the year. It now insisted that the increased traffic should be considered in deciding its percentage of the pooled business.[27] The trunk-line pool, however, had reached the end of its resources. Gould, acting through the Lackawanna, had made compromise impossible and both the Lackawanna and the Vanderbilt lines were cutting indiscriminately. The chairman of the pool, acting upon instructions, informed the Lackawanna that all of its western connections would refuse to move its freight on through waybills, and that freight would have to be rebilled at Buffalo. Any reduction in rates made by the Lackawanna would therefore fall upon it alone since its western connections would accept for their services their proportion of the through tariff rate west of Buffalo. They would accept no rate cuts.

The order immediately went into effect. Gould now recognized that he had gone as far as he could. Since he could no longer cut rates without exacting a corresponding reduction from competitive lines, he intervened to stabilize rate conditions. The Lackawanna board met and authorized him to offer the trunk lines a proposal for arbitration.[28] Gould acted promptly. Before twenty-four hours had passed he had already made overtures. Sloan, as president, agreed to refer outstanding questions to arbitration, and the Lackawanna withdrew its legal proceedings.

The fight was over, or so it seemed, and the trunk lines could breathe a sigh of relief. They could breathe as easily, probably, as did the Western Union board in August of 1877 after they had bought Gould's Atlantic & Pacific. Gould himself was optimistic. "I think," he remarked, "that [it] is a great thing. I think it will help to restore confidence not only here, but among foreign investors." And then he declared, probably as an afterthought, "I have made up my mind to hold on to the stocks whose value I know. . . ." [29] The mainspring of Gould's interest in this settlement was thus clarified. It was made with an eye upon the stock market. Gould was heavily involved in the market and a settlement by eliminating the rate war would elevate the price of railroad stocks which he held in abundance.[30]

Gould was now in his turn to be surprised and confounded. He was now the arbitrator and compromiser. He was trying to conserve something from a threatened wreck. No longer in an aggressive mood, he now wanted peace and harmony. The New York Central insisted that, while it was willing to maintain rates, it would not lose a pound of business regardless of rates. "We have partly recovered our lost business," said an official, "we intend to get it all back, and we will not relinquish a pound of the freight we have recovered." [31] Vanderbilt saw no reason to restore rates merely to save the Gould lines, and it was not only the Lackawanna which was now involved, but the Wabash as well.

The settlement in mid-January which engendered such optimism from Gould proved temporary. Within two weeks the rates in trunk-line territory between the Mississippi and the seaboard were again demoralized, and in early February a meeting of the presidents was again called. The war of rates had been exceptionally severe upon his ill-fated Wabash; Gould therefore appeared personally as president of the Wabash to urge harmony. The new rate situation was more serious than anything which had gone before. One railroad man remarked that "the situation had reached the stage where every route knew that rates had to be restored or everything would go to pot." [32] Probably more to save the Wabash than the Lackawanna, Gould again decided to accept the decision of the arbitrators on the Lackawanna's share of the existing traffic. Since written and formal agreements had not settled the rate disputes, the meeting of February 7 adopted another plan. An agreement for the restoration of rates and a promise to maintain such rates was signed personally by all the presidents. The trouble again appeared to be settled, and a well-informed trade journal stated flatly that the agreement had restored rates.[33]

Gould was indeed anxious to establish harmony. He had attended the meetings of trunk-line presidents called for the purpose of stopping rate wars, a thing in itself unusual. He also called upon Fink, the eastern trunk-line commissioner, at his office. None had ever seen him there before. "Mr. Gould's hand," in the words of one current observer, "[was] seen everywhere." [34] Early in March the arbitrators, in a typical arbitration compromise, fixed the award of traffic to the Lackawanna at more than the 10 per cent which the trunk lines had originally offered, but less than the 20 per cent for which the Lackawanna had originally fought.

Nevertheless the rate-cutting continued, and it was not the Gould lines that did the cutting. Strange to say, it was the Vanderbilt lines. Vanderbilt did not intend to delude himself again by Gould's specious promises. He therefore continued to cut rates out of St. Louis, Peoria, and other western points. Not only the Wabash but also the Pennsylvania and the Erie were now complaining.[35]

Fink vainly called upon the presidents to honor their February promises. Long patient and hopeful, he called another meeting for March 13; but he was no longer hopeful. The observation of a financial writer probably reflected Fink's beliefs. "Of course,"

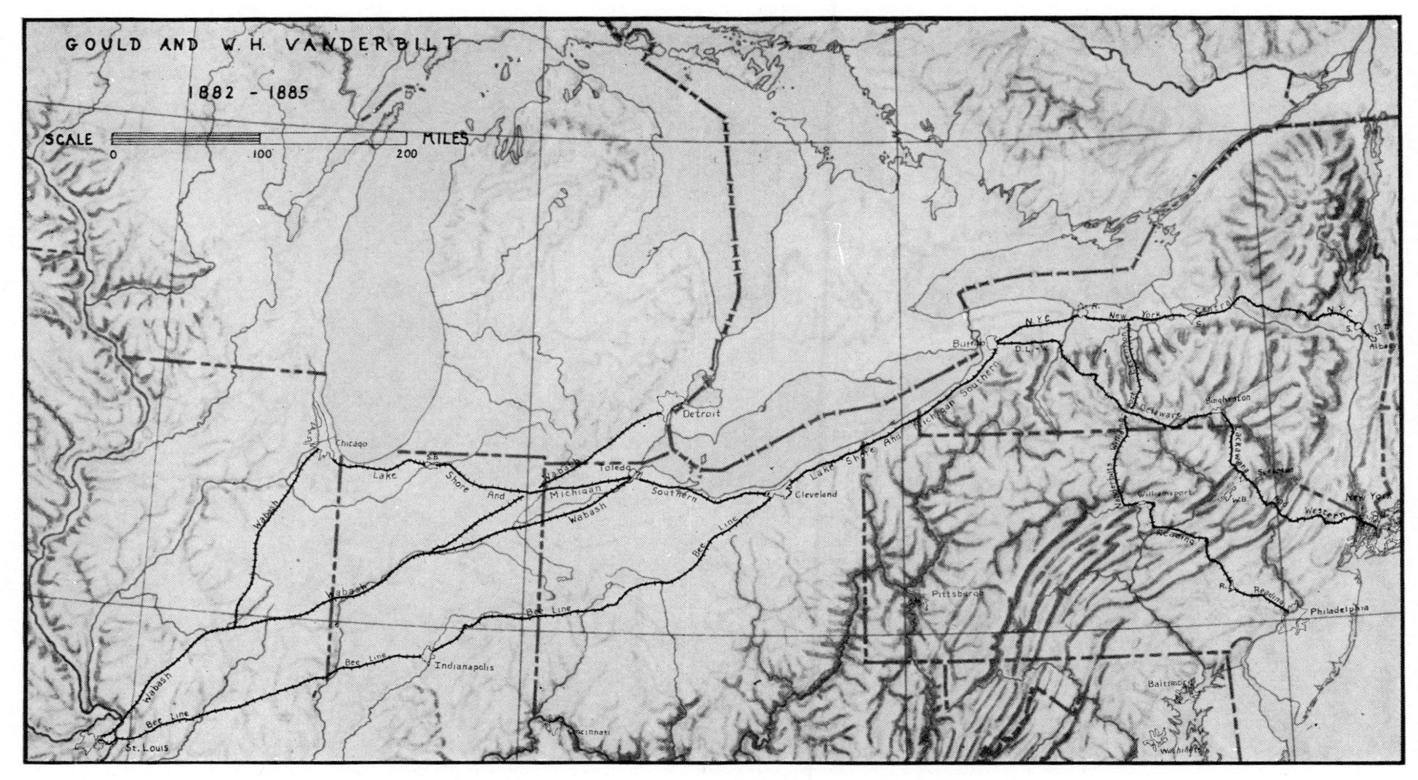
GOULD AND W. H. VANDERBILT
1882 - 1885
SCALE
0
100
200
MILES
Chicago
Detroit
Toledo
Cleveland
Buffalo
Binghamton
Williamsport
New York
Philadelphia
Pittsburgh
Baltimore
Indianapolis
St. Louis
Cincinnati
Lake Shore And Michigan Southern
Wabash
Bee Line
N.Y.C.
New York Central
D.L.W.
Delaware
Reading
Western

wrote this observer, "these gentlemen will meet, partake of the usual conciliatory champagne and oysters, shed potential tears, promise to do so no more, and within twenty-four hours, go to work cutting rates, merrily as ever." [36] Peace was now out of the question. The rate war in the first eleven months of 1883 had produced such fatal results that not even Gould himself could undo his work. At the end of that year, he could have prided himself on his success in diverting a large volume of traffic from the New York Central and the Pennsylvania to the Lackawanna. Gould, however, was mistaken: Vanderbilt was in a fighting mood and would tolerate no interference from Gould or the eastern trunk lines in his struggle to recapture the diverted business.

The meeting of March 13 was, therefore, not a meeting of peace but a council of war. It was probably called because of the Pennsylvania which insisted upon carrying out its pool obligation not to cut rates, but at the same time did not propose to lose any business. It had complained to the pool repeatedly. To use the language of its annual report for 1883 published just before the meeting, the roads with "inferior facilities" attracted business at low rates, and used the "undue" traffic thus secured as a basis for getting "an unfair proportion of the pooled traffic." [37] The Pennsylvania proposed to meet this competition and to reduce rates through the mechanism of the existing trunk-line association. The presidents in their March 13 meeting, therefore, agreed to cut eastbound grain rates. The Pennsylvania was not satisfied with this initial cut and insisted upon a further reduction. Commissioner Fink in announcing the additional cut stated that it had been ordered upon demand of the Pennsylvania.

Gould was disappointed over the trend of events. The persistent rate cuts were injurious to both the Lackawanna and the Wabash. The pool, he said, was "a rope of sand," and a clearing house might do better.[38] The break in rates since the early summer of 1883 was reducing the earnings of the low-cost lines and eliminating the earnings of the high-cost lines. The construction company of the leading high-cost competitor—the West Shore —was already in receivership, and the West Shore itself was soon to follow. The Wabash receivership came even sooner, late in May of 1884. Almost simultaneously came the announcement that the Wabash had made an open cut in rates between St.

Louis and Chicago. Although the Wabash was in receivership, the order emanated from Gould headquarters. When a new traffic manager took over affairs early in August, the Wabash was carrying approximately 50 per cent of the eastbound business—a percentage far greater than the pool allotment.

In his contest with eastern trunk lines, Gould was therefore largely unsuccessful, though his investment in the Lackawanna stock was profitable. The road as an operating unit was well managed, and despite some unprofitable lease contracts, was conservatively capitalized. It had also a rich and growing anthracite business. Gould's efforts to increase its earnings through construction of the Buffalo extension were without success. He made a characteristically bold effort to capture a large part of the through traffic from the Erie and the New York Central. His success, however, was temporary, and his eventual failure brought on a devastating railroad war, which was settled only after a prolonged contest by the intervention of a man who had a compelling sense of responsibility to the army of investors who had followed his leadership. That man was Morgan. It was not however until the summer of 1885, after the war had reached a climax in the form of dividend reductions by the soundest railroads, that Morgan, taking advantage of the competitive problems of the two leading trunk lines, could exact from each sufficient concessions to bring about an agreement.

In eastern territory, therefore, Gould was defeated. He and Vanderbilt carried on a rate struggle for almost two years—a period longer than any other major rate war had lasted. It was a war, furthermore, which reduced rates to the lowest point in history. Gould never re-established his position in eastern territory, and gradually sold out his holdings in the Lackawanna. Morgan ignored him in making the West Shore settlement in the summer of 1885. He was no longer able to use the Wabash as a means of whipping other eastern lines or even of threatening them with dire consequences. Gould, in short, was no longer a major factor in eastern railroad affairs.

NOTES FOR CHAPTER XVIII

1. See Chapter XI, pp. 218-9 for details.
2. The explanations are found in the annual report, Wabash, 1880, cited in *Chron.*, Jan. 15, 1881, 71.

3. For details on these transactions, see *Ry. World*, May 22, 1875, 330; Sept. 22, 1877, 897; Sept. 21, 1878, 906. A detailed history of the issue of the Atlantic's financing of the purchase of the Bee Line's stock is given in London *Railway News*, April 23, 1887, 692.
4. New York *Evening Mail & Express*, Oct. 31, 1881.
5. For Vanderbilt's intention on this point, see Phila. *North American*, Dec. 13, 1882.
6. Interview of Vanderbilt with Shenandoah *Mining Herald*, cited in Phila. *Press*, Jan. 13, 1883; Jan. 16, 1883.
7. New York *Tribune*, March 24, 1882; March 31, 1882.
8. Vanderbilt made this statement to a reporter of the Phila. *Press*, cited in New York *Tribune*, Jan. 13, 1883. For details on the new route, see Phila. *North American*, March 20, 1882; New York *Times*, Dec. 12, 1882; Phila. *Press*, June 12, 1883.
9. The powerful influence of the Pennsylvania at Trenton had "long been conceded," according to a New York dispatch to the Phila. *Press*, Feb. 17, 1882.
10. *R. R. Gaz.*, Feb. 24, 1882, 123.
11. For a statement of the history of its denial, see the New York *Times*, Feb. 21, 1882.
12. Known hereafter as the Nickel Plate.
13. This is the statement in the Phila. *Press*, July 19, 1888.
14. Chicago *Tribune*, Oct. 9, 1882.
15. New York *Times*, Oct. 31, 1882.
16. Phila. *Press*, Oct. 30, 1882.
17. *Wall Street Journal*, July 16, 1924. For a fuller account of the Nickel Plate incident, see *The New York Stock Exchange*, Vol. 1, 380, 299 ff., edited by Edmund C. Stedman, Stock Exchange Historical Co., New York, 1905.
18. *R. R. Gaz.*, March 16, 1883, 170.
19. This agreement is summarized in *R. R. Gaz.*, Dec. 8, 1882, 762.
20. Ibid., Nov. 24, 1882, 719.
21. Ibid.
22. Ibid., May 12, 1882, 292.
23. New York *Herald*, April 20, 1883.
24. New York *Tribune*, March 15, 1883.
25. *R. R. Gaz.*, July 6, 1883, 443.
26. New York *Tribune*, Nov. 9, 1883.
27. On these negotiations, see ibid., Jan. 10, 1884; *R. R. Gaz.*, Jan. 11, 1884, 30.
28. Phila. *North American*, Jan. 18, 1884.
29. New York *Tribune*, Jan. 18, 1884.
30. For Gould's market position, see Chapter XXIV, pp. 486-9.
31. New York *Tribune*, Feb. 5, 1884.
32. Ibid., Feb. 8, 1884.
33. *R. R. Gaz.*, Feb. 15, 1884, 135.
34. *Bradstreet*, Feb. 23, 1884, 120.
35. See on these rate cuts, New York *Times*, March 12, 1884; March 14, 1884; New York *Tribune*, March 11, 1884.
36. New York *Herald*, March 12, 1884.
37. Annual report, Pennsylvania, 1883, 32-3.
38. New York *Tribune*, March 28, 1884.

CHAPTER XIX

Gould Fights the Burlington

IN WESTERN as in eastern territory, in the period following the end of 1881, Gould's problems were largely dominated by a single personality. In the East, it was Vanderbilt; in the West, it was Perkins. In the renewal of the contest with Gould, Perkins was no longer a subordinate official. As president of the Burlington, he was the leader of an able group, vigorous, yet cautious; aggressive, yet careful not to extend themselves unduly.

When the Burlington built the Denver line in 1882, it delivered a blow at the heart of the Union Pacific's traffic. Ever since its main line had been completed in 1869, that road had encountered no serious competition on through business. The cloudless sky, however, was soon darkened. The Burlington, although the first, was by no means the most important of these competitors. To the north in the summer of 1881, the Northern Pacific had just received encouragement from two sources. It had succeeded first in selling $40,000,000 of bonds. A controlling interest in the road, furthermore, had been acquired by Villard, who was also the dominant factor in the Oregon Railway & Navigation Company. That enterprise had a monopoly on the transportation business in the Columbia Valley. Villard was an enterprising promoter, and in control of these two lines he proceeded upon a plan to complete the Northern Pacific to a connection with the Navigation Company. In two years this task was accomplished and the Union Pacific was flanked on the north.

On the south Gould had tried unsuccessfully to even scores with Huntington by expanding his lines to the coast. Huntington, however, continued to build and expand, and by 1883 had established his own route to New Orleans. The Union Pacific was flanked on the south.

From the Mississippi Valley, in the area served by the Burlington, entered another candidate for transcontinental honors. The

Northwestern in the early eighties began to move across the Missouri River into Nebraska. With these lines as a spearhead it held over the head of the Union Pacific the threat of an extension to Ogden unless that line met its views.

Midway between the Union Pacific on the north and the Huntington lines on the south loomed still another threat. There Strong was aggressively leading the Atchison westward to the coast.

In addition to through transcontinental business, the Union Pacific's earning power was dependent upon a large volume of local traffic. The Colorado business in the early eighties was the product of a mining boom. A heavy volume of westbound mining supplies and equipment made this business especially lucrative. The Union Pacific had a monopoly on the mineral traffic of Utah. The Nebraska area, rich in wheat and cattle, was served in competition with the Burlington system.

Months before the Burlington's Denver extension became a reality, the Atchison joined its fortunes with the Frisco—a road with frustrated transcontinental ambitions. The plans had been stopped by excessive financial burdens assumed in the early seventies. When the road was reorganized, it created a separate company—the Atlantic & Pacific—to build its transcontinental extension. Early in 1880 the Frisco entered into an agreement with the Atchison to build the Atlantic & Pacific westward. Both roads agreed to buy its stock and bonds, the necessary cash to be raised from the stockholders of the two parent companies.[1] By the end of 1881 the combined managements of the two parent roads were pushing ahead with the line. One of these roads, the Frisco, was also expanding in Missouri, Arkansas, and northern Texas, the center of Gould's southwestern territory. Gould offered to make a pooling arrangement but the offer was declined.

Both Gould and Huntington were anxious to stop the onward march of the new transcontinental line. They could not buy control of the Atchison; the stock was closely held by aggressive Boston businessmen. Early in 1880, however, Perkins expressed the fear that Gould and Huntington might purchase control of the Frisco, and thereby block the new outlet to the Pacific Coast.[2] Perkins's fears were justified. Gould acted first. In January, 1882, he began negotiations for acquisition of the Frisco's stock. Discovering that little stock was available, he asked its president, E. F. Winslow, at what price he would sell his holdings. The answer was curt and sharp: "It is not for sale." [3] The search for a solution was carried on by Huntington who, ascertaining that the firm of J. & W. Seligman & Co. had a substantial block of the stock, asked Gould whether he would be interested in buying. The transaction was made quickly and on the 24th of January Gould on behalf of himself and Huntington bought a little less than one-half of the Frisco's stock.[4] The ambitious program of the Atlantic & Pacific Railroad was curtailed. The road would be built westward only to the Colorado River. To that point from the west Huntington would build a line and give the Atlantic & Pacific a part of the Southern Pacific's business.

From Gould's standpoint, this was not a happy solution. It was possible that business which could be sent east over the Central Pacific and Union Pacific might now be diverted to the Southern Pacific-Atlantic & Pacific route.

Gould must have been dissatisfied with the outcome of his venture into this new enterprise. Although he accepted a position on the board of the Frisco, he did not long hold the stock.[5] This was Gould's first major business transaction with Huntington after the resumption of good feeling ushered in by the agreement of November, 1881. Their relations thereafter cooled, and it was not long until they clashed again on many a business front in the Southwest.

While Gould was trading with Huntington in the effort to stop the growth of one new competitor of the Union Pacific, he was opening up a battle in Colorado which eventually stimulated the growth of another, i.e., the Burlington. In building its line to Denver, the Burlington looked forward to the co-operation of the Denver—still managed by Palmer. Although Gould had been elected to the board in December of 1880, he had never attended a meeting. The Denver early in 1881 had become a competitor of the Union Pacific, and it was therefore obvious that Gould in the Union Pacific would therefore not be on the friendliest terms with that road. It was possible, nevertheless, that as a member of the board of the latter he might follow a neutral, perhaps a conciliatory, policy in stabilizing the competition between the two properties.

The possibility of a friendly alignment between the two roads was rendered impossible by another adverse interest which characterized the Gould empire. Palmer, the president and a large stockholder of the Denver, was a competitor of Gould in the Republic of Mexico. Independently of the Denver, Palmer had promoted an enterprise to build a road from Laredo to the City of Mexico. He and his associates had in fact outbid Gould and his associates, and they had organized a construction company to build the road. Palmer, although an able operating man, had little of the speculative following which Gould enjoyed. When, because of the declining trend of speculative and business activities which developed late in 1881, the subscriptions to the stock of the construction company were not paid, the company was unable to secure funds.

The Denver stock, meanwhile, which had advanced in the boom markets in the spring and summer of the year to a high of 113 had reversed its trend, and by late December had dropped to below 80. Gould, however, had sold his holdings at the high prices, for in June he declared publicly that he had no interest in the stock.[6]

Late in December, 1881, Gould delivered an assault upon the stock, and its price soon declined to 66, reaching 50 in mid-March.

By this market raid, Gould made a new enemy. Palmer was now anxious to retaliate. When the Burlington reached Colorado in the spring of 1882, it found a warm friend, anxious to co-operate to protect its own interests and also to strike at the enemy. Indeed, it was believed that the Burlington would actually acquire control of the road.

In view of the unfriendliness between the Union Pacific and the Denver, it is not surprising that even before the Burlington reached the the city of Denver, a local rate war in Colorado broke out. When the Burlington arrived, it was not sufficiently sure of its competitive ground to enable it to follow a definitive rate policy. More as an experiment than anything else it agreed to form a pool applying to all traffic to and from points between Colorado and the Mississippi River.[7] In entering this pool the Burlington underestimated the amount of traffic which shortly thereafter it was able to obtain. Many Colorado shippers who had consigned their eastbound freight via that road discovered that, owing to its small percentage of the pool business, more than half of the freight so consigned had to be diverted to the Wabash and the Alton. The Denver merchants were dissatisfied and the Burlington recognized that its "only salvation was to withdraw from the pool." [8] No serious rate war nevertheless occurred in the first six months of 1882.

Meanwhile negotiations for a new pool and the avoidance of a war of rates were actively considered. On July 15 the Burlington traffic representative in Colorado informed Perkins that, after a prolonged and continuous two-day session, a one-year pool had been made.[9]

It now looked as though the rate harmony which for so many years had prevailed in southern Iowa and in southern Kansas would be duplicated in the area between the Rocky Mountains and the Missouri River. Such however was not to be the case. Gould and the top executive officials of the Union Pacific concluded that rate stabilization would facilitate the Burlington's expansion program in Nebraska and Colorado. Gould accordingly instructed the Union Pacific's executives not to sign the pool contract unless the Burlington agreed to refrain from building extensions in northern Colorado.

Meanwhile, in the absence of a pool agreement, the Denver and the Burlington entered into friendly relationships to the detriment of the Union Pacific. The Denver was giving the Burlington all of its eastbound business, whether consigned or not, and according to a leading Burlington traffic official, the Union Pacific felt this loss in business "very *keenly*." [10] By late August the two roads were approaching open warfare. The Union Pacific was diverting some of its eastbound freight at Council Bluffs from the Burlington to other lines, and the Burlington, as a retaliatory measure, was considering the idea of diverting some of its freight from the Union Pacific to the Atchison. It appeared to the Burlington officials that the truce on the war of rates could not be much longer maintained.[11]

By mid-September, however, the officials of the Burlington and the Union Pacific resumed negotiations. The Union Pacific backed down on its proposal that it would not enter a pool unless the Burlington refrained from building in Colorado and Nebraska. The Union Pacific's traffic chief now declared that his road had wanted the Burlington to agree not to build for a period of one year only. He therefore inquired whether the Burlington would agree with the Union Pacific not to build into the territory of the other without previous consultation. In this way a rate war could be averted and each road earn a reasonable profit. The Burlington recognized that the promise of the Union Pacific to build no new lines would be worthless unless Gould agreed to bring all his lines in the territory under the terms of the agreement. A Burlington officer accordingly suggested that if the Missouri Pacific could be included in the proposed territorial understanding he would favor the arrangement.[12]

Although the negotiations for a territorial understanding were fruitless, the roads did finally establish a pool. The Union Pacific gave ground, for under the terms of the pool the Burlington received 30 per cent of the business, although in the spring it had expressed its willingness to accept a minimum of 25 per cent. The Union Pacific received 50 per cent and the Atchison the remainder.[13]

The pool appeared to be a master stroke. It seemed that the invasion of a new trunk line would after all not seriously alter existing conditions. The Union Pacific would give up a part of its business to the Burlington, the rate structure would remain normal, and both roads would carry a reasonable share of a growing traffic.

This result did not, however, follow. For, just as the negotiations for the conclusion of the Colorado pool were treading their way over the tortuous path of intercorporate competition, the Gould specter suddenly emerged at Kansas City. At that point the Burlington still depended upon the Hannibal for a connection. Although Gould was on the board of the Hannibal he had sold out his stock, and control of the road remained uncertain. Suddenly, in September, 1881, under the leadership of John Duff, a Boston stockbroker, the stock was cornered and in a few days its price rose from \$96 to \$200 a share. Gould and Sage had been selling short in a small way and both immediately took their market losses.[14] Duff found it impossible, after the shorts had settled for their commitments, to sell the remainder of his stock in the open market at any reasonable price. Here seemed to be an opportunity for the Burlington. Duff offered the stock for sale at $50 a share but Perkins and his advisers declined the offer.

Before the end of March, Duff had changed his mind and notified the Burlington that he was no longer interested in selling. "All trades [are] off," he declared.[15]

Although Perkins and his associates declined to pay $50 a share for the Hannibal shares, by the late summer of 1882 they were willing to pay $42. In view of the other advantages of the Hannibal to the Burlington, Perkins was now ready to make a trade. Just about the same time, however, Gould and his associates, Sage, Dillon, and F. L. Ames also decided to buy the Hannibal stock. Gould was as difficult to follow as ever. After blandly assuring the Burlington that he was not interested in the Hannibal, he stepped in and bought just as the Burlington was about to make the purchase.[16]

The purchase of the Hannibal by the Gould interests was a blow to the Burlington and produced consternation in the mind of Perkins. Perkins was ready for the worst and believed indeed that the worst was about to be realized. He was certain that the Hannibal would be used as part of the Wabash, and that road, he observed, would take good care to keep itself informed of all that the Hannibal and the Burlington did, "while the dark tricks of the Wabash would be carefully hidden from our view." He therefore insisted that the Burlington must build to Kansas City. If thereafter Gould retaliated by building to Chicago, then the Burlington would "consider the fences down in all directions and . . . build wherever and whenever we think it will pay, especially to Salina, to Lexington, and north of the Union Pacific in Nebraska."[17] Gould meanwhile renewed his oft-repeated threat to build a Chicago line. As late as February, 1883, the president of the Hannibal insisted that Gould had assured him that the extension would be constructed. Officials of the Burlington were also fearful of this possibility. One of the Burlington directors even suggested the idea that the road announce its plans to build extensions into the Missouri Pacific country, thus meeting threat with threat. Forbes, however, was not convinced of the wisdom of such a game. "I suppose," he wrote to Perkins, "you have several other things to do besides playing a game at Bluff with the great Jay Hawker & chief thief." [18]

While both contestants thus threatened to take action or to retaliate against each other, nothing happened. Both in fact misunderstood each other's motives. It may well be true that Gould might have followed the policies anticipated by Perkins in the fall of 1882. With all his experience with Gould, Perkins, nevertheless, had failed to consider the most important factor that motivated Gould's policies—his interests in the Western Union.

Gould made his first approach to Perkins in January, 1883, through a confidential agent. Although no definite decisions were reached, Gould's agent informed Perkins that Gould was preparing to leave the country to be gone for two years and that, among other things, he would like to settle the Hannibal-Burlington controversy. Gould did not want to build to Chicago, nor did he want the Burlington to build to Kansas City. Perkins informed Gould's representative that the Burlington above all was interested in a secure existence at Kansas City. The Gould messenger then stated that he thought the Burlington could buy the Hannibal stock, and he further dropped a hint that Gould had said something about telegraph relations, which he, the Gould agent, did not understand.[19]

The message was the first indication that Gould would trade the Hannibal in connection with a Western Union contract.[20] The hint was not lost upon Perkins. Ten days later the agent turned up with another note from Gould. Gould was willing, he said, to make a general settlement, and he thought the Burlington could buy the Hannibal stock at the cost to Gould plus 6 per cent.

Shortly thereafter at a meeting of the Burlington's board, a committee was appointed consisting of Perkins and Paine, with power to buy the Hannibal upon substantially the terms offered by their present owner, upon condition that a reasonable amount of preferred should be obtained in exchange for a Burlington guarantee of not more than 5 per cent, and if necessary, to agree upon a lease of the Hannibal.[21]

Early in April when the Wabash officials were making their unofficial proposals, Gould returned from Florida. The pace of the negotiations quickened. A long series of telegrams and letters followed each other in rapid succession. The early exchanges resulted only in serious misunderstanding. Coolidge, a board member of the Burlington, as well as of the Atchison, intervened with a telegram to Gould suggesting that the Burlington had already yielded a great deal and that since the differences between Gould and the Burlington were so slight and a telegraph and railroad war was so serious, that he hoped Gould would excuse him for interfering. "I should not do so but I think the negotiations ended without it." [22]

Further negotiations followed, and on April 27 a contract was finally made.[23] Despite all the fears of Perkins and Forbes, the Hannibal was now safely in the hands of the Burlington. Gould, in negotiating the sale of the Hannibal stock, had confounded both his business associates and business enemies. Perkins had believed that the Hannibal would be used to build up the fortunes of the Wabash and tear down those of the Burlington. The president of the Hannibal had been assured that the extension to Chicago would be built, thus increasing the strategic power and competitive strength, if not the financial strength, of the Hannibal. Sage was led to believe that the Hannibal would be used in such a way as to improve the competitive position of an Iowa road in which he was interested. Gould, however, did none of these things. Instead, he sold the road on terms which, while they left his associates little profit, gave him, as the largest owner of the Western Union stock, a reasonable price in the form of an increase in the competitive strength of the Western Union.

Another source of unfriendliness between Gould and Perkins was now removed. Though by the terms of the Colorado pool the Burlington could, if it wished, extend its lines beyond Denver, in the six months which had elapsed since the date of that agreement it had not done so. Rate stability now seemed assured.

Surface appearances were again misleading. Palmer now decided to build to a connection with the Central Pacific at Ogden. He thus invaded Union Pacific territory, in which no competition had heretofore existed. What Gould had threatened to do in November of 1879, Palmer made up his mind to accomplish late in 1882. If a transcontinental route consisting of the Denver-Denver & Rio Grande Western—the name of the new Utah extension—and of the Burlington were formed, the threat to the Union Pacific would be serious. Yet the current financial and trade judgment did not so consider it. Government officials, in accordance with normal expectations, reflected the views of the populace. The government directors of the Union Pacific, reporting early in 1883, stated that the road compared favorably in all respects with any other. The storm of criticism that broke out against the Union Pacific management, only a little more than a year after the publication of this report, presents a curious insight into the legitimacy of hindsight criticism.

Neither was informed railroad and financial judgment of any help to the careful observer. In the spring of 1883, shortly before the outbreak of the rate war, the president of the Union Pacific expressed the bland assurance that everything was well. The Burlington, he said, had been in Denver for nearly a year and yet the Union Pacific had done more business than ever before.[24] An authoritative financial journal well thought of in banking circles and, incidentally, a strong critic of Gould and his policies, expressed the same convictions.

The staid and stolid investor of New England accepted these assurances at their face value. They were encouraged to do so furthermore by the representations of a valuable public servant—Adams of Massachusetts. He traveled over the Union Pacific system and returned to relate, with enthusiasm, wonderful stories of its strength. The Union Pacific was the Broadway of the country and the main artery of the nation's railroad system. When the Union Pacific stock was dropping, he ascribed the decline to the iniquitous short sellers. He urged people to buy.[25] They bought, and by the end of 1883, 4,800 of the road's 7,000 stockholders came from New England.[26]

The stock market alone spoke in the clear language of truth. While government, public representatives and journalistic sages spoke with assurance, the stock market told a different story. Superficially, optimism was warranted. The Colorado pool had divided traffic among the existing railroads, and rates were stable. It is true that the pool was soon to expire; but, as it is so easy to say when there is nothing else to say, there was no reason to believe that the agreement would not be renewed. Yet in the early fall Union Pacific stock was pressed for sale, one broker reporting that enough stock was pressed for sale "to sink a ship."[27] Early in 1883 the price was still about 100, while a few days later it dropped to 91. The decline was baffling, especially to the New England security holders, who appeared to have a "most profound belief" in its value.[28]

The selling could not be attributed to Gould. He had sold his holdings in the booming months of 1880. One need not go too far afield in search of the identity of the sellers. They came from the ranks of those who spend their waking hours and many of their sleeping hours in interpreting facts in the light of their future possibilities. They were men of financial and business imagination. At times they interpret events and trends inaccurately, and they are called speculators. This is particularly so if their decisions bring losses to others as well as themselves. Such losses are usually exposed in strong and occasionally in vituperative language. Their successes are not well understood, although the results of such successes soon become the well-established facts of the day.

The story which the declining quotations were revealing, the story which the prudent and confident New England investor refused to accept as the truth, soon was expressed in terms of events, for the war of rates soon began. Palmer's Utah extension was finished to a connection with the Central Pacific in April of 1883. An understanding for rate maintenance between the Union Pacific and the new line lasted only a short time. The effort to establish a pool failed and the war followed almost immediately. The rate war soon spread to western trunk territory. In mid-July the Burlington, Atchison and Denver reduced passenger fares between Denver and Pueblo.[29]

Meanwhile the Denver's management was changed. The new board included a number of Burlington friends, thus boding no good for Gould. The new management, in co-operation with the Burlington, assumed the offensive in diverting traffic from the Union Pacific. In the fall of 1883 an official of the Burlington told a Denver executive that whenever his road wished to open a rate fight, the Burlington's line between Denver and the Missouri River could be used.[30] The Burlington, furthermore, forwarded its Utah and California business over the Denver-Denver & Rio Grande Western instead of the Union Pacific. The latter tried to get some of that business from the Burlington by giving that road some of its eastbound business at Omaha. The Burlington's representative raised strong objection to such a proposal. In a short time, he observed, the Union Pacific would so manipulate the Burlington's westbound freight that shippers would send their business all the way by the Union Pacific. "I don't believe," wrote the officer, "our giving business to the Union Pacific at Denver will make them any more friendly to, or put a dollar into the coffers of, the B & M," i.e., the Burlington.[31]

The breakdown of rates between the Missouri River and Utah came in November when a twenty-five-cent rate was established, thus heralding one of the most devastating of all western rate wars. By the summer of 1884, the war had cost the Union Pacific more than $20,000,000 in gross business.[32]

The war was also costing the Denver heavily and in view of its impaired finances it could ill afford the continuous and heavy losses in revenue. Frederick Lovejoy, its president, asked Adams, recently appointed a member of the Union Pacific board, to intervene.

Adams's reaction genuinely shocked Lovejoy. Adams assumed a belligerent tone. If he managed the Union Pacific, he would "force the fighting until some results of a permanent nature were reached." He would look forward to peace only until one party or the other "was thoroughly worsted." Adams rarely used such violent language. "I should certainly strike your road as hard as I could, wherever I could reach it, and I should expect that you with equal certainty, would return my blows." Adams concluded that at the end of the war either one road or the other would dictate terms.[33]

Despite these views, he believed that the course of the Union Pacific had been forced upon it by the Burlington associating itself "in what [seemed] such a thoroughly aggressive way with the Denver." [34] Perkins on the contrary was convinced that the Union Pacific "was deliberately the aggressor in the Utah fight" and had entered the struggle on the absurd theory of Adams, with the expectation that the Burlington and the Atchison would refuse to aid the Denver while the Union Pacific was engaged in destroying it.[35]

The transcontinental rate war harmed the Union Pacific (whose stock Gould was now rebuying on a substantial scale) and also Gould's other railroads. With a reduction in rates from the west to Omaha, the rates to Kansas City would also have to be reduced. The Missouri Pacific, in order to participate in traffic moving from the Union Pacific at Kansas City, would therefore have to reduce its Kansas City-St. Louis rates.

Gould recognized that the Burlington in alliance with the Denver and the Atchison was inflicting heavy damage on his roads. He looked around for an opening to strike back at the Burlington, and, as usual, he discovered a point from which he could deliver a counterattack. That point was the weakened position of the Iowa Pool, which for more than a decade had worked so well. Gould had never surrendered the idea of interfering with its smooth functioning. Early in 1879 before he acquired control of the Wabash, for example, he declared he was "very desirous" of breaking the Pool at that time.[36] By the summer of 1883 the Pool had developed many defects. Two roads—the St. Paul and the Wabash—had been added, and the traffic was now divided between five lines. Of these roads, the Rock Island and St. Paul, with no lines west of the Missouri River, had a common interest in building up the traffic volume of the Union Pacific at the expense of the Burlington.

On December 3, 1883, Gould's hope for the break-up of the Pool was finally realized. On that day a twenty-five-year contract between the Union Pacific, Rock Island and St. Paul—known as "the Tri-Partite"—was made public. Under its terms the Union Pacific agreed to send its eastbound business over the lines of the Rock Island & St. Paul, while the others agreed to send their westbound business over the lines of their ally. The Union Pacific, furthermore, fixed the rates on eastbound traffic, and its two allies on westbound. The Iowa Pool in substance although not in form—the formalities were soon to come—was dissolved.

Meanwhile the rate war on the far western end of the Union Pacific in Utah continued. Suddenly the traffic officials of the Union Pacific asked for terms of peace, and following brief negotiations, a new pool, the Utah Traffic Association, was formed. The pool divided the business between the Missouri River and the Utah points, and between the Utah points and the Pacific

Coast. The first public declaration of the terms of peace came in the form of a wire sent to Gould by the general manager of the Union Pacific.[37] Gould was neither president nor an operating officer of that road though he was still on its board, and a member of its executive committee. While he had repurchased some Union Pacific stock, he was still a small stockholder. He was nevertheless in charge of the negotiations.

Gould soon learned that it was easier to destroy than to rebuild. The Union Pacific's new allies refused to follow his lead. These roads, acting in their own interests, refused to recognize the terms of the Utah peace. They declined to approve the settlement unless the Burlington agreed also to make a satisfactory division of its Nebraska business.[38] The fellow members of the Union Pacific in the Tri-Partite, therefore, continued to accept Utah business at cut rates and insisted that the Union Pacific take its pro-rata share. Late in February the Union Pacific began to cut rates in eastern Nebraska, as well as in Colorado. In March the Burlington made a sensational discovery that E. P. Vining, the Tri-Partite commissioner, had, apparently as an officer of the Union Pacific, engaged a person at a small salary to make secret rate cuts against the Burlington. "We want," wrote Vining, "to annoy and demoralize the B & M and their business as much as possible and with as little loss to ourselves as possible." And, he continued, "Do all that you can to increase the ill-will." [39]

Perkins and his fighting traffic assistant were ready for an immediate fight and proposed in conjunction with the Atchison "to knock the bottom" out of Colorado rates, and to terminate the pools east of the Missouri River.[40] Such a policy was too drastic for Forbes. While the rate cuts continued to spread, and the Atchison came out openly in support of the Burlington, Forbes in a succession of meetings with F. L. Ames, Adams and other Union Pacific stockholders arranged informal settlements and temporary truces. The Burlington was now willing to make some concession to the eastern connections of the Union Pacific, though it refused to make any concession on its right to extend lines into new territory. It would build, if necessary, to Ogden or to Montana, and thus share in the growing mineral business with the Union Pacific or if necessary in its own interests to extend its lines into the lucrative Columbia Valley.

It was some time before a final settlement of the war of rates was effected. Gould's Tri-Partite alliance to isolate the Burlington was a drastic failure. Perkins emerged from this contest the undisputed victor. "It is a noteworthy fact," wrote one observer, "that in every case where the Chicago, Burlington and Quincy has gone into a contest, it has worsted its opponents. Wherever this powerful corporation gets a hold, someone has said, no grass will ever grow." [41]

Gould's general policy in western territory must be set down as a failure. By his violation of the territorial agreement of 1880 through the construction of the Missouri Pacific line to Omaha, he invited the Burlington to invade the Union Pacific territory. By his dispute with Palmer of the Denver, he created a close ally of the Burlington in Colorado and thus facilitated the establishment of a competitive line over the Burlington and its new associate from Ogden to Omaha. These were the two moves that, from the Union Pacific standpoint, constituted the primary blunder. Whether it was a blunder to Gould's business interests as a whole is another matter. The Missouri Pacific may have benefited from the Omaha extension, and if this was so, Gould as the largest stockholder of the road benefited correspondingly. Gould may have also profited personally from his operations in the Denver stock.

Gould furthermore came out second best in his contest with Huntington. He had acquired control of the Texas & Pacific in order to build a line to the Pacific Coast. In this attempt he failed. Although Huntington gave him many promises in the agreement of November, 1881, he delivered only a few crumbs of traffic. Huntington built his own route to New Orleans, and diverted the transcontinental business in accordance with his own interests.

Neither was Gould successful in blocking the transcontinental ambitions of the Atchison. The part-interest which he bought in the corporation through which the Atchison was building its transcontinental line served no useful purpose. When in the summer of 1884 Huntington became involved in financial difficulties, as he continued to do from time to time until almost the end of his business career, he solved them in part by selling a Southern Pacific line to the Colorado River to the Atchison system. As a result, the Atchison and the Burlington were able in the summer of 1884 to organize a fast freight service from the Middle West to the Pacific Coast. The new line did not carry much traffic immediately, but in the course of years it came to be a powerful factor in the transcontinental business.

Gould's policies finally led to the greatest railroad rate war that had yet occurred in the Far West. The cost to the Union Pacific was heavy. It was a cost which the Union Pacific could not sustain, and was a primary factor in producing the financial reverses which led to the suspension of dividends in 1884. Almost twenty years passed before the financial wreck was rehabilitated. Not until then, did the Union Pacific stock return to the price at which it sold at the top of the market boom in 1881 or reacquire the investment status which it lost in the middle eighties.

NOTES FOR CHAPTER XIX

1. Details of this agreement are found in *Ry. World*, May 1, 1880, 420; the annual report of the Atchison, 1884; and Poor's *Manual of Railroads*, 1885, 845.
2. Burlington archives, Perkins to Forbes, Nov. 14, 1880.
3. Phila. *Press*, Jan. 18, 1882.
4. New York *Tribune*, Jan. 26, 1882; Crocker to Huntington, Feb. 4, 1882, M. M.
5. New York *Times*, March 7, 1887.
6. Chicago *Tribune*, June 2, 1881.
7. The experimental nature of this pool is referred to in Burlington archives, Potter to Perkins, April 17, 1882. The organization of the pool is noted in *R. R. Gaz.*, Jan. 27, 1882, 61.
8. Burlington archives, Potter to Perkins, April 17, 1882.
9. Ibid., July 15, 1882.
10. Ibid., July 31, 1882.
11. Ibid., Aug. 29, 1882.
12. Ibid., Sept. 18, 1882.
13. Details of these negotiations are found in Phila. *Press*, Oct. 12, 1882; Oct. 17, 1882; *R. R. Gaz.*, April 21, 1882, 242; June 9, 1882, 351; July 21, 1882, 447; and Oct. 20, 1882, 652.
14. Chicago *Tribune*, Sept. 8, 1881.
15. Burlington archives, unsigned letter dated March 22, 1882.
16. Ibid., memorandum, Sept. 13, 1882, unsigned, although from the tenor of the argument there is little reason to doubt that the author was Perkins; also Perkins to J. L. Gardner, Jan. 20, 1883.
17. The above presentation of the views of Perkins and the quotations are based upon and taken from a letter in the Burlington archives, Perkins to Geddes, Sept. 16, 1882.
18. Ibid., Forbes to Perkins, March 3, 1883.
19. Ibid., Perkins to Gardner, Jan. 20, 1883.
20. See Chapter XXIII, pp. 455-6 for details.
21. Burlington archives, "Memo at Board Meeting," dated Feb. 15, 1883.

22. Ibid., Coolidge to Gould, April 14, 1883.
23. For details on these negotiations, see an unpublished manuscript, "The Hannibal & St. Joseph, 1870–1883," by the author, in the Newberry Library, Chicago, Illinois.
24. New York *Times*, May 30, 1883.
25. Boston *Advertiser*, Dec. 19, 1882.
26. Phila. *North American*, Dec. 25, 1883.
27. Ibid., Oct. 19, 1882.
28. *Bradstreet*, Dec. 15, 1883, 376.
29. *R. R. Gaz.*, July 20, 1883, 486.
30. Burlington archives, Potter to Perkins, Dec. 28, 1883.
31. Ibid., Aug. 6, 1883.
32. This is the estimate in the Phila. *North American*, Aug. 2, 1884.
33. The letter from Adams to Lovejoy, from which the above quotations are taken, is dated Dec. 4, 1883, and is found in the Burlington archives.
34. Ibid., Adams to Perkins, Dec. 17, 1883.
35. Ibid., Perkins to Forbes, Dec. 31, 1883.
36. Ibid., W. F. Sapp to Hon. W. C. James, Jan. 27, 1879.
37. New York *Times*, Feb. 2, 1884.
38. *R. R. Gaz.*, Feb. 8, 1884, 118.
39. Burlington archives, E. P. Vining to D. M. Carne, March 8, 1884, enclosed by Perkins in letter to Forbes, March 17, 1884.
40. Ibid., Perkins to Forbes, March 17, 1884.
41. New York *Times*, July 6, 1884.

CHAPTER XX

Gould Holds in the Southwest

In less than two years, by acquisition and construction, Gould had established the broad outlines of the through routes between St. Louis and Kansas City gateways and the Rio Grande and Gulf Coast. By connection with the Huntington properties he had also completed the first east-and-west line through Texas and the first transcontinental line south of the Missouri. Except for the El Paso route of the Texas & Pacific, he accomplished this program in less than a twelve-month period. Where railroads in the Missouri Valley had failed to develop a through route to the Rio Grande and the Gulf Coast, Gould had succeeded. Similarly, where Texas roads had failed to develop routes to the Missouri Valley, Gould had also succeeded.

By the end of 1881, the Gould southwestern system took on definite outlines. It consisted of one east-west line and three major north-south lines. The former extended from Texarkana to El Paso. Of the north-south lines, one extended from New Orleans to St. Louis, consisting of the Texas & Pacific to Texarkana and the Iron Mountain beyond. The other was represented by the International from Houston to north Texas and to a junction with the Texas & Pacific. The third extended from Laredo on the Rio Grande, north over the International and beyond via the Kansas & Texas to the upper Mississippi River gateways.

The completion of these north-south routes after years of delay produced a decided impression on the railroad strategy in this vast area. Previous to the Gould invasion the traffic interchange between the Missouri Valley and Texas, Arkansas and Louisiana had been well stabilized. The northern roads in St. Louis and Kansas City traded their southbound business with noncompetitive connections—the Iron Mountain and the Kansas & Texas. And the southern roads terminating in north Texas exchanged their northbound business with the same lines. There was thus a mutuality of business interests. The two northern lines frequently threatened to build south and the Texas lines north, but neither followed their threats with action. Gould suddenly appeared and did both, thereby seizing control of the through routes between the south and the north. Gould thus cut off his northern competitors from a southern outlet and his southern competitors from a northern outlet. The Alton, the Burlington, the Frisco, and the Atchison lost their independent connections to the south, and could now reach western Louisiana, Arkansas, and the eastern section of Texas only over Gould lines.

The transformation in railroad strategy was important to the northern trunk lines; but to the southern lines—competitors of the Gould roads—the effect was even more momentous. The northern roads had an abundance of traffic in their own territory that did not compete with the Gould lines. If Gould discriminated against their southbound traffic, they had means of retaliation. The southern lines however were not so strong. Their through traffic was largely competitive with the Gould lines. Their only effective weapon was a price war. The Houston & Texas Central [1] and the Gulf, Colorado & Santa Fe [2] were the major southern roads whose connections to the north were cut off. Both roads extended from the Gulf Coast to northern Texas. The Gould lines were therefore their competitors as well as their connections. The Gould Texas lines on movements beyond their termini could offer better service if the traffic were handled over their lines instead of over non-Gould roads.

It was imperative, therefore, that the latter open up independent connections. The two roads unfortunately competed with each other for local movements between north and south Texas points, and they could not, therefore, sink their differences to face the common enemy. In the summer of 1882 the Gulf decided to move alone. Its officers proposed to the Alton that if it built south from Kansas City to the Indian Territory, the Gulf would build north from Fort Worth. Both roads would then jointly build a line across the area.[3] The Alton management, however, was in no expansive mood, and the negotiations proved fruitless. The officers of the Gulf also talked with the Burlington management about building a line in the Indian Territory.[4]

While aid from these sources was not forthcoming, relief suddenly appeared from an unexpected source. South and west of the southern end of the Iron Mountain was a small line with a heavy cotton traffic that served as a lucrative feeder to the Iron Mountain. Hardly had Gould acquired the Iron Mountain, than this feeder, the Texas & St. Louis, decided upon a program of expansion. Early in 1881 it planned to move west to Dallas and Fort Worth, south to Waco and beyond to the Rio Grande, and north and east to Cairo, Illinois, and by traffic arrangements with the Illinois Central to Chicago.

Gould fought the new road aggressively. In order to break up the projected route to the north, he endeavored to acquire control of the Gulf—an essential link. The road was conservatively financed. Because of its light debts its stock was valuable. It was therefore not possible for Gould to buy control at a low price. The stock was owned by merchants and moneyed men of Galveston.[5] The management showed the same ability to handle its own affairs and to ignore the Gould technique of threats that Perkins had displayed on behalf of the Burlington. When necessary to cut rates to meet Gould's moves, it did not hesitate. When Gould leveled his threats of parallel construction, it did not shiver as did Vanderbilt. From the very beginning Gould refused to co-operate with the Gulf. He controlled its northern and eastern outlets, and his refusal to honor tickets sold by the Gulf inconvenienced the public and impaired its earnings. The Gulf replied in kind and refused to honor tickets sold by the Gould lines. Tactics of this kind finally led early in 1882 to a general rate war.

The war involved Gould's main routes through this area—the International and the Texas & Pacific. In May the managers of the contestants met and established a pooling arrangement. The rate war was over, or so it seemed. The Gulf, however, remained adamant, and refused to accept its allotment of traffic. It did 75 per cent of the business out of Galveston and purposed to get all of it.

Far from entering into peaceful arrangements with the Gould lines, the Gulf announced another expansion plan. Gould had refused to accommodate the Gulf's through business, believing perhaps that this pressure would depress the market value of the stock. Instead of surrendering or compromising, the Gulf's management seized the offensive. With renewed determination it decided to build an extension through the Indian Territory, this time to a connection with the Frisco.

Rather than invite a competitor into Kansas & Texas territory, Gould thought it better to give way. He was now making concessions, but the concessions came too late. His patience in awaiting a suitable opportunity to buy a desirable property at a low price did not in this case succeed.

In the spring of 1886 the Gulf stockholders finally sold—but not to Gould. They delivered their stock to the Atchison on a stock exchange basis. Gould was thus confronted with powerful competition on the business moving from the Southwest to Kansas City and points east. This transaction gave a strong competitor of the Missouri Pacific in southern Kansas an entrance into Texas. The through line thus created built up a competitive route which surrounded the Missouri Pacific system at numerous points on the south and west. It was a development, the first of a number that in time was to break the Gould monopoly on business between Texas, Oklahoma, and the Missouri Valley.

Neither was Gould able to seize control of the other north-and-south connection of the competitive through route. A large part of the stock of the Houston was closely held. Huntington, as part of his expansion rampage, early acquired control of the road. It appeared that he might even build to St. Louis and thus challenge Gould in the very heart of his system. Huntington however had overextended himself. The panic of 1884 brought on a personal crisis and he was soon forced to relinquish some of his properties. The Houston, however, despite a spectacular battle remained in control of his Southern Pacific system.

If Huntington by acquiring the Houston upset Gould's plans on one part of his system, he delivered a smashing blow on another. Gould's Texas & Pacific had at great speed pushed through the construction of the Rio Grande division, and in order to avoid a battle with Huntington had concluded an agreement designed to regulate the traffic interchange with the Huntington road at El Paso. Huntington soon decided that it was to his benefit to send eastbound traffic over his south Texas line rather than over the Texas & Pacific—the El Paso agreement to the contrary notwithstanding. Gould fumed but did nothing. He had exhausted his ammunition in the Southwest. His properties were in poor physical and financial condition, and Huntington knew it. While the traffic of the Texas & Pacific lagged, that of the Southern Pacific mounted.[6] The Texas & Pacific's El Paso line was virtually a stub, and since its local traffic was light, the line soon became a financial derelict.

For a time Gould thought of expanding into the Southeast. The most convenient stepping stone would be Memphis, Tennessee. Gould's Iron Mountain skirted the city some miles to the west but did not reach it. A small independent east-west property, the Memphis & Little Rock, connected the Iron Mountain with Memphis. Gould's program to bring that line into his southwestern system produced a sensational succession of lawsuits.

The Memphis & Little Rock had long competed with the Iron Mountain, and rate wars had sapped the earnings of both properties.[7] Gould decided to get control and to eliminate this competition. In conjunction with Sage, and also with Marquand, his new southwestern associate, he bought over 90 per cent of the stock, for which he paid a high price. The bonds of the reorganized road carried an interest rate beginning July 1, 1882, of 8 per cent. This interest rate, thought Gould, was too high. He cast about for ways and means to accomplish a reduction, and thus make his stock more valuable. He soon devised a plan. The state of Arkansas in March, 1882, had secured a judgment against the road on an old claim. The first mortgage bondholders paid the judgment and secured an assignment of the claim. They then applied for the appointment of a receiver and, had they been successful, the stock for which Gould had paid a good price would have lost most of its value. Gould was prepared. Before receivership proceedings became effective the road confessed judgment on a small note to Sage. The bondholders had never heard of the note, judgment having been confessed only fours days after the note was given. The Gould clique got in first, and the court appointed a receiver friendly to it and unfriendly to the bondholders.

Gould then made a bold stroke. He entered suit challenging the validity of the mortgage and asked the court to annul the bonds. He questioned the right of a corporation which had purchased a property to mortgage the very property acquired in order to obtain the purchase price. If the mortgage was invalid and the corporation had no equitable title to the property, it would appear to follow that it should return the property to its creditors. This, however, Gould on behalf of the company refused to do. The attempt on Gould's part to destroy the rights of the creditors and to seize the property without any consideration, led a federal judge to use some vigorous language. "The case is phenomenal," wrote the judge, "in the audacity of the attempt to induce a court in equity to assist a corporation in repudiating its obligations to its creditors, without offering to them the property it acquired by its unauthorized contract with them. . . . Every stockholder of the corporation, when he acquired his stock, took it with notice explicitly embodied in his certificate that his interest as a stockholder was subordinate to the rights of the holders of the mortgage bonds. It is now contended that if there is any obligation on the part of the corporation to pay for the property it purchased it is not to pay what it agreed to, but to pay a less consideration because the property was not worth the price agreed to be paid. The court will not compel the bondholders to enter into any such inquiry." [8] Though the complaint of Gould was dismissed, more litigation followed.

While these proceedings were making their way through the intricate maze of legal channels, the clique (Gould, Sage, and Marquand) was making threats. If the bondholders of the Little Rock, asserted Sage, would not make a friendly arrangement, then a new line costing only about 50 per cent of the road's first mortgage bonds would be built to Memphis.[9] The bondholders eventually reorganized the road and secured control, and Gould was compelled to build a duplicate line to Memphis. Despite this and other forays into new territory, Gould exercised considerable restraint in expanding his southwestern system. He used better judgment in managing the strategy of his southwestern system than he had of either the Wabash or the Union Pacific. He was careful to preserve his transregional connections as independent units. His southwestern connections were friends rather than competitors.

The parent company of the southwestern system was the Missouri Pacific, and in all stages of consolidation negotiations its predominant position was controlling. Gould personally owned a large percentage of its stock. By unifying the corporations under his leadership, he controlled the system. In view of the Kansas & Texas lease to the Missouri Pacific, it was not necessary that he personally own many shares of the lessor. So long as the latter continued to pay interest, the Missouri Pacific's control was undisturbed.

With respect to the Texas & Pacific, the case was not so clear. This company was considered more prosperous. It was not described in the 1881 boom market (as had been the Kansas & Texas) as worthless stuff. When the high hopes for the road were blasted by the rush of events in 1883 and 1884, its security holders organized for action. They succeeded in getting two traffic experts to make an investigation of the division of the through rate with the Missouri Pacific, as a result of which the Texas & Pacific obtained a larger percentage of the rate.[10]

They accomplished little. They were informed investors and thus understood the technique of balance sheets and income statements. Though acquainted with the art of measuring financial results, they had little conception of the nature of railroad traffic, and they almost certainly had no understanding of Gould's methods.

Regardless of the large non-Gould holdings, these two roads were operated as parts of the Gould system and were included in its reports. The first report of the Missouri Pacific system was unintelligible. It was only after the passing of many years that the accounting profession was able to devise principles which made it possible to present truthful reports of a consolidated enterprise where the business of constituent companies was intermingled. Gould had no purpose to serve in presenting clear reports of each part of his system. Since his ownership of the southwestern roads was concentrated largely in Missouri Pacific stock, it was obviously to his interest to reduce the earnings of the other system companies and to increase those of the Missouri Pacific.

The method by which the earnings of the Missouri Pacific were bolstered and those of the Texas & Pacific, the Kansas & Texas, and the International were reduced, can, for the purposes of convenience in discussion, be classified as follows:

1. By overcharging or undercharging of payments for terminal services.
2. By inequitable divisions of through rates for services rendered in moving through traffic over system routes.
3. By shifting of through traffic in such a way as to move it over one part of the system instead of another.
4. By inadequate maintenance in order to provide cash to pay interest, thereby concealing the financial condition of the property.

1. *Payments for Terminal Services*

Under the lease of the Kansas & Texas to the Missouri Pacific, for example, all the terminal charges payable to the Missouri Pacific were "exacted and paid." The Kansas & Texas, on the other hand, originated a large volume of business. The expense of collecting and distributing the traffic was constant. If it moved over the Kansas & Texas exclusively, the road received the full revenue of that haul. In this way it was reimbursed for the heavy outlay in picking up the traffic. If, however, the traffic was delivered to the Missouri Pacific, that road received a large part of the revenue and should have, therefore, reimbursed the Kansas & Texas for its expenses in picking up the business. According to the investigating committee representing the latter's security holders, the Missouri Pacific made no "equitable allowance." [11]

2. *Division of Through Rates*

The Missouri Pacific shipped traffic eastward to St. Louis and beyond over the Wabash long haul to Toledo. On a typical movement the Missouri Pacific hauled grain 200 miles, and the Wabash more than 400 miles. On one such shipment it received twenty-five cents per hundred pounds, and the Wabash received ten cents.[12] It is obvious that the Missouri Pacific received more and the Wabash less than each deserved. Or, to take another illustration, Texarkana was a point of interchange between the Iron Mountain and the Texas & Pacific. The Iron Mountain, with a haul of 490 miles, received more than 70 per cent, and the Texas & Pacific with a haul of 1,487 miles, received less than 30 per cent of the gross. A large increase in the division of the through rate to the Iron Mountain occurred in 1883, and was due to a change in the basis for dividing the rate made by the Missouri Pacific without the authority of the Texas & Pacific board. Had the old basis remained in force, then, according to a well-informed critic of the Gould management, the Texas & Pacific in 1885 and 1886 would have been "in sound financial condition." [13] Gould flatly denied these charges.

3. *The System Shifting of Through Traffic*

The International originated traffic in Texas which could be sent north and east over either the Kansas & Texas or the Iron Mountain. Most of the traffic, according to the former's investigating committee, was sent via the Iron Mountain. In 1887 the Kansas & Texas, for example (it was estimated), was "wrongfully deprived of at least $1,000,000 through manipulation of the traffic in favor of the Missouri Pacific Company." [14]

4. *Low Standards of Maintenance*

The evidence on standards of maintenance is conclusive. In 1884 and 1885, while security holders' committees were actively negotiating with Gould, the wretched condition of the Texas & Pacific became clear to all. Contrary to public statements made on behalf of the Gould interests in 1880 and 1881, both the New Orleans and the Rio Grande divisions were built of iron and not of steel rails.[15] Gould himself stated after the road passed into receivership that the road was laid with iron rails, "and bad ones at that." [16] In the spring of 1885 passengers on the New Orleans division said that after a ride on the property, they left the trains "feeling black and blue from the effect of being banged about, . . ." [17] The Kansas & Texas, according to a representative of a trustee of one of its bond issues, was "a physical wreck," and interest was paid from cash that should have been used to improve the property." [18]

A curious instance of Gould's lack of interest in normal standards of railroad operation is revealed in his reaction to a complaint of a passenger on one of the Texas roads. The president had asked Gould for new equipment, explaining that passenger cars leaked. Gould replied that the trains be run in dry weather only, and suggested that passengers provide themselves with umbrellas.[19]

Despite these practices, and in the face of vigorous protests against them, Gould in the middle eighties continued to hold his southwestern system intact. The first attack upon it came from the wary holders (largely Philadelphians) of the Texas & Pacific income and land grant bonds. In 1875 as a means of easing its financial position, the company had issued some $8,000,000 of these bonds, and by subsequent proviso, it was authorized if cash was unavailable to pay the interest in scrip. On July 1, 1882, the company defaulted in its cash payments and in July of the year following it also defaulted in the payment of the scrip. Most of the bondholders accepted this double blow with apparent equanimity, and certainly in silence. A few, however, were not disposed to take this beating without a struggle. They consulted counsel and were informed that the failure of the company to pay in scrip automatically entitled them to cash payments. This was more than Gould had bargained for, so he called the board together and decided to pay the interest in scrip. The rebellious bondholders in their turn were now dissatisfied. They entered suit to get their interest in cash, recalling to Gould his frequently reiterated statements that no more scrip would be issued.

The earnings of the property meanwhile declined rapidly. It was not certain that the company would be able to pay the interest on June 1, 1884. Despite the fact that the Missouri Pacific owned none, and Gould but little stock of the Texas & Pacific, its policies were dominated by the Missouri Pacific. The road was managed under an operating contract, the details of which had never been published. It was executed without submission to the Texas road's shareholders or directors. In the middle of May the Missouri Pacific announced that the bond interest due June 1 by the Texas & Pacific would be paid. The latter company, it was stated further, had no floating debt. The interest was paid not, however, by the Texas & Pacific but by the Mercantile Trust from funds advanced by the Missouri Pacific. The trust company instead of destroying the coupons surrendered them to the Missouri Pacific which, in turn, held them as security for advances to the Texas & Pacific. The latter had fulfilled its obligation to its bondholders, and the bondholders therefore had no further claim. It had not, however, fulfilled its obligation to the holder of its bond coupons—the Missouri Pacific—and that road consequently did have a claim against the Texas & Pacific. As a holder of the coupons, it could apply for a receiver. The bondholders had no claim and could not apply for a receiver. Here was another financial device which produced consternation in the ranks of the bondholders.

Gould tried to belittle the affair. It was not a new idea, he said. Other roads had done the same. Drexel & Company, for example, had bought the coupons of the Reading.[20] Neither was it anything new, he emphasized, in the relations between the two roads; it had been done two or three times before.[21] Gould could have said that the practice went back even further. Early in 1882, Marquand, the president of the Memphis & Little Rock and representative of the Gould interests, had adopted the practice. The scheme subordinated the rights of the bondholder to the interests of the controlling group. It was one of the many financial devices introduced into American corporate life designed to retain corporate control. This particular one put Gould ahead of the mortgage bondholder. An influential foreign observer described the device as a serious blow at the integrity of the mortgage bond.[22]

The purchase of the coupons of the Texas & Pacific produced a storm of opposition among its bondholders. Before that opposition could be crystallized, however, Gould, anticipating their moves, declared that the coupons would be canceled. In the middle of July a committee appointed by the Texas & Pacific board recommended the funding of the coupons maturing over the next four or five years into new bonds. The bondholders rejected the proposal. By October they succeeded in uniting their ranks and appointed a committee of five to make an investigation and to recommend a policy. The committee was requested to ask for the removal of the Missouri Pacific interests from the board and to insist upon the appointment of new executives.

Gould refused to surrender. Although the road's earnings had declined, it was a property essential to his southwestern system. By excessive division of the through rate and by favorable terminal allowances, the Missouri Pacific probably realized a good return from the business with the Texas & Pacific. Instead of retreating Gould took the offensive and announced that the unpaid Texas & Pacific coupons would remain uncanceled. Negotiations extending over many months followed. It was not until March of 1885 that a settlement permanent in intention but temporary in fact was finally negotiated. Like so many of his arrangements he succeeded only in surrendering advance ground recently occupied, as a means of bringing pressure to bear upon the other side. The compromise plan approved the funding of 50 per cent (Gould some nine months before had proposed 100 per cent) of the maturing coupons of the Rio Grande and of the New Orleans divisions for four years. The security holders' committee had asked Gould for a majority on the board, and for the right to appoint its own vice president and general manager.[23] Gould gave the committee only as much representation as he himself had. Each side had four members, and Roberts, president of the Pennsylvania, was appointed as a neutral member. Gould had consistently opposed the demand by the committee for an examination of the accounts between the Texas & Pacific and the Missouri Pacific. By controlling and revising the accounts the security holders intended to separate the interests of the two properties and thus to secure an independent management. Gould agreed only to a revision of the amounts; he did not agree to permit this revision to lead to an independent management. He, therefore, retained control of the road.[24]

The investigating committee, like most such, both public and private, made its recommendations upon the basis of the record. It sought to plug up the holes which had been made by the shrewdness of an able and resourceful individual. The committee, finding that through rates had not been fairly divided, insisted that experts be appointed to examine the through rates between the Texas & Pacific and its connections. The experts recommended that they be adjusted to make them fair. This meant simply that the Texas & Pacific would get more and the Missouri Pacific less than each was then getting. Again, in order to prevent Gould from exploiting the use of bond coupons as collateral for intercompany loans, it was stipulated that the coupons should be held in trust, and not kept alive once they were turned in under the funding agreement.[25] The adoption of these recommendations did not interfere with Gould. As conditions changed and demanded new remedies, he rose to meet them.

During these months of negotiation, Gould retained his grip

on the southwestern roads. Contrary to expectation, he was not handling the Missouri Pacific as he had the other roads. He had decided to become a railroad manager. To accomplish this it was necessary that he retain his majority interest in the Missouri Pacific and control the Kansas & Texas. Though he had faced many problems in controlling the Texas & Pacific, he had few at this time in controlling the other. That road was heavily bonded. Its strength lay largely in its control of local traffic in the Indian Territory. In the seventies and early eighties it had a monopoly of the business. In the middle eighties, competition began to deplete its revenues. First the Frisco and later the Atchison secured franchises and rights of way through the territory. By 1887 the profits of the Kansas & Texas began to drop.

From 1881 to 1885, however, the road remained profitable to the Missouri Pacific system. Its bondholders were watchful and in 1884 they exerted pressure to exact a more equitable division of the through rate. Since the bonds were paying interest, they had no legitimate complaint; but they were sufficiently enterprising to arrange for a committee representing the lessor and the lessee roads. The committee in 1885 secured a slight change in the division of the rate. Three years later another committee expressed in cautious language the belief that the road did not receive "the consideration for origination of business which it might have done had that point been advocated by some representation of a distinctive Missouri Kansas & Texas interest." [26]

Outside of this futile through-rate investigation, Gould encountered no obstacle in retaining full control of the Kansas & Texas. The road remained an integral part of the system until Gould early in 1888 decided for the time being to surrender it to the receivers. By that time, however, the road was no longer profitable.[27] While Gould in the early and middle eighties was clear about the Kansas & Texas, he hesitated about the destiny of the Wabash. In 1881 and 1882 he considered selling out his Wabash stock. Its preferred dividend had never been earned, and it is even questionable whether the fixed charges were earned in the boom year of 1881. In that year and in the year following, Gould had rebought some of the stock which he had sold in 1880. His holdings in 1881 and 1882 were probably small. By the spring of 1883, however, he appears to have concluded that the Wabash was essential to the prosperity of the Missouri Pacific. "A year or more ago," he declared at this time, "I had an idea of selling [referring to this Wabash stock], but I have since made up my mind that the Wabash is necessary to the southwestern system." [28]

By 1883 he perceived that more traffic was moving east—that is over the Wabash—and less south, down the Mississippi. The river route from St. Louis to New Orleans, which he had established with so much optimism in the spring of 1881, was in fact a product of boom times and high railroad rates. By 1883 eastern railroad wars had reduced eastern rates to record low levels. The river route became unprofitable and Gould recognized that an ever-increasing proportion of traffic would move east by rail. With the Wabash he could co-ordinate his operating policies, provide for expeditious terminal handling of the St. Louis-East St. Louis area, and, above all, divide the rates in such a way as to help the Missouri Pacific.

To retain control over the road, it was necessary that he finance the company's deficits, though he was as usual loyally supported by Sage and Dillon. Through the year 1882 and the early months of 1883, the Wabash, in order to finance current needs, sold commercial paper bearing the endorsements of Gould, Sage, and Dillon to recognized commercial paper houses.[29] The financial load of the Wabash, however, was growing too heavy even for Gould and his associates to carry. The road, Gould said in the fall of 1882, requires "more care than I bargained for; but I mean to do the best I can for it and work it out." [30] Since the road was heavily mortgaged, it could sell no more bonds. In addition to divisional liens and a large general mortgage, it had also issued car trust obligations. It was therefore necessary to develop a financial scheme which would enhance its credit standing without at the same time unconditionally engaging the earnings of the Missouri Pacific in its rescue. The Wabash at a secret meeting adopted a resolution authorizing the issue of $10,000,000 6 per cent collateral bonds. The bonds were issued under mysterious circumstances. Gould in a circular, personally signed, declared that $4,000,000 would be used to pay the car trust obligations, and another part sold to liquidate the floating debt. The bonds would be guaranteed by the Iron Mountain. With this guarantee, Gould anticipated little difficulty in selling the bonds. They would be secured, he said, by $18,000,000 of collateral. The public had never heard of these assets. The annual report, issued some weeks later, first identified them, and they were found to be largely unmarketable. One report, characterized by an observer as an "astonishing story," declared that the Iron Mountain had bought all the bonds at fifty cents on the dollar, and that the Wabash used the proceeds to pay Gould and Sage advances. This story was denied only to be followed by another which credited a Philadelphia banking firm with the purchase of the bonds at ninety.[31]

Gould created a good publicity build-up for the bonds. He stated that he was the largest stockholder of the Wabash. This was correct, for in the spring of the year he had bought large amounts of Wabash stock at prevailing low prices. He also announced that he had bought some of the bonds. This he said should be sufficient answer "to the malicious and unfounded reports recently circulated." [32] The bonds nevertheless did not sell.

In order to protect the Iron Mountain in its guarantee of Wabash securities, Gould had the Wabash execute secretly a new general mortgage of all its properties in favor of the Iron Mountain. The mortgage was not recorded at the time. Only on the eve of receivership was it recorded and its existence made known. In this way, and others to be described hereafter,[33] Gould laid his plans in advance with the purpose of perpetuating his control over the Wabash—receivership or no receivership—or, to adapt Mussolini's remarks about the League of Nations prior to his campaign for the conquest of Ethiopia, with receivership, without receivership, or against receivership.

Despite all these critical problems and the rate wars of 1884, Gould held his southwestern system intact. Through the panic of 1884 in the midst of a heavy load of personal obligations, when for a time it seemed he was about to collapse, he succeeded in maintaining his through southwestern routes, rates and divisions. The Missouri Pacific controlled the system, and Gould by majority stockholdings continued to control that road. He controlled the Texas & Pacific and the Wabash by minority holdings. Neither security holders nor judges, neither business reverses nor market fluctuations, neither receiverships nor reorganizations broke his grip on these properties.

NOTES FOR CHAPTER XX

1. Known hereafter as the Houston.
2. Known hereafter as the Gulf.
3. Chicago *Times,* May 24, 1882.
4. Burlington archives, Potter to A. E. Touzalin, May 18, 1882.
5. Ibid.
6. Some details on the rise in Southern Pacific traffic are given in *Ry. Review,* May 16, 1882, 254, citing a compilation of a Pacific Coast journal.
7. See, for example, *Public,* July 27, 1877, 57.
8. *R. R. Gaz.,* Feb. 15, 1884, 138.
9. The story of this transaction may be followed in ibid., various issues between 1882 and 1887; see also New York *Tribune,* June 29, 1882; April 14, 1884; April 15, 1884; New York *Times,* Feb. 12, 1884; Feb. 17, 1884.
10. Statement of the Receiver, Texas & Pacific, before the Subcommittee on Labor Troubles in the South and West, Report No. 4174, House of Representatives, 49th Congress, 2nd Session, May 5, 1886, Part 2, 185.
11. The report of the investigating committee is in *Chron.,* Sept. 1, 1888, 257-60.
12. New York *Times,* April 26, 1885.
13. This point is made in Henry Clews's *Weekly Financial Circular,* July 15, 1886. This circular was issued by a banking firm which in its clients' interests closely followed the activities of Gould's southwestern roads.
14. *Chron.,* March 24, 1888, 371.
15. *Ry. World,* Oct. 15, 1887, 998.
16. Phila. *Press,* June 4, 1886.
17. Ibid., March 9, 1885, from its New York correspondent who credits these remarks to a passenger.
18. This statement was made by Wheeler H. Peckham, counsel for Union Trust Company, according to the New York *Times,* Sept. 27, 1888; and New York *Tribune,* Sept. 27, 1888.
19. S. G. Reed, A *History of Texas Railroads,* 355; St. Clair Publishing, Houston, 1941.
20. *Chron.,* June 7, 1884, 680.
21. Phila. *North American,* June 6, 1884.
22. London *Economist,* Jan. 31, 1885, 133.
23. Phila. *Press,* Nov. 19, 1884.
24. On the development of these plans between June 1884 and March 1885, see *Chron.,* June 7, 1884, 680; July 26, 1884, 97; Nov. 29, 1884, 607; *Bradstreet,* March 7, 1885, 151; *Ry. World,* March 7, 1885, 224.
25. *R. R. Gaz.,* Nov. 28, 1884, 860; Dec. 19, 1884, 908.
26. *Chron.,* Sept. 1, 1888, 257.
27. For details see Chap. XXVII, pp. 538-41.
28. Phila. *Press,* May 18, 1883.
29. *R. R. Gaz.,* Dec. 1, 1882, 744; New York *Times,* Jan. 20, 1884, declared that it was a "fact well known" . . . that Gould had endorsed Wabash paper for a long period.
30. Phila. *Press,* Oct. 30, 1882.
31. Good accounts of the issue of these bonds are found in *Bradstreet,* April 21, 1883, 248; April 28, 1883, 264.
32. *R. R. Gaz.,* April 27, 1883, 274.
33. See Chapter XXI, pp. 414-7.

CHAPTER XXI

Gould's Empire Crumbles

THE system which Gould controlled in 1881 extended from Boston to Ogden, Utah. To retain control of all the roads would require sums which were not at his disposal. Control implies the ability to influence corporate policies. A management may have little or no stock in a company, but if the shareholders have confidence in the company's management, they will deliver their proxies to the officials and permit them to determine the destinies of the enterprise. Control, furthermore, is not based on membership on the board of directors. Gould for some years was on the Northwestern, Frisco, and the Rock Island boards. On none of these boards did he accomplish anything useful in behalf of his railroad interests.

Gould lost control of a property only when his opponents eliminated him from company management. Loss of control involved change of executives and a reversal of corporate policies. His dominance of his railroad empire was as temporary in its term as it was rapid in its establishment. It was no sooner completed with the acquisition of the New England late in 1881 than the process of liquidation began. First was the loss of the Central of New Jersey. Gould's interest in the affairs of another eastern railroad was also short-lived. He had entered upon control of the New England amidst a great acclaim. Although he had said little publicly, the president and some board members had spoken glowingly of the potential increase in traffic. Their expectations arising from the affiliation of the property with the Gould system were, surprisingly enough, borne out by results. By the end of the first year of Gould control, the through business was indeed so heavy that it interfered with local passenger and freight trains, and for a time in 1882 an average of 300 cars of through freight daily was refused.[1] At the road's annual meeting in December of that year when Gould and Roberts of the Pennsylvania were elected to the board, the directors in order to handle the business proposed to add more double track.

This heavy through traffic fitted in well with Gould's other plans. He moved the business at reduced rates over routes consisting of the Wabash, Grand Trunk, Lackawanna, Erie, and the New England. Even though neither the Erie nor the Grand Trunk was under his influence or control, he could make contracts with both for the movement of business at low rates because of the roads he did control. Since both were weak roads their standard of service was lower than that offered by their competitors, and only by quoting lower rates could they secure more traffic. Just as it had been the fate of Gould to learn by experience that local traffic was the core of railroad earnings, so it was necessary for the management of the New England to learn by the same cruel test that through traffic was not necessarily profitable traffic.

If they were not disillusioned by the end of the first year of Gould control, they were certainly disheartened and appalled by the end of the second. The price of the stock which had advanced to 84, when Gould acquired control, had dropped to less than 20. Not until publication of the annual report did they learn definitely that more business at lower rates spelled only disaster. In 1883 traffic increased, but most of the increase was received from connections. The rates on this business were so low and the cost of movement so high that, according to the receiver, the road had to spend about $225 in order to carry an increased gross of $100.[2] In liquidating his stock Gould turned trader. To sell he decided first to buy, thereby pushing the price higher. When in the middle of October the New England's unfavorable report for the preceding year was published and showed a deficit after fixed charges, the price of the stock went up instead of down. To facilitate the purchase of more stock at low prices, Gould sent a publicity agent to Boston to attack the road's policies. The price of the stock declined and Gould bought to secure a low average book cost. Before the end of the year the stock rose to 37 and he sold out.[3]

At the annual election in December, 1883, Gould, notwithstanding, was re-elected to the board. The company was then in a financially desperate position. It had incurred a heavy floating debt of about $2,000,000 and had sold second mortgage bonds to finance a program of betterments. When Gould was asked to make loans to the company, he blandly suggested that it be placed in receivership. Such a proceeding, he declared, would lead to an advance in the price of the stock. It is on record that one wealthy investor even took Gould's line of reasoning seriously. "Why," this person wrote in a communication to a New York paper, "who ever heard of a corporation being placed in the hands of a receiver in order that it might advance the price of the stock." [4] Gould had no further interest in the road. He resigned his directorship, retired from the exercise of any controlling influence in the property, and, according to one commentator, wished the management a Happy New Year.[5] And thus ended Gould's connection with his second eastern railroad property.

Even though Gould had thus trimmed his empire in the East, he retained his interest in the Lackawanna, although in the strict sense of the word he never did control the road. From time to time he was able to carry through his policies, especially in the course of the rate wars in 1883 and early 1884. Yet Sloan, the president, was at all times the active manager and controlling influence in the road's affairs.

Gould's influence in the properties west and south of Toledo in 1883 and early in 1884 remained dominant. In the Wabash he had a large block of common stock, bought in March and April of 1883, in order to facilitate the lease to the Iron Mountain. He controlled the Missouri Pacific by stock ownership, and including the shares owned by Sage, Marquand and a number of his other associates, could vote a large majority. Ownership and management of this road were in the same hands. In the third property, the Texas & Pacific, neither the Missouri Pacific nor Gould owned much stock. Neither did Gould have any substantial interest in the securities of the Kansas & Texas. Despite his nominal interest in the securities of these roads, his control of their policies was not seriously challenged. His fifth major property was the Union Pacific in which by 1884 he had been the dominating factor for a period longer than in any other road.

In 1884 these five roads appeared to be essential parts of a unified railroad system. The Wabash, the Missouri Pacific route from St. Louis to Kansas City, and the Union Pacific from Kansas

City and Omaha to Ogden appeared to form a natural through route. Gould tried to direct traffic along the Kansas City route and away from that formed by the Union Pacific at Omaha with connections which competed with the Missouri Pacific and Wabash. His efforts to divert traffic to the latter roads led to the fateful decision by the Burlington to extend its line to Denver. The Union Pacific despite the damage inflicted by this Gould-stimulated Burlington extension remained a close ally of Gould's roads.

The Wabash and Missouri Pacific continued to control the St. Louis terminal facilities. The Wabash, like the New England, was a victim of an excessive reliance upon through traffic and, more than any other eastern trunk line, was severely punished by the rate wars of the eighties. In 1882 and 1883 the road maintained a showing of earnings by reduction in the standard of maintenance and by charging operating expenses to capital account. As its condition became a matter of general knowledge, the securities were pressed on the market, and in the opening weeks of 1884 the stock dropped to below $20 a share. Gould, at that time a large stockholder as well as the holder of its commercial paper, insisted that "its financial condition [was] good and the property intact." [6]

Early in 1883 through the Iron Mountain lease, he had already revealed his determination to retain his hold on the road. Its financial burdens were, however, becoming ever more pressing, and the obligations he and his associates had assumed ever more heavy. By the middle of May he faced the most desperate financial crisis in his business career. Sage for the first time in many years was also in trouble and for a time was unable promptly to meet all of his obligations. Both men therefore found it impossible to finance further the deficits of the Wabash. In the middle of April the board met. There was a full attendance; the meeting was a prolonged one and in response to a request for information, the secretary declared that the meeting was of no public interest, that a receivership was not considered, and that no attention had been given to the payment of interest due June 1. Yet considerable doubt was expressed that the interest would be paid.[7]

Fears of receivership were frequently expressed, though officials and others close to Gould insisted that a receivership was neither possible nor advisable. Humphreys, formerly president, declared that he had sold no Wabash stocks or bonds himself and advised his friends not to do so.[8] Connor, Gould's brokerage partner, who probably saved him from insolvency in the critical days of May, 1884, announced there was no foundation for such rumors. "How," declared Connor, "can such an application [for receivership] be made? The road has paid its interest so far, and not being in default, no such step could be taken. . . . It is all stuff." [9] With this view that receivership was legally impossible many agreed since under the lease to the Iron Mountain a default must have lasted for six months before it could be canceled and a receivership requested. Finally Gould himself on the very eve of the receivership declared that reports of such an impending proceeding were "all folly . . . we have paid all interest on its bonds so far, and I know of no cause why we should not continue doing so in the future." [10]

If these remarks were made for the purpose of influencing Wabash stock, they were made in vain. Gould and his associates were no longer able to raise the funds to meet the road's pressing requirements. Suspension of interest payments on June 1 would eventually lead to receivership. Despite its financial weakness the road was essential to Gould, and a receivership might lead to its loss. The arch-enemy of Gould among the metropolitan dailies asserted that if the general mortgage bondholders and preferred stockholders of the Wabash would now unite, they could take control away from Gould.[11]

The Gould critics hailed with delight and perhaps with a sense of relief the declaration of the Wabash receivership at the end of May. It seemed that the Gould system had received a body blow. On the face of things it looked as though the holders of general mortgage bonds, most of whom were English citizens, supported and led by experienced financial personnel, could take control and eliminate Gould from the property in which they had invested so much and Gould so little.

Again, as so many times before, the Gould opponents underestimated his resourcefulness. Despite his preoccupation with such a variety of pressing affairs in April and May, he found the time to work out a program designed to transfer the jurisdiction of the road to the hands of the court, and at the same time prevent the security holders from seizing control. He first relieved the solvent Iron Mountain, the guarantor of the Wabash obligations under the lease, from any liability. Under the lease contract the guarantor could default in interest without confessing insolvency, because it had agreed to pay interest only out of the lessor's earnings. Late in May the lessee-guarantor announced that the earnings of the lessor were insufficient to pay interest. The Iron Mountain and hence the Missouri Pacific were saved from loss.

Gould's next problem was to save himself from liability. The Wabash had a floating debt of about $2,000,000 for supplies, unpaid wages and taxes. More important to Gould, however, was the fact that the Wabash had promissory notes in the amount of about $2,300,000, some of which matured late in May and others in June. They were endorsed by Gould, Sage, Dillon, and Humphreys. If called upon, the latter two would probably be unable to meet their obligations as endorsers. Gould and Sage knew that if the Wabash did not pay these notes at maturity they would have to pay. To Gould this additional obligation in the critical days of late May and early June would have been dangerous, if not fatal.

Gould, strangely enough, in an effort to seek a way out of this crisis sought a Wabash receivership. A receiver could subordinate existing debts to a new debt called receiver's certificates which could be issued by the receiver to raise cash to pay the maturing notes. If a receiver was to be appointed there was, however, no time to lose. A few days after the denials of receivership and defaults, the Wabash executive committee met and resolved to apply for a receivership. After a nine-day search an acceptable judge was found—Judge Brewer of the Kansas Circuit. Another difficulty was now presented. Creditors generally applied to the courts for a receiver; but the road's creditors, as the Gould apologists pointed out, had no rights in court. The Wabash had paid its interest. Even if a default did occur, under the lease a six months' grace was allowed before a receiver could be appointed.

Gould was also equal to this situation. If there was no creditor ready to ask for a receivership, Gould on behalf of the Wabash was ready, and so the Wabash made the application. On May 30, in an ex parte proceeding and with no notice to any interested party, the application was granted, and Humphreys and Thomas E. Tutt—Wabash stockholders—were appointed receivers. The court's action on the application of the corporate mortgagor was a record-shattering precedent. For years to come the question was destined to be discussed, argued and reargued. The problem finally came to the United States Supreme Court, and Chief Justice Fuller conceded that the bill placing the Wabash in receivership on application by its own counsel was "without precedent"; and that "the concession to a mortgagor company of the power through its own act to displace vested liens by unsecured claims [is] dangerous in the extreme." [12]

This language was expressed years later and obviously exerted no influence on Gould's policies. Gould took immediate advantage of the receivership to solve his own financial problems. On the very day that the court acted, application was made and granted to sell receiver's certificates to raise funds to pay the maturing notes endorsed by Gould and his co-endorsers. So ingratiating was the court, that in order to avoid the "personal inconvenience and injury" that might result from publicity, the names of Gould, Sage, and Dillon as endorsers were not made public.[13] Thus through court courtesy, Gould's obligation as endorser of the bankrupt Wabash notes was concealed from his creditors.

To the public, uninitiated in the significance of these legal technicalities, Gould's control of the road was over. Critics and investors in expressing this opinion were, however, jumping to conclusions. It was not until the end of June that they came to realize the full possibilities of Gould's actions. The bitter daily critic denounced the receivership as another Gould trick, quite worthy of his genius. Gould, it was contended, was trying to set aside the lien of the general mortgage. If he succeeded, the public could well believe that there was less security in a mortgage bond on a Gould road than there was in a floating debt, especially if Gould happened to hold the floating debt.[14] This observation was correct. The floating debt of the Wabash was superior to the lien of the bondholders, and Gould had set a precedent which for many a year was to plague mortgage bondholders. While the latter received no interest, to say nothing of principal, Gould and his friends became the fairy godchildren of the judiciary.

Security holders now began to recognize that the Wabash in receivership was as effectively under Gould's control as out of receivership. The reaction on English financial opinion was even more severe than it had been fifteen years before in connection with the Erie. In the use of strong language and outspoken denunciation of his work, the remarks of an informed English journal were unprecedented. Said this writer: "There are few frauds on earth so black as that which is associated with the name Wabash, and few men, we are pleased to say, so black as Mr. Gould himself, the president of this wretched swindle."

Gould, furthermore, declared this same writer in a spirit of unrestrained condemnation, was "indeed, the imperial Autolycus of the Western World. . . . Like the Ishmaelite of old, his hand is against every man, and every man's hand is against him. . . . But to attempt to sketch the character of Mr. Jay Gould in its true colors would be futile, since no language is equal to the task. . . ."

And as a final blast, in referring to his public statements during the previous two years that the Wabash would eventually resume preferred dividends as contrasted with the sworn testimony of Hopkins (an operating official) in petition for receivership, that the road had not earned its operating expenses for two years, it declared that Gould "would seem to have been roundly lying all through the peace in order to successfully pioneer one of the most disgusting, barefaced swindles on record." [15]

On this side of the water the Wabash receivership was also condemned. A leading weekly financial journal unleashed a strong attack upon Gould's policies. This paper in 1879 and 1880 had seen little to criticize. In 1884, after the debacle, and with a beautiful sense of hindsight philosophy, it delivered an amazing castigation. It described the history of the Wabash under Gould control as "one of the most remarkable and interesting that [had] ever occurred in American railroading. It [was] even phenomenal, embracing in a comparatively short period nearly every phase of kite-flying, watering, stock jobbing, bankruptcy of the company and assessment of stockholders." [16] This critic and many others did not fully comprehend the situation. They seemed to believe that Gould was anxious only to recover his investment in the Wabash at the expense of bondholders and stockholders. They believed that the Wabash as part of the Gould empire was a thing of the past, and that it was on its way out. The critics were soon to be undeceived.

The Wabash receivership was by no means the only Gould exploit in the stirring days of May and June, 1884. Gould was threatened not only on the east but also on the far west of his far-flung system. There the Union Pacific had displayed a magnificent record. Investors with their eye on the past had found an ideal investment. In the midst of the depression of the seventies, its stock passed from a nondividend-payer to a 6 per cent payer, and after the merger of 1880 the dividend was continued.

Meanwhile the road's expansion policy was financed by a continuous succession of bond issues. These debts produced a heavy burden of fixed charges. Its strength was further impaired by the rise of competition from other roads. The rate structure of the Union Pacific accordingly weakened, and the ton-mile rate dropped. In 1883 and 1884 the earnings upon any sound basis of accounting would have reflected a decline sufficiently serious to warn the investing public. In the absence of supervised statements by a public authority, Gould was free to use his genius for misleading accounting methods. Dillon must have been impressed by Gould bookkeeping, for, when in 1884 the company passed the dividend, he belittled the significance of the event. It was, he said, "mainly a matter of bookkeeping."[17]

Even so informed a student of Gould's career as Adams was oblivious to the financial effect of these policies. It was not until after he had assumed the presidency that Adams recognized the nature of Gould's bookkeeping and denounced the road's earnings report issued in 1883. "They were deceptive," he said, "they misled me and a good many others, because a change in the methods of bookkeeping made the comparisons with the previous year utterly valueless. These approximate statements were a fraud —that is, owing to the change in bookkeeping."[18]

Yet in 1882 and 1883 when the silent but informed businessman-investor, the man who thinks much and talks little, was selling his stock, Adams recommended the stock for purchase.[19] In so doing, Adams apparently did not consider the operations of the Thurman Act of 1878. The law required the Union Pacific, as one of the subsidized roads, to set aside for the purpose of paying the government bonds advanced to aid in construction of the road, 25 per cent of its net income and all of its gross revenue derived from the movement of government traffic. On various pretexts Gould as the controlling power had not set these sums aside. There was nothing secret about the law nor about the views of the Union Pacific concerning the law. The obligation was there and eventually would have to be met. Perhaps Adams never gave the matter a second thought. There is no evidence that in approving the stock as a conservative investment, he made any reference to his potential liability. *Quis custodiet ipsos custodes?* (Who will guard the guards themselves?)

This failure to heed the dictates of the Thurman Act brought the road's affairs to a climax. Early in 1884 the stock was still selling at about 80. Early in April the report spread that Congress was about to enforce the Thurman Act and to compel the Union Pacific to make its payment into the sinking fund. On the basis of another report that a House committee would recommend an increase in the contributions from 25 per cent to 37½ per cent, the price of Union Pacific broke sharply.[20] Before the end of the month the situation in Congress rapidly reached a crisis. The House passed an amendment to the Thurman Act to increase the sinking fund contribution to 55 per cent. The sales of Union Pacific increased, and by the end of the month the price of the stock dropped to nearly $60 a share. In the first week of May the situation grew even more critical. The House bill was referred to the Judiciary Committee of the Senate. There Senator George F. Edmunds, long a critic of the Union Pacific, presented a report asking the president to request the attorney-general to execute the penalties against the road for paying unauthorized dividends, and against any official who had voted for such dividends. The report was turned over to Senator Hoar, and he was asked to bring it before the Senate for a vote on the sixth of May.

The situation now confronting Gould was desperate. He had been an official of the Union Pacific for the period in which the road had paid unauthorized dividends. His personal loans were heavy, and he was beset by a group of traders who were trying to bring about his downfall.[21] The passage of the bill at this critical period probably would have meant a death blow to Gould. He had bought substantial blocks of Union Pacific at prices slightly below 90, and passage of the law might reduce the stock to nominal values. Penalties, furthermore, would have subjected him to fines sufficiently heavy to induce his creditors to call their loans and insist upon immediate payment.

Gould was again equal to the occasion. The panic did not unnerve his iron courage. He again revealed his mastery of men and once more showed his ability to select the proper man at the proper time to do the job. He understood well the temper of public opinion, and he recognized that the Senate would pay scant attention to his requests. He did not represent any body of public opinion nor could he generalize his personal troubles and financial problems and assert that they were part of a problem of an army of investors.

On the Union Pacific board, however, there was a person well fitted to present the public view and to explain how any measure taken against the Union Pacific would harm the public. That man was Adams. He was a citizen of distinction and with a large following among public-spirited citizens and investors. The board of directors, all of whom were involved, accordingly selected Adams to avert or postpone the introduction of the Edmunds resolution. Adams, in the words of Senator Hoar, was a man "of unimpeachable moral and business character. . . ." [22] He could not, however, fathom the motives of others. "An entirely honest man himself, morally speaking," wrote Perkins of Adams, "he, nevertheless, suspects everybody less stupid than himself of not being honest." [23] Adams was the ideal man to convince the Senate that passage of the Edmunds bill would be detrimental to the public welfare. At the "urgent solicitation" of the board he left for Washington. His approaches to Senator Edmunds not being satisfactory, he addressed himself to other members of the committee, finally securing a hearing from Senator Hoar. Adams's arguments followed traditional lines. First was a plea of personal self-defense. He was assured, he said, by directors and officials of the Union Pacific, that the property was all right. His position, he said further, was not enviable. He had endorsed the stock and the company's management. In the country's present critical financial condition, he declared, the passage of the resolution would "destroy the entire value of the stock, create a panic, completely discredit Jay Gould, and bring to ruin" many holders of Union Pacific securities.[24] The argument of Adams brought some opposition on the floor of the Senate. Senator Van Wyck of Nebraska, for example, remarked sarcastically, that one must speak in bated breath for fear that this institution of credit—the Union Pacific—would tumble, and that care must be taken not to impair the value of its stock on the market.[25]

Adams's use of the time-worn innocent-investor argument, however, won the day. Senator Hoar agreed, on behalf of the committee, to postpone action to the twentieth of May. Prolonged negotiations followed. The twentieth of May came and passed and no action was taken; but Adams eventually succeeded in making one of the most unusual agreements on record with a representative of a legislative body. With no legal authority, without informing any of the law-enforcing agencies, such as the attorney-general or the Department of Justice, Senator Hoar on behalf of a Senate committee made an agreement with a corporation which was believed to have been violating the law for a period of about six years. The legislative committee approved the agreement; the agreement was designed to enable the railroad to comply with the law, and as carried out made any executive action to enforce compliance with the law unnecessary. A legislative committee, in short, made an arrangement for the enforcement of a law, and thus took over the function of the executive branch of the government.

The arrangement negotiated between Senator Hoar and Adams eliminated Gould and his group from the management of the property. Dillon, his close associate, agreed to resign the presidency. The company agreed to pay no dividends until after Congress met in December, to permit the government to retain the revenue derived from government traffic, and to pay the United States Treasury approximately $700,000 due under the Thurman Act for the year 1883. The agreement of the Union Pacific, which of course was unilateral, since the committee could not pledge either the Senate or the Executive, was submitted to the Judiciary Committee on the seventeenth of June. It was accepted by the committee on that date. The plan was presented to the Union Pacific board the next day and was promptly accepted.

The dividend was passed, Dillon resigned, and Adams was elected president. Adams well deserved the title of the Angel of the Union Pacific, although it was not bestowed upon him. Gould was saved. He still had a large block of Union Pacific, and by this extraordinary arrangement with a Senate committee, the way was open for a rising market in Union Pacific stock. The Gould-staged bull market in the two following months was led by that stock.

When Gould, as the dominant factor in the Union Pacific policies departed, the property was in an unenviable condition. It had a volume of unfinished construction work on hand. The Oregon Short Line almost two years in building was still unfinished, and other extensions were in the course of construction. The road's physical condition was poor. Its main lines were almost entirely unballasted, and its equipment largely obsolete. Finances were also poor. Payment of unearned dividends left the company with little cash, and with slight reserves against emergencies. The interest charges on the debts incurred in building many lines had been charged to capital account; they were soon to appear as interest and thus increase the company's heavy fixed charges. The borrowing capacity was almost exhausted; earnings were falling, with the war of rates promising to reduce them further; and the stock dropped to below $30 a share.

Thus did Gould lose a valuable part of his railroad empire of 1881. By the summer of 1884 he had lost all his eastern properties as well as his transcontinental line. Besides the main stem of the combined Missouri Pacific-Iron Mountain system, he was left with only two major roads, the Kansas & Texas, and the Texas & Pacific. His hold on the latter was weakening. In order to maintain his grip, he had in 1884 adopted an ingenious scheme which aroused the bondholders.[26] Another agreement made in March, 1885,[27] did not settle fundamental problems. It was difficult for investors to conclude that their optimism in 1880 and 1881 had been unjustified. They believed that the road needed only a respite; and that if given a little leeway, would soon earn enough to pay both interest and dividends.

The plan for readjustment of the road's finances provided little cash to spend on its impoverished property. Gould, however, was not concerned. He held none of the bonds and looked upon his small stock investment from the standpoint of the Missouri Pacific. Even though the financial plan was unsound as a means of restoring the road to financial health, it was sufficiently sound from the standpoint of Gould. On the face of things he held control by the narrowest of margins, since on a vote of the board on a critical issue, he could command only eight out of the seventeen votes. Hence, before the end of 1884, loss of control seemed inevitable. In September a committee of the board went over the line and decided that the road could no longer pay interest, and in December the company went into the hands of a receiver. On taking over the property that official discovered that more than 20 per cent of the rolling stock was unserviceable, that only a few miles were laid with steel track, and that the road needed badly a large number of new ties.[28]

It appeared that Gould would lose control. Here again, as in the case of the Wabash, external appearances were deceptive, for Gould prior to the receivership had secured a commanding position in the Texas & Pacific. To enable the road to pay interest, the Missouri Pacific had made loans, thereby making itself a floating debt creditor for about $1,250,000.[29] Repeating the Wabash precedent, Gould used this small debt as a basis for another scheme to acquire control of the property in receivership at an insignificant price.

Of the major properties in his railroad system, there were only two left intact. One was the parent, the solvent Missouri Pacific. The other was the Kansas & Texas leased to the Missouri Pacific. A large block of its stocks and bonds was held in Amsterdam.[30] The Dutch bondholders were suspicious of Gould's control. Probably impressed by the decline in price of the securities of the Gould roads, they became suspicious of Gould's willingness or ability through the Missouri Pacific to continue the payment of interest on their bonds. They therefore did the unusual. Before any financial difficulties developed, and while the road was still paying interest, they appointed a committee. The committee found no evidence of any unfair arrangement of system traffic or of property undermaintenance. The committee consisted of bankers and brokers, not engineers and operating men. They saw what they were supposed to see and looked only for the obvious.

In 1885 Gould thus enjoyed secure control of both the Kansas

& Texas and the Missouri Pacific. He appeared to have lost the Union Pacific, the Wabash and the Texas & Pacific. A perennial metropolitan critic, in viewing his system, was impressed by the appalling magnitude of the stocks and bonds issued by his five major properties. This volume of securities, "with but a few exceptional classes of the bonds, are in utter discredit. Not one of these companies," it continued, "can put out a report which commands confidence; some scarcely pretend to give reports; two are bankrupt; a third is not far from it; a fourth is flourishing amid ruin with a fictitious appearance of prosperity, and its stock, while quoted at a high figure in the market, no one dares touch; the fifth, nominally controlled by the government, which built it, had contributed to our history little more than a record of scandals and corruption. Everywhere the lines run, they mark bankruptcy, fraud, deception; there is no sound spot anywhere, because far as they run to north and south and wide as they stretch from east to west, a single hand is over them all, under whose blighting shadow everything rots." [31] And that hand was the hand of Gould.

NOTES FOR CHAPTER XXI

1. Boston *Transcript*, cited in *Ry. Review*, Dec. 2, 1882, 687.
2. The annual report is analyzed in *R. R. Gaz.*, Dec. 14, 1883, 830, and the statement of the receiver with respect to the terms on which the road did its through business is in ibid., Feb. 8, 1884, 120.
3. Boston *Transcript*, Jan. 3, 1884, is authority for the statement that Gould sent an agent to Boston for the purpose of attacking the New England.
4. New York *Herald*, Jan. 6, 1884.
5. *Bradstreet*, Jan. 5, 1884, 10.
6. New York *Tribune*, Jan. 18, 1884.
7. Ry. *World*, April 19, 1884, 368.
8. New York *Herald*, April 25, 1884.
9. New York *Times*, May 9, 1884.
10. New York *Mail & Express*, May 12, 1884.
11. New York *Herald*, June 2, 1884.
12. 145 U. S., 95, 6.
13. Atkins vs. Wabash, *Federal Reporter*, Vol. 29, 165, 1886.
14. New York *Herald*, June 23, 1884.
15. These remarks were made by the London *Railway Times*, cited in ibid., July 22, 1884.
16. *Chron.*, Aug. 16, 1884, 183.
17. *Bradstreet*, Oct. 4, 1884, 216.
18. *Ry. Review*, Sept. 6, 1884, 464.
19. Burlington archives, Perkins to Forbes, in a letter dated May 23, 1884, wrote that Adams had induced many people to buy the Union Pacific stock.
20. New York *Herald*, April 3, 1884.
21. See Chapter XXIV, pp. 493-5.

22. *Congressional Record*, June 21, 1884, 5436.
23. Burlington archives, Perkins to Forbes, May 23, 1884.
24. This argument of Adams, including the quotation, is based upon an analysis in the New York *Times*, July 31, 1884; another account appeared in the New York *Tribune*, Dec. 5, 1890.
25. *Congressional Record*, June 21, 1884, 5432.
26. See Chapter XX, pp. 404-5.
27. See Ibid., p. 406.
28. Report No. 4174, House of Representatives, 49th Congress, 2nd Session, Statement of the Receiver, Texas & Pacific, May 5, 1886, before the Subcommittee on Labor Troubles in the South and West, Part 2, 172-3.
29. Ibid., 184.
30. Amsterdam held $18,000,000 of stock out of $46,000,000 outstanding, according to an analysis made by a New York broker, as reported in the Phila. *North American*, Aug. 7, 1884.
31. New York *Times*, Jan. 18, 1885.

CHAPTER XXII

Gould's Empire Reorganized

Of the three major railroads which Gould lost in 1884 and 1885, only two were of importance in the building of his southwestern system. He was not interested in the third, although this, the Union Pacific, appears to have been the most important in 1879–81. It was the prospective traffic which it would turn over to the Wabash that seemed at the time to give the latter such a high value. The Union Pacific, however, discovered that it could do little for the Wabash since its own traffic needs allied its fortunes with the direct Omaha-Chicago lines.

It was in the development of the southwestern system that Gould placed more and more of his time, energy and capital. The two roads—the Wabash and the Texas & Pacific—whose control he apparently had lost, were essential to its prosperity. Gould accordingly arranged his affairs in such a way as to enable him at reasonable cost to reacquire control of both of the roads. To achieve this, he was forced to take the leadership in their corporate reorganization and to enter the intricate field of mortgage foreclosures, rearrangement of capital structures, cancellation of corporate leases, and many other financial problems. He was obliged, furthermore, to deal with different classes of security holders; with bankers and brokers, partners of investment houses, presidents of trust companies and railroad companies, not only in this country, but also abroad, especially in England, Germany, and Holland. These men possessed wide experience in financial matters and a thorough understanding of the possibilities. Many also had a strong investor following. Despite all this talent, Gould usually came out the victor. He took an advance position in his efforts to reorganize properties to the point where they could earn fixed charges and become solvent. Because of their realistic thoroughness some of these methods were violently criticized.

Of the two major roads which required financial surgery, the most important both as to size and complexity was the Wabash. Despite its reorganization in the middle seventies its financial structure had not been radically changed. Its property was still covered by separate first mortgages on various parts of its line, to which second mortgages were later added. Under the administration of Gould the company added a large number of feeders and branches, mostly on a lease basis. By 1880 almost every bit of property was covered either by a first mortgage or a rental contract which had the same effect as a mortgage. To these liabilities Gould in 1881 added a general mortgage with a lien on the entire property subject to the existing mortgages. Unlike most instruments of this kind, the lien embraced *only* the property which was then owned by the company. The securities and the contracts representing the rights of the Wabash to use bridges, tracks, tunnels and terminals were not embraced in the lien of the general mortgage bonds. Without these contracts the Wabash system could not operate.

Evidences of these rights were kept by the Wabash in the treasury. Their existence might, it is true, have been discovered by inquiring observers; inquiring observers, however, are always few. When the Wabash in the spring of 1883 announced its intention to issue collateral trust bonds protected by a portfolio of securities, including contracts conveying title to some of these strategic rights, financial observers were surprised. Gould was not surprised.

Despite his preoccupation with so many critical problems, Gould shortly after the Wabash receivership was ready with a plan of reorganization. The bondholders had hardly grasped the essentials of the problem before Gould was ready with a proposal. His plan was drastic, and to the junior mortgage bondholders, it threatened disaster. He proposed that the general mortgage be foreclosed, and that in exchange for the bonds, the new company issue an equal amount of noncumulative debentures on which no interest be paid unless earned. With Gould's finesse in the art of bookkeeping, investors could look ahead to many years of no income. This was not all. Gould proposed that the stock be assessed $6 a share to raise $3,000,000; with an equal amount to be raised by the sale of debentures. The $6,000,000 or thereabouts thus raised would be used to pay the company's floating debt and to retire the collateral trust bonds pledged as security. The plan would drastically reduce the Wabash's fixed charges.[1]

It was a good plan for the company, and an even better plan for Gould. The company's notes held by Gould would be paid in cash. While this was an advantage for the Wabash and Gould, it was a devastating blow to the general mortgage bondholders. Gould recognized that the success of the plan depended upon the approval of the English bondholders. Appreciating that his position as the chief executive of the Wabash might interfere with the acceptance of his proposal, he resigned as president. Joy, who stood high in the confidence of British investors, succeeded him.

Shortly after his elevation to the presidency, Joy, accompanied by O. D. Ashley, secretary of the Wabash, left for Europe. Joy was certain that the reorganization plan would be successful. Both he and Gould, however, were soon to be disappointed. In the United States and in England the plan was assailed in inflammable language. In this country a trade journal, which in the few months preceding had gradually changed its attitude toward Gould from one of friendliness to outspoken hostility, attacked the plan violently. "One reads the details of this remarkable plan with a feeling of wonder whether the federal judiciary of the United States is really the law department of Mr. Gould's southwestern railroad system, or whether there is actually any law in the country at all." [2] A leading English paper remarked that since the new debentures had no proprietary rights, the general mortgage bonds became junior to the collateral trust bonds. In this way Gould and his group would reacquire control —"a monstrous proposal, monstrous in its audacity, and in its unblushing demand for yet more money." [3] The most revealing criticism came from one who was in a position to appreciate the ingenuity of the author of the plan. This man was a banker—the chairman of the London Wabash Bond and Shareholders Committee—who, on the basis of twenty-five years of experience, declared he was "amazed almost with a feeling of admiration at the prodigious swindle which [had] been perpetrated upon the unfortunate bondholders." [4] Joy failed to get approval of the plan and within a few weeks returned to the United States. Like other experienced railroad men, he was deeply discouraged. Perkins of the Burlington, for example, observed that the Wabash was "floundering about and trying to make settlement with its creditors and reorganize," though he doubted whether the effort would succeed.[5]

Gould, meanwhile, busied himself with another aspect of the reorganization. The Wabash leased lines carried little traffic. Gould moved to solve the problem of unprofitable leased lines with complete disregard of corporate amenities. He proposed to the court that the Wabash discontinue immediately the operation of all such lines. After a delay of almost a year, Judge Brewer finally handed down one of those inscrutable decisions which seemed to deny something that, for all practical purposes, it did not deny. Although Gould's request for permission to abandon unprofitable lines was rejected, and although the court declared that it would not sever branches from a railroad system, it nevertheless upheld the right of the lessor or the holder of a mortgage whose rent or interest was unpaid to insist upon repossession or foreclosure. This was not "sloughing off" branches, asserted the court: If disruption did come, it would come to those who have a "legal right" to do so.[6]

The decision simply transferred the initiative from Gould to the unfortunate security holders. Under this decision, Gould could pass the interest or the rent, and then invite the security holders to repossess their property. During the next two years the creditors of company after company took title to property either by foreclosure or by eviction proceedings. Many of the weak lines which for so many years were to be such disturbing factors in the railway world were born of acquisitions and subsequent reorganizations similar to those of the Wabash.

These problems of public interest were of no concern to Gould any more than they were to corporate reorganizers of later years. They were, however, of great help to the Wabash, since, by permitting the lessor-owners or mortgage creditors to repossess their unprofitable branches, the earnings on the other routes of the system were increased. Before Judge Brewer handed down his decision authorizing the Wabash to adopt this policy, the English and the American bondholders' committee had succeeded after "long and tedious negotiations"[7] in working out a modified plan of reorganization which the London committee agreed to recommend to its bondholders. The general mortgage bonds, instead of being exchanged for unsecured debentures, would be exchanged dollar for dollar for new mortgage bonds. The interest would be reduced from 6 per cent to 5 per cent, and for five years would be income bonds, the interest on which would not be paid unless earned. The new bonds were made more palatable by getting fair representation on the board of directors. These were insubstantial variations from the original plan. Gould had previously, as in the Texas & Pacific, given representation on the board to the creditors, and he knew from experience that the privilege could have little effect on corporate policy. In this modified plan, he adhered to his major premises: the new junior bonds would pay no interest, and assessments would be levied on the stock sufficient in amount to redeem the floating debt.

It seemed, nevertheless, that Gould's new plan despite the slight changes would succeed. Joy was asked to return to England to secure approval. The bondholders, however, rejected the plan, and in addition decided to appoint an investigating committee. Despite failure, negotiations continued. Within less than three months a third plan emerged. The right of the general mortgage bondholders to secure representation on the board was more clearly defined. One-half of the board would be elected by the bondholders, and the other half by the shareholders. The president of the road would be elected by agreement between the two groups of board members, and failing that, by the trustees of the bondholders. It was still provided that the floating debt should be paid from funds raised by an assessment on the stockholders. It was suddenly discovered that the floating debt had been underestimated by about $900,000. Since the existence of such a large debt would "be fatal" to the success of the plan, the committee suggested that the problem be referred to another committee.[8]

This committee for the first time discovered the real value of the collateral trust bonds. The pledged securities, it was now recognized, were highly important, and the committee, therefore, raised embarrassing questions regarding their ownership. After hard bargaining it finally succeeded in reaching an agreement that all the securities should be subject to the new general mortgage.[9]

This was a notable victory for the bondholders. The committee, having tasted blood, now wanted more, and demanded that an investigation of the property be made. Joy deprecated such a move, insisting that if Gould should turn hostile, he could injure the Wabash by diverting the business of the southwestern lines from it to the lines of its competitors.[10] This threat was typical. It made no impression on the British bondholders who proceeded with their plans and appointed a committee to come to the United States to investigate the road. By this show of firmness the committee made a strong impression on Gould. He was not anxious to divert his business from the Wabash to a competitive line. He continued to negotiate and on the first of September reached an agreement for a new plan. The foreclosure of the two junior mortgages which Gould had originally suggested was included, but the preference in treatment of the collateral trust bondholders over the general bondholders was discarded. Each group would get dollar for dollar in the debentures of the new company. The floating debt would be exchanged in part for a new issue of debentures. The stocks were still to be assessed, and the proceeds used to pay off the balance of the floating debt.

The plan, involving the purchase of the property at foreclosure sale, was to be carried out by a purchasing committee. Joy was appointed chairman. The committee at that time appeared to be unimportant and almost everybody ignored it. This fulfilled Gould's wishes. He had plans and, as the months rolled on in 1885 and well into 1886, he used the purchasing committee to carry out such plans.

Everything was now arranged for the grand climax. Gould, convinced that the path was clear, had declared months before that reorganization was "virtually assured." [11] The plan, he said, had been accepted by a sufficiently large number of bondholders and stockholders to insure success. On April 26, 1886, the sale of foreclosure was held and the success of the plan seemed assured. Acquisition of the property by the purchasing committee heralded the approaching end of the receivership—an event which was hailed by one railroad periodical as "the closing scene in one of the most complicated reorganization movements ever attempted in this country." [12]

The other steps necessary to complete the reorganization, said the secretary, would be taken as rapidly as circumstances permitted. The other steps were soon revealed. The senior bondholders—those holding first and second mortgages on the main system line, from Kansas City to St. Louis, and from St. Louis to Chicago and to Toledo—had not participated in the reorganization proceedings. Perhaps they believed that they were not involved in any plans which called for reduction in principal or interest on the part of the junior security holders. They were soon disillusioned. Within less than a month the purchasing committee requested them to make their contribution to the cause. They were asked to reduce their interest rate to 5 per cent and to exchange their overdue coupons for new bonds.

This proposal was submitted in a pamphlet issued by the purchasing committee in which for the first time the traffic realities of the Wabash system were officially presented. The competitive situation of the Wabash was described as critical. The road served a territory which was crossed by every eastern trunk line. "All roads from Chicago to the seaboard, except the Michigan Central," declared the committee, "cross it. All roads from that city southwest, south and southeast cross it, and they radiate from Chicago like the sticks of a fan. . . . There is no point on its lines not subject to competition as intense as competition can be. There are parallel roads on all sides, and roads crossing it at all points." [13]

The security holders now knew the worst. Gould, in the hour of desperation, flooded their minds with gloom even as five years before, in the hour of triumph, he had flooded their minds with cheer. They were told, furthermore, that the floating debt had increased about 100 per cent in the two years since the beginning of the receivership. This large debt, according to the committee, had a lien on the property superior to that of the first and second mortgage bondholders.

The first mortgage bondholders learned also that aside from the danger of the floating debt, the strength of their lien was impaired by its very exclusiveness. By contract and in equity, the first mortgage bondholder was entitled to the full satisfaction of his claims. To enforce his rights, he could if necessary seize the property. If the line served as a part of a through route with other lines, each of which was covered by a separate first mortgage, then his rights of property repossession were of little value. The strength of the bond lay in the fact that the secured property was a part of the railroad system. The exercise of the right of foreclosure might prove a dangerous gesture. The bondholders, probably for the first time in the country's financial history, were presented with this paradox. Though they seemed to be strong, their position was weak, and this weakness was not overlooked by financial observers. There seemed to be "little doubt that it would be a financial mistake," declared one writer, for the first mortgage bondholders "to enforce their equitable rights to the extent of disrupting the continuous system." [14] Here was one of the earliest recognitions on record of the subordination of primary legal rights of the mortgage contract in a system pattern.

Despite this gloomy picture, opposition immediately developed. A meeting of the underlying bondholders on the line east of the Mississippi was held early in July. Ashley, secretary of the purchasing committee, was present and invited the fullest investigation of the company's accounts. The bondholders appointed a committee which decided to confer with the purchasing committee and make recommendations. The committee did not take long to consider the suggestion of the purchasing committee. In less than a month its report and recommendation were ready; it voted to recommend to the bondholders the acceptance, subject to some slight modifications, of the committee's proposals.

Although the committee thus approved the suggested reduction in interest charges from 7 to 5 per cent, the bondholders were not bound. The recommendation, therefore, produced no important change. Even before this committee was organized, another group of bondholders decided to oppose the reorganization plan. They objected to the proposed reduction in fixed charges on the underlying bonds as calculated to aid the collateral trust and general mortgage bondholders. The lead was taken by the Chicago division bondholders who pointed out that that division had earned all its interest charges.

These bondholders asserted that the existing receivers had

been appointed as a result of a proceeding in which they had no interest. The case was presented before a judge who had already made a record of judicial independence. Judge Walter L. Gresham, afterward Cleveland's Secretary of State, had already gone on record that courts had been too liberal in granting receiverships.[15]

A number of other bondholders who had also begun court proceedings to oppose the Gould-sponsored plan of reorganization joined hands with the Chicago group. The judge acted with reasonable promptness. After listening to the evidence he instructed the receivers early in August to prepare a report on their management of the Chicago division.[16]

Gould recognized that he had a fight on his hands, and that he had no means of exerting pressure upon the senior bondholders. Neither he nor his allies had any holdings of these bonds. Sage, Humphreys, and Dillon, the co-endorsers on the Wabash notes, had holdings of the Wabash stock, as did Hopkins. Sage had also some of the Wabash general mortgage bonds. It appeared therefore that Gould was helpless—but, as always with respect to Gould, appearances were misleading. He soon discovered another device, novel in character, which appeared to give him the necessary leverage.

The new financial mechanism involved the functioning of the purchasing committee. That committee, although presumably independent, was, to use the expression of a critical Wabash security holder, "under the thumb of Jay Gould." [17] It administered the details of the reorganization, managed the property until formally released by the court, and received the company's revenue and paid its expenses. The decree accompanying the foreclosure sale in April had required the receivers to pay and discharge the receivers' obligations. Instead, the receivers bought their obligations, and kept them alive; the committee then held the certificates as a prior lien against the property. When the certificates were paid off, their former holders had no claim against the road. The purchasing committee, however, having paid off the receivers' certificates with the funds of the company, had a lien against its property, superior to that held by the underlying bondholders.

Even this was not the whole story. The purchasing committee

had succeeded in inducing Judge Brewer to issue an order authorizing the receivers, who were business friends of Gould, to pay interest on senior bonds only as requested by the purchasing committee. The committee did not wait long in taking advantage of the new order. With the co-operation of the receiver, it would hereafter pay interest only to those senior bondholders who agreed to the proposals to reduce interest charges. The committee then declared that if the dissenters did not agree, the resulting litigation would be "long and expensive." [18]

These proceedings met with an abrupt check in December, 1886. Judge Gresham, in "probably one of the most important decisions ever entered in a railroad case in this country," [19] condemned the Wabash receivership. The bondholders' application for the appointment of an independent receiver was granted, and, what was equally important, the court appointed the distinguished judge, Thomas M. Cooley, to the position. The new receiver was authorized to take possession of the property east of the Mississippi River and to displace Gould's two associates. The decision was a "complete surprise" to Wall Street,[20] and the price of Wabash securities declined sharply. Gould's associates in the reorganization of the property were pessimistic. Joy, who had spent so many months in this country and in England to work out the reorganization, stated that all plans of the purchasing committee having failed, the Wabash system would be broken up.[21]

Gould himself entertained no such thoughts. The Wabash was just as essential to the Missouri Pacific in December of 1886 as it had been before. He was therefore ready with a renewed proposal calculated, despite Judge Gresham's decision, to expedite the progress of the reorganization. He proposed, through the purchasing committee, to pay the accumulated unpaid interest on the first mortgage bonds if the court would transfer title to the property to the purchasing committee. Judge Gresham refused to agree. On the first of January, 1887, in accordance with the orders of the court, the existing receivers relinquished the roads east of the Mississippi to Judge Cooley. The eastern and western lines of the Wabash were again independent as they had been prior to the merger of 1879.

The underlying bondholders now delivered a counterattack.

Appearing before Judge Brewer in the St. Louis Circuit Court—the court in which the Wabash receivers were appointed in May, 1884—they demanded that the court order a distribution to them of more than $1,300,000, which, they said, represented the surplus earnings of the Chicago division. They insisted that these earnings had been used to finance deficits on other parts of the system. The decision of Judge Brewer was one of the most unusual in judicial history. He answered the request of the bondholders at great length and with considerable warmth. He defended the receivers whom he had appointed against the charges by Judge Gresham. The purchasing committee, he insisted, bought the property under conditions prescribed by the court, and the court therefore had no moral or legal right to saddle any such burden upon the committee. He therefore dismissed the petition of the first mortgage bondholders.[22]

Gould on his part pressed his attacks and carried his demand for the release of the main eastern lines upon the payment of the accumulated interest to the United States Supreme Court. The nonassenting bondholders also put in their counterclaim. The struggle in the courts was only shadow boxing, neither side believing that its proposal would be successful. Nothing came of these thrusts and counterthrusts. Gould was convinced that the determined opposition which had wound up successfully in the far-reaching decision of Judge Gresham could not be swayed by either frontal or flank attacks. He recognized that he could not use the floating debt or the collateral trust bonds to secure a strategic position in the reorganization. He still held the stock which he had bought in the spring of 1883 in connection with the Wabash lease to the Iron Mountain. Since then he had bought additional stock and was now probably the road's largest stockholder.[23]

Gould concluded that it was impossible to eliminate the opposition of the underlying bondholders, and he accordingly prepared a new plan. It proposed the creation of a first mortgage upon the main lines of the road east of the Mississippi River between St. Louis, Chicago, and Toledo. Existing first mortgage bonds would be exchanged for new bonds. The bonds, except those on the Detroit division, would also receive their past-due interest in cash.

A second mortgage, while covering the same lines east of the Mississippi River, would also include a first lien on the road's equipment. The existing second mortgage bonds, and branch line bonds, would be converted into the new second mortgage bonds. Upon foreclosure, the lines east of the Mississippi would be united with those west of the river.[24] The plan appeared to be fair to the underlying bondholders. All previous devices designed by Gould to force the underlying bondholders into a plan not of their own choosing had failed. It seemed now that the reorganization was virtually completed.

Some of the investors, however, refused to accept the terms. One group of first mortgage bondholders conceived the idea that they were entitled to a lien on the equipment. They therefore decided to fight the plan. Their committee insisted that since every division on which the bonds had a lien had earned its interest, the bondholders should make no sacrifice. They declared, furthermore, that the equipment should be divided among the first mortgage bondholders. The court decided in favor of the bondholders. The equipment belonged to the bondholders, and must be apportioned among them on an equitable basis. In the absence of any other basis, it was suggested that the mileage be used.[25]

This was the most sweeping victory which any group of bondholders had ever secured against Gould. With this decision to support them, the bondholders decided to make a wholesale attack on the plan. They determined that in order to get full value, they would bid at the foreclosure sale and compete against the purchasing committee. This was a unique situation. The minority bondholders' committee asked its followers to deposit 25 per cent of their holdings with a trust company to be used to bid for the property. If it outbid the purchasing committee, it could retain title to the property and dispose of it to a competitor of the Wabash. If its bid were exceeded by the purchasing committee, the bonds could be sold at a profit.[26]

The foreclosure sale, climaxing almost five years of complicated negotiations, and unprecedented in many respects in financial history, took place on May 15, 1889. The minority committee bought three main-line divisions, while the purchasing committee bought the other divisions. It appeared for a moment that the property east of the Mississippi would be split in two parts, each hostile to the other. To prevent this, the purchasing committee had no alternative but to make a bid for the entire road including all the divisions as one unit. The bid was made and the entire property was sold to the purchasing committee.[27] Thus ended one of the most successful minority bondholders' suits in American corporate history.

The sale put a heavy burden on the Wabash. Before the reorganization could be completed and title passed to a new company it was necessary to buy out the dissenting bondholders. To accomplish this the committee on behalf of the new company was obliged to issue between $5,000,000 and $6,000,000 of bonds. The first mortgage bonds, in consequence of the successful fight made by the minority bondholders, rose to a premium. The minority bondholders received, instead of the 5 per cent bonds given to the assenting bondholders, one hundred cents on the dollar of their bonds in cash. By July the details of the reorganization were completed; the receiver turned the property over to the purchasing committee, and the latter turned it over to a new company, which had also acquired the properties west of the Mississippi. The new Wabash railroad thus succeeded the old Wabash as the owner of the consolidated line between Toledo, Kansas City and Omaha.

The long fight to reorganize the road was over. Gould's initial efforts to acquire control at a low price, via the floating debt, were unsuccessful. His failure was not due to his own lack of shrewdness or foresight or trading ability, but rather to the forthright independence of an able judge who had unhesitatingly condemned the passive acquiescence of a brother member of the judiciary. Judge Gresham by eliminating the friendly receivers in favor of an outstanding independent receiver for the lines east of the Mississippi eliminated most of Gould's trading advantages. Gould was forced to deal with the dissenting underlying bondholders on a basis of their respective rights and privileges. Even then he was successful in inducing most of the first and second mortgage bondholders to accept a reduction in interest charges from 7 to 5 per cent. In his efforts to reduce the interest charges paid on the junior mortgage bonds and to raise a fund from the stockholders for the purpose of improving the property and to provide part of the reorganization expenses, he was successful. The general and collateral trust bonds were exchanged partly for unsecured debentures and partly for income bonds.

The fixed charges of the reorganized company were substantially less than those of the old. The company, furthermore, was strengthened by the elimination of the leased lines that were designed originally to serve as the basis of new through routes. Competition having removed the possibility of establishing such routes, the properties were left as they had been before, as little deserts, surrounded by green fields of rich traffic.

Gould retained control of the policies of the new company, thereby serving well the interests of his enlarged Missouri Pacific system. As a stockholder, he gained little, since the price of the stock was not improved by the reorganization. According to the secretary of the purchasing committee, Gould by the summer of 1886 had lost $6,000,000 or $7,000,000 in Wabash securities.[28]

While Gould considered the Wabash as an indispensable eastern outlet for his southwestern system, he believed it equally essential to retain the Texas & Pacific as an important feeder of eastbound traffic. Gould's hold on the Texas & Pacific was weaker than his hold on the Wabash. Although he found it more difficult on the Texas & Pacific to acquire control of key bits of railroad and terminal properties, he did nevertheless succeed in creating a floating debt, this time in favor of the Missouri Pacific. The floating debt was secured by a peculiar obligation in the form of a bond secured by a general mortgage, subject to the other system mortgages, and by a lien on some terminal property in New Orleans. It was a bond about which almost nothing was known. It appeared on its face to have considerable strength, because it had, presumably, an exclusive lien on the New Orleans terminal facilities essential to the effective operation of the Texas & Pacific. In fact, the terminal properties were unimportant, they were poorly located, and represented only a slight investment. It was nevertheless through the exploitation of the putative value of these bonds that Gould, in the first stage of reorganization, endeavored to acquire a controlling position with a nominal cash investment.

Both in physical layout and in the complexity of the financial structure, the Texas & Pacific problem was simpler than that of the Wabash. The former did not have a complex assortment of leased lines and feeders. The road consisted of three divisions, each serving a separate territory. The middle division, built by (T. A.) Scott in the period prior to Gould control, was the most productive portion, extending from Shreveport to Texarkana, and from that point to the commercial center of north Texas at Fort Worth. The second division was the old New Orleans Pacific from New Orleans to Shreveport. The third, the Rio Grande division—the longest and least prosperous of the system—ran from Fort Worth to El Paso. This was the line which Gould, with the co-operation of Scott, had built in such a hurry. From this line an extravagant flow of business had been anticipated. As a fact, almost the precise opposite occurred. Even the gloomiest prognosticator could hardly have predicted the nominal flow of business over this division. Upon completion of the Southern Pacific lines to New Orleans in 1882, the transcontinental traffic was "wholly lost." [29] Of its extensive mileage, only 160 miles had any population or originated any traffic.

The financial structure of Texas & Pacific corresponded to its simple physical layout. On the middle division there rested a small first mortgage followed by a larger second mortgage. Another first mortgage covered the New Orleans Pacific, and still another the Rio Grande division. There was also a financial curiosity in the form of an *Income and Land Grant* mortgage, secured by a first mortgage on land grants and a junior mortgage on the rest of the property. Finally, there was an enticing tidbit in the form of the General and Terminal Mortgage with a first lien on some New Orleans terminal property. This was the collateral held as part security for the Missouri Pacific's advance, which, in Gould's opinion, made the loan "perfectly safe." [30]

Of the three divisions, the middle division was the most profitable. Since most of these bonds were held in Philadelphia,[31] it is not surprising that a citizen of that city, General I. J. Wistar, assumed the leadership in organizing these bondholders. Gould made proposals to Wistar which, although never published, threw the general into the Gould camp. Scarcely more than three months after the receivership the general arranged for a meeting in Philadelphia. There he informed the bondholders that a committee of its choosing, which had investigated the condition of the company, had been unable to find anything unfair in the road's management.[32] Gould received a whitewash.

To informed people it should have become evident that Gould was preparing another of his financial moves. The financial public, made cautious through experience, was already on the watch. The perennial financial critic, for example, hardly more than a week after the receivership, issued its warning. The security holders of the road, it declared, should organize immediately for their protection, unless they were "willing to see their rights trampled upon, and the control of the property put entirely beyond their reach in the hands of Mr. Jay Gould, or his alter ego, the Missouri Pacific. There has been much parade made of the Philadelphia interest in the property, but to those who have observed the methods practiced with other roads, the hand of Gould seems clearly discernible in the Texas & Pacific operations, and it appears like a determined effort to get control of the property for a merely nominal consideration."[33]

Although many groups were organized in the few months following the receivership, none made any substantial progress except the Wistar committee with which nearly all of the middle division bonds had been deposited.[34] The Wistar plan reduced interest charges from $1,970,000 to approximately $1,115,000. The reduction was made possible by foreclosure of all the mortgages except that of the small first lien on the middle division. All other bonds would be changed either for new first mortgage or income bonds.

Gould's interest, however, lay in the distribution of the common stock. The plan proposed an exchange of three shares of the old company for one of the new and offered the stockholder of the old company the right to buy at $15 per share the stock of the new. Finally, it liquidated the floating debt of $1,800,000 held by the Missouri Pacific through the issue of new stock at $20 per share, i.e., five shares of stock for $100 of debt.[35] This was the extraordinary part of the plan: For the Missouri Pacific's claim, whose validity never had been established, it was proposed to issue $9,000,000 par value of stock. To put it another way, the Missouri Pacific would buy this amount of stock at $20 a share. And even though the present stockholders bought new stock at

$15 a share, they could not hope to acquire control of the property.

Again Gould had taken advantage of a small debt, created under questionable conditions, in order to dominate a property with a small investment. The plan was immediately assailed. "So bold a plan to squeeze out stockholders and get possession of a company," cried one critic, "has seldom been proposed, and it would be far cheaper for stockholders to pay a cash assessment of 10 per cent on their present holdings, and thus put over $3,000,000 in the treasury, than to be practically wiped out by this plan proposed in the Gould interest." [36] The Rio Grande division bondholders denounced this provision of the plan as a "freeze out." [37]

The Wistar proposal, as the first in the field, acquired all those strategic advantages which normally accrue to the first constructive plan in any field of negotiations. Other groups of security holders now rushed their plans. The Rio Grande division bondholders appointed a committee, of which Charles N. Fry, president of the Bank of New York, was the most prominent member. Only in the treatment of the floating debt and of the stock were there any important differences from the Wistar plan. The Fry group proposed that the floating debt be exchanged for junior mortgage bonds. Gould's Missouri Pacific would thereby receive a slight equity in the new company. The stock was to be assessed, and the voting power placed for three years in the hands of the reorganization committee.

This plan, representing the views of the weakest of the system bondholders, made only a slight impression. Another, however, submitted some weeks thereafter by a committee headed by Robert Fleming, and representing security holders of all divisions, met with a different reception. This plan was designed to remove the basis of Gould's strong position in the reorganization by buying up the bonds of the middle division. With the help of a strong underwriting syndicate, including Drexel, Morgan & Company, it proposed to buy these bonds at a price close to par. With the bonds out of the way, Wistar and his group would have little to say in formulating the plans of reorganization. This plan "somewhat staggered" the Wistar committee,[38] and probably also staggered Gould himself. If it were successful it would place the reorganization in the hands of a man who, it was clear to Gould, was no friend of his. The dominating force in the house of Drexel, Morgan & Company, at least in the field of railroad financing, was Morgan, the man who, in carrying out in such a masterful manner the reorganization of the West Shore, had ignored Gould's suggestions.

After weeks of discussion, Wistar found the basis for a common interest with this group. The two committees shook hands, merged their interests, and produced a new plan. The new committee consisted of four representatives from the Wistar and three from the Fleming group. The essentials of the Wistar plan, calling for a reduction in fixed charges as had been originally proposed, were retained. The stock to be outstanding under the new compromise plan, however, was increased from $32,000,000 to $40,000,000. The proposal of Gould to utilize the floating debt of the Missouri Pacific as a means of getting control of the property was dropped. An assessment on the shareholders of $10 a share in exchange for a second mortgage bond with a market value of about fifty cents on the dollar was also suggested. The floating debt was paid in cash. Of the stock, the Missouri Pacific received the right to buy approximately $6,500,000 at $20 a share.

The plan did not meet with success. The income and land-grant mortgage bondholders organized a committee, and asserted that in addition to their third mortgage lien on the eastern division they also had a claim on other parts of the property. The stockholders also submitted a plan which, however, made little impression. The land-grant bondholders created considerable difficulty. It was necessary to make concessions to induce them to approve the plan, thus delaying its final consummation. After making adjustments essential to harmonize the minority, the fixed charges were reduced to $1,287,000—a substantial reduction.[39]

Since the Missouri Pacific was not given the right to acquire large blocks of stock, it was clear that Gould had not succeeded in acquiring control of the reorganized company. He was, nevertheless, free, if he so chose, to buy stock in the open market. Early in 1886 the stock fluctuated, in the heavy trading, between $7 and $15 a share. Gould bought large blocks at these levels although of course he did not advertise his activities. Early in

1888, when the company was about to reorganize its affairs, it was believed in some informed quarters that the company would be independent of Gould.[40] These views were mistaken. Gould, at the annual meeting, was elected chairman of the executive committee. At that time he announced that with the stock he personally owned, he and his group would control the new road. It was not until October of 1888 that the road was released from receivership, and it was not until the spring of 1889 that the new directorate was reorganized in accordance with the stockholdings of the controlling interests. It was only then that the strategic position of Gould was fully revealed. At the annual meeting he personally voted 84,000 shares, and 189,000 by proxy, including those of Sage and the Missouri Pacific.[41] Since there were 400,000 shares outstanding, these two blocks gave Gould control.

The reorganization of both the Texas & Pacific and the Wabash were completed at about the same time. Gould had succeeded in rebuilding his railroad system in its essential parts. In 1884–85 his unified system from Toledo to El Paso and from St. Louis to New Orleans seemed about to crumble. Four years later it was again reunited. By that time, however, profound changes had occurred in other parts of the system. The Missouri Pacific proper had transformed itself from a small compact property into a far-flung network reaching through southern and central Kansas to Denver, and comprising many extensions and branches in Arkansas, Texas, and Louisiana. On the other hand, the system had lost the Kansas & Texas—a line connecting western Kansas with northern Texas. In the late eighties, Gould was making a strong effort to reacquire the road. In this effort, made with the same patience, the same technique, and the same persistence that had characterized his efforts to acquire control of the Wabash and of the Texas & Pacific, he was about to fail.[42]

Aside from his trading operations, Gould had lost little in the receivership and subsequent reorganization of the two southwestern roads. He had sold out both his Texas & Pacific and Wabash stocks at the top of the boom in 1880 and 1881. He had bought back large blocks of Wabash after the price had dropped substantially, at what appeared to be reasonable prices. They turned out, nevertheless, to be high prices, and at his death his holdings showed heavy paper losses. He rebought the Texas &

Pacific stock at much more attractive prices. In both cases he succeeded well, as a railroad man and as a financier. He reorganized the properties in such a way as to reduce their fixed charges and to give him control over their policies. As a trader in the purchase of stocks at low prices, he was, however, unsuccessful.

NOTES FOR CHAPTER XXII

1. This plan is summarized in *Chron.*, Aug. 22, 1884, 117.
2. *Bradstreet*, Aug. 2, 1884, 72.
3. London *Standard*, cited in Herapath's *Ry. Journal*, Aug. 30, 1884, 970.
4. Ibid., April 18, 1885, 411.
5. Burlington archives, Perkins to W. W. Baldwin, Dec. 9, 1884.
6. For summary of this decision, see *Bradstreet*, May 2, 1885, 301. The case is reported in *Federal Reporter* Vol. 23, 866, 1885.
7. New York *Herald*, Feb. 18, 1885.
8. *Chron.*, May 9, 1885, 571.
9. Ibid.
10. *Bradstreet*, May 9, 1885, 317.
11. Phila. *Press*, Nov. 30, 1885.
12. *Ry. World*, May 1, 1886, 409.
13. From Circular of the Committee, cited in *Chron.*, June 5, 1886, 695.
14. New York *Tribune*, June 7, 1886.
15. For the views of Judge Gresham on receivership, see *Ry. Review*, March 13, 1886, 124.
16. The instructions of Judge Gresham to the receivers are noted in *Ry. Review*, Aug. 7, 1886, 414.
17. London *Railway News*, July 24, 1886, 132.
18. Atkins vs. Wabash, *Federal Reporter* Vol. 29, 168, 1886.
19. *Bradstreet*, Dec. 11, 1886, 377.
20. New York *Tribune*, Dec. 8, 1886.
21. *Ry. Review*, Jan. 15, 1887, 35.
22. The decision of Judge Brewer is reported in *Federal Reporter* Vol. 30, 333, 1887.
23. In the summer of 1889, after the organization of the new Wabash, Gould, according to the New York *Times*, May 16, 1889, owned "enormous blocks" of Wabash stock; and, according to *Stockholder*, June 21, 1889, he held approximately 25 per cent of the common stock of the road, at a cost to him of about double the then existing market price. Although he was probably the largest stockholder, the majority of the stock, nevertheless, was still held in England. New York *Times*, Aug. 13, 1890.
24. For details on this plan, see *Chron.*, Oct. 29, 1887, 573.
25. New York *Tribune*, Feb. 5, 1889.
26. For details on the proposal of the minority bondholders, see Phila. *Press*, April 20, 1889.
27. *Chron.*, May 18, 1889, 663.
28. London *Railway News*, July 24, 1886, 132.
29. This is the phrase used by I. J. Wistar, Chairman, Texas & Pacific Railway Reconstruction Committee to the Committee of London Bondholders, as cited in the New York *Tribune*, June 29, 1886.
30. Phila. *Press*, June 4, 1886.
31. *Autobiography of Isaac Jones Wistar*, 492-4, Harper and Brothers, New York, 1937.

32. Phila. *Press*, March 6, 1886.
33. *Chron.*, Jan. 9, 1886, 61.
34. *Autobiography of Isaac Jones Wistar*, 492-3.
35. The exact amount of floating debt is differently stated in different sources. The amount of $1,800,000 is presented by *Chron.* which has a record for accuracy in these matters. The Phila. *Press*, which reported minutely on the progress of the plan, puts the floating debt at $1,500,000; and a circular of the committee of the Rio Grande Division bondholders at $1,600,000. See *Bradstreet*, June 12, 1886, 403.
36. *Chron.*, May 1, 1886, 550.
37. *Bradstreet*, June 12, 1886, 403.
38. Ibid., July 31, 1886, 74.
39. *Chron.*, Dec. 17, 1887, 821.
40. See Phila. *Press*, April 13, 1888.
41. Ibid., March 19, 1889.
42. For details, see Chapter XXVII, pp. 543-6.

CHAPTER XXIII

Gould Monopolizes Western Union

GOULD'S stroke in acquiring the Western Union in 1881, far from being accepted as a masterpiece of corporate strategy, was almost universally regarded as a serious blunder. Besides the chorus of public condemnation of the company as a monopoly and a public oppressor, there was the conviction in financial circles that the new water-logged combination would not be able to pay dividends. In fact, according to many, it would seem that the company was headed for disaster. If it could earn enough to pay a 6 per cent dividend upon an inflated stock base, the telegraph business must be decidedly profitable. New capital would be attracted, competition would increase, and the rate of profit decline.

Gould knew this danger. Despite his preoccupation with the many problems of railroad strategy, he acted with promptness and energy to forestall some of the competition. First he made an agreement with the Pennsylvania which removed the outstanding differences with that company. Threat and counterthreat, suit and countersuit, all vanished in an atmosphere of harmony. Scott, president of the road, was then associated with Gould in financing the construction of the Texas & Pacific. Precisely what proposals passed between Gould and the Pennsylvania officialdom, and the agreements reached, are not known. Shortly after his acquisition of the Western Union, Gould did travel to Philadelphia to visit the road's officials, and thereafter the friction between the two properties disappeared.

Gould then moved quickly to the next major competitive problem, the Baltimore & Ohio, a road which under the direction of Garrett maintained an independent policy with respect to the express, sleeping-car and telegraph services. The company had no exclusive contracts with the Western Union and had encouraged every promising competitor of the telegraph monopoly. When Gould merged the American with the Western Union, he did not long hesitate in opening negotiations with the Baltimore & Ohio for the acquisition of its telegraph system. A reversal in policy was of course no novelty to Gould. What explanations he made to the Baltimore & Ohio management, what alluring promises he extended, are not known. An agreement for a union of the railroad's telegraph lines with those of the Western Union was almost consummated, and it was only the intervention of Garrett that knocked these negotiations, all but completed, "into a cocked hat." [1]

Garrett soon renewed the struggle against the Western Union. The Baltimore & Ohio's telegraph lines early in 1881 were still confined largely to its own system, and the company had not yet taken advantage of the law which authorized a railroad to enter the general telegraph business. Instead, the road allied itself with the Mutual Union Telegraph,[2] which had just begun business (December, 1880) with a capital stock of only $20,000. Early in 1881, however, the company announced plans to extend its property, so that in the course of time, it would do about 90 per cent of the profitable telegraphic business of the country.[3] To finance its program, it sold $5,000,000 of bonds. Each bondholder would receive a stock bonus equal to the par of the bonds. By the fall of the year the company had succeeded in attracting a number of important capitalists, including Keene and Vanderbilt.

The biggest stroke by the Mutual Union, however, was its lease of the Baltimore & Ohio's wire system in September, 1881.[4] The Western Union officials were aware of the significance of this event, and took active steps to meet the menacing competition. Some of their acts were discreditable, and although Gould's name was not directly mentioned, there is little doubt that his influence was dominant. The Western Union, through Erastus Wyman, a member of the board, supported by the vice president and general manager, bribed a clerk in the office of the contractors who were then building the lines of the Mutual Union in order to secure a copy of the railroad-telegraph contract. Wyman seems to have had a glib and ready tongue, and was indiscreet in expressing the motives of the Western Union management. "We will get these Mutual Union folks on the rock yet," he said.[5] He declared that he wanted the newspapers to make a "stink" so as to impair the credit of the Mutual Union; then he would get a Mutual Union bondholder to sue for a bill of discovery and thus get the construction contract into court.[6]

The Mutual Union continued to expand and soon increased its financial strength and attracted new leadership and capital. Before the end of 1881 its promoters succeeded in interesting a New York banker, George F. Baker, who only a few years before had created a sensation in government bond circles. Baker was a man of deep silences. More than thirty years later, at the height of his power as one of the richest and most influential men of his time, he was still unknown. An observer in 1913 remarked: "Like the Man in the Iron Mask, George F. Baker, the New York banker has the unusual distinction of being important, yet unknown." [7] Baker bought the controlling interest in the First National Bank soon after the Panic of 1873, and shortly after this he became its president. In the United States Government Bond Syndicate of 1879, Baker, in conjunction with another bank, made a stroke which gave his bank a national reputation. There was some fear that the new bonds would not sell well, and that perhaps only foreign banks would bid for the issue. The Baker-led syndicate, however, responded to the government offering with an "unparalleled" subscription—the largest single subscription ever made for a government loan in any country.[8] Baker had also participated in a number of successful railroad bond issues. He was also the leader in the Tide Water Pipe Line which fought John D. Rockefeller to a standstill.

The association of Baker with the Mutual was followed almost immediately by announcements of plans to extend its business throughout the country. Although Baker assumed the leadership of new enterprises, he was not the kind of man to engage in a fight in an effort, regardless of losses, to sustain his position, or to maintain his personal dignity. Like most bankers, he was peculiarly sensitive to the interests of his immediate followers; to those who in response to his leadership had bought securities. Gould therefore played his hand accordingly. By the fall of 1881 Gould was probably the most successful litigant in American history. His court suits had been almost phenomenally successful.

He always "knew the judge." When he wanted secretly to change the terms of a corporate trust, he found a judge to do his bidding. When he wanted to prevent some friendly interests from paying the rental on the New York Elevated, he found a judge to help him carry out his policy. When he needed the help of the court to appoint friendly receivers for the Manhattan Elevated, receivers who were on his corporate pay roll, he found a judge to accommodate him. When he wanted to exert competitive pressure on Field by denying to him the right to repossess his elevated property, he found a judge who would fulfill his wish. He was at the height of his judicial power in the fall of 1881, when he recognized that it was necessary to take strong action in an effort to defeat the growing strength of the Mutual Union.

In again entering the courts of the land as a means of furthering his objectives, he followed the technique in which he had been so successful. His name appeared in none of the early suits. Individuals unimportant in the business community—clerks and others unknown, equipped with a few shares of stock—suddenly appeared in the courts and challenged the legality of the Mutual Union's policies. It was alleged in one suit that the company was violating the Page patent which had been exploited for years in litigation. In another case it was alleged that the Mutual Union had violated its charter by the issuance of stock without compensation. These suits embarrassed the Mutual Union. The preliminary injunctions, as usual, were granted. The company's legal position was under a cloud and careful businessmen were reluctant to enter into contracts with a concern whose right to exist was seriously challenged. Gould had correctly interpreted the character of Baker. Baker, instead of fighting back as had Cornelius Vanderbilt, entered into negotiations for a settlement. He recognized more quickly than other early Gould opponents, who his real antagonist was, and it was not long before an agreement was made. The Mutual Union then had outstanding 100,000 shares of stock and of this amount Gould, after buying from Baker 13,000 shares at $5 a share and an additional 8,500 shares from the construction company at the same price, agreed to ask the court to discontinue the lawsuits. After the court had acted favorably, Gould was privileged to buy an additional 10,000 shares at $10 a share. Gould and Baker furthermore agreed to trustee their joint holdings.[9]

It is not clear whether this was an arrangement between the two men personally or between them on behalf of the companies. Baker and his group insisted that the arrangement was personal. Gould advertised it as calculated to eliminate the competitive difficulties between the two companies. Despite the nature of the agreement, it came to the public in the form of an announcement that the two companies had combined, that the earnings were to be pooled, and that any excess earnings were to go to the Western Union.[10] There was of course no such close union. Baker apparently believed that if he sold Gould a block of stock that Gould would not continue to oppose the company's policies. Baker probably was aware of the fact that Gould had frequently been on both sides of a corporate contract, and that he had frequently represented adverse interests. He apparently believed that if Gould purchased some Mutual Union stock at a low price, his interest in promoting the welfare of that company would be greater than his loss as a stockholder of Western Union.

Whatever the intentions of Gould and Baker, later events belied the existence of any close union between the two companies. "Scarcely a week has passed" since the date of the announcement of the contract, declared a contemporary observer, . . . "without something turning up which was strangely incongruous with this reported agreement."[11] The conflict was soon brought to a climax in a quarrel between the Western Union and one of its leading customers, the Associated Press, which took strong exception to certain contracts upon which the Western Union insisted, and transferred an important part of its business to the Mutual Union.

It became clear to Baker that in relying upon the agreement with Gould he had erred. Even before the conflict over the Associated Press, Gould had already acted. Without transferring the Mutual Union stock to the name of the Western Union, he sold the stock to the latter company at its cost to him. The Western Union board and its law committee formally passed upon the transaction, and the company assumed the obligations incurred by him in the purchase of the securities.[12] Within a few weeks, Gould purchased additional shares on the market at an average price of $6 to $10 a share, and these he also transferred to the Western Union.

By the summer of 1882 the Western Union controlled 40,000 shares out of a total of 100,000 outstanding. Under normal conditions this would have been sufficient for control; indeed under some conditions, the ownership of as little as 15 per cent is sufficient to effect control. In this particular instance, however, 40 per cent was not enough. If Gould was quiet and effective, Baker was equally effective and equally silent. Baker, recognizing the danger, moved quickly. He personally owned 20,000 shares of Mutual stock, and with most of the balance of non-Gould stock owned by loyal followers, he succeeded in enlisting the support of holders of more than 50,000 shares. Thus Baker outmatched Gould. If Gould had placed 40,000 shares with Western Union, then he (Baker) would place 50,000 with the Central Trust Company as depository. The three trustees to administer the new trust were George W. Ballou, the first president and promoter of the Mutual, A. P. Potter, president of a small bank, in whom Baker had great faith, and Baker himself.

Gould was thus on the defensive. Baker, as usual, said little. Indeed in the very nature of the case, it was not necessary that he say or do anything .The next step was Gould's, and his action, as usual, was prompt and decisive. He asked for an injunction, which was immediately granted, to restrain the trust company and the trustees. However Gould's record as a successful litigant was coming to an end. The lawsuit device was now to be used against him. "An exhaustless crop of suits" were springing up against the Western Union, noted a contemporary observer.[13] The Western Union was being sued in the states of Pennsylvania and New York on the ground that its charter was invalid, and Gould perhaps anticipated the sting of defeat in this litigation.

In this maze of legal entanglements and competitive aggression, the Western Union early in December, 1882, was facing another threat. Forbes, the veteran chairman of the Burlington, decided that the time had come to extricate his road from a Western Union contract which, in his own language, was then "bearing so heavily" upon the road.[14] The contract executed in 1872 for a twenty-five-year period had about fourteen years more to run. Garrett, of the Baltimore & Ohio, who was now one of

Gould's most persistent enemies, stood ready to pro rate business with the Burlington's 4,400 miles of wire, mile for mile.

So momentous did Forbes consider the impending struggle against the Western Union that he ignored the advice of his physician who had ordered him to take a rest in Florida. Forbes's judgment was warped by his personal dislike of Gould as a stock-market trader. He was particularly savage in his characterization of Gould's management of the Western Union which, he believed, embraced the censorship of clients' messages. Upon one occasion, perhaps in a moment of exasperation, he asked Garrett why the editor of the New York *Times* who had "brought Tweed down to his marrow bones" could not win additional credit "by getting Gould into his proper quarters, the P—, a place I will not mention for fear of the law of libel." [15]

It is therefore not surprising that he adopted measures characteristic of the Gould tactics that he had so roundly denounced. Although he had determined to engage in a struggle against the Western Union, he did not wish to make a definite commitment. Accordingly, when he decided to intervene in a lawsuit in New York challenging the validity of the Western Union charter, he did so through a third person for whose account he would buy a few shares of Western Union. This device of acting through a small security holder who appeared in court in the interests of the public welfare had been successfully used by Gould in his campaign to acquire control of the Manhattan Elevated. Forbes, however, had neither the skill nor the trading following of Gould, and his efforts to locate a person, who would intervene in the Western Union suit, were not successful. Among others, Forbes tried to enlist the aid of George Jones, editor of the New York *Times*, a consistent critic of Gould and his corporate policies. Forbes asked Jones confidentially whether he would be willing under proper indemnities to have his name used as a stockholder in joining the Western Union suit.[16] This approach was unsuccessful.

While Forbes was thus laying the groundwork for an intervention in the Western Union suit, he was also devising schemes to break the Burlington's Western Union contract. In addition to putting the road's counsel to work, Forbes engaged outside aid. He sent Richard Olney, an outstanding young attorney, a copy of the contract, instructed him to keep it for his own eye and then to return it carefully. "Our hope is to break it on some flaw," wrote Forbes, "either on its merits or its want of confirmation by our Board, or under the law of Congress" which permitted the railroads to do a public telegraph business.[17] Olney, replying in a lengthy communication, pointed out to Forbes that it would be possible to invalidate that section of the contract which gave the Western Union the "exclusive right of way" upon the Burlington, and that, even though the other provisions of the contract were sustained, the contract with the monopoly clause excluded would seriously impair its value.[18]

The Burlington's board, however, was not wholly in accord with Forbes's actions. The "prevailing opinion" among the board, as reflected in a meeting held in late December, was to the effect that "not much could be gained" by joining in the Western Union attack. The board, nevertheless, did believe that it would be worth while to understand whether the road was really tied to the Western Union so that it could not trade with the Baltimore & Ohio or with anyone else.[19]

Gould, it may be safely assumed, was well aware of the legal loophole that Forbes's counsel had so solicitously uncovered. As usual, he had plenty of ammunition in his corporate armory. The decision in this telegraph war in which Forbes so actively intervened was not to be decided in the courts of law, for Gould had another club in his trading closet. In September, 1882, he had acquired control of the Hannibal which owned the line serving as an outlet for the Burlington to Kansas City and the Southwest,[20] and it is probable that Forbes's bitterness against Gould late in 1882 may be ascribed to his control of this road. In the months that followed Gould's purchase of the Hannibal, suspicions, reports, and guesses of his intentions were widespread. Gould, sojourning in Florida, maintained however a policy of silence.

The competitors of the Western Union meanwhile solicited the Burlington in an effort to get an increasing share of its telegraph business. An official of the Postal, for example, explained the advantages of the company's new mechanical contrivances,[21] while the Baltimore & Ohio proposed that it be given the opportunity to build on part of the Burlington's right of way.[22]

Gould, upon his return from Florida, almost immediately opened negotiations with the Burlington's officials. The Burlington wanted the Hannibal, and Gould wanted the Burlington's telegraph business. To the Burlington the perennial Gould problem again emerged. How far should it yield to the Western Union in order to close the Hannibal trade? The negotiations in the form of personal conversations, telegrams and letters lasted for several weeks. The Burlington in the end acquired the Hannibal and surrendered on the Western Union, and Garrett was again defeated. Gould, as in so many other instances in his career, surrendered his less vital interests in behalf of the more important ones. He enhanced the strength of the Burlington against the Wabash in the struggle for the southwestern business. On the other hand, by assuring to the Western Union control of the telegraph business of the Burlington, he strengthened its competitive position.

While Gould was trading with the Burlington, he continued to press the suit against Baker. He did not, however, get the permanent injunction he requested. The judge refused to be stampeded into a decision.

Gould tried another device. He asked the attorney-general to bring suit in the name of the people to invalidate the charter of the Mutual, on the ground that most of its stock had been issued without any consideration. It was the same device that he had used successfully on another attorney-general. The new attorney-general granted the application against the Mutual.[23]

This time, however, Gould was not to have his way smoothed by weakness in the opposition. The attorney-general was not the same complaisant personality as the one who, little more than a year before, had been so easily influenced. The Mutual Union was also free to fight its own case before the attorney-general. Within a few weeks after he accepted the application of Gould to sue the Mutual, he also accepted an application to bring action on behalf of the people to invalidate the charter of the Western Union.[24]

Both the Western Union and the Mutual were now ready for a fight. Both were about to file affidavits demonstrating the inequities, and uncovering the financial and trade secrets, of the other. The success of Gould in litigation was weakening. In January, 1883, he lost his contest with Baker, the court dissolving the temporary injunction to restrain the transfer of the Mutual's stock to Baker and his co-trustees. The Western Union, said the court, was not a party to the contract of March, 1882, and therefore Gould's sale of his Mutual stock to Western Union dissolved the contract.[25]

Gould recognized that Baker was a determined foe and a man of means who had gathered behind him a group of associates and followers. The Mutual Union, furthermore, had become powerful and had made an alliance with some of Gould's foes, including Garrett of the Baltimore & Ohio, and Vanderbilt of the New York Central. The company had also acquired exclusive rights of way on 25,000 miles of road, occupying territory that the Western Union wanted to occupy. Some of the latter's railroad contracts were made "very troublesome" to the Western Union, and to embarrass that company further, the Mutual Union pressed numerous suits to prevent it from using its wires freely.[26]

Although Gould was ready to compromise he could not do so on his own terms. An understanding was reached, and although the terms were hard, Gould signed. The Western Union leased the Mutual Union and agreed to pay annually $500,000 as rental. Of this amount $300,000 represented the interest on bonds, $50,000 the sinking fund, and $150,000 a dividend on its stock. Each company agreed to withdraw the suits pending against the other, either in its own name or in the name of its security holders. Baker was taking no chances on any future ingenuity of Gould. He made Gould agree on behalf of himself and the security holders of the Western Union, so that no party in interest could create further trouble in the courts and upset the contract.

Thus a dangerous competitor of the Western Union was eliminated. Garrett of the Baltimore & Ohio was again defeated. The Mutual and the Baltimore & Ohio, however, were not the only competitors of the Western Union. The latter's profits and dividends had attracted still others. Even though they did not develop the same early strength of the Mutual Union, nevertheless they constituted a threat to the monopoly. Soon after the Western Union merger of 1881, Keene, a former trading associate of Gould, gathered around him a number of capitalists and organized the Postal Telegraph Company[27] which succeeded in acquiring control of a number of efficient mechanical devices.

Another small competitor of the Western Union, the American Rapid Telegraph, also the owner of a number of improved devices, was organized in the summer of 1880. Shortly after the Western Union merger, it decided to expand. The capital stock was increased to $10,000,000 of which $6,000,000 was offered to its shareholders at par.[28] The company's capital stock was thus not watered. It proposed to sell the stock for cash and to use the proceeds to build a telegraph plant.

Another enterprise, the Bankers' & Merchants' Telegraph, was organized in April, 1881. It, too, avoided stock watering, financing requirements from the sale of stock at par or higher. This small property was prosperous, and in the last two quarters of 1882, paid a 2 per cent quarterly dividend.

The Southern Telegraph was another small company organized in the south. Considerable difficulty was experienced in financing its requirements.

Another venture, the Commercial Telegraph, organized in 1883, was designed to invade the Western Union's monopoly, exercised by its affiliate—Gold and Stock Telegraph Company—in the handling of stock exchange quotations. Its entrance into the business was heralded by a rate war; rates dropped 50 per cent.[29]

Each company followed an independent course, and each did business in a selected territory. Except for the Baltimore & Ohio, none was able to secure any important railroad contracts, the very business which accounted for the prosperity of the Western Union. Gould, before the end of 1881, had succeeded with the help of counsel in perfecting the exclusive telegraph railroad contract. The new contract was so ironclad that future competition against the Western Union was exceptionally difficult. Gould of the Western Union made contracts with Gould as president or policy-maker in the multitude of railroads which he then controlled.

By the spring of 1883 the competitors of the Western Union, although profitable, were doing business on a restricted scale. The very fact of their ability to operate profitably led them to think in terms of expansion, to fight the well-entrenched Western Union. If a number of companies singly could do a successful business, then in co-operation each with the other, they could do even better. If the business was successful on a small local scale, it would succeed even more so on a large and national scale. Volume would increase, overhead decline, and increased profits develop.

The expansion of the Western Union, climaxed by the lease of the Mutual Union, appeared to lend force to the desirability of unifying the interests of the independent telegraph ventures into larger and more powerful concerns. The leadership of this movement was assumed by a stockbroker, A. W. Dimock, who had been successful in the inflation boom of 1879 to 1881. Like most traders, including Gould, he was unable to interpret the broad secular down-swing which began in 1881. At the peak of his career in 1881, he and a number of associates acquired control of the Bankers' & Merchants' Telegraph, and shortly thereafter of the Southern Telegraph. No sooner did Dimock acquire control of these two properties, than he entered upon a program of rapid expansion. By September, 1883, he dominated a group of companies which owned wires from New England, through New York, Philadelphia, and Washington to many points in the Southeast. The combination made plans to extend even farther. Early in 1884 it bought the Lehigh Telegraph, serving eastern Pennsylvania, and the Commercial Telegraph, thus giving it a share of the growing stock-ticker business.

The Bankers' & Merchants' Telegraph was an imposing combination. Like many other rapidly expanded consolidations, it was financed on an extravagant scale. In accordance with established custom, it was built in a period of booming prosperity when capital could be readily obtained. Unfortunately, this was also a period of high prices and of inefficient labor. Although the combination had increased in size, it had decreased in financial strength. Mortgages were placed upon its constituent properties. It was also proposed to increase its capital stock from $1,000,000 to $10,000,000.

Dimock's company early in 1884 was a formidable competitor of the Western Union, and, according to Dimock at least, by far the largest.[30] Dimock felt certain of his competitive strength. There was no danger, he insisted, of his company merging with the Western Union. The stock was fully paid and the company's business was sound.

It is strange how confident every independent telegraph company was of its future success. Each was certain it would never sell out to the Western Union. The Western Union in the pre-Gould era had been equally certain that it would acquire no property of Gould's. Gould, however, defeated all these expectations. Soon after Green, president of the Western Union, declared early in 1881 that the company would fight it out with Gould's American Union, the Western Union merged with that property. When, less than two years later, the president of the Mutual declared that his property was and would continue to be independent of the Western Union, and Green declared that the report of the consolidation of the two properties "was absolutely without foundation,"[31] the Western Union under Gould's leadership bought the property. A few years later when Garrett, speaking for the Baltimore & Ohio, insisted before a Congressional committee that his telegraph property would remain independent, his statements carried the same conviction as did the statements of the other Western Union competitors. The Baltimore & Ohio's telegraph, however, succumbed to the superior strength of the Western Union and to the trading genius of Gould.

During 1883 and 1884 not only the Bankers' & Merchants' Telegraph but also two others took steps to enlarge the scope of their operations. The Postal under Keene had not been successful. The stockholders were not satisfied with his administration, and in August of 1883 the management as well as the capital structure was changed. A number of directors resigned and their seats were taken by others, the most prominent of whom was John W. Mackey. A large block of stock was pooled, and Mackey and George S. Coe, president of the American Exchange National Bank, were appointed trustees. The stock was placed in trust for three years. During this time no member of the pool could sell.[32] The new directors were men of affairs and of considerable wealth. They purchased additional stock and with the funds thus raised the company launched an expansion program to carry the lines from Chicago to St. Louis. Mackey, like Baker, had a following among investors and men of means. Unlike Baker, he was essentially a businessman. Baker was a shrewd banker and a skillful trader. Mackey was a business pioneer, inured to the taking of great risks. He had already acquired a fortune in the silver business, and understood the necessity of making heavy commitments and accepting correspondingly heavy financial responsibilities. He was a practical businessman, furthermore, in the sense that he looked farther ahead than did the investor or trader, recognizing that a long period of construction and preparation is imperative before large returns can be realized. Like Garrett he was a man of independent character, unimpressed by Gould's schemes. Rather, he made it clear that the newly reorganized Postal would fight the dominant Western Union with rate cuts which that company with its heavy capitalization would find it difficult to meet. To the critical public the forthcoming competition was not particularly edifying and promised little in substantial rate reductions.. To one observer the idea of the bonanza kings from the Pacific Coast "coming to the rescue of the dear public to assist it in squeezing thirty or forty millions of water out of a modest eighty millions of capitalization [was] enough to split the sides of Jack Falstaff." [33]

Mackey, however, was true to his word and the subsequent wars with the Western Union produced a permanent reduction in rates. Furthermore, he was not content with expansion in the land telegraph business. He realized that every telegraph company competing with the Western Union was at a handicap in competing with that property for transatlantic telegraph traffic. Since the pooling agreement in the spring of 1882 between the Gould cable company and its competitors, every transatlantic message to and from the United States passed over the wires of the Western Union. Neither the Baltimore & Ohio nor the Postal had any independent cable connection. Garrett of the former company tried to break up this arrangement. In these efforts he secured the aid of John Pender, chairman of one of the English cable companies, and popularly known as the English cable king. Pender traveled to New York but his negotiations were disappointing. Mackey, however, was not as naive as Pender. He perceived that he could make no deal with Gould, and even before Pender had concluded his negotiations, Mackey was busily making arrangements for a new independent cable. With the co-operation and financial help of James Gordon Bennett, publisher of the New York *Herald*, he signed the contract for the building of two Atlantic cables, the construction to be finished by June of 1884.[34]

Thus the new competition begun in 1883 brought an era of declining profits for the Western Union. Although the company maintained its 7 per cent dividend, its earnings declined sharply. Its competitors, flush with money, were taking a large part of the business. The pressure upon Congress, meanwhile, to do something to increase competition, became too strong to be ignored. Early in 1883 a bill was introduced into the House of Representatives to authorize an examination of the nation's telegraph services.[35] Another bill was introduced to revive a proposal, frequently suggested, of a postal telegraph system. In the Senate a resolution was passed early in 1884 instructing a committee to determine whether telegraph costs had been "injuriously affected" by the Western Union merger agreement and stock dividend; by contracts with cable companies and by the leasing of telegraph and cable lines. The committee was directed to ascertain whether the Western Union had made rules for the transmission of press news, or had introduced discriminations which had the effect of "restricting the free and independent use of the telegraph by the press." [36] All these proposals, as well as some others, drifted off into investigation and ended in vapid speeches. Gould did not appear before the investigating committees; but he was ably represented by Green, president of the Western Union, who was liberal in supplying the committee with a vast fund of information, some useful, some irrelevant. Gould was also well represented by counsel, particularly John F. Dillon, a man who found legal justification for almost every move made by Gould.

Hardly had the House and Senate committees begun their investigations than the Western Union was confronted by a new threat. In January of 1884, timed almost to the week with these Congressional inquiries, the Baltimore & Ohio initiated an expansion policy. A new concern, incorporated in August, 1883—the National Telegraph—had made exclusive contracts with the West Shore and the Nickel Plate. The Baltimore & Ohio purchased control of this company, and later in the year also made telegraph contracts with another railroad. Garrett declared that his road proposed "to make a complete and perfectly equipped telegraph system that will cover the entire business area, North, South, East and West." [37]

True to his word, Garrett began a policy of construction which exceeded that of the Western Union or of any other telegraph company in a comparable period. Within four months the Baltimore & Ohio built twenty thousand miles of wire. The Mutual had built many lines primarily to accommodate merchants with leased wires, and the Postal had built many lines in the Far West and Southwest. The Baltimore & Ohio, however, boldly attacked the Western Union by building lines into the larger metropolitan areas in which most of the business was done. It could not, however, get permission to build lines on a Gould road without its consent. The cost of building under this handicap was high.

In addition the Baltimore & Ohio found that in some cases it could not even build on the rights of way of those railroads which had no relationship to Gould. In Massachusetts, for example, a bill was introduced to authorize any telegraph company to enter upon a railroad right of way and build structures in accordance with specifications approved by the railroad commissioners. The Baltimore & Ohio under the terms of this bill proposed to erect a telegraph line by using the tracks of the New England. This road was in receivership and the stockholders were bitter over the condition in which Gould had left their property. Gould was gone, but his influence remained. The evil that men do lives after them. Gould had loaded the New England with an exclusive contract and the court in charge of the receivership declined to disturb it.[38]

Despite all this the Baltimore & Ohio expanded vigorously. Its program was well financed, over $3,000,000 of construction cost being charged to operating expenses. This was sound financial practice and in accordance with the policies followed by some of the best managed enterprises of the country. By midsummer of 1884, the road was serving territory from which the Western Union derived 75 per cent of its total revenue.[39]

Here were three powerful competitors of the Western Union. The Bankers' & Merchants' Telegraph was particularly strong in New England and through a subsidiary had some influence in the South. The Postal, although expanding more slowly, was making steady strides in the West. The lines of the Baltimore &

Ohio covered the system of the railroad itself, the line between New York and Chicago owned by the West Shore and the Nickel Plate, and a number of other lines in the East and Middle West. The transatlantic cable owned by Mackey and Bennett operated in co-operation with the Baltimore & Ohio, as well as the Postal.

Of these three, the Bankers' & Merchants' Telegraph was financially the weakest. Its support came from men involved in stock-market speculation which culminated in the sharp break of May, 1884. At that time the property's construction program was unfinished. Such a property in the face of a depression, with business falling off, and fixed charges increasing, is in a dangerous position. So it was with the Bankers' & Merchants' Telegraph. It was one of the first casualties in the Panic of 1884. The president, personally, was not able to meet his obligations, and failed. He owned much of the company's stock, which he had pledged as collateral for personal loans. The effort of his creditors to sell the collateral broke its price from close to $150 to less than $50 a share. The stock was offered to the Western Union and refused.[40]

The company was thus left deserted in the midst of an uncompleted construction program, bereft of any financial support. Here was an ideal situation for a corporate union of the three opposing units of the dominant company. It was a situation of which Gould had taken repeated advantage. All that was needed was leadership, supported by adequate funds. The funds were available. Mackey, the aggressive leader of the Postal, was a capitalist. Although he had suffered some losses, he was still a wealthy man. Garrett was also a capitalist and, what was more important, the credit of the Baltimore & Ohio was of the best.

It seemed for a few months in the summer of 1884 that a combination between these three companies was about to be formed. In the first week of June, when Gould's finances were still critical, the Postal and the Bankers' & Merchants' Telegraph entered into a twenty-five-year contract for the joint operation of facilities, the pooling of receipts, and for interlocking directorates.[41] Here was another opportunity for the Baltimore & Ohio to increase the opposition to the Western Union. By joining the new group it would have succeeded in creating the strongest competition which the Western Union had ever encountered. Negotiations for a union were begun on July fourth and an agreement was reached on the thirty-first. The three companies agreed to pool their earnings, and although each company retained its corporate independence and assumed no responsibility for payment of the fixed charges of either of the other two, the joint properties were to be operated as a unified enterprise. The business would be managed by a joint board comprising, among others, Garrett, Mackey, and Bennett.

On the surface this new combination appeared able and ready to make a real fight against the Western Union, to force it to reduce rates, to raise its standard of service, and perhaps to force a reduction if not a suspension of dividends. The property controlled by this combination was extensive; its wires reached many large cities and hence extended through territory doing about 80 per cent of the paying telegraph business.[42] Soon after its organization telegraph rates of all three companies were reduced to the lowest existing level, which were those of the Postal, and about 50 to 65 per cent lower than those of the Western Union. Nevertheless, the combination was expected to earn from $1,200,000 to $1,500,000 per year.[43]

The combination in all respects save one was stronger than the American Union which in 1881 had forced the hand of the Western Union. It reached more important commercial centers; it had a better balanced strength in different parts of the country; it was led by capitalists who had a strong following among investors rather than speculators. Its leaders, Garrett, Bennett, and Mackey, were in position either personally, or through the sale of securities, to furnish the needed capital. Unlike the American Union, the combination did not have many exclusive railroad contracts.

In order to strengthen its position among the railroads, the Baltimore & Ohio endeavored to accomplish by negotiation what Gould early in 1880 had achieved by bold action. The lines of the new combination reached the Union Pacific at Omaha. David H. Bates, president of the Baltimore & Ohio's telegraph system asked Adams, president of the Union Pacific, to enter into a business arrangement. Adams was the reforming president of the Union Pacific. It was expected that he would reverse the policies of Gould and thus bolster the financial strength of the road. Six months after Bates had made this initial request, he had received no reply. Then Adams, strange as it may seem, courteously referred his request to the Western Union for consideration.[44]

Both Adams and the Baltimore & Ohio found that the Union Pacific was bound by a contract made with the Western Union in July, 1881, which was more exclusive than the one which Gould had so unceremoniously broken in February, 1880. The Baltimore & Ohio appealed the case to the Commissioner of Railroads who informed the Union Pacific that it must accept the business of the Baltimore & Ohio. It must, that is to say, accept business from that company as it did from any other individual or corporation; but it was not bound to make any mechanical connections with the Baltimore & Ohio or to enter into any credit relations with it.[45] This was precisely the stand of the Union Pacific and of the Western Union. Despite this setback, the combination seemed to be on the road to success. Success, however, did not long continue. In many critical moments of his career, Gould had the good fortune of being confronted with poor business opposition. Again he was in luck. In the fall of 1884 the powerful combination against the Western Union suddenly and with almost no warning collapsed. In the first week of September the Baltimore & Ohio, asserting that the Bankers' & Merchants' Telegraph could not carry out its financial agreement, withdrew from the pool. The latter company had been financially weakened by the bankruptcy of its owners. Gould and his associates when faced with similar conditions tided a property over with the use of their own funds. In 1874 Gould took the lead in extricating the Union Pacific from financial embarrassment. In times of need, he had repeatedly lent money to the Wabash, the Missouri Pacific, and other properties. These loans were of course well secured. Gould served himself in extending these loans, but at the same time he kept the property afloat and retained control.

No such leadership sustained the telegraph pool in the fall of 1884. The employees of the Bankers' & Merchants' Telegraph failed to get their wages on time, and the creditors talked of receivership. The stock could have been bought at nominal prices, or the members of the pool and their stockholders could have made loans to the company. It was not so to be, and the most formidable opposition that ever had been organized against the Western Union dissolved. The Baltimore & Ohio declared the pooling contract at an end. The decision of the road was a grave mistake. Apparently its managers believed that the Bankers' & Merchants' Telegraph would continue its existence as a separate corporation, and that even though a receiver was appointed, it would continue to function. The bonds were held by strong financial interests, including the Mutual Life Insurance, the Central Trust, and the Bank of Commerce. Again Gould's financial ingenuity, patience, and sense of accurate timing were underestimated. Both the Bankers' & Merchants' Telegraph and its major subsidiary, the American Rapid Telegraph, were placed in receivership. The receiver for the latter had indeed little to receive. Although it had issued mortgage bonds, such was the negligence of the bondholders that its property, on October 18, 1883, was for all practical purposes delivered to its corporate parent. A contract was made by which the poles and wires of parent and child were joined in such a way that it was difficult to ascertain which belonged to which. Each party received the right to string its wires on the other's poles.[46]

The creditors of the Bankers' & Merchants' Telegraph meanwhile were making plans to build it up as a strong unit in the telegraph business. They secured the appointment of an able executive, General James G. Farnsworth, as receiver, and also enlisted the services of a number of promoters and capitalists to provide some money by the sale of stock. Some of these were Gould's enemies, particularly Woerishoffer, the hardy trader who had bested Gould in the bear market of 1884, and Josiah C. Reiff, long a Gould critic. The plan of reorganization of the Bankers' & Merchants' Telegraph called for a foreclosure sale of the properties on July 10, 1885.

While these plans were on foot, Gould apparently did nothing. His silence, however, should have warned his watchful competitors of impending danger. Gould had made a close study of the reorganization proceedings. He was looking for a weak spot. He rarely failed to make a discovery, and this was not one of the exceptions. He learned that one of the largest individual bondholders of the Bankers' & Merchants' Telegraph was Edward S. Stokes, and that the vice president of the American Rapid Telegraph had a grudge against Stokes. He also knew of the contract of October 18, 1883, by which the properties of the two corporations had been intermingled. Perhaps Gould could induce the receiver of the American Rapid Telegraph to force the Bankers' & Merchants' Telegraph to return its property, and thus be relieved of the contract of October 18, 1883. Early in June the receiver did in fact enter suit. He asked the court to order an investigation of the properties of both companies in order to determine the precise ownership of the poles, wires and other telegraph facilities. Such an investigation would be a slow proceeding.

Gould, however, was planning bolder moves. Those who were sponsoring the reorganization of the Bankers' & Merchants' Telegraph were suspicious of him. They probably believed that in some way he could negotiate a contract adverse to the interests of that company. Prudently, somewhat as Cornelius Vanderbilt did in February of 1868, they appealed to the courts to prevent such a move. Judge Shipman, in charge of the receivership, had promised the Bankers' & Merchants' Telegraph that no contract with the American Rapid Telegraph would be made without first giving the former a reasonable chance to protect itself. This arrangement with the judge was no more successful in thwarting Gould's plans than the series of injunctions secured years before by Cornelius Vanderbilt. Gould played upon the personalities involved. He discovered a new tool in the person of Frederic May, who succeeded in bringing together Gould and the receiver of the American Rapid Telegraph. They met on Gould's yacht, and an understanding was reached. What Gould gave the receiver is not clear. In any event, the receiver gave Gould a curious contract authorizing the Western Union to act as his agent. The existence of this contract was not known to anyone interested in the Bankers' & Merchants' Telegraph. Not any of the company's bondholders or stockholders, the reorganization manager, the bondholders' trustee, not even the federal judge in charge of the receivership who had also approved the plan of reorganization and set the day on which the foreclosure was to take place, had any knowledge of the contract. Gould was careful to preserve that state of blessed ignorance.

Gould was now armed with a deadly weapon. An ordinary person might have used this contract as a basis for negotiation with its opponent and made some countermoves before the judge. He might have tried to block or at least to delay the foreclosure sale. Gould did none of this. He ignored the receiver and the receivership estate, as well as the court jurisdiction. Gould presented the judge with a petition asking His Honor to instruct Farnsworth, the receiver for the Bankers' & Merchants' Telegraph, to hand over to the Western Union, as agent for the receiver of the American Rapid Telegraph, the property of the latter. Whose property it was, nobody knew, since it was then the object of judicial investigation. Neither the receiver for this company nor for the Bankers' & Merchants' Telegraph could identify the property. Gould, strange to say, was able to identify it. He listed the property in the complaint, so that the judge without further ado or investigation granted the petition. The order of judicial approval was immediately given to General Eckert, operating vice president of the Western Union. Eckert lost no time in serving the judge's order upon Farnsworth. The latter looked at the order, and his answer was obvious. He replied that he could not readily distinguish the wires of the two companies. The answer of Eckert, acting under instructions from Gould, was not so obvious. If Farnsworth could not distinguish the wires, he, Eckert, could. Eckert promptly cut all the wires of the Bankers' & Merchants' Telegraph except those leading to Washington.

The business, if not the property, of the Bankers' & Merchants' Telegraph was thus, with a single blow, destroyed. It was an outrageous proceeding, but from a business standpoint it was effective. Gould, like Frederick the Great who invaded Silesia without warning, acted first and explained later. Frederick the Great, in political and military life, has had many predecessors and successors. Gould in business and financial life has had few. The proceeding was condemned in violent language. The chairman of the reorganization committee denounced it as highway robbery. "I challenge," he said, "any one to produce a more iniquitous proceeding under the cover of law since the days of Barnard, Tweed, and Sweeny." [47] The voluble Col. Robert G. Ingersoll, in his capacity as counsel in one of the many damage suits which followed this proceeding, spoke in even more challenging terms. "I do not believe," he thundered at the court, "that since man was in the habit of living on this planet anyone has ever lived possessed of the impudence of Jay Gould to make such a request of a judge." [48] And Stokes, a large security holder of the decapitated telegraph company declared, "It was deliberate high-handed robbery. They don't seem to respect God, Judge or devil. . . ." [49]

At one blow Gould destroyed one of the most powerful competitors of the Western Union. The blow was sharp and sudden; more important, it was fatal. Damage suits were begun, eminent counsel was retained, eloquent speeches were made, and furious editorials were written. The earning power of the property, however, was reduced to a figment. The foreclosure sale was not held as scheduled and the equity money was not furnished. Thus did Gould eliminate, at almost no cost to himself or the Western Union, one of the latter's three most powerful enemies.[50]

The other two members of the telegraph pool of 1884 still remained and offered competition as serious as ever. The strength of the Postal was exercised largely through its transatlantic cable. The activities of the Baltimore & Ohio precipitated the rate war of 1885 and 1886. Gould insisted that the Baltimore & Ohio could not long maintain this reckless form of competition, since it was losing $50,000 a month. The Baltimore & Ohio, however, declared that since it had charged many of its improvements to operating expense, its costs were low, and that even with a rate of 50 per cent below that of the Western Union, it still could operate.

While the Baltimore & Ohio was losing money, the Western Union also was seriously affected. Its losses arose not only from land, but also from cable competition. Early in 1886 it reduced the price of cable service to twelve cents a word, thereby creating a unique price war. The Commercial Cable declined to follow Gould all the way down and reduced its rates only to twenty-five cents a word. The company requested its customers to support it in this drastic rate war, pointing out that Gould and his group were interested, not in reducing rates, but in driving it out of existence. Many businessmen supported Mackey and continued to buy service from his company at a price 100 per cent higher than that paid by Gould's customers.

This rate competition on land and sea was followed by disastrous financial effects to the Western Union. In March, 1886, it passed its dividend. It was the threat of such an eventuality that led many of the small stockholders to appeal to Vanderbilt late in 1880 for protection. Cornelius Vanderbilt probably would have listened to no such complaint; he probably would have acted on the premises of sound business principles, as did Gould in 1886. Gould did not consult the temporary interests of the shareholders for an immediate dividend, but rather the permanent welfare of the company and the many years of dividends to come in the future. The 1886 annual report of the Western Union explained the reduction clearly. Said the report, "Whilst the volume of traffic has continued to increase, the tables show a material reduction in revenues, principally in the cable, gold and stock and commercial news earnings. . . . Notwithstanding continued reductions in rates, the earnings from land lines service have been well maintained, the falling off in earnings from messages transmitted over the land lines being less than the increase from wire rentals."[51]

The rate wars had by the end of 1886 weakened the company's financial position. The company had during the years of the Gould regime substantially increased its fixed charges, while its earnings declined. The published earnings furthermore were overstated. Gould, as elsewhere, adopted an opportunistic bookkeeping system. When conditions demanded a showing of reduced earnings, he charged additions and improvements to operating expenses. With respect to the Western Union, it was to his interest in 1884 and 1885 to increase published earnings. He therefore provided an interesting "construction account" to which he charged items which were properly chargeable to operating expenses. In 1886 the account amounted to some $6,000,000.[52]

In the period 1879 to 1886 the Western Union had increased its poles and wires by 100 per cent. The number of messages had increased about 75 per cent, and its gross revenue about 60 per cent. Expenses, however, had increased more than 100 per cent, thus reducing its profits nearly 20 per cent.[53] This was the bill which the rate wars presented to the Western Union stockholders.

The future of Western Union as the year 1886 ended looked dark. In Congress another effort was being made to secure help from the government in the struggle against the dominant telegraph enterprise. Late in February the House ordered a committee to make an investigation and submit a report on legislation needed to prevent a telegraph monopoly.[54] The Baltimore & Ohio continued to press the rate war on an increasing scale and rates dropped to record low levels. The Postal followed the lead of the Baltimore & Ohio. Rebates and discriminations were rife and special contracts with important customers became the normal order of the day.

The Baltimore & Ohio, however, was losing heavily not only in the telegraph but also in the express business. Although its railroad business was also declining, it still appeared to be an imposing financial enterprise. Since it had sold its stock for cash on a scale equaled only in railroad circles by the Pennsylvania, its stock was not watered. For years it had maintained dividend payments and built up a substantial surplus. Its past was excellent; its future appeared assured. Its stock sold at high prices and yielded only a small return on its market value.

These considerations appealed to many investors both in this country and abroad. The impaired strength of the company was not evident to those who read financial reports and who accept past records at their face value. Gould did not accept this test. As a man of business, he was an untiring investigator and close observer. He knew that the Baltimore & Ohio was losing heavily in the telegraph business and openly said so. He also knew that for some years the road's management had lived on past tradition. It was not aggressive; it had opened no new territory; it had not made satisfactory traffic agreements with its connections; and it had not, for a number of years, replaced its equipment and other property with new facilities.

Gould therefore used sound judgment in refusing to excite himself over the continued war of rates. He declined to make any move in order to buy out his competitor. In the summer of 1885 some meetings were arranged in London between Garrett and other telegraph men. It seemed that Robert S. Garrett, son of the elder Garrett, having seen Gould at work in the Atlantic & Pacific and in the American Union, desired to emulate him and to sell his telegraph property at a high price. He had, however, none of Gould's bargaining ability. His ideas of a selling price were fanciful, and nothing happened.[55]

Gould refused to bid aggressively for the Baltimore & Ohio. Time was on his side. He waited for an offer, and the offer soon came. The Baltimore & Ohio management was anxious to sell. The weakened character of its management was revealed in the bungling procedure followed to find a buyer for the property. Henry Ives, a broker in New York City with no strong following and who had been involved in a number of irregularities, secured an option for the purchase of a large block of the Baltimore & Ohio stock. The stock was owned or controlled by the president of the property, Robert S. Garrett, who had built up the road. The existence of the option became a matter of public knowledge. Ives bought an option which he could not exercise. He did not have the means to conclude such a transaction, even though he may have made exaggerated representations to Garrett about his connections. Gould, however, was not so easily deceived. When Ives offered him the opportunity to buy the option, he declined. He did not have enough data on the finances of the Baltimore & Ohio, he declared. Neither did he know enough about its floating debt, the condition of its branch roads, and its relations with its connections.[56] He had no opportunity to examine its books. Since his experience with accounting made him familiar with the tricks of that eminent art, he refused to make any commitments based upon the results of accounting without a thorough knowledge of its premises. Gould insisted that Ives had better buy the stock first and then he could do business with him.

Within a few days Gould was called upon by another person purporting to represent the anxious sellers of the Baltimore & Ohio stock. This time it was Alfred Sully,[57] a financier of some note. He had mediated between the various groups of Reading security holders, and was generally credited with having made the reorganization of that road possible. Gould again refused to purchase.

Meanwhile the war of rates continued. Gould remained confident of the competitive position of the Western Union. Although the company paid no dividends its position in the industry was strong. The company, declared Gould about this time, had "withstood all competition and all opposition, and [had] grown stronger in spite of both." [58] He did not, however, overlook the power of the Baltimore & Ohio. He watched Ives, who continued his plans for the acquisition of control of the road. Gould apparently encouraged him. He probably believed that if

Ives with his scant resources would buy control on a shoestring, he would soon be compelled to unload his stock, and on a declining market he would be able to buy at low prices.

Ives, meanwhile, bought control of an important connection of the Baltimore & Ohio—the Cincinnati, Hamilton & Dayton. To secure and establish this control, Ives had borrowed extensively; partly, although indirectly, he had borrowed from Gould himself.[59] Although he had not secured control of the Baltimore & Ohio, it seems that by mid-July he had entered into some sort of agreement by which he was given the opportunity to sell the company's telegraph lines and to use the cash proceeds for the purpose of making part payment on Baltimore & Ohio stock. With that payment made, he probably could borrow additional sums with the stock as collateral. In late July, Ives apparently made an offer to sell the telegraph lines to Gould for a cash consideration of $3,500,000. Gould after considering the offer rejected it. From a careful search, he learned that the Baltimore & Ohio had only two years before sold a bond issue payable in sterling, secured by a lien on railroad facilities and telegraph rights. Gould thus could not get a clear title, and refused to purchase.[60] He was in no hurry to act. His patience and his refusal to become entangled in the adventures of promoters were justified by the public demonstration of the financial weakness of the Baltimore & Ohio. Its imposing book surplus turned out to be a financial mirage. It was invested in part in obsolete property, and included uncollectable advances to such subsidiaries as its own telegraph company. The debt of the latter to its parent approximated $3,875,000, although according to some reports the debt would reach $7,000,000.[61] Suddenly the Baltimore & Ohio found itself begging for help, unable without outside assistance to carry its floating debt. Morgan, who had tied his business destiny to the maintenance of railroad stability, announced his intention of purchasing a large block of its securities. For the first time in many years the accounts of the road were made available to outsiders and the road's true condition thus revealed. Among the conditions precedent to the extension of financial help was the sale of the road's telegraph lines. In a swift and simple transaction the property was sold to the Western Union. The discussions were carried on between Morgan and Gould—two negotiators who were accustomed to making rapid decisions. Thus passed away the last powerful competitor, but one, of the Western Union.

The acquisition of the Baltimore & Ohio's telegraph system represented a milestone in the progress of the Western Union. The new addition was almost nation-wide in extent. The wires covered from Portland, Maine, to South Carolina, up to St. Paul, and down to Texas. The increase in its competitive strength facilitated negotiations for the purchase of a number of smaller telegraph enterprises. Including these additions, the Western Union succeeded in acquiring in one year, in mileage of lines and wire, a property about twice as great as the entire plant which any competing telegraph system ever controlled.[62] Gould had succeeded in enhancing the competitive strength of the Western Union to such a degree that the Postal was relegated to an inferior status. Mackey, the man of business that he was, recognized that he could no longer indulge in rate wars with his powerful competitor, and he quickly proposed a truce. The Postal agreed with the Western Union to do away with the rebate system and to abolish the ten-to-fifteen-cent rate. The Western Union agreed not to cut rates against the Postal. There was no point in Gould's eliminating a competitor which would do the Western Union no harm. Each agreed to cultivate relationships on a service basis and on a given rate structure. The Postal by that time had extended its lines to serve many important cities, and through the part ownership by Mackey in the Atlantic cable, the Postal was enabled to give an efficient, well-rounded cable-telegraph service.[63]

Agreement had thus been reached on the land-telegraph business. The two-way price system in the cable business lasted only about a year, and in September of 1887 the Commercial Cable finally cut its rate to the level of the Western Union's.[64] It was not until July of 1888, approximately nine months after acquisition of the Baltimore & Ohio, that the cable rate war was settled and the way opened for a final peace agreement between the two remaining telegraph companies.

Gould was now master of the telegraph business. His success shocked both the commercial and the political world. A conservative financial daily described the Western Union as a concern which followed a "monopolizing and aggressive course. . . ."[65]

Further aggressive efforts were made by the federal government to strike at the Western Union. The new Postmaster-General, the distinguished Philadelphia merchant, John Wanamaker, pressed for the adoption of an elaborate government postal telegraph system. Nothing, however, was done. Gould had successfully confounded legislative investigators, political critics, and financial skeptics. The watering of the Western Union stock in 1881 and the increase in fixed charges on the transatlantic cable lines convinced financial observers that it could not survive real competition. The aggressiveness of the Baltimore & Ohio seemed to seal its financial doom. It appeared that the Western Union would go the way of the Wabash, the Texas & Pacific, the Union Pacific, and the Erie. Gould would drain the treasury, surfeit its financial structure with bonds and stocks, and leave the company a financial derelict. He would then bid the enterprise good-by and look for greener financial pastures.

These rational expectations were all confounded by the succeeding events. Out of the Western Union, Gould made the greatest success of his career. His accounting as usual was questionable, and was resorted to on a major scale to help him out of speculative troubles in 1884 and 1885. He was aggressive in buying up competitors and paid the market price readily when necessary to eliminate powerful opposition which threatened to become more powerful. Thus he bought out the Mutual Union at a price dictated largely by the seller. Baker, in association with Morgan, was later to become one of the leaders of the banking community. He was the dominant factor in control of the Mutual Union, and later became a Gould admirer. Gould on the other hand was not aggressive in the purchase of the Baltimore & Ohio telegraph lines. In all cases he was realistic. He was aggressive at the proper time, and he was also patient and receptive in his negotiations at the proper time. He succeeded in buying or eliminating his competitors. By extraordinary means he excluded one competitor at no cost to the Western Union, and by ordinary measures, for cash or stock, he bought out others.

After elimination of all save one of his competitors, Gould was able to steer his Western Union away from the path of rate wars into the highway of rate stability and increased sales volume. In times of trouble the Western Union passed its dividends to conserve its resources, and in times of prosperity it resumed its dividends and achieved a strong investment rating for its securities. In the Western Union, Gould, contrary to expectations of contemporaries, critics, and friends alike, was a successful man of business.

NOTES FOR CHAPTER XXIII

1. Testimony before Committee on Post Offices and Post Roads, on the Postal Telegraph, Report No. 577, Senate, 48th Congress, 1st Session, 1884, 246, Green.
2. Known hereafter as the Mutual Union.
3. This was the statement made in an advertisement in the New York *Times*, April 26, 1881.
4. New York *Times*, Sept. 1, 1881.
5. Phila. *Press*, Oct. 25, 1881. Wyman made this remark in a letter to the contractor's employees.
6. Ibid.
7. *Literary Digest*, Jan. 25, 1913, 190.
8. New York *Tribune*, April 18, 1879.
9. Ibid., Nov. 30, 1882.
10. *Bradstreet*, May 27, 1882, 328.
11. Ibid.
12. New York *Times*, Nov. 7, 1882.
13. *Bradstreet*, Jan. 6, 1883, 8.
14. Burlington archives, Forbes to Perkins, Dec. 9, 1882.
15. Ibid., Forbes to John W. Garrett, Dec. 15, 1882.
16. Ibid., Forbes to George Jones, Dec. 10, 1882.
17. Ibid., Forbes to Olney, Dec. 15, 1882.
18. Ibid., Olney to Forbes, Dec. 20, 1882.
19. Ibid., W. J. Ladd to Forbes, Dec. 20, 1882.
20. For details on the importance of the Hannibal to the Burlington and of the competitive rivalry between Gould and the Burlington for acquisition of its control, see an unpublished manuscript by the author, "The Hannibal & St. Joseph, 1870–1883," in Newberry Library.
21. Burlington archives, A. W. Beard to Forbes, March 25, 1883.
22. Ibid., Potter to Perkins, Feb. 4, 1883.
23. *Chron.*, Nov. 15, 1882, 576; Dec. 2, 1882, 638.
24. New York *Times*, Dec. 16, 1882.
25. New York *Tribune*, Jan. 3, 1883.
26. Testimony before the Senate Committee on Education and Labor as to the Relations between Labor and Capital, Report No. 1262, Senate, 48th Congress, 1885, 917, 2nd Session, Green.
27. Known hereafter as the Postal.
28. For details of the company's expansion plans, see Springfield (Mass.) *Republican*, cited in *Ry. Review*, April 2, 1881, 183.
29. New York *Times*, letter from J. S. Moore, Jan. 14, 1887.
30. In a letter of A. W. Dimock to the Committee on Post Offices and Post Roads, Senate, Feb. 15, 1884, in Testimony before Committee on Post Offices and Post Roads, on the Postal Telegraph, Report No. 577, Senate, 48th Congress, 1st Session, 1884, 163-4.
31. *Chron.*, Oct. 7, 1882, 393.
32. Ibid., Aug. 18, 1883, 175.
33. Boston *Transcript*, Aug. 22, 1883.

34. New York *Times*, Feb. 5, 1884; *Chron*., Oct. 20, 1883, 424.
35. New York *Herald*, Aug. 6, 1883.
36. These quotations are taken from the text of the resolution presented in ibid., Feb. 21, 1884.
37. Phila. *Press*, Jan. 30, 1884.
38. New York *Tribune*, April 29, 1884.
39. Testimony before Committee on Post Offices and Post Roads, on the Postal Telegraph, Report No. 577, Senate, 48th Congress, 1st Session, 1884, 130, R. Garrett.
40. New York *Herald*, June 8, 1884.
41. For the text of this contract, see *Chron*., June 14, 1884, 707.
42. New York *Times*, July 18, 1884; New York *Herald*, July 19, 1884. This percentage, however, was challenged by an official of the Western Union. While the combination insisted that the miles of wires controlled amounted to one hundred and twenty thousand, a Western Union official declared that it controlled only sixty thousand miles.
43. *Iron Age*, July 24, 1884, 17.
44. Land-Grant Telegraph Lines, Report No. 3501, House of Representatives, 49th Congress, 2nd Session, 1886, 3, D. H. Bates.
45. Ibid., 150-53, J. E. Johnston.
46. New York *Herald*, July 14, 1885.
47. New York *Times*, July 12, 1885.
48. New York *Herald*, May 22, 1886.
49. New York *Times*, Jan. 27, 1885.
50. Accounts of the details of these proceedings are found in the New York *Times*, New York *Tribune*, and New York *Herald*, on various dates in July, 1885. Detailed accounts of the litigation initiated by the receiver of the Bankers' & Merchants' Telegraph for damages against the Western Union are found in New York *Herald* from May to July 1886. The New York *Herald* published in full the vivid and revealing addresses of counsel.
51. *Chron*., Oct. 16, 1886, 458.
52. *Stockholder*, Dec. 6, 1886.
53. New York *Tribune*, Oct. 14, 1886.
54. Military & Postal Telegraph, Report No. 178, House of Representatives, 50th Congress, 1st Session, 1888, III.
55. On these negotiations, see *Bradstreet*, Aug. 1, 1885, 73; Aug. 8, 1885, 89; Aug. 15, 1885, 98.
56. Phila. *Press*, March 13, 1887.
57. *Stockholder*, March 16, 1887.
58. Ibid., June 29, 1887.
59. New York *Tribune*, June 25, 1887.
60. Baltimore *Sun*, cited in *Stockholder*, July 27, 1887.
61. *Bradstreet*, Oct. 15, 1887, 678.
62. Annual report, Western Union, 1888, cited in *Chron*., Oct. 13, 1888, 439.
63. For details on the settlement of the rate war between the Western Union and the Postal, see New York *Herald*, Oct. 28, 1887.
64. Ibid., July 21, 1888.
65. *Journal of Commerce*, cited in New York *Herald*, Oct. 18, 1887.

CHAPTER XXIV

Gould Trades: To 1884

To THE army of security holders, in the years following his association with the Erie, Gould's activities in corporate acquisitions, in acquiring and selling the control of railroad systems, in securing mastery of the telegraph combination and of the elevated rapid-transit system of New York City were subsidiary to his stock-market operations. Gould conducted his business negotiations during most of his business career with an eye on their stock-market effects. A success in business was not a finished product until it was also a success on the stock market. His trading operations in the seventies have already been surveyed. As a trader he was not, on the whole, successful. In 1878 he seriously misjudged the market. The price declines then reflected the selling of the nonimaginative investor who, upon seeing all the grave economic disasters, adjusts his mind and purse to the assumption that these conditions are permanent. Gould, as a security trader, could probably not be charged with committing such a sin, although his mind appeared to have been warped by a sense of futility over the impending resumption of specie payments, scheduled to go into effect January 1, 1879. He adjusted his trading policies to reflect that judgment. In the rising market of 1878 he made large short commitments, and his losses were heavy. By the end of 1878, and in the first few weeks of 1879, he had lost a large part of the speculative following, and his persistent critics considered him a lame duck. How he retrieved his financial losses and rose to a position of business supremacy has already been examined.[1]

In the two years which followed, his interests veered to the business side and he became in a few months one of the leaders of the railroad industry. He bought numerous properties in a broad program not originally conceived as such, but gradually growing upon him, of acquiring working control of all of them.

In the course of time as the securities appreciated in value and as his paper profits grew to immense proportions, he resumed his position as a speculative trader. During these years he gave few public interviews, and much of what the newspapers and the financial press said about him was mere surmise. Gould did not want company. His speculative following in 1879 and 1880 was not of his own making. They grouped around him not because he beckoned but because they followed him naturally in pursuit of speculative profits. The speculators were to pay a high price in the subsequent three years for the profits made in the first three years.

By 1881 Gould had established his trading leadership; and his losses in 1878 were forgotten. Beginning with a cash fund which in February of 1879 (after the sale of the Union Pacific stock to the syndicate and the settlement for his losses on his short sales) probably did not exceed $3,000,000, Gould in the next two years established a fabric of market values for which there was at that time no equal in the country. His purchases were made in a rising market, the strongest since the Civil War inflation. The rise although not continuous, nevertheless created favorable conditions for the pyramiding of security purchases. The increase in the market value of each successive acquisition furnished the means for the purchase of more securities. The sensational advance in Wabash and in the Kansas City in the spring of 1879 created a market value which Gould utilized to finance the purchase of Kansas & Pacific and of additional blocks of Wabash. The heavy rise in the price of Kansas Pacific securities in the summer provided him with additional credit to secure funds for the purchase of the Denver Pacific bonds. His purchasing power was also increased by profits from construction companies and from Union Pacific dividends.

In the speculative boom of his southwestern securities, he made additional purchases. Although some of these acquisitions were made on a cash basis, there is little question that he depended heavily on bank credit. By 1881 he and his associates had acquired interests in the Mercantile Trust and were elected to the board. To the big three, Sage, Gould, and Dillon, board members, there was added Green of the Western Union, Humphreys of the Wabash, Marquand, a large stockholder in and a promoter of the International and of the Iron Mountain, and Garrett of the Baltimore & Ohio. Although Gould's holdings in the stock of this bank were never "very large," [2] there is no doubt that part of his financial load was carried by this bank. Additional financial support came from stockbrokers with whom he transacted business. Since the market from 1879 to 1881 was advancing, there was no reason why stockbrokers should have denied him credit. Collateral loans grew ever more sound, and brokerage failures were few and far between. Gould in his urge for expansion did little to curtail his brokerage debts. It appears probable that until the summer of 1881 his time was so preoccupied with his amazing program that he had little time to watch the growth of his debit balances, and that he permitted himself to become overexpanded. Early in 1881, at about the time his purchase of the Western Union was consummated, he was still adding to his holdings. He had out-generaled Keene in the Western Union pool, and Keene had therefore joined with the bear contingent to depress the market. In this group was Smith, for almost ten years estranged from Gould, Addison Cammack, and C. H. Osborne. Keene was the unquestioned leader on the one side, and Gould on the other. "It [was] Keene against Gould, with their respective followings," remarked a contemporary observer.[3]

Despite the dullness of the market, the Gould group permitted stories to spread of the profits to be made in the forthcoming market. Traders, in the language of one financial writer, "were apparently converted to the new belief (belief in higher prices) propounded by Jay Gould and Russell Sage, the high priests of the New deal." [4]

By the end of April the market had responded little to the buying activities of Gould and other optimistic traders. Many indeed were disappointed and sold their stocks freely, while others who had bought Gould's securities remained hopeful. The boom in southwestern stocks began shortly thereafter. Price increases were large, and although the rise was confined to a short period, profits were such that Gould's program of exchanging the Iron Mountain for the Missouri Pacific and the International for the Kansas & Texas was an unqualified success.

Gould's tactics in promoting this move were sound, as they were in numerous other speculative tilts in the ensuing three years. These tactics made a deep impression upon the minds of contemporary observers, analysts, brokers, and traders. His general strategy, however, was unsound. He had overloaded himself with many stocks, and although in the early summer of 1881 he had substantial profits, they were largely on paper. Hardly had he completed his southwestern consolidation program than the booming market reached a climax. The assassination of President Garfield in July produced a sharp reaction and inaugurated a change in trend which was generally overlooked. Few observers recognized the break as the beginning of a three-year downward market. Said one writer, "Reactions are always liable to occur; but it really looks as if panics or even serious declines might almost be considered things of the past." [5]

Gould had no opportunity to unload, to reduce his commitments, and to make himself unassailably solvent. In the early stages of the long decline, he set the pattern of his trading operations during the entire period. The break in prices was so sharp that reliable observers insisted that Gould was selling out as fast as possible; and some even believed that having foreseen the evil days, he had sold out his southwestern stocks and a good deal of his Western Union.[6]

Gould, however, exercised no such foresight and displayed no such sound market judgment. Neither in word nor in deed did he reveal any comprehension of the changing business and economic trends. Who the sellers are at the end of a long buying wave has always remained unanswered, although this is not to say that the question never can be answered. Gould maintained his position as a leader of the group working for higher prices. It was a local and limited action not indicative of a change in mind, nor revealing any recognition of the change in economic forces.

Late in December the market suffered another drop. Although Gould was probably next to Vanderbilt the largest holder of railroad securities in the country, he was accused of being the author of the break. Since the majority of traders were as usual operating for the rise, and since almost all investors were anxious to see the prices of their securities rise uninterruptedly, blame for the losses inflicted on thousands of security holders who were seeking a scapegoat was placed upon the shoulders of Gould. "The immediate cause," (for the market break) declared one financial reporter, was given in a monosyllable, " 'Gould.' " [7]

The sense of exaggerated power credited to Gould at this time was widespread. Perhaps some of the remarks of financial journalists may be pardoned in an effort to build up reader interest at a time when other financial events were lacking. There must nevertheless have been deep feeling behind the following expressions which refer to the sharp market break in December, 1881, when Gould played his trick on the Denver stock: "It was a striking instance of the immense power which one man can exercise. Jay Gould has done more in a single week, without the aid of a solitary bear event or disaster, than all the Vanderbilts, Mills, Cammacks, Keenes, Sages and Osbornes were able to accomplish with the assistance of an assassination, a change of administration, a tight money market, a railroad war, a short crop, a drought, and a flood, so long as the little dark man was not in sympathy with them." [8]

The feeling of hostility to Gould as a wrecker of values was accentuated. Traders awaited word from him before determining their market position. Following his signal to buy or sell, many journals of opinion and chroniclers of events renewed their attacks upon the integrity of his statements. When Gould proclaimed that he was in favor of lower prices, observers concluded that he was anxious to buy stocks cheap, and when he proclaimed himself in favor of higher prices, they concluded that he wanted to sell out his holdings. In truth, except for occasional market forays, he was for most of 1881 and the early months of 1882 on the rising side of the market. Meanwhile, the prices of his major holdings—Missouri Pacific and Western Union—dropped sharply. Early in February, 1882, therefore, he announced in a formal statement that he was now a buyer of stocks. "It was a rather sudden turn—sudden enough, indeed, to take one's breath away; but we are getting used to that," was the remark of the editor of one of the more conservative journals.[9] To elevate the general list and therefore his own Missouri Pacific and Western Union, Gould had formed an understanding with Keene and some other operators. Despite his great need, the time set for a rising movement was not propitious. A panic threatened in Paris and many operators who had joined their interests with Gould sold out and left him almost alone in the field. In the face of adverse European news, the export of gold and the rise in money rates, together with the short sales by some market traders, Gould almost singly held up the market "as it were, by main strength." [10]

Gould far from being a wrecker of existing values was now on the defensive in supporting such values. He was a leader in fact of a group struggling for higher security prices. In this effort, he was for many weeks unsuccessful. The market throughout the most of February and early March was in a turmoil. The attack on Wabash was particularly heavy. The sharp break reached a climax in mid-February, and again Gould traced the pattern which was gradually becoming familiar to many close observers, of holding up the price of Missouri Pacific and Western Union, while doing little to maintain the prices of his other securities.

Another sharp selling wave on the twenty-third of February was sufficiently extensive to encourage Gould to repeat publicly that he was on the side of higher prices. The last decline, he said, was "without reason; the sacrifice of stocks foolish. . . ." [11] It is apparent that Gould's advice at least to some extent was generally followed, and for a few days the market was again stabilized. By the beginning of the second week in March, however, prices again buckled. By the end of the week the situation looked serious to those who had large lines of stocks to carry on borrowed money.

That the situation was disturbing to Gould, there is little reason to doubt. Over the week end, therefore, he conceived another plan, unprecedented in scope and effective in execution. On Monday morning he called a group of friends to his office and displayed $53,000,000 (par) of stock certificates taken from his vaults. They were not, Gould explained, used as collateral for loans; they were free treasury assets. The collection was worth more than $40,000,000 at market prices, as collateral he could use them to borrow $30,000,000. Reports were that Gould had another $20,000,000 which he did not exhibit. Despite the fact that he was forced to sustain the value of his holdings, it was again insisted that he was still for the most part a trader. . . . "For no one in the slightest degree acquainted with Wall Street imagines in his wildest dreams that Mr. Gould has them (his securities) to keep as permanent investment, or for any other purpose than to sell." [12]

His motive, however, was simple and obvious. There is little doubt that Gould exhibited his securities to convince the public that he was not selling. Gould's tactics proved successful and the exhibit was followed by a market stampede. The market moved upward and a part of Gould's paper losses were recovered.[13] This tactical advance engineered by Gould exhausted itself in a few weeks. The Gould leadership was strong and the financial community excited. Aside from a venture into Northern Pacific on the short side, a move to which he was to return some months later in the spring of 1883, he did little in the market for the remainder of the year. His operations during this period were a puzzle to the financial community. He concealed his plans well; his own brokers knowing nothing of what he was doing.[14] The general market resumed the decline which Gould had interrupted by his March coup. Though the selling was not as heavy as it had been in the initial break from July, 1881, to March, 1882, it was persistent and in the course of months the erosion of values was serious. It is probable that in the late months of 1882 Gould accumulated additional lines of stocks. By the middle of January, 1883, he publicly announced his adherence to the rising side of the market,[15] and privately he talked about restoring confidence, which presumably meant a rising stock market.[16] A few weeks later when Union Pacific was selling at 95 he bought a large block at private sale,[17] and a few days thereafter he announced that he had a "moderate interest" in Union Pacific.[18] At about this time the rate situation was stabilized. Although the Burlington had been in Denver for more than six months, the threat of a rate war had not materialized. Gould consequently believed that what he called a "moderate interest" in Union Pacific would probably prove a profitable commitment.

At the same time he increased his holdings in Western Union. According to Green, president of the company, Gould's holdings since the merger had advanced from $20,000,000 to $30,000,000. "Indeed," remarked Green, "I know that [Gould] has not got any other stock that he prizes so highly." [19]

The problem of the Wabash was meanwhile becoming burdensome. To retain the road as an integral part of his southwestern system, he was compelled to buy large blocks of stock. Even these purchases could not long sustain the market, and by the middle of May the market again began to decline. He learned at about that time that the war of rates, which had just begun because of the completion of the Denver's Ogden extension, would be extended and that this would lead to a slash in Union Pacific's earnings. Gould apparently then sold out his small amount of Union Pacific and assumed a short position in the market; becoming, in the words of one of his newspaper critics, "the most active, persistent and formidable bear on Union Pacific of all the crowd of speculators. . . ." [20]

It remained difficult, as it had for almost two years, for him to sell any substantial part of his holdings. His knowledge of the inside forces of the market, his mastery of market technique, his wide understanding of security distribution, his ease of securing credit, his command of the large speculative following upon whom from time to time he could unload some of his securities, were of little use to him. All of these factors are of importance only if one is in accord with the trend of underlying economic forces. His unsound strategy was his major error, and from it came most of his trading losses. In the summer of 1883 he first undertook seriously to dispose of some of his holdings. For the first time since the beginning of the decline he appears to have observed that prices were on the downward march, and that it was necessary in order to solve some of his pressing financial problems to undertake some heroic measures. He was then, as one observer remarked, "plainly in a more uncomfortable position than it [was] usually his luck to get into." [21] A circular of a leading broker, and a close Gould follower, referred to his desire "to realize as best he [might] upon large amounts of securities in which he [was] interested." [22]

Vanderbilt also was faced with heavy paper losses on his large holdings in eastern railroad securities. Leading Vanderbilt stocks had taken such a severe price drubbing that Vanderbilt sought the aid of Gould in maintaining price levels. Both were so loaded, however, that the proposed joint action appeared to one banker like the "blind leading the blind." [23]

Gould was now convinced that the market would continue to decline. It should not be surprising that under these circumstances calling for general liquidation, Gould adopted a contradictory trading policy. While he was heavily long of stocks which he was holding permanently, he was short of others. Early in August the price of Wabash, Texas & Pacific and Kansas & Texas dropped sharply, though the most serious was the break in Western Union. Ever since Gould had acquired a large interest late in 1880, he had succeeded in keeping the price above 80, but in the summer of 1883 the stock was forced to new low levels. His satellite stocks also dropped to new lows, and it was therefore no wonder that he could state with some semblance of sincerity early in September that the market could not be "cheaper than at present." [24]

Though by now Gould must have been convinced that the market could not advance, he could do little to liquidate his holdings. He was hesitant about selling his Wabash for fear that control of the property might be captured by adverse railroad interests and since his holdings in Texas & Pacific and Kansas & Texas were not substantial, their liquidation would be of little help.

Gould was indeed fearful for the first time in his business career of disposing of his holdings in his major properties—the Missouri Pacific, the Western Union, and the Manhattan. Although observers did not recognize the fact, he was anxious to become a businessman in his own standing. He was therefore unable to assume the bold speculative leadership necessary to take full advantage of the downward trend in the security markets. This responsibility was taken by a trader of whom mention has already been made, Woerishoffer, who soon became "the great bear king of Wall Street." [25] One is tempted to say that the task of leading the bear traders was not one of any exceptional risk, since the forces operating for a decline were so obvious that profits on the short side were almost inevitable. That of course is hindsight reasoning. To many informed people, writers and actors in the business drama who lived through the eight or nine months preceding the sharp financial breakdown in the early summer of 1884, the trend was not so clear. According to a leading metropolitan newspaper, indeed, except for the silver question, "the dangers of a commercial or financial panic [had been] well passed." [26] Some months later, shortly before the financial revulsion of May, Vanderbilt, who was in a position to reflect the opinions of influential businessmen, remarked that it was foolish to sell stocks. All large institutions, he declared late in March, 1884, hold some dividend paying stocks, and he added, apparently in an off-hand way, perhaps bonds, too. Trust companies and savings banks are buying stocks and carrying them. "A person is a fool to sell," he said.[27]

Gould by the force of circumstances, paradoxical though it may appear to be, was for a time forced to assume the leadership of the forces operating for a rise in the market. He was not prepared to envisage the possibility of a panic. Although he recognized that it was essential to liquidate and to reduce his heavy loans, he recognized, also, that before he could liquidate it was necessary for securities to rise. By the fall of 1883 he had been unable to sell much of his 50,000 shares of Wabash, and he declared about a month later that he never owned more Wabash than he did then.[28]

The stock market continued to falter in January, 1884. Gould, contrary to his policy of silence followed in the years of accumulation between 1879 and 1881, became decidedly voluble. If he were handling the Union Pacific, he declared, he would advance it 15 per cent on the faith of the Tri-Partite agreement. "The stock," he declared further, "[is] very cheap, and will doubtless go up." [29] This statement was followed by a sharp decline in prices. Days later, after his views were widely publicized, additional buying came in and the Union Pacific rose to $80 a share. Within a week however the buying gradually fell off and the general list which had moved ahead cautiously in the wake of the Union Pacific's spurt was demoralized by a break of the West Shore bonds and the receivership of the North River Construction Company. This latter was the company whose stock represented the profits realizable, if any, from the building of the West Shore. Prices retreated rapidly and soon sank to new low levels since the lows of the seventies. Meanwhile Gould's financial obligations were growing heavier. Trust companies were reported to be calling loans, and Gould was obliged to look for additional accommodation abroad where, according to press reports, he secured a collateral sterling loan of £250,000.[30] His solvency depended upon his ability to maintain the market value of his Western Union and Missouri Pacific in which his holdings remained large. The price of the former had declined, though not in proportion to the decline in the general list; Gould maintaining its price, as one observer remarked, "with a grasp of iron." [31] The terms of his loans became ever more stringent. The collateral was marked down substantially below the market price, at least 25 per cent. Some loans gave the creditors the right to lend the collateral, and when Gould discovered that some of it was being lent to traders to facilitate their short sales, he hurried to pay off those particular loans.

The January market rise proved to be abortive, and again Gould resorted to issuing public statements. Before the end of the month, he insisted publicly that good stocks and bonds were selling below their value. "Shrewd moneyed men are buying them. . . ." Stocks were oversold and cornered. Such stocks, he declared, included the Union Pacific, Western Union and the Vanderbilt stocks, among others. The Wabash, he said, was improving and its financial condition was better than a year ago. The market, he continued, would soon advance. Once, he said, he had bought Northwestern at 14, and in eighteen months it had sold above par.[32]

Whatever effect these public outpourings may have had on the speculative public, they did disclose to the sophisticated trader the seriousness of his financial condition. No accumulation of securities can be normally carried out in a floodlight of publicity. This breaking of Gould's policy of silence which had characterized his major operations must have revealed his grave financial position to Woerishoffer and to the other major traders. Gould was on the alert for every selling opportunity, superintending his trading operations through financial news agencies and an army of brokers estimated in some quarters to exceed two hundred, who reported to him instantly the buyers and sellers of stocks. "No such minute supervision of the dealings [had] ever been known," [33] remarked one writer.

He even took occasion to threaten suit, which again was something new. Expressing irritation over the spread of rumors, he declared that if they were traced to their source, the grand jury would be invoked.[34] A few days later he declared that he had placed in his lawyer's hands material which would facilitate the prosecution of those who were spreading gossip about his financial embarrassment.[35] Little attention was paid to these threats. The feeling of pessimism was intensified by a resumption of the heavy decline in the Villard stocks. Suddenly, the entire stock market reversed its trend and moved upward, the rise being led by the weakest stocks. On one day late in January, the price of Oregon Railway & Navigation opened at 88, and then moved upward to 119. A large supply was then rushed to the market and the price broke sharply to 95. The upward twist elevated the Union Pacific, for which Gould was seeking a market. On a Saturday morning almost 25 per cent of the turnover of 665,000 shares was represented by the Union Pacific, and in a week's time its price advanced from 76 to 82.

The market flare-up was a characteristic trading stroke of Gould. It was carried out as part of the negotiations with an embarrassed company which agreed to make a contract on hard bargaining terms, in order to get essential funds to avoid financial disaster. The Oregon Transcontinental's maturing loan of $1,-500,000, was secured by collateral in the hands of traders who were operating on the side of lower prices. They expected the debtor to sell the securities in order to pay the loan; the resultant decline would enable them to cover their line of short stocks. Or probably, they were counting upon accepting payment of their loans in collateral and not in cash. These securities were attractive, moreover, to an interest other than Gould. Forbes, who had made large commitments in Villard securities both personally and for the account of the Burlington, had planned to come to the support of the company.[36] Gould, however, acted more decisively. Through a syndicate he raised $4,000,000 and advanced sufficient funds to pay the loan. The concern then requested the creditors, who were selling stock short, to return the collateral. The traders were forced to enter the market to get the stock, and Gould no doubt helped things along by buying some shares for quick sale. This new advance was also short-lived. It did not enable him to liquidate much of his major holdings, though his victory in this limited engagement must have yielded him substantial profits.

After trapping these traders Gould stepped aside for a few days and awaited results. Little additional outside buying came in, and the market again turned dull. Gould then made another move. He decided once more to intervene in the eastern railroad situation in an effort to settle the existing rate wars, and soon succeeded in arranging a meeting of eastern railroad presidents on the seventh day of February. Each railroad president, personally, declared that railroad rates would be maintained. This settlement opened up vistas of railroad prosperity.

Gould now lined up a strong buying contingent, including Vanderbilt, the holder of perhaps the largest supply of liquid finds. On the very day of the meeting of the railroad presidents, Vanderbilt was buttonholed by a newspaper reporter. The bull market, he said was going to last; the stocks were not in Wall Street, and he, himself, had been buying for two weeks. New York Central, Lake Shore and Northwestern were cheap. New York Central particularly, he said, was even better than United States Government bonds. "In a year or two, we may have no Government. We must have railroads." [37] This may seem a curious statement, coming from one reported to be the largest single holder of government bonds. It was nevertheless a reflection of the confidence then, and for many years thereafter, entertained in good railroad securities. About a quarter of a century later another businessman, Henry Clay Frick, declared in a similar moment of exuberance that railroad bonds were the Rembrandts of investment. Vanderbilt also paid his respects to the bears; . . . "their doom [was] sealed," [38] he said.

Gould also convinced Field, who was especially impressed by his Oregon Transcontinental coup. "I don't know of anything else," he declared, "that is hanging over the stock market except possibly the West Shore matters, and I am told that they are in a fair way of adjustment. . . . I really believe that the tide is turning; . . ." [39]

This array of financial leadership was enough to turn the market in February. For three weeks prices moved ahead slowly but with no rampant advances in any particular stock. There was no evidence of artificiality, except perhaps the Lackawanna, whose price appeared so firmly held that a corner appeared almost inevitable. Late in February, as the market turned dull, Gould decided upon another venture. He was then one of the leading stockholders of the Lackawanna, owning probably about 70,000 shares.[40] Market operations in the stock were conducted by

Stephen Van Cullen White, Deacon White, as he was generally known, an active, plunging trader, and like so many traders who had no qualifications as men of business other than their ability to plunge heavily in the face of grave risks and market uncertainties, he eventually lost his fortune in an attempt to corner a commodity. Now at the top of his business career, he was in the midst of a successful market operation in Lackawanna, his second successful move to corner the stock in little more than a year.

Late in February, White joined with Gould, Sage, and Sloan in conjunction with others to form a pool in the stock with himself as manager. By the first of March, the market became aware that the stock was again cornered. A gap of about $10 per share developed between the price for regular delivery and the price for cash. The latter represented the price which short traders had to pay in order to secure a supply of stocks to make delivery immediately in response to the call from those who owned the stock. Although Gould's association with the pool cannot be stated as a definite fact,[41] the rise in the stock was nevertheless an important factor in his liquidation program.

The rapid rise in Lackawanna, even though it appeared to be artificial, temporarily stemmed the process of liquidation; though after the advance promoted by the corner the list again turned dull. The floating supply of stock, the supply available for trading, was reduced. Though it was conceded that Gould and Sage were holding up prices by "brute force," it was clear that some real support was coming in from investment demand. It was about this time that Vanderbilt in declaring his confidence in the future of the market insisted that institutions were buying. Though Vanderbilt was using his "spare" money, as he declared it, to sustain his own stocks, he was cautious and insisted that he did not intend to "run unnecessarily in debt." [42] Gould's trading prestige was also gradually returning, and his position was again described in extravagant language. "He is," declared one source, "undeniably the most potent person in the speculative ranks." [43]

Gould felt satisfied with the market and left for Florida for a vacation. The liquidation of securities, however, had by no means been stopped. Savings banks and other financial institutions which had bought stocks were awaiting, as indeed Gould himself was, for a good market on which to sell. Still the market did not rise. The dullness was broken by a sharp break in the price of wheat and, among Gould's stocks, Western Union by the first of April broke below 70. It was still a 7 per cent stock, and a return of 10 per cent on such an investment seemed to some to be "ridiculous." [44] By mid-April prices were dropping sharply and Gould's southwestern stocks had been reduced to the level of speculations. His finances were so weakened that he no longer had the power to sustain even his Western Union. By early May its price broke to 60, and the price of Missouri Pacific to 80, while the Wabash stocks, both common and preferred, had almost no value. Under the force of pressure from creditors and brokers he had no alternative to liquidation. He was selling as a speculator caught with insufficient margin.

The final panic break was, as usual, accompanied by a number of specific events. First was the failure of the Marine Bank, and of Grant & Ward. This was followed by the collapse of the Metropolitan National Bank, whose president, G. I. Seney, had made a fortune by his timely sale of Nickel Plate stock to Vanderbilt. The effect of the market break upon the value of Gould's stocks was severe. Missouri Pacific dropped from 78 to 68, Union Pacific from 45 to 39, and Western Union from 54 to 49. Earlier in the year Western Union had sold at 80. Thirty points on his holdings of $40,000,000 of Western Union meant a drop of $12,000,000 in the collateral supporting his debts.

Woerishoffer and the other bear traders now delivered a savage attack against the Gould stocks. It was at this time that Connor proved his loyalty to Gould when he stood in the breach and bought thousands of shares of Western Union. Woerishoffer, Cammack, and Smith staked their existence on Gould's downfall. Connor is said to have bought a block of 10,000 shares of Western Union several times within an hour,[45] and Gould was said to have bought 30,000 shares in three hours.[46] Profits of the bear traders were heavy. It was estimated for example that Smith, Gould's former associate and reputed to be the largest trader in Western Union, realized a profit of $500,000.[47]

Gould's position was critical. His debts were heavy and his collateral suspected. It is probable that in the last two weeks of May the stock of the Missouri Pacific which sold at a low of just above 60 did not have collateral value at the banks of more than

20; while other southwestern rails, Texas & Pacific, Kansas & Texas, and Wabash, were worthless for collateral purposes. His Western Union under the prevailing conditions probably did not have a collateral value of more than 25 or 30. Had his loans been called he probably would have been unable to pay.

In the midst of these difficulties a rumor spread that the Fourth National Bank had called a large loan on Gould, and had sold the collateral which happened to be the Missouri Pacific stock.[48] The price of Missouri Pacific dropped and it appeared for a time that there were no bids, but the decline was finally halted just above 60. Gould's position steadily grew more acute. Another of his major assets suitable for collateral, the stock of the Western Union, would probably be affected by a competitive situation which was then just reaching a head. The Baltimore & Ohio Telegraph was laying plans to complete a pooling agreement with two major competitors of the Western Union. It would not be at all surprising that under those conditions additional selling by frightened holders would drive the Western Union even below its current record low price of $50 a share.

Gould's critics were quick to recognize his impaired position, and for the first time since he rose to business power in 1879, they were able to anticipate with some degree of probability his coming collapse. "Is the load which Gould is carrying too heavy for him?" [49] asked one editor. Despite his heavy loans it was declared that he might be forced to borrow more, in default of which it would be necessary to throw over his Western Union and his other shares, "for whatever they would bring." [50] The other New York City leading journalistic critic asserted that the bear traders had finally reduced Gould to a position of impotence. "An impartial view of the present crisis of his securities, would indicate that the boys had not only got him under, but were walking up and down on his prostrate form." [51]

Gould had been defeated as a trader in a long speculative bout lasting about three years. During this period he had at times made heavy trading profits, though his losses far outbalanced his gains. His position at this time was not substantially different from what it had been at the end of 1878. In the ensuing three years he had become a major factor in the business world. His investment had increased to a peak where, with the exception of

Vanderbilt, it was greater than that of any man in the country. A fair estimate would give him a dividend and an interest income of about $6,000,000 a year. And yet his trading activities appeared now about to drive him into insolvency, and at a time when his investment income was not seriously endangered. Although he had no income from his heavy holdings in his Wabash and Texas & Pacific, he still had a return of about 6 per cent on about $40,000,000 of Western Union and 7 per cent on about $12,000,000 of Missouri Pacific. He was also credited with bond holdings of about $8,000,000 in Iron Mountain, $6,000,000 in Texas & Pacific, and $5,000,000 in Kansas & Texas, together with miscellaneous bonds of about $9,000,000. He also had industrial dividend-paying properties including the profitable stock of the St. Louis Bridge.

In May of 1884, nevertheless, his speculative activities had brought him to the brink of disaster. He was indeed, as Connor said more than a year later, "in deep water." [52] In this hour of need his friends failed him, and he decided to ask help from his enemies. While his friends failed him, his foes rescued him. He called a meeting of his foes—the bear traders, led by Woerishoffer—who were short of Missouri Pacific and Western Union. As early as February the short interest in Western Union had been estimated at about 100,000 shares.[53] Because of his heavy debts, estimated by one of his biographers at $20,000,000,[54] it was impossible for Gould to raise funds to force up the price of Western Union and Missouri Pacific, and thus force the shorts to cover. Gould decided to follow the philosophy of Samson: if he had to go down he would at the same time break his adversaries. Bringing a copy of an assignment to the meeting, he declared that unless the traders made an agreement with him, then and there, he would announce the next day that he was unable to meet his engagements. This is the same kind of threat which Cornelius Vanderbilt adopted in 1868, at a time when his large block of Erie stock had lost its value as collateral. When the banks threatened to call his loans, secured by the Erie, he threatened to sell his New York Central.

Gould's scheme was successful, and in this moment of desperation he revealed his superiority as a man of courage and resourcefulness, even though he revealed himself also as an unsuccessful trader. He was a success in business negotiations, though a failure in security trading.

The short traders needed the Western Union stock to deliver on their short contracts in order to realize their paper profits in Western Union. By selling the short traders the 50,000 Western Union, Gould obtained the sorely needed cash. What Sage, Vanderbilt, and his other friends could not give him, what the banks were unable to give him even if they were so inclined, his foes readily gave him. His enemies were certain that he would fail; the help thus extended to him would, in the opinion of these traders, "be transient in its effects as a glass of brandy given to a dying man."[55]

Gould now not only had ready cash; he also had a large interest in Missouri Pacific. Including the holdings of Sage, Marquand, and his other allies, he controlled a large proportion of the stock. The way was, therefore, open for a corner. With this large supply of cash, so generously supplied by his short-selling opponents, Gould found no difficulty in booming the price of Missouri Pacific, and within a few days the price leaped upward to the middle seventies. The traders who had just covered their Western Union and were still short of Missouri Pacific were panic-stricken. They competed in the market with Gould's purchases, and it took only a small part of Gould's newly found millions to force the stock up to par. By the middle of June Missouri Pacific was cornered, the short traders were routed, and Gould, unable in May to sell any Missouri Pacific in the sixties, was able in July to sell large amounts in the nineties.

Gould by shrewd personal negotiations had thus saved himself and had restored his finances. There is, nevertheless, some doubt that the traders, led by Woerishoffer with whom Gould made the Western Union deal, had permitted themselves to become the victims of Gould's market tactics. It is just as probable that Gould convinced them that there would be more profit on the up rather than on the down side of the market; that with these funds on hand, Gould could put the market up and that they could then buy and participate in the profits.[56]

Whatever the fact, the effect upon Gould's position was clear. He was now at least solvent, though his solvency was by no means assured. His loans were still heavy and even in the first week in June, after Missouri Pacific had crossed the middle eighties, reports stated with considerable confidence that Gould was still borrowing on collateral at the rate of 2 per cent a month.[57] In the weak market of the following two weeks, the price of Western Union and Union Pacific remained depressed and their collateral value at the banks was substantially below their market value. Even after the sharp rise in Missouri Pacific, Gould's finances were, therefore, still strained and he was compelled to borrow further. His critics were still jubilant, and to one of them Gould seemed "to be following fast in the footsteps of Mr. Villard, and hastening toward the same termination—namely, a grand collapse." [58]

In early July there was a widespread belief that his insolvency had only been delayed, and financial institutions rushed to deny any connection with him. When it was reported that Kidder, Peabody & Co. had extended a $2,000,000 credit to Gould, the report was denied. The Mercantile Trust on whose board Gould had served for a number of years hastened to announce that it had no loans with him, and early in July he retired from the directorate.

Gould meanwhile stuck grimly to his task. He was confronted with many perplexing problems in these dark and dreary days. By a show of resourcefulness, of bold and skillful use of his securities and by the manipulation of his leading stocks in the market, he was able to command sufficient cash to pay off his most pressing obligations. Unlike Villard in the previous summer he did not hold on to every bit of property and go down quiescently with the decline in their market value. He had resources, in shrewdness of personal dealings, in the thoroughness of his knowledge of market technique, and in his ability to engage in successful tactical operations which Villard did not have. Gould survived the supreme crisis in May of 1884. His securities were restored to a position of bankable collateral and his personal position was relieved.

By the middle of July, he had succeeded in increasing the price of his Missouri Pacific; although further efforts to elevate the price of his other securities and to liquidate a part of his collateral had been stopped by the break in late June. By early July he was busy laying plans for another market program to ease his financial stringency. In a public statement, he declared that money was growing easy. Security prices, he continued, were "ridiculously low." [59]

The market resumed its advance in the third week of July under the leadership of the Missouri Pacific and the Lackawanna. The leadership, however, soon switched to the Union Pacific, and by early August the stock market was "in a raging fever of advance. . . ." [60] While the general list advanced between 8 and 10 per cent, the price of Union Pacific rose daily with almost mechanical regularity until by the end of August its price had almost doubled.

How much Union Pacific Gould was able to unload is not known. On top of the boom, he said, he had not been selling stock; in fact, he insisted, he was buying and that he expected to see the price "much higher." [61] Suddenly, within a day or so thereafter, the price of Union Pacific declined. Gould now learned that some large interests were selling out, including Tilden, the Democratic presidential candidate in 1876.

The break in Union Pacific in late August proved to be the end of the summer rise. As much as any other market in the history of his business career, this was one of Gould's own making. He made the market for Missouri Pacific from late May till mid-June, and also for Union Pacific from early July to late August. He had now accomplished what he had set out to do; he had liquidated enough of his holdings to pay some part of his debts and to relieve the pressure of his creditors.

Gould was now a changed man—physically and mentally. The horrors of his financial and trading experiences in the summer months had overtaxed his physical and nervous energies, and in the years following he could no longer keep up the same ceaseless grind on so many active business fronts. His experience had also changed his financial outlook. When he had finished with the summer markets, he declared he would no longer borrow money for speculation.[62] He had by this time learned a lesson which others had learned in the same way—apparently the only way in which lessons of this kind are taught, by repeated instruction in the school of experience. Scott of the Pennsylvania in the middle seventies, Stanford in the early eighties, and Huntington in the middle nineties were others who after long experience decided to remain no longer in debt.

NOTES FOR CHAPTER XXIV

1. See Chapters IX-XVII.
2. This is the language used in the New York *Times,* July 15, 1884, by Louis Fitzgerald, president of the Mercantile Trust, at a time when the bank was seriously criticized because of its close association with Gould, and when there was reasonable probability of losses to the bank from Gould's paper. For this reason perhaps Fitzgerald's belittling of Gould's holdings cannot be accepted as entirely reliable.
3. *Bradstreet,* Feb. 5, 1881, 72.
4. Phila. *North American,* Feb. 14, 1881.
5. Ibid., July 20, 1881.
6. *Bradstreet,* Aug. 20, 1881, 120.
7. Phila. *North American,* Dec. 21, 1881.
8. Ibid., Dec. 23, 1881.
9. *Bradstreet,* Feb. 4, 1882, 72.
10. Ibid.
11. New York *Commercial Advertiser,* Feb. 24, 1882.
12. *Bradstreet,* March 18, 1882, 168.
13. A commentator writing many years later, presumably from memory, or upon the basis of remarks made by others to him from their own memory, remarked that Gould in January was short of pretty much the entire list; and that Gould made a trading profit by covering his stocks. *Wall Street Journal,* June 12, 1924. There may be some truth in this statement. The trading profits he may have made, however, represented an infinitesimal part of the paper profits he realized from the later advance in the bulk of his permanent holdings, primarily Missouri Pacific, Western Union and Manhattan.
14. This is the judgment of a New York correspondent of the Phila. Press, Nov. 13, 1882.
15. Phila. *North American,* Jan. 16, 1883.
16. Burlington archives, Perkins to Forbes, Jan. 20, 1883.
17. Phila. *North American,* Feb. 12, 1883.
18. New York *Times,* Feb. 15, 1883.
19. Phila. *North American,* Feb. 24, 1883.
20. New York *Times,* June 10, 1883.
21. *Bradstreet,* Aug. 25, 1883, 120.
22. Circular of Henry Clews & Co., cited in *Ry. Review,* Aug. 4, 1883, 459.
23. Burlington archives, Griswold to Forbes, Feb. 14, 1883.
24. Phila. *North American,* Sept. 3, 1883.
25. So designated in the Phila. *Press,* Oct. 8, 1883.
26. New York *Tribune,* Oct. 16, 1883.
27. New York *Times,* March 27, 1884.
28. Phila. *North American,* Nov. 23, 1883.
29. Ibid., Jan. 7, 1884.
30. Ibid., Jan. 21, 1884.
31. *Bradstreet,* March 1, 1884, 136.
32. Phila. *Press,* Jan. 23, 1884.
33. Ibid., Feb. 4, 1884.
34. *Iron Age,* Jan. 24, 1884, 19.
35. New York *Tribune,* Jan. 23, 1884.
36. Burlington archives, Perkins to Forbes, Jan. 29, 1884.
37. New York *Times,* Feb. 7, 1884.

38. Ibid.
39. New York *Tribune*, Jan. 29, 1884.
40. In denying that he sold any of the stock in this road, Gould declared he owned 73,000 shares. *Railroad Herald*, March 18, 1884, 17.
41. New York *Tribune*, Sept. 23, 1891, states definitely that Gould supported White in his original Lackawanna ventures.
42. New York *Times*, March 27, 1884.
43. *Bradstreet*, March 29, 1884, 200.
44. This is the adjective used by the New York *Tribune*, April 2, 1884, in characterizing the drop in Western Union.
45. This is the statement of a financial reporter in the Phila. *Press* of July 21, 1891, some years after the event.
46. Ibid., Jan. 20, 1888.
47. Phila. *North American*, May 16, 1884.
48. Phila. *Press*, May 21, 1884; Phila. *North American*, May 21, 1884.
49. New York *Herald*, May 24, 1884.
50. Ibid., May 27, 1884.
51. New York *Times*, May 25, 1884.
52. Phila. *Press*, Nov. 30, 1885.
53. Phila. *North American*, Feb. 25, 1884.
54. Murat Halstead and J. Frank Beale, Jr.: *Life of Jay Gould*, 85.
55. Ibid.
56. That this was the effect of the arrangement was the statement made after Gould's death by his persistent newspaper critic, the New York *Times*, Dec. 4, 1892. The agreement, according to this source, made Woerishoffer a bull on the market. The Phila. *Press*, May 11, 1886, asserts, on the contrary, that Woerishoffer lost in the Gould-created June rise.
57. New York *Times*, June 8, 1884.
58. New York *Herald*, June 11, 1884.
59. New York *Mail & Express*, July 14, 1884.
60. *Bradstreet*, Aug. 2, 1884, 72.
61. Phila. *North American*, Aug. 23, 1884.
62. This remark is noted in Phila. *Press*, Sept. 1, 1887.

CHAPTER XXV

Gould Trades: September 1884–1886

Gould in the fall of 1884 was again successful as a man of business. Although his prestige as a trader had been impaired by the events of May and June, it was restored by the turn of events in July and August. His position as a man of wealth was dependent upon the maintenance of the market value of his holdings in Missouri Pacific, Western Union, Manhattan, and Union Pacific. While his holdings cannot be determined even with approximate accuracy, it is nevertheless clear that he had not finished his program of liquidation. He had arranged his affairs, paid off some loans, rearranged others, and above all he had escaped insolvency. He was still, however, interested in a rising market—in fact a rising market was essential to enable him to pay his debts and retire from the speculative markets.

His liquidation program was frustrated by the recurrence of the market decline which he had succeeded in stemming in the summer of 1884. Business deterioration and severity of railroad competition, which had occasioned so much of the trouble in 1883, was intensified in the fall of 1884. The rate wars continued. They were not to be solved by Gould nor by agreements among independently owned corporations led by aggressive personalities. They were destined to be solved by the emergence of a commanding figure in the railroad industry, by a personality who had the loyalty and confidence of a large army of investors. This Gould never had. His following consisted largely of traders ever ready to engage in some transaction promising large speculative profits. The man who more than any other was beginning to command the loyalty of investors and who was destined soon to emerge from his position as a junior member of a banking house into a position of national eminence was Morgan.

By the fall of 1884, however, his time had not yet arrived. The forces which were to produce a new wave of rate wars, and to bring on a renewed break in railroad security prices were deep and far-reaching. Vanderbilt and the Pennsylvania were at sword's ends over the West Shore and the South Pennsylvania projects. Both the Grand Trunk and the Lackawanna refused to pool, and in January, 1885, the eastern pool broke down.

Though Gould looked with some concern upon this development, he did nothing. The market was dull and narrow, and although he still had large blocks of Wabash, Union Pacific, and Lackawanna for sale, it was impossible to unload any further. The Wabash stock was unsalable; the market for Union Pacific stock was not of the best; the buying from New England was almost entirely gone. Much of the stock was in the hands of speculators and traders, who took advantage of slight price advances to dispose of their holdings.

The market for the Lackawanna, however, was strong. Gould apparently believed that it was possible to lead the market out of its dullness with the Lackawanna as a market leader. In the third week in January, with the price in the lower 80s, Gould transferred 10,000 shares of stock to his name.[1] Almost immediately after the announcement of this news the market moved forward with Lackawanna in the lead. There was, however, no sign of investment buying. The war among the anthracite roads, the rate wars among eastern trunk-line properties, the persistent gunfire exchanged between the Pennsylvania and the Vanderbilt interests, furnished the background for a drab business picture. The effort made by Gould and other market operators to interpret the rise in terms of a forthcoming boom in trade brought in some buying, but the sophisticated traders were emboldened by the rise to enter into a considerable number of short-selling contracts. A distinguished journal declared flatly that those people who believe that the rise in security prices was discounting trade prospects would soon be "undeceived." [2]

It is probable that Gould took advantage of the rise engendered by the upward movement of the Lackawanna to sell some of his holdings in Western Union and Union Pacific.[3] He found, however, that he had too much company on the selling side, and in order to discourage such selling, he adopted another unique tactical trading trick which caught the attention of an admiring financial community. Since the break of Western Union to below 50 in May of 1884, the price of the stock in the middle of February, 1885, despite all Gould's efforts, was still in the lower 60s. In the midst of his selling campaign he learned that John Jacob Astor was also selling. To an ordinary trader, to a man of the type of Jay Cooke, in the early seventies, or of Villard in the early eighties, a supporting program would probably represent the counterattack. When Cooke's friends sold Northern Pacific bonds in 1872 and 1873, Cooke bought to support the market, and when Villard's friends sold Northern Pacific and Oregon Transcontinental in the summer of 1883, Villard also bought. When, however, Astor sold Western Union, Gould sent his faithful Connor into the board room to sell, and not to buy. Connor sold 12,000 shares. It was another Gould stage play, representing, in the language of one of the financial writers of the day, "simply one of those surprises for which Mr. Gould is famous. . . ." [4] In the next three days the price of Western Union broke from 63 to 58. Though this price decline might have interfered with Gould's program of further liquidation, outside liquidation on the declining market was assuredly discouraged.

In the face of the weakness of Western Union and Missouri Pacific, Lackawanna rose by the middle of February to 100. It was not clear whether White was leading another move against the short interest or whether Gould was directing the movement. In any event, at the higher prices, Gould sold.

By the second week of March the opportunity had gone. The reduction in the New York Central dividend to a 4 per cent annual basis and the continued cutting of rates discouraged even the most optimistic trader. The New York Central's dividend reduction was a hard blow to investor confidence. Many investors had come to look upon the stock as exempt from ordinary risks; they considered it as a sort of bond on which 8 per cent interest was owed.[5] By the end of the month a heavy price break was the prelude to a decline which lasted for the entire month of April. Gould, recognizing that liquidation was impossible, left the financial district for a trip to the South. In May the decline, led by the strong investment stocks, continued. Gould meanwhile had returned and issued his customary batch of hopeful statements.

The trading community recognized that he was their leader, and that since the break in the markets of May, 1884, he had been a major factor in every important change. "Whatever may have been the diversified opinions of speculators at large before," declared the financial column of a New York newspaper, "recent occurrences have solidified them into one generally accepted belief, that Jay Gould is and has been the main and principal support, the chief thinker and mover in nearly all the speculative deals for more than a year, and that others who at times have seemed to be chiefs were only lieutenants possessed of ability to obey orders with [sic] discretionary power." [6] Gould nevertheless misinterpreted the business and railroad situation. The dissolution of the pool had produced a spirit of helplessness. Adams, then president of the Union Pacific, has left a touching account of the utter degradation of spirit among the officers present at one of the last pool meetings. They were assembled, he said, in the office of Fink, the pool commissioner. "It struck me as a somewhat funereal gathering. Those composing it were manifestly at their wits' ends. They evidently felt, one and all, that something had got to be done; yet no one knew what to do. Everything had been tried and everything had failed. Mr. Fink's great costly organization was all in ruins, and no one felt any faith in new experiments. Yet if events were allowed to take their course unchecked the result was inevitable. They all reminded me of men in a boat in the swift water above the rapids of Niagara. They were looking one at another in blank dismay, and asking 'What next?' and no one could tell what next." [7]

It was clear to all, including even those who see only upon the basis of established facts, that prolonged war was inevitable. The trunk-line situation was reduced to utter prostration. Eastbound rates from Chicago to New York dropped to a level which inflicted a loss to the carrying railroad of from $1.50 to $1.80 per ton.[8] Even the highly profitable ore traffic was carried at losing rates,[9] while grain rates from Chicago dropped to a fraction above two mills per ton mile.[10]

The suicidal rate war was pressed by all the eastern trunk lines. With elimination of pools, co-operation among the roads was not possible. It was a free-for-all fight, and the situation soon grew desperate. "It seemed to my mind," said one railroad president, "as though something was absolutely necessary to be done to save the railroads of this country from utter ruin and destruction. . . ." [11] The leading journal of the iron and steel industry declared that the war had "more of the characteristics of the Commune than of a conservative management which commands the confidence of investors." [12] The rate war was described by another observer, a few years after the event, as "one of the most unrelenting and bitter railroad wars ever seen in this or in any other country." [13]

It seemed as though the railroads, strong and weak alike, were drifting in mid-ocean, without a savior in sight. Formal organizations, traffic divisions, and informal agreements had failed. No personality in whom people had sufficient confidence, to whom railroad managements and investors alike could entrust their problems, had come forth to solve the situation.

Here entered the paradox of paradoxes. Gould was convinced that he was the leader in whom investors and railroad managements would repose their confidence and to whom they would entrust their properties in the belief that thereby they would receive fair treatment. As one who commanded the policies of particular railroads, he was quick to take advantage of any opportunity afforded him to enrich the revenues of those roads. He apparently believed, nevertheless, that as a measure of desperation, in the absence of anything better, railroad managements and investors would respond to his leadership.

In mid-May, accordingly, personally and by letter, he asked the trunk lines if they would co-operate in the restoration of rates. He sent a wire to president Roberts of the Pennsylvania, stating that Sloan of the Lackawanna, and John A. Stewart, trustee of the West Shore, were willing to join in such an effort. Roberts replied that he would be glad to co-operate. Gould also wired King, president of the Erie, and King declared that he, too, would co-operate. He sent a wire to Rutter, president of the New York Central, who referred it to a vice president. The latter in a long and involved letter declared that the Pennsylvania and the Erie were not really co-operating. They had, he said, expressed only "a willingness to co-operate." It was the sort of letter which might be expected from an attorney or some judicially minded person, and not from an active businessman schooled in making decisions. The letter must have been carefully drafted in an effort to throw the onus for the continued conflict upon competitive properties.

Justification of the New York Central's point of view was revealed by the end of the week. Despite the co-operative offer made by the Pennsylvania, that road within a few days ordered a sharp reduction in passenger rates.[14] Roberts had sized the situation up better than had Gould, recognizing, as Gould evidently did not, that Vanderbilt had left his childish things behind him. He had now grown to full intellectual maturity. He was clad in fighting armor, and it must have been a shock to Gould to learn that Vanderbilt would no longer conciliate.

Gould as a leader in eastern trunk-line circles was therefore a failure. His settlement effort was recognized for what it was—a scheme to elevate the stock market. "Never did such a stock-jobbing scheme fall flatter," declared one financial writer, who as a rule was more sympathetic to Gould than were many others.[15]

Losses no longer appalled Vanderbilt; he was becoming inured to them. His income and the value of his estate had dropped sharply. The New York Central had reduced its dividend by 50 per cent, and for months the road had earned little more than interest.[16] The war of local rates between the West Shore and the New York Central continued in all its bitterness. The former did not earn operating expenses. Out of his rich experience Gould found justification for the following sweeping conclusion: "No such railroad war was ever before seen; it has been the bitterest in all my experience."[17]

Gould's initiative, far from settling the rate war, probably increased its severity. The slashing rate cut by the Pennsylvania was followed by a hurried conference at the offices of the Trunk Line Commissioners. No road showed any evidence of compromise. The Pennsylvania was particularly aggressive. A prominent official of that road spoke sarcastically of both Gould and Vanderbilt. Surely, said this officer, Gould favored restoration of rates; today he wants to aid in the settlement of the rate war, and thirty days from now he is just as likely as not to be on the other side of the fence. Vanderbilt will not consent today, continued the official, but within thirty days he "may move heaven and earth" to do this.[18]

All hands now appeared to be united in a confession of insolvency. Another meeting of presidents, convened at the suggestion of the Grand Trunk, accomplished nothing. The representatives of the West Shore and the Lackawanna were not even present. The meeting emphasized to the mind of one writer "the apparent hopelessness of a solution of a Trunk Line difficulty in the near future." [19] Representatives of the railroad pool meanwhile appeared before a Congressional committee, and suggested that Congress protect the railroads from wrecking each other.[20]

From this impasse, the solution came from an unexpected quarter. As in political history, so in industrial and financial history, the unexpected frequently happens. The emergence of great political characters as viewed in the perspective of historical development can be satisfactorily explained. To statesmen who carry the responsibility for the making of policies, such crystal-clear visions are not often possible. In fact there is little evidence of the clear-cut, hindsight vision of the historian being adopted as a matter of positive policy by the statesmen struggling in the morass of daily routine work for a light to the future. And so it is in many a field of financial and industrial history. The appearance of Rockefeller in the early seventies to stabilize an almost hopeless price war in the oil industry, the emergence of Carnegie as a cost-reducing factor in the steel rail industry, the leadership of Harriman in the late nineties as a rebuilder of the Union Pacific which government expert representatives insisted had little value, and whose securities were being sold by well-informed investors—all these events were unexpected.

And so in the summer of 1885 there emerged a striking business personality who infused new life into a business corpse. This personality was that of Morgan. Morgan, although not yet nationally known to the general public, had already created a large following of investors. He had sold large blocks of railroad and United States Government bonds both in this country and abroad. The market appreciation on government bonds had won him many business friends. Morgan was not a market trader, nor did he dominate the policies of business enterprises to benefit himself personally. He was on the boards of the New York Central, the Western Union, and numerous other properties, as a banker and as the representative of investors. Investors knew that; they believed that they could rely upon him, and he was confident that they would follow him.

When he returned from Europe in May, 1885, he began negotiations almost immediately for the settlement of disputes between the Pennsylvania and the Vanderbilt groups over the West Shore and the South Pennsylvania. In these discussions Gould was ignored. With the knowledge of pending negotiations, informed buying produced a substantial rise in the stock market. Gould, with no such knowledge, took advantage of the opportunity to sell.

Here was a market tailor-made for Gould, one for which he had long waited. Here was his opportunity, almost heaven-sent, to enable him after a prolonged period of four years to complete his liquidation. He sold more of his Lackawanna, and also of his Union Pacific of which early in May, 1885, he still had 50,000 shares.[21] Toward the end of the second phase of the boom late in July, Adams, the Union Pacific president, stated publicly that Gould was selling many of his stocks, including Union Pacific.[22]

Gould's policy of selling his speculative holdings on this Morgan-sponsored rise was accompanied by an almost unconcealed show of resentment against the railroad settlement in which he had been ignored. He was a man of influence and a leading factor in the southwestern picture, but whether or not he knew it, he had lost his power in eastern territory. To think that Morgan had thus succeeded where he had failed must have been galling, and his sense of personal frustration warped his business judgment. His actions indicate that he went beyond his liquidating program. While the general list was buoyant in late July, the Gould stocks were heavy, and rumors spread that Gould was short of leading stocks.[23] By late July he had become pessimistic. Some weeks before, he had predicted the return of prosperity and a rise in market values, but now, he insisted, the market was on the verge of calamity. After Union Pacific declined to less than 50, Connor, his leading broker, sent out tips to sell.[24] Gould openly expressed his contempt for the Morgan efforts. His market influence by this time waned almost to the vanishing point, and those who had followed his judgment profited little. The general list advanced, particularly the Vanderbilt stocks, but the Gould stocks declined. Union Pacific broke sharply. It was known late in July, when Gould assumed the lead in an effort to puncture the boom, that he had sold his Union Pacific, and this was the stock which he had stated only two months before he had inventoried at a price of 90 and which would soon reach that point.[25]

Security buyers, however, were watching closely the activities of Morgan, and they grew ever more confident that he would follow up the West Shore agreement with an all-inclusive rate settlement. Despite the fact that little was accomplished in adjusting the rates to a satisfactory level, the market continued its advance in July and August. The buyers may not have liked the continuing rate wars, but they were confident that Morgan would soon be as successful in ending the general war as he had been in settling the Pennsylvania-Vanderbilt differences.

Morgan unlike Gould did not make a settlement overnight—a settlement which although superficially successful was fundamentally delusive, proposed mainly as a means of affecting the stock market. Morgan, in preparing the ground carefully, communicated with railroad presidents and their traffic executives. By September he had secured no results and despite the West Shore settlement, rates continued to decline. In mid-August the demoralization at Chicago and other western points was as severe as at any time since the beginning of the war, and three weeks later Chicago-New York grain rates reached another record low.[26]

The renewed rate war dampened speculative and investment hopes, and selling in the security market again appeared. The Vanderbilt stocks were particularly weak and Gould by late August and early September was still unable to complete the liquidation of his speculative holdings. The market did not long remain depressed. Morgan continued his efforts to reach an agreement, and by the last week in September results began to appear. For the first time in the history of the war there were indications of an early peace. The trunk-line presidents met on September 22. Although they did not organize a pool, they did unanimously agree to raise westbound rates.[27] Since the increase was not scheduled to go into effect until October 1, railroad earnings would not be immediately affected.

The security markets nevertheless revived. Reports persisted that Morgan would cement corporate relationships in eastern territory by throwing the Reading under control of the Pennsylvania. At this time, however, he was not successful in eliminating the Reading sore spot. The stockholders and junior bondholders of the road still entertained great hopes of the future earning power of their property. Before consenting to follow Morgan's leadership, security holders were destined to travel through a valley of bitter experience and disastrous financial losses. It was not until the middle nineties that Morgan finally achieved that mastery which made him the leader of American security interests.

The possibility of a general settlement was nevertheless widely entertained throughout the fall. Early in October the security market entered into another boom which soon surpassed in scope and virility the summer rise. Gould now had the opportunity of unloading the rest of his Union Pacific. For some weeks he had been publicly reported as pessimistic on the future market position of that stock. Its price, however, rose 50 per cent between August and November, and Gould finally liquidated his commitments. He no longer found it necessary to conceal his true market position. He insisted that prices were too high, and that only the cheapness of money allowed manipulators to advance prices.[28] The surprising strength of the market trapped a number of venturesome short traders, and two of the determined market antagonists of Gould finally failed. One was the redoubtable Smith, his old Erie associate; and the other, Soutter, who had aided Kneeland in the fight in behalf of the Metropolitan against Gould. Both traders made large profits in the violent market break in the spring of 1884; both overstayed their markets.

Professional traders, armchair prognosticators and interpreters failed to appreciate the real market position. Instead of a corrective reaction the market entered into a new burst of strength, for Morgan had succeeded by early November in promoting a settlement of the eastern railroad war that to many observers had all the earmarks of finality. The agreements which had been made at intervals in the preceding three decades were usually preceded by concessions. A pool was usually arranged and the traffic divided. The efficacy of such traffic divisions had been almost destroyed by the spring of 1885, and Gould was among the railroad men early to appreciate the fact.

Morgan made a sincere effort to produce a communion of interest by attacking the general causes of unsettlement, and avoiding the mistakes which had been made in earlier efforts. Morgan reached the conclusion that it was possible to make an all-around settlement, even though each cause of irritation was not removed. He was mistaken, however, in placing undue reliance upon administrative machinery. The agreement which was made by trunk-line presidents on November 5, 1885, contained some distinct improvements over the earlier pacts. This was not an ordinary understanding for the division of business. Each line pledged itself to act with its associates on all rate-making actions, and to take no independent action on any question which affected the welfare of the others. The agreement made another revolutionary advance. The eastern trunk lines for the first time assumed responsibility for maintaining through rates with their western connections and definitely pledged themselves to refuse to divide rates or extend traffic facilities to any connection which refused to maintain rates.

The elaborate machinery to enforce the agreement made a profound impression on some observers. The contract was declared "not only ironclad, but copper-bottomed and steel-riveted in its traffic details." [29] The first result of the settlement was satisfactory. Rates were restored to the figure prevailing before the beginning of the general smash more than a year before.

The effect of this new contract upon the market was spectacular. Except for a short interval in late August and September the market had been rising almost steadily since June. On many stocks the price had recovered a large part of the losses suffered in the panic smash of May, 1884; on a number of others there had been no reaction worthy of notice throughout late September and the entire month of October. The announcement of the new trunk-line contract produced another violent rise. The public was in on a large scale and speculation ran wild. Gould was able finally to complete his liquidation. Despite all rumors to the contrary, he was selling out. It was difficult for financial analysts to adjust themselves to this new arrangement in the last stage of the advance in December, 1885. When Vanderbilt died suddenly the correspondent of an authoritative London weekly, after describing Gould as "the biggest toad in the puddle," [30] insisted further that he was selling the market short.

Gould's announcement early in December, when the market was still moving dizzily upward, that he had decided to retire was consequently taken lightly. One trade observer flatly remarked that the statement was of little importance.[31] He had announced his retirement from speculative activities a number of times before, and this announcement, it was believed, was probably part of some as yet undisclosed venture. Gould's trading career was finished. If he had intended seriously to take the leadership in breaking the rising market which set in in the summer of 1885, he must have been disappointed; although it is probable that he had no such intention. He was happy that he had successfully unloaded his speculative holdings, after a long, patient, grinding campaign lasting over four years. His retirement was genuine. Early in the spring of 1886 when questions were raised about his retirement, he testified before a Congressional committee that he had neither bought nor sold stocks since the beginning of the year.[32] Some two months later, approached by a reporter, Gould insisted that he had neither bought nor sold a share of Western Union nor of any other stock, for that matter, since the first of January. "I am out of the Street, and nothing whatever could induce me to go back into it." [33]

In the second half of 1886 another market rise developed, and again Gould denied any participation in security trading. The boom was ushered in by another Morgan move. Settlement of the Pennsylvania-Vanderbilt war in the summer of 1885 had not realized all the anticipated results. The major deterrent was the financial condition of the Reading. Though its traffic density was heavy, its financial structure was overburdened with bonds. In the middle eighties it was in receivership for the second time. Meanwhile Gowen had lined up with Garrett of the Baltimore & Ohio. Gowen wanted a line to Pittsburgh, and Garrett a line to New York. Both projects were aimed at the Pennsylvania, and the latter retaliated on both fronts. By building the Schuylkill Valley lines, it competed with the Reading for a share of its anthracite traffic. It fought the Baltimore & Ohio by refusing to allow that road to use its New York line. Rate and passenger fare cuts followed.

In 1886 Morgan renewed his efforts to reorganize the Reading, and by mid-September, 1886, "without parade, almost without suspicion," [34] the troubles of this eastern property under his careful handling were solved. Gowen retired from the property. A voting trust was set up whose policy, in the words of a director, would be the prevention of "disastrous warfare" between the Reading and the Pennsylvania, or other roads.[35] The security markets responded immediately, and prices rose rapidly. Trading in Reading was enormous. On one day soon after the settlement 25 per cent of the volume of the stock exchange was in securities of that company. The market rise proved to be one of the most extraordinary in history. The railroad settlement had been accomplished in a background of favoring conditions. Money was easy, and a supply of money under the then existing banking system was a market factor of great importance. Eastern railroad earnings had been improving, and there was also general expectations that a pool of the granger roads would improve their earnings. The lead given by the Morgan-Reading settlement soon resulted in a "fever of speculation." [36] By the end of November the weekly volume of trading was more than double that of two weeks before. Speculation in some respects exceeded anything ever before witnessed in Wall Street.

Again, as in the market of the year before, the Gould stocks did not participate in the rise. In the face of the upward movement Gould stuck to his decision. Six months later he insisted again that he had been out of the market since January, 1886. "I shall never under any circumstances," he emphasized, "be a speculator again." [37]

In mid-December the market collapsed. Gould had stated only a few days before that the market "was the wildest speculation he had ever seen." [38] Money rates rose from 6 to 75 per cent; and two days after that to 100 per cent. This was followed within the next three days by a drop of 2 per cent. It was one of the most skillfully executed stock-market breaks on record. The manipulation of money rates was evidence that some person or group with large resources was behind the break. This, together with the remarks made by current observers, friendly and unfriendly, led to the conclusion that the spectacular market revulsion was engineered by Gould, or with his direct connivance and support. To the bitter New York press critic there was no doubt that Gould was selling. Gould himself said, "I am glad that I am no longer in Wall Street." [39]

As speculator and trader, Gould in all probability ended his career in 1885. Speculation had brought him to the edge of disaster. Masterful trading negotiations with his trading foes in June, 1884, not shrewd trading, saved him from collapse. A new personality, Morgan, grappling with old forces, had created selling markets which enabled Gould to liquidate. He took opportunity of these advantages and regained some of his losses. His net trading loss was, however, heavy. As a stock-market trader he must be classed as a failure.

NOTES FOR CHAPTER XXV

1. Phila. *Press*, Jan. 23, 1885.
2. London *Economist*, Feb. 28, 1885, 255.
3. Phila. *Press*, Feb. 14, 1885, estimated that in the previous week Gould had sold at least 50,000 shares of Western Union and Union Pacific.
4. Ibid., Feb. 15, 1885.
5. *R. R. Gaz.*, Sept. 12, 1884, 670.
6. New York *Tribune*, May 18, 1885.
7. Report of the Select Committee in Interstate Commerce, Senate, 49th Congress, 1st Session, 1886, 1207-8, Adams.
8. Phila. *Press*, May 21, 1885.
9. *Iron Age*, June 11, 1885, 16.
10. *Bradstreet*, May 9, 1885, 316.
11. M. E. Ingalls, president, Cincinnati, Indianapolis, St. Louis & Chicago, cited in *Ry. Review*, April 11, 1885, 170.
12. *Iron* Age, May 7, 1885, 24.
13. *Stockholder*, September 6, 1887.
14. New York *Tribune*, May 26, 1885; Phila. *Press*, May 25, 1885.
15. Phila. *Press*, May 25, 1885.
16. Early in January, 1885, the New York Central informed the Railroad Commissioners that it was earning only its interest. *Bradstreet*, Jan. 17, 1885, 39. Since then conditions had become worse.
17. New York *Tribune*, May 24, 1885.
18. Phila. *Press*, June 1, 1885.
19. *Bradstreet*, June 13, 1885, 396.
20. Ibid., May 30, 1885, 364.
21. *Chron.*, May 9, 1885, 570.
22. Phila. *Press*, July 29, 1885.
23. *Bradstreet*, July 25, 1885, 57.
24. Phila. *Press*, July 25, 1885.
25. Ibid., May 16, 1885.
26. *Iron* Age, Sept. 17, 1885, 23; *Bradstreet*, Sept. 12, 1885, 169.
27. Ibid., Sept. 26, 1885, 201.

28. Ibid., Oct. 3, 1885, 217; Oct. 10, 1885, 233.
29. Phila. *Press*, Nov. 6, 1885.
30. London *Economist*, Dec. 26, 1885.
31. *Iron Age*, Dec. 3, 1885, 25.
32. Labor Troubles in the South and West, Report No. 4174, House of Representatives, 49th Congress, 2nd Session, 1886, Part 2, 64, Gould.
33. New York *Tribune*, July 5, 1886.
34. New York *Times*, Sept. 19, 1886.
35. *R. R. Gaz.*, Sept. 24, 1886, 664.
36. London *Economist*, Dec. 25, 1886, 1605.
37. Phila. *Press*, June 25, 1887. Many years later a writer in the *Wall Street Journal*, Nov. 15, 1924, declared positively that Gould participated in this market. This writer believed that history had not recorded "a Wall Street operator of larger courage or one that could be a better appraiser of stock markets, their quality and their capacity, than was J. Gould." On the market of 1886, he continued, Gould sold most of his stocks in the rising market, sold short, and lost heavily. But he changed his mind, bought at higher prices, and made "the biggest winning that ever came to him in any market." It is impossible to assess the value of statements of journalists made years after the event. It is possible, despite all visible evidence to the contrary, that the statement may be true; that Gould had spoken an untruth to a Congressional committee in May and to a newspaper reporter in July; that in fact, he was heavily engaged in the market, first on the down side, then on the up. It is not probable, however, that he could have kept these operations secret; that he could have denied them openly. All these things are of course probable. The statement of this journalist may perhaps be set down as a lapse of memory. The evidence supporting this conclusion is not satisfactory.
38. *Bradstreet*, Dec. 18, 1886, 393.
39. New York *Tribune*, Dec. 16, 1886.

CHAPTER XXVI

Gould Expands in Kansas and Colorado

THE Missouri Pacific in 1884 was confined largely to the state of Missouri. In addition, through stock holdings and lease contracts it controlled an extensive system in Arkansas, Texas, and Oklahoma. It had also preferential arrangements with the Texas & Pacific (commanding outlets to New Orleans and El Paso), and with the Wabash (extending the system to Chicago, Toledo and Detroit). The road had extended little after its first burst of growth in 1880 and 1881. Although it thereafter acquired a number of branch lines and built some feeders in the coal fields of southern Missouri and Kansas, its mileage early in 1885 was not substantially higher than four years before.

The territorial stability of the Missouri Pacific was part of the general equilibrium in the Missouri Valley. The roads east of the Missouri had not built lines west, and the roads west of the river had not built lines east. In southern Kansas, the Atchison served a territory free from competition. It had a written understanding with the Frisco, its partner in the construction of the Pacific Coast extension, whereby each road agreed not to build any lines in southern Kansas without permission of the other. The Atchison also had agreed not to expand east of the Missouri, and the Missouri Pacific not to expand in southern Kansas.

The Burlington's Denver extension was the first major factor which undermined this equilibrium. The war of rates that followed the Burlington's invasion of eastern Colorado was followed by the Tri-Partite compact and the dissolution of the Iowa Pool.

The competitive forces unleashed by the Burlington extension and the dissolution of the Iowa Pool were too powerful to be settled by compromise and concession. The consummation of the Tri-Partite in the waning days of 1883 stimulated Perkins's plans to add hundreds of miles in Union Pacific territory in northern Nebraska and eastern Wyoming.[1] Owing largely to the conciliatory approaches of Forbes, however, these construction programs were not immediately carried out. Forbes placed great faith in his ability to work out by personal conversations with F. L. Ames and Adams some arrangements which would block the moves that threatened to break the earning power of the participating companies. The rate truce he arranged failed. Adams felt strongly, even bitterly, about the Burlington's plans to extend its lines into Union Pacific territory. The Burlington, he thought, was planning to take advantage of the Union Pacific's weak financial position to drive it into insolvency. Perkins now learned for the first time that Adams, who was soon to become president of the Union Pacific, was considering the advisability of selling the Central Branch (since 1880 leased to the Missouri Pacific) and the St. Joseph & Western (successor to the Denver City) to the Missouri Pacific and to the Rock Island respectively. To the Burlington, such a program involved serious dangers. Two of the most aggressive roads in the Missouri Valley area would thus be introduced into the trans-Missouri region. Perkins, with remarkable power of penetration, peered through the façades Gould had set up to conceal his interests in Union Pacific policy. The Central Branch occupied a rich region in Kansas. He suspected that Clark, the operating manager of the Union Pacific, was playing into the hands of Gould with no regard for the real interests of that road.

Forbes, however, continued his policy of caution. He suggested that in the tight condition of the money market it was unlikely that any large construction program would be undertaken by the Burlington, the Union Pacific, or by any Gould road. He would be slow, he continued, to spend any money in occupying new ground in anticipation of a competitive battle, and, he concluded, it would be better to save money now, conserve financial strength, and carefully to avoid any measures that might involve any large new expenditures.[2]

The expansion forces were, however, only momentarily checked. A road, by getting more business from new territories, could carry more traffic at a slight increase in cost. Railroad managements thought, as did theoretical economists, in terms of static relationships. They assumed that while one factor changed, all the other factors would remain the same. They reasoned that while a particular road expanded and invaded new territory, the other roads would stand idly by. Or perhaps if they did not stand by, all the roads, having each other's territory, would again be able to reach an understanding and thereby arrest any downward movement of rates.

Another factor which modified the fundamentals underlying these territorial understandings was the sudden increase in population in western Kansas. The trunk lines had built their mileage largely in the eastern half of the state. West of the 100th meridian the state was considered a desert country, incapable of producing crops or supporting a large population. Some settlers had gone into this area shortly after 1870. Their failures had been disastrous. In 1884 and 1885, however, the situation changed for the better. Rainfall in the arid zone increased and stories spread that the climate had permanently changed. This widespread opinion was reflected in a rush of people to the arid plans of western Kansas and Nebraska and eastern Colorado. In two years, more than $30,000,000 was invested and a real-estate boom was on.[3] The desert area which had experienced so many disasters suddenly attracted many people and much money. The most significant phenomenon, however, was the rush of railroad capital into this hitherto unproductive area.

The investment of heavy capital in response to a temporary influence should not surprise the trained observer. Few indeed are the businessmen and political and military leaders, for that matter, who look ahead many years in an effort to align current trends with long-term influences. Those financial opportunities which are likely to bring results in one or two years are normally preferred to others which bring larger results in twenty years. The immediate effects normally impress businessmen and investors. It was, for example, the guarantees afforded to the railroads' earning power by the Transportation Act of 1920 which led to the investment of billions of dollars by institutional investors in the following decade, and it was the unbounded confidence in the future of the utility holding companies which led to the spectacular rise from 1925 to 1929. Investment and financial growth come in spurts and they are the result largely of short-term influences.

As the depression influences waned in the closing months of 1884, and as the tempo of returning prosperity was quickened in the early months of 1885, the deep-seated desire to maintain rate and territorial stability clashed head-on with the aggressive forces motivating railroad expansion. In the spring of 1884 the Burlington and the Union Pacific had agreed to build no roads without notifying each other,[4] and in the following summer Cable of the Rock Island, in justifying the organization of the Tri-Partite, declared that there were "already more roads than were needed both east and west of the Missouri River, and to build additional roads meant ruin to all existing lines." [5]

Forbes expressed himself in a tone of savage denunciation: "The tribe of Hinckleys, Cranes, Graves, Villards, and other cranks and thieves led by Hopkins and Gould, have built and will build Roads wherever fools with money will follow, and where three Roads stimulated by contracts, are thus built to do the work of one, it, in the very near future, leads right up to a necessity for the nearest solvent Railroad to buy the other useless ones. . . ." [6]

Against these judgments making for caution in railroad expansion policies was the policy of the determined managements of the Burlington, Northwestern, St. Paul and the Rock Island, and of course the aggressive personality of Gould. Early in 1885, the St. Paul and the Rock Island were preparing to strike for a greater share in the Colorado, Utah and the Pacific Coast traffic. Under the Tri-Partite these roads could cut on westbound traffic and the Union Pacific was obliged to participate. Adams had repeatedly expressed his determination to achieve peace in western territory, but under the Tri-Partite he was helpless in the hands of his eastern allies.

While these forces were in their developmental stage, Perkins thought that he saw an opportunity to stabilize the situation anew, without at the same time seriously endangering the interests of the Burlington. He was convinced that Adams did not know what he wanted. What the Union Pacific, as well as the Burlington and the Northwestern (the other two eastern roads with lines west of the Missouri River) needed was a peaceful arrangement among themselves, with the Rock Island and the St. Paul being held at bay on the eastern side of the river. If this situation could be maintained for another five-year period, the western lines could so thoroughly occupy the country that the temptation to build by any other road would be slight indeed.[7] A detailed plan for co-operation between the Burlington, Union Pacific, and Northwestern designed to promote these objectives was presented by Perkins in a letter to Adams in March of 1885. Perkins proposed, as a basis for bargaining, that the Union Pacific agree to give the Burlington, and perhaps also the Northwestern, all the business not covered by the Tri-Partite, and that it alone or with the Northern Pacific, lease the Oregon Railway & Navigation Company. The major roads would then agree to divide the territory. Unless such an arrangement were made, Perkins declared, there would be a trial of strength; the Burlington would expand north into Nebraska and beyond, and the Northwestern and the Union Pacific would inevitably follow. The Union Pacific, according to the Perkins proposal, would also put two Burlington men on its board of directors and eliminate the Gould element.[8] Though the plan was not approved, Perkins continued to negotiate. In May he succeeded in completing an arrangement between the roads west of Chicago, designed to stabilize rates for a six months' period. It now appeared as though the rates "were in a fair way to be reasonably maintained west of Chicago for some time to come." [9]

The agreement was not final until approved by the Burlington's board of directors, and this approval was never secured. For, before it could be carried into effect, Gould had acted and in his customary way broke the pillars of the agreement. The Missouri Pacific system was not interested in these problems. From its St. Louis and Kansas City anchors, the road extended southwest and not west into Kansas and Colorado. Gould did not choose to assume a passive attitude. This was a policy alien to his temperament. In compliance with the letter of the agreement, he did not invade the Atchison's territory in southern Kansas. He was not prepared, however, to go along with the spirit of the understanding, and to remain passive and refuse to share in the rich traffic of southern Kansas, crossed and recrossed by his major Kansas competitor. He therefore turned aggressive, though indirectly and unobtrusively. The Missouri Pacific, with which the Atchison had made the agreement, performed no act of aggression. The aggressive move was made by Gould personally. Viewing the southern Kansas railroad field in the early eighties, he observed the growth of a small road—the St. Louis, Fort Scott & Wichita,[10] organized to build a line between Fort Scott and Wichita. The line was opened for business in July of 1881. In 1882 Gould acquired a majority of its stock at $10 a share. It was not clear whether the Atchison was aware of Gould's interest. If it was, it did nothing to counteract it. Perhaps the Atchison was not aware of Gould's ability to interpret financial and industrial agreements to his own advantage. In any event, the Atchison at first pursued a passive policy, but when the Wichita in the spring of 1883 began to build west into its territory, it grew restive. The company's management became convinced that the Missouri Pacific was financing the Wichita's extension, and, according to a Boston observer, a quarrel appeared to be imminent.[11] Meanwhile the road continued to expand. It was not until the summer of 1884 that Hopkins, an official of a number of Gould's railroads, was appointed president of the property, thus making it clear for the first time (certainly to the outside public) that the road was under the Missouri Pacific influence.

While Gould was thus expanding through the media of the Wichita in southern Kansas, he was also moving along different lines in northern Kansas and southern Nebraska. In this section, the Missouri Pacific in 1885, aside from its extension from Atchison to Omaha, controlled only a nominal mileage. However, it operated, though it did not own, the Central Branch. The road was poorly maintained; most of the track in 1884, for example, was still laid with its original iron rail, and, in the opinion of the Kansas commission, was so battered that both life and property were "in constant jeopardy in transit over them." [12] Gould persisted in his efforts to buy the road, and Adams was not entirely unfriendly to the proposal. Perkins feared that Gould's acquisition would be followed by its extension to Denver. He finally negotiated an understanding with Adams, not reduced to writing, and never submitted to the respective boards, by which Adams agreed not to sell the road nor to take other territorial action without previous notice and consultation.

By the spring of 1885, therefore, Perkins believed that he had succeeded in stabilizing competition in Kansas and Nebraska.

Late in May, however, he learned that a new railroad company organized in Kansas to build a line to Denver, with Gould's name attached to it, had just been announced in the public press. He was certain that Gould by taking this step "intended to bulldoze the Union Pacific into making such arrangements about the Central Branch as might be agreeable to the Missouri Pacific." [13]

Meanwhile the rate structure began to soften. The St. Paul withdrew from one of the traffic pools and slashed rates on dressed beef from Omaha. "It [seemed] as though the St. Paul road," wrote a Burlington official, "was bound to wreck itself and everybody else if it [could]." [14] Trouble continued to accumulate, and within a few weeks after the St. Paul's action, the Atchison announced its withdrawal from the transcontinental pool.

The rate wars were followed by breakdowns in territorial stability. Plans which had long been maturing were now put into execution. The Burlington had long considered the idea of building an extension to the Twin Cities. Ever since the St. Paul in the early eighties had completed its line to Omaha, "making practically a new line all the way from Chicago," the Burlington considered the wisdom of allowing "so powerful a competitor" to secure a foothold in the Burlington's country without the latter retaliating by going north.[15] In 1885, adopting the same tactics that had been followed in Nebraska, the road arranged for the building of a St. Paul line through a corporate affiliate—the Chicago, Burlington & Northern. The Burlington executed a contract for the interchange of traffic with this newly organized concern and agreed to purchase its bonds with the understanding that they soon would be exchanged for the stock at par. It also acquired a large block of the stock of its affiliate.[16]

This was an invasion of the territory of the Rock Island and the St. Paul, the two allies of the Union Pacific in the inglorious Tri-Partite pact. The Burlington's invasion was described by a leading Chicago railroad journal as "the most important recent event in the western railway field." [17]

Both the St. Paul and the Rock Island reacted promptly. A few months thereafter the directors of the former met secretly in New York City, and, according to a leading eastern railroad journal, decided to begin work on the extension from central Iowa to Kansas City.[18] This retaliatory move was likely to hurt the Gould system, since the line would penetrate local territory served by the Missouri Pacific and the Wabash.

The Rock Island, like the St. Paul, was not prepared to permit invasion of its territory by the Burlington without retaliation. Its management, stirred even more than that of the St. Paul, became actuated by an "indefinite desire to extend itself in all directions." [19]

The opening gun in the battle for territorial expansion in the West had now been fired. The Burlington had invaded the territory of the St. Paul and the Rock Island, and the latter two had invaded the territory of the Burlington. The battle in the Missouri River Valley had not yet spread to wider areas. It was still possible to limit the warfare to the three major contestants. There was no compelling reason why the Union Pacific and the Burlington should not remain at peace in the broad territorial stretches of Kansas, Nebraska, and Wyoming.

This reasoning, however, did not reckon with Gould. It is not clear what pressure Gould exerted upon Adams to force a violation of his personal understanding with Perkins, with reference to the Central Branch. Adams had repeatedly declared that the breakdown in rates in territory common to both the Burlington and the Union Pacific was due to the Burlington. His Central Branch policy might also have been occasioned by the Gould pressure which Perkins had so frequently described as "bulldozing." Gould might have threatened to parallel the Central Branch with a Denver extension in competition with the Union Pacific. There is considerable support for the latter idea in the fact that Adams had considered the building of a proposed extension of the Central Branch to a connection with the Kansas Pacific.[20] A few months before Adams had sent out surveyors to work up the prospective right of way, the story spread that a new Colorado company was planning to build east from Denver to a connection with the Gould-controlled Wichita in southeastern Kansas. Perkins believed this story was true, although he qualified his judgment with the reservation that perhaps Gould was going into the venture in order to force Adams to sell the Central Branch to Gould.[21]

By early fall of 1885 Gould had bought up a number of small lines in eastern Kansas, and with the aid of some local construction he was ready to proceed with the building of a new line to Denver. The new company, the Kansas Western, capitalized at $10,000,000, announced plans to build through the Central Branch country. Adams presumably found his position uncomfortable. He had sent out surveyors to make plans and to submit reports. Gould, however, needed no such help. He was not interested in reports which to him represented a waste of time, since he and his associates had often examined this territory. Before Adams was ready to execute his plans, Gould had acquired feeders, had partially built some new lines and had let out contracts for the construction of others. By these actions he was invading Union Pacific territory. Adams hastened to ward off the invasion. In September, 1885, the Central Branch lease of 1880 was modified. Gould agreed not to build into Union Pacific territory nor to construct roads in Kansas or Nebraska competitive with the Central Branch. The latter, together with the Union Pacific, agreed not to build lines competitive with the Missouri Pacific. Both Gould and Adams thus relinquished the idea of building a new Denver route.

The Missouri Pacific, freed from Union Pacific rivalry, was now at liberty to expand in northern Kansas and southern Nebraska in competition with the Burlington. The Union Pacific, freed from Missouri Pacific competition, could more effectively fight its territorial battle with the Burlington in Nebraska.

Forbes, however, was not convinced of impending danger to the Burlington. He believed that Adams had been overhasty in striking hands with Gould, thereby giving him a legal contract "upon so flimsy a guarantee as Gould's promise that 'the said line will not build competing lines.' Gould [had] as many aliases as a London professional thief and in fifteen minutes [would] find a substitute to do his bidding if he [saw] his interest in it." [22] Perkins, on the other hand, was disturbed. He proposed to Adams that the Burlington and the Union Pacific jointly build several lines and thereby minimize the cost of construction. "We deprecate premature construction and all talk of war," he wrote.[23]

Peace had, however, become impossible. It had become difficult for a major road to remain conservative, to refuse to build into new territory and to insist that the wisest policy was to refrain from incurring new burdens. While Gould by the modified Central Branch lease had thus paved the way for the opening of a potential Union Pacific-Burlington war, he was also preparing the ground for another competitive battle in southern Kansas. This struggle involved the Atchison. The territorial understanding with the Missouri Pacific had been beneficial to both properties. Much of the Atchison's earnings came from its hold on the business of southern Kansas. That region produced a large and profitable long-haul wheat traffic. Through its lines in that area, the Atchison profited also from the cattle traffic of Oklahoma.

Gould in acquiring and laying plans for expansion of the Wichita was invading the heart of the Atchison citadel. He had pushed the building program of the Wichita until the road reached a point in southern Kansas close to the major gateway for the valuable Oklahoma cattle traffic of the Atchison. The Atchison had made no move against the new competition, although by 1885 it was clear that the road was a Gould project. The Atchison was losing business, not only to the Wichita, but also to a number of new local lines in southeastern Kansas. If the Atchison retaliated, a war of rates was inevitable, and in such an eventuality the Atchison would have to absorb the entire cost. Much of its traffic moved east beyond the Missouri River. The Atchison had no through line into that territory, nor did it have any traffic alliances with roads which would absorb part of a rate reduction. The Wichita, under Gould control, had an outlet beyond the Missouri River in the Missouri Pacific, and beyond the Mississippi in the Wabash. That line was ready to cut rates and arrange through routes and divisions so as to benefit the Missouri Pacific.

It was vital for the Atchison, in order to meet this potential competition, to have an eastern line of its own. Aside from the acquisition of the Gulf, it had expanded little in the eighties. It was now destined to seize the offensive and to push into new territory. The road's management had discovered that in business, as well as in international politics, the doctrine of defense by aggression, although strictly illogical, is nevertheless eminently practical, and that in the face of an almost unanimous desire for peace, war becomes inevitable. The fight of Gould against the Burlington and the Atchison was thus partly responsible for the most promiscuous paralleling and duplication of railroad mileage in the country's history.[24]

The surveys of the Atchison in 1884 for a Chicago line led to no action. The Gould aggression in extending the Wichita through southern Kansas, however, helped the Atchison to recognize the necessity for action. The company, declared its president, had been "much too conservative during the last few years." [25] The management furthermore was convinced that the traffic agreements by which it served Chicago and the Middle West were unsatisfactory. Gould, among others, had demonstrated that a traffic agreement was practicable only if both parties had equal powers to enforce it. It was the history of such contracts, observed the Atchison wistfully in its 1886 annual report, that they were effective only so long as it was to the interest of the parties concerned to make them so, and broken as soon as they became burdensome to either party. It discovered, as did the democratic countries, one by one, from 1939 to the fall of 1941, that a policy of nonaggression invited attack from an aggressor. To defend its territory the Atchison concluded that it would be necessary to invade the territory of its opponents. "It would seem to be a fact," declared the management of this property in justification of its new policy, "that we had tempted these invasions by our own inertness rather than challenged them by an aggressive disposition." [26]

The decision to expand was reached at about the same time by the Atchison and by almost all the major lines east of the Missouri River. Each road suddenly realized that a policy of aggressive invasion was the only safe defense. The president of the Rock Island, who in the summer of 1884 had decried the building of competitive mileage, was now leading his property in a program which carried it to eastern Colorado and to southern Kansas. The Burlington, deflected by Gould's sharp trading from expansion in Kansas in the heart of the Missouri Pacific country, launched a program of construction north of the Platte River in the center of the Union Pacific territory. The St. Paul hesitated long in initiating a trans-Missouri expansion; and as late as the summer of 1887 the board was still considering the idea. It decided finally to depend upon traffic agreements for the interchange of business with roads which competed in its own territory. This was a historical decision. For the next quarter of a century its policy remained unchanged. It finally built in a period and under conditions which forced the road into a receivership at the height of the boom of the 1920s.

Through the Wichita, Gould had at small cost secured access to the traffic of southern and eastern Kansas. To the south of that line, the promoters of a local line, the Denver, Memphis & Atlantic, had been successful in securing subsidies from counties, cities and townships.[27] The management was confident of the future, and during the next year planned to build in Kansas about 1,000 miles of road. In his plans to parallel the Atchison and to extend the Missouri Pacific to Denver, Gould did not overlook the possibilities of this enterprise. In the fall of 1885, in the very heyday of its corporate expansion, he announced plans to parallel this road, just as he was then laying plans to do the same to the Union Pacific.[28] It is impossible to learn when he acquired control, or what pressure he placed upon the promoters to dispose of their interests. Although the first public statement of the control of this property by Gould was not made until October, 1886, there is little reason to doubt that Gould followed the same policy which he had with respect to the acquisition of the Wichita—he acquired a substantial interest but said nothing.

Following his Wabash tactics of 1879 and 1880, Gould endeavored to buy control of existing stub lines and feeders. By acquiring these roads, he was able, he thought, to ward off threatened competition which might result from their acquisition by other roads. On the other hand, some of the lines had light traffic density and thereby became a burden on the system. Gould understood this risk, but his mind was fixed more largely on corporate strategy. The justification of this policy was presented in a circular sent to the shareholders of the Missouri Pacific. The local lines were necessary, he said, "to protect the present traffic" of the company, and "insure its future growth." [29] Some of these roads, remarked a close observer, seemed to have little value, "except as a basis for future extensions." [30] It was the Wabash all over again.

In some of the Kansas acquisitions, however, Gould was more fortunate than he was with the Wabash. The Wichita, for example, turned out to be, in the language of the counsel of its promoters, "a perfect gold mine."[31] After Gould acquired the majority of the stock, he recognized its financial possibilities and adopted policies to insure that profits of the road remain with the Missouri Pacific.

Aside from the corporate formalities, Gould's program of branch-line acquisition was completed by the end of 1885. So were the agreements and understandings which removed the Union Pacific and the Burlington as potential competitors. By that time the grand program of railroad construction of 1886 and 1887 had begun. It was the greatest period of railroad construction in the history of the country. No new through routes were opened. Between each producing and consuming area major trunk lines had already been laid out. Though there was general recognition that competitive construction would result in financial losses, the lines were built. The forces of competition proved to be superior to all considerations of reason.

Building was confined almost entirely to western territory. For the most part, except for the Atchison's Chicago line, the program was concentrated in the area west of the Missouri River and east of the Huntington lines in California. The geographical center, as well as the origin of the expansion program, was in Kansas. It was in that state that Gould's silent aggression through a number of ostensibly independent corporations set the stage for the giant expansion of competing lines. It was in Kansas that the Atchison, finally recognizing the weakness of a defensive policy, lashed out in a battle against Gould.

As the year 1886 opened, there was "a prospect for increased business, and consequently for increased revenue, never exceeded in the history of the company" (i.e., the Missouri Pacific).[32] This language, which was applied by Gould to the destiny of his own railroad enterprise, could with equal truth be applied to the other western railroad properties. The crops were good; in Kansas they were exceptionally good. On the basis of short-term reasoning the prospects were excellent. It was therefore easy to sell bonds and stocks. Apparently all factors combined to make the next two years the banner period in the history of American railroad building. But they also served to lay the basis for financial disaster to railway investors.

Both of the major Kansas contestants, the Atchison and the

Missouri Pacific, laid plans on an extravagant scale. The Atchison, late in 1885, proposed to build 2,400 miles in Kansas alone.[33] The Missouri Pacific projected the construction of approximately 2,000 miles, and proposed to use its recent acquisitions as a base for a new line to eastern Colorado. There it made a contract with the Denver road which let it into the Colorado mountain country and made it a competitor of the Atchison. In order to accommodate the prospective increase in traffic which would rise from this new affiliation, the Denver agreed to build a third rail on its narrow-gauge road west from Pueblo. By the time the Missouri Pacific's extension was completed the third rail had also been finished. The Missouri Pacific now had a through line from the Missouri Valley to an independent connection with the Huntington system at Ogden. The Atchison, in turn, recognizing the implications of the new development, abandoned its trackage agreement with the Denver, and built a parallel line from Pueblo to Denver.

The Missouri Pacific, meanwhile, actively prosecuted its construction program. By the summer and early fall of 1886, Gould was personally supervising the building of over 1,000 miles of the Missouri Pacific. "My chief business at present," he said in September, "is to attend to the affairs of the Missouri Pacific." The cost, he continued, would be low, approximately only $12,000 a mile. The track would be laid with the best grade of steel, and oak ties would be used.[34]

The Atchison also proceeded actively with its plans. By April it had already let contracts for the building of 345 miles in Kansas, with another 811 miles to be built before the end of the year.[35] In October the company announced an increase in the number of branch lines to be built in Kansas from eighteen to fifty-two; an increase in common stock of its Kansas subsidiary from $48,000,000 to $154,000,000, and in the length of the road contemplated in that state, from 2,400 to 7,274 miles.[36]

The extravagant plans of the Atchison and the Missouri Pacific were supplemented by equally ambitious proposals of the Rock Island. The president of the latter in the fall of 1886 had publicly proclaimed the unwisdom of duplicate railroad construction. He could not, however, sacrifice his road and the interests of his stockholders to a general principle. It was essential, he insisted, that the road command a sufficient volume of traffic from the productive areas of the West. The road was also influenced by the necessity of getting a supply of coal. The management therefore decided in 1886 to extend its lines from the tip of northeastern Kansas, through the state and beyond into Pueblo where it would reach the center "of the best coal district in the west . . ." [37] and also an active lead and zinc-smelting center, which then provided about 22 per cent of the traffic of the state of Colorado.[38] Within the next three years the Rock Island, by this expansion policy, increased its mileage from 1,400 to 3,000 miles.

In part, these building programs in Kansas were stimulated by local public authorities. Kansas was one of the last states in the Union which continued to vote subsidies, both in cash and bonds, for the purpose of aiding railroad construction. The voting of public aid in 1886, when these construction programs were proceeding so rapidly, was "quite startling." [39] The race for subsidies, especially between the Missouri Pacific and the Rock Island, was unique in western railroad history. There was open bidding, both in the state legislatures and in local legislative bodies. Little is known about the detailed lobbying and negotiations between the public authorities and the railroad managers. Some of the branch lines were poorly built, some were unnecessary, and some were built along lines which were different from those contemplated in the agreement with counties or townships.[40] The subsidies reduced the cost of construction, and served in part to explain the speed with which the railroads pushed through the construction of such a large mileage in such a short time. Nearly all the lines built in 1887 by the Atchison, for example, were aided by the counties through which they passed, and so great was the help in some cases that the subsidies paid for the cost of construction.[41]

Subsidies also helped to induce investors to finance the program. It was the first time in many a year that the railroad investors were presented with proposals to advance money in partnership with governmental bodies. Because of these subsidies the cost of construction would be reduced. Indeed, on a statistical basis, Gould could demonstrate when the construction program was completed, that under his administration the bonds and

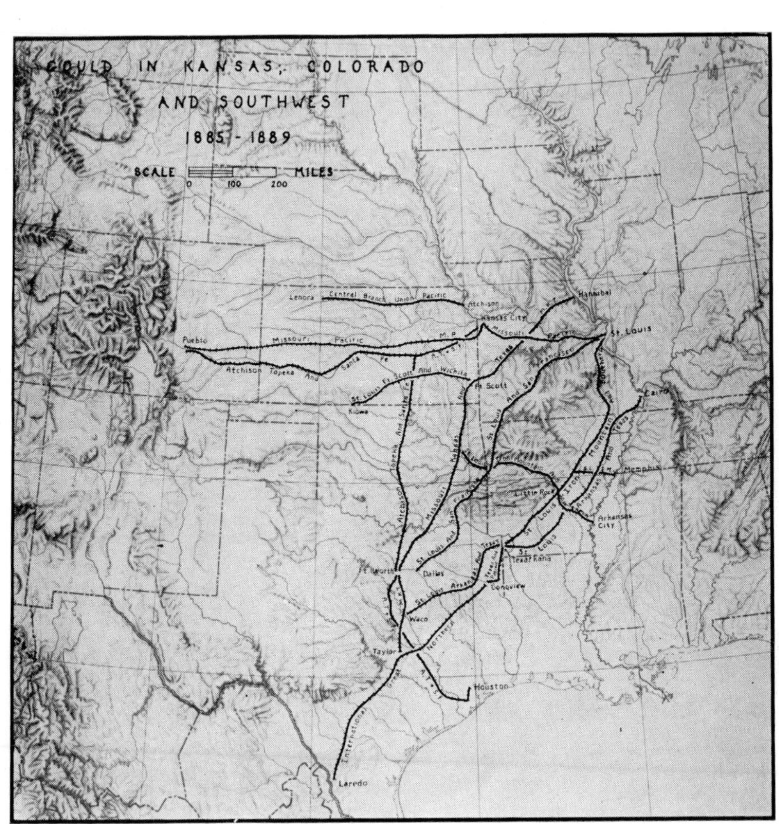
GOULD IN KANSAS, COLORADO
AND SOUTHWEST
1885 - 1889
SCALE
MILES
0
100
200
Lenora
Central Branch Union Pacific
Atchison
Hannibal
Kansas City
Missouri
Pacific
St. Louis
Pueblo
Missouri Pacific
M. P.
Atchison Topeka And Santa Fe
St. Louis Ft. Scott And Wichita
Kiowa
Ft. Scott
Texas
St. Louis And San Francisco
Atchison Topeka And Santa Fe
Cairo
Memphis
Little Rock
Iron Mountain
Arkansas City
St. Louis
Texarkana
Ft. Worth
Dallas
St. Louis Arkansas And Texas
Longview
Waco
Northern
Taylor
Great
International
Houston
Laredo

stocks outstanding per mile on the Missouri Pacific had been greatly reduced.

These programs of the Missouri Pacific and other roads were, in many respects, the most remarkable in American railroad history. Adams, president of the Union Pacific, observed that corporations had "contracted the madness, and [had] built hundreds of miles of road almost paralleling each other." [42] The programs attracted the attention of railroad interests throughout the country. Roads were built over tenantless prairies, in advance of population and of transportation-supporting industries. They were built by companies which had decided to engage in a wild race to pre-empt territory. There was no thought of securing an immediate return upon the investment. It was a war of defense by aggression. In the strict economic sense of the word, the building of these duplicate lines might be called speculative ventures, and yet they were financed by orthodox financial methods. While much of the mileage built through more settled regions, both in the Middle West and in the industrial East, were financed by speculative construction companies and by the sale of bonds at substantial discounts, these ventures penetrating an inhospitable country supported by little traffic—the very center of the plain areas in which numerous disastrous crop failures had frequently occurred—were financed mostly by sales of stock and bonds at high prices.

When the program was completed before the end of the eighties, the state of Kansas had only a few points at which the farmer could not find a station within from twelve to fifteen miles of his home to market his produce.[43] Kansas then contained a greater railroad mileage than New York, with a population of almost six million, to say nothing of its large manufacturing industries, and its location as the country's chief commercial center. It had more mileage than the state of Pennsylvania with the population of five and a quarter million to say nothing of its great steel, coal, and miscellaneous manufacturing industries, and a state which furnished more than fifty times the passenger and freight business of Kansas. Kansas, furthermore, had 1,050 miles more mileage than all the New England states combined, with their aggregation of more than five million people, to say nothing of their numerous transportation manufacturing industries.[44]

The program had been inaugurated in a period of prosperity. In accordance with expectations, the westward flow of population and the extensive railroad construction increased the earnings of the Kansas lines in 1886. In the following two years, however, western Kansas returned to an arid condition. The rains failed; crops were exceptionally poor; the livestock was starved, and what little was left was rushed to the market. Crops in other sections of the country, however, were good. Prices of wheat and corn and livestock dropped, and produced a heavy depression in agricultural values. The stimulus given to railroad traffic by the good crops of previous years, and the traffic stimulated by railroad construction was lost by the fall of 1887. Gould in the summer of the following year stopped building on the Missouri Pacific.[45] Other roads had already halted. The drop in business accompanied, if not primarily caused, by the depression in agriculture, superimposed upon the increase in parallel lines throughout the West, was followed by a break in rates without precedent in western railroad history. The western territorial equilibrium which served as a basis for railroad prosperity collapsed. A decline in traffic, combined with a demoralized rate structure, led to a wholesale passing or cutting of dividends in the late eighties, and paved the way for receivership and reorganization in the early and middle nineties. Before these results of the partially Gould-stimulated expansion program can be considered, it is necessary to analyze the Gould construction program in the southwestern part of his railroad system, in the states of Arkansas, Louisiana, and Texas.

NOTES FOR CHAPTER XXVI

1. Burlington archives, Holdredge to Potter, Jan. 14, 1884, presents the projected Burlington construction program in great detail.
2. Ibid., Forbes to Perkins, May 20, 1884.
3. An excellent description of the movement, including industrial, real-estate and railroad developments, is found in a series of articles by Frank Wilkeson in the New York *Times*, March 17, 1889; March 24, 1889; March 31, 1889. See also, by same author, *Harper's New Monthly Magazine* for April, 1886, 795.
4. Burlington archives, Perkins to Adams, Nov. 17, 1884.
5. R. R. Cable of the Rock Island, to commissioner of the Western Trunk Line Association, cited in *Ry. Review*, Aug. 16, 1884, 428.
6. Burlington archives, Forbes to Perkins, Aug. 25, 1885.
7. Ibid., Perkins to Potter, March 27, 1885.

8. Ibid., enclosing a letter from Perkins to Adams, March 19, 1885.
9. Ibid., Perkins to Ladd, May 11, 1885.
10. Known hereafter as the Wichita.
11. Boston *Transcript*, May 12, 1883.
12. Report of Board of Railroad Commissioners of Kansas, 1884, 84.
13. Burlington archives, Perkins to Adams, May 20, 1885.
14. Ibid., Potter to Perkins, May 28, 1885.
15. Ibid., Perkins to Hughitt, Feb. 17, 1888.
16. Annual report, Chicago Burlington & Quincy, 1885, cited in R. R. *Gaz.*, April 30, 1886, 308.
17. *Ry. Review*, Aug. 8, 1885, 376.
18. *R. R. Gaz.*, Jan. 29, 1886, 83.
19. Ibid., Sept. 11, 1885, 590.
20. *Ry. Review*, March 28, 1885, 150.
21. Burlington archives, Perkins to Potter, Dec. 23, 1884.
22. Ibid., Forbes to T. S. Howland, Oct. 19, 1885.
23. Ibid., Perkins to Adams, Dec. 18, 1885.
24. There is a curious effort, in a secondary source, made by an uncritical hero-worshiper, to fix the responsibility for the territorial war upon the Atchison. In an effort to dramatize the situation, a synthetic interview is presented between Gould, on behalf of the Missouri Pacific, and Strong on behalf of the Atchison. The Gould line is alleged to have kept its pledge not to invade the territory of the Atchison; and Gould, to avoid duplicate construction, is alleged to have suggested that he would take half of the lines already built by the Atchison through its newly formed subsidiary, the Southern Kansas Railway. This interview and offer is found in *The Story of the Railroad*, by Cy Warman, 121. There is no basis for this presumed interview. The evidence is convincing that Gould was the aggressor.
25. *R. R. Gaz.*, Oct. 29, 1886, 748.
26. Annual report, Atchison, Topeka & Santa Fe, 1886, 29.
27. *Ry. Review*, April 19, 1884, 205; Aug. 22, 1885, 404.
28. Ibid., for details, Sept. 12, 1885, 440.
29. *Chron.*, Jan. 23, 1886, 125.
30. *Bradstreet*, Jan. 23, 1886, 57.
31. St. Louis *Globe Democrat*, cited in New York *Tribune*, Oct. 10, 1886.
32. This was the language of Gould in the 1886 annual report of the Missouri Pacific, 7.
33. *Ry. Review*, Nov. 28, 1885, 582.
34. New York *Herald*, Sept. 20, 1886.
35. *Ry. Review*, April 24, 1886, 200.
36. Ibid., Oct. 16, 1886, 556.
37. Ibid., Dec. 10, 1887, 712.
38. Ibid.
39. Annual report, Board of Railroad Commissioners, State of Kansas, 1884, 4.
40. See, for example, ibid., 1887, 137-9.
41. *Ry. Review*, April 7, 1888, 191.
42. *R. R. Gaz.*, Dec. 21, 1888, 841.
43. This is the opinion of a traffic official of the Missouri Pacific, in State of Missouri, Statements and Testimony of Railroad Managers and others before Committee on Railroads and Internal Improvements of the Extra Session of the 34th General Assembly of Missouri, Jefferson City, 1887, 230.
44. Annual report, Board of Railroad Commissioners, State of Kansas, 1890, 8.
45. Phila. *Press*, July 18, 1888.

CHAPTER XXVII

Gould Contracts and Expands in the Southwest

In the middle eighties the Missouri Pacific system connecting St. Louis and Kansas City with Arkansas, Oklahoma, Louisiana, and Texas was the major system in the Southwest. Two north-and-south non-Gould lines operating between north Texas and the Gulf Coast had been unable to extend their lines further north, thus to make connections with the middle-western lines. One of these, the Houston, was in the hands of Huntington, who through a personal holding company, the Southern Development Company, held a majority interest in its stock. It was not clear what Huntington had in mind in acquiring control. Whatever may have been his objectives, they were frustrated by a serious personal financial reverse in the summer of 1884. Instead of expanding he was forced to contract. On the far western end he had to sell a part of his lines in California to another railroad, thereby permitting that road to compete more effectually for California business. His associates refused to extend their financial support, thus compelling him to relinquish those extensive plans which he had matured for the building of an all-rail transcontinental artery.

The other non-Gould north-south Texas line was the Gulf. The road's sturdy management refused to deal with Gould or any of his properties. The other major competitor of the Gould southwestern lines was the Frisco. Since 1881 the road singly and in conjunction with others had planned the construction of a connection with either one or the other of the non-Gould lines in northern Texas.[1] Gould defeated these plans and, in conjunction with Huntington, succeeded early in 1882 in securing an interest in its stock and representation on its board.

In 1885, therefore, the railroad business in Texas with the exception of the Gulf and a number of smaller roads was controlled by Gould and Huntington. Although they had occasionally cooperated, their interests repeatedly clashed. Early in 1885, for example, a rate war broke out, but by July the contestants came together and organized a pool covering the Texas traffic.[2] The pool soon broke down. Gould and Huntington, however, negotiated a compromise arrangement providing for a new five-year pool, subject to withdrawal upon sixty days' notice.

It looked as though peace was now to prevail in the Texas railroad industry. While Gould was preparing for peace in Texas, however, he was making ready for war in Kansas. In defying the Atchison in that area, Gould precipitated a struggle, the limits of which he probably did not appreciate. The Atchison offensive of 1886 and 1887 struck at the vitals of the Gould system, not only in Kansas and eastern Colorado but also in the Southwest. For more than two years the road had been negotiating with the Gulf to build an extension from northern Texas. Before the end of 1885 the construction was under way, and in the spring of 1886 the Atchison acquired the Gulf by an exchange of stock. Acting defensively to check Gould the Atchison may have paid a high price. Perkins of the Burlington expressed the opinion that though he had no detailed knowledge, the Atchison in acquiring this road had taken on "a pretty long line of railroad at a pretty high price." [3] The price was high and the blow struck by the Atchison was quick and sharp. The Atchison now had a through route to the Gulf Coast. For the first time Gould was faced with a competitor that controlled a line from traffic-producing regions in Texas to Kansas City. Within the next two years, with the completion of the Atchison extension to Chicago, Gould was confronted by a competitor with a through line of its own from the Gulf Coast to Chicago.

The Atchison, furthermore, challenged for the first time the monopoly position of the Kansas & Texas in the Indian Territory. If the Atchison maintained rates and shared the existing business with the Kansas & Texas, earnings of the latter might indeed be reduced, although not sufficiently to impair the margin of safety for interest. If as a measure of retaliation for Gould's aggression in Kansas and Colorado it reduced rates, the effect on the Kansas & Texas might be disastrous. Its financial structure was weak and its physical condition poor.

The invasion of Oklahoma and Texas by the Atchison paved the way for another damaging blow to the Gould system. The Atchison had no outlet of its own to St. Louis. The Frisco, however, with which the Atchison for a number of years had worked closely, did have such an outlet. An extension of the Frisco south to north Texas would connect the road with the northern terminus of the Gulf. Such a line which had been "long contemplated and earnestly desired" [4] would give the enlarged Atchison system an outlet to St. Louis. The Kansas & Texas would be flanked on both sides: on the west by the Atchison and on the east by the Frisco. The Texas rate stabilization which had been established in the fall of 1885 could no longer be retained. As a new line the Atchison decided to do what almost every other new road had done; the Lackawanna in 1883, the Wabash in 1880 and 1881, and the Baltimore & Ohio after completion of the Chicago extension in 1874. It cut rates and after a period of some months the road would secure enough traffic to give it a good bargaining position in a pool. Shortly after the Atchison and its allied Frisco completed their extensions to north Texas, the rate war began. It was inaugurated by Huntington's Houston which, anticipating a rate cut by the Atchison, took the initiative and opened "an animated war of freight rates." [5] The war was short and sharp, and in two weeks an understanding was reached and rates were restored.

Gould must have realized that this settlement was only a truce and that in a short time additional wars would break out. In preparing countermoves to meet these attacks, Gould again thought in terms of establishing new through routes. His mind turned to grand competitive schemes, ignoring again, as he had so many times before, the cost elements and the relative importance of through traffic vs. local. His new lines in southern Kansas served rich grain and hog-packing districts. Growing markets for these products existed in the Southeast—in the territory beyond Memphis east of the Mississippi River. He could reach these areas over his existing system lines only by a circuitous route, east to St. Louis and south to Memphis where connection was made with southeastern roads.

He therefore conceived the idea of building a direct connection between the Kansas & Texas and the Iron Mountain at a point many miles below the Kansas City-St. Louis line of the Missouri Pacific. As if to carry out the very purpose he had in mind, local Arkansas promoters had already constructed a number of small roads paralleling the Arkansas River from the western part of that state to the southeastern section. Three separate local companies with a complementary traffic relationship were involved. Together these roads formed the Arkansas Valley route; they were nevertheless separately owned and operated. One of them with a large debt was in receivership, and Gould with his usual trading ability recognized its strategic value. He therefore purchased a majority of the outstanding bonds of the property, and with these bonds at the foreclosure sale secured full control. He could now make terms with the other two roads which could not exist except by the use of the road he just bought. Within a few months he had carried out his purpose. The other two roads sold out and by the spring of 1887 Gould and his group were elected to the boards of the three companies. Shortly thereafter the companies were merged with and formally taken over by the Missouri Pacific.

This Arkansas Valley route terminated at Fort Smith, Arkansas, on the west. Gould made arrangements for construction of an extension to connect Fort Smith with the north-and-south line of the Kansas & Texas in the Indian Territory. Upon the completion of this extension Gould would control a new short line from Kansas and eastern Colorado to tidewater. The new route would give Kansas City an outlet to tidewater by a route of 900 miles via Memphis and down the Mississippi River open all the year, against a route of 1,400 miles via St. Louis and Chicago. Nothing could overcome the advantages of this short route, asserted the operating manager of the Missouri Pacific; and Gould himself declared that he expected to take business to tidewater over this route from points as far north as Omaha.[6]

To facilitate the movement of this traffic, Gould rushed through the extension of the Iron Mountain to Memphis, thereby making the system independent of the Memphis & Little Rock which had given him so much trouble in his efforts to acquire control at what he considered to be a reasonable price.[7]

Thus Gould again succeeded in attracting wide publicity for a new competitive route with great possibilities. The enlarged Gould system in Kansas and Colorado, it was widely asserted, would as surely succeed in diverting traffic over the new Arkansas route to tidewater as the Union Pacific only five or six years earlier had promised to divert traffic over the enlarged Wabash.

Despite its valuable strategic position, Gould had meanwhile permitted the physical condition of the Kansas & Texas to deteriorate. "With inconsiderable exception," declared the 1892 annual report of the reorganized road, "it may be stated that no part of the line was ballasted or fenced; a large portion of the permanent way was laid with iron rails; most of the bridges were of the old pattern, wooden structures inadequate for sustaining heavy trains and exposed to constant danger from fire. The southern terminus of the main line was at a water-tank in the bush eighty miles from tide-water; an interval of sixty-seven miles interrupted the continuity of the main line in its most important part, and three small pieces of track were built with the company's funds as feeders for a rival line whilst entirely separated from contact with its own." [8] The road was an essential part of the system through route between Kansas City and the Southwest, and between southern Kansas and the Southeast, and was also a link connecting the Texas & Pacific's transcontinental line with southern Kansas and western Missouri. Gould was therefore anxious to maintain control. The price of retention seemed, however, to be excessive. Its fixed charges were out of line with comparable properties, and existing earnings were threatened by new competition.

It was probably late in 1887 that Gould made up his mind that the Kansas & Texas was too burdensome for the Missouri Pacific. By that time he had sold out most of his stocks and bonds in the road.[9] Late in 1887, furthermore, the price of its securities began to drop. There were of course others besides Gould who understood the reasons which contributed to their price decline, although, as usual, people in the financial district, who are presumed to know most about these matters, knew in fact comparatively little. William Dowd, president of the Bank of North America, and a member of the Kansas & Texas board of directors, stated blandly that he had examined the company's books "quite thoroughly," and discovered that the company "had laid down a large amount of steel rails, so that it [was] now in first class condition."[10] Neither was the stock exchange of any help to the innocent investor. A large part of the company's stocks and bonds were held in Holland, and its securities were therefore listed on the Amsterdam Stock Exchange. When prices dropped, this Exchange could discover no better remedy than the appointment of an investigating committee, thereby to defend the "holders of securities against the alleged machinations of bear traders. . . ."[11]

The price decline led to the usual rumors. One was that the company would default in the payment of its December coupon; a story that was promptly denied. Sage pronounced it as ridiculous; the coupon and the next semi-annual coupon as well, he said, would be paid.[12] Gould declared that the company had no floating debt, and a receiver, he insisted, had "never been dreamed of except on the street. . . ."[13]

The denials were similar to those which were made in May, 1884, prior to the appointment of the Wabash receiver. In this case, as with the Wabash, Gould had made up his mind to act, although he was not yet ready to show his hand. To enable him to retain control in the face of an impending receivership, he needed time to place himself in a strong strategic position. In view of the company's heavy fixed charges, possession of a large block of stock would be of little help. He could, it is true, buy some of the junior mortgage bonds. These, however, were outstanding in amounts far too large even at prevailing prices to enable him to secure a controlling interest, at bargain prices.

Accordingly he resorted to the device of the floating debt—that curious instrument which had done such good service in the receivership and reorganization of the Wabash and of the Texas & Pacific. Toward the end of the year 1887, the security holders were assured, on what appeared to be the best of authority, that the company had no floating debt.[14] Gould found little difficulty, nevertheless, in creating one, and by early April only a few weeks after the public had been assured that the company had none, it turned up with an $800,000 item borrowed from the Missouri Pacific. Gould asserted further that "additional large advances" would have to be made until the earnings improved.[15]

Even before the formal announcement of the new debt to the Missouri Pacific, the company's bondholders and stockholders began to discover the truth. They discounted at their proper value the assurances of Gould and of corporate officers that nothing was fundamentally wrong. They appreciated at face value the superficial judgments of the Amsterdam Stock Exchange authorities, and they determined to find out the truth for themselves. Late in March they organized a committee headed as usual by a banker. The committee was authorized to secure proxies in order to elect a new board and thus get control of the new company.[16] The committee, after unsuccessfully trying to secure information from the company, communicated with Gould. Gould, as bland and assured as always, was willing to be generous. If the committee, after acquiring control of the road on behalf of the stockholders desired to operate independently, the Missouri Pacific would give it fair treatment; and that was an important factor in its success, asserted Gould.[17] The harmony between Gould and the committee led to a vigorous upward movement in the prices of the road's securities. "No other securities," referring to the non-Gould securities, commented a friendly Philadelphia newspaper, "have shown any such buoyancy." [18]

If the work of the committee in securing information from Gould, despite the latter's professed spirit of co-operation, was unsuccessful, its efforts in securing proxies, on the contrary, was highly successful. The annual election was close at hand and it was clear to Gould that he would be forced to relinquish control. He accordingly called a meeting of the old board of directors and revealed the purpose of the newly created debt. The Kansas & Texas owned all the stock of the International. These securities and others held in the company's treasury had a value of about $3,000,000.[19] At the board meeting resolutions were passed transferring these securities to the holder of the $800,000 floating debt.

Shortly thereafter the annual meeting of the Kansas & Texas was held. The Gould interest was not even represented and the new management assumed control. Resolutions were passed denouncing the actions of the Gould board, and appointing an investigating committee. The committee made an elaborate investigation and discussed numerous facts, many of which had already been known. The disclosure could not, however, save the Kansas & Texas. Receivership was essential to give the management the necessary time and capital to rehabilitate the road both physically and financially.

Receivership of the Kansas & Texas made it more than ever necessary for Gould to retain control of the International. Since the stock of that road belonged to the Kansas & Texas, it was inevitable that despite anything he could do, the Kansas & Texas could by paying the small floating debt take over the stock. With the International lost to the Gould system, traffic would go north over the lines of the Kansas & Texas to Hannibal and beyond over the Burlington. The International's rolling stock was badly run down and the company did not have enough cars to carry the available traffic. Of the locomotives still available, a number of the engines were literally worn out.[20] The company was also in exceptionally poor financial condition, and for a number of years had operated at substantial deficits. In the fall of 1888 the company upon one occasion had only $23,000 in its treasury to meet supply vouchers, including pay rolls, of between $150,000 to $200,000.[21]

In the summer of 1888, some months after the Kansas & Texas had been taken over by its shareholders and the lease to the Missouri Pacific canceled, it seemed inevitable that the Kansas & Texas would acquire control of the International. Although its stock was held by the Kansas & Texas, Gould's appointees remained in control. In order to give him an interest in subsequent legal proceedings, Gould advanced funds to the road to enable it to pay its bond coupons which otherwise would have defaulted. Gould kept the coupons alive and received notes from the company evidencing his advances. By November 1 he had thus accumulated a claim against the company of about $500,000. This claim, together with the unpaid coupons which he held as a lien against the road, was sufficient to give him a standing in the courts as a security holder. He then permitted the International to default.

Gould was now a floating debt creditor. What he could not do as a first mortgage bondholder he could well do as the holder of unsecured promissory notes. To exploit the notes to the maximum degree, it was essential that Gould secure a judgment in a state court in Texas, and then use this judgment as a means of securing a federal receivership.[22] The execution of this plan precipitated a spectacular corporate and political battle which resulted in an elaborate legislative investigation of Gould's transactions and led to a series of clashes with the Kansas & Texas and its leading stockholders and bankers.

In order to obtain the desired judgment, Gould carefully prepared the way by securing local counsel who "knew" the judge. The petition to the Texas court was drafted by J. F. Dillon, and forwarded to the solicitors of the International. Gould had the International call a meeting of the directors and at that meeting a resolution was adopted authorizing one of its solicitors to confess judgment on behalf of the International. Two days later, February 11, 1889, the climax of a long-prepared campaign by Gould to precipitate the International into a federal receivership took place in a Texas court. Toward the end of the day after everybody apparently had left, Gould's solicitor, acting in behalf of the International, quietly asked the court for a judgment. Unfortunately, however, somebody had talked. Local officials of the International had openly bragged that shippers, small creditors, and others who had claims against the International (approximately 260 damage suits against the road were pending) would get nothing. One of the attorneys for the small creditors kept his ears and eyes open, and being suspicious that Gould would make some sudden move in the courts, took particular care to be present at all proceedings. The Gould solicitors were not aware of Gould's motives; they were acting only on orders to secure judgment for a debt of the International to Gould. When the solicitor for the miscellaneous creditors, therefore, objected to the granting of the judgment and filed interventions, it was "like a clap of thunder out of a clear sky." [23]

By a narrow margin, Gould thus missed his aim. The judge postponed the case for a number of days, thereby giving the Kansas & Texas the opportunity to marshal its forces for a fight against Gould. Inasmuch as the six months' grace period under the terms of the mortgage had not yet expired, the Kansas & Texas could, after assuming control of the property, pay the interest, discharge Gould's outstanding obligations, and thereby add the International to its own system. The Kansas & Texas called a shareholders' meeting for April first with a view of electing a new board. It now seemed that despite all Gould could do, the International was about to be lost to his railroad system.

Gould was again equal to the occasion. Through a new Texas friend he secured access to the state's attorney-general, who was informed that the International and Kansas & Texas were competitors, and that their control by a single interest would suppress competition. Gould's attorney, who communicated with the attorney-general, admitted later to a state investigating committee that while he had appealed to a public officer in the name of the state of Texas, he did not disclose the fact that he was aiming to promote private ends.[24] Gould's plan was successful, and the shareholders' meeting of the International called by the Kansas & Texas was, upon application by the attorney-general, enjoined. Meanwhile, the state court in charge of the receivership, after an investigation into the validity of the Gould claim, had issued a judgment in his favor. Gould had again blocked the Kansas & Texas and prevented it from taking control of the International.

With the property of the Kansas & Texas in poor physical condition, with numerous parts of its main lines disconnected from each other, with no terminals on the northern and southern ends of its line, Gould could await developments. In reorganizing the property, the creditors, he could assume, would eventually come to him. It was generally expected that the road would remain part of the Missouri Pacific system. The weekly financial Gould critic, for example, observed that although the road was not absolutely essential to the Missouri Pacific, it was "hardly within the range of probabilities that no strong effort [would] be made to keep it within that system." [25] About two years before when the road was still under control of the Missouri Pacific, Forbes of the Burlington remarked that in his opinion neither Gould nor his successor "when he is used up will let go their grip on it." [26]

In his struggle to reacquire control, Gould originally paid little attention to the stock which had only a nominal value. Ahead of the stock were numerous high-interest-bearing bond issues. The liens were conflicting, and the loss of any part of the property secured by one bond might prove harmful to the property as a whole. The line north of Denison, due in part to the Gould policy of diverting business to the Missouri Pacific, had relatively little traffic. If the bondholders succeeded in their foreclosure proceedings and seized the northern lines, the section south of Denison would find the best resting place in Gould's southwestern net. Another group of bondholders held the lien on the southern and more productive part. Although the southern lines earned more than the northern, the bondholders nevertheless could not afford to lose the latter.

The weakness of the northern bondholders was such that they decided early in the fall of 1888, even before the company formally went into receivership, to trade with Gould. The Union Trust Company, on behalf of this group, submitted a plan to exchange three shares of Kansas & Texas for one share of Missouri Pacific, with the stock paying an assessment of $10 a share. Approximately $4,500,000 would be raised, of which $3,500,000 would finance the improvement of the road's physical condition, and the balance, aside from reorganization expenses, would be used to discharge the debt to the Missouri Pacific. The interest charges under the plan approximated $2,270,000.

Another plan submitted on behalf of the stockholders reduced the interest charges to $1,420,000 but set up a preferred stock, the dividend on which would call for the payment of more than $1,000,000. Gould opposed these as well as a number of other plans, primarily because they did not call for a sufficiently large reduction in prior charges ahead of the new common stock.

Gould was ready to retransfer the road to the Missouri Pacific if the interest charges were reduced to a figure considerably less than $1,500,000. His scheme involved also the elimination of the common stock; but the stockholders and many bondholders opposed this feature on the ground that it would lead to endless litigation.

The Kansas & Texas management, meanwhile, assumed the aggressive by acquiring a Kansas City line, and this prompted Gould to change his mind about the importance of the stock. Even though the road was in receivership, he thought that with stock control he could stop the management from following policies detrimental to the interests of the Missouri Pacific. Since almost 50 per cent of the stock was held abroad, he sent an agent there to get proxies for the 1889 annual meeting. The president of the road, partly through overhearing a chance conversation, sent a competitive agent and, accordingly, both sailed for Europe on the same boat. The Dutch bondholders, remembering their experiences of 1879, did not repeat their mistake of succumbing to the lure of Gould's promises, and transferred their proxies to the existing management.[27]

Gould underestimated the financial stamina of the stockholders. The stockholders' committee was a strong one. At its head was F. P. Olcott of the Central Trust Company, a leading competitor of the Gould-affiliated Mercantile Trust. On the Olcott committee was also Harry K. Enos, a representative of the Standard Oil Company, whose president and guiding genius was Rockefeller. The latter was a large holder of the securities of the Kansas & Texas, one source describing him as the largest holder.[28] This was the first time that Gould encountered Rockefeller, and in this original contact Gould found himself outdistanced, outguessed, and outplayed. In the fall of 1889, in the midst of a series of claims and counterclaims from various security holders' committees, when the problems confronting the would-be organizers seemed almost to defy solution and when it appeared, in the language of one commentator, that "one of the most difficult problems in railroad organization that has ever appeared" [29] was still far from a solution, the Olcott stockholders' committee, appeared suddenly in December of 1889 with an entirely new plan. It was a plan which only strong financial interests could carry out. At one stroke it solved the intricate problem posed by the conflict of interests between the northern and southern bondholding groups. The plan proposed to retire the northern division bonds, and to levy a 10 per cent assessment on the stock. This was Gould's original idea and both he and Sage enthusiastically supported the plan. Gould said that the plan had been suggested by him some years ago, and that if the proposed assessment had been accepted the cost of reorganization and receivership could have been avoided.[30] The support given the plan by the Gould group led observers to express the thought that the road would soon be a part of the Missouri Pacific system. It was "pretty well understood" in Wall Street, reported one newspaper observer, that the road surely would be included as part of the Missouri Pacific,[31] and Gould himself remarked categorically that the Kansas & Texas was "a natural ally of the Missouri Pacific." [32] He therefore hastened his assurances and approval of the plan and, together with Sage and his associates, deposited his bonds in support of the plan.

Gould probably thought that upon failure of stockholders to pay the assessment he could get sufficient stock to control the company after reorganization. He did not apparently appreciate the financial power, the fixity of purpose, and the sound judgment of Rockefeller and his associates. A syndicate was organized to guarantee the subscription to more than $22,000,000 of new bonds to pay off the bonds on the northern division and to guarantee the payment of the assessment on the stock. The reorganization committee set up in the agreement had two Standard Oil men and one Gould man. The agreement provided that the committee should name the directors for two years. Even though Gould's interests were represented by only one of the six members of the committee, a well-informed financial journal remarked that it was "presumed, though not definitely stated, that there [was] to be some sort of alliance between the M. K. & T. and the Missouri Pacific." [33]

Gould misconceived the powers behind the reorganization, just as the contemporary writer did. He did not, however, have to wait long before he was enlightened. At the next meeting of the board the Rockefeller representatives predominated, and Enos was elected president.[34] At the next annual meeting in the spring of 1891, Rockefeller was elected to the board.

In the reorganization plan which thus elevated the Rockefeller interest to control, the fate of the International apparently had also been settled. It was agreed that the Kansas & Texas and the Missouri Pacific should each own one-half of the stock of the road, and that one-half of the judgment held by Gould against the road should be turned over to the Kansas & Texas. It was further agreed that the traffic relationships between the Missouri Pacific and the Kansas & Texas should be governed by a ten-year contract with the International to be operated jointly in the interests of the two controlling properties. When Gould learned later that the Kansas & Texas was no longer his and that, accordingly, the valuable traffic interchange between north and central Texas and Kansas City was lost, he resorted to his well-established method of respecting an agreement in letter but not in spirit. Late in February of 1890 at a time when Gould discovered the enormity of his error in believing that he had reacquired control of the Kansas & Texas, he bought at auction all except a few of the qualifying shares of the International. This was in accordance with the reorganization plan, although under the terms of the plan it was not essential for the sale to be conducted at such an early date. Gould moved fast to acquire control of the stock, the title to which, of course, was not entirely in his hands.

The reorganization plan providing for an assessment on the stock contained the conventional provision that if any shareholder did not pay the assessment, the committee or someone representing the committee could pay it and take up the stock. Gould in an effort to acquire control of the International decided to exploit the possibilities of this presumably innocent provision. The plan contained an expiration date, and in order to purchase the stock, a stockholder must have paid the assessment on a certain date. Gould had physical possession of the stock and on the very last day he delivered 50 per cent of the stock to the Kansas & Texas. The stock was deposited so late that it was impossible for the Kansas & Texas to deposit the money at the time stipulated in the plan of reorganization. Gould proposed, accordingly, to make a deposit adversely and thus get the stock for himself.

The scheme was promptly challenged by the Kansas & Texas, and additional lawsuits were begun. The argument on this specialized technicality lasted all day before a judge in the state supreme court. An injunction was secured against all parties concerned. Rockefeller, however, was not interested in prolonging a technical lawsuit, and before the judge could hand down a decision, he reached a private settlement. All suits were withdrawn and the International stock was sold to the Missouri Pacific for one-half of Gould's judgment against the former road.[35]

Despite numerous defensive measures, Gould failed to protect the western flank of his southwestern system. He had been forced to build parallel lines both in eastern Oklahoma and in southeastern Louisiana in order to carry traffic which had been lost through his failure to reacquire the Kansas & Texas. What was lost on the western part of the system was made up, however, at least in part, by another corporate trade on the eastern part.

One of the earliest competitors of the Gould lines on the traffic from Texas to the upper Mississippi Valley at St. Louis was the reorganized St. Louis, Arkansas & Texas, which under its new ownership was equally as aggressive as it had been prior to the reorganization. The company resumed the program of its corporate predecessor for the building of a road between St. Louis and Cairo. The management had attempted to induce the Burlington to build that extension to a connection with its own lines. To Perkins, however, the proposal was unattractive; . . . "with all the other fish we have to fry at present, it was hardly worth our while to do so. . . ." Perkins therefore suggested that the other road build the connection.[36]

The management of the St. Louis, Arkansas & Texas was in the hands of Colonel S. W. Fordyce—one of those personalities which have done so much to expand both the railroad and industrial plant of the country. When the road was reorganized in 1886 he was selected to operate the property by a committee clothed with authority to appoint the board for a period of five years. The company's treasury securities, consisting of second-mortgage bonds and stocks, proved unsalable. Fordyce decided nevertheless to improve the property, and in order to buy steel rails and other equipment, placed his personal endorsement on more than $3,000,000 of corporate paper. The paper was held by Carnegie.[37]

Fordyce probably believed that the prosperity of 1886 and 1887, to which the construction activities of the western railroads contributed, would last for some years. He therefore decided that he would be able to sell securities in amounts sufficient to meet the Carnegie obligation. Although the traffic of the road increased, the profits did not. The extensions, both actual and proposed, into the Gould territory, led to a war of rates, and both the earnings of the Gould roads and of this road were adversely affected. As November, 1888, approached, Fordyce recognized that he would have insufficient funds to meet the road's interest. Despite the money already spent on improvements, some parts of the line were still in poor physical condition; and in order to place the road in working order, from two to three million of additional cash was needed. The company's financial condition in the fall of 1888 became so serious that for a while the company could not meet its current pay roll.[38]

Fordyce, although an able operating man, was helpless. He was in a corner and sought a way out to relieve himself of his personal financial obligations; and the logical candidate for the position of reliever was Gould. Gould had long desired to acquire control, though there was no necessity for acting quickly to save the property from a trunk-line competitor. He could bide his time, and in the fall of 1888 the critical moment arrived.

Fordyce in negotiating with Gould possessed precisely what Gould wanted. He had some junior securities which gave the holder the right to control a majority of the members of the board of directors. Gould bought the junior securities, thus giving the company sufficient money to pay its interest, liquidate its floating debt, and make improvements. Sage, Gould's son George, and Louis Fitzgerald, president of the Gould affiliated Mercantile Trust, were elected to the managerial committee.

The rate war between the Gould system and the purchased road came to a quick end. The latter stopped work on the St. Louis extension, and arranged to use the line of the Iron Mountain for an entrance into St. Louis. The Gould purchase was a great stroke for the Missouri Pacific, substantially increasing its competitive strength.

On the face of things the first mortgage bondholders of the company were not interested in the managerial change, and they therefore ignored the new acquisition. Perhaps they might even have been pleased since the passage of control provided sufficient funds for the payment of the November, 1888, coupon, which in the absence of the new control might not have been paid. In this feeling of confidence they were mistaken. There was plenty of experience which should have taught them the unwisdom of closing their eyes to change in control, if the change was effected by a man who had shown his knowledge and ability in taking full advantage of any opening offered to reduce the capital charges ahead of his holdings of junior securities. The first mortgage coupon was due in May, 1889. The trustee was the Central Trust Company, headed by Olcott, who was then serving as chairman of a group of junior security holders of the Kansas & Texas. The Central Trust, under the provisions of the first mortgage, had issued some peculiar coupon-bearing certificates which were obligations against itself as trustee. Upon his assumption of control, Gould appointed the Mercantile Trust Company as the road's fiscal agent. He now repeated the financial device which he had used some years before on the Texas & Pacific. The Mercantile Trust honored the first mortgage interest coupons in cash; but the coupons, instead of being canceled as received, were held alive. In the hands of the trust company, representing some Gould interest, the coupons served as a lien against the railroad company. After about $140,000 out of a total of $490,000 was paid, the Central Trust refused to recognize as obligations any coupons held by the Mercantile Trust.

By making this small payment, Gould apparently planned to place himself again in one of those strategic positions which were so dear to him. In addition to involving the Central Trust which, in connection with the Kansas & Texas activities, was blocking his efforts to reacquire control of that road, Gould was also actuated by the desire to reduce the interest rate on the first mortgage bonds of the St. Louis, Arkansas & Texas. His persistent critics were surprised, as they had so often been before, at the ease with which he played the same game over and over to a new and inexperienced audience. His weekly financial critic which had persistently assailed him for a score of years renewed its attack in an interesting editorial entitled "A New Tale With an Old Moral." "To be fooled once or even twice by a certain set of circumstances," it asserted, "does not argue perhaps a lack of sagacity; but to be fooled over and over again by the same conjunction of facts subjects one at least to a charge of infatuation." [39]

The Central Trust Company, in view of its potential liability under the first mortgage of the road, acted promptly. Within a few days it moved for a receiver, and the application was granted. The large German bondholdings were represented by a committee representing leading American financial institutions. Of the $16,000,000 outstanding first mortgage bonds, German bondholders held about $12,000,000.

Gould, as usual, found any number of strategically sound arguments to bolster his position that the first mortgage bondholders of the company should and must accept some sacrifice in the form of a reduction of interest. He discovered that the first mortgage bond, like the Wabash general mortgage bond of 1880, was protected by a lien which did not cover the entire system. It covered only the property at the time it was executed and did not include the extensions acquired since that time. He insisted, furthermore, that the actions taken by the Mercantile Trust in May, 1889, did not constitute a default in interest. Any apparent default was due entirely to the acts of the Central Trust.[40]

Before many months passed Gould made another move to enable him to exert further pressure on the first mortgage bondholders. The receivers petitioned the court for permission to divide the company's revenue between the company's lines in Arkansas and Missouri on one hand and its lines in Texas on the other. The Texas lines would receive 60 per cent of the through rate and those in the other two states would receive 40 per cent. The Texas lines produced most of the traffic. The Arkansas and the Missouri lines, however, were parallel to and competitive with those of the Missouri Pacific. If Gould could acquire the Texas lines he would have little need for the others, and they would be left helpless with little or no earning power. The system as a whole, in the opinion of an English commentator, would "disintegrate." [41] The petition of the receivers was approved by the court.

Despite the initial victory, Gould was nevertheless unsuccessful in his efforts to dominate the reorganization. It is needless to examine the dispute between the security holders. In the reorganization of the company, though Gould and Sage exchanged their stocks and bonds for a respectable block of common and preferred stock of the new company, they did not acquire control. Gould's holdings, however, were sufficient to make his son, Edwin, vice president; and thereafter the reorganized company—the St. Louis & Southwestern—became a friend, not a foe.

After completion of the expansion and construction program, and despite the loss of the Kansas & Texas lines, the Gould railroad system was one of the largest in the country west of Chicago. In 1891 when the program was fully effective, it controlled more than one-fifth of the 80,000 odd miles in this area.[42] Although there were many competitors in the Central West, there were, aside from the independent Kansas & Texas, only two major competitors in the Southwest. One was the combined Atchison-St. Louis San Francisco system; the other was dominated by Huntington. On the western part of the Missouri Pacific in central and southern Kansas, another competitor, the Rock Island, had appeared. Although it stood on the brink of the southwestern area and threatened for a time to extend its lines farther south and west, it did not during the lifetime of Gould carry out this threat. In the Southwest, Gould, Huntington, and the Atchison were dominant. If this triumvirate could be brought together and their relations harmonized, the competitive and territorial stability, which Gould in 1885 had disturbed, could be re-established. Such a harmony of interests in the late eighties and early nineties was essential to enable the railroads to retain sufficient earnings to cover their interest charges, to say nothing of dividends. By the end of 1891 their dividends had been largely eliminated. The wave of competitive expansion in the late eighties had produced a financial collapse even before the advent of the nineties. The three dominant interests recognized the danger and endeavored to bring their properties into harmony. In view of the background of Rockefeller as the leader of the Standard Oil trust, there is little reason to doubt that the Kansas & Texas would fall in line with any program of stability.

NOTES FOR CHAPTER XXVII

1. The earliest notice of such a project is in *Ry. Review*, Jan. 22, 1881, 32.
2. *Bradstreet*, July 4, 1885, 9.
3. Burlington archives, Perkins to Geddes, May 11, 1886.
4. Annual report, St. Louis & San Francisco, 1886, 8.
5. R. R. *Gaz.*, July 15, 1887, 478.
6. These declarations are found in *Ry. Review*, June 11, 1887, 345.
7. For details on the building of the Arkansas Valley route and the accompanying transactions, see, in addition to the sources already mentioned, *Ry. Review*, Nov. 26, 1886, 684; Dec. 11, 1886, 666; Dec. 25, 1886, 696; May 7, 1887, 271; New York *Tribune*, Dec. 8, 1886.
8. Annual report, Missouri, Kansas & Texas, 1892, 7.
9. This statement was made categorically in the Phila. *Press*, Feb. 27, 1888.
10. *Chron.*, Nov. 5, 1887, 613.
11. Ibid., Dec. 17, 1887, 820.
12. *Stockholder*, Oct. 29, 1887.
13. Ibid., Nov. 1, 1887.
14. This was the statement of the president of the Bank of North America, *Chron.*, Nov. 5, 1887, 613, and also of responsible officials of the Missouri Pacific.
15. Ibid., April 21, 1888, 511.
16. *Ry. World*, March 31, 1888, 301; New York *Tribune*, March 27, 1888.

17. *Ry. World*, May 19, 1888, 467.
18. Phila. *Press*, April 29, 1888.
19. This was the estimate of R. V. Martinsen, the non-Gould president of the Kansas & Texas, New York *Times*, Sept. 25, 1888.
20. Report of the Joint Committee of the 22nd Legislature, State of Texas, appointed to investigate the Receivership of the International & Great Northern Railroad, 1891, Judge Felix J. McCord, 338; and Thomas R. Bonner, 151.
21. Ibid., Bonner, 151.
22. Gould's counsel were not accustomed to state receiverships; and therefore desired to avoid them. This was the opinion of Judge Alex. G. Cochran, one of Gould's attorneys familiar with Texas court procedure. See ibid., 271, N. W. Finley.
23. Ibid., 26-27, testimony of H. M. Whitaker, solicitor for the Missouri Pacific.
24. Ibid., 73, testimony of Charles T. Bonner, another Gould attorney in Texas.
25. *Chron.*, Nov. 3, 1888, 555.
26. Burlington archives, Forbes to Perkins, Dec. 29, 1886.
27. New York *Times*, April 8, 1889.
28. Ibid., Nov. 27, 1892.
29. *Bradstreet*, Aug. 17, 1889, 526.
30. New York *Tribune*, Dec. 20, 1889.
31. Ibid., Dec. 21, 1889.
32. Phila. *Press*, Dec. 6, 1889.
33. *Chron.*, Dec. 21, 1889, 825.
34. Ibid., June 7, 1890, 801; May 31, 1890, 771.
35. For details on this incident of the International Great Northern plan see *Ry. World*, Feb. 27, 1892, 204; New York *Tribune*, Feb. 19, 1892; New York *Times*, Feb. 19, 1892; Feb. 24, 1892; *Chron.*, Feb. 27, 1892, 366.
36. Burlington archives, Perkins to Wert Dexter, Dec. 26, 1888.
37. S. G. Reed, *A History of Texas Railroads*, 415.
38. New York *Times*, Oct. 3, 1888.
39. *Chron.*, May 11, 1889, 601.
40. These contentions were presented to the court in the suit filed by the Central Trust and summarized in *Ry. Review*, Dec. 7, 1889, 710.
41. London *Railway News*, Sept. 21, 1889, 518.
42. This is the computation made by *Bradstreet*, April 18, 1891, 243.

CHAPTER XXVIII

Gould Stabilizes Rates

THE program of railroad construction outlined in the two previous chapters permanently changed the western railroad equilibrium. The roads east of the Missouri crossed the river, and the roads west of the river crossed to the territory on the east. Gould's southwestern system no longer was the only line which connected Chicago and the Middle West with Texas. The Atchison was a new competitor, and the Rock Island having thrown its lines west across the state of Kansas into Denver, and south to the Kansas-Oklahoma boundary, was another disturbing factor. In the Northwest, the Burlington had invaded southern Minnesota by acquiring a working interest in the affiliated Chicago, Burlington & Northern. The construction of the Canadian Pacific and the provision of through routes over the road and its connections, and the development of railroad-owned steamship lines on the Great Lakes from Duluth were other factors which upset the delicate balance of territorial equality established prior to the events of the middle eighties.

The construction and expansion programs stimulated in large part by the policies of Gould introduced new forces which in a short time broke down almost the entire rate structure, both through and local. Demoralizing disturbances sufficient in extent to reduce earnings and impair financial structures had formerly been confined to eastern territory. These disturbances had been brought under control by various devices. The textbook of recorded experience served no useful purpose however in teaching western railroad men the perils of rate cuts. They themselves had to undergo the experience personally before they could be made to adopt most of the measures the eastern railroad men had adopted. When rate wars had produced their baneful effects upon railroad earnings and finances in the West, it was Gould who for the first time in his career assumed leadership in an effort to stabilize rates and maintain values. It was a unique position for a man who in the popular eye had for so many years been considered a railroad wrecker. He was now to come forth in a new role—that of railroad stabilizer.

The rate wars in western territory began even before the competitive railroad construction of 1886–87 was well under way. Early in 1885, months after Adams had assumed the presidency of the Union Pacific, a rate dispute between the Union Pacific and the Central Pacific led to the cancellation of the Pacific Mail subsidy, and to a diversion of the Union Pacific's westbound traffic from the Central Pacific to the Oregon Short Line. Huntington on behalf of the Central Pacific retaliated by exacting local rates on traffic interchanged with the Union Pacific.[1] Traffic pools organized some weeks later failed to produce any settlement, and by November the continued unfriendliness among the transcontinental lines led Huntington to seek a way out. In a letter to Adams, referring to the "unpleasantness" among the managers of these roads, he suggested a meeting in New York "to see if something [could not] be done that [would] work more to the satisfaction of all than the arrangements heretofore made." [2] Perkins was dissatisfied with Huntington, and although he could not see how he could compromise, he would "meet Huntington and talk." [3] Adams was sure that if railroad presidents would only come together peace would reign eternally. "They got to fighting," he wrote, "simply because they [would] not meet." If the houses of the railroad presidents could be built in one block, "a sort of Presidents' Road," they could walk down to their offices in the morning "and I would be willing I think to wager my head that there would not be one quarrel then where there are five quarrels now." However Adams appreciated that his views probably would not be accepted. "I simply am a go-between," he declared, "carrying out my high mission among the railroads of the country. Here again I am acting simply as the friend of peace. Probably, before we get through, both parties will unite in pitching into me. Nevertheless, so it was of old!" [4]

These conferences among western railroad men, however, proved fruitless. Early in 1886, transcontinental rates collapsed, and the transcontinental pool gave way. This war was settled by the end of the year. The year 1886 had been prosperous; the collapse in business which followed the panic in the spring of 1884 having been short-lived.

Competitive construction completed largely in 1887 laid the basis for the rate cuts which reached their full force in 1888. By January, rates between Chicago and St. Paul and Minneapolis, for example, were demoralized. A responsible railroad official referred to "the worse than absurd waste of revenue [then] going on,"[5] a waste which threatened the solvency of both the Burlington and the Northwestern.[6] In the Missouri Valley the rate war also raged. In Kansas the new railroad commission had begun its rate-reduction program. The rates voluntarily initiated by the active contestants, however, were "considerably lower" than those ordered by the commission.[7]

The competitive situation was intensified by the fact that not all of the roads had extended their lines beyond the Missouri. Two important properties, the Alton and the Chicago, St. Paul & Kansas City,[8] served the area between Chicago and Kansas City. They originated no traffic from points beyond the river and could secure such business only by quoting lower rates. Late in 1887 the Alton reduced grain rates from Kansas City, and the Burlington followed with corresponding cuts from Omaha. This forced the roads serving other Missouri River points to do likewise. A few weeks later the Alton, in co-operation with its eastern connections, reduced rates to Toledo and Detroit. This action forced the Wabash, in order to hold its share of the traffic, to meet the cut. In the first quarter of 1888 the rate cuts were so drastic in Illinois, Wisconsin, Iowa, Minnesota, and Missouri that it became difficult for many of the lines even to earn their operating expenses.[9]

The reduced earnings engendered by these rate cuts were anticipated by the security markets in the summer of 1887. Though the Gould stocks were hard hit, Gould himself was cheerful. In the spring he insisted that the local business of the Missouri Pacific was exceptionally good,[10] and in the fall he reiterated this judgment. The Missouri Pacific, he said, thus far in 1887 had made $3,000,000 more than in 1886, and the system was $5,000,000 ahead.[11] His public expressions of confidence in the future of the road were shown by a statistical exhibit to the company's shareholders in a statement which accompanied the September dividend check. The statement called attention to the increase in mileage and decrease per mile of the company's debts. In 1881 on a per-mile basis the outstanding stock was about $27,000 and the bonded debt about $39,000, while by the end of 1887 the corresponding figures were $10,700, and slightly over $20,000.[12]

This was a remarkable showing and was calculated to make an impression on the informed but unreflective investor. Though the facts were correct, they did not point to the truth. Each mile is not standardized in its traffic density and traffic diversity. One mile moves more traffic and more higher-rated traffic than another. One mile, in short, has a larger profit than another. Some of the branch lines built, as Gould himself stated a few years later, hardly earned their interest charges.[13]

This type of reasoning made little impression on the experienced investor. The reasoning probably did not ring true to Gould himself, and perhaps it may not be too improbable to believe that Gould, knowing the truth, prepared a statement of this kind in order to facilitate the sale of part of his holdings. The security markets were not even temporarily buoyed by the statements, and the price of Missouri Pacific continued to weaken.

The rate wars meanwhile continued in all parts of the West. Indeed they became more violent than ever. Early in 1888, the rates in the Northwest were described as "seriously demoralized." [14]

The competitive methods which produced these results called forth forebodings among railroad leaders. Adams observed that he had discovered "a depth of railroad morals among freight agents lower than had ever previously existed, and that is saying much." He referred to the "sneak-thief and pick-pocket methods of management." [15]

It came to be generally realized that the rate wars with their adverse effects on railroad revenue and on values of railway securities were principally the work of traffic executives and subordinates. The evil genius was the traffic salesman who was not responsible to the stockholding body. Charged with the responsibility of getting business at any price, he took his orders seriously and cut rates, granted rebates, and introduced discriminations.

The losses that followed the completion of the building program were not the result of financial abuses. There was no stock watering, and no construction companies. Stocks and bonds were sold for cash at reasonable prices. Losses to security holders nevertheless were substantial. The drop in values which had begun in the spring of 1887, and which was quickened in the latter months of the year, swelled into a crescendo in the early months of 1888. In January the price of Missouri Pacific suddenly declined; the reason, remarked a writer in a New York daily, was "mysterious." It was difficult to determine the earnings of the system. They were published annually, but the system was so complex and the relations of the constituent roads were so mixed up, that only an expert could figure out what the system was doing even if he had all the necessary data.[16]

In the midst of these uncertainties, Gould after a five months' absence, returned to the country. His return was signaled by a renewed break in the price of Missouri Pacific. The explanation was given by events. For the first time since the road came under Gould control, it reduced its dividend. Gould nevertheless insisted that Missouri Pacific was worth $150.[17] He followed this with a statement a few weeks later, reiterating his expressions of hope and confidence. The Missouri Pacific, he said, was bonded and capitalized at a per-mile figure lower than that of any leading road.[18] If only the short sellers understood the real situation, he observed two days later, there would be panic. There were few stocks afloat in Wall Street, he insisted. They were held more than ever by investors.

The Missouri Pacific's earnings and dividends were symptomatic of the western railroad picture. The Missouri Pacific was the first in the field of dividend reductions, just as it had been first in railroad expansion. Within a few weeks the Atchison reduced its quarterly dividend. The cycle of dividend reductions thus begun in the spring continued throughout the fall. In September the St. Paul passed, and within a few weeks the Atchison made another cut. At the next meeting in January, 1889, it completed the cycle of devastation and passed its dividend. This was followed by a reduction of the conservative Illinois Central dividend.

In the face of these casualties, Gould emphasized that, "intrinsically," Missouri Pacific stock was cheap. If only the western roads, he said, could get the rates of six years ago, "they would hardly know what to do with the money earned. . . ." [19] The drastic dividend reductions were nevertheless financial facts of primary significance. Their importance could not be minimized by expressions of hope and confidence. Railroad leaders, recognizing the dangers involved in the rate wars, began to look for a solution. There seemed to be no satisfactory alternative to agreement. The leading roads, first in one section of the country, then in another, turned toward co-operation in the hope that it would succeed where competition had failed.

Division of traffic or revenue among roads to remove the incentive to rate-cutting had in 1887 been made illegal. It became necessary accordingly to work out some new arrangement designed to bring an end to rate disturbances.

By fall, in consequence of dividend reductions, the problem assumed national significance. Thoughtful observers began to realize that no single company or railroad could possibly settle these demoralizing wars. Some believed that only Congress could arrive at a solution. Others believed that unified action could be achieved only by the trusteeing of the majority holdings of the leading railroad stocks; while still others asserted that some outstanding personality, in whom railroad investors had confidence, must take the lead. The New York City financial weekly, whose views carried considerable weight in financial circles, stressed that "the situation [required] some authority over and above these differing managements, strong enough to force a permanent arrangement of present rivalries, and to compel future principles of living and lines of growth which shall not be destructive of one another. Some such power as this must come in before lasting order [could] be brought out of the Western chaos." [20] The Moses to lead the railroads out of the financial wilderness, it continued, was Morgan.

The time for Morgan had not yet arrived. In the area south of the Union Pacific, in the Missouri Valley and in the Southwest to the Pacific Coast, the railroad industry was dominated by three systems and by three personalities. These were, respectively, the Southern Pacific, the Atchison, and the Missouri Pacific; and the men involved were Huntington, Strong, and Gould. Here the clash of personalities, particularly between Strong and Gould, was the most violent. Since each property was of equal importance, none could individually settle rate disputes. Gould could not employ any of his abilities in the fields of financial and corporate strategy in an effort to settle this problem. Inasmuch as the Southern Pacific stock was closely held by Huntington and his associates, Gould could not gain control. There was some possibility that he might be able to acquire control of the Atchison. The road's large shareholders in New England were not, however, willing to trust their property to Gould.

If competition was to be stabilized by common action, it was essential that some plan be devised to secure agreement among independent companies, separately owned and separately operated. And it was during this period (the summer and fall of 1888) that ideas were devised, plans drafted and arguments presented that set the pattern for discussion in years to come. Ideas for unified action among the large carriers still remained in the discussion stage. Some were incorporated in the tentative plan for railroad consolidation in 1921, and others in the so-called final plan of consolidation of the Interstate Commerce Commission in 1929.[21] The leadership in drafting the plans of railroad harmony was assumed jointly by Gould and Huntington. Beginning with the summer of 1888, and lasting for about three years, these two, first working by themselves, and later jointly with the presidents of other roads, evolved one scheme after another in an effort to devise machinery to eliminate discriminatory rates and promote a stable rate schedule.

One of the earlier plans was a railroad clearing house. In its development, in the working out of details, and in the struggle for its adoption, Gould took the lead. For some weeks in November he met with Huntington, Adams, Strong, and others in closed session.[22] The plan which was revealed late that month was almost breath-taking in its universality. Nothing like it had ever been presented. All existing freight and passenger associations were to be abolished and their functions taken by a clearinghouse. Each road west of the Mississippi River would be represented, and the clearinghouse would take over the rate-making authority of all the roads. It would also prescribe the divisions on all through business. The suggested agreement struck at the very root of the stabilization problem by declaring "that the bidding for business by means of private concessions shall cease. . . ." [23]

This sweeping grant of power to a new body and the surrender of all managerial control over rate-making was the most radical step in railroad unity of action ever suggested. In concentration of managerial authority, and in the centralized placing of responsibility, it was a close parallel to the industrial trusts. These were anathema to the popular mind, and so was the proposed railroad clearinghouse. The plan nevertheless was supported by some who could not possibly be classified as Gould supporters. Adams, president of the Union Pacific, declared it should have been in effect ten years before. The plan was not a trust, he insisted.[24]

The opposition, however, was immediate and overwhelming. In less than a week after its publication, its doom was certain. Gould, quick to learn, saw the light and tried to evade responsibility for its failure. He had not invented the scheme, he said; he had only approved a trial test.[25] The plan disappeared. In the discussions which took place in the fall and early winter of 1888, Gould succeeded in completing plans in southwestern territory for joint action with Huntington and Strong. In co-operation with representatives of the Rock Island and the Burlington, an agreement was reached to increase the rates 25 per cent. Huntington, in announcing the schedule, remarked that "something was really needed to end this difficulty [referring to the rate war], for the situation was becoming serious." [26]

In his efforts to work out an agreement covering the other parts of western territory, Gould was not successful. He was now to learn that his financial ingenuity and ruthlessness in interpreting agreements in accordance with their strict letter instead of their spirit, had cost him the support of many railroad officers. Many refused to attend meetings or join in plans if they were arranged or proposed by Gould.[27] Despite this there was agreement on the necessity for co-operation. While Gould was busily engaged in canvassing schemes with his southwestern associates, those railroad men who were not in sympathy with him succeeded in interesting Morgan. Since the West Shore settlement in the summer of 1885, he had led one railroad after another into various plans to stabilize eastern railroad conditions.

Late in 1888 Morgan, responding to the confidence placed in him, invited the presidents of western roads to his home. At the first meeting, a preliminary draft was drawn up. It was accompanied by another even more important arrangement: that rates should be restored on January 1 for sixty days. It was expected that in the meantime a plan for permanent stabilization would be presented. The meeting had been arranged, and the documents drawn, largely by the bankers. The bankers were anxious to solve the immediate problem: how to terminate the rate war. They accomplished their immediate objective. One banker, with confidence born of ignorance of the vital problems involved, declared exuberantly, even before a definite plan had been drawn up, "The work is already done so far as the prevention of rate wars is concerned. You will hear of no more rate wars.[28]

In drafting the agreement designed to enlist the support of the western railway world, Morgan ignored Gould. A new organization was formed, the Interstate Commerce Railway Association, vested with jurisdiction over western competitive traffic. To the association was given the responsibility of maintaining "reasonable, uniform and stable rates." Power was given to punish any employee found guilty of rate-cutting, and the railroad presidents pledged themselves to discharge this responsibility.[29] It was impossible, however, to obtain the assent of all the western roads. One of the most conservative, the Illinois Central, refused to sign. By a resolution of its board, the road decided only to give the new arrangement its "moral support as far as may be consistent with the best interests of the company."[30] Not so strange was the reluctance of Gould to sign on behalf of the Missouri Pacific. Even in his desire to secure some measure of rate stability, he had his eye on competitive realities. He refused to sign on the ground that a road, the Kansas City Ft. Scott & Memphis, controlling a line running southeastward from Kansas City to Memphis, and thus competing with Gould's newly established Arkansas route, refused to sign. The officers of the other road insisted that they would not sign until they received a guarantee that the Missouri Pacific and its southeastern connection, the Richmond Terminal, would not manipulate rates. Gould instead of reaching some amicable agreement was ready with another of his ingenious suggestions. He proposed that if any line outside of the agreement (this included the Richmond Terminal) refused to sustain rates, the new association could authorize its members to meet the competition. This would prevent the sacrificing of local rates on the member lines. The plan was impractical and met with no support.[31] It was not until February 22, 1889, that the agreement was finally signed.[32]

Even before the association was formally approved and before it could commence to function, rate cuts broke out anew. The rate rise, sponsored by the Morgan meeting, was lost early in February. Rates, however, were soon restored and an armistice followed. Railroads and shippers watched each other to see who would cut rates first. No shipper could permit those doing business on a competing road to get a rate reduction; nor could a railroad agree to permit another road to reduce its rates. By early March traffic conditions improved and the Missouri Pacific appended its signature to the agreement. Within a week thereafter, rate cuts again broke out. It was initiated in the Northwest by the same road, not a member of the new association, which had taken the lead in the previous two years—the Chicago Burlington & Northern, now described by one writer as the "prince of destroyers of railway harmony." [33] Other roads followed. The smaller lines, the Wisconsin Central and the Stickney line, insisted that they would make rates as low as any others. The old charges and countercharges followed.

The market for railroad securities again weakened, and Gould began to lose hope. The railroad business, he said, as the rate war was breaking out, was the worst he had seen it in thirty years.[34] The Interstate Commerce Railway Association meanwhile had been formally organized and its administrative agency had issued a number of decisions. These were minor in character and did not test the ability of the new agency to function as a rate stabilizer. The first major case involved the Alton. The road refused to obey the directive, and its vice president issued an intemperate statement denouncing the association as "a colossal fancy of some eastern bankers whose sole excuse for foisting it upon the practical managers of the West was the supposed necessity of doing something to satisfy demands of Wall Street." [35] In the emergency growing out of the withdrawal of the Alton, the association authorized member roads to follow their judgment in meeting the Alton's reductions. This was an open invitation to war. Rate cuts followed again in rapid succession.

Against this dreary background Gould recovered his confidence. Describing himself as "bullish" on the general situation, he insisted that he hadn't sold a share of Missouri Pacific stock for a year;[36] yet within a few weeks the price of Missouri Pacific renewed its decline. It was soon learned that the road had been unable to complete its plan of financing through the issue of bonds and stocks. Loss of confidence in railroad earning power had left it with an unfinished program of construction and expansion. In order to meet its obligations it borrowed between $7,000,000 and $10,000,000 from Gould and Sage. To informed investors and traders this was a dangerous sign. It was the debt owed Gould and his associates, personally or indirectly, which precipitated although it did not cause the financial breakdown in the Wabash, the Texas & Pacific, and the Kansas & Texas.

In the midst of these rate and stock-market disturbances, a new development suddenly occurred which intensified the difficulties of the Missouri Pacific. The Northwestern had extended its line to Wyoming and had made plans to build its road to Ogden for connection with the Central Pacific; and probably even beyond to Los Angeles, which would make it a new transcontinental rival.[37] Its completion to Ogden and beyond would be a heavy blow to the Union Pacific; it would produce another division of the business, and introduce still another rate-disturbing factor.

Railroads, having been seriously hurt, had however learned their lesson. Instead of building new lines they entered into traffic agreements, which, at least momentarily, would serve the interests of the participants equally well. Of these agreements, one destined to become a permanent influence in the railroad life of the country was concluded in October, 1889, between the Northwestern and the Union Pacific. Although the two roads agreed to interchange traffic on a preferential basis, it was not an exclusive contract. Because of the agreement the Northwestern pledged itself not to extend its lines as planned.

The contract was hailed by an authoritative western railway

journal as "one of the most important compacts in recent years," [38] while Adams, president of the Union Pacific, wrote that the two roads had now become "in all essential through traffic respects one company. They will protect and sustain each other; and, in case of attack, make common cause." [39] The Northwestern was a Vanderbilt road and so was the Lake Shore-New York Central system. It was expected that the Vanderbilts, who controlled a major system to New York and Boston, would now be able to control a through line from coast to coast. The Missouri Pacific was placed on the defensive. Gould reacted immediately, and concluded an agreement with the Denver, which virtually extended its line to Ogden, and from that point via the Huntington system to the Pacific Coast.

Gould also opened an attack on the Union Pacific-Northwestern contract on the ground that it was in violation of the Interstate Commerce Railway Association agreement. The latter, officially recognizing the validity of the protest, stated explicitly that the traffic contract had been made in defiance of the spirit and even of the letter of the compact. This was too much for Adams of the Union Pacific, and shortly thereafter both that road and the Northwestern resigned. This was the death blow to the association.

There was nothing further to hinder the development of competitive forces. Formidable economic conditions, however, gave assurance to the prospect that rate reductions would be avoided. The heavy wheat and corn crops produced record movements on some of the western roads. The general manager of the Missouri Pacific reported that he had never seen anything to compare with the traffic now moving. Traffic for the first two months of 1890 was described as "phenomenal." [40] There was therefore no justification for a decline in rates. Business was heavy and the plant and equipment inadequate to carry the traffic. There was every reason to expect that the rise in traffic would be followed by a rise in earnings.

That, however, was not to be. The industry was in the throes of forces which led almost insistently to additional rate wars. There is nothing unusual about this phenomenon. In the following half century of American business history, many industries were afflicted in times of prosperity with the plague of indiscriminate price cuts. Even in the booming 1920's, such industries as radio, rubber, paperboard, electric refrigeration and others, faced with a rapid rise in business, cut prices. Although volume expanded, earnings declined.

The renewal of rate wars, despite appearance of prosperity, was ushered in by the St. Paul in February, 1890. Almost all other roads had already manipulated rates, insisted its officials. The St. Paul's reduction was met by its competitors, and within a few days radical rate cuts appeared in the Missouri Valley from Kansas City to the Twin Cities.[41] The war immediately spread to points west of the Missouri. Those reductions were met by its competitors. It was however the cut in the St. Louis-Kansas City passenger rate—the Missouri Pacific's bread and butter [42]—which led to the general rate-slashing.

There was no administrative machinery to set in motion in an effort to stop these disturbances. The presidents of the western roads therefore acted informally and called a meeting to settle the war by agreement. Gould however had returned again to his accustomed technique. He thought he saw in this disturbed situation a means of helping the Missouri Pacific at the expense of the other roads. Hence neither he nor any other representative of the Missouri Pacific attended the meeting. The meeting produced no results. Cable of the Rock Island insisted that Gould was responsible for the failure. Gould, he said, could "settle the whole Western railroad rate war in five minutes if he wants to." [43] Perhaps in the heat of the moment, and in a spirit of resentment, Cable gave Gould more credit than he was entitled to, but there is no gainsaying the fact that Gould's influence was exerted against the side of stability.

Another meeting of the presidents meanwhile was held in Chicago early in May. Every western line was represented, either in person or by letter. Although the presidents remained in continuous session for a week, no agreement was reached and the rate war continued—in fact it grew worse. In any event, rate cuts were intensified. In passenger fares, chaos prevailed.[44] It became evident to western railroad officers and financial observers that Gould was the chief disturbing factor. "It is conceded," wrote a hostile Gould critic, "that the question of a speedy restoration of rates depends, to a great extent, upon the course that Jay Gould will pursue."[45] The Atchison officers took the lead in an effort to bring Gould to terms. At one time it was reported that the management of that road gave him twenty-four hours to decide upon peace or war. Gould at the time was ill; but through his son he made overtures to the chairman of the Atchison. Congratulating him on the acquisition of the Frisco, he expressed the hope that the southwestern roads might live in peace and harmony. Gould's son, George, stated publicly that his father wanted the Missouri Pacific to be brought into harmony with the Atchison, and that the road would restore rates as soon as the differences with other western roads were adjusted.[46]

Gould thus found that the road to rate stabilization was a thorny one. He found it difficult to operate in the spirit of harmony, in which mutual concessions were imperative. Although he had observed that no competitive advantage that he could secure for the Missouri Pacific would be as profitable as an all-around agreement, it was difficult for him to apply this lesson. He had spent a lifetime in a contrary pattern. He had learned from experience that competitive advantages led to corporate profits and to increases in security values. He was now living in a new environment in which this sequence was no longer true. When rate cuts were renewed in February, 1890, security prices were as badly demoralized as railroad rates. When in early May, on the contrary, it seemed that the railroad presidents would be able to end the rate wars, stock values increased to an extent which led at least one writer to declare that this period was "among the most remarkable occurrences that Wall Street [had] seen in some years."[47]

After cessation of the violent rate wars of the early part of the year, Gould set himself to work to create a more permanent administrative framework for the maintenance of rate schedules in the southwestern area. After weeks of negotiation, he succeeded in forming what he called his "ideal" association—the Southwestern Railroad & Steamship Association—which included all lines south of Kansas City and west of the Missouri River. The administrative organization consisted of an executive committee of five "with powers as autocratic as [were] those of the Czar of Russia." This committee was controlled by the representatives of Gould, Huntington, and the Atchison lines.[48] The decision of a majority of the executive committee was final. Gould apparently tied himself hand and foot. He could order no change in rates on the Missouri Pacific which would hurt his competitors, except with the consent of the new association's executive committee. It was a short, clearly written contract. A financial writer who had examined the other compacts made in the previous decade, declared it to be "one of the shortest and strongest documents of the kind ever formulated." [49]

Gould had taken the leadership in drawing up this agreement. He had long contended for a firm compact and was satisfied with it. A few weeks later he concluded an arrangement with the Atchison for the limiting of new extensions and for the maintenance of rates.[50] This was the kind of agreement which the Atchison thought that it had with Gould in the early eighties. For some time thereafter Gould and the Atchison group worked in harmony. Since Huntington also had been working closely with Gould, it appeared that these executives might be able to work out an arrangement that would dominate the Southwest and pave the way for the promotion of rate stability, and the return of railroad earning power.

The conclusion of the agreement thus strengthened the prospects of all the southwestern roads. Beyond that it increased the personal prestige and power of Gould as a railroad leader. When the southwestern presidents met about a month later after the formulation of the new agreement, a spirit of peace and harmony prevailed like a "flock of turtle doves," remarked an observer.[51] With the same volume of traffic the roads found they were earning more than at any time since the passage of the Interstate Commerce Act almost four years before. Gould felt encouraged to resume his activity in behalf of co-operation and united action as an alternative to competitive rivalry. He again brought forth his clearing-house plan, suggesting that it could be used as a vehicle for the unified operation of all the western railroads. A group of New York bankers, dissatisfied with the obsolete Interstate Commerce Railway Association, appointed a committee of railroad presidents to devise a plan for a new association on lines somewhat similar to the clearing-house idea. The committee planned to discuss the subject with Gould and Huntington, among others.

Active consideration meanwhile was given to another Gould proposal. He had originally brought this idea to the attention of railroad presidents in November and December of 1888 in the conferences which preceded the formation of the presidents' agreement. At that time he advocated the abolition of all freight agencies of individual roads and the establishment of a single agency at each important traffic center. That agency would bill traffic in such a way that each line would receive its proportion of through and competitive business. Gould estimated that in addition to maintaining the rate structure, the scheme would produce an annual saving of between $2,000,000 and $3,000,000.

This line of reasoning was taken up in the summer of 1890 by A. F. Walker, chairman of the Interstate Commerce Railway Association, and elaborated before the Senate Committee on Interstate Commerce. Walker referred to the increasing expense of solicitation, to the unnecessary increase in competitive train service, which he said was sapping the revenues of carriers everywhere. Through trains were being duplicated in all directions. These unnecessary expenses involved in unregulated competition amounted "to millions of dollars annually; probably fifty million would be far within the mark." [52] This was the beginning of an argument which has lasted from that day to the present.

Walker, a few months after presenting these views to the Senate Committee, issued a call for a meeting to reconstruct the association and to remedy existing conditions, which, he said, in a short time would make "receivers the managers of most of the western roads." [53] He insisted further that the roads should discard independent action in making competitive rates, and should put the subject into the hands of a central agency, responsible only to the presidents and directors of the member lines. Walker was talking the language of Gould, and emphasizing the latter's arguments advanced over the past two years. Walker was calling a meeting to renew or to rebuild an existing organization in order to establish an administrative framework along lines which Gould had just completed in the Southwest. It seemed again, as it had two years before, that Gould would be able to take the leadership in the West, and work out a proposal upon lines similar to those he had already perfected in the Southwest. Whether or not he would have been able to impose his ideas on other western presidents cannot of course be established. Before the railroad presidents could be called together to consider the new proposals, however, Gould had already taken other steps which again upset the western equilibrium. Again he moved in the direction of competitive acquisition. Again he moved for the purpose of acquiring advantages for the Missouri Pacific. Again he demonstrated his inability to work in harmony and in peace in the light of a settled pattern. And again he justified the opposition of those western railroad men who had persistently fought any proposals designed and sponsored by him. Gould probably thought that he could not be certain whether one policy or another could be successful; whether a policy of a competitive advantage or competitive stability would prevail. So he decided to experiment.

NOTES FOR CHAPTER XXVIII

1. See on this point Phila. *Press*, March 20, 1885; March 23, 1885.
2. Burlington archives, Huntington to Adams, Nov. 5, 1885.
3. Ibid., Perkins to Adams, Nov. 9, 1885.
4. Ibid., Adams to Perkins, Nov. 9, 1885.
5. Ibid., Perkins to Hughitt, Feb. 24, 1888.
6. Ibid., Perkins to H. B. Stone, May 4, 1888.
7. The quotation is from the language used by Railroad Commissioners of Kansas, cited in *R. R. Gaz.*, Jan. 13, 1888, 32.
8. Known hereafter as the Stickney road.
9. This is the opinion of the president of the Wabash Western—the company which owned the lines of the Wabash west of the Mississippi River—in the 1888 annual report of that road, cited in *Ry. Review*, March 30, 1889, 173.
10. Phila. *North American*, April 27, 1887.
11. Kiernan's News Agency, cited in *Stockholder*, Sept. 14, 1887.
12. *Chron.*, Sept. 17, 1887, 369.
13. *Stockholder*, Sept. 26, 1891.
14. *R. R. Gaz.*, Feb. 10, 1888, 98. The phrase "totally demoralized" is used by *Chron.*, Feb. 4, 1888, 145, in discussing the rates between Chicago and St. Paul, Chicago and Omaha, Chicago and Kansas City, and Chicago and St. Louis; and Hughitt, president of the Chicago & Northwestern referred at about the same time to "existing disastrous conditions." See Burlington archives, letter of Perkins to Albert Fink, Feb. 9, 1888.
15. *Bradstreet*, Oct. 18, 1890, 662.
16. New York *Times*, Jan. 22, 1888.
17. New York *Tribune*, March 25, 1888.
18. *Stockholder*, April 25, 1888.
19. Ibid., Oct. 22, 1888.
20. *Chron.*, Sept. 29, 1888, 368.
21. 159 Interstate Commerce Commission Reports (1929), 522.
22. New York *Times*, Nov. 28, 1888.
23. *R. R. Gaz.*, Nov. 30, 1888, 796. The plan was published also in New York *Times*, Nov. 28, 1888.
24. New York *Sun*, Dec. 16, 1888.
25. New York *Times*, Dec. 4, 1888, citing *Stockholder*.

26. New York *Herald*, Nov. 25, 1888.
27. For evidence on this point see New York *Tribune*, Dec. 16, 1888. The lack of faith in Gould's leadership was also evident upon other occasions. See for example, New York *Tribune*, Feb. 24, 1889, which credits an unnamed railroad man as having said, in referring to Gould's voting trust scheme, that the scheme may be good but that the railroad men would not try it.
28. *Iron Age*, Jan. 10, 1889, 63.
29. For summary of text of plan, see *Chron.*, Jan. 12, 1889, 67-8.
30. This is the wording of the resolution approved by the board of directors, cited in New York *Times*, Feb. 21, 1889.
31. *Bradstreet*, March 2, 1889, 143.
32. Burlington archives, "Memorandum" on Interstate Commerce Railway Association, dated June 26, 1889.
33. Boston *Transcript*, Feb. 11, 1890.
34. Phila. *Press*, March 14, 1889.
35. *Stockholder*, July 20, 1889.
36. Phila. *Press*, Sept. 14, 1889.
37. San Francisco *Bulletin*, cited in *Ry. Review*, March 31, 1888, 176.
38. *Ry. Review*, Oct. 26, 1889, 620.
39. Dodge Papers, Adams to G. M. Dodge, Oct. 23, 1889.
40. New York *Times*, March 9, 1890.
41. *R. R. Gaz.*, Feb. 14, 1890, 120; Feb. 21, 1890, 136.
42. So said Gould in New York *Times*, April 30, 1890.
43. Ibid., April 28, 1890.
44. This was the language of *Chron.*, May 17, 1890, 679.
45. New York *Times*, May 23, 1890.
46. Ibid., May 28, 1890.
47. *Bradstreet*, May 3, 1890, 280.
48. New York *Tribune*, Sept. 19, 1890.
49. Ibid., Sept. 30, 1890.
50. New York *Times*, Nov. 22, 1890.
51. *Ry. World*, Nov. 1, 1890, 1039.
52. The arguments of Walker are summarized in *Ry. Review*, July 5, 1890, 386.
53. *Bradstreet*, Oct. 18, 1890, 662.

CHAPTER XXIX

Gould Experiments

By 1890 Gould's holdings had become well stabilized. He had the controlling interest in three dividend-paying enterprises—the Missouri Pacific, the Manhattan, and the Western Union. The stocks of the latter two were desirable investments. Neither had any substantial competition; the Manhattan in fact had none. In the spring of 1891 the Manhattan bought control of another transit line: the Suburban Rapid Transit Company. Morgan, who represented the interests of the owners of the latter, was so satisfied with the investment caliber of the Manhattan stock that he recommended an exchange of that stock for the Suburban's. The Manhattan, whose control was acquired by Gould at the end of a receivership, was on a 6 per cent dividend basis. Its credit was one of the best and the Morgan firm bid actively for the opportunity of buying its bonds for resale to customers on a low yield basis. Morgan joined the board of directors, and Gould could say with considerable pride that the Manhattan, financially, was one of the best properties in the country.

Western Union was also prosperous, and had likewise achieved a position of relative freedom from competition. From the host of competitors that sprang up to challenge the water-logged Western Union in 1881, only the Postal remained.

Aside from his third major holding—the Missouri Pacific—Gould had numerous interests in widely scattered industrial and railway auxiliary properties. His holdings in the St. Louis Bridge and Tunnel properties were valuable. These were merged with others in the area, and in exchange for his stocks he secured interests in the enlarged and financially profitable Terminal Railroad Association. In this case again, as in many others, he worked hand in hand with Morgan.

In industrial enterprises Gould also occupied an important position. He was an extensive stockholder in coal-mining properties in Missouri, Kansas, Oklahoma, Texas, Iowa, and Illinois. The leading outlet for bituminous coal at that time was found in the railroad industry. As Gould extended his railroad system he purchased coal lands, transferred them to new companies, and then made the latters' stock valuable by contracts made with his railroads. From the Wabash, for example, he secured profitable contracts for the purchase of coal in Illinois and Iowa; while in southeastern Missouri he organized a coal company which sold coal to the Missouri Pacific.[1] It is impossible to state how profitable these coal companies were. Although data on their earnings and dividends are scanty and fugitive, it may be inferred, but not with any degree of certainty, that for a time at least the coal companies succeeded in selling merchandise to the railroad companies controlled by Gould at prices in excess of the prevailing market. At other times, as a result of price wars in this competitive industry, the price of coal fell below cost, and on such occasions the Gould-controlled coal companies operated at a loss.[2] His major railroad holdings were represented by the Missouri Pacific stock. On this stock a dividend of 6 per cent was paid from 1880 to 1882. It was later increased to 7 per cent, in April, 1888, reduced to 6, and in the following July to 4, only to be passed in the fall of 1891. The dividend record of the Missouri Pacific was unique. In the decade of the eighties its stock stood on the same plane with the stock of some well managed properties. The investment rating of its securities was superior to those of Huntington's far-flung transcontinental lines. A considerable body of investment opinion throughout the eighties looked confidently to the elimination of the Missouri Pacific dividend. The collapse in 1884 appeared to lend substance to these expectations, yet those who sold the stock were disappointed.

In seeking an explanation of the good earnings of the Missouri Pacific in the eighties two factors must be considered. Gould in the first place followed policies which consistently favored the Missouri Pacific as against his other railroad properties. In the movement of traffic, in the division of rates, and in the distribution of terminal allowances, the Missouri Pacific was favored, and the Wabash, International, Kansas & Texas, and the Texas & Pacific—to place the most charitable interpretation on Gould's policies—were not favored. The earnings of the Missouri Pacific were bolstered and the earnings of the other properties were impaired.

In the second place, prior to the expansion program of 1886–1887, the Missouri Pacific was well protected from excessive railroad competition. Between Kansas City and St. Louis, aside from the excessively circuitous route of the Frisco, the road had only the competition of the Alton, the favored connection of the Atchison. The rates on the Missouri Pacific, therefore, changed little in the early and middle eighties. There were few price wars, and the relatively stable rates, accompanied by a rise in traffic, disturbed only by occasional local crop failures, produced a rise in earnings.

The Missouri Pacific was thus able to pay a dividend at the very time when its associated companies produced only financial disaster for their security holders. The demoralizing rate wars of the late eighties, however, introduced a chain of events which led to the interruption in the forward march of the Missouri Pacific's earnings. In this environment Gould was helpless in the face of the forces which he had done so much to unleash, and for the first time he resorted to a policy designed to replace competition by co-operative action between independently owned and operated properties. It was a new field of activity to Gould. Previous co-operative moves were part of a program of expansion, and were normally accompanied by aggression in territory not covered by the agreement; or, after a lapse of some months, were followed by further moves into the very territory in which stability had been achieved.

In 1887–88, however, when his building program came to an abrupt halt, as did the program of almost all western railroad competitors, Gould made no further aggressive moves. It has already been shown how in the following two years he made an effort to achieve through agreements with other roads a stability in rates which he, in company with almost all other railroad men, had hoped would lead to stable earnings. In this he was disappointed. Despite the leadership taken by railroad men and bankers the rate stability lasted only a few weeks. The competitive forces soon expressed themselves again in repeated rate wars. By the end of 1890 Gould was convinced that stabilization by rate agreements would not of itself serve as a means of solving the problem of transforming higher revenues into higher profits. Gould was not certain which policy to follow. It was evident that competition carried to extreme limits without any basis for united action would be suicidal. On the other hand, a commitment in behalf of the principle of co-operation would not be advisable if the Missouri Pacific were weakened. He seems to have decided therefore, some time in the summer or fall of 1890, to experiment with both policies. In the Southwest, after reaching an agreement with Huntington and the Atchison lines through the Southwestern Association, he prepared a plan for co-operative action among all the roads in this territory. His interest in co-operation, however, did not lead him to overlook the necessities of his own properties, and he decided to strengthen at the same time the position of the Missouri Pacific. His expansion program had placed the Union Pacific in an unenviable position. That road, at its eastern termini of Omaha and Kansas City, had traded traffic with roads which, except for the Burlington, were friendly connections. Since these roads had no lines west of the Missouri, they had no competitive interests which clashed with those of the Union Pacific.

Now, with the Rock Island in Kansas, the Northwestern in Wyoming, and the St. Paul in Kansas City, the Union Pacific found it necessary to change its policy. It could no longer trade with all friendly connections. To Gould the Union Pacific's traffic agreement with the Northwestern obliged each road to trade with the other exclusively. The Rock Island and the St. Paul were also dissatisfied, and they urged that the Union Pacific permit them to use its bridge at Omaha jointly. A refusal would lead them to build a bridge of their own. In May of 1890 an arrangement was made whereby in return for an annual rent, plus the assumption of a proportion of the joint expenses, the Union Pacific permitted the other companies to use the bridge for both freight and passenger business. By use of the bridge and the auxiliary tracks, the Rock Island secured a route to Denver, and the St. Paul, by using the Rock Island's line, also obtained a part of the transcontinental traffic. The business of both roads was transferred to the Union Pacific at Denver for further movement.

It was an arrangement which suited all three participating

roads. The Northwestern raised no objection, but Gould was not happy. To the extent that the Rock Island and the St. Paul moved more business, the Missouri Pacific moved less. Gould although dissatisfied made no aggressive move. In October, 1890, however, at the very time when he was working out the agreement for the maintenance of rates in southwestern territory, the Union Pacific made a further move. Adams demanded that eastern connections increase the compensation of the Union Pacific for the movement of business to and from the Missouri River. "Our proportion of the through rate has been too low," he said. "Our connections have been taking the lion's share. We have been accepting a pro-rate on the basis of 60 cents to the Missouri River from Chicago. Formerly those roads pro-rated with us on a 75-cent basis. Rates from Chicago to the Missouri River have been restored by our eastern connections, but they still want us to pro-rate on the 60-cent basis. This we will not do. The Northwestern readily consented to allow us the increased division, and we simply notified the other roads that they must allow us the same, or we would have to refuse to do any through business with them." [3] The Union Pacific's eastern connections refused to grant the demand, and on November 1 all divisions with the Union Pacific were withdrawn. The Union Pacific therefore was obliged to pay local or higher rates over all eastern connections except the Northwestern.

The Missouri Pacific, at least from the standpoint of ability to compete for transcontinental traffic, was placed in a weak position. By virtue of the joint bridge arrangement, the Rock Island and the St. Paul could pick up traffic from the Union Pacific at Denver, carry it over non-Union Pacific lines to the Missouri River, and then beyond via their own lines to Chicago. The Northwestern could carry traffic exclusively for the Union Pacific between Chicago and Omaha. The Missouri Pacific was a loser.

Gould therefore looked upon the Union Pacific as an enemy of the Missouri Pacific. Early in 1890 he had no interest in the company's stock. If he acquired control of the road he might introduce an unstable factor by making it more difficult to eliminate disastrous rate wars. To a lesser extent he had open to him the same choice of policies which were available a decade earlier as a result of his acquisition of the Wabash. It would appear that after a decade of experience with the disturbing character of competitive as contrasted with co-operative policies, Gould would have chosen a different course. He decided nevertheless to acquire control of the Union Pacific.

That road was then burdened with a heavy debt. A substantial part of its bonds had been issued in the early seventies for the purpose of retrieving past financial mistakes, and the proceeds had therefore not been invested in plant and equipment. Proceeds of additional securities had been invested in property which brought slight return. In 1889, furthermore, it impaired its financial strength (from the short-run point of view) by a blunder in financing the acquisition of a controlling interest in the Oregon Railway & Navigation Company—a line which afforded the Union Pacific an outlet to Portland. The Union Pacific, after raising part of the funds by the sale of bonds, discovered that it could sell no more bonds on favorable terms, and accordingly withheld their sale pending the return of a more suitable money market. Meanwhile it borrowed money on the bonds as collateral. The money market, instead of improving, became worse; the floating debt remained and even increased.

The paralyzing rate wars and the disturbance in railroad earnings made it impossible to pay the floating debt. The liquidation in the security markets was intensified by events in the British investment market. In order to raise cash the bankers sold railroad securities on American exchanges. The market turned weak in early summer, and became acutely so in September and October. Despite the purchase of bonds by the United States Treasury and the resultant increase in the surplus reserves of the banks, security liquidation developed. By late October and early November a panic was on. Bank reserves dropped below the legal minimum; loans were called, and the stock market suffered from the most violent break in prices since May, 1884.

November, 1890, found Gould in a comfortable position. According to different estimates he had anywhere from $15,000,000 to $20,000,000 in cash, available for investment.[4] When the stock market crashed Gould was ready to buy. The price of Union Pacific was low, partly because of the general market weakness and partly because of the road's floating debt. In 1890 he and his associates, particularly Dillon and Frederick Ames, bought stock. The fate of the company was in the hands of its floating-debt creditors. Gould attacked the company's credit, at first secretly, then openly, through an interview in a New York paper. Adams sought aid from both Drexel, Morgan & Company and the Vanderbilt interests. If they agreed to take over the floating debt, they could take over the management. They refused.[5] Gould assumed this responsibility. He made an arrangement with some of the leading creditors, and agreed to lend the road enough money to meet its January coupons and stave off receivership. Adams resigned and Gould and his followers assumed control. Dillon, president under the Gould control in the 1874–84 decade, again became president.

The Union Pacific acquisition, although perhaps the most valuable, was by no means the only addition to the list of Gould's holdings in the panic weeks of 1890. From the southeastern end of the Missouri Pacific at Memphis, Tennessee, ramified the lines of the Richmond Terminal system. On the face of things, looking at the map and without examining any of the complicated underlying traffic realities, an observer might conclude that if a community of interests were built up between the Missouri Pacific and this property, a new traffic route could be established between southern Kansas and southeastern points. Those in charge of the policies of the Richmond Terminal, though not operating railroad men, were hard traders. Since Gould could come to no satisfactory agreement with them, he took advantage of the low prices, and bought about 15 per cent of its stock.[6] In December he and Sage were elected to the board.

This news was greeted with enthusiasm and anticipation of good things to come. A newspaper in Atlanta declared that Gould would soon go on the board of a road which connected with the Richmond Terminal and give the latter an entrance to the seaboard at Savannah. This road—the Central of Georgia—also had connections with a steamship line operating from Savannah to New York City. Gould, this newspaper declared, would "be the power in the Richmond Terminal system" and would give the Central of Georgia an "enormous" amount of traffic from the Missouri Pacific.[7]

Gould's power in railroad affairs was now substantially increased. A Philadelphia paper reporter friendly to Gould observed that Gould was the "master of our railroad system," [8] and a New York writer was certain that Gould had "not only the key to the situation, but something more." He had a plan to settle vexatious railroad questions which would stabilize values, and his work from this time on must be constructive.[9] The Burlington management, however, was not impressed. "I guess," wrote Forbes, "we can get on quite as well with the new as the old rule." [10]

While Gould had thus strengthened his position in the railway industry, he continued his search for a solution to the problem of eliminating rate wars by developing the possibilities of co-operative action. In common with others he was convinced that such action was essential. There was scarcely an important annual railroad report of a western line which did not refer to the urgent necessity of concerted action. That of the St. Paul, for example, declared: "Unrestrained competition will, in the end, destroy all competition," [11] while the Burlington's report insisted that "without some method of effective co-operation competing lines must become bankrupt, and in the end consolidated." [12]

Gould was alive to the necessities of the situation. After the southwestern pool had been completed in mid-October, he became active in working out a plan for joint railroad action. On the very first day of the panicky market of November 11, he announced approval of Walker's suggestions for the replacement of competitive solicitors by joint agencies.[13] He also enlisted the aid of Morgan, who talked things over with him both at St. Louis and later at his (Morgan's) office in New York City.[14] Gould worked out his views in a memorandum which he asked railroad presidents to sign. The memorandum contemplated a number of far-reaching innovations. Those lines which did not enter into the agreement would be blacklisted. Business would be divided among the several roads, and the building of parallel lines would be prohibited for five years.[15] Though Gould succeeded in securing the signatures of a number of presidents, he accomplished nothing.

Morgan then issued a call for a meeting of western railroad presidents at his home on December 15 to draft a new plan. If Gould believed that because of his accretion of corporate power he could enlist the confidence of railroad presidents, he was soon to be undeceived. The idea that he would step out of his activities as a competitive businessman interested in initiating policies calculated to advance the interests of his own railroads in order to save the general situation was too novel to be widely accepted. The "public is a little shy," remarked one of the leading railroad journals, in believing that Gould could inspire a reform which would eliminate rate-cutting on the western and southwestern roads. Perkins, Cable, and Hughitt, among others, were not impressed by Gould's reforming activities. When the railroad presidents met at Morgan's house, therefore, it was not at all surprising that Morgan presented a plan, prepared, not by Gould, but by others. Morgan stated that a simple and comprehensive, although ineffective, plan had been agreed upon by the Vanderbilts and the Pennsylvania, and that based upon this he had prepared another. His plan included the suggestion that a committee should establish and maintain uniform rates between competitive points. This was a statement of objective rather than of ways and means. Everybody subscribed to the idea. The new committee would administer the joint agencies for securing traffic at competitive points. This was Gould's pet hobby. Morgan's plan also contemplated the dismissal of any company official who changed an established tariff. This was also a favorite idea with Gould, who long had advocated the use of sanctions without which, he declared, the agreement could not be made to function.

Morgan, in including provisions in the agreement calculated to please Gould, was playing the traditional part of the conservative banker, who is frequently cast in the role of an arbitrator. He thereby solves many a business dispute, especially if the dispute involves conflicting personalities or varying interpretations of a particular contract. In this case the differences between Gould and the other presidents arose from deep-seated competitive forces. Railroad executives looking to their own property interests did not appreciate the necessity, as did Morgan, of making concessions for the purpose of pleasing Gould or any other competitor. The draft of the agreement, as finally approved, eliminated the joint soliciting agencies of the traffic pool. Instead the plan set up an agency which on application by a railroad could make an equitable division of business between the lines interested, "upon such basis and upon such lawful manner" as was deemed advisable. The agreement contained no provision calling for the elimination of the construction of duplicate railroad lines. A body known as the commissioners, headed by a president, served as the supervisory agency to carry out the agreement, although its decisions were subject to review by an advisory board. The agreement declared that the decisions made either by the commissioners or the advisory board should not be construed to deprive the directors of any road of their right to fix rates and make rules and regulations affecting their own business.

Although the agreement had dropped most of the provisions for which Gould had so long contended, he expressed himself as satisfied. In many respects the new arrangement was similar to the one adopted two years before, and which within a few months had so ingloriously collapsed. There were, however, several new features. Withdrawal from the association could be made only by formal action of the presidents themselves. Penalty for infraction of the decisions of the association was made more severe. The member roads agreed to discharge any officials found guilty of cutting rates. The new plan was not greeted with the same enthusiasm as had been accorded the first. Perhaps the railroad presidents themselves were not particularly hopeful. They said nothing for publication, though to sophisticated observers the railroad meeting was a disappointment. It "fell awfully flat," declared the New York critic of Gould and Morgan, and of Drexel, Morgan & Company.[16] To make the new arrangement work it was necessary that its spirit more than its letter be obeyed. Compacts and agreements had characterized the railroad industry for more than ten years. While some lasted longer than others, each had collapsed.

Meanwhile the Missouri Pacific's earnings were declining. It was apparent that the road would soon be obliged to follow its three major competitors—the Union Pacific, the Atchison and the Southern Pacific—and pay no dividends. In order to maintain earnings it was essential that Gould use his newly acquired power over the Union Pacific to promote rate stability. If that road were exploited for the purpose of benefiting the Missouri Pacific, he would be following the same tactics which had repeatedly unsettled railroad rate structures in the seventies and eighties. Such a policy would invite retaliation by roads losing traffic to the Missouri Pacific. Such retaliation involved dangers far more serious than those of former years. In the earlier period competitive tactics left a number of small lines so helpless, that they were in no position to retaliate. By the late eighties and early nineties, however, most of these companies had by consolidation and acquisition been eliminated. The competition now was mainly between powerful railroad properties.

Despite these dangers Gould announced his aggressive policy, not in words but in deeds. Scarcely had the presidents met in Morgan's home than, as the dominant factor in the Union Pacific, he made his first move, announcing that the joint arrangement by which the Rock Island and the St. Paul were authorized to use the Omaha bridge was invalid. Both roads had announced that they would soon move cars across the bridge to Denver and the Pacific Coast. The bridge contracts, said Gould, were "the most ridiculous he ever met in his railroad experience." [17] Before he took a definite position and declared these contracts illegal, he secured able legal judgment confirming his position. John F. Dillon was still counsel for the Union Pacific. In the spring he had approved the contract as being within the jurisdiction of the company's charter. In the winter he committed a right-about-face and concluded that the contract was beyond the powers of the contracting parties. Cancellation of the contract was strongly resisted by both the Rock Island and St. Paul, and the case went to court.

In using the Union Pacific as a competitive weapon, Gould did not overlook another obvious opportunity to aid his Missouri Pacific—he also canceled the traffic agreement between the former and the Northwestern. It was a risky, though a highly promising policy. Wherever he could, he had the Union Pacific divert its trade eastbound from the Northwestern to the Missouri Pacific. The Northwestern, with the co-operation of the Vanderbilt interests, then renewed oft-threatened plans to build from Wyoming west. The New York Central and the Northwestern managements, for example, made a trip over the latter's lines to determine the feasibility of such expansion.[18]

These moves and countermoves involved the Missouri Pacific only in its western territory in Colorado, Missouri, and Kansas.

In the Southwest there was still a strong prospect that Gould would unite his interests with those of the Atchison and the Huntington lines. These roads controlled three of the five members of the executive committee of the southwestern pool. If they could decide upon a basis for the division of traffic among themselves, it was probable that rates could be stabilized. In the first few months of 1891, active negotiations proceeded in an effort to arrive at a solution. From time to time trouble was encountered and it seemed that rate stability never would be reached. Early in February the roads between Chicago and St. Louis reduced their rates to southwestern points from 10 to 30 per cent, with the Atchison taking the initiative.[19] Early in April the Texas Railroad Commission reduced rates, thus making it even more difficult for the larger railroad properties, even if they arrived at a solution, to keep rates stable. Nevertheless, negotiations continued. It was proposed that the properties combine their interests in a joint-ownership plan. The major stockholders would delegate certain powers to a board of arbitration with power superior to that of individual boards of directors. The board would represent joint ownership, and would act through power received directly from the stockholders.[20] Both Gould and Huntington were in favor of the scheme.

These men, however, were hard bargainers, and each insisted upon a division of the business unacceptable to the other. Gould, in order to give the Missouri Pacific a more adequate share of the available traffic, followed a policy of expediency. Due to a change in the tariff, large shipments of sugar were available for movement from the eastern seaboard to western markets. The basis of distribution of this traffic among the western roads was important. Gould believed that if the Missouri Pacific could get the lion's share of the business, its earnings would increase and his bargaining position against Huntington improve. The road therefore cut rates on sugar from forty-eight cents to forty cents, and since the other roads refused to meet these reductions, it hauled most of the traffic. It was not a secret cut since the tariff had been duly filed with the Interstate Commerce Commission. It was, nevertheless, a sharp trick which Gould and the Missouri Pacific played on the other western roads. Gould thus, in order to carry out some competitive deal in the Southwest, had been the first to violate the agreement made by the western railroads in mid-December to maintain rates.

The first quarterly meeting of the advisory board of the new Western Traffic Association was scheduled for the fifteenth of April. Its serious problem was the action to be taken on the sugar rate cuts. The board stated officially that the matters to be considered at its first meeting were "of such importance that, if unacted upon at an early date, the integrity and life" of the association were threatened.[21] Nevertheless, neither Gould nor Huntington nor any of the representatives of their roads attended the meeting. The members who did attend, only to find that because of the absence of a quorum no business could be done, were bitter. One member was particularly outspoken: "It was a dirty trick on the part of Mr. Gould," he declared, "to allow us to go out there [Chicago] for nothing." [22]

The board called another meeting in early May which Gould attended. He was now all for compromise. Admitting that the Missouri Pacific had cut sugar rates, he expressed willingness to abide by any decision the board might make, though he personally disclaimed any responsibility for having made the cut. That was done by the traffic manager on his own responsibility. Here was a beautifully clear case for punitive action by the board, and the board found it easy to punish the offender. It decided that the Missouri Pacific had violated the agreement and should discharge the guilty party. The decision was accepted with good grace and the road promptly discharged the traffic manager. It is needless to say that Gould soon arranged to give the "goat" another position.

Despite the cuts in sugar tariffs, the rate situation in the first half of 1891 was well stabilized. There was then less rate-cutting and underhanded competition, and perhaps fewer secret rebates, than there had been for some years. It is not possible to measure the extent to which this movement could be attributed to the new association. Railroad traffic at the time was moving in good volume. Stable rates, however, did not mean higher rates. Most states had already established regulatory commissions which were closely watching the rate structure, and that meant lower rates.

Though Gould had made advances to the Union Pacific to enable it to pay its interest, the floating debt kept mounting. Its ownership was widely scattered. Some of the notes had been placed with locomotive and car companies, while others were held by commercial banks and trust companies—some by Drexel, Morgan & Company, and of these a portion was endorsed by Gould and some of his associates.

In the first half of 1891 the Union Pacific safely passed through each crisis and, despite the increase in the size of its debt, no pressure was exerted by creditors. In April at the annual meeting, the company was authorized to execute a new mortgage to secure bonds of $25,000,000, of which $10,000,000 would be sold immediately. Gould of course strongly supported the bond issue. "There can be nothing better than the security we propose," he declared, and he continued, "Of course I shall take some of the bonds. I don't know a better security." [23] The money markets however were not receptive, and none of the bonds were sold. The heavy interest payments due on July 1 were met in part from funds advanced again by Gould. Early in August a sudden drop in price of Union Pacific stock heralded the arrival of a climax. While Gould was then in the Far West, a number of the holders of the floating debt demanded payment.[24] With the market for railroad securities almost closed, it seemed impossible to raise large sums of money. One alternative to receivership remained: Holders of the Union Pacific might be induced to accept notes running for a three- to five-year period in exchange for their demand notes. Those who refused to accept the exchange, provided they did not represent a substantial percentage of the floating debt, would be paid in cash.

Gould in the Far West announced that he was prepared to organize a syndicate to carry out the plan. If the notes could not be sold, the syndicate would advance the funds, and Gould and Sage, respectively, for their personal accounts, agreed to lend $5,000,000 and $1,000,000.[25] The effort, however, failed and it was Morgan who came to the rescue. Though he was not the banker for the Union Pacific, his firm was one of the holders of the floating debt. A $2,000,000 Union Pacific note held by the Morgan firm moreover was endorsed by Gould.[26]

Within less than a week after Morgan had agreed to undertake the task, a realistic plan had been submitted to the Union Pacific's board. Almost all of the treasury securities of the borrowing road were to be trusteed as collateral for a proposed note issue. The par value of the collateral was about $40,000,000; while the face value of the new securities amounted to $24,000,000. The par value of the collateral did not, however, represent its market value. Some securities had no market. They were stocks or bonds of small roads with no independent earning power. Their earnings were associated with the earnings and policies of the Union Pacific, which owned all of their stocks.

It was neither possible nor necessary at that time to sell $24,000,000 of securities. The plan was based upon the idea that many of the holders of the floating debt would exchange their paper for new notes because of their confidence in the integrity and judgment of Morgan. Creditors trusted him, and distrusted Gould. Many banks acceded to the suggestion of Morgan, and exchanged their holdings for the new notes. Gould agreed to take $1,000,000, and in exchange for this subscription, he was relieved from his endorsement on some Union Pacific paper held by the Drexel, Morgan firm.[27]

By mid-September holders of about $14,000,000 of the paper had agreed to accept the new notes. To finance essential needs it was necessary to sell only between $5,000,000 and $6,000,000 to new investors. The cash thus raised would be used to pay off those creditors who needed the cash. The $14,000,000 accepted by the creditors included Gould's commitment, and Gould also agreed to buy $1,000,000 of the new notes. Morgan encountered difficulty in selling the notes and it appeared that the Union Pacific crisis was not yet over. Gould tried to wiggle out of his commitment—at least so Morgan believed. He said that Gould was "juggling with the property"; he was reported to be "indignant" and to have informed Gould that unless he acted frankly he would be hustled out of the road.[28] According to another story Morgan told Gould to come to his office. Gould said he was ill, to which Morgan replied that he would be in his office all day. Gould came, and when he left Morgan's office after an hour's conference Morgan, according to this account, "looked angry and Gould sulky." Within an hour or two, however, it was announced that Gould had subscribed to the new notes.[29]

Though the crisis had been surmounted, Gould's power over the Union Pacific was weakened. He could no longer as the controlling factor in its affairs, even had he owned the majority of the stock, exploit the Union Pacific for the benefit of his favorite child—the Missouri Pacific. The policies of the Union Pacific were in the hands of the creditors' committee, and that committee was dominated by Morgan.

Gould meanwhile was confronted with increasing difficulties in handling the Missouri Pacific. It was no longer possible to use either the Wabash or the Texas & Pacific to bolster the earnings. Both properties were watched by aggressive minority interests. Although he individually was the largest holder of the Wabash stock, a sizable proportion was concentrated in the hands of foreign investors. The holders of the income bonds were also well organized, and did not propose to permit the Wabash to reduce its earnings in order to help the Missouri Pacific.

The same situation prevailed on the Texas & Pacific, though here the minority stockholders were not so well organized. On this property, also, there was an income bond. The road's inability to pay interest on that bond presented a threat to Gould's control. The income mortgage provided that if by 1892 interest was not paid the income bondholders could, through the trustees, take possession and operate the property.

The loss of the western arm of the southwestern system, controlled by the Kansas & Texas, proved to be another damaging blow to the Missouri Pacific. The Kansas & Texas had become an aggressive competitor. The most serious factor in impairing the earnings and financial strength of the Missouri Pacific, however, was the war of rates. All Gould's efforts in the direction of cooperation had been fruitless and the rate wars continued. The two presidential agreements had accomplished little. Though the southwestern pool had more promise, it finally broke on the rock of Huntington's independence. It was clear that the pool despite some apparent success was but a hollow shell.

By the summer and fall of 1891 Gould had found it impossible to raise rates from their low levels. The Atchison by this time had passed its dividend; the Southern Pacific had never paid one, and the Missouri Pacific had also reduced its dividend. The break in earnings had demoralized the market for railroad securities and had made it difficult for the Missouri Pacific to complete its financial program. Gould and some of his associates therefore made personal advances. In the spring of 1890 the Missouri Pacific succeeded in floating one of those ingeniously arranged bonds, designed to attract the investor who wanted to combine security with profit. The road offered the stockholders the privilege of buying a collateral trust bond at 95 with a bonus of one share of stock for each bond. Based upon the market price of the stock, the 5 per cent bond cost the Missouri Pacific stockholder about 87; or he could keep the stock, pay 95 for the bond, and hold the stock for a rise in value.

The financial problems of the Missouri Pacific were for the moment solved—but only for the moment. Rates were still low. Even though earnings were declining, the Missouri Pacific continued to pay dividends. Soon the road needed more funds—and the road was forced again to borrow. The money markets being closed, the company again borrowed, directly from Gould and Sage.

The new loans, made in the routine course of business, were not known to the financial community. Meanwhile the security markets reflecting the increase in railroad traffic due to large cereal grain crops, indulged in one of those exuberant upward movements which anticipate something that never happens. The rise in the market was stimulated by heavy London buying which in September reached "enormous proportions." [30] Investors who sold in the fall of 1890 were buying in the fall of 1891. The rise was so pronounced that professional traders were astounded. Newspapers assured the investing public that the upward rise was based upon a record crop, that, to use the language of one of them, "A bull movement with such a basis has the most solid of foundations." [31] The newspapers as so often before were playing the game of informed sellers, of which Gould was one. In the general rise the price of Missouri Pacific advanced, attaining a level in mid-September only slightly below the highest prices reached in 1889 and 1890. How many shares Gould sold in the rise is not known.

The realities of the situation were revealed in late September. In June Gould had insisted that Missouri Pacific was "intrinsically cheap," and that it was selling "far below its real value." [32] Its floating debt, however, had again been increased, and it was soon revealed that Gould and Sage had advanced funds to the road. These fatal words, remarked the financial-weekly Gould critic, "form the epitaph which can be found on the tombstone standing over every distressed property which [had] fallen into the same management during the past twenty years." [33] The dividend was passed and within a few days the price of the stock broke sharply from more than 76 to less than 55.

Almost at the end of his career, all of Gould's railroad properties had become non-dividend payers. He was still in control of four of the five major properties which constituted the basis of his railroad empire of ten years before. One of these, however—the Union Pacific—was in the hands of a creditors' committee, and until liquidation of a large debt had been completed, no dividends could be paid. The Wabash and the Texas & Pacific although controlled by Gould through the stockholdings of himself and his associates, could pay no dividends until the interest on their income bonds was met. Finally on his major enterprise—the Missouri Pacific—the dividend had been passed.

Over the next few months the railroads continued to carry a large grain traffic—much of it for export. The securities markets late in 1891 and early in 1892 resumed their advance, and the stocks of the Gould roads participated. It was one of the most active and buoyant markets since the rapid rise in 1880 and 1881.

Gould, however, appreciating the forces which made it impossible for the railroad industry to transform the rise in gross into a rise in net, succeeded in selling out most of his holdings in the Union Pacific, Richmond Terminal, and the Atchison, as well as a considerable part of Missouri Pacific. Even while the market was still rising, the underlying factors in the railroad industry were already at work to reduce earnings. By early February, 1892, the market began to retreat. Some spectacular moves in individual securities served to maintain an appearance of a rising market. Late in January the decline was arrested by a sudden spurt in National Cordage, one of the leading industrial speculative securities of the day. A few days later the market received another stimulant in a sudden advance in coal securities. While the financial analysts were writing about the "inevitability" of the rising market, share prices weakened. The stock market in the summer and fall of 1891, having anticipated nothing, now reversed itself and proceeded to predict that which railroad men had been expecting for some time. In the face of heavy traffic from the fall of 1890 to the fall of 1891, railroads were too busy to compete by cutting rates. As the heavy traffic movement was completed, the incentive for renewed rate-cutting again came to the fore.

Before these rate cuts broke out, the annual election of the Union Pacific was held late in April, 1892. Some security holders had by this time lost their confidence in Gould's leadership. The foreign stockholders especially were dissatisfied. They announced their determination to oust Gould, and initiated a drive for proxies. A substantial block of foreign-owned stock was placed in the hands of a representative in Amsterdam, who made efforts in this country to secure the support of Amsterdam shareholders. As Gould had sold most of his stock it was expected that he would lose control.

Contrary to expectation, the Gould slate at the annual meeting was victorious. The fight was close and the Gould ticket won by the narrow margin of 10,000 votes. The victory was achieved by a last-minute switch in proxies representing a large block of foreign-owned stock. There were some charges of bad faith on the part of a foreign banking house which delivered the proxies to an American firm friendly to Gould instead of to an unfriendly firm.[34] Despite the outcome Gould was not elated. In fact he professed indifference. The result was a personal triumph for his son, George, who had played the leading role in securing the switch in foreign proxies that made victory certain.

Continuance of the Gould influence on the Union Pacific board did not materially aid either that road or the Missouri Pacific. Whatever help either could give to the other; whatever operating economies could be accomplished by their joint management; whatever traffic could be diverted by the Union Pacific to the Missouri Pacific, was more than absorbed by the heavy losses arising from the renewal of rate wars. Hardly had the Union Pacific's new board been approved than a wave of rate cuts appeared. At the April quarterly meeting of the Western Traffic Association, the western railroad presidents appeared ready to accuse Gould face to face of responsibility for the rate trouble. Gould, however, did not attend and the meeting was adjourned. In the Southwest the Missouri Pacific and the Atchison renewed hostilities. In the Missouri Valley the Burlington cut rates on wool. In the mountain territory in Colorado and Utah, both the Burlington and the Rock Island asked the advisory board's permission to reduce rates. The board met in May but accomplished nothing. It issued orders which were not obeyed. Gould was not the only recalcitrant. His old enemy Perkins of the Burlington was also a rate-cutter, and Huntington did not even pretend to obey the board's orders.

The climax came early in July. Although traffic had declined, business moving over the Missouri Pacific, Union Pacific, and the Atchison had increased; while business moving over the Burlington and Rock Island had decreased.[35] The non-Gould roads looking at this showing, insisted that the Gould lines must in some manner be manipulating rates. "Gould is at his old tricks again," said the representative of some of the western roads.[36] Early in July charges and counter-charges, affirmations and denials, constituted the main business of the board. The Burlington was dissatisfied with several of the decisions and demanded a change of rules of the association. Should its demand not be met the Burlington would withdraw. Its demand was not complied with, and in giving notice of withdrawal it asserted that for a long time it had had information on the underhand cutting of rates by the Missouri Pacific.

This was the beginning of the end of the elaborate efforts to stabilize rates and to remove discrimination by joint action of independently owned and operated railroads. Road after road left the association. The Western Traffic Association was now a corpse and required only a formal funeral to validate its disappearance. Before the end of November the funeral was held and the association formally decided to disband.

Gould returned to his old habits—both the Missouri Pacific and the Union Pacific became the leading rate-cutters of the West. It must have been clear to Gould nevertheless that he could not expect prosperity in the midst of a rate war. By this time he had learned that he could not follow contradictory policies at one and the same time. He could not acquire other properties and become a rate disturber, and at the same time lead the roads in active co-operation and become a railroad harmonizer.

His position to the last continued doubtful. He had experimented in the last few years of his life, first with one policy, then with another. He must have felt that a policy of thorough cooperation had never been attempted. He had strongly sponsored the elimination of individual soliciting agencies in the belief that competition of the roads' solicitors was the main cause of rate-cutting. He had repeatedly suggested the merits of this idea to the presidents, individually, and to the administrative board of the two Morgan-sponsored railroad associations. The first association had ignored his views. Although the second had taken his views more seriously and had appointed a committee to draft a plan, nothing was ever done.

The outburst of renewed rate-cutting by the Gould roads in October and November of 1892 upon the dissolution of the association may have been the beginning of a new experiment. Because of his liquidation program Gould was well supplied with liquid assets. Perhaps he believed that a break in the market was about to ensue, and that he could purchase railroad securities at bargain prices. Meanwhile he could intensify the war of rates, reduce railroad earnings and drive securities to even lower levels. If the Missouri Pacific lost in the general smash-up and could not pay fixed charges, he would be ready to advance the necessary sums to enable it to meet its obligations. He may have felt that such a policy was necessary to discipline the recalcitrant roads. Perhaps had he lived a few years longer, he might have been able to carry out some of these policies, with results probably as sensational as those which characterized his appearance in the security markets in the spring and summer of 1879.

Gould, however, was a sick man. He had never fully recovered from his distressing experience in the summer of 1884. He had lost that mastery of expression and equanimity of temper that had so impressed many of his contemporaries. A number of temperamental outbursts at board meetings and in newspaper interviews in the late eighties and early nineties had been unprecedented in his career. Increasingly long vacations on his private yacht accomplished little in improving his health.

When he passed away in December of 1892, his position as a man of business remained obscure. He had disclosed neither his motives nor his possible campaign. In the railroad industry in which strong competition had to be faced his properties passed their dividends. In the telegraph and transit industries in which almost all competition was eliminated, his properties maintained their dividends. In view of the value of his holdings on the brink of a widespread business depression, it is interesting, though hardly profitable, to speculate on what his plans might have been. In control of the Union Pacific, he might have challenged the United States government and built a road competitive with the Union Pacific, in this way weakening the government's second-mortgage lien on the main line of the road. At the low prices in the middle nineties he might have been able to acquire control of the Atchison and other properties. In view of Huntington's financial problems it was even possible that he might have been able to negotiate an agreement with that leader.

Both Gould and Huntington, however, rarely compromised. Gould's concessions in the interests of rate stability were short-lived and ineffective. Huntington was still dominant in his territorial sphere, and trading with him was as difficult as ever. Gould, moreover, was prematurely exhausted. He had been in failing health for almost a decade. His incessant activities had taken their toll. Especially after his reacquisition of Union Pacific control in 1890 his energy was unequal to his responsibilities. His son, George, took over in numerous cases, including the fight for the retention of the Union Pacific in 1891, and his active participation in the affairs of the St. Louis & Southwestern.

Gould's death had long been anticipated, and his actual passing produced only slight effects in stock market and business circles. After his death, there was no one to carry on his work. Although he left his cash, current assets, and stock holdings, he left no plans. His death paved the way for Harriman and Morgan. They were free to take up the burden of the western roads in such a way as to create new common interests. This in turn made possible a stabilization of rates which a generation of plans, conferences, and associations had failed to achieve.

NOTES FOR CHAPTER XXIX

1. *Ry. World*, Sept. 6, 1885, 926.
2. For some data on Gould's coal investments, see Chicago *Tribune*, Jan. 17, 1883; New York *Times*, Oct. 9, 1888; Kansas City *Times*, cited in New York *Times*, Feb. 22, 1890.

3. *R. R. Gaz.*, Nov. 7, 1890, 778.
4. Phila. *Press*, Sept. 10, 1891, states definitely that he had $20,000,000 in cash; and that in the six months following the panic he invested $15,000,000 in stock.
5. *More They Told Barron*—Notes of Clarence W. Barron; edited and arranged by Arthur Pound and Samuel Taylor Moore, 115-16, Harper & Brothers, New York, 1931.
6. John H. Inman, president of the Richmond Terminal, said that Gould had told him that he had acquired 100,000 shares out of 700,000 outstanding. The management owned 150,000 shares. New York *Times*, Nov. 19, 1890; New York *Sun*, Nov. 21, 1890. A few months later Inman stated that Gould had increased his holdings to "probably" around 30,000 shares. New York *Times*, Feb. 14, 1891. It is not possible to reconcile this conflict of evidence.
7. Atlanta *Constitution*, cited in New York *Times*, Dec. 19, 1890.
8. Phila. *Press*, Nov. 23, 1890.
9. New York *Tribune*, Dec. 15, 1890, in an article signed I.H.B.
10. Burlington archives, Forbes to Perkins, Nov. 22, 1890.
11. Annual report, Chicago, Milwaukee & St. Paul, 1890, 12.
12. Annual report, Chicago, Burlington & Quincy, 1890, 18.
13. New York *Sun*, Nov. 12, 1890.
14. Phila. *Press*, Nov. 9, 1890.
15. Phila. *Public Ledger*, Dec. 4, 1890.
16. New York *Times*, Dec. 21, 1890.
17. Ibid., Jan. 4, 1891.
18. New York *Tribune*, April 18, 1891.
19. Ibid., Feb. 7, 1891.
20. This scheme in its dim outlines was sketched by vice president Crocker of the Southern Pacific, in discussing the course of negotiations in southwestern territory. *Ry. Review*, April 18, 1891, 374.
21. New York *Tribune*, April 16, 1891.
22. Ibid., April 18, 1891.
23. Statement of Boston News Bureau, cited in *Stockholder*, April 30, 1891.
24. This was the statement made by the solicitor of the Union Pacific in New York *Tribune*, Sept. 9, 1891.
25. New York *Times*, Aug. 8, 1891. The New York *Tribune* of the same date reported that the syndicate, in addition to Sage, Gould and Dillon, would have representatives of the Mercantile Trust, Drexel, Morgan & Company, and Kuhn, Loeb & Company.
26. *Stockholder*, Sept. 28, 1891.
27. Phila. *Press*, Sept. 26, 1891.
28. New York *Times*, Sept. 27, 1891.
29. Phila. *Press*, Sept. 27, 1891.
30. *Bradstreet*, Sept. 19, 1891, 604.
31. New York *Times*, Sept. 20, 1891.
32. *Stockholder*, June 30, 1891.
33. *Chron.*, Sept. 26, 1891, 418.
34. New York *Tribune*, Sept. 28, 1892.
35. Details are in *R. R. Gaz.*, June 17, 1892, 458.
36. New York *Times*, June 10, 1892.

CHAPTER XXX

Conclusion

In assessing the importance of a business leader, his contribution to the industry and to the public welfare must be considered. This is particularly true in an examination of business success in the free-enterprise economy of the period following the Civil War. Argument is still hot between those who deny and those who defend that system as the best means of affording to the community a high standard of living. Although it is probable that the unregulated capitalistic economy of the nineteenth century has been weakened, there is still no agreement upon the extent to which a regulated economy can exist without destroying the profit motives which make a free-enterprise system possible.

It is therefore particularly profitable to examine the contributions made both in terms of business advance and public service which were made by Gould in the generation following the Civil War. Gould was, and still remains, a business type. He had his virtues and he had his faults. His defects have been exaggerated beyond their true significance. Gould possessed a cold-blooded unscrupulousness which enabled him to take full advantage of the primitive nature of the art of corporate finance and the status of corporate law, and to adapt to his purposes the low state of political morals prevailing at the time.

What positive contribution did he make to the transportation and telegraph industries with which for the better part of his business life he was so closely associated? What contribution did he make to the well-being of the general public? How did he promote the general interests of the community? To many conservative businessmen of the time, interested primarily in the promotion of stability and in the maintenance of the earnings of well-established enterprises, Gould was a wrecker of existing values, "a destroyer of the peace," [1] to use the language of one of the careful businessmen of the time. He sold stocks short to depress their value and then frequently outwitted his short-selling associates by buying them back at low prices, even while his associates were still selling. This he did on a large scale with the Western Union Telegraph, and on a smaller scale with other corporations. He made contracts not to build railroads into the territories of his rivals, only to violate them when it was profitable for him to do so. He made rate agreements only to break them. He issued statements on security values merely to confute his opponents in the stock markets.

Strange to say, these very misstatements and continuous violations of the spirit if not of the letter of the contracts, enriched his contribution to the public welfare, even though they impaired, at least temporarily, the earning power of a large section of the railroad industry. Perhaps even stranger is the circumstance that the very factors which temporarily injured the industry, did in fact over the longer period aid it, and enhanced both its permanent value and its long-term earning capacity. Gould's violation of the understandings prohibiting the building of new roads, for example, led to the extensive rate wars which depressed rates and reduced railroad earnings. The reduction of dividends in 1884 and 1885 by eastern, and in the late eighties by western, railroads followed by the extensive receiverships in the early and middle nineties, were largely the result of the rate wars and the promiscuous building of new railroads. Yet the reduction in rates was of extraordinary benefit to consumers and producers. Although the immediate effects were disastrous to corporate earnings, the long-range effects were beneficial, not only to shippers and consumers but also to the railroads themselves. The depressed rates increased operating efficiency and lowered costs. This paved the way for a rise in traffic made possible in part by reduced rates. The lowered rates were permanent. The traffic and managerial alliances and understandings of the middle nineties and of the first decade of the present century, and the waves of railroad consolidations and acquisitions, did not produce any substantial rate increases.

It is however necessary to point out that for a part of his career, Gould was instrumental in raising rates. His acquisition of control of the Union Pacific, possessing the only transcontinental route of the seventies, was followed by the introduction of monopolistic policies. In the depression of the middle and late seventies, transcontinental rates over the combined Central Pacific-Union route were raised sharply through the united efforts of Huntington and Gould. Also, discriminations between shippers, classes of traffic, and geographical areas were imposed in order to increase railroad earnings.

Except for this phase of his career Gould, in quest of business advantages for the companies with which he was associated, fought for reduced rates. Together with McHenry, he was the leading factor in the reduction of rates on crude and refined oil that brought the cost of oil transportation down to the low levels of the late sixties and early seventies. Rockefeller took advantage of the railroad competition that Gould and McHenry initiated in order to exact the maximum business concessions for his refineries, and rates thus reduced were not increased. In fact the rate structure on the petroleum traffic was further corroded in the following decades. Gould's control of the Erie railway was also featured by the rate battles with Commodore Vanderbilt.

The most far-reaching effects on the railroad rate structure, however, were reflected in 1879 and in the eighties, following Gould's brilliant expansion program. In these years he repeatedly broke up rate structures and territorial agreements. He furthermore destroyed established rate and traffic pools in rapid succession. From 1879 until the late eighties, when the pursuit of this policy brought earnings and stock values to the lowest point attained since the late seventies, he consistently followed this policy of intransigeance. His activities produced widespread business unsettlement and contributed to the creation of a group of foes who characterized him as a corporate wrecker and business disturber.

Aside from his association with the Erie, Gould first instituted this policy in a major sense soon after he gained control of the Wabash. In one incident after another he took the aggressive. The rate depression in the Missouri Valley and in the Middle West was due in considerable degree to his policies.

The invasion of southern Iowa by the Wabash in 1880; the construction by the Missouri Pacific of the line to Omaha in 1881; the ill-concealed extension into the Atchison territory in southern Kansas through the instrumentality of a partially controlled subsidiary; the invasion of the Leadville territory in Colorado through the Union Pacific; and the elaborate construction and expansion program in the Southwest—all contributed in the late eighties to the largest railroad-building program and to some of the most violent rate wars in American railroad history.

When Gould initiated his policy of rate-cutting and railroad construction in 1879, competitive railroad relationships in many parts of the country had become reasonably well stabilized. Gould broke up this stabilized rate and territorial structure. The eventual result was the construction of the Burlington's line to Denver, and the emergence of competition with the Union Pacific on transcontinental traffic. The rate wars that followed the Burlington invasion of the Union Pacific territory permanently reduced rates. The same results followed in eastern and central Kansas, where the Atchison eyed closely the Gould invasion of its lucrative traffic-producing country. The Gould aggression was partly responsible for the Atchison's counter-measures, primarily the construction of the Kansas City-Chicago extension and the transformation of the road into a new transcontinental system. Again, to use another example, the conflict of Gould with the Gulf was followed by the merger of that property with the Atchison. With the aid of additional construction in Oklahoma, this union produced a new competitive through route between the Missouri Valley and the Gulf Coast.

By reducing rates with apparent abandon as a means of achieving results, Gould impaired the fortunes not only of his competitors but also those of his own properties. Though the security holders of many roads may have lost, the public was a major gainer. The record building construction in 1879–81 and in 1886–87 were in part the consequence of competitive fears inspired by the Gould policies. Gould was in this sense a public servant. The building program in the eighties, of the Atchison, the Union Pacific, the Burlington, the Rock Island, the Northwestern, and the St. Paul, reflected to a considerable degree adjustments to his rate-cutting, business-disturbing policies.

Although in this sense Gould rendered a public service, he accomplished nothing in the raising of railroad service standards or in reducing costs. His roads during his lifetime and for two generations thereafter had an unsavory reputation. To the operating man accustomed to efficient car and train movements and to the shipper accustomed to expeditious deliveries, the Gould railroads were by no means a blessing. A Gould road in the Southwest was a byword for poor service. To the operating man and shipper the poor service of a Gould road was compared with the good service of the Atchison. Enough detail has been presented in preceding chapters to establish the conclusion that the Gould roads were poorly maintained; in fact usually drastically undermaintained. And an undermaintained railroad cannot render a high standard of service.

Neither did Gould introduce any mechanical improvements in the railroad industry nor for that matter in the telegraph industry. Gould was no inventor and had no mechanical ability; and unlike Westinghouse, for example, he made no contribution to the mechanical arts of the day. He had none of the driving genius for new and better things which characterized the activities of Rockefeller and Carnegie.

Having thus considered his accomplishments in one field, and his failings in another, attention must be directed now to another phase of his business activity in which the truth lies hidden in a complex business and financial organization. Gould throughout his life was attacked by group after group of security holders. From the beginning of his experience with the Erie it was his destiny to be associated with properties which had passed through receivership and reorganization. Except for the Union Pacific, and also for the Lackawanna in which he had only a minority interest, every major transportation property with which he became associated had a history of financial reverses. To an extent this was true even of the Union Pacific. Although the road had not gone through receivership prior to Gould control, the price of its securities had fallen to low levels and its original promoters after suffering heavy financial losses had lost control. The other properties prior to Gould control had either been in, or had narrowly escaped, receivership. The Kansas & Texas, the International, the Iron Mountain, the Texas & Pacific, the Denver, the Kansas Pacific, the Wabash, the Hannibal, and a number of smaller lines which were acquired by the larger properties were included in this category. Many of these roads after a number of years under Gould control drifted back into the receiverships from which they had so recently emerged. The drop in the market value of their securities which accompanied their financial embarrassment was usually laid to the evil genius of Gould. He was the scapegoat of the unsuccessful, as were the bankers and the utility magnates in the depression of the 1930's, and the Federal Reserve Board in 1920 and 1921.

To some extent this conclusion was justified. Gould in promoting rate wars and in invading local territories occupied by other railroads contributed to the financial difficulties of many roads and to that extent security holders were correct in ascribing their losses to Gould. The complaints of the losers were loud and long, and were registered in the daily press and in other organs of public opinion. They were also reflected in the documents presented before the courts and legislative committees by opponents of Gould and his policies. It is clear that losses were incurred and it is therefore easy to conclude that those who followed Gould lost money, and that the loss inflicted by the Gould policies represented a loss to the community.

This conclusion, however, does not represent the entire truth. To arrive at a conclusion reflecting financial and economic realities, it is essential to examine the source from which capital necessary for expansion in a dynamic capitalistic society is derived. The flow of capital into the production of goods and services necessary to meet consumer demands was only slightly affected in the seventies and eighties by governmental policies. The process of capital creation thus reflected the free play of economic influences. Gould operated largely in the railroad industry in which the demand for capital was exceptionally heavy. Except for a limited number of companies, the funds needed for the construction of new roads were secured by the sale of bonds and stocks. Funds were secured in part from individual and institutional savings. Such a source of capital creation is normal and this supply in conjunction with the demand for capital from borrowers produces what economists call a "natural" rate of interest. There are, however, other methods of creating purchasing power essential to capital formation. Expenditures by government for capital purposes out of the proceeds of bond issues sold to the banks became a normal feature in the 1930's and 1940's. Whatever objection there may be to this practice, the fact remains that billions of dollars of capital expenditures have been thus financed.

Purchasing power for capital improvements is also created by changes in capital values. The nature of these values and the extent to which they contribute to the growth of capital in a capitalistic economy should be properly appraised. Those who take the lead in creating capital from this source are frequently condemned as speculators or as the recipients of unearned gains. These profits are on occasion exceptionally large, although the losses under adverse economic conditions are even larger. Since the number who are successful in this phase of business are relatively few, there seems to be a presumption of inequity, or perhaps even of dishonesty, by those who are successful. This hypothesis may be a major reason for the failure to examine this problem adequately and to assess the contribution made by participants in this field of business to the public interest in a capitalistic economy.

A rise in the market value of assets consisting either of land and its improvements, or of stocks and bonds representing the capitalized earnings realized from the use of land and improvements thereon, produces an increase in the purchasing power of the holders of such property rights. Some of the holders may have bought such rights at one price level and held them throughout the period when they sold at a lower price level, awaiting their return to the original, higher cost level. To those people the increase in market value from the lower price level may represent no increase in purchasing power. There are others, however, who purchase securities at the low prices prevailing normally in a period of depression. It may be contended that the buyers gain only that amount which the sellers lose. This does not necessarily follow. Those who sell the securities have already made their contribution to the economic well-being of the community. The cash they paid for their securities or for other evidence of property rights has already been expended by the borrowers and transformed into capital. The capital exists in the form of railroads, telephone, telegraph, machines, or tools which are creating services for the consumer. The new security purchasers make additional commitments. Their investments are not transformed immediately into capital formation. Such investments transfer purchasing power to the original holders, who have now become sellers. To determine the economic benefits to the community coming from the increased capital values, it is essential to consider the disposition made of these greater values on the part of buyers. If the buyers hold the securities through the rising capital market; if, that is to say, they never sell the securities they have made no important contribution to the public welfare.

The buyers of the securities at the depression-made low prices may, however, sell their securities at the high capital values established in the boom era. When the securities are converted into cash, the purchasing power of the holders is correspondingly increased. If that purchasing power is then transferred to those businessmen who are active producers for transformation into capital goods, then a substantial economic benefit has been realized. If the holders sell their securities at high prices and use the proceeds to buy new securities directly from the corporations which use the cash to install capital improvements, the productive wealth of the community is increased.

Those who buy and sell such securities in periods of low and high prices, respectively, are frequently described as speculators or as suppliers of "equity" capital. The first is a questionable and the second a praiseworthy description of the functions of the role of this kind of capital creator in the period of recovery from a general depression. It is then generally recognized that fixed charges have become too heavy for many corporations to carry. What is needed under these conditions, it is therefore contended, is capital which carries no interest charges. In the later stages of cyclical recovery, in the midst of an economic boom, the services of the supplier of equity capital are not so generally recognized since by that time funds for capital needs are relatively easy to obtain. Conservative people, particularly those representing financial institutions such as banks and insurance companies, stimulated as they are by a record of good earnings over a period of years, are willing to provide capital yielding low returns. This is especially true if such returns are fixed contractually in terms of dollars. The borrowing corporations in turn are desirous of making such contracts. They can thereby make substantial profits from the difference between the interest paid and the profits expected to be realized from the use of the borrowed funds. Those who buy stocks at high prices in the latter stages of a boom and who lose part of their capital are frequently described as speculators; while those who buy at low depression prices and sell at the high boom prices are frequently described as investors. Ordinarily those who have not bought the securities at the low depression prices are so impressed by the record of boom-time earnings, presumably so well established as to insure their indefinite continuance, that they are led to buy the securities at the higher boom prices.

Those who followed Gould in the purchase of securities at the low depression-born prices and in the early period of recovery, made exceptional profits. It is perhaps not so clear, however, that those who made these gains were not so voluble in their praise as were those who were so expansive in seeking a scapegoat for their losses. Gould above all was a leader in the field of speculative capital and in this phase of business activity he performed a service to society. It was also in this field that he made his greatest personal gains and contributed most to the public weal. In this field he did not, however, realize the maximum potential gains. He made many mistakes, as do most businessmen in this and other fields. In the early recovery from the depression lows of 1877 he was on the wrong side of the market and his short sales produced heavy personal losses. After the successful resumption of specie payments in January, 1879, he changed his mind. He financed his early buying ventures by the sale of a substantial block of Union Pacific stock to the Sage-Keene syndicate. His purchases in the spring and summer of 1879 of the Kansas Pacific, Wabash and other securities, which he bought at an accelerated tempo, have been examined. In his buying program, it is an established fact that Gould had a large following. Sage, Humphreys, (S.) Dillon, Field, Tilden, G. M. Pullman, Marquand, J. S. Seligman, Keene, Woerishoffer, Sloan, T. A. Scott, W. L. Scott and Hopkins, among many others, participated with him in the purchase of securities at depression prices. Each of these capitalists had his own following, and though it is not possible to establish the extent of the group that followed his leadership, it is a reasonable assertion that their numbers could be counted in the thousands.[2]

Gould also had a following abroad, particularly in Holland, where his purchase of Denver & Pacific bonds in the summer of 1879 created a favorable impression among capitalists. As early as 1875, his leadership in reversing market trends by using Union Pacific stock as a vehicle, created much good feeling there.[3]

Aside from the Union Pacific stock, the securities which Gould purchased on a large scale in 1879 and 1880 had little investment following. Although the roads responsible for the issue of these securities were strategic from the standpoint of their importance to the economic life of the community, they had yielded slight returns to the original investors. Since they were financially weak, their properties were in poor physical condition. It is therefore not surprising that conservative capitalists, such for example as Forbes, referred to these properties contemptuously as the "broken-down" railroads. The prices of these securities were exceptionally low. Gould's market judgment in 1879 and 1880 was excellent, and those who followed his lead realized substantial profits. It is of more than passing significance to observe that those capitalists who were associated with Gould in these two luscious years were not among his bitter critics. Among his followers during this period were a number, Woerishoffer for example, who later disagreed with him on the problems of market trading. Woerishoffer gained and Gould lost in the panic markets of May, 1884, whereas Gould profited and Woerishoffer lost by reason of Gould's sale of his Denver stock and the failure of Woerishoffer to sell his in the booming markets of 1881. Neither man condemned the other because of his market losses.

With a view of presenting a picture of the market appreciation of the securities in which Gould and his army of followers were interested, the following table, "Market Values of Stocks in Gould Properties, 1879–1881," was prepared.

Notes to Table I

1. Early in 1879 Central Branch Union Pacific stock had no value. At that time an official of the Burlington was unable to secure a quotation for the bonds of the Central Branch. See Burlington archives, Tyson to Perkins, Jan. 9, 1879. The price of $10 per share is therefore reasonable.
2. This is the price per share paid by Gould for 6,250 shares, according to testimony before the Pacific Railway Commission. See Executive Document No. 51, 50th Congress, 1st Session, 1887, p. 663.

TABLE I

MARKET VALUES OF STOCKS IN GOULD PROPERTIES—1879–1881

Name of stock	Low price per share 1879 *	No. of shares outstanding Dec. 31, 1878	Average price per share 1881 * **	No. of shares outstanding Dec. 31, 1881	Mkt. value in $ of outstanding stock based on low price per share, 1879	Mkt. value in $ of outstanding stock based on average price per share, 1881
Central Branch Union Pacific, com.	10 [1]	10,000	250 [2]	10,000	$ 100,000	$ 2,500,000
Central of New Jersey, com.	45 [3]	185,632	96.6	185,632	8,353,440	18,006,304
Hannibal & St. Joseph, com.	13¼	91,687	74.1 [4]	91,687	1,191,931	6,784,838
Hannibal & St. Joseph, pfd.	34	50,830	109.7	50,830	1,728,220	5,591,300
Manhattan Elevated, com.	21⅜ [5]	130,000	36.18 [6]	130,000	2,730,000	4,680,000
Missouri Pacific, com.	($3,800,000) [7]	8,000	103	299,589	3,800,000	30,857,049
Internat'l Grt. North'n, com.	5 [8]	55,000	.....	...... [9]	275,000	......
Missouri, Kansas & Texas, com.	5⅜	214,050	44	399,714 [10]	1,070,250	17,587,416
St. Louis, Iron Mt. & So'n, com.	50 [11]	214,598 [12]	.....	...... [13]	10,729,900	......
Texas & Pacific, com.	10 [14]	70,185	60.5	281,277 [15]	701,850	17,157,897
Union Pacific, com.	57½	367,623	120.4	507,623 [16]	21,322,134	60,914,760
Denver Pacific, com.	5 [17]	40,000	.....	......	200,000	......
Kansas Pacific, com.	9⅛	96,899	.....	......	872,091	......
Wabash, St. Louis & Pacific, com.	....	......	48.3	200,000 [18]	......	9,600,000
Wabash, St. Louis & Pacific, pfd.	....	......	88.2	200,000 [18]	......	17,600,000
Wabash, com.	17¾	160,000	.....	......	2,880,000	......
St. Louis, Kans. Cy & North'n, com.	7	120,000	.....	......	840,000	......
St. Louis, Kans. Cy & North'n, pfd.	25½	120,000	.....	......	3,120,000	......
Western Union Telegraph, com.	99.3 [19]	155,265 [20]	85.5	800,000 [21]	15,371,235	68,800,000
				TOTAL	$75,286,051	$260,079,564

* Fractions eliminated and prices raised to the higher integer.

** The average 1881 price is computed as follows: the monthly highs were averaged; the monthly lows were averaged; the two averages were added; the sum of these two were then divided by 2.

3. This is the price paid to Keene by Gould for the stock of the Central of New Jersey early in 1881, according to Chicago *Tribune*, Jan. 12, 1882.
4. This average price does not include September, 1881, when, as the result of a corner, the price of the common stock reached a high of $350 per share.
5. This is the average of the high and low prices for July, 1881.
6. This is the average of the high and low prices for October, 1881, when Gould bought most of his Manhattan Elevated.
7. The price per share is based on the *reported* price (never confirmed by the participants) paid by Gould to Commodore Garrison for the latter's holdings of Missouri Pacific. It is assumed that this price covered the purchase of the entire 8,000 shares outstanding; though in view of the small minority interest, the price is not entirely accurate.
8. The price of $5 a share for International Great Northern is assumed, since no market price for 1879 has been found. Inasmuch as the property was sold at auction in July 1879, the price of $5 a share probably overestimates its market value.
9. By the end of 1881, 164,700 shares of Missouri, Kansas & Texas had been issued for 82,350 shares of International Great Northern stock on the basis of the exchange of two shares of the former for one share of the latter. Hence the value of the International Great Northern's stock by the end of 1881 was reflected in the value of the stock of the Missouri, Kansas & Texas.
10. Of the 399,714 shares of Missouri, Kansas & Texas outstanding by the end of 1881, 378,750 represent the shares equal to its own 214,050 shares outstanding on December 31, 1878; and the 164,700 shares issued for 82,350 of International Great Northern. The remaining 20,964 shares were issued by construction companies for the building of new mileage. The large capital gains realized from the stocks for the construction companies are not reflected in this tabulation.
11. This is the price per share paid to Messrs. Allen and Marquand by Gould in December, 1880, according to *R. R. Gaz.*, Dec. 17, 1880, 678.
12. Number of shares outstanding on December 31, 1880.
13. Since almost all of the St. Louis, Iron Mountain & Southern's stock had been exchanged for the stock of the Missouri Pacific by December 31, 1881, the market value for 1881 is reflected in the market value of the Missouri Pacific.
14. The price of $10 a share for Texas & Pacific is assumed. No market quotation for 1879 has been found. Since the company's financial condition approximated that of the Missouri, Kansas & Texas, whose stock sold at a low of 5⅜, a price of $10 for Texas & Pacific stock is probably a fair reflection of its value early in 1879.
15. This is the number of shares outstanding on June 30, 1882, since the fiscal year ended on that date.
16. 504,522 shares of Union Pacific on December 31, 1881, were issued for the shares of the old Union Pacific, Kansas Pacific and Denver Pacific. There were actually outstanding 507,623 shares; the balance of 3,101 shares reflect some minor adjustments.
17. The 40,000 shares of Denver Pacific had no value in 1879 in the opinion of the Pacific Railway Commission. The five-dollar nominal value assigned to this stock is undoubtedly in excess of its market value.
18. The 200,000 shares each of Wabash, St. Louis & Pacific common and preferred were exchanged for the Wabash common and the St. Louis, Kansas City & Northern common and preferred. There were actually outstanding on December 31, 1881, a total of 269,210 shares of common and 230,332 shares of preferred of the Wabash, St. Louis & Pacific. The additional 69,210 and 30,332 shares of common and of preferred, respectively, were exchanged for the securities of other companies—mostly in connection with the re-

organization of companies in receivership. The appreciation in the market value of these receivership securities through their exchange for the shares of the Wabash is thus not included in this table.

19. This is the monthly average of the high and low prices of Western Union Telegraph stock for the last six months of 1880. Although Gould had traded in the stock since 1875—and perhaps earlier—he was not closely associated with it as a buyer for purposes of acquiring control until the summer of 1880.
20. Number of shares outstanding June 30, 1880.
21. The increased number of shares reflects the stock created in consequence of the merger in 1881 of the Western Union Telegraph with the American Union Telegraph and the Atlantic & Pacific Telegraph companies. To a slight but indeterminate degree the stocks of the latter two telegraph companies represent some cost to the holders who exchanged them for the Western Union Telegraph stock; and to this extent the market appreciation of Western Union Telegraph is exaggerated.

This table is by no means accurate or all-inclusive. It does, however, indicate the shape and trend of things in the depressed markets in the spring of 1879 as compared with the boom markets in 1881. The table compares the low price registered in 1879 generally prevailing in the spring months of the year when Gould began his buying program, and an average of the 1881 prices. The high prices of 1881 with some exceptions were not duplicated for a twenty-one-year period.

This tabular compilation bristles with hypotheses. Almost every figure can be challenged. It is obviously incorrect to assume that Gould or any of his followers bought a large part of the stocks at the lowest prices prevailing in 1879, and it is of course equally inaccurate to assume that all of the stocks were sold by Gould or his followers at the high 1881 prices. If there is a margin of error which leads to the exaggeration of the appreciation in the market value of securities in this period, it is probably more than adequately balanced by the profits realized by the Gould-following in many securities that are not included in the tabulation. Such omissions embrace the appreciation in the stock of the Denver, in the junior bonds of the Kansas Pacific and the Wabash, and of the numerous small roads that were embraced in the latter system. Nor does the compilation reflect the gains realized from the activities of the construction companies. Although the Lackawanna was not, strictly speaking, a Gould property, it is nevertheless true that Gould and many in his group realized large profits from trading in that stock. One of the most stable security values created through the Gould leadership—that of the various corporations involved in the St.

Louis terminal area—is ignored. It is therefore reasonable to conclude that this table reflects fairly the increase in the market value of the securities of the Gould railroads in the boom period between 1879 and 1881.

In these years, characterized by a rapid expansion in the nation's productive plant, thousands of miles of railroads were built by the Gould roads. Few of these properties enjoyed a high credit rating. They therefore had to finance their needs in the speculative markets. Gould was a leader in this field, and hundreds of communities owed their early facilities to his speculative leadership. A substantial portion of the speculative funds employed in the building of new lines came from those who had reaped capital gains from the purchase and sale of Gould securities. The reorganization of the Texas & Pacific in the mid-eighties, for example, disclosed the large number of Pennsylvania citizens who followed the lead of Scott and Gould in the purchase of its securities. Tilden, Marquand, Field, and Sage were heavy buyers of securities sold to finance railroad construction. The volume of Gould railroad mileage built during the first part of the boom of the eighties was by no means inconsiderable. Taking the four-year period of 1879–82, inclusive, as a basis for study, the new mileage built by the Wabash-Kansas & Texas-Missouri Pacific-Iron Mountain-International-Texas & Pacific-and Union Pacific systems (excluding the Lackawanna, where the building of the Buffalo extension was also financed to a great extent by capital of Gould and his following) amounted to 4,231.29 (See Table II). Assuming a cost of $20,000 per mile,

TABLE II

MILES OF ROAD BUILT BY GOULD RAILROADS 1879–1882

(Excludes construction in Republic of Mexico)

1. Texas Pacific	1,010.00
2. Union Pacific	1,249.87
3. Wabash	462.01
4. International Great Northern	256.71
5. Missouri Kansas & Texas	588.2
6. Missouri Pacific	466.5
7. St. Louis Iron Mountain & Southern	198.0
	4,231.29

NOTE: The mileage of the first three roads is based on letters from these companies. The mileage of the last four is based on data in Poor's *Manual of Railroads*.

probably on the low side in the strong commodity markets in the early eighties, this construction involved an investment of $84,-620,000.

A substantial part of the funds invested in the stocks (and bonds) of the Gould railroads in the early eighties was later lost. Similar losses flowing from investment in state government bonds sold to finance public works in a boom period were incurred in the wake of the panic of 1837, and far more extensive losses were inflicted from time to time by default and repudiation of European governments as the result of disastrous wars and even more disastrous peace treaties. There is, however, a notable difference between the nature and the distribution of the losses from private securities as contrasted with those from government securities. Risks in the former group are assumed and losses absorbed by the investor. Except for government subsidies, the investor cannot transfer the loss to any other group; he assumes the risk and either takes the profits or absorbs the loss. Losses arising from improper financing of government needs, however, are usually taken by the taxpayer. It is only in the event of the destruction of the government or of a breakdown in the economy, that the investor is forced to take the loss either in the form of default or repudiation, or in the guise of a worthless currency in which the debt is repaid.

Except for the destruction of a country's economy, or the devaluation of its currency, the issues of government bonds for nonproductive purposes thus remain a permanent liability upon the community. Bonds issued by corporations on the other hand are reduced or eliminated in the course of time as the unprofitable character of the capital in which the funds have been committed is revealed. So it was with many of the bonds of the Gould-controlled railroads—the Wabash, the Kansas & Texas, the International, and the Texas & Pacific during the lifetime of Gould, and those of the Missouri Pacific after his death. Some of the bonds were exchanged for stock. No longer was the public taxed to finance the payment of interest on an unproductive debt. The unproductivity of the debt in many cases was the result not of the economic disutility of the capital, but rather of the decline in railroad rates. That is to say, the unfortunate investment made by the bondholder gave the public a railroad facility at a low price. It was the combination of fixed capital which could be converted to no other use and of depressed rates that frequently undermined the safety of the investment. The security holders, followers of Gould, who sold at the top prices of 1881 realized good capital gains. Those who reinvested such gains in the Gould railroads eventually lost part. Distribution of profits and losses among Gould followers was highly unequal. While Sage for example invested a major part of his profits in railroad bonds which maintained their value even in depression, Field invested his in the stock of the Manhattan Elevated at high prices. His loss was fatal.

Whatever the loss of the followers of Gould and to Gould himself, the public benefited from his activities as a man of business in the railroad industry and in the field of speculative capital. As a leader in the railroad industry he built many new roads; he broke down local territorial monopolies, destroyed traffic pools, and wrecked railroad rate structures. As a leader in the arena of speculative capital, he transformed millions of dollars of paper profits into productive wealth in the form of new railroads. Gould made fortunes for many of his followers, and produced losses for others. What his followers in the security markets gained, many did not permanently retain. The public did gain permanently, so far as anything permanent can be assumed to exist in economic life. Through the use of funds obtained from speculative followers and which could not have been obtained from investors, he built many new railroads. At the same time, in the process of disturbing existing business values, he reduced permanently the price of railroad service. To Gould, as much as to any other single business leader, goes the credit for that far-reaching reduction in rates that characterized the growth of the American economy in the generation after the Civil War.

NOTES FOR CHAPTER XXX

1. Burlington archives, Harris to W. W. Murphy, April 23, 1877.
2. An example of an individual investor who profited by following Gould's leadership is furnished by a New York surrogate who said publicly that Gould told him to buy Union Pacific stock at 40, after which the price rose rapidly; and that, through the advice of Sweeny, one of Gould's political followers, he profited also from the purchase of the stock of the Cleveland & Pittsburgh. *Wall Street News*, March 15, 1882.
3. *Ry. Review*, June 12, 1875, 118.

Index